Human–Computer Interfaces and Interactivity:

Emergent Research and Applications

Pedro Isaías
Universidade Aberta (Portuguese Open University), Portugal

Katherine Blashki
Noroff University College, Norway

A volume in the Advances in Human and Social Aspects of Technology (AHSAT) Book Series

Information Science
REFERENCE

An Imprint of IGI Global

Managing Director:	Lindsay Johnston
Production Editor:	Jennifer Yoder
Development Editor:	Hayley Kang
Acquisitions Editor:	Kayla Wolfe
Typesetter:	James Knapp
Cover Design:	Jason Mull

Published in the United States of America by
Information Science Reference (an imprint of IGI Global)
701 E. Chocolate Avenue
Hershey PA, USA 17033
Tel: 717-533-8845
Fax: 717-533-8661
E-mail: cust@igi-global.com
Web site: http://www.igi-global.com

Library of Congress Cataloging-in-Publication Data

Human-computer interfaces and interactivity : emergent research and applications / Pedro Isaias and Katherine Blashki, editors.
    pages cm
  Includes bibliographical references and index. ISBN 978-1-4666-6228-5 (hardcover) -- ISBN 978-1-4666-6229-2 (ebook) -- ISBN 978-1-4666-6231-5 (print & perpetual access) 1. Human-computer interaction. 2. People with disabilities. I. Isaias, Pedro, editor of compilation. II. Blashki, Kathy, 1961- editor of compilation. QA76.9.H8H86 2014
  004.01'9--dc23
                                2014013852

This book is published in the IGI Global book series Advances in Human and Social Aspects of Technology (AHSAT) (ISSN: 2328-1316; eISSN: 2328-1324)

British Cataloguing in Publication Data
A Cataloguing in Publication record for this book is available from the British Library.

For electronic access to this publication, please contact: eresources@igi-global.com.

Advances in Human and Social Aspects of Technology (AHSAT) Book Series

Ashish Dwivedi
The University of Hull, UK

ISSN: 2328-1316
EISSN: 2328-1324

Mission

In recent years, the societal impact of technology has been noted as we become increasingly more connected and are presented with more digital tools and devices. With the popularity of digital devices such as cell phones and tablets, it is crucial to consider the implications of our digital dependence and the presence of technology in our everyday lives.

The **Advances in Human and Social Aspects of Technology (AHSAT) Book Series** seeks to explore the ways in which society and human beings have been affected by technology and how the technological revolution has changed the way we conduct our lives as well as our behavior. The AHSAT book series aims to publish the most cutting-edge research on human behavior and interaction with technology and the ways in which the digital age is changing society.

Coverage

- Human Development and Technology
- Human-Computer Interaction
- Cyber Behavior
- Technology Dependence
- Cultural Influence of ICTs
- Technology Adoption
- Philosophy of Technology
- Gender and Technology
- ICTs and Social Change
- ICTs and Human Empowerment

IGI Global is currently accepting manuscripts for publication within this series. To submit a proposal for a volume in this series, please contact our Acquisition Editors at Acquisitions@igi-global.com or visit: http://www.igi-global.com/publish/.

Titles in this Series

Evolving Issues Surrounding Technoethics and Society in the Digital Age
Rocci Luppicini (University of Ottawa, Canada)
Information Science Reference • copyright 2014 • 349pp • H/C (ISBN: 9781466661226) • US $215.00 (our price)

Technological Advancements and the Impact of Actor-Network Theory
Arthur Tatnall (Victoria University, Australia)
Information Science Reference • copyright 2014 • 320pp • H/C (ISBN: 9781466661264) • US $195.00 (our price)

Gender Considerations and Influence in the Digital Media and Gaming Industry
Julie Prescott (University of Bolton, UK) and Julie Elizabeth McGurren (Codemasters, UK)
Information Science Reference • copyright 2014 • 357pp • H/C (ISBN: 9781466661424) • US $195.00 (our price)

Human-Computer Interfaces and Interactivity Emergent Research and Applications
Pedro Isaías (Universidade Aberta (Portuguese Open University), Portugal) and Katherine Blashki (Noroff University College, Norway)
Information Science Reference • copyright 2014 • 325pp • H/C (ISBN: 9781466662285) • US $200.00 (our price)

Political Campaigning in the Information Age
Ashu M. G. Solo (Maverick Technologies America Inc., USA)
Information Science Reference • copyright 2014 • 359pp • H/C (ISBN: 9781466660625) • US $210.00 (our price)

Handbook of Research on Political Activism in the Information Age
Ashu M. G. Solo (Maverick Technologies America Inc., USA)
Information Science Reference • copyright 2014 • 498pp • H/C (ISBN: 9781466660663) • US $275.00 (our price)

Interdisciplinary Applications of Agent-Based Social Simulation and Modeling
Diana Francisca Adamatti (Universidade Federal do Rio Grande, Brasil) Graçaliz Pereira Dimuro (Universidade Federal do Rio Grande, Brasil) and Helder Coelho (Universidade de Lisboa, Portugal)
Information Science Reference • copyright 2014 • 376pp • H/C (ISBN: 9781466659544) • US $225.00 (our price)

Examining Paratextual Theory and its Applications in Digital Culture
Nadine Desrochers (Université de Montréal, Canada) and Daniel Apollon (University of Bergen, Norway)
Information Science Reference • copyright 2014 • 419pp • H/C (ISBN: 9781466660021) • US $215.00 (our price)

www.igi-global.com

701 E. Chocolate Ave., Hershey, PA 17033
Order online at www.igi-global.com or call 717-533-8845 x100
To place a standing order for titles released in this series, contact: cust@igi-global.com
Mon-Fri 8:00 am - 5:00 pm (est) or fax 24 hours a day 717-533-8661

Table of Contents

Section 2
Inclusion and Accessibility

Section 3
Emerging Technologies

Detailed Table of Contents

Section 1
Design Approaches and Interfaces

Chapter 1
Visda Goudarzi, University of Music and Performing Arts Graz, Austria

This chapter presents a contextual inquiry of climate scientists during data analysis tasks. Eighteen scientists volunteered for requirement-gathering interviews and focus groups. The interviews have been analyzed in order to determine the implications for a complementary audio interface based on sonification. Results show that climate scientists depend heavily on visualizations, and the amount and complexity of data to be displayed are huge. Climate metaphors are assessed to help develop an intuitive sound design of the interface. The outline and basic properties of the audio tool could be determined. Furthermore, user preference of sound for the auditory display has been evaluated. The volunteers evaluated the sounds aesthetically and associated them with climate parameters. The stimuli, which have been chosen as the sonically most appealing and associated with the same parameter, are considered the optimal ones for the auditory interface.

Chapter 2
Aslı Günay, Middle East Technical University, Turkey
Çiğdem Erbuğ, Middle East Technical University, Turkey
Paul Hekkert, Delft University of Technology, The Netherlands
Natalia Romero Herrera, Delft University of Technology, The Netherlands

Human-computer interaction and holistic user experiences are considered crucial concepts in the design of interactive products, where interactive self-service kiosks require special attention, as they are different than any other type of consumer and personal products. The public nature of self-service kiosks suggests that social context may have an important role in understanding the experience of users when interacting with such products. Yet, this is hardly reflected in the development of self-service kiosks in which usefulness and functionality are still the basic, and usually the only, concerns. This limited discussion hinders innovation when redesigning this type of product. This chapter firstly studies the major factors affecting users' interactions with self-service kiosks, followed by the influence of presence or absence of other people on user experience with interactive self-service kiosks looking at the relationships between different social contexts, feelings, and task performances; it then elaborates on task performances. The studies conducted to explore these relations reveal that interactions with interactive self-service kiosks are specialized according to different task qualities that these kiosks serve as well as the social context, which highlights the necessity to take into account the inseparable context during the design of these self-service kiosks. They emphasize that not only the product interface but also other product features, product body, and context should be shaped by these task qualities and the social context. Hence, suggested design implications go beyond traditional usability and technical issues, considering social context as a key issue to address innovative self-service kiosk designs.

André Constantino da Silva, UNICAMP, Brazil & IFSP –Campus Hortolândia, Brazil
Heloísa Vieira da Rocha, UNICAMP, Brazil

Multimodal interaction is a proposal to turn the interaction between humans and machines more natural, increasing the usability, flexibility, and convenience of one application. Improve an application with multimodal features impacts on its architecture and, to describe the main components to treat the multimodality, some architecture models are proposed in the literature, including for Web multimodal systems. E-Learning environments are Web-based systems and need a good usability, flexibility, and convenience: requirements that can be improved with implementation of multimodal features on them. Since they have their own peculiarities, we need a more specific multimodal architecture model described in such a way to reuse the components built for multimodal systems and to connect them with the e-learning environment components. This chapter proposes an architecture for multimodal e-learning environments. A viability study was done in the Ae, an e-learning environment developed using a component-based development process, with components to treat the pen and touch modalities.

Jacob Nielsen, University of Southern Denmark, Denmark
Gunver Majgaard, University of Southern Denmark, Denmark

How can we merge interactive design processes and the development of interactive prototypes for first-semester students without prior programming experience? The authors provide a selection of relevant contructionism-inspired programming tools and provide indications on how one of them can enrich a user-centred design project for first-semester software and IT engineering students. They do this by describing the experiences from two runs of a HCI course and the concurrent semester projects. The students developed interactive touch-based learning apps for children in the fourth to sixth grade using App Inventor. Most of the project groups managed to do three iterations of specifying requirements, doing conceptual design, physical and interactive prototyping, and user evaluation. The groups implemented quite complex programs with multiple-screen switching, multiple interfaces, media such as pictures, animations and sound, database connection, Web-server connection, and integrated sensors, such as camera, accelerometer, etc. The students did a lot more project iterations and spent more time on the creative designs in real-life situations than the authors expected. This also allowed for the students' professional reflections on their prototypes, usability, interaction, and the design processes. All in all, this gave them a more profound real-life experience in the user-centred design process. The authors compare the two runs and suggest how to introduce contructionist prototype programming in a HCI course curriculum and conclude that contructionist programming tools can be a valuable addition to the teaching of HCI, and they suggest that further research should be conducted to explore how to best integrate these tools in order to optimize the students' learning capabilities.

Chapter 5

João Silva, University of Lisbon, Portugal
Pedro Isaías, Universidade Aberta (Portuguese Open University), Portugal

Football teams can explore the benefits of Websites and increase their popularity through the creation of a well-designed Website that will attract users. The fact that football is the leading sport in most countries constitutes an advantage, as it becomes an appealing subject for Internet navigation. This chapter explores the type of relationship that the supporters of Sporting Clube de Portugal have with the football team on the club's official Website. This objective demands an analysis of the characteristics that a Website is required to have in order to attract and engage its intended users. Through a survey conducted via different social media and email communication, this study asked Sporting Clube de Portugal's supporters about their engagement with the Website. In addition, this chapter presents the features that users consider to be most important in a football club Website.

Section 2
Inclusion and Accessibility

Chapter 6

Renate Motschnig, University of Vienna, Austria
Dominik Hagelkruys, University of Vienna, Austria
Ján Struhár, University of Vienna, Austria
Kamila Balharová, Pedagogical and Psychological Counseling Center Brno, Czech
*   Republic*

Human-Centered Design requires end-user consideration and involvement in all steps of the human-computer interface design, but how can this be accomplished if the primary user group is users with special cognitive and affective needs? Would "classical" tools and techniques be sufficient or would they need to be adapted and complemented with special effort? This chapter shares the strategies the authors adopt and the experiences they are gradually gaining in including users with dyslexia in the design of the LITERACY Web-Portal. LITERACY is a project of the European Union aiming at improving social inclusion of youth and adults with dyslexia. The authors hope this case study provides insight on and gives courage for inclusion of end-users even though—or particularly because—they have special needs.

Chapter 7

Alma Leora Culén, University of Oslo, Norway
Anna Karpova, University of Oslo, Norway

In this chapter, the authors consider a researcher's perspective in projects involving design of assistive technologies for and with children who have moderate to severe limitations, such as cognitive impairments, impulse control issues, strongly reduced vision, or speech problems. The secondary objective is to introduce the concept of vulnerability in such complex design contexts, exploring it in relation to researchers, the user group, and other stakeholders. They argue that awareness of diverse risks can lead to a design process that reduces or even eliminates some of these risks, empowering both researchers and users in the process. The case used as a basis for discussion is that of an iPad app design for and with children in a special education class, and later, with children in occupational therapy.

Chapter 8

Web services are an emerging technology that has attracted much attention from both the research and the industry sectors in recent years. The exploitation of Web services as components in Web applications facilitates development and supports application interoperability, regardless of the programming language and platform used. However, existing Web services development standards do not take into account the fact that the provided content and the interactive functionality should be accessible to, and easily operable by, people with disabilities. This chapter presents a platform named myWebAccess, which provides a mechanism for the semi-automated "repair" of Web services' interaction characteristics in order to support the automatic generation of interface elements that conform to the de facto standard of the Web Content Accessibility Guidelines 2.0. myWebAccess enhances interaction quality for specific target user groups, including people with visual and motor disabilities, and supports the use of Web services on diverse platforms (e.g., mobile phones equipped with a browser). The Web developers can build their own design templates and the users of myWebAccess can create a personalized environment containing their favourite services. Thus, they can interact with them through interfaces appropriate to their specific individual characteristics.

Section 3
Emerging Technologies

Enterprise 2.0 has been part of the business sector vocabulary for quite some time now. Web 2.0's revolutionary philosophy and applications have been absorbed by various areas of society. The success of the business sector benefits from a client-oriented approach, so when the benefits of a user-centric Web became evident, adopting it was the natural next step. Enterprise 2.0 presents advantages mainly in two areas: within organizations, as they enable communication through new dynamic methods of communication and interaction, in order to enhance efficiency and productivity; and between companies and customers, suppliers, and partners, as they increase both revenue and customer satisfaction and promote cooperation and co-creation to improve services or products. This chapter illustrates the reality of Small and Medium Enterprises' (SMEs) adoption of Web 2.0. An online questionnaire was developed to assess numerous SMEs in Portugal to understand if and how Web 2.0 implementation is taking place.

In the context of human-driven design and environmental sustainability, the authors have developed a computer-based platform concept for studying and co-designing places (i.e. socially meaningful locations). The Visual IHME platform provides a photo-based, interactive spherical panorama environment with a set of co-creative interaction tools such as discussion boards, questionnaires, and polls on-screen. All creative content can be pinned to specific spatial spots on the image. In a preliminary end-user evaluation of the concept demonstration, the authors found that the participants valued the co-design platform, though many doubted the role of this kind of social technology in terms of real impact on issues that are important to people. They discuss how co-design platforms like Visual IHME can have an impact on environmental sustainability and the evolving role of human-computer interaction research and design in addressing sustainability problems.

Chapter 11

How does design of emerging embodied technologies enrich the HCI learning processes? The authors introduce a model for embodied interaction and use it in the development of a painting app for children based on the motion sensor Asus Xtion Pro (similar to Kinect). The development of the app was part of a HCI course for engineering students. The motion sensor was interesting as a design tool, because it appealed to full body interaction. The development exemplified and unfolded the embodied elements: multiple modalities, physical, bodily, social, and symbolic interaction in a situated environment. Subsequently, the authors introduce a physical-digital toolbox, illustrating the span of parameters within the model for embodied interaction: robot technology, tangibles, wearables, interactive surroundings, and bigger objects.

Section 4
Mobile and Ubiquitous Computing

It is the goal of ubiquitous computing (UbiComp) to hide computers from the users. Instead, everyday objects embedded with computer processing capability become smart objects that act as interfaces to computer software. A challenge with this new paradigm of computing is to create natural and obvious ways for people to interact with objects and receive output from the computer software that these objects serve as interfaces to. In this chapter, a solution is proposed whereby virtual user interfaces are added to smart objects. These virtual interfaces are viewed in augmented reality through personal viewing devices which also allow people to interact directly with them. The implementation of UbiComp environments and personal viewing devices is described in order to illustrate the use of current technology in creating user-friendly UbiComp environments.

Chapter 13

Yu-Horng Chen, University of Taipei, Taiwan
Yih-Shyuan Chen, St. John's University, Taiwan

This chapter investigates the research projects and prototypes related to currently available mobile applications used in wayfinding and navigation. The advancement in small-screen devices, mobile computing and modelling counterpart, location awareness techniques, and wireless technologies have improved screen resolutions and provided technical solutions for delivering textual, 2D, and 3D information to a mobile device. After investigating small-screen representations and the related navigation content and mobile interface design from the previous cases, two suggestions are presented in this chapter in order to enhance the design for future mobile wayfinding systems: 1) pseudo-3D representations and 2) personalised and on-demand services.

Section 5
User Experience

Chapter 14

Hsiu-Feng Wang, National Chiayi University, Taiwan
Pei-Yu Wang, National Chiayi University, Taiwan
Ching-Chih Liao, Ming Chuan University, Taiwan
Yu-Yin Lin, National Chiayi University, Taiwan

This chapter examines children's aesthetic preferences for learning Web pages designed for them. It applies Berlyne's theory of aesthetic preference to these Web pages: a theory that suggests that people prefer a medium level of stimuli to a low or high level of stimuli. The experiment employs a 3 x 2 x 2 between-subject design; it explores perceived visual complexity, gender, cognitive style, and aesthetic preference. A total of 120 children (60 boys and 60 girls) aged between 11 to 12 years-old take part in the experiment. The children are asked to rate learning Web pages of different levels of perceived visual complexity for aesthetic preference. These Web pages have been created by the authors. The results of the experiment show that overall the children prefer Web pages that display a medium level of perceived visual complexity to those that display a high or low level of perceived visual complexity. Thus, the results support Berlyne's theory. However, when aesthetic preference is analysed with respect to gender, it is found that different levels of perceived visual complexity have an impact on boys' aesthetic preferences but not girls'. In other words, Berylne's theory is only partly supported. Likewise, Berylne's theory is only partly supported when aesthetic preference is analysed with respect to cognitive style. Here, imagers prefer a high level of perceived visual complexity and verbalisers prefer a medium level of perceived visual complexity. This chapter should be of interest to anyone who designs learning Web pages for children.

Chapter 15

In the Web of devices, information and services are designed for multi-device use. As each device has its specific characteristics, inter-device adjustments and adaptations result in inconsistent inter-device (system) models. They are perceived by users on visual and functional experience layers as well as on information architecture and prevent users from building transparent mental models. Evidence from case studies reveals the nature of cognitive information processing in this situation of rich user experience. Consistency design rules seem to be insufficient to overcome the rich user experience problems, as users' exploration of inconsistencies lead to interaction problems. In consequence, a systemic intermedia perspective is needed. This is explored in this chapter.

Chapter 16

If line-shape information was physically presented by virtue of some kind of mechanical interface, man-machine communication would be enhanced in the sense of multi-modal interactions. In order for such interactions to be available with ease, they should be realized as simple, small, and cheap devices even though suffering from a bit of performance decrease. Thus, the authors have studied a mouse-like computer-human mechanical interface. The idea is that slippage stimuli on a fingerpad would be effective enough to provide users a piece of motion information, and that the mechanism for slippage can be embodied in mouse interfaces. Here, to enhance the slippage perceptual performance, raised-dots were considered to be useful, and thus, a series of psychophysical experiments were carried out by using raised-dot planes with the period of 1.5, 3.1, 12.5, 30, and 50 mm, together with a without-dot flat plane. It was confirmed that the perceptual lengths were well formulated by a power law: they were proportional to the power of both speed and length. The exponential constants with the length factor were a little less than 1 corresponding to the ideal linear relationship. While the ones with the speed factor were in negative, nearly 0 corresponding to the ideal undisturbed relationship. Then, it was found that the pathway length perceptual accuracies for the raised-dot planes were much superior to that for the flat plane from the viewpoint of (1) length-related perceptual length contractions, (2) speed-induced perceptual length contractions, and (3) perceptual length random errors. This is shown in this chapter.

Preface

Human Computer Interaction (HCI) is the broad area covered by this book. Namely, this book aims to address the main issues of interest within the Culture and Design of interaction between humans and computers at the interface level, especially in Internet applications (i.e. Web interfaces, game interfaces). In particular, this book will emphasise emergent and innovative aspects of design, development, and implementation of interfaces for interactivity between humans and the technologies they routinely use. Significant evolutions have emerged since Web 1.0 and novel aspects emerge for Web 3.0 applications.

In addition, this book aims to explore and discuss innovative studies of technology and its application in the implementation of interactivity in interface design and development (through Web 1.0 to 3.0) and welcomes significant research in Human-Computer Interfaces and Interaction. This book aims to address a range of approaches including, but not limited to, the conceptual, technological, and design issues related to these developments.

The book is mainly intended to support an academic audience (academics, university teachers, researchers, and postgraduate students at both Master and Doctorate levels). In addition, this book will be of benefit to public and private institutions, HCI developers and researchers, HCI enterprise managers, professionals related to Information Systems and ICT sectors, and those who seek to reach an audience/user via media or technology.

The chapters were divided into the following five sections, for the purpose of structure and organization: "Design Approaches and Interfaces," "Inclusion and Accessibility," "Emerging Technologies," "Mobile and Ubiquitous Computing," and "User Experience."

The initial section concerning design approaches and interfaces is composed of five chapters and explores a broad range of issues.

SECTION 1: DESIGN APPROACHES AND INTERFACES

Chapter 1, titled "Contextual Inquiry for a Climate Audio Interface" by Goudarzi, presents a contextual inquiry of climate scientists during data analysis tasks. It introduces sonification (the use of non-speech audio to convey information) and its usage to generate a multi modal interface to scrutinize climate data. The author states the advantages of the auditory (sound for one auditory display was assessed) perception and the circumstances that are most appropriate for the usage of sonification in an information swarming world. The research project (syson.kug.ac.at) has the main purpose of incorporating a user-centered design process to develop sonifications. Therefore, an extensive investigation of daily basis research work of scientists has been performed. This study was performed with the help of 18 scientists who volunteered for requirements-gathering interviews and focus groups. The participants assessed the sounds aesthetically and associated them with climate factors. The author focuses on data from climate models and measurements. This data is a good model domain for sonification because of the typically large and multivariate data sets, which are difficult to visualize. The data was assessed on different levels, the quantitative data was assessed by in progress use of software tools, and qualitative analysis was performed with the aid of workflows that the scientists followed, including typical tasks that have to be solved in the data analysis process.

In chapter 2, "Changing Paradigms in our Interactions with Self-Service Kiosks" by Günay, Erbuğ, Hekkert, and Herrera, the main factors that affect users' interactions with self-service kiosks are examined. The public nature of this type of kiosk implies that social context may have a significant role in understanding experience of users when interacting with such products. Here, human-computer interaction and holistic user experiences are seen as vital concepts in the design of interactive products. The influence of presence or absence of other people on user experience with interactive self-service kiosks is studied. In this chapter, the significance of considering social context in the design of interactive self-service kiosks is concluded. Through the literature review, the author states that user experience with self-service kiosks can be affected by the presence of other people, either in a positive or negative manner. Understanding and considering the users' anxieties about the presence of other people is crucial while designing self-service kiosks.

Chapter 3, "Multimodal User Interface in E-Learning Environments: A Proposed Architecture" written by Silva and Rocha, presents a structural design for multimodal e-learning environments. The authors suggest an architecture for multimodal e-learning environments based on common architectures for multimodal systems and specificities of e-learning environments. Taking into consideration the W3C multimodal architecture, Web-accessible multimodal interfaces architecture, and the architecture of multimodal systems, the authors redesign the Ae architecture model, an e-learning environment developed by using a component-based development method, with components to treat the pen and touch modalities. As a result, a viability study was performed in Ae. These learning environments are systems used to aid teaching and learning activities through the Web, allowing a huge interaction between its users. The Ae has flexibility to permit the administrator install only a set of tools; as a result, tools that do not follow the institution rules or overload the server can be removed. As new directions, the authors want to employ new components into the model and revise the multimodal e-learning environment on mobile contexts, the impact of multimodality on learning activities, and the connection between modality and the courses.

In chapter 4, "Constructionist Prototype Programming in a First Semester HCI Course for Engineering Students," Nielsen and Majgaard provide a variety of relevant constructivism-inspired programming tools that can help first-semester students without previous programming experience and examine how MIT App Inventor (which is, according to the authors, a "fourth generation visual programming language for developing interactive Android mobile applications" that allows "the user to navigate and set up different interface elements through a drag-and-drop interface") can improve a user-centred design project for first-semester software and IT engineering students. The authors concluded that using a constructivist programming tool (i.e. App Inventor) as a prototyping tool has definite benefits with concerns to the first-semester students' learning. The major benefit is that this tool takes the focus away from some of the tiresome parts of programming, with this allowing the students to put into practice even advanced functionalities within a much shorter time than usually they do. Consequently, the students are more capable to use more time on the design process and the user involvement and thus do more project iterations by having more time in these stages they gain a more insightful experience in the user-centred design process. The authors consider that these constructivist programming tools are an important addition to the teaching of Human-Computer Interaction and suggest that additional research need to be made to examine better ways to integrate them in learning environments.

Chapter 5 with the title "Website Interaction between a Football Club and its Supporters: The Case of Sporting Clube de Portugal," authored by Silva and Isaías, focuses on the notion that football teams can take advantage of Websites and enhance their popularity through the creation of a well designed Website, in order to attract more users. With this notion in mind, the authors' purpose with this chapter is to investigate the type of relationship that the supporters of Sporting Clube de Portugal (a Portuguese football team) have with the football team on the team's official Website by presenting an outline of the Internet's current situation and an analysis of how football can gain from its advantages. Consequently, the authors present the characteristics that a Website must have in order to draw attention and engage its intended audience. Which characteristics should be present on a quality Website and on a football team Website are examined, and the chapter establishes the type of relationship that occurs between football and the Internet. The empirical data presented in this chapter was gathered through a survey performed via different social media and email communication with the purpose to ask Sporting Clube de Portugal's supporters regarding their engagement with the team's Website.

This next section concerns different inclusion and accessibility issues throughout three chapters.

SECTION 2: INCLUSION AND ACCESSIBILITY

Chapter 6 explores the strategies the authors adopted and the experiences they are increasingly obtaining in including users with dyslexia in the design of the LITERACY Web-Portal. This chapter titled "Including Dyslexic Users in the Early Design of the LITERACY Portal" is authored by Motschnig, Hagelkruys, Struhár, and Balharová and presents the strategies and requirements that maximize end-user inclusion in all aspects of the design process of a literacy Web-portal. The authors' purpose is to develop an advanced online portal, which can assist both dyslexic youths and adults. This portal "is destined to provide personalized e-learning programs, useful tools, and methods for helping people with dyslexia to improve their abilities in reading and writing." In addition, this chapter demonstrates some actual techniques and steps to incorporate end-users with dyslexia in order to serve as an example or inspiration on how to achieve and exploit end-user inclusion for increased usability of a Web-portal. With the concern of inclusion as a main goal for this Web-portal, the authors applied the Human-Centered Design approach, which includes users' insights at early design stages. By using this method, the authors are able to find out about the specific needs and preferences of the users and then can eradicate potential problems before they appear. This iterative approach allows the reduction of the cognitive load and the enhancement of the user experience.

Chapter 7, "Designing with Vulnerable Children: A Researcher's Perspective," written by Culén and Karpova, focuses on special education needs. The authors discuss challenges, lessons learned, and rewards from a design process concerning children who live with cognitive, motor, or sensory disabilities and who, consequently, need special education. The main goal of this study is to reveal a researcher's perspective in projects involving design of assistive technology for and with children with moderate to severe limitations. In this research, an iPad application design for and with the children in a special education class and in another stage with the children in occupational therapy is used. In addition, the chapter aims to present the notion of vulnerability in intricate design environments by exploring its relation to studies, the user group, and other stakeholders. The authors state that the knowledge of vulnerabilities may lead to a design process that can decrease or eliminate risks and as a result empowering both researchers and users.

Chapter 8, titled "Supporting Accessible User Interfaces using Web Services" by Bouloukakis, Basdekis and Stephanidis, presents a platform called myWebAccess, which provides a mechanism for the semi-automated "repair" of Web services' interaction characteristics in order to support the automatic generation of interface elements that conform to the standard of the Web Content Accessibility Guidelines 2.0. This platform improves interaction quality for a specific target user groups, such as people with visual and motor disabilities and also supports the use of Web services on diverse platforms including mobile phones equipped with a browser. One of the essential characteristics of the platform is Web services management and operations management, where operations can be added, edited, and made accessible to the end users. The myWebAccess has been developed using the MVC (Model-View-Controller) architecture to sustain multiple design templates. In addition, the authors assessed the proposed platform by analyzing Web services reusability and interoperability with assistive technology solutions. In addition, the use of the platform has demonstrated the adjustment of the repaired services in different context of usage. To sum up, this work focuses on the development of Web services as components in a Web interface in order to support the development of accessible and multi-channel Web interfaces.

The third section presents emerging technologies through three chapters.

SECTION 3: EMERGING TECHNOLOGIES

With the title "The Impact of Enterprise 2.0 on SMEs," chapter 9, authored by Antunes and Isaías, explores, in general, Web 2.0 technologies and, in particular, enterprise 2.0 (E2). This chapter presents the scenario of Small and Medium Enterprises' (SMEs) adoption of Web 2.0 in Portugal. In order to illustrate the reality of SME adoption of Web 2.0 applications, an online questionnaire was performed to identify if and how Web 2.0 implementation is occurring. The empirical study was applied to Portuguese SMEs that have been distinguished with the status of "SME Excellence" awarded by IAPMEI (a Portuguese acronym that means SMEs and Innovation Support Institute). The sample was comprised by 438 companies, from a population of 1481 companies that were awarded with the "SME Excellence" between the years of 2010 and 2011, and the results presented in this chapter were based on 99 valid questionnaires. The authors concluded that regardless of the size of the sample, the results expose an early, but fast-moving stage in the adoption of E2 technologies (39% of respondents had a low familiarity with the notion of E2.0, while about 30% assumed that they already use these technologies in work context). The results provided an important illustration of what is the reality of Web 2.0 implementation in this particular scenario (the elite Portuguese SMEs).

Chapter 10 titled "Visual IHME: Co-Designing Meaningful Places for Sustainability," authored by Niemelä, Kivinen, Kulju, Tammela, Ikonen, and Korhonen, explores the context of human-driven design and environmental sustainability, how Human-Computer Interaction (HCI) can influence and improve sustainability behaviours. Following this context, the authors developed a computer-based platform concept for studying and co-designing socially meaningful locations named Visual IHME (this word come from Finnish and is an acronym for "IHmislähtöiset MEnetelmät" – human-driven methods). This platform was developed with the purpose to examine, understand, co-create, and share meanings bound to or growing from specific locations. Visual IHME platform has been developed in two phases. In the first phase, the platform was built as a virtual travel application demonstrator for a travel agency, which according to the authors facilitates "users to virtually move in a panoramic environment projected on a big screen, receive detailed information from various services or other points of interests related to the location, leave comments or guidance to the other travelers or service providers, and get online or recorded video guidance related to the specific location." In the second phase, the platform was developed to improve support co-ideating and research purposes with the integration of different co-design features well known from social media in the panorama of Visual IHME. All this research reflects the authors' goal to develop and apply technology deeply from the human point of view. With this study, the authors aim to study how this kind of human-computer interaction application can work for environmental sustainability.

Chapter 11, "Teaching Design of Emerging Embodied Technologies" by Majgaard, focuses on the question, How does design of emerging embodied technologies enrich the HCI learning processes? With this question in mind, the author presents a model for embodied interaction; this model is employed in the development of a painting application for children. The author explores how a design of emerging embodied technologies, such as Asus Xtion Pro created by fifth semester engineering students (similar to Microsoft's Kinect), can enhance the HCI learning processes in engineering education. This work resulted in a painting application prototype where the users used their hands for painting, painted in different colours, and used pencils in different sizes. This prototype was tested by four school children from the third grade. With these tests, the students receive insights regarding usability issues, creative ideas (such as painting using feet instead of hands), and unexpected playful use. Accordingly with the author, this development demonstrated the following elements: multiple modalities, physical, bodily, social, and symbolic interaction in a situated environment. In this research, the author tried to examine the relationship between new technologies, embodied and natural interaction, and learning activities.

Two chapters concerning mobile and ubiquitous computing were joined together in the fourth section.

SECTION 4: MOBILE AND UBIQUITOUS COMPUTING

Chapter 12, with the title "Augmented Reality Interfaces for Smart Objects in Ubiquitous Computing Environments" by Yew, Ong, and Nee, deals with the challenge to generate natural and obvious procedures for users to interact with objects and receive output from the computer software that these objects serve as interfaces to. Taking in consideration the fact that daily objects embedded with computer processing capability become smart objects, in this study the authors present a solution through which virtual user interfaces are added to smart objects. Furthermore, it proposes a framework for executing UbiComp (Ubiquitous Computing) environments that allows for virtual graphical user interfaces to be added to objects (these objects known as smart objects are instilled with computing and networking capacities) in the environment. By using Augmented Reality (AR) technology, every smart object acquires a virtual user interface that is amplified onto the user's view of the physical environment, which can be seen through a personal viewing device. With this, the user does not have to change his focus from the environment to be capable of accessing interactivity and complex functionality of the environment. This results in a person being able to get into an environment and instantly see the objects that are providing services and functionality beyond their physical capability.

Chapter 13 on "A Study of Mobile Guide Applications in Wayfinding Context" by Chen and Chen examines research projects and prototype associated to currently available mobile applications used in wayfinding systems and navigation context. The authors state that the main purpose of this study is "to investigate various available representations and interface that have been developed, the representations and techniques that could be delivered to different small-screen devices, as well as the representations and illustrations that could be understood by a wide audience." For that reason, they present some mobile guide designs. After examining small-screen representations, the related navigation content and mobile interface design from previous cases, the authors propose two approaches in order to improve the design for future mobile wayfinding systems: pseudo-3D representations and personalized and on-demand services. The peudo-3D representations are a method that can be used for visualising city information and images, as well as transmitting to a mobile device in a short time. The personalized and on-demand images are "a system with various visualisations and functions which could be selected and operated (e.g. Google Maps) for different users and under different conditions [and] may be one of the ways to design a mobile guide."

This last section is about user experience, and comprises three chapters.

SECTION 5: USER EXPERIENCE

The study presented at chapter 14, "The Impact of Perceived Visual Complexity, Gender, and Cognitive Style on Children's Aesthetic Preferences for Learning Web Pages," by Wang, Wang, Liao, and Lin, evaluates children's perceived aesthetic preferences for Websites designed for them as end users. In this study a total of 120 participants (60 boys and 60 girls) aged between 11 and 12 were asked to rate 3 self-designed children's learning Websites for perceived aesthetic preferences. These participants were randomly selected from amongst 6th grade students at a primary school in Taichung, Taiwan, and they had received computer lessons at least once a week and mentioned that they frequently use computers for entertainment (i.e. gaming) and browsing the Internet at home. The Websites presented to the children had been developed according to whether they exhibited a high, medium, or low level of visual complexity. The authors, taking in consideration the results of this study with the children, concluded that visual complexity has a significant impact on children's perceived aesthetic preferences towards e-learning Websites. Overall, the children favoured Websites that presented a medium level of visual complexity to those that displayed a high or low level of visual complexity.

Chapter 15 titled "Intermedia and Transmedia User Experience with Multi-Touch Apps," authored by Kritzenberger, focuses on multi-device environments design. The research presented in this chapter is part of a research agenda on examining inter-media and trans-media interaction processes; with the research question, how the inter-media transformation of a conceptual design model from one media platform to another media platform influences user experience, as base, the author performed case studies (10 persons, ages 25-30) where the users had to solve typical tasks of newspaper reading. Here two case studies with inter-device consistency in multi-display environments, in which the users' mental models were examined, are presented. Moreover, it makes a formative evaluation by monitoring the user behavior in scenario-based user testing situations and thinking out loud (which gave feedback into the process of mental model formation during the interaction process) in a user experience lab. After the initial observation was done, it examines the qualitative data from the transcriptions and video protocols. The results of these case studies with news apps gives insight into the nature of rich user experience in inter-media design contexts of applications on different platforms.

With the concept that man-machine communication can be improved, chapter 16 with the title "Length Perceptual Characteristics on Raised-Dot Slippages" authored by Nomura and Iwabu, studies a mouse-like computer-human mechanical interfaces. The notion is that slippage stimuli on a fingerpad would be useful to offer users a portion of motion information, and consequently, the mechanism for slippage can be materialized in mouse interfaces. To perform this research and to develop the slippage perceptual performance, raised-dots were considered to be helpful; therefore, a sequence of psychophysical experiments were performed by using raised-dot planes with the period of 1.5, 3.1, 12.5, 30, and 50 mm, together with a without-dot flat plane. By introducing the raised dots, the authors have examined sliding pathway perceptual characteristics via index fingerpad cutaneous sensation in the passive-touch framework.

Pedro Isaías
Universidade Aberta (Porteguese Open University), Portugal

Katherine Blashki
Noroff University College, Norway

Section 1
Design Approaches and Interfaces

Chapter 1
Contextual Inquiry for a Climate Audio Interface

Visda Goudarzi
University of Music and Performing Arts Graz, Austria

ABSTRACT

This chapter presents a contextual inquiry of climate scientists during data analysis tasks. Eighteen scientists volunteered for requirement-gathering interviews and focus groups. The interviews have been analyzed in order to determine the implications for a complementary audio interface based on sonification. Results show that climate scientists depend heavily on visualizations, and the amount and complexity of data to be displayed are huge. Climate metaphors are assessed to help develop an intuitive sound design of the interface. The outline and basic properties of the audio tool could be determined. Furthermore, user preference of sound for the auditory display has been evaluated. The volunteers evaluated the sounds aesthetically and associated them with climate parameters. The stimuli, which have been chosen as the sonically most appealing and associated with the same parameter, are considered the optimal ones for the auditory interface.

INTRODUCTION

For the last centuries, throughout the evolution of modern science itself, the main tool for data display and basis for numerous analysis methods has been data visualization. Today, with the growth of information technology, the amount of data available to be explored and observed has expanded and needs innovative data scanning methods. Auditory displays have been explored as a complimentary tool and can potentially help scientists, depending on the amount of data, data structures, and the tasks within the research con-

text. Sonification, the use of non-speech audio to convey information (Kramer, 1999) has still un-explored potential for application in science. Numerous sonification tools have been developed for specific scientific problems (e.g., sonification for EEG data Analysis (Hermann, 2002), sonification of data from computational physics (Vogt, 2008), or sonification of earthquakes' data (Aiken et al., 2012)), but to date few have been adopted within the scientific domain they are intended for.

Within the field of human computer interaction (HCI), auditory display has not been explored as much as other ones, primarily graphical interfaces.

DOI: 10.4018/978-1-4666-6228-5.ch001

(Frauenberger, 2009) analyzed 23 proceedings of the International Conference on Auditory Display (ICAD) on four themes: design process, guidance, rationale, and evaluation. He describes that all papers introduce the application domain, but contextual information is not playing a role in the design process. After the in-depth view on design issues, he looks at the field of design in sonification from HCI community's point of view using an online survey. The results of this research show that the design process for auditory display is mostly unstructured and it provides limited support to reuse the design knowledge created. Another issue is that methodologies and existing guidance in audio domain are often tied to a specific context and reusing them is only possible within the restricted context (Flowers et al., 1996).

The research project (*syson.kug.ac.at*) aims at incorporating a user centered design process to develop sonifications. Therefore an extensive investigation of the day-to-day research work of scientists has been performed, as is described in this paper. In the research project, we focus on data from climate models and measurements. Climate data are a good model domain for sonification because of the typically large and multivariate data sets, which are difficult to visualize completely. Furthermore, the time-based nature of the data implies a straight-forward direction of reading as sound, which evolves in time as well. General advantages of the human auditory system, e.g., an extremely precise resolution in the time and frequency domain (Bregman, 1990) can be utilized in the data display. Other advantages of using auditory display in the context of climate research have been found with the contextual inquiry discussed in this paper.

Examples of sonification in the context of climate research are (Halim et al., 2006) presenting a "rain prediction auditory icon". They used auditory icons to display the probability of rain based on weather conditions of previous 48 hours. Another example is (Bearman, 2011), using sound to represent uncertainty in UK climate projections data. He compares different visual and sonic methods of representing uncertainty in spatial data. He shows; when handling large volumes of spatial data, users can be limited in the amount that can be displayed at once due to visual saturation (when no more data can be shown visually without obscuring existing data). Bearman presented that using sound in combination with visual methods may help to represent uncertainty in spatial data. This idea can be expanded into other data sets to help represent uncertainty when visual representations are not sufficient. In addition to scientific examples, many projects exist where sonification of climate data was used in an artistic context, e.g., (Polli, 2004) sonification of storm data from weather models.

NEEDS' ASSESSMENT

In order to assess the needs of climate scientists with regard to their data analysis methods we investigated their research context applying different methods: as master-laymen condition we conducted interviews for a contextual inquiry implying task analysis; for investigating the master-master communication we observed focus groups. Based on the collected data, we applied different evaluation techniques: from simple quantitative analysis and a reflection of the workflows to experimental qualitative analysis of, e.g., the metaphors used in communication and the visualization types used for analysis.

We recruited eighteen volunteers from the staff of Wegener Center for Climate and Global Change (www.wegcenter.at). One participant was excluded from the evaluation, as he is not involved in research. Details about the test participants can be found in Table. 1. Interviews have been conducted in German, the native language of all participants, audio-recorded and partly transcribed for analysis. All participants received headphones as an acknowledgement for their participation (meanwhile encouraging the research lab with additional audio infrastructure.)

Contextual Inquiry

We visited climate scientists in their workplace to capture their activities, workflows, and the environmental factors while analyzing data. Interviews took about an hour and consisted of three parts. After a short introduction on the project, the participant's personal background and qualifications were assessed. The central part of the individual interview session consisted of a walk-through of a self-chosen data analysis task. The task should have been completed by the participant recently, where s/he had been faced with raw data and wanted to understand it better to find out something (successfully or not), and which s/he discussed with colleagues or presented at a meeting. Finally, expectations about an auditory display were collected, including a recording of what the data in the task would sound like, which data sets would be most useful for the participants to sonify, and how and if they would use sound at their work.

Task analysis is an established technique in HCI (Crystel et al., 2004) therefore we decided to explore different data analysis tasks that climate scientists are regularly involved in. The approach is challenging because each scientist uses an individual set of programs and performs different tasks, due to different habits and background. Therefore we conducted a usability study in a non-classical sense, following (Karat et al., 1992).

Focus Groups

Focus groups were conducted to observe more specific information about the communication between the experts. Participants belong to three different research groups (see Tab. 1). Each user group participated in a facilitated discussion where they shared ideas and opinions on their work, i.e., a focus group. Participants brought their own task results, as had been demonstrated in the contextual inquiry, and were asked to briefly present and discuss them with the other members of the group. The focus groups took about one hour each and were observed by the interviewers without interfering.

EVALUATIONS

The data were evaluated on different levels. As quantitative information, we assessed the current use of software tools. Qualitative analysis was done on the workflows that the scientists follow, including typical tasks that have to be solved in the data analysis process. Furthermore, the visualizations that were involved in the tasks were categorized to get an overview of their strengths and weaknesses. Finally, the language content of both the contextual inquiries and focus groups was collected and analyzed in the search for metaphors used in climate science. Additionally, the observation of the task and focus group discussions allowed drawing conclusions on the interactions and expertise of the users with the existing tools.

Quantitative Analysis of Software Tools

A brief quantitative analysis of different software that the climate scientists use for data analysis and/ or visualization is conducted, including their own assessment of their capabilities (beginner, intermediate, or expert). IDL, Interactive Data Language, is the most used software due to historic reasons at the institute. While IDL is a commercial program, open source languages such as Python and R are also gaining usage, according to what the participants reported informally.

In general, it could be seen that most participants were familiar with coding themselves rather than using ready-made software packages, and are used to scripting on the command line level. Another observation is that some basic applications have not been declared for this list by most participants, probably because they are so basic and/ or "just" command-line tools, notably ncview[1], a netCDF visual browser (where

Figure 1. A general workflow from the observed tasks

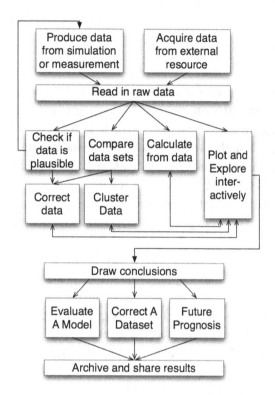

netCDF is the typical data format for climate data). Ncview is a simple open source project for quick data visualization that most scientists use for a quick-check of their data. We decided to build our sonification tool on top of ncview to enable our users to interact with the data visually and sonically on the same tool.

Work Flow Analysis

Figure 1 shows a common workflow summarizing the data analysis process in all three user groups. The task of data analyzing is very similar and can probably be generalized to other scientific disciplines as well.

The first step is the acquisition of data, either from external research institutions or from their own simulations. This data has to be read into their software environment. Then, often, the data is plotted, or otherwise checked for its plausibility,

e.g., by scanning through the numbers by hand. Often, some data is derived from the raw data by calculations following some hypothesis. Following the results of these steps, and potential plots of data, the original data are corrected or clustered. Results at this stage are always plotted and/ or explored interactively. From this, conclusions are drawn. The conclusions are specific to climate science, and can consist of either the evaluation of a model, the correction of a data set, and/ or some future prognosis. Finally, results are archived and shared – for which usually the plots serve as a basis in discussions and publications. The analysis shows that visual inspections are the key parts of the workflow. Therefore we argue that an additional auditory display can be helpful for the scientists to explore data from other perspectives.

The commonalities in each step (Data gathering, Data Analysis, Drawing Results) of the users actions will help define features of the audio interface.

Analysis of Existing Visualizations

The visualizations that were used and discussed in the tasks of the contextual inquiry were collected and categorized. Out of 30 visualizations, we found 12 line charts (out of which 7 are time series, 4 height profiles, and one other), 8 maps, 4 bar charts, 4 scatter plots, and 2 pie charts. In general, all but one of the visualizations were color-coded. While we rated 23 of them subjectively as self-explanatory, 5 are very difficult to understand. Furthermore, independent of their complexity, we rated 8 plots as very confusing, because either there are many data sets involved, or differences are hard to find (e.g., when a sequence of similar maps are placed one next to the other). The mean number of data sets that the scientists tried to compare with each other was 47 (!), with single tasks going up to 400 (25 different climate models, that were color-coded, compared in 4 different altitudes of the atmosphere and in 4 different regions, i.e., in 16 sequential plots.)

Obviously, the amount and multi-variance of data is challenging for the scientists in the analysis and communication of their results. This is also reflected in a citation by a participant (#12): „*This was really a huge challenge: how to display [the data] was the really difficult part.*" Therefore an additional display channel, e.g., sonification, might be useful to relieve and support the visual sense.

Contextual Analysis and Metaphors

As a further qualitative analysis, both the interviews from the contextual inquiry and the focus groups have been analyzed for their language content (Mayring, 2010). Two goals were envisaged with this basic assessment. First, a climate terminology will help realizing a domain-specific description of the sonifications that are understandable in the field. Second, identifying metaphors can help building a metaphoric sound identity for the sonification (Vogt et al., 2010).

All "non-trivial" words, i.e. nouns, adjectives and whole phrases have been counted for each person using it at least once. The context of the word was included in ambivalent cases as commentary. Personal statements or comments on the sonification have not been taken into account.

In a quick check on the correlation of mentions of words, a small trend to using similar vocabulary within the same research group could be seen. The difference of the focus of the research groups is reflected in the language. The richness in vocabulary, i.e., the number of different words mentioned by each person, does not correlate with his/her experience in the field, but with the general talkativeness of the person.

In the next step of analysis, the words have been grouped. The categories for the groups have been determined iteratively, where final categories emerged while trying to group the data as far as possible. For instance, the words "(to) plot, display, diagram, visualization, illustrate, graphics, ..." where grouped into the category "plot".

The categories most often cited in the interviews are "data analysis", "simulation", "description of climate phenomena", and "data properties", which is not surprising because of the task the participants have been asked to show. Comparing the master-master communication in the focus groups and the master-layman communication in the personal interviews, it turned out that in the latter condition the scientists talked more about general phenomena and less about data analysis.

The top-20-sub-categories used by the subjects in interviews and focus groups are listed in Table 3. The words have been translated to English by the authors. The total maximum possible is 25, i.e., when all 17 interviewees and all 8 speakers in focus groups used it. This listing shows that

1. Climate scientists use visualization as a basis of their work (e.g., number 1 "look at" and 2 "plot");
2. Temperature is the most important climate parameter they are interested in (number 6);
3. In terms of working style, programming is the daily job of most of the scientists (e.g., climate model, program structure);
4. And the mathematics used is often rather basic, e.g., "difference" is still in the top 10, the most important basic method when comparing data sets amongst each other.

Regarding the generalized categories "data" and "climate phenomenon", it turned out that for data analysis the most important method is correlating or finding relations between two data sets. Also visual analysis is often used. Next, preparatory steps are important, including for instance data acquisition, listing, simple calculations, calibration, and transformation of grids, sorting and retrieval. When describing phenomena, subjects mostly use comparisons; followed by logical, emotional (good/bad, interesting), and aesthetical statements (beautiful/not).

In general, few metaphors have been found in the collected words. Even in the master-to-layman condition, the participants used the standard vocabulary of science. In the contextual analysis these terms cannot be interpreted as metaphors, but become metaphoric when shifted to the auditory domain. Therefore we attempted to collect such "metaphoric" climate terms.

- Climate data is inherently dynamic: climate scientists "run a simulation" or collect time series data; Therefore, in general, the time axis can be used as direction of reading for the playback independently of further processing, filtering, amplification, etc., that depend on the specific sonification design.

- Periodicities and any associated type of wave phenomena play an important role in climate science and can directly be linked to sound oscillation and rhythmic phenomena.

- Resolution is a big topic in climate science, when comparing different data sets with each other or trying to find phenomena at a certain range; resolution in audio is given by the sampling rate. It can be changed by interpolation, that the scientists are used to as well, e.g., when fitting a plot.

- Missing data play a large role in climate science; an obvious analogy is making them hearable as breaks, which can be used for a quick scanning of the completeness of a data set.

- The ensemble in climate science is a group of data sets resulting from different runs of a simulation. Because a single outcome is always the product of random processes, only the ensemble of many simulations can be regarded as trustworthy; in music, an ensemble is a group of different instruments – the metaphor can be used by mapping, e.g., different models on different sound colors.

- Noise – climate scientists who work with measurement data or with simulation data both know about the signal-to-noise ratio; one participant called the atmosphere "noisy", when a high amount of greenhouse gases was to be found there; the scientists search for long-term trends within the noisy/ random behavior of everyday weather. These ideas can directly be associated with noise in sound.

- Obvious mapping strategies comprise the height dimension in climate data (altitude) to the height in sound (pitch), but also temperature has a very tight association to mapping to pitch; the geographical spread can be used for spatial rendering of audio.

- Weather phenomena are linked to typical sounds and can be used, e.g., rain or wind sounds.

- On a more conceptual level, terms as for instance "extreme", "dramatic" or "beautiful" will have to be transferred to the sound design and evaluated in listening tests by the future users.

- Furthermore, the control of the audio interface will involve actions that climate scientists are used to anyway, e.g., calibrating or filtering data/ sound.

Sonification Platform

Classical approaches of data sonification (Hermann et al., 2011) consist of audification, parameter mapping, earcons and auditory icons, and model-based sonification. All possible methods of digital signal processing can be used for creating sonifications, e.g., wave shaping, FM synthesis, granular synthesis, physical modeling, and spatial rendering. Depending on different tasks, a combination of all of them will be built into the audio tool.

From the quantitative analysis of software tools we decided to build our system on top of ncview, a simple open-source command line tool, that most of the climate scientists at Wegener center are comfortable with. From the workflow analysis we identified three main categories of tasks that could involve sonification and have to be implemented in the audio tool: quick-scans (checking the plausibility of data), comparing different data sets in details (including different options of zooming, filtering, and overlapping), and creating sound files to present the data in simple standard format (stereo). The system shall work interactively with a GUI and can be calibrated for personalized sound settings. The analysis of visualizations that are used showed that the amount and dimensionality of data being displayed within one analysis is huge and the resulting plots often confusing. The audio display should therefore serve as an additional information channel to the visualizations.

The contextual analysis gave hints on how the cognitive process of understanding data is implemented in every-day climate science; statistical methods, programming individual applications, and visualizing at all stages of the process are key factors. The discussion of metaphors shall be used to create the interface as intuitive as possible for climate scientists. These results are probably most relevant for the sound design, but also most difficult to transfer. Mappings will follow simple intuitive basics, e.g., temperature to pitch, location to spatial rendering, etc., and the sound design shall evoke climate associations that are straightforward, e.g., as known from climate conditions.

The sonification framework we are implementing provides an application-programming interface (API) which connects data I/O, visual and auditory display. A standalone application provides both a graphical user interface and a text-based shell. The application can easily incorporate libraries running on the Java Virtual Machine, such as our sound synthesis layer and the NetCDF interface. Furthermore, third party numerical computing libraries can be easily integrated into the application to enable more complex computing. Communication with external clients such as Ncview is possible through the OSC protocol. The framework functions as analysis tool for the

climate scientists and development environment for the sonification designers.

Sound Design

In the current stage of the project, conceptual links between climate science and sound have been elaborated and first sonification designs have been developed. Aesthetical preference of the climate scientists and the intuitive mapping of climate characteristics to sound parameters are very crucial and be- ing explored in two sets of experiments.

For these experiments 24 sound samples of 10 seconds duration each were used. We chose these sounds from a database so that each three would constitute a group thematically or metaphorically connected to one of eight climate parameters determined in workflow analysis: Temperature, Precipitation, Air Humidity, Pressure, Geopotential height, Refractivity, Radiation, Wind. The reason for this selection was to provide a broad range of sounds which can be used to elucidate whether the climate scientists will be able to associate these sounds to parameters of their domain, and whether this association is unanimous.

Each experiment was divided into two sections; the purpose of the first stage was mainly to evaluate the sound samples (stimuli) aesthetically, and the second part for mapping the stimuli to the climate parameters. Altogether each experiment took between 35–45 minutes. The participants were given identical settings, listening to the stimuli via the same type of headphones.

Participants were presented eight groups of three stimuli. After listening to each group of each three, they were supposed to indicate which of the three they liked the most on a scale from 1 ("not at all") to 9 ("very much"). Furthermore they were asked to describe the characteristic that they liked about it. In the second round, they heard the same 24 stimuli one after another but with a random order. They were handed a list of climate related parameters and for each sound sample, they were asked to chose which parameter best correlates to the sample they just listened to. Each sound stimulus is about 10 seconds and there was a 10 seconds break between successive stimuli to give the participant time for evaluation or mapping.

In order to control the effect of auditory experience and music knowledge on evaluating the aesthetics of sounds, the experiment was repeated on two different groups of participants. The first group are the domain scientists (the climate scientists), and the second group are all sound experts from Institute of Electronic Music and Acoustics in Graz (http://iem.kug.ac.at). The first group is taken as our experimental group (EG) and the sound experts as control group (CG). The project and the goals of the experiments were briefly explained to both groups before the experiments. Additionally, the climate parameters were briefly explained to the sound experts since they did not have the domain knowledge.

Most of the sounds used in these two experiments were recorded sounds from nature (rain, wind, earthquake, etc.) The reason we chose these is that they are the closest to the climate phenomenon and they are more bearable to listen to in the long run [the soundscape book by Schafer]. Further-more, we added some synthesized sounds to the mix to rep- resent more abstract climate parameters such as radiation and refractivity.

The hypothesis was that the experimental group (EG) would rate all stimuli lower than control group (CG) because of not being used to actively listening to non-musical sounds. Surprisingly the EG rated most stimuli (70%) higher than the CG did. That shows a general openness of the participants to an auditory interface. The only stimulus that was rated significantly higher by the CG is number 16 (see Figure 2). The reason could be that this stimulus is the most synthetic sound and furthest to natural sounds within the corpus.

Parameter Mapping

In the second round of experiments, each participant was supposed to map the sound samples to one of eight climate parameters mentioned above. The hypothesis was that each group of three stimuli represents one specific climate param- eter (by our own judgement as sound experts). The results (see Figure 3) show that for most categories (6 out of

Figure 2. The aesthetically preference of stimuli by EG and CG

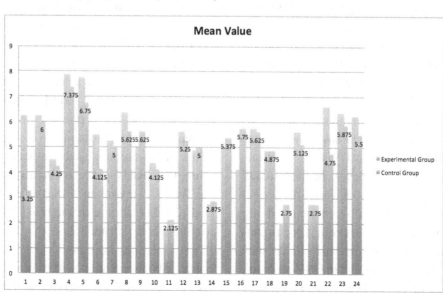

8), the EG and the CG mapped the same parameter to the sounds. Two parameters (Temperature and Geopotential Height) have not been mapped to the stimuli often enough or have not been mapped to the same sounds by both groups. The authors assume these difficulties arose from the fact that these parameters, unlike for example wind, do not have straight forward sound cor- relates in everyday experience. On the other hand, the same could be said about radiation which was mapped consistently, perhaps because we have stronger cultural conventions as what may appear (in a movie, etc.) as a sound correlate of radiation.

Therefore further research and experiments are essential to find optimal soundscapes for these parameters and to understand their metaphorical implications better. At least we could start with sounds that are perceptually closer to the ones that were elected most by participants, even though they were not significantly chosen. E.g. stimulus number 14 has been mapped to Geopotential Height by 7 EG participants but was not the most preferred sound among the group of three (13, 14, 15). In future work, we could create sounds that have similarities to 14 but not having all auditory characteristics of it.

FUTURE RESEARCH DIRECTIONS

The interaction design and sound design of our sonification tool is part of an iterative approach. The initial needs assessments and user tests made the work process and the terminology of climate scientists clear. Furthermore, the experiments discussed in this chapter evaluated our primary sound design, which leads to a more advanced soundscape and improvement of the auditory display. The next steps are to evaluate the dynamics of sounds and see how and if they correlate with related climate phenomena. Those experiments should be designed within the tool to give the participants the option to interact with the user interface and adjusting the sound dynamically while analyzing data. To intensify the interdisciplinary work setting within the project, we would also bring in both sonification experts and domain scientists from climate science to work together using our sonification platform and create sonifications collaboratively in the form of several workshops and training sessions.

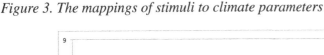

Figure 3. The mappings of stimuli to climate parameters

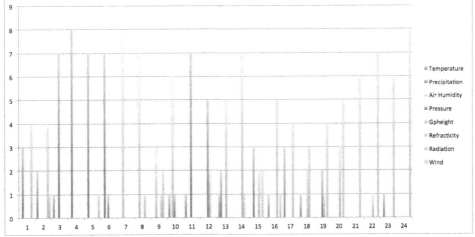

CONCLUSION

In this chapter we introduced sonification - the use of non-speech audio to convey information - and the use of it to create a multi modal interface to analyze climate data. We discussed the advantages of our auditory perception and the conditions that are suitable for the use of such a powerful technique (sonification) in an information-overloaded world. In terms of the systematic design process, we also consider tracking both the sound design process from our side as well as the interaction of the climate scientists with the framework. Several aspects found in visualisation, such as overlaying graphs, highlighting regions, showing differences and error boundaries, adding threshold guides, adding labels to particular parts of a plot, and so forth, were studied in terms of potential analogues in the auditory domain.

We hope that this chapter touches the surface to encourage data scientists to use multi-modal interfaces in the complex tasks of data analysis to extract features and patterns that are hidden while using one modality.

REFERENCES

Aiken, C., et al. (2012). Shaking up earth science: Visual and auditory representation of earthquake interactions. In *Proceedings of the 18th International Conference on Auditory Display*. Atlanta, GA: Georgia Institute of Technology Publishing.

Bearman, N. (2011). Using sound to represent uncertainty in future climate projections for the United Kingdom. In *Proceedings of the 17th International Conference on Auditory Display*. Budapest, Hungary: Academic Press.

Bregman, A. S. (1990). *Auditory Scene Analysis: The Perceptual Organization of Sound*. Cambridge, MA: MIT Press.

Crystal, A., & Ellington, B. (2004). Task analysis and human-computer interaction: approaches, techniques, and levels of analysis. In *Proceedings of the Tenth Americas Conference on Information Systems*, (pp. 391-397). New York: Association for Information Systems.

Flowers, J. H. et al. (1996). Desktop Data Sonification: Comments on Flowers et al. *ACM Transactions on Applied Perception*, 2(4), 473–476. doi:10.1145/1101530.1101545

Frauenberger, C. (2009). *Auditory Display Design*. (Unpublished PhD Thesis). Queen Mary University of London, London, UK.

Halim, Z., et al. (2006). Sonification: A Novel Approach towards Data mining. In *Proceedings of IEEE International Conference on Emerging Technologies*. Peshawar, Pakistan: IEEE.

Hermann, T., et al. (2002). Sonifications for EEG data analysis. In *Proceedings of the 8th International Conference on Auditory Display*, (pp. 37-41). Kyoto, Japan: The International Community for Auditory Display.

Hermann, T. et al. (2011). *The Sonification Handbook*. Berlin: Logos Publishing.

Karat, C., et al. (1992). Comparison of empirical testing and walkthrough methods in user interface evaluation. In *Proceedings of CHI92 Human Factors in Computing Systems*, (pp. 397-404). New York: ACM Publishing.

Kramer, G. et al. (1999). *The sonification report: Status of the field and research agenda (Technical report)*. National Science Foundation.

Mayring, P. (2010). *Qualitative Inhaltsanalyse*. Beltz Publishing.

Polli, A. (2004). Atmospherics/Weather works: A multi-channel storm sonification project. In *Proceedings of the 10th International Conference on Auditory Display*. Sydney, Australia: Georgian Institute of Technology.

Vogt, K., et al. (2008). Exploration of 4d-data spaces. Sonification of lattice QCD. In *Proceedings of the 14th International Conference on Auditory Display*. Paris, France: International Community for Auditory Display Publishing.

Vogt, K., & Höldrich, R. (2010). A metaphoric sonification method - towards the acoustic standard model of particle physics. In *Proceedings of the 16th International Conference on Auditory Display*. Washington, DC: International Community for Auditory Display Publishing.

ADDITIONAL READING

Barrass, S. (1997). Auditory Information Design. Ph.D. Thesis, Austrialian National University.

Ben-Tal, O., & Berger, J. (2004). Creative aspects of sonification. *Leonardo*, *37*(3), 229–232. doi:10.1162/0024094041139427

Bregman, A. S. (1990). *Auditory Scene Analysis: The Perceptual Organization of Sound*. Cambridge, Massachusetts: The MIT Press.

Brewster, S. A. (1994) Providing a structured method for integrating non-speech audio into human-computer interfaces. PhD thesis, University of York, York, UK.

Chai, W. (2006). Semantic segmentation and summarization of music. *IEEE Signal Processing Magazine*, (March): 124–132. doi:10.1109/MSP.2006.1598088

Cherryand, E. C., & Taylor, W. K. (1954). Some further experiments on the recognition of speech with one and two ears. *The Journal of the Acoustical Society of America*, *26*, 549–554.

Chowning, J. M. (1977, June). The simulation of moving sound sources. *Computer Music Journal*, *1*(3), 48–52. doi:10.2307/3679609

Chowning, J. M. (1980). Frequency modulation synthesis of the singing voice. In M.V. Mathews and J.R.Pierce, editors, Current Directions in Computer Music Research Cambridge, pages 57–63. MIT Press.

Diniz, N., Demey, M., & Leman, M. (2010) An interactive framework for multilevel sonification. In B. Bresin, T. Hermann, and A. Hunt, editors, Proceedings of ISon 2010, 3rd Interactive Sonification Workshop, KTH, Stockholm, Sweden, April 7.

Dolson, M., & Laroche, J. (1999). Improved phase vocoder time-scale modification of audio. *IEEE Transactions on Speech and Audio Processing*, *7*(3), 323–332. doi:10.1109/89.759041

Duda, R. O., & Hart, P. E and.Stork, D.G. (2001) Pattern Classification. Wiley-Interscience, New York, USA.

Ferguson, S. (2009). Exploratory Sound Analysis: Statistical Sonifications for the Investigation of Sound. Ph.D. Thesis, The University of Sydney.

Flowers, J. H., Buhman, D. C., & Turnage, K. D. (1997). Cross-modal equivalence of visual and auditory scatter plots for exploring bivariate data samples. *Human Factors*, *39*(3), 341–351. doi:10.1518/001872097778827151 PMID:9394628

Grond, F., & Hermann, T. (2011). Singing function, exploring auditory graphs with a vowel based sonification. Journal on Multimodal User Interfaces.

Hand, D. J., Manila, H., & Smyth, P. (2001). *Principles of Data Mining: Adaptive Computation and Machine Learning*. Cambridge: MIT Press.

Hayward, Ch. (1994). Listening to the Earth Sing. In G. Kramer (Ed.), *Auditory Display. Sonification, Audification, and Auditory Interfaces* (pp. 369–404). Reading: Addison-Wesley.

Hermann, T. (2002). Sonification for Exploratory Data Analysis. Ph.D. Thesis.

Hermann, T., Bovermann, T., Riedenklau, B., & Ritter, H. (2007). Tangible Computing for Interactive Sonification of Multivariate Data. In *International Workshop on Interactive Sonification,* York, UK.

Hermann, T., & Hunt, A. (2005). An introduction to interactive sonification. *IEEE MultiMedia, 12*(2), 20–24. doi:10.1109/MMUL.2005.26

Hermann, T., & Ritter, H. (1999). Listen to your data: Model-based sonification for data analysis. In G.E.Lasker, ed., Advances in intelligent computing and multimedia systems, pp. 189–194. Int. Inst. for Advanced Studies in System research and cybernetics, Baden-Baden, Germany.

Kramer, G., Walker, B. N., Bonebright, T., Cook, P. R., Flowers, J. H., Miner, N., & Neuhoff, J. G. (1997). *Sonification report: Status of the field and research agenda. Technical report.* National Science Foundation.

Nesbitt, K., & Barrass, S. (2004). Finding Trading Patterns in Stock Market Data. *IEEE Computer Graphics, 24*(5), 45–55. doi:10.1109/MCG.2004.28 PMID:15628100

Pollack, I., & Ficks, L. (1954). Information of elementary multidimensional auditory displays. *The Journal of the Acoustical Society of America, 26*(1), 155–158. doi:10.1121/1.1907300

Pulkki, V. (1997). Virtual sound source positioning using vector base amplitude panning. *In Journal of the Audio Engineering Society, 45*(6), 456–466.

Rath, M., & Rocchesso, D. (2005). *Continuous sonic feedback from a rolling ball.* IEEE Interactive Sonification.

Speeth, S. D. (1961). Seismometer Sounds. *The Journal of the Acoustical Society of America, 33,* 909–916. doi:10.1121/1.1908843

Sterne, J. (2003). *The Audible Past: Cultural origins of sound reproduction.* Durham: Duke University Press.

Tukey, J. W. (1977). *Exploratory Data Analysis.* Reading, Mass.: Addison-Wesley.

Tzanetakis, G. (2002). Manipulation, Analysis And Retrieval Systems For Audio Signals. PhD thesis, Princeton University.

Walker, B. N. (2002). Magnitude estimation of conceptual data dimensions for use in sonification. *Journal of Experimental Psychology. Applied, 8*(4), 211–221. doi:10.1037/1076-898X.8.4.211 PMID:12570096

Walker, B. N., & Lindsay, J. (2006). Navigation performance with a virtual auditory display: Effects of beacon sound, capture radius, and practice. *Human Factors, 48*(2), 265–278. doi:10.1518/001872006777724507 PMID:16884048

Ware, C. (2000). *Information visualization: Perception for design.* Morgan Kaufman, San Francisco.

Williamson, J., & Murray-Smith, R. (2005). Sonification of probabilistic feedback through granular synthesis. *IEEE MultiMedia, 12*(2), 5–52. doi:10.1109/MMUL.2005.37

Worrall, D. (2009) Sonification and Information - Concepts, Instruments and Techniques. PhD thesis, University of Canberra.

KEY TERMS AND DEFINITIONS

Auditory Display: The use of sound to communicate information from a computer to the user.

Interaction Design: About shaping digital things for people's use, alternately defined as "the practice of designing interactive digital products, environments, systems, and services.

Multimodal Interaction: Provides the user with multiple modes of interfacing with a system.

A multimodal interface provides several distinct tools for input and output of data.

Sonic Interaction Design: The study and exploitation of sound as one of the principal channels conveying information, meaning, and aesthetic/emotional qualities in interactive contexts. Sonic interaction design is at the intersection of interaction design and sound and music computing.

Sonification: The use of non-speech audio to convert information.

Sound and Music Computing: A research field that studies the whole sound and music communication chain from a multidisciplinary point of view. By combining scientific, technological and artistic methodologies it aims at understanding, modeling and generating sound and music through computational approaches.

User Centered Design: A process (not restricted to interfaces or technologies) in which the needs, wants, and limitations of end users of a product, service or process are given extensive attention at each stage of the design process.

ENDNOTES

1   http://meteora.ucsd.edu/~pierce/ncview_home_page.html

Chapter 2
Changing Paradigms in Our Interactions with Self-Service Kiosks

Aslı Günay
Middle East Technical University, Turkey

Çiğdem Erbuğ
Middle East Technical University, Turkey

Paul Hekkert
Delft University of Technology, The Netherlands

Natalia Romero Herrera
Delft University of Technology, The Netherlands

ABSTRACT

Human-computer interaction and holistic user experiences are considered crucial concepts in the design of interactive products, where interactive self-service kiosks require special attention, as they are different than any other type of consumer and personal products. The public nature of self-service kiosks suggests that social context may have an important role in understanding the experience of users when interacting with such products. Yet, this is hardly reflected in the development of self-service kiosks in which usefulness and functionality are still the basic, and usually the only, concerns. This limited discussion hinders innovation when redesigning this type of product. This chapter firstly studies the major factors affecting users' interactions with self-service kiosks, followed by the influence of presence or absence of other people on user experience with interactive self-service kiosks looking at the relationships between different social contexts, feelings, and task performances; it then elaborates on task performances. The studies conducted to explore these relations reveal that interactions with interactive self-service kiosks are specialized according to different task qualities that these kiosks serve as well as the social context, which highlights the necessity to take into account the inseparable context during the design of these self-service kiosks. They emphasize that not only the product interface but also other product features, product body, and context should be shaped by these task qualities and the social context. Hence, suggested design implications go beyond traditional usability and technical issues, considering social context as a key issue to address innovative self-service kiosk designs.

DOI: 10.4018/978-1-4666-6228-5.ch002

1. INTRODUCTION

Over the last decade, design literature is moving its focus from product to user, where special attention is given to user experience in relation to product interaction (Desmet & Hekkert, 2007; Schifferstein & Hekkert, 2008). Design for user experience addresses issues beyond the traditional usability and technical concerns, and involves hedonic and emotional experiences and benefits like pleasure in products (Jordan, 1999; 2000). Most research on user experience has focused in the private domain of consumer products although it is known that experiences also affect the interaction of public products like interactive self-service kiosks where the interaction is automated by technology. Such interactive self-service kiosks offer generic interactions, which are often experienced as unfamiliar and alien to potential users. In particular, automated teller machines, ticket vending machines, food or drink dispensers, self-service check-in or check-out kiosks are placed in a context where users have to use them in limited time and in presence of other people around. Regarding this distinctive interaction, social context, which is handled hereby as the presence or absence of other people, is expected to have a significant influence during users' experiences with the self-service kiosks. However, holistic studies related to self-service kiosks are rare and primarily focused on pragmatic aspects with minimal attention to user experience (e.g. Maguire, 1999; Zhu, Nakata, Sivakumar, & Grewal, 2007)

Social psychology literature hints that the effects of other people's presence, i.e. social influence, are of great importance while people are conducting tasks. It is comprehended that even the mere presence of other people has an effect on task performances (Zajonc, 1965). Diverse tasks have been examined while attempting to understand and demonstrate the reasons and results of the effects of the presence of other people (Allport, 1924; Dashiell, 1930; Triplett, 1898). However,

the point of interest has not been the products or the relationships between them; rather different motor and cognitive tasks have been in question (Strauss, 2002). Acknowledging the significant effect of social context in the interaction with self-service kiosks, the following paper presents the results of three empirical studies evaluating the use of self-service kiosks beyond usability issues. In the subsequent section, context and social context related theories are introduced. Then, the empirical studies investigating the importance of presence of other people during users' experiences with self-service kiosks are described. After, feeding from these inputs, possible design interventions are discussed.

2. AN UNDERSTANDING OF THE SOCIAL CONTEXT

User experience is encapsulated as the awareness of the affective phenomenon stemming from the users' interactions with products like the stimulation of senses, attribution of values and meanings, and elicitation of emotions (Schifferstein & Hekkert, 2008). This gives insights into the diversity of factors involved and the different disciplines dealing with the term 'experience'. A large body of literature among different disciplines indicates that experience is a complex and multidimensional phenomenon. It is affected greatly from the users' internal state, products' or systems' features, and context (Hassenzahl & Tractinsky, 2006).

Context takes an important place and has been addressed numerous times in diverse disciplines, such as HCI, design, sociology, psychology, and so on, as an important aspect effecting individuals' experiences (Cooper, 1991; Dourish, 2004; Suchman, 1987). Considering HCI and design literature, ignoring the usage context of a product or system has been reported as a major problem eventuating in usability studies (Chamorro-Koc, 2007). Context is a dynamic concept encompassing various relationships between the situation, goal, action, and interaction. These relationships bring about different understandings to the users. So, it is an important part of user experience and it gives meaning to the experiences (Pullman, 2002). Different contexts bring about different interactions, resulting in different comprehension and knowledge of product use, meaning that users' understanding of a product is not only related to the product's features; it is prompted by the product's contextual information, as well. Context encompasses social, experiential, cultural, and other contextual factors which influence how people relate to products (Hekkert & Van Dijk, 2001). It can be said that people's interactions with products are informed by and situated in a specific context, culture, condition, and experience (Suchman, 1987). This hints that how people relate to the products depend also on the specific context of use with the people around or not.

Forlizzi and Battarbee (2004) focused on the social context. They addressed the importance of users' experiences with products within the context of social interactions. Regarding their approach, user experience can be referred as co-experience when it is shared and created with other people.

In social psychology, social influence can be explained by the alterations in an individual's ideas, affective experiences, and behaviors due to interaction with other people (Rashotte, 2007). Especially social psychology literature provides a wealthy research work explicating the social influence. The focus has been mainly on how attitudes, feelings, and manners of people are influenced by the physical or imagined presence of other people. It is seen that even the smallest social context "one person with another" brings about changes in the arousal levels, alertness, attentional processes, and social valuation (Guerin & Innes, 1984). Also, changes in person's performances have been in consideration. Influence on the performances have been investigated majorly under the term 'social facilitation' which was pulled away from its real meaning over time addressing both facilitation and impairment. Diverse evidences have been

found showing that the presence of other people can either improve (Allport, 1924; Triplett, 1898) or worsen (Dashiell, 1930) task performances.

Additional researches have revealed that there are different variables playing a role in how people are affected by the presence of other people (audiences, co-actors, etc.); such as the type of task being conducted (Dashiell, 1930). Researchers have tried to classify different variables under common theories regarding the sources of social facilitation. Activation theories and attention theories are the mostly addressed ones. Activation theories highlight the arousal and drive processes as the social facilitation source; whereas, attention theories approach to the social facilitation reasoning the attentional processes.

Activation theories include generalized drive (Zajonc, 1965), alertness and monitoring (Guerin & Innes, 1985; Zajonc, 1980), evaluation apprehension (Cottrell, 1972; Henchy & Glass, 1968), challenge and threat (Blascovich, Mendes, Hunter, & Salomon, 1999) perspectives. Briefly, according to the generalized drive hypothesis, the apt response of a person is brought about during the presence of others. That is to say, if the task is simple, easy, and repeated many times, then the performance would probably be enhanced. Oppositely, if the task is complex, difficult and novel to a person, then the performance would probably go inferior. According to the alertness hypothesis, when other people are present, a person cannot know how to act which triggers alertness in that person and the corresponding preparedness for an unanticipated situation. Thus, the increase in alertness gives rise to facilitation in task performances. In terms of monitoring hypothesis, the unfamiliarity of the person who monitors an individual or the unfamiliarity of the situation leads to increase of uncertainty and arousal of the individual. According to diverse evaluation apprehension approaches concern about being evaluated (Henchy & Glass, 1968) and learned drive (Cottrell, 1972; Cottrell, Wack, Sekerak, & Rittle, 1968) could bring about changes in activation, arousal and changes in behaviors. Challenge and threat approach have dealt with the simplicity and internalization of the tasks and the task performance; and, cardiovascular processes have been consulted to explain the influence. So, if a person is conducting an easy and well-learned task, this results in a regular cardio-vascular process as observed usually when there is a challenge. Nevertheless, if a person is performing a difficult task, the cardio-vascular response resembles to the response when the person is under a threatening situation, which leads to an inferior performance.

Attention theories encompass the distraction- conflict theory, which is related to allocated attention and distraction due to the presence of others (Sanders & Baron, 1975). Sanders, Baron and Moore (1978) presented that there occurs an arousal in the presence of other people, but because of the conflict in the attention. Again relationships have been established between easy tasks- increased performance and difficult tasks-impaired performances. Despite the reason of the changes is an arousal, this theory is usually investigated under attention theories since the reason of the arousal is related to the attentional processes. Overload in the cognition can be also observed if there are people present when a person is performing a task (Baron, 1986). The overwhelming information coming both from the task being conducted and the people around causes distraction, and correspondingly, decrease in performance in complex tasks.

There are also other theories and studies which do not fit in the above mentioned classification. Social comparison and self presentation theories have also been introduced accounting for the social facilitation. Baumeister (1982) asserted that when there are people present, people are motivated by a desire to please them and to construct a certain public image. Bond (1982) acclaimed that when performed tasks are difficult, the will for the favorable self presentation results in being ashamed, stressed, and so, in inferior performances. However, on easy tasks, more attention can be given,

leading to better performances. Latané (1981) revealed that the number, strength and immediacy of the effects increase the social impact on an individual. In other words, the amount of the other people present, their relevance and prominence would promote the social facilitation effects. In addition, he mentioned that when the number, immediacy and strength of an impact are distributed over several targets, the social impact on an individual would decrease.

Apart from the aforementioned studies, there are also a number of researches in both social psychology discipline (Diener, 1979; Festinger, Pepitone, & Newcomb, 1952; Latane & Darley, 1970; LeBon, 1895; Zimbardo, 1969) and other disciplines (Bearden & Etzel, 1982; Ratner & Kahn, 2002) which are not related to task performance directly; yet, they show that when other people are present, individuals tends to act differently than they are alone.

Despite the rich body of research about social influence in social psychology, there are only few studies about the effects of other people on user experience in HCI literature, especially regarding the self-service kiosks. Benford and Giannachi (2012) pointed out that daily interactions have changed and turned out to be performative with the proliferation of computers in public areas since those interactions are observed by other people. Due to the social context in public areas, social embarrassment might hinder people from approaching to the self-service kiosks as Brignull and Rogers (2003) exemplified with large public displays.

3. USER EXPERIENCE ISSUES WITH SELF-SERVICE KIOSKS

The brief review above demonstrates the importance of considering social context in the design of interactive self-service kiosks. It can be assumed accordingly that user experience with self-service kiosks can be highly affected from the presence

Figure 1. The stages during the exploration of user experience with self-service kiosks

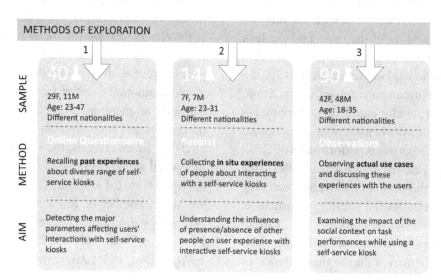

of other people, either in a positive or negative way. The effects can be on diverse dimensions of user experience. Bethinking all these issues, the authors aimed to answer three questions by conducting three studies following a method as shown in Figure 1. These questions were:

- What are the major parameters affecting users interactions with self-service kiosks?
- How users' interactions with the self-service kiosks are affected during the presence and absence of other people?
- How users' task performances change according to different social contexts?

3.1 Methods of Exploration

3.1.1 Online Questionnaire

For understanding the major parameters effecting user – self-service kiosk interactions, a questionnaire was distributed using an online survey platform. It grounded on recalling the past experiences about diverse range of self-service kiosks.

The questionnaire included a brief introduction about the aim and content of the study, and short demographics questions. It proceeded with three main parts. In the first part, eight different self-service kiosks were presented enquiring frequency of use and main concerns of using them or not, ranging from security, social pressure, product design, to technical problems. This part was designed to stimulate the participants to recall their interactions with different self-service kiosks, and desirably, eliciting the role of social context in these interactions. In the second part, participants were requested to remember two very bad and two very pleasant experiences with self-service kiosks. Questions were asked regarding the type of self-service kiosks, usage time, context, interaction, concerns, and feelings. In order to facilitate the recalling and expression of feelings, the PMRI tool was used (Vastenburg, Romero Herrera, Van Bel, & Desmet, 2011); in addition to an 'other' option incase participants would feel differently and would want to express their feelings in other words. In the final part of the questionnaire, participants' suggestions to improve the user experience with self-service kiosks were collected.

A total of 40 participants responded to the questionnaire (29 Female, 11 Male), ages ranging between 23 and 47. The sample was composed of participants from different nationalities (13 Turkish, 7 Dutch, 5 Iranian, 4, Italian, 2 German, 2 Bulgarian, 1, Hungarian, 1 Spanish, 1 Latvian, 1 Greek, 1 Chinese, 1 Russian/Swedish, and 1 Colombian) in order to eliminate the probability of finding evidences related or specific to a certain group/nationality since social influence might differ from culture to culture.

3.1.2 Booklet

For understanding how users' experiences could change regarding the presence or absence of other people, a booklet study was conducted. Hereby, participants mentioned about their fresh and situated experiences just after interacting with any type of self-service kiosks. This was necessary since people have hard time to remember their previous experiences and might only recall overall feelings related to them. Moreover, the social context was more explicitly investigated by asking direct questions.

The booklet started with an introduction about the aim and content of the study. Participants were instructed hereby to fill in the booklet every time after using self-service kiosks.

Participants were instructed to describe up to 7 experiences of interacting with a self-service kiosk or as many as they experience within 2 weeks. Afterwards, they were asked to send the booklets back to the researcher. To describe an experience, participants were first asked to indicate the type of self-service kiosk used. The booklet then was divided into two parts, pre-use time and use time: time in the waiting line (if there was a line of people before them) and time while interacting, respectively. The first part of the experience, which is related to the waiting time, asked to report the amount of the people in the queue before the participant and the feelings elicited during this stage. The PMRI mood chart was used again to collect participants' feelings during this pre-use stage. In the second part of the experience, similar

questions were asked and the same mood chart was given. Nevertheless, the focus was on the 'use' stage rather than the 'pre-use'. Finally, in the last part of each experience, questions related to the effects of presence of other people during the experience and suggestions related to both the social context and product properties were asked. During this stage, to understand the effects on task performances, pre-defined task performances were presented: duration of use, ease of use, ease of remember, number of errors, satisfaction. This provided standardization among the answer types, facilitating the comparison and analysis.

Participants were expected to report their experiences with one or many self-service kiosk types.

Booklets were handed out to 14 participants (7 Female, 7 Male). Ages were ranging between 23 and 31. Participants were from different nationalities (2 Dutch, 2 Turkish, 2 Italian, 2 Mexican, 2 Korean, 1 German, 1 Argentinean, 1 Colombian, and 1 Chinese).

3.1.3 Observations

Finally, in order to further investigate the impact of the presence or absence of other people on task performances, observations were done involving the realization of one familiar task and one unfamiliar task in three different social contexts during interacting with one specific type of self-service kiosk – public coffee machine: when no one present apart from the user, when there was a queue, and when there were scattered people around.

For the familiar task, participants bought a cup of coffee according to their preferences; whereas, for the unfamiliar task, a specific type of coffee with specific sugar and milk settings were assigned. This final stage also included a short questionnaire and interviews with participants to be able compare their actual use with their perceived effects of the social contexts and perceived task performances.

90 participants were involved during this stage (42 Female, 48 Male). More specifically, 30 par-

ticipants were present for each of the three social contexts. Ages were ranging between 18 and 35. The sample was composed again of participants from different nationalities.

3.2 Themes of Experience

Content analysis was the main analysis method for all of the stages. Experiences gathered from the participants were read through, important segments were coded and then themes were generated. Both inductive and deductive coding were done. I.e., the codes were not predefined before the data analysis, they emerged from the data, but some of the assigned codes were familiar from the literature.

For answering the initial question, collected experiences were categorized according to meaningful segments and the most recurring patterns, which constitute the themes about user experience with self-service kiosks: major parameters, task qualities, social context types, feelings, task performances. Before proceeding with the details of the themes, it would be beneficial to explain each of them very shortly.

Major parameters refer to the main concerns of the users while interacting with self-service kiosks. In other words, major parameters are the main factors effecting how users interact with these products. *Task qualities* theme is about different task types and task specific concerns. *Social context types* incorporate the diverse situations about the absence or presence of other people. *Feelings* theme, as the name implies, is about the feelings elicited by the users while interacting with self-service kiosks. Finally, *task performance* refers to the duration, accuracy, and completion of the tasks.

3.2.1 Which Factors Affect Our Interactions With Self-Service Kiosks?

Understanding the major factors affecting users' interactions with self-service kiosks was the primary aim; hence, *major parameters* theme was

examined in detail. Usability, functionality, social context, usefulness, and pleasure in use appeared as major parameters. Table 1 demonstrates the content of each parameter. The numbers in parentheses refer to the number of statements of each major parameter. In 23 out of the 91 experiences social context, i.e. the presence or absence of other people, was the major parameter affecting the interactions, either in a positive or negative way.

It is seen that with 25%, social context took an important place among all other factors affecting users' interactions with self-service kiosks. Actually, it can be said that it had almost as much significance as the de facto pragmatic aspects like usability and functionality. The prominence of these pragmatic aspects could be anticipated as they directly affect the realization of the goals while interacting with all types of products; yet, the weight of the social context showed the necessity to consider social context especially in such publicly used products.

3.2.2 Does The Interaction Differ According To The Types Of Kiosks?

While the major factors affecting users' interactions with self-service kiosks and social context's place among them were investigated, it was seen that experiences were not only affected by social context but also by task qualities, which were categorized under the *task qualities* theme. Three different task types appeared from the mentioned experiences, which are: simple task, money related task, and time limited task. To clarify, *simple task* refers to the users' interactions with self-service kiosks during which they dealt with the task itself and there were no additional concerns apart from finishing the task such as buying a cup of coffee from a public coffee machine. *Money related task* comprises the tasks during which the monetary issues and security due to dealing with money is important such as withdrawing money from an ATM. *Time limited task* included the tasks during which the time is an important concern for the

Table 1.Major parameters affecting users' interactions with self-service kiosks (Numbers represent the number of statements)

Usability (33)	• fundamental aspects related to the comprehension and use of the products
Functionality (28)	• circumstances when a self-service kiosk functioned properly or mulfunctioned
Social Context (23)	• circumstances when the presence/absence of other people affected the feelings and interactions of users
Usefulness (4)	• availaility of certain features beyond the main functions to enhance the experience
Pleasure in Use (3)	• hedonic aspects during the experiences

participants such as buying a train ticket from a ticket machine when being in a rush to catch the train. Actually, these qualities did not always appeared orthogonal since multiple concerns and situations could be observed at a time; yet, the most prominent concerns were considered hereby while defining the task qualities in order not to deviate from the main focus of the study. Figure 2 shows that the effects of the presence or absence of other people appear differently in different task types. Simple task involves all the major parameters which were demonstrated in Table 1. Mainly, usability, technical problems and social context were in the foreground. Usefulness, pleasure in use and functionality were also apparent. However, not all of the factors are present in the other task categories. Money related and time limited tasks incorporate similar concerns though their percentages are different. It is seen that the social context is equally important in all tasks. It is important to note that the total number of statements and experiences in each task are uneven since these task-related categories were not pre-defined; they were generated after gathering experiences.

3.2.3 What Are The Possible Social Contexts And Their Emotional Outcomes?

In order to understand how users' experiences could change regarding the presence or absence of other people, various feeling were investigated in relation to diverse task qualities and diverse social contexts. There were five diverse social contexts mentioned by the participants, which were named shortly as: no one, queue, queue manners, people around, queue and people around. *No one* was about the experiences during which no one was present apart from the participant as a user. *Queue* related to the experiences during which there occurred a queue behind the participant, but when there was no specific reaction from the queue. *Queue manners* was about the experiences when attitudes and behavior of the queue affected the participants. *People around* referred to the experiences when there was no queue behind the participant, but when there were just scattered or passerby people around. *Queue and people around* encompassed the social context when there were both queue and people around.

NodeXL program (Smith et al., 2009) was used to visualize these relationships (Figure 3). The gray circles refer to the changes in task performances; whereas, the colored ones represent the feelings. Feelings represented with blue are about negative feelings and with pink are about positive feelings. Lilac color refers to the situations when participants felt neutral. Also, the sizes of the circles are in relationship with the number of being stated. Furthermore, some participants mentioned about feelings without talking about how their task performances changed. These statements were referred as 'undefined effect'. This does not mean that social context did not affect them; but, no effect was mentioned.

Figure 2. Major parameters affecting users' interactions with self-service kiosks (Numbers represent the number of statements)

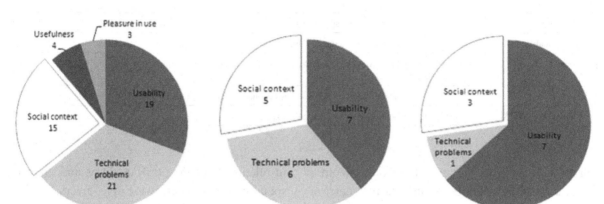

It can be seen in Figure 3 that the relationships are multidimensional. Multiple feelings were elicited sometimes, resulting in certain changes in interaction with the self-service kiosks, or vice versa. Mainly negative feelings were elicited in different task types during the presence of other people.

While conducting simple tasks, participants mostly felt neutral, relaxed, and calm considering all of the apparent types of social context types. This mainly influenced their duration of use, ease of use, and satisfaction. The negative feelings observed hereby were related to feeling irritated, tense, and ashamed. Participants were diversely affected from different negative feelings. They felt either less satisfied, did more errors, or tried to have shorter usage times.

During money related tasks, negative feelings were more dominant due to the queue and people around together with the queue. Participants mostly felt tense, which affected their ease of use and number of errors. Sometimes, they felt irritated and scared. In certain situations they felt positively, as well. Yet, these were the situations when there was no one around and when there were people scattered around. When they felt relaxed

and calm, their duration of use was longer. They did not feel pressure to use faster in these cases.

When time related task was being conducted, feeling tense was prominent. They also did errors, had difficulty in use and remember. They did not mention about change in duration of use due to these negative feelings. Yet, when they felt calm and neutral, they mentioned that their duration of use was perceived longer.

More specifically, the presence of the queue, people around apart from the queue, and manners of the people (angry, impatient, complaining, rushing, and so on) in the queue caused mainly negative feelings in the user when interacting with a self-service kiosk. These feelings caused participants to use the self-service kiosks fast, more prone to errors, with more difficulty in use and remember, and with less satisfaction. Sometimes, they even quitted their actions or refrained from the actions that they wanted to perform. Having company reduced the negative feelings of the presence of other people in one experience. Nevertheless, especially when a place was perceived as insecure due to the location and time, users felt secure if there were people in the queue or around.

In order to further investigate the impact of the presence or absence of other people on task

Figure 3. Feelings and task performance relationships in different tasks

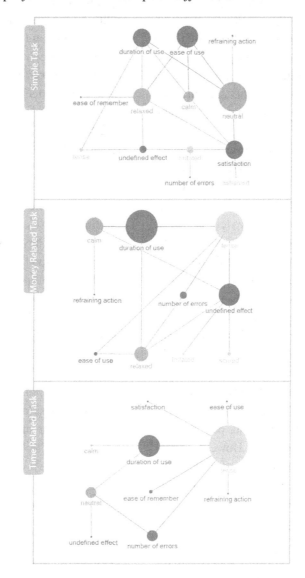

performances, three of the social contexts were focused on as aforementioned briefly: when no one was present apart from the user, when there was a queue, and when there were scattered people around. These task performances are discussed below concentrating on number of errors, durations of use, and perceived effects.

3.2.4 What Are the Social Context's Effects on Number Of Errors?

Grounding on the observations, some tendencies were found and certain interpretations were done about interactions with self-service kiosks. While participants were conducting specific unfamiliar tasks, the fewest errors were observed when the participant was alone. It can be interpreted in two different ways. Firstly, owing to eliciting comparatively more positive feelings than the conditions when there were other people, fewer errors were done. Secondly, participants might be able to concentrate more on the task since no one was around. These two interpretations might have a close link, too.

Nevertheless, surprisingly, fewer errors were done when there was a queue than when there were people around in a scattered way. This might not be expected addressing the feelings elicited. It was presumed that if more negative feelings were elicited, then inferior task performances would be brought about. This time, although the most negative feelings were observed when there was a queue, slightly fewer errors were done compared to the condition when there were people around in a scattered way. Thus, it can be inferred that because of the waiting people, participants would try to focus more on the task and try to finish it more quickly and accurately. Moreover, the people around in a scattered way could distract the participants more since, in the queue, people were behind the people in a neat way. However, when it was in the scattered way, they were more in the sight of the participants and in more dynamic way, which can distract the participants. Therefore, both the feelings and the concentration (either because of not being distracted by other people or because of the pressure of other people) would account for the trends of errors in diverse conditions while conducting the unfamiliar task.

Furthermore, participants conducted the familiar tasks almost in similar durations in different social contexts. This implies that the effects of the social context on number of errors while conducting a familiar task is less than the situations while conducting an unfamiliar task. This finding is corresponding to the majority of the literature presented previously which claimed that worse performances are observed if the tasks are unfamiliar. However, unlike this majority of the literature, no specific facilitation effects were found in the familiar tasks.

Dwelling on the number of errors to interpret the big picture, it can be said that the participants did more errors respectively when there were people, no matter how, than when there was no one.

3.2.5 What Are the Social Context's Effects on Duration of Use?

When focused on the duration of use, certain inclinations and patterns were encountered. In unfamiliar tasks, participants used the product fastest when they were alone. This is reasonable bearing in mind the number of errors done in this condition. Comparing the durations of use during the presence of other people, it was seen that participants finished their tasks quicker when there was a queue. This might have a link to the number of errors, as well. Resembling patterns were seen looking at the number of errors and durations in the unfamiliar task. Nonetheless, the trend of duration in the familiar task was not resembling to the number of errors done while conducting this task. It can be inferred that although being familiar to the task, because of pressure from the other people (again in order to use the product as fast and as accurate as possible), participants used the product fast, but with more self-confidence and less concentration due to the familiarity, which brought about more errors. Furthermore, it was seen that participants finished the familiar tasks in a shorter time than the unfamiliar tasks. This could be expected referring to the familiarity.

In brief, the differences between the duration trends in unfamiliar and familiar tasks can be elucidated addressing to the diverse aspects and variables incorporated in the study, such as self-confidence levels of participants due to the familiarity/ unfamiliarity of the tasks, concentration due to the familiarity/ unfamiliarity of the tasks, the amount of the people around, and how they were situated.

3.2.6 What Are The Social Contexts' Perceived Effects?

Participants thought that there was a small effect of the social contexts on different task performance aspects. However, as above demonstrated, it was observed from their experiences that the accuracy of use had a close link to the social contexts. Also, there was an effect on durations, too. Apart from these, according to the participants, there was no obvious effect of the social context on their ease of use, ease of remember regarding the steps in the tasks, satisfaction, and finishing the task. Nevertheless, considering the previous findings, it can be inferred that participants could have been even much more affected than what they reported. This might be because of difficulty of noticing and conveying these more implicit and latent experiences. Also, task performances such as ease of use, ease of remember, and satisfaction cannot be easily observed as duration and errors.

4. DISCUSSION

The findings above demonstrate the importance of considering social context during users' interactions with self-service kiosks. In addition to the above presented relationships, diverse product properties were also of great importance in being affected from the social context.

While investigating relations between social context, feelings, and task performances, it was observed that feelings could be elicited both due to the social context and to the properties of the self-service kiosks and related concerns towards these products. In other words, a person could elicit certain feelings because of the people around and this could affect how she or he interacts with the self-service kiosks. Also, the self-service kiosk properties could cause certain feelings which intensify or diminish the affection from the presence of the other people. As can be seen in Figure 4, social context may appear as differ-

ent patterns of presence considering queue, other people apart from the queue, and the manners of those people. Generally, social influence; i.e. being affected from the social context, was more obvious respectively in money related task, time related task, and simple task. During money related tasks, all types of social context affected users' interactions with self-service kiosks. Nonetheless, interactions during conducting time related tasks were influenced by the absence of people, presence of queue and queue's manner. That is to say, people that were scattered around and just passing by had little influence on those interactions. During simple tasks, majorly queue and queue's manner had effects on users' interactions with self-service kiosks.

4.1 Task-Based Design Interventions

Experiences and suggestions that participants mentioned included examples about self-service kiosk features, which pointed out possible design implications that could eliminate, or at least reduce, the negative effects of the social context. Figure 5 summarizes the findings from both studies, translating social context into design implications that would provide a good track for innovation.

It can be seen that in all different task types usability, usefulness, functionality, and privacy of usage are important, which are shown as prominent dimensions during interactions with self-service kiosks. Among the initial pragmatic aspects such as usability, usefulness, and so on, privacy of usage was closely related to social presence as participants did not want their actions and especially their errors to be seen by the other people no matter which task they were conducting. For instance, they mentioned that sound feedback should not be too loud or the information on the screen should not be possible to be seen by the others. Only when a technical problem occurred, they wanted the visibility of that information to be known by others; so that, others would not think that they were not able to use the self-service

Figure 4. Users' interactions with self-service kiosks in relation to different social context types and task qualities

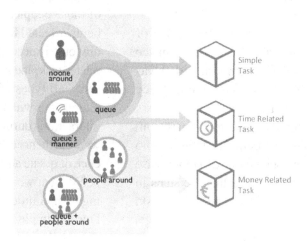

kiosks. Apart from these common dimensions, pleasure in use, security, and familiarity appeared differently in diverse tasks, which are discussed separately below. These dimensions might also seem far reached and may not be strictly specific to the related task type; yet, this categorization explains the most pertinent dimensions and task type relationships.

Simple Task: Participants looked for pleasure in use more in simple tasks, when they did not have any major concerns except from finalizing their goals. In order to achieve the prominent dimensions in simple tasks, enjoyment and usability of the self-service kiosks seemed to provide these dimensions. The possible implications could address primarily self-service kiosks' interfaces. They should not be perceived too serious and

Figure 5. Prominent dimensions in different tasks and corresponding design implications that could be done

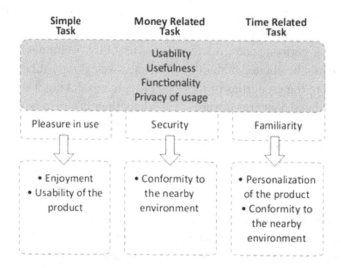

mechanic, which would make the users feel less serious to conduct the tasks wrong and fell less stressed. Moreover, usability of the self-service kiosks can be enhanced by presenting relevant information about how to use the system on top part of the kiosks in a visible way for the people in the queue. In this way, they can learn how to use it beforehand, which in turn reduce the negative effects of the social context while they start using the kiosks. Also, as the people in the queue would concentrate on the presented information, the user can feel calmer when interacting with the self-service kiosk.

Money Related Task: When the participants were conducting money related tasks, they had concerns about money, and so, with security. The self-service kiosks' location or isolation, in addition to interface, feedback possession, feedback conformity (visual or sound), and so on, gained urgency. Particularly, participants demanded different solutions for different times in a day. Mainly, they did not want too many people around when the location of the self-service kiosks felt comfortable and secure. However, when it was night and they were alone, the presence of other people was wanted to a certain extent. That's why, possible implications could be more on the nearby environment. Conformity of the self-service kiosks to the nearby environment during different times in a day should be considered. For example, isolation from the context considering the self-service kiosk's distant location, semi-closed form and unobtrusive feedback for other people than the user might be achieved first.

Time Related Task: In time related tasks, familiarity appeared to be important because especially the precipitancy of the people in the queue made the participants felt tense and tried to use the self-service kiosks faster. However, when they were familiar to the products, they were able to use them more quickly without doing so many errors and without feeling that much negatively. Hence, possible design implications would imply providing personalization and conformity to the

nearby environment. Users of the self-service kiosks could either personalize the interface or the interaction. To illustrate, they could interact with the self-service kiosks through their personal devices, which would shorten the time they pass in front of the self-service kiosks, and the duration they are affected from the social context. Moreover, the more the self-service kiosks suit to the nearby environment, the less the participants would feel negatively.

Apart from familiarity, visibility of the information on the self-service kiosk's interface to the other people could be considered to a certain extent. When there is a technical problem, this would eliminate the thoughts of hectic people in the queue that the problem is caused by the user, which accordingly can reduce the time and social pressure on the user.

4.2 General Recommendations for Designers

Apart from the task-specific design interventions, some generalizations and recommendations can be made to the designers of self-service kiosks to provide better and richer interactions, which also ground on social context's effects. These recommendations are listed below.

- Privacy and usability should be given equal importance while designing self-service kiosks.
- The clarity of information is of great importance to accelerate the comprehension and usage of the self-service kiosks, and to eliminate errors and other problems during the interaction. Hence, the chances of doing mistakes and eliciting negative feelings due to being seen by other people while doing these mistakes would be eliminated or reduced.
- The visibility of information is important both from the user's and the other people's perspectives. The information on the self-

service kiosk should be understood by the user immediately. However, the scope of the information provided to the user should be visible to the other people to a certain extent. The information about the technical problems should be visible to the other people in order to eliminate the thoughts that these problems are caused by the user.

- General information about the self-service kiosks such as the product types in vending machines, basic instructions, and so on could be visible to the people waiting in the queue, so that other people can concentrate on this information rather than the user. Hence, the pressure on the user can be relieved to a certain extent, and also, the people in the queue can learn the main steps of and the products in the self-service kiosks beforehand. So, in their turn, they could also understand and use the product more easily, resulting in being less negatively affected from the social context.

- In order to provide quick and easy understanding, feedback types gain importance. In some products sound feedbacks are being implemented and they usually do facilitate understanding. However, they do not necessarily bring about positive user experiences since they usually annoy the users considering the presence of other people. If it is vital to use sound feedbacks, they should not be too loud to be heard by the other people. Also, more pleasing sounds should be selected in order not to convey information to the other people around as if the user has done so serious mistake.

- The orientation, size and angle of the screen in self-service kisosk are of great importance. The display should not be seen easily by other people.

- Both the interaction and the appearance of the self-service kiosks should be pleasing. It is natural that pleasure in use brings about positive user experiences; however,

this might be even more important to eliminate or reduce the negative effects of the social context. It is acknowledged that the accuracy of use especially in self-service kiosk is of great importance because they usually serve the function of doing transactions and buying necessary things; yet, if a user makes a mistake, the negative effects of this mistake on the user experience concerning the social context could at least be reduced by pleasing interactions. The user could elicit fewer negative feelings and do fewer prospective errors during that interaction.

5. CONCLUSION

Large body of literature in diverse disciplines mentioned that context is a crucial factor impacting on people's experiences. As social psychology literature shows, other people in the context affect people's arousal levels, attentions, decisions, performances, and so on. Feeding from this literature, three studies were conducted to understand the influence of the presence or absence of other people while people are interacting with self-service kiosks. It is revealed that interactions with interactive self-service kiosks are different than human-computer interaction with any other type of consumer and personal products. Interactions with interactive self-service kiosks are specialized according to different task qualities that these kiosks serve for, which highlight the necessity to take into account the inseparable context during the design of these self-service kiosks.

In summary, understanding and considering the users concerns about the presence of other people is crucial while designing self-service kiosks. As can be understood from all the previously mentioned research findings that it is difficult to make generalizations about the effects of the presence of other people due to all different contexts, tasks and personal characteristics, but it is possible to comprehend certain aspects and relationships in user experience with these products. It can be deducted that though the presence of other people is desired in few cases as explained above, there is hardly a facilitating effect of the presence of other people on users' task performances. Generally, the presence of other people results in negative feelings and inferior task performances. However, if the user is familiar to the product and tasks, the negative effects of the social context diminishes, but usually still exists. It is significant to note again that feelings, though playing an important role, are not always the mere reasons of being affected from the social context. Feelings are highly interlinked with different phases of the experience; hence, it might be sometimes difficult to distinguish the mere reasons and moments of the elicited feelings. Conversely, it is found out that when there is no people around, users were more likely to feel neutral and positive; hence, resulting in facilitation of task performances. Only in the money related tasks the positive effects caused due to the absence of other people decrease. Money related tasks yields bit diverse results since security is much more important than in the other tasks. Moreover, some cases are found where the presence of other people reduces the negative effects on feelings and task performances. When there is company, users may perceive less the social pressure.

It can be asserted that a new task-based approach considering the social context in relation to different task qualities should be pursued while designing the self-service kiosks to provide better human-computer interactions; which implies the design of more experience based innovative solutions. This could be done by understanding the distinctive influence of people in the context in which users' interactions with self-service kiosks are realized. So, self-service kiosks should be pulled away from providing only one-way interaction and dominant interfaces, and undergo a differentiation in their entire bodies, contexts, and corresponding interactions. As a result, designers of these interactive self-service kiosks can support their designs with related contextual elements such as abovementioned semi-private form and location for money related tasks; familiar interactions and pre-interaction opportunity for time related tasks; and more pleasant interfaces for simple tasks.

6. FUTURE PROJECTIONS

The importance of pursuing a holistic approach rather than limiting the focus on pragmatic issues and taking social context into account in human-computer interactions, especially when such a publicly used product is in question, is now understood. Nonetheless, it is acknowledged that considering all user experience dimensions in different self-service kiosks in all different social contexts at a time is formidable. This situation designates new gaps, and so new opportunities to uncover which may give direction to future researches and design solutions in this area.

Firstly, different self-service kiosks like train ticket machines, snack dispensers, ATMs, and information kiosks, can be studied and compared. Diverse self-service kiosks are touched upon hereby and also general trends within different self-service kiosks and related tasks are revealed. However, feelings and task performances for each product category can be examined separately and compared regarding the absence and presence of other people. This would bring about more specific and exact results about differences between different tasks and concerns.

Secondly, taking the feelings at the heart of a research can bring about different directions for future design solutions. So, feelings can be examined in a further research to classify which feelings are elicited due to the social context and effect the task performances, and which feelings are elicited as a result of the task performances related to the social context. To clarify, the former can be epitomized by feeling tense or scared due to the presence of other people and doing errors accordingly. The latter one can be exemplified by feeling ashamed and stupid due to doing errors in front of other people. Although all above mentioned feelings are caused due to presence of other people, the hierarchy in occurrence time is different. This can be investigated to provide better understanding and richer information to inform design of the self-service kiosks.

Furthermore, target-group specific solutions can reveal interesting results, as well. Studies can be carried out to understand how the effects of the social context change considering different user groups. For instance, elderly people would be incorporated who might be affected more from the social context.

Other studies can be conducted with self-service kiosks in order to comprehend the impacts of the presence of other people on how users perceive the aesthetics of the self-service kiosks and assign meanings to them. These can provide certain design opportunities and directions, too, and also help to constitute a broader understanding of the effects of the presence of other people on user experience with self-service kiosks.

To sum up, all these aspects show the gaps and possible directions towards which the design of self-service kiosks may incline.

REFERENCES

Allport, F. H. (1924). *Social Psyshology*. Boston: Houghton Mifflin.

Baron, R. S. (1986). Distraction-conflict theory: Progress and problems. *Advances in Experimental Social Psychology*, *19*, 1–40. doi:10.1016/S0065-2601(08)60211-7

Baumeister, R. F. (1982). A selfpresentational view of social phenomena. *Psychological Bulletin*, *91*, 3–26. doi:10.1037/0033-2909.91.1.3

Bearden, W. O., & Etzel, M. J. (1982). Reference group influence on product and brand purchase decisions. *The Journal of Consumer Research*, *9*(2), 183–194. doi:10.1086/208911

Benford, S., & Giannachi, G. (2012). Interaction as Performance. *Interaction*, *19*(3), 38–43. doi:10.1145/2168931.2168941

Blascovich, J., Mendes, W. B., Hunter, S. B., & Salomon, K. (1999). Social facilitation as challenge and threat. *Journal of Personality and Social Psychology*, *77*(1), 68–77. doi:10.1037/0022-3514.77.1.68 PMID:10434409

Bond, C. F. (1982). Social facilitation: A self-presentational view. *Journal of Personality and Social Psychology*, *42*(6), 1042–1050. doi:10.1037/0022-3514.42.6.1042

Brignull, H., & Rogers, Y. (2003). Enticing People to Interact with Large Public Displays in Public Spaces. [INTERACT.]. *Proceedings of INTERACT*, *03*, 17–24.

Chamorro-Koc, M. (2007). *Experience, Context-of-Use and the Design of Product Usability*. (Doctoral dissertation). Queensland University of Technology.

Cooper, G. (1991). Context and Its Representation. *Interacting with Computers*, *3*, 243–252. doi:10.1016/0953-5438(91)90015-T

Cottrell, N. B. (1972). Social facilitation. In C. G. McClintock (Ed.), *Experimental Social Psychology* (pp. 185–236). New York: Holt.

Cottrell, N. B., Wack, D. L., Sekerak, G. J., & Rittle, R. H. (1968). Social facilitation of dominant responses by the presence of an audience and the mere presence of others. *Journal of Personality and Social Psychology*, *9*, 245–250. doi:10.1037/h0025902 PMID:5666972

Dashiell, J. F. (1930). An Experimental Analysis of Some Group Effects. *Journal of Abnormal and Social Psychology*, *25*(2), 190–199. doi:10.1037/h0075144

Desmet, P. M. A., & Hekkert, P. (2007). Framework of Product Experience. *International Journal of Design*, *1*(1), 57–66.

Diener, E. (1979). Deindividuation, Self-awareness and Disinhibition. *Journal of Personality and Social Psychology*, *37*(7), 1160–1171. doi:10.1037/0022-3514.37.7.1160

Dourish, P. (2004). What We Talk About When We Talk About Context. *Personal and Ubiquitous Computing*, *8*(1), 19–30. doi:10.1007/s00779-003-0253-8

Festinger, L., Pepitone, A., & Newcomb, T. (1952). Some consequences of deindividuation in a group. *Journal of Abnormal and Social Psychology*, *47*, 382–389. doi:10.1037/h0057906 PMID:14937978

Guerin, B., & Innes, J. M. (1984). Explanations of Social Facilitation: A Review. *Current Psychology (New Brunswick, N.J.)*, *3*(2), 32–52. doi:10.1007/BF02686548

Hassenzahl, M., & Tractinsky, N. (2006). User Experience - A Research Agenda. *Behaviour & Information Technology*, *25*(2), 91–97. doi:10.1080/01449290500330331

Hekkert, P., & Van Dijk, M. (2001). Designing from Context: Foundations of the VIP Approach and Two Applications. In P. Lloyd & H. Christiaans (Eds.), *Designing in Context: Proceedings of Design Thinking Research Symposium*. Delft, The Netherlands: DUP Science.

Henchy, T., & Glass, D. C. (1968). Evaluation apprehension and the social facilitation of dominant and subordinate responses. *Journal of Personality and Social Psychology*, *10*(4), 446–454. doi:10.1037/h0026814 PMID:5708047

Jordan, P. W. (1999). Pleasure with Products: Human Factors for Body, Mind and Soul. In W. S. Green, & P. W. Jordan (Eds.), *Human Factors in Product Design: Current Practice and Future Trends* (pp. 206–217). London: Taylor and Francis.

Jordan, P. W. (2000). *Designing Pleasurable Products*. London: Taylor and Francis.

Latané, B. (1981). The psychology of social impact. *The American Psychologist*, *36*(4), 343–356. doi:10.1037/0003-066X.36.4.343

Latané, B., & Darley, J. M. (1970). *The unresponsive bystander: Why doesn't he help?* New York: AppletonCentury-Crofts.

Le Bon, G. (1895). *The Crowd: A Study of the Popular Mind*. Retrieved from http://etext.virginia.edu/toc/modeng/public/BonCrow.html

Maguire, M. C. (1999). A review of user-interface design guidelines for public information kiosk systems. *International Journal of Human-Computer Studies*, *50*(3), 263–286. doi:10.1006/ijhc.1998.0243

Rashotte, L. (2007). Social Influence. In G. Ritzer (Ed.), *The Blackwell Encyclopedia of Sociology*. Retrieved from http://www.blackwellreference.com/subscriber/tocnode.html?id=g9781405124331_chunk_g978140512433125_ss1-154

Ratner, R. K., & Kahn, B. E. (2002). The impact of private versus public consumption on variety-seeking behaviour. *The Journal of Consumer Research*, *29*, 246–257. doi:10.1086/341574

Sanders, G. S., & Baron, R. S. (1975). The motivating effects of distraction on task performance. *Journal of Personality and Social Psychology*, *32*(6), 956–963. doi:10.1037/0022-3514.32.6.956

Sanders, G. S., Baron, R. S., & Moore, D. L. (1978). Distraction and social comparison as mediators of social facilitation effects. *Journal of Experimental Social Psychology*, *14*, 291–303. doi:10.1016/0022-1031(78)90017-3

Schifferstein, H. N. J., & Hekkert, P. (Eds.). (2008). *Product Experience*. Amsterdam: Elsevier.

Strauss, B. (2002). Social Facilitation in Motor Tasks: A Review of Research and Theory. *Psychology of Sport and Exercise*, *3*(3), 237–256. doi:10.1016/S1469-0292(01)00019-X

Suchman, L. A. (1987). *Plans and Situated Actions: The Problem of Human-Machine Communications.* Cambridge, UK: Cambridge University Press.

Triplett, N. (1898). The Dynamogenic Factors in Pacemaking and Competition. *American Journal of Technology, 9,* 507–533.

Vastenburg, M. H., Romero Herrera, N., Van Bel, D., & Desmet, P. M. A. (2011). PMRI: Development of a Pictorial Mood Reporting Instrument. In *Proceedings of the 2011 annual conference extended abstracts on Human factors in computing systems,* (pp. 2155-2160). Academic Press.

Zajonc, R. B. (1980). Compresence. In R. B. Paulus (Ed.), *Psychology of group influences* (pp. 35–60). Hillsdale, NJ: Erlbaum.

Zajonc, R. B. (1980). Social Facilitation. *Science, 149,* 269–274. doi:10.1126/science.149.3681.269 PMID:14300526

Zhu, Z., Nakata, C., Sivakumar, K., & Grewal, D. (2007). Self-service technology effectiveness: the role of design features and individual traits. *Journal of the Academy of Marketing Science, 35*(4), 492–506. doi:10.1007/s11747-007-0019-3

Zimbardo, P. G. (1969). The human choice: Individuation, reason, and order versus deindividuation, impulse, and chaos. *Nebraska Symposium on Motivation. Nebraska Symposium on Motivation, 17,* 237–307.

KEY TERMS AND DEFINITIONS

Context: Context is a dynamic concept encompassing various relationships between the situation, goal, action, and interaction. It encompasses social, experiential, cultural, and other contextual factors which influence how people relate to products.

Self-Service Kiosks: Self-service kiosks are interactive products and systems which are used by public such as automated teller machines, ticket vending machines, food or drink dispensers, self-service check-in or check-out kiosks.

Social Context: Users' experiences with products are affected from the context of social interactions, which addresses the social context. In a more basic sense, social context can be explained as the presence of other people whether it is real or imagined.

Social Facilitation: Social facilitation refers to the changes in an individual's performance due to other people's presence. Although the term was about the impairment in performance when the term was coined initially, it started to encompass both facilitation and impairment.

Social Influence: Social influence is the changes in an individual's ideas, affective experiences, and behaviors due to interaction with other people.

Task-Based Design: Task-based design is about putting emphasis on task qualities in addition to other aspects like product features or social context. I.e., tasks which users conduct while interacting with products and systems should be considered while designing these products and systems.

User Experience: User experience is the awareness of the affective phenomenon stemming from the users' interactions with products like the stimulation of senses, attribution of values and meanings, and elicitation of emotions.

Chapter 3
Multimodal User Interface in E-Learning Environments:
A Proposed Architecture

André Constantino da Silva
UNICAMP, Brazil & IFSP –Campus Hortolândia, Brazil

Heloísa Vieira da Rocha
UNICAMP, Brazil

ABSTRACT

Multimodal interaction is a proposal to turn the interaction between humans and machines more natural, increasing the usability, flexibility, and convenience of one application. Improve an application with multimodal features impacts on its architecture and, to describe the main components to treat the multimodality, some architecture models are proposed in the literature, including for Web multimodal systems. E-Learning environments are Web-based systems and need a good usability, flexibility, and convenience: requirements that can be improved with implementation of multimodal features on them. Since they have their own peculiarities, we need a more specific multimodal architecture model described in such a way to reuse the components built for multimodal systems and to connect them with the e-learning environment components. This chapter proposes an architecture for multimodal e-learning environments. A viability study was done in the Ae, an e-learning environment developed using a component-based development process, with components to treat the pen and touch modalities.

INTRODUCTION

Devices, such as smartphones and tablets, are becoming increasingly popular; most of them have touch screen displays, access to the Internet, and enough computing power to process Web pages. The number of input hardware on conventional computers (desktop and laptops) is increasing, with

computing devices equipped with touchscreen devices, microphones, and cameras. Most of the computational devices have an output display, but the size can vary widely. But others output data is possible as voice synthesis and tactile feedback.

One of the mobile devices that are gained repercussion is the tablet, a small and easy-to-carry computational device with a screen between 7 to

DOI: 10.4018/978-1-4666-6228-5.ch003

10 inches in which users interact using fingers. Another device is the Tablet PC (Tablet Personal Computer), a device with height as similar to a notebook and had an input device similar a pen, called stylus. The paper and pen metaphor implies that tasks performed before in paper, like draw or manuscript writing, can be more natural in the Tablet PC than in another computing devices. Some Tablet PCs have touch and pen-sensitive screens, allowing users interact using pen or fingers. Resuming, the Tablet PC has the following hardware characteristics: (i) Pen-sensitive screen; (ii) Screen that allow different positions; (iii) Wireless network access by WLAN (Wireless Local Area Network) and bluetooth technology; (iv) Microphones and embedded loudspeakers; (v) Keyboard (some models the keyboard are detachable); (vi) Batteries. The Tablet PC´s peripherals allow users interact in different ways, using: hands and keyboard to typewriting; fingers and touchpad to move the mouse pointer; fingers and a virtual keyboard on the touchscreen to typewriting; fingers and touchscreen to trigger an action in a user interface element; hand holding a pen, a pen-sensitive screen and a virtual keyboard to typewriting; hand holding a pen and a pen-sensitive screen to handwriting; voice and recognition software to trigger actions; and other combinations.

Nowadays, computers, tablets, Tablets PC, smartphones, video game console are connected through the Internet. The Internet is a global system of interconnected computer network with standards protocols that allow different technologies to change data. The mainly Web technology, the HTML, evolved and the improvement defined to the last version, the HTML5, are related with support multimedia, keep it easily readable by humans and consistently understood by computers and devices (Berjon *et al.*, 2012). HTML5 adds the new <video>, <audio>, and <canvas> tag elements, as well as the integration of Scalable Vector Graphics (SVG, a vector image format for two-dimensional graphics based on eXtended

Markup Language - XML) content and MathML (Mathematical Markup Language is a XML based-format to describing mathematical notations) to integrate mathematical formulae into Web pages. These features are designed to make it easy to include and handle multimedia and graphical content on the web without having proprietary plugins and APIs (Application Programming Interface) installed.

But Web sites and Web applications are still designed to be used with keyboard, mouse (or trackpad in laptop computers) and a high resolution medium sized monitor. One kind of Web application is e-learning (acronym of electronic learning) environments, systems used to support teaching and learning activities that must have good usability and accessibility to support diversity of users and contexts. The e-learning environments had several technological changes in the last two decades, either in changing their user interface, either in the number of available tools, shaped by technological advances and the user´s needs. But the actual version of e-learning environments does not receive input data from many modes to control the application; they only consider trigger actions by keyboard or mouse.

e-Learning environments are designed taking account the user will interact using keyboard, mouse, and high resolution medium-sized screen. But nowadays the users can interact touching a screen with their fingers, with their voices, using a pen, doing gesture with their hands or with body movements. Shneiderman (2002, pg. 21) describe that "The new computing technologies would include wall-sized displays, palmtop appliances, and tiny jewel-like fingertip computers that change your sensory experiences and ways of thinking." Kugler (2008), supported by reports from Gartner Group, describes one of the big challenges for the Information Technology and Communication (ICT) field in the next 25 years are non-tactile and natural interfaces, and automatic translation of speech. This challenge, coupled with the tendency to change the mouse gradually for emerging alternative interfaces for working with facial recognition, motion and gestures (Hayes, 2008) brings new challenges to Human-Computer Interaction (HCI), as Preece *et al.* (1994) already pointed: how to account for rapid technological change? How ensure that the design provide good HCI whilst exploiting the potential of new technology and functionality?

In the context of rapid advances of the technologies for human interact with computers, to design a software whose lifetime will cover decades, requires to design an user interface that also must fits the evolution of time and enable good user experiences over the years. So it is necessary to go beyond than providing access using available devices. It is necessary to consider that the number of peripherals is increasing over the years and these peripherals should allow users to interact with applications differently than usual. The user can use more than one peripheral, allowing her to input data in more than one mode. Multimodal systems are present in the HCI literature to allow users interact with more than one mode, supporting multimodality. Multimodality can aim increase the usability, accessibility, convenience, and flexibility of an application (Dumas, Lalanne & Oviatt, 2009), four desirable requirements for e-learning environments; so e-learning environment can benefit from multimodality. But we believe that other benefit emerges: support a large number of educational contexts. Non-multimodal e-learning environments do not take the advantage of the modality used by the user. For example, in the case of pen-based devices, in these environments are not possible to handwrite or sketch using the pen, turning difficult to adopted e-learning environments in contexts where users have pen-sensitive devices.

To turn easier to understand and build multimodal systems some works present general architecture model for these systems. But to build a multimodal e-learning environment it is not a trivial task, it is necessary to deeply understand the e-learning environments, their use and their tech-

nology, and define an architecture that considers components of multimodal interaction, of native e-learning environments on the Web platform restrictions. To define these components and their communications we propose an architecture for multimodal e-learning systems; and we validate the architecture through the implementation of components to treat the pen and gesture modalities; modalities available at Tablet PCs.

The next section presents a literature review about multimodal systems and architecture for this kind of systems. After we present our proposal to an architecture model for multimodal e-learning systems and some use cases. Finally we discuss some future works and conclusion.

BACKGROUND: E-LEARNING ENVIRONMENTS AND THEIR ARCHITECTURE

The actual versions of e-learning environments, such as Moodle (2013), TelEduc (2013) and SAKAI (2013), take advantages of the Web to offer content with text, images, audios and videos in a hypertext document. Chat, forums, portfolios, repositories are tools found on e-learning environments, and tools those explore the audio and video resource to user communication, such as instant messenger and video-conferences, are becoming common among the environments.

The e-learning environments are built to Web so they have a common architecture model: the client-server (Figure 1). Client is responsible to render the user interface through a browser. The server is responsible to process all client's requests and data persistence. It is in the client side that the user interacts with the application using input and output hardware. The input data from user peripherals (mouse and keyboard) is treating by the GUI Controller component and, if its needs, it will send a request to the server; the output data, i.e. the page rendering on the user display, is treated by the Application GUI component.

Figure 1. E-learning environments´ architecture model highlighting components for manage tools, sessions, courses and users data

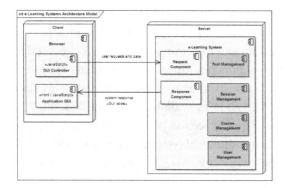

An action done by the user in the client side should trigger a request in the server side (treated by the Request Component on the server side), and the server will response with a new page through the Response Component. The programmer defines, for each page, the mapping between the user action and the server response; so it is considered deterministic.

In Figure 1 we highlighted some e-Learning environments´ components that manage data about which tools are available in the server (Tool Manager), about the users, their profiles and preferences (User Management), about registered courses (Course Manager) and, if the user is logged, which page the user is accessing (Session Management).

The server knows few about the input and output devices in client side. All the communication done between server and client is using HTTP protocol and HTML to specify the page interface. The low coupling between client and server allows different technologies to communicate on the Web, but can impact on the page adaption in the server side.

Besides the client-server architecture model, a Web application can adopt another architecture model to define and structure the client or server components. A software architecture encompasses the definition of its general structures, describ-

ing the logical components that make up the system and the connectors between them (Shaw & Garlan, 1996), and it is influenced by quality requirements (Kazman & Bass, 1994). So the defined architecture impacts on software quality: it aim to improve the scalability, maintainability, performance, reliability and other nonfunctional requirements.

For example, the Ae environment (2013), an e-learning environment developed by a consortium of Brazilian universities using J2EE technology, has a layered component-based software architecture model (Beder *et al.*, 2007) with the following layers:

- **Presentation Layer:** Provides the application user interface;
- **System Layer:** Provides an interface for the application functionality, that is, it is a façade for the application business rules;
- **E-Learning Layer:** Provides the component interfaces that implement the application's business rules, which can be used by various applications and which use services and functionalities from the infrastructure layer to implement the business rules;
- **Infrastructure Layer:** Implements a set of infrastructure services such as data persistence;
- **Common Services Layer:** Have the public services that can be utilized and accessed by all other architecture layers, except by the presentation layer.

Each developed tool following the Ae architecture model has one or more components for each layer. Usually, the presentation layer is treated like a unique component for each tool, and one component for the system layer, but it is not a rule in the Ae architecture. Beder *et al.* (2007) describe the advantages of a component-based software architecture considering the nonfunctional requirements:

1. **Abstraction:** Explicit separation between the specification and the implementation of functionalities. The implementation details of a functionality are hidden from the clients, facilitating the incorporation of changes or the inclusion of new functionalities with the minimum impact on the other parts of the system (Flexibility and Maintainability); and

2. **Uniform Composition:** In order to assemble functionalities implemented by distinct components, there must be communication between these components' provided and required interfaces, thereby providing uniform composition. The composition is accomplished by the connectors that recognize the interfaces of the various components and can make the adaptation from one interface to another (Interoperability). In this way, it is possible to reuse components (Reusability) developed by other educational institutions, bringing increased productivity and quality of the produced software. (Beder *et al.*, 2007, p. 22)

The current version of Ae environment is based on SAKAI nucleus (2013), so the course and user management, user authentication, and session management are from SAKAI environment; they have functionalities to manage data about courses, users, and where an online user is browsing. To define what a user can do in a page (e.g. Marie, a student, post a blog message in a course about HCI), it is necessary analyze data about who is the user (Marie), which role she has (a student), which course she is browsing (a course about HCI) and which tools she has access in these context (blog tool). In Figure 2 is presented the Ae architecture model highlighting these components in the system layer.

The Ae e-learning environment have flexibility to allow the administrator install only a set of tools, so tools that do not follow the institution rules or overload the server can be removed. This flexibility allows developers and community to produce tools

similar as software plugins; they can be installed in any server and be separately distributed. The flexibility to choose tools is given for teacher too, who can choose which installed tools will be available in her course. These flexibilities are not trivial to treat, since the environment development team needs to specify how the environment will discover new tools and their functionalities.

The e-learning environments were designed to conventional computers (desktops and laptops), with keyboard, mouse (or touchpad in the case of laptops), a high resolution medium-sized display. To browsing among the e-Learning environment´s pages, the user uses the mouse to click over an interface element or use some keys of the keyboard to trigger an action. For example, to activate a link, the user click over the link and the browser will send a request for the server that will response with the page that will be rendered in the client. The link element is unique over the mouse pointer´s corner, so it is simple to determine which reaction the browser needs have. We can conclude that the interaction is deterministic and each mode per time and their architecture cannot, initially, support multimodality.

Conventional computers have enough processing power to manipulate multimedia content, and the environments allow users to publish content in many media. Some limitations of the environments make difficult to produce content, as audio or video, and publish it on the e-learning environments. For example, to produce a video and publish it, it is necessary, after do the record, go to the environment and upload the file. Other approach is to use videos available on dedicated sites, such YouTube but it is necessary to browse in the site to find the media, copy their URL (or HTML code that shows the video) and paste it on the environment´s tool; a difficult task for people whom know few about Internet and technology.

Beside these problems, the environments have a good usability considering the technology restrictions of the conventional computers.

Figure 2. The Ae e-learning environment architecture highlighting components for manage tools, sessions, courses, and users data

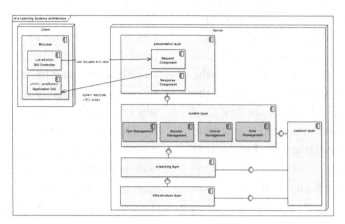

Despite which e-learning environment used, most of the courses publish content to read, sometimes videos to watch, exercises to do, forums to discuss some subjects. Most of the delivered activities have the purpose to write a text in a text editor outside the environment and send the file through the environment or build collectively a text in a wiki tool. Since the non-multimodal e-learning environments are not sensitive about which modality the user is interacting, some of these tasks are hard to be completed in devices without keyboard and mouse, e.g., participate in the writing process in a wiki tool. And does not take the advantages of the modality used, e.g., is not possible to handwrite or do sketches in pen-based devices or trigger features by voice. So the interaction continues the same: focused on mouse and keyboard to input and output in a high resolution medium size screen and sometimes the use of alert sounds. This is a limitation of the environments in your ages: many hardware peripherals to interact supporting different input and output modes.

For example, computers equipped with pen are become common nowadays, e.g., Tablets PCs, a device with height as similar to a notebook and had an input device similar a pen. The paper and pen metaphor implies that tasks performed before in paper, like draw or manuscript writing, can be more natural in the Tablet PC than in another computing devices. Pen-based Computing or Pen Computing refers to a computer user-interface using a pen, rather than devices such as a keyboard or a mouse. User interfaces for pen computing can be implemented in several ways, like using the pen as a pointing input device; in this case the user can interact with the e-learning systems as similar and deterministic as using a mouse, but with more limitations: the hand over the screen can decrease the usability. But the user takes better advantages over the pen-based interaction when the application is developed considering direct manipulation, handwriting or gesture recognition.

When the user moves the pen in the screen, the pen´s trace should result in electronic ink that must be treated by the application to be rendered and stored. But desktop applications, that running in the Tablet PCs, do not treat electronic ink; it is necessary special applications to treat the electronic ink to have benefices of the pen-based interaction.

MODALITY AND MULTIMODALITY

Some models of Tablet PCs are equipped with touchscreen, so user can interact with the keyboard, mouse, track pad, pen or using her fingers. Since the touch is become common to interact with digital application, mainly on mobile devices, e-learning environments need to be improved to manipulate data from this input device. And it is not possible to combine data from more than one modality to trigger actions, and the environments cannot process more than one modality per time: they are unimodal systems; since they do not do a flexible use of input or output modes (Oviatt, 2002). Bernsen (2008) defines unimodal interaction systems as systems that use the same mode for input and output and a system of multimodal interaction as it is a system that uses at least two different modes for input or output.

Modality is the term used to define a mode in which a user´s input or system´s output are expressed.

The communication mode or mode refers to the communication channel used for two different entities that interact (Alty & McCartney, 1991). Nigay and Coutaz (1995) define modality as an interaction method that an agent can use to reach a goal, and that modality can be specified in general terms as "speech" or in more specific terms as "using microphones".

Bernsen and Dykjær (2010, p. 68) discuss that "The dictionary's term "modality" is not overly informative. One of its senses is to be a manner of something, another, the so-called sensory modalities of psychology (vision, hearing, etc.)". The authors define modality as:

A modality, or, more explicitly, a modality of information representation, is a way of representing information in some medium. ... a modality is defined by its medium–carrier–sensor system triplet and its particular "way" of representation. It follows that a modality does not have to be perceptible by humans ... We need those "ways", or

modalities, because humans use many and very different modalities for representing information in the same medium. We use, e.g. the graphics medium (everything visible) to represent text, images, facial expression, gesture and more. These are different modalities represented in the same medium. (Bernsen & Dykjær, 2010, pp. 68-71).

By this definition, Bernsen considers that Graphical User Interface (GUI) interfaces are multimodal: haptic input and graphical output, and both use a variety of modalities. For Bernsen & Dykjær (2010, p. 69) "GUI-based interaction is a useful multimodal interaction paradigm which, because it came first historically, is just better explored, and more familiar to most people, than most other kinds of multimodal interaction.". Bernsen presents a taxonomy for elementary modalities that can be used to build multimodal interfaces and reach multimodal interaction, e.g., typed text, manuscript text, gesture and body movements. Bernsen´s basis are haptic, graphical, and acoustic media; dominant media on computational systems. Bernsen describes that two modalities not are equivalent; they differ in relation to the strengths and weaknesses of expressiveness and in their relationship with the perceptual systems, cognitive and emotional human being.

Several modalities have become research topics in recent decades; among them we can mention the voice, handwriting recognition, touch, and gestures. Touch modality is a haptic modality that employs haptic sensors for identifying one or more regions of a surface in which one or more fingers come into contact. Touchscreens have become common especially on mobile devices. On touchscreens, the act of touching the surface with a finger (a tap) can trigger an action on the object drawn in the region where the touch was performed. It is possible to have a continuous sequence of touches on a region, for example, a double tap, similar as double-clicking the mouse, or tap and hold; both can be used to trigger a functionality of the object. Some peripherals can distingue more than one touch per time:

Multi-touch (or multitouch) denotes a set of interaction techniques that allow computer users to control graphical applications with several fingers. Multi-touch devices consist of a touch screen (e.g., computer display, table, wall) or touchpad, as well as software that recognizes multiple simultaneous touch points, as opposed to the standard touchscreen (e.g. computer touchpad, ATM), which recognizes only one touch point. (Teiche et al., 2009, p. 2)

Karpov *et al.* (2008, p. 156) define gesture as "an expressive, meaningful body motion, i.e., physical movement of the fingers, hands, arms, head, face, or body with the intent to convey information or interact with the environment". Gesture can have information, e.g., the gesture that compose a signal language or when using gestures to supplement a speech.

There are in HCI area researches to develop and evaluate system for each described modality here, and to use modalities combined. Mayes (1992) defines multimodal interaction systems as a system with the capacity to communicate with the user by different communication modes, using more than one modality, automatically gives or extracts mean. According to Oviatt:

Multimodal interfaces process two or more combined user input modes (such as speech, pen, touch, manual gesture, gaze, and head and body movements) in a coordinated manner with multimedia system output. They are a new class of interfaces that aim to recognize naturally occurring forms of human language and behavior, and which incorporate one or more recognition-based technologies (e.g., speech, pen, vision). (Oviatt, 2002, p. 418)

Lalanne *et al.* (2009) describe that multimodal interaction systems, or multimodal systems, allow users to interact with computers though many data input modalities (e.g., speech, gesture, eye gaze) and output channels (e.g., text, graphics, sound, avatars, voice synthesis). Bersen (2008) defines "a multimodal interactive system has both input and output, and uses at least two different modalities for input and/or output". According Bangalore and Johnston (2009), multimodal interfaces enable that user´s input and system´s output to be expressed in the way or in the ways they are better adjusted, given a task, user´s preferences, physical, and social environment characteristics where the interaction is happen.

Multimodal interaction is a research proposal to turn the interaction between humans and machines more natural, i.e., more close to the interactions between two humans, and have the benefits to increase the usability, flexibility, and convenience (Lalanne *et al.*, 2009). To Bernsen (2008) the main question of multimodality is to create something new, because "when modalities are combined, we obtain new and emerging properties of representations that could not be considered individually by the modalities". Larson (2013) proposes three general questions to answer to determine if a web application has improved by employing a new method of data entry: the new way needs to add value to the web application, the application must leverage the strengths of the new mode interaction and nullify their weaknesses, and users need to have the necessary hardware and software for the new mode.

Multimodal systems need to process all input done by the user to identify and process the desired action and generate the output using the appropriate modes. Dumas, Lalanne and Oviatt (2009, p. 11) describe that "Fusion of input modalities is one of the features that distinguish multimodal interfaces from unimodal interfaces" and "Fission techniques allow a multimodal application to generate a given message in an adequade form according to the context and user profiles" (Oviatt, 2009, p. 13).

Dumas, Lalanne and Oviatt (2009) present a generic architecture for multimodal systems composed by the components: i) input recognizers & processors, ii) output synthesizers, iii) fusion engine, iv) fission module, v) dialog management, and vi) context, user model and history manager. The last four components (components iii, iv, v, vi) compose the Integration Committee. The authors define how these components communicate with each other:

… input modalities are received though various recognizers, which output their results to the fusion engine in charge of giving a common interpretation of the inputs. A fusion machine gives an interpretation for the data and it communicates it to the dialog manager, in charge of identifying the dialog state, the transition to perform, the action to communicate to an application, and/or the message to return through the fission machine. The fission machine returns a message to the user through the most adequate modality or combination of modalities, depending on the user profile and context of use. For this reason, the context manager, in charge of tracking the location, context and user profile, closely communicates any changes in the environment to the three other components, so that they can adapt their interpretations. (Dumas, Lalanne & Oviatt, 2009, p. 11)

To implement multimodal system for web it is necessary consider both multimodal architecture and Web architecture. Gruenstein, McGraw and Badr (2008) present a framework to aim to develop multimodal interfaces for web, the WAMI Toolkit. The framework defines tree client-side components (Core GUI, GUI Controller and Audio Controller) and more four server-side components (Web Server, Speech Recognizer, Speech Synthesizer, and Logger). The user interacts with the Core GUI, described at HTML and JavaScript, and the Audio Controller, a Java Applet to receive the audio input. The collected data is sent to the server to be treated by the Speech Recognizer and the Web Server components. The components Core GUI, GUI Controller, Audio Controller, and Speech Recognizer can be classified as the input recognizers & processors of the Dumas *et al.*'s architecture, and the Speech Synthesizer can be classified as output synthesizers. The WAMI toolkit is focused on speech plus keyboard and mouse modes, but the authors describe that the framework can be expanded to include other modes through definition of new components.

WEB MULTIMODAL SYSTEMS

The W3C Multimodal Interaction Working Group (MMI-WG) is developing a standard framework for such applications since 2002 and it purposes a recommendation in 2012 (W3C, 2013) with three components to compose the Runtime Framework and more one called Modality Components which recognizes the input data and running a markup language. The Modality Components interact with the Interaction Manager component through the event-based MMI life-cycle API. The Interaction Manager is one of the Runtime Framework components, who is responsible to sends and receives all messages from Modality Components, and queries and updates the Data Component as needed. The Data Component contains the public data model for the multimodal application. The Delivery Context is another Runtime Framework component; it is responsible to store static and dynamic device properties, environmental conditions, and user preferences; properties which can be queried and dynamically updated (as the Dumas *et al.*'s context, user model, and history manager component). The Interaction Manager component essentially contains the multimodal application and it maintains the dialog flow, current state, and public data (as the Dumas *et al.*'s dialog management).

An important aspect of the W3C Multimodal Architecture is that each modality component runs its own markup language document, but McCobb (2013) points out that W3C XML languages directly not support multimodal authoring and there is a lack for standard to combine the XML that represent various modalities into a single document when all modalities are rendered on the client.

Due the difficulties to build a multimodal system and the technology to build Web pages, the actual e-learning systems do not have multimodal interface. One step forward is to have an architecture model. To propose an architecture for multimodal e-learning environments we will use as basis the Ae environment due the characteristic of have well-defined interfaces for each environment´s component, turning easier to build an e-learning system with multimodal interface, but the functionalities to manage users, courses, and roles are in any e-learning environment.

ARCHITECTURE FOR MULTIMODAL E-LEARNING ENVIRONMENT

Considering the W3C Multimodal Architecture (W3C, 2013), Web-Accessible Multimodal Interfaces architecture (Gruenstein, McGraw & Badr, 2008) and the architecture of multimodal systems (Dumas, Lalanne & Oviatt, 2009), we redesign the Ae architecture model (Figure 2) and propose an architecture for multimodal e-learning environments (Figure 3).

Due to the fact that the browser has the responsibility to show the GUI components in the client side, the input recognizers & processors and output synthesizers components needs to be distributed in the client and the server. Input recognizers components are added to treat the data input from the client side, these components receive the data input stream and describe it in the proper XML format. In Figure 3, there are components to treat data arising from pen gestures. More components need to be added to consider other interaction modes.

The input data is sent to the server by modality components and the server has the responsibility to process this data through the recognizers (the recognizers components are not showed in Figure 3 but they are integrated with the request component) and the integration committee will gives a mean for the data. So, the fusion and fission machines will be on the server. The fusion machine will be called when the server receives the data from the client-side components, and the correspondent action is invoked on the Ae´s system component. After the fission machine will be called to the system produce the response for the request.

E-Learning environments are complex systems, composed by a lot of tools and features. The user usually deals with a set of the functionalities related with the tool she is using, and some features she can use. For example, the student is reading a material published in a content tool but want to write a message to the teacher. The student can invoke the new message screen without to change to Mail tool; the user just can say "send a mail message for the teachers saying that I just finished the activities". But user cannot delete an item in the tool without specify clearly which item is: she cannot say just "delete it", unless she is seeing the item. So the Dialog Management component needs to be integrated with Tool Management and Session Management to identify the meaning to given for a user request and system response. The data about functionalities needs to be updated each time the user browsing to another tool or another course, since some functionalities change when the user browses to another tool or course. But some functionalities, e.g., change the course, logoff, needs to be available every time. This is a peculiarity of e-learning systems and complex systems; in the literature the multimodal system have the same features during all the user interaction.

Another characteristic with impact on tasks that can be performed by users is related with the available tools in the server. It is necessary a

Figure 3. Architecture for multimodal e-Learning environments

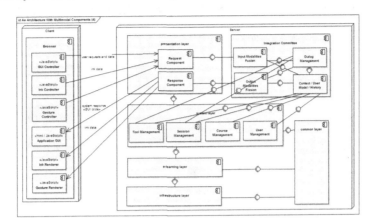

mechanism to tools inform for the dialog management about the functionalities the user can trigger. One solution is writing code to describe the tool´s functionalities and process it on the tool´s deployment. The tool developers need specify and write the code about the tool´s functionalities in the developing time.

The Context, User Model, and History component needs to interact with Tool Management, Session Management, Course Management, and User Management components of the environment that will provide useful data for update the context model in the integration committee and necessary data about the tasks users can perform.

In Figure 3 is presented components to treat the input data from pen and gestures. The actual environments do not support electronic ink, so we used components from our previous work (da Silva & da Rocha, 2013) where we developed a pen-based blog tool for e-learning environments that allow users to handwrite posts or sketches and do comments using pen (Figure 4). To implement the InkBlog, we specified the InkEditor, an electronic ink editor, composed by two client-side components: InkController and InkRenderer (Figure 5). The pen input data is received by the InkController, who transform each point of the trace into coordinate points following InkML format (Chee *et al.*, 2011). The user can choose

the trace´s color and the width selecting the options in the right side (Figure 4a). When the user points to and presses the pen into a color or width button, the next traces will have the brush attribute set to look likes the selected options. The InkRenderer, another InkEditor´s component, draws the traces of the handwrite posts in the user screen. The InkController and InkRenderer components are an input recognizer & processors and output synthesizers, respectively.

To treat data from gesture, both from pen or touch, we developed the GestureEditor, composed by GestureController and GestureRenderer, respectively, input recognizer & processors and output synthesizers components. In Figure 6 we present the GestureEditor with the user drawing a gesture for post a new InkBlog message in the current course.

The GestureController and GestureRenderer were built using the same technology of InkController and InkRenderer: HTML5, JavaScript and InkML. The InkML was used since the gesture is a simple draw and can be represented using the InkML format.

Use Case

Consider the following case with the user interact with the environment without multimodal

Figure 4. Using InkBlog in the Ae Environment to (a) handwrite a reasoning to prove the better case of an algorithm in a Computer Theory course and (b) displaying a post about Graph Theory

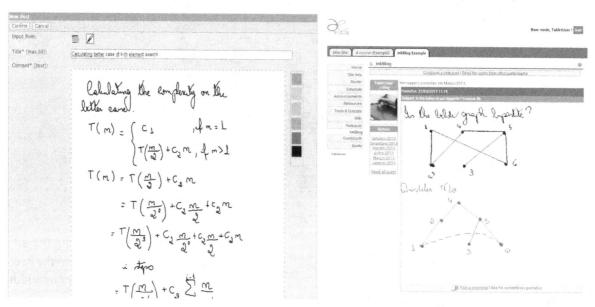

interaction: Marie is an undergraduate student and she had a Tablet PC that she uses to browse into Internet and to handwrite class annotations using a proprietary application. In this semester, Marie is doing the Computer Theory course and the teacher adopted an e-learning environment to support the teaching and learning activities. In the adopted environment, the teacher usually publishes slides, articles, suggested books to read, activities and exercises. In the middle of the course, Marie read the content and started to do exercises. To resolve the exercises is necessary to write equa-

tions, a hard task to be done using keyboard and mouse, but Marie uses a proprietary tool to write equations using the pen in the Tablet PC. But she had some doubts in the exercises resolution and due to the environment restrictions, she asks for help sending a mail message and attached the file in a format that she thinks the teacher had software to open it (e.g., .pdf format). She also posted her resolutions on the blog tool as pictures (.jpg format) to share her reasoning with the other students.

John is the Marie´s teacher on the Computer Theory course. He read the Marie´s message asking for help, and to answer her, he printed the attached file writing over the document. He preferred to print her resolutions due he needs to write new equations and correct some equations written by Marie. After to do the annotations, John scans the sheets and responses the Marie´s mail attaching the file with scanned sheets. Marie read the John´s message and now knows how to correctly resolve the exercises.

In this context, the use of InkBlog will brings some efficient to the process, reducing time and resource. Marie could write her solutions direct on the InkBlog as posts, and the teacher writes

Figure 5. InkBlog components used in a handwritten or sketched post

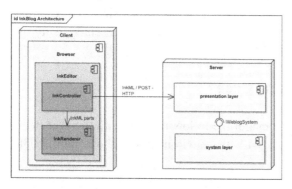

Figure 6. Using GestureEditor in the Ae Environment to open the new InkBlog message dialog

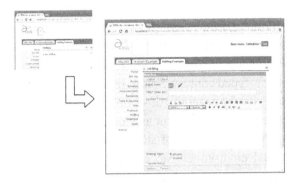

him suggestions and explanations as comment for her posts. If she want, it is also possible to use the voice to trigger some features, e.g., change the color of the ink, ask for undo the last trace, and change the ink width while she is writing.

But it is necessary a more detailed vision to understand the improvement given by a multimodal interaction. For example, Marie wants a new blog message, so she uses the browser to access the environment, do the log in, goes to the Computer Theory course page, select the blog tool and click in the "New post message" button. If the environment has gesture recognition, she can draw a symbol, e.g. "B" letter (Figure 6) over the environment page with the pen to trigger the new blog message action. But the reaction of the environment will depends the page where the Marie draw: if it is over a course page, the new post will be publish in this course, but if the user draw over her space page, the environment needs to ask which course the new post will be published. This example shows the necessity to consider the context (in this case, the page where the user is) to give the meaning for the user´s request and the integration between the multimodal components and the environment components on the Figure 3.

Another example is delete an item published in a tool. The user can draw the letter "D" or draw an "X" to trigger the action to delete an item, but, to execute the operation, the environment needs to know which item the action is to be done. The

draw can be done over the page that shows one item, or can be done over the page that shows many items or a page that this gesture does not have a meaning. In the case of a page with many items, the environment needs to ask for the user to mark the items to be deleted.

When Marie was writing their responses using InkBlog, she used the pen to write her answer and to change the color or line thickness. If the environment had components to receive and treat touch input, she can use her fingers to trigger the functions about colors or line thickness, or can use the pen to do a selection and after move the selected sketches with the fingers.

Consider the context of mobile devices where the user interacts with the environment with touchscreen. In non-multimodal e-learning environments, the user cannot use the microphone available in the smartphone to interact with the system (e.g., said to system to change the color). Actually, if the user uses zoom to focus on a screen part, and it is necessary to go to another screen part to trigger an action, the user will need to do a lot of movements to go and turn back between these two parts; so the efficient is low. In a multimodal system the user does not need to do these movements, just asking by voice the desirable feature.

FUTURE RESEARCH DIRECTIONS

Dumas, Lalanne and Oviatt (2009) describe that multimodal user interfaces have multiple input streams, are continuous and probabilistic, needs parallel processing, and are distributed and time-sensitive architectures. Since we are using a component-based architecture, the presentation layer and the multimodal components can run in proper servers, meeting the constraints of distributed and time-sensitive architecture and increasing the scalability and performance.

Through the analysis of works about fusion machine and using the BRETAM model for determining the maturity in the field, Lalanne *et al.* (2009) comment that software tools and architecture models for multimodal interaction are at the Maturity stage, the last one of the model. By BRETAM model, when a concept is in this stage means that the theories were assimilated and used routinely without questions.

But it is important to merge the architecture model for multimodal interaction with the software architecture. Here we merged the architecture model for multimodal interaction with an e-learning environment, including interfaces between components to change data to be used to give a meaning for user input data. We believe that the proposed architecture can be used in other e-learning environments, since we started from a generic architecture for e-Learning environments.

Here we implemented components to treat input data from pen and touch and consider the case of do gestures with pen or touch. For transfer gesture data from client to server we used the InkML format, but future works can improve these components to use the GestureML - Gestural Markup Language (Ideum, 2013) to change data between client and server and among the other components. Other modalities can be treated by defining components for treat them. For example, with components to receive audio input, actions for change the color or thickness line can be triggered by voice when the selection and can be done using a pen or a finger.

Different from existing examples of multimodal systems, which ones the data is recognized to typed text and stored in the database, the e-learning systems need to store data from the modalities, not only store typed text. So multimodal e-learning environments join functionalities from multimodal systems and multimedia systems to the user interaction and produce content. For example, if the user is interacting with a pen, the generated electronic ink can be used to trigger action such item selection or can be used to produce content such a sketch in a blog tool. The user can trigger a delete action over a Portfolio item or can record an audio content, like a podcast post.

Some tools access data from other tools, e.g., the search tool. The search tool needs to read the content stored in other tools and return for the user each occurrence. Search tool in e-learning environments uses string compare techniques, so this tool needs access recognizers when searching in non-typed content. Some studies must be done to verify the necessity of search mechanism must have non-typed content as input.

Another context of study is using the multimodal environment accessed by mobile users. The possibility of access the environment in any place brings some challenges e.g. the influence of context (physics and social) to choose available modalities to interact. Considering that the user will have many devices, she may choose which the best device and modality available in the device to use to reach her goal.

Multimodality can aim increase the usability, accessibility, convenience, and flexibility of an application (Dumas, Lalanne & Oviatt, 2009), due one modality can reduce the weaknesses of the other modality. This is true when you have all modalities considered in design time available to the user, where the application is built considering these modalities. But it is important to consider that in certain contexts, e.g. context awareness, some modalities cannot be used, or the user does not have the desire to use it. In these cases, the interface needs to have good usability to allow user to reach her goal. We think that the interface needs to have good usability for each modality and for each combination of modalities. The design and evaluation methods need to consider this if the application is context awareness.

Allow user access the environment with any modality brings a pedagogical difficult for the teachers. In non-multimodal e-learning the teachers know about the hardware used (keyboard, mouse, and medium size display). But in the case of multiple devices, the teachers need to elaborate their courses thinking about this variety: are they will force use a specific device? When? Or write different exercises, evaluation criteria and content?

CONCLUSION

e-Learning environments are systems to support teaching and learning activities through the Web, allowing course participants communicate with each other, build and publish content and manage the virtual space. The current versions have been designed taking into account that users will interact on a conventional computer (desktop or laptop) equipped with keyboard, mouse or track pad, and a medium size high resolution display.

With the increasing of interaction styles (e.g., touch and voice) on conventional computers and the increasing of computational power in mobile devices (e.g., touch and gesture), the environments are accessed by users using interaction styles that were not considered in the design time. A solution is adopting a multimodal interface to increase the usability, accessibility, and convenience of e-learning environments in this new context. The first impact is on the e-learning environment architecture, which needs components to deal with many channels and do the data fusion and fission.

We proposed an architecture for multimodal e-learning environments based on generic architectures for multimodal systems and specificities of e-learning environments. Due the Web platform, it was necessary to have components in the client to receive the input data and render the result. Another need was integrate components of multimodal architecture with components of the e-learning environment, e.g., the context, user model, and history management of the multimodal architecture with the Tool Management, Session Management, Course Management, and User Management components of the e-learning environment.

A viability study of the proposed architecture was done in the Ae, an e-learning environment developed using a component-based development process, with components to treat the pen and touch modalities. These both modalities can be used as pointing device, so their actions can easily be mapped for mouse´s actions. As future work we want to implement components for other modalities and study the multimodal e-learning environment on mobile contexts, the impact of multimodality on learning activities and the relationship between modality and courses.

ACKNOWLEDGMENT

The authors thank the CAPES and CNPq for financial support and for FAPESP through TIDIA-Ae Project (n. 05/60572-1), which provided the equipment.

REFERENCES

Ae Project. (2013). *Ae - Aprendizado Eletrônico Environment*. Retrieved October 20, 2013, from http://tidia-ae.iv.org.br/

Alty, J., & McCartney, C. (1991). *Design of a Multi-Media Presentation System For A Process Control Environment*. Paper presented at the Eurographics Multimedia Workshop, Session 8: Systems. Stockholm, Sweden.

Bangalore, S., & Johnston, M. (n.d.). Robust Understanding in Multimodal Interaction. *Computational Linguistic, 35*(3), 345-397.

Beder, D. M., Silva, A. C., Otsuka, J. L., Silva, C. G., & Rocha, H. V. (2007). A Case Study of the Development of e-Learning Systems Following a Component-based Layered Architecture. In *Proceedings of the 7th IEEE International Conference on Advanced Learning Technologies*, (pp. 21-25). Los Alamitos, CA: IEEE Computer Society. doi: 10.1109/ICALT.2007.4

Berjon, R., Leithead, T., Navara, E. D., O'Connor, E., & Pfeiffer, S. (2012). *HTML5 - A vocabulary and associated APIs for HTML and XHTML W3C Candidate Recommendation*. Retrieved March 25, 2013, from http://www.w3.org/TR/html5/

Bernsen, N. O. (2008). Multimodality Theory. In D. Tzovaras (Ed.), *Multimodal user Interfaces: From signal to interaction* (pp. 5–28). Berlin: Springer. doi:10.1007/978-3-540-78345-9_2

Bersen, N. O., & Dykjær, L. (2010). *Multimodal Usability*. London: Springer-Verlag. doi:10.1007/978-1-84882-553-6

Chee, Y., Franke, K., Froumentin, M., Madhvanath, S., Magaña, J., & Pakosz, G. … Yaeger, L. (2011). *Ink Markup Language (InkML) W3C Recommendation*. Retrieved October 20, 2013, from http://www.w3.org/TR/InkML

Community, S. A. K. A. I. (2013). *Sakai Project | collaboration and learning - for educators by educators*. Retrieved October 20, 2013, from http://sakaiproject.org

Da Silva, A. C., & da Rocha, H. V. (2013). Ink-Blog: A Pen-Based Blog Tool for e-Learning Environments. *Issues in Informing Science and Information Technology*, 10, 121–135.

Dumas, B., Lalanne, D., & Oviatt, S. (2009). Multimodal Interfaces: A Survey of Principles, Models and Frameworks. In *Human-Machine Interaction* (pp. 3–26). Berlin, Germany: Springer. doi:10.1007/978-3-642-00437-7_1

Gruenstein, A., McGraw, I., & Badr, I. (2008). The WAMI Toolkit for Developing, Deploying, and Evaluating Web-Accessible Multimodal Interfaces. In *Proceedings of 10th International Conference on Multimodal Interfaces* (pp. 141-148). New York, NY: ACM. doi: 10.1145/1452392.1452420

Hayes, B. (2008). Gartner's Seven IT Grand Challenges. *Communications of the ACM*, 51(7), 10.

Ideum. (2013). *GestureML*. Retrieved October 20, 2013, from http://www.gestureml.org/

Karpov, A., Carbini, S., Ronzhin, A., & Viallet, J. E. (2008). Two SIMILAR Different Speech and Gestures Multimodal Interfaces. In D. Tzovaras (Ed.), *Multimodal user Interfaces: From signal to interaction* (pp. 155–184). Berlin: Springer. doi:10.1007/978-3-540-78345-9_7

Kazman, R., & Bass, L. (1994). *Toward Deriving Software Architectures From Quality Attributes* (Technical Report, CMU/SEI-94-TR-10). Software Engineering Institute, Carnegie Mellon University. Retrieved October 20, 2013 from http://www.sei.cmu.edu/reports/94tr010.pdf

Kugler, L.(n.d.). Goodbye, Computer Mouse. *Communications of the ACM*, 51(9), 56.

Lalanne, D., Nigay, L., Palanque, P., Robinson, P., Vanderdonckt, J., & Ladry, J. (2009). Fusion Engine for Multimodal Input: A Survey. In *Proceedings of the 11th International Conference on Multimodal Interfaces* (pp. 153-160). Cambridge, MA: ACM. doi: 10.1145/1647314.1647343

Larson, A. (2013). *Should You Build a Multimodal Interface for Your Web Site?* Retrieved October 20, 2013, from http://www.informit.com/articles/article.aspx?p=29024

Mayes, T. (1992). The 'M' Word: Multimedia interfaces and their role in interactive learning systems. In Multimedia Interface Design in Education (pp. 1-22). Berlin, German: Springer-Verlag.

McCobb, G. (2013). *The W3C Multimodal Architecture, Part 2: the XML specification stack*. Retrieved October 20, 2013, from http://www.ibm.com/developerwo rks/web/library/wa-multimodarch2/index.html

Moodle Community. (2013). *Moodle.org: Open-source community-based tools for learning*. Retrieved October 20, 2013, from http://www.moodle.org

Nigay, L., & Coutaz, J. (1995). A Generic Plataform for Addressing the Multimodal Challenge. In *Proceedings of the 13ʰ Conference On Human Factors in Computing Systems* (pp. 98-105). New York, NY: ACM Press / Addison-Wesley Publishing Co.

Oviatt, S. (2002). Multimodal Interfaces. In A. Sears, & J. Jacko (Eds.), *Handbook of Human-Computer Interaction: Fundamentals, Evolving Technologies and Emerging Applications* (pp. 413–432). Lawrence Erlbaum.

Oviatt, S. (2003). Advances in Robust Multimodal Interface Design. *IEEE Computer Graphics and Applications*, *23*(55), 62–68. doi:10.1109/MCG.2003.1231179

Preece, J., Rogers, Y., Sharp, H., Benyon, D., Holland, S., & Carey, T. (n.d.). *Human-Computer Interaction: Methods for User-Centred Design*. Addison-Wesley.

Shaw, M., & Garlan, D. (1996). *Software Architecture: Perspectives on an Emerging Discipline*. Upper Saddle River, NJ: Prentice Hall.

Shneiderman, B. (2002). *Leonardo's Laptop: Human Needs and the New Computing Technologies*. Cambridge, MA: MIT Press.

Teiche, A., Rai, A. K., Yanc, C., Moore, C., Solms, D., & Çetin, G. … Sandler, S. (2009). *Multitouch Technologies*. Retrieved October 20, 2013, from http://nuicode.com/attachments/download/115/Multi-Touch_Technologies_v1.01.pdf

TelEduc Project. (2013). *TelEduc. Ensino a Distância*. Retrieved October 20, 2013 from http://www.teleduc.org.br

VandenBos, G., Knapp, S., & Doe, J. (2001). Role of reference elements in the selection of resources by psychology undergraduates. *Journal of Bibliographic Research*, *5*, 117–123.

W3C. (2013). *Multimodal Architecture and Interfaces*. Retrieved October 20, 2013 from http://www.w3.org/TR/2012/REC-mmi-arch-20121025/

KEY TERMS AND DEFINITIONS

Architecture: Encompasses the definition of its general structures, describing the logical components that make up the system and the connectors between them (Shaw & Garlan, 1996).

E-Learning Environment: Virtual Learning Environments or Learning Management Systems are web systems used to support teaching and learning activities; usually they have functionalities to publish content, to allow communication among participants and to manage the course.

Gesture: Is an expressive, meaningful body motion i.e. physical movement of the fingers, hands, arms, head, face, or body with the intent to convey information or interact with the environment (Karpov *et al.*, 2008, p. 156).

Human-Computer Interaction (HCI): A discipline concerned with the design, evaluation and implementation of interactive computing systems for human use and with the study of major phenomena surrounding them (SIGCHI, 1992).

Modality/Modalities: A mode in which a user´s input or system´s output are expressed.

Multimodal Interaction Systems: Systems with the capacity to communicate with the user by different communication modes, using more than one modality, automatically gives or extracts mean.

Multimodality: The use of at least two different modalities.

Pen: An instrument for writing or drawing with ink or similar fluid. Digital pen is an input device which captures the handwriting or brush strokes of a user.

Touch: To bring a bodily part into contact with so as to perceive through the tactile sense. For computer devices, refers to the ability of a surface to recognize the presence of a point of contact with the surface.

Web Multimodal Systems: Web systems that support multimodal interaction.

Chapter 4

Constructionist Prototype Programming in a First Semester HCI Course for Engineering Students

Jacob Nielsen
University of Southern Denmark, Denmark

Gunver Majgaard
University of Southern Denmark, Denmark

ABSTRACT

How can we merge interactive design processes and the development of interactive prototypes for first-semester students without prior programming experience? The authors provide a selection of relevant contructionism-inspired programming tools and provide indications on how one of them can enrich a user-centred design project for first-semester software and IT engineering students. They do this by describing the experiences from two runs of a HCI course and the concurrent semester projects. The students developed interactive touch-based learning apps for children in the fourth to sixth grade using App Inventor. Most of the project groups managed to do three iterations of specifying requirements, doing conceptual design, physical and interactive prototyping, and user evaluation. The groups implemented quite complex programs with multiple-screen switching, multiple interfaces, media such as pictures, animations and sound, database connection, Web-server connection, and integrated sensors, such as camera, accelerometer, etc. The students did a lot more project iterations and spent more time on the creative designs in real-life situations than the authors expected. This also allowed for the students' professional reflections on their prototypes, usability, interaction, and the design processes. All in all, this gave them a more profound real-life experience in the user-centred design process. The authors compare the two runs and suggest how to introduce contructionist prototype programming in a HCI course curriculum and conclude that contructionist programming tools can be a valuable addition to the teaching of HCI, and they suggest that further research should be conducted to explore how to best integrate these tools in order to optimize the students' learning capabilities.

DOI: 10.4018/978-1-4666-6228-5.ch004

INTRODUCTION

How can we integrate interaction design and development processes without prior programming experience? Within our HCI course we used MIT App Inventor as a prototyping tool for programming. App Inventor is a fourth generation visual programming language for developing interactive Android mobile apps, which allows the apps to be run on all Android-enabled devices. The students used the iterative interaction design method as described in "Interaction Design - beyond human-computer interaction" (Rogers, Sharp, & Preece, 2011). When introducing the methods of interaction design to young software engineering students, it becomes, in our experience, a great challenge to integrate user-centred design processes and development of interactive prototypes. Software engineering students at the beginning of their studies usually have mixed backgrounds with regards to programming experience; some have much experience in several programming languages, while others never wrote a single line of code. This study investigates if an easy-to-use prototype tool – in our case App Inventor – can be used for successfully linking analysis, design and implementation, and in this way give the students a broader picture of what it means to do interaction design with both simple and later on more advanced prototypes. In similar courses we have successfully used GameMaker as a prototype tool as introduction to iterative design processes and game design (Majgaard, 2012b). Within this course we did not want to put focus on game design, instead we wanted to focus on the development of interactive learning tools on tablets.

From a didactical point of view we coupled classroom teaching and real-life experiences. Within their projects they had to design and develop interactive prototypes for learning targeted at schoolchildren aged 10-12 years. The students had between one and three interventions with the target group. Our learning model was based on learning by doing and reflections on actions (Bateson, 2000; Dewey, 2008; Schön, 1983). Dewey (2008) introduced the ideas of experimental learning, which takes place outside the classroom, and he is famous for the expression, "learning by doing". Knowledge gained and supported by experience is richer than academic classroom teaching. In our case, the students tested their prototypes on schoolchildren two or three times during the semester. In the iterative design process the students evaluated and reflected at the end of each iterative cycle.

As research method we use Design-based Research (Akker, Gravemeijer, McKenney, & Nieveen, 2006; Majgaard, Misfeldt, & Nielsen, 2011). The method supports digital educational research and allows for strong retrospective analysis of educational designs. The empirical data is based on class discussions and semester project documentation.

Our goals with this chapter is to give our reader a view on how App Inventor and similar fourth generation programming languages can effectively be used to obtain student-centred experimental learning in an interaction design course.

BACKGROUND

How do we best introduce the programming process? Seymour Papert (Papert, 1993) suggested that children learn while they are constructing and experimenting. Papert coined the concept of constructionism, which combines Piaget's constructivism and an experimental learning strategy. Within this section we describe several technologies that are more or less consequences of the initial ideas of Seymour Papert and which can all be considered constructionist tools. We present these technologies as a part of our research in the quest for finding a technology suitable for our HCI course and the required application area specified by our partner company, MC Nordic, as stated in the settings and case section.

Logo

Papert introduced Logo programming of digital turtles and the children intuitively learned about geometry. The turtle drew a trace on a piece of paper dependent on how it was programmed. The programming instructions were for example {move (100 units)}; {turn (90 degrees)}. The idea was to provide a "low floor" (easy to get started) and a "high ceiling" - opportunities to create increasingly complex projects over time (Resnick, 1996). In the late 90s we also used turtle programming on first semester students as a basic introduction to programming concepts. We provided the students with a special turtle class. The students then used the turn and move methods to construct small programs. The students drew all kind of shapes, rectangles, circles houses etc. This was inspired by Caspersen (Caspersen & Christensen, 2000), who used turtles to achieve a better and more intuitive learning of e.g. instructions, parameters, loops and methods. Basically we wanted the students to experiment, learn from errors and induce a need for more abstract programming construc-tors. Even though the turtle programming from a pedagogical view was successful it was limited to drawing shapes.

Lego Mindstorms

Lego Mindstorms® is also used to provide an understanding on how to sense and interact with the physical world from a programming angle. Within our institution we have, since the release of the first RCX version, been using Lego Mind-storms as a platform for teaching our students about autonomous robots, and how to build the physical and the mechanical parts as well as the robot control. We have especially been focusing on the interaction between morphology and control as well as the interaction between multiple robots and human-robot interaction. The programming of Lego Mindstorms can be done in third generation languages such as e.g. C or python or the visual

LabView powered NXT programming language. Mitchell Resnick was inspired by Papert's ideas and the Lego building blocks (Resnick et al., 1998) when he and the MIT Media Lab participated in the development of Lego Mindstorms, which also borrowed the "Mindstorms" name from the title of Paperts book (Papert, 1993).

I-Blocks

At our institution our research has also been heav-ily inspired by the work of Semour Papert and Mitchel Resnick, and one of the authors of this chapter, Jacob Nielsen, developed several genera-tions of a user-centred, user-configurable modular robotic system (I-BLOCKS) that allows a user to configure a system of technological modules, both defining the physical manifestation and the system behaviour while constructing (Nielsen & Lund, 2008). In other words, the user physically programs a technologic device through assembling a structure of modules. The overall research ques-tion in this work has been how to create systems that provide an easy interface to somewhat complex paradigms (Such as e.g. wheeled, learning robots (Nielsen & Lund, 2003), technological sensor and actuator tools (Nielsen & Lund, 2008), musical composition (Nielsen, Jessen, & Bærendsen, 2008), spelling, grammar, mathematics etc.), and which are flexible enough to allow the users to experiment trough manipulation within a given paradigm and thereby allowing them to create many different kinds of emergent behaviours. The term, physical programming, is actually one that fits very well with the user's activity with such a system, although this term does not capture the learning value of the experimentation through manipulation that goes on while figuring out how to use such a system. Compared to e.g. Lego Mind-storms, the I-BLOCKS provide a truly distributed behavioural system where the user experiences a direct and immediate consequence of his actions while constructing. There is no PLAY button to press in order to execute the program. All the sub-behaviours of the individual modules are active at all times and are responding immediately to the behaviours of their neighbouring modules, the user's actions and the sensor data available due to changes in the environment.

Sifteo

Sifteo cubes are interactive cubes for playing and learning. They are an example of modular tangibles. Sifteo is a combination of interactive blocks and screen-based interfaces. They perform small animations and display pictures, letters, numbers and other symbols. Each Sifteo package consists of 3-6 Sifteo blocks. Each block is clickable, contains a colour display and a number of motion sensors. Each block is just under 4x4 cm. The blocks are connected wirelessly to a computer via a USB radio link. Sifteo applications are executed from a special computer-based Sifteo-runner program. Children interact while connecting, shaking, tossing, and turning the cubes. The children can also collaborate with each other while interacting with the cubes.

Our students have been developing new software for the cubes in order to explore new ways of interacting and they developed interactive paper dolls (Majgaard, 2012a).

Scratch

Scratch (Lifelong Kindergarten Group, 2003; Maloney et al., 2004; Maloney, Resnick, Rusk, Silverman, & Eastmond, 2010) is a web-based visual programming language that was developed by Mitchel Resnick et al. at MIT media lab. In their paper, "Scratch: Programming for all" (Resnick et al., 2009), they state that with Scratch they wanted to develop an approach to programming that would appeal to people who had not previously imagined themselves as programmers. They wanted to make it easy for everyone, of all ages, backgrounds, and interests, to program their own interactive stories, games, animations, and

simulations, and share their creations with one another. Scratch has been developed to have a feel similar to LEGO, where the grammar is based on a collection of graphical programming blocks. Children (and adults) snap these blocks together to create programs. The connectors ensure correct syntax, so that you can only snap blocks together if it makes sense syntactically. The main users of Scratch are right now children aged 8-16, which indicates how a user-friendly environment and a more visual manipulative and explorative approach to programming invites a whole new audience into the world of software development.

App Inventor

MIT App Inventor ("App Inventor," 2012) is a visual block programming language for developing mobile applications for the Android platform. App Inventor was originally provided by Google, but is now maintained and developed further by Center for Mobile Learning, MIT. The visual blocks programming language is very similar to Scratch - using jigsaw puzzle-like blocks for representing different elements such as definitions, text and text handling, lists, math and numbers, logic, control and colours.

App Inventor consists of two parts - a browser-based part in which you design your interface, and a Java-based program called blocks editor, in which you puzzle together the program behaviour – see Figure 1.

App Inventor allows the user to navigate and set up different interface elements through a drag-and-drop interface. Here you can insert standard interactive GUI elements such as buttons, lists, labels, text input fields, canvases, sliders etc. Also, the interface editor gives access to using the different multimedia capabilities of the android device such as the camera, camcorder, image gallery, sound and video players, and other device-specific sensors such as GPS, accelerometer and gyroscope as well as social capabilities such as texting, phone calls, picking contacts, tweeting etc.

Figure 1. a) App Inventor's browser-based interface editor. b) The Java-based blocks editor

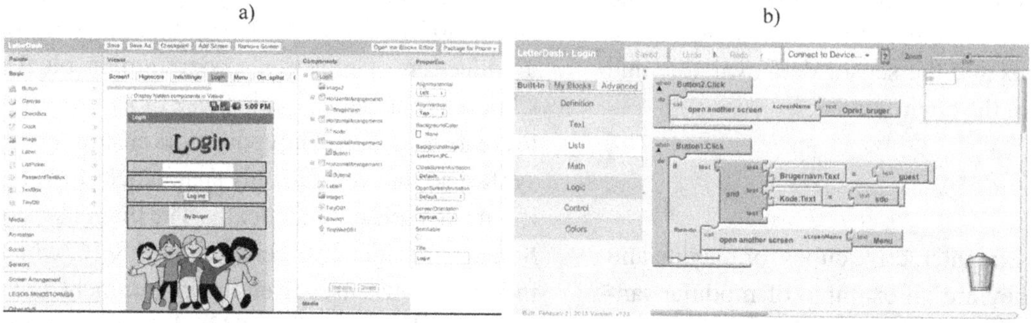

Besides those, App Inventor also allows access to web databases and more specific operations such as Bluetooth communication, text to speech, barcode scanning and web HTTP POST and GET requests for communicating with a web server.

The App Inventor interface editor even provides access to the Lego Mindstorms interface, closing the circle of the different technologies described in this section.

From a programming perspective App Inventor provides the user with the blocks editor, where a user will see a representation of the elements of the interface he built in the My Blocks section of the editor. With these elements the user can construct the controls of his application such as e.g. the response of pressing a button, filling data into a list from a web database, drawing polygons on the canvas or any other behaviour that would normally be reachable with a textual programming language.

Grover and Pea (Grover & Pea, 2013) have successfully been using App Inventor in a four-day workshop for middle-school children (aged 13 years). Wolber (2011) has used App Inventor in a course on "Computing, Robots and the Web" as an introduction to programming concepts for university students. He states that the brick language reduces beginners' syntax problems and that the students almost immediately build apps with real-world utility.

Arduino

As stated at the Arduino website ("Arduino," 2013) –"Arduino is an open-source electronics prototyping platform based on flexible, easy-to-use hardware and software. It is intended for artists, designers, hobbyists and anyone interested in creating interactive objects or environments". Among the Arduino products are processing boards, different sensor boards, output boards, such as sound, light (LED), motor-controllers and finally communication boards for Bluetooth, Wi-Fi, Ethernet, ZigBee etc. The Arduino platform comes in different series, and with different amounts of processing power, and is supported by a customised software, IDE, based on the processing language, where the user builds "sketches", which are their metaphors of the programs that are made on this platform. Arduino is also programmable by a software platform called ModKit Micro, which again is a visual programming language similar to Scratch and App Inventor. As the Arduino platform is open source, there are numerous sites offering different Arduino-powered technologies, software examples etc. and there are numerous forums and YouTube videos on people's creations to be found. This platform allows people with only little programming- or technological skills to invent and demonstrate quite complex technologies.

The technologies described above are the ones we, as writers of this chapter, are most familiar with, but it is just a small selection of the huge amount of "constructionist tools" available. It is our belief that there is a strong tendency in the world right now to design and produce technologies and interactive construction tools with "a low floor and a high ceiling" allowing non-experts to easily enter and learn about the technologic world (hardware, software and even mechanics) through hands-on, manipulative and explorative interaction. This DIY (Do It Yourself) tendency has also been known in part as the "Maker Culture" and is by some considered a consequence of the current financial crisis (Lahart, 2009).

BENEFITS AND CHALLENGES OF RUNNING A HCI-COURSE AT FIRST SEMESTER OF AN ENGINEERING EDUCATION

Our new software engineering education was intentionally designed to have user-centred design as a first semester theme. We did this, because we wanted to give the students an early impression of the importance of how to work with the users and the direct and indirect benefits of this with regards to the design of new interactive solutions. Letting our students discover how involving users early in the design process would allow them to evolve and adapt their design ideas into effective applications and good user experiences. This again, would be of great value to the rest of their studies as well as their succeeding professional life. In general, there is a tendency in the Danish software industry to request these user-centred qualities of software engineering and computer science from students leaving our educational institutions due to several large-scale software projects that did not succeed in meeting the user's expectations and demands.

One critical point in teaching HCI and user-centred design is to assure the aforementioned discovery of the benefit of involving the users in the design process. Often, this discovery is made through multiple iterations of the cycle of designing, prototyping and evaluating with the users starting with simple, non-technological prototypes and continuing with more complex implemented software solutions. As written in the introduction, software engineering students at their first semester do not necessarily have the skills or experience necessary to implement even simple interactive applications. In order to do that they would at least need to complete a course on programming graphical user interfaces and before that maybe a course in object-oriented programming. So this contradiction between students' prerequisites at first semester and our wishes for more design iterations, which would require implementing quite advanced software, had to be solved somehow. Looking at the different technologies mentioned in the background section, it appears that they all offer the user a low complexity entry barrier as well as a high ceiling with regards to what can actually be made. We linked this knowledge with the wishes from our partner company, stating that the end product should be implemented and tested on a touch-device, and to that end we selected App Inventor.

SETTINGS AND CASE

As stated previously, our target group for our research was first-semester software and IT engineering students. The main learning goals for the HCI course were for the students to be able to plan and conduct a user-centred design process, that is, iteratively investigate users, their needs and praxis through interviews and observations, establish requirements and do conceptual designs followed by physical prototype designs and evaluate those with the users as illustrated in Figure 2. The book used in the course is Interaction Design: Beyond Human - Computer Interaction. (Rogers et al., 2011).

Figure 2. The interaction design life-cycle model as illustrated in Rogers et. al., 2011

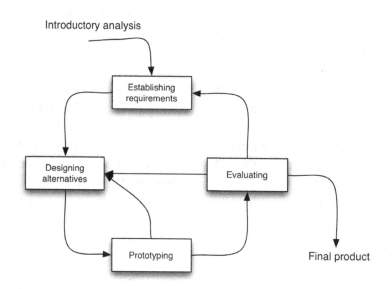

In parallel with the HCI course, the students were taking courses that introduced them to software engineering, information technology, basic object-oriented programming and study techniques, project work and communication as well as one integrating semester project, in which the students work on a user-centred design project where they try to include some of the theory and practical experiences learnt in all the courses, but with the main focus being HCI and user-centred design. Therefore, there was a close relationship between the HCI course and the semester project, and the HCI teacher also had the role of project supervisor on most of the student semester projects.

The semester was attended by approximately 70 engineering students, which were divided into 12 project groups for the semester project on behalf of a Belbin self-perception test. These groups were each assigned one school teacher and his/her respective class from four different Danish municipal schools.

The semester project case was described in collaboration with a locally founded company, MV Nordic, which produces communication and learning apps for the Nordic school systems. One of the first pedagogical decisions with regards to the project target group was that it should be easy for our students to collaborate with the users, and that the user environment should be somewhat known to them. The municipal schools were an easy choice due to the fact that we already had a lot of collaboration with quite a few of them and had contacts in several schools in the vicinity of the University campus. Having pupils as users and co-developers would, in the teacher-groups experience, be advantageous to our students due to the fact that the pupil target groups, especially from 4th grade and up, are easy to get a lot of feedback from, are eager co-designers and first and foremost they work with learning material that should be well-known to our students beforehand.

MV Nordic, specified the 4th to 6th grades as an interesting target group, and suggested touch-based learning apps for Danish language education as a relevant theme. The company also suggested that the main focus of the application should be the pupils´ communication with each other and the teacher, and that it should be possible for the teacher to obtain an overview of the pupils' use of the system as well as their learning progression. In addition, the company stated that increased motivation should be one of the key objectives with regards to the user experience of the prototype applications. All these suggestions were rooted in one of the company's own current focus areas.

The project lasted 15 weeks and after being introduced to the project case, the students had their first meeting with the teachers at the respective schools the following week. During this first meeting the teachers of the schools were presented more specifically to the project case and thereafter each of them teamed up with a separate student group. This was the students' first meeting with part of the user group – their contact person and curriculum expert – and from thereon they were responsible for the planning of the coming interventions with the users.

The settings and case from the teachers' point of view was actually quite similar to that of the students. As written in the introduction, our studies for the development of this course are based on the design-based research methodologies, more specifically educational design research (Akker et al., 2006). So, we did a lot of preliminary research on both literature and technical platforms as described in the background chapter before choosing app inventor as a plausible link between the needs of our partner company and the students' current skills. In our study we consider each run of the course: design, development and evaluation of a prototype as illustrated in Figure 3. This way our course is developed through annual iterations. The Figure (2) is inspired by a display of the CASCADE-SEA study (McKenney, Nieveen, & Akker, 2002) in (Akker et al., 2006), which illustrates both the cycles, number of people involved and the different contexts of the process. With our work only few people (3 teachers) were involved in the needs and context analysis, while the design, development and formative evaluation of each of the course prototypes involved teachers, students, schoolteachers and pupils.

The following is a list of challenges we used as measuring points of the success of designing and running these prototype courses. The challenges became apparent during the iterative process, and here we ordered the list, such that the challenges surfacing first, are placed first in the list:

- Integrating app inventor lessons into a HCI course curriculum
- Aligning the course book contents with the multi-iteration projects
- Evaluating the level of knowledge needed in order for the students to develop their own App Inventor programs.
- Identifying when students would benefit from going from simple (paper) prototypes to advanced (digital) prototypes.
- Identifying the optimal or minimum amount of development iterations in order for the students to understand the importance of the cyclic design process.
- Identifying improved learning outcomes, in a new course with no comparison possible.

In the following we will provide our answers to at least some of these challenges, while remembering that our course design-process has only just completed its 2nd cycle and that our answers may only yet be indicative and subject to change with the testing of new alternative directions and technologies in the coming years.

FIRST-RUN COURSE CURRICULUM

Within the original course description, the main academic learning objectives of the 5-ECTS Interaction and Interaction Design course are that the student at the end of the course should be able to:

- Plan a user-centred design process
- Investigate the users, their needs and their practice through interviews and observa-

Figure 3. The iterative design process of the HCI course described in this chapter

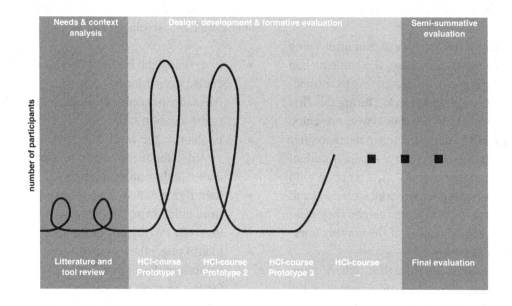

tions, and present the results in ways suitable for making design decisions.

- Involve users in design and evaluation in suitable ways
- Design interactions to fit with the users' needs and practices
- Apply fundamental design rules for user-friendly designs
- Describe different types of interactions
- Use selected types of interactions
- Plan and conduct evaluation of interaction design and present the results
- Develop simple digital prototypes
- Reflect on interactive design processes and the meaning of good design

As also written above, the course is run in parallel with the 10-ECTS semester project on user-centred design, which allows the students to work more thoroughly with the theories and methods of the course. The course is evaluated through a pre- and post-test (Nielsen & Majgaard, 2013) as well as a multiple-choice examination and the oral presentation and examination of the student semester projects.

The specification of the above learning objectives were based on previous similar HCI-courses in other engineering educations as well as literature and the course book selected. The inclusion of a constructionist programming technology was not yet decided at this time. The course plan for the first run was established a few weeks before the

Table 1.

Week	#	Lesson
36	1	Introduction to the course: What is interaction design, understanding and conceptualizing interaction.
37	2	The interaction design process.
38	3	Establishing requirements.
39	4	Design, Prototyping and Construction.
40	5	Cognitive aspects.
41	6	Social interaction.
43	7	Emotional interaction.
44	8	Interfaces.
45	9	Data collection.
46	10	Data analysis, interpretation and presentation.
47	11	Evaluation.
48	12	Course résumé and exam preparation.

beginning of the course and the new education. A brief version of this is presented below:

The subjects within the above plan are largely based on the chapters of our course book (Rogers et al., 2011), but rearranged to fit better with the project, so that the students right from the beginning get a good idea about the interaction design process and how to do the initial analysis and establish a first set of requirements and start designing and prototyping.

As can also be seen from the plan above none of the lesson subjects includes App Inventor teaching, and this posed a challenge for the responsible teacher, and therefore extra lessons – disguised as workshops - had to be included in order to get the students started using App Inventor. These lessons were placed rather late in the semester in the beginning (2nd) and end (23rd) of November because we as teachers decided it would be a good idea to wait introducing App Inventor before it was actually needed in their projects.

SELECTED FIRST-RUN PROJECT DISCOVERIES

This section describes the findings we as teachers did during the students' semester projects the first time this course was run at our new education. The findings are primarily based on our observations and divided into three overall iteration sub-sections, although the process for our students contained several sub-iterations within each of these iterations, and as such much more than three iterations were made during the project period.

Iteration 1

Most of the student groups did a lot of initial research and brainstorming together with their assigned schoolteachers on their first meetings. The overall outcome of this was mainly specifications of the main challenges within the teachers' curriculum. These challenges were, among others, *understanding what you read, learning grammar through sentence analysis – finding subject, sentence verb and object etc. in order to do proper punctuation, analysing different kinds of texts – e.g. fairy tales and novels and doing graphical novels.* For most teachers it was a challenge for them to give feedback to all the pupils when doing exercises in class and although they knew immediate feedback would improve the pupils' learning they had no proper tools to do so.

As part of iteration 1 most of the student groups arranged an observation day, where they would come and observe a Danish lesson in order to get to know the pupils as well as gaining a deeper understanding of the teaching environment, their current use of IT-equipment, the teaching materials, the teaching styles of the teachers, the levels of the pupils and also the pupil-pupil and pupil-teacher communication.

For our students these first meetings with both teachers and pupils were eye openers. Most could not believe that so little had changed since they were at the same age, and first and foremost they had all believed that IT-equipment had a much more prominent place in today's teaching environments.

As a result of our students' first findings they had to present a project proposal, which in many cases was now quite different from the case proposed by MV Nordic. This was mainly due to the students' wish to solve the more relevant and often more specific problems that they had discovered through the first meetings with the users. Only a few groups chose to follow the suggested focus on pupil-pupil and pupil-teacher communication.

Iteration 2

For most of the student groups, the 2nd iteration involved evaluation of simple technologic or paper-based prototypes with the user group. In the beginning, the students were quite hesitant with regards to going back to paper and pencil as they had just started on an IT- or Software Engineering education and they expected that they would be spending more time in front of their PC. A few groups actually presented almost fully described concepts and wanted to know when they could start implementing them and bring them to the schools. Those who went with paper and paint and e.g. the wizard of OZ method (Rogers et al, 2011) got some very productive feedback and according to their reports the pupils had no problems imagining they were playing with a real application.

Figure 4 shows one group's different version prototypes of the same application where they use different layouts, themes etc.

The main results of iteration 2 were the students' discovery of simple prototypes being efficient tools for validating specific interaction patterns, the learning material, graphical themes, structuring and layout of user interfaces etc. Those who went with paper prototypes got a lot of de-sign feedback from the pupils due to the informal sandbox environment these prototypes create. The groups that started out with App Inventor prototypes at this stage did also receive a lot of useful feedback, but were usually more focused on a specific design and because of that they did not cover as large a design area.

Iteration 3

During the 3rd iteration most student groups started implementing their first App Inventor prototypes. Quite a few students complained about having to use a "non-textual" programming environment, and how they would loose flexibility and not be able to implement things exactly how they wanted to. Many of them thought of App Inventor as a children's tool for learning how to program, and actually felt that they were not able to do any real programming using this tool. From our supervision meetings with the student groups it was soon quite clear that the main part of those who complained about not using a textual programming language were those who had no or only little experience in programming. However, most of those who had some experience in programming were also able to see the advantages of using App Inventor – mainly because they already knew the difficult and tedious parts of its textual alternatives. With some guidance from the supervisors and through the App Inventor workshops held by the HCI teacher, the students were shown different project-related examples and solutions. These examples e.g. included how to set up and use a TinyWebDB for storing data online, how to use multiple screens, how to use lists as databases, how to set up and customise the interface using canvas elements instead of buttons, text fields etc. Also, the App Inventor cafés worked as a forum, where those who were already enthusiastic about and actively using App Inventor helped those who were still in doubt about its potentials and its ability

Figure 4. One project group's example of three different paper prototypes with similar content but different layout and interaction styles

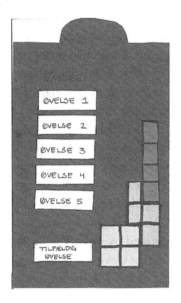 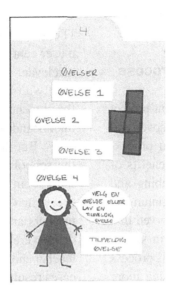 

to support their application ideas. So despite of the initial reluctance to use App Inventor, a lot of creative prototype solutions were actually implemented with this tool, and the resemblance to a "real" programming language became clearer and clearer to the students, the more they got into the environment and the blocks language and the more they learned about the Java programming language in their introduction to programming classes. This was first and foremost so, because App Inventor is basically constructed and structured like many of the c-inspired textual programming languages available today and uses the same concepts of variables, functions and control structures, although with a graphical representation instead of textual. So when the students learned about these components in their Java course, they could often draw parallels to the relevant App Inventor blocks.

Most groups ended up implementing quite large programs with multiple screen switching, multiple interfaces, media such as pictures, animations and sound, database connection, web-server connection, integrated sensors – such as camera,

accelerometer etc. This was all done within a few weeks.

In the schools, the evaluation of the digital prototypes provided the students with a lot of user data succeeded by numerous design changes, prototype tweaks etc. The learning process for the student groups in this phase mainly included getting experience with interviewing 4th to 6th graders – i.e. learning how to have specific goals with your evaluation, formulate and ask relevant open questions and how to create a safe and informal environment for the pupils. Also, many groups commented back that they had had a lot of positive feedback from their attached teachers. One group who worked with an app for creating graphic novels did a usability test where they observed pupils that had been instructed in how the application worked and some that had received no instructions. All test persons had difficulties of some sort during the test – e.g. navigating around the application and finding out how to use the camera. Figure 3 illustrates the main interface of that specific application in the final prototype version, where the user has taken a picture and added some graphics and text, stating that he wants to engage in a snowball fight. The App Inventor blocks code shows the main procedure of drawing graphics or text in their app.

Understanding the Iterative Process

One of our main goals with the student project was for the students to be able to discover and understand that a user-centred design process should be iterative and to learn the benefits of evolving a product rather than describing and defining everything from the very beginning of the project. During iteration 2 we observed that a few of the groups had difficulties in seeing why they would have to go through this process of designing, prototyping and evaluating more than one time, because they thought they had the perfect idea for an application, which they just needed to implement. An example that illustrates how we as project supervisors tried to illustrate why more iterations would be necessary: at one of the project supervision meetings one of these groups were asked to show what their application would look like when implemented, and almost none of the group members agreed on the layout. From that point they started understanding, that having a common conceptual idea is not the same as knowing how to lay out every bit and piece of e.g. the user interface.

In general, there have been a lot of questions during the semester as to how many iterations would be enough, and it has been challenging for the students to discover themselves all the smaller iterations they have actually done during the larger iterations 1, 2 and 3 described above. Some groups also had trouble accepting, that they would not necessarily build a final product during the project period, but in the end most groups were indeed very satisfied with their final prototype, and this was partially due to the number of iterations they made and partially due to the user involvement.

Benefits of User Involvement

Our presumptions that first-semester software and IT engineering students would benefit from doing a user-centred design project with real users and a relevant project subject were indeed correct. Like with the iterative process, it was hard for the students at the beginning of the semester to understand why it was important to involve the users. But through the different interventions at the schools we, as supervisors, could see that the student groups really learned something new every time they were together with their contact teachers and classes. At the beginning, the students were mainly informed by talking with the teacher and by observing the class, which in many cases resulted in a shift of focus in the design as opposed to what had be proposed by our partner company. With the evaluation of the first simple paper or App Inventor prototypes the student groups got substantial feedback on their design and were able to do several changes or additions to the design each time they had been in contact with the pupils or teacher.

All of the prototype versions implemented did not necessarily reach the pupils in the schools, mainly because the student groups had obtained a level of self-criticism on behalf of the paper prototype evaluations. The groups that did a substantial amount of work with the physical paper-based prototypes often had a clearer picture of how to make their concept into a digital prototype, and as a result they were much more focused in their 3rd iteration phase.

Usefulness of the Prototype Tool

App Inventor's usefulness as a prototype tool has been proved at several levels during the students' projects. It has been quite easy for the students to build quite complex programs in a short time.

If one should compare the complexity of the implemented App Inventor applications held up against the students' current levels of program-

Figure 5. a) Graphic novels application interface. b) app inventor code example

a)

b)

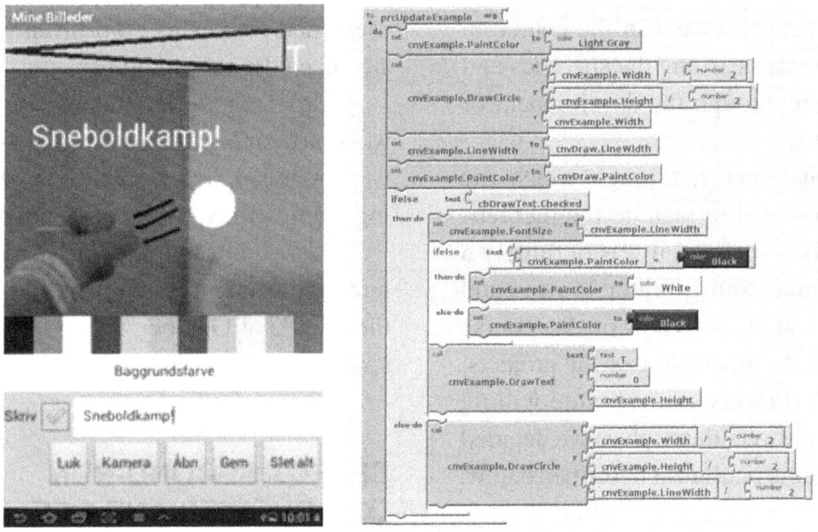

ming expertise and the time they actually spent implementing the applications, there is no doubt that they would not have been able to reach even half that complexity with a textual programming language such as Java, which was the language they were taught the basics of on 1st semester. Not all students were able to do this discovery during the project, because they did not have the relevant expertise with textual programming languages to do such a comparison. Chances are, however, that they will make this discovery in the coming semesters.

One of the weaknesses of App Inventor, which is still in its beta-stage, is that it does not yet support collaborative programming very well. It is e.g. not possible to import parts of another program into your own project. Another limitation is the redrawing speed of the blocks editor. When working with complex programs with many blocks many students complained about the slowness of the program. Also, the interface editor still lacks some graphics abilities in order to allow you to make programs that will look professional. At one point during the semester we decided to install our

own local App Inventor service at the university because the students were experiencing a lot of down-time of the MIT App Inventor server mainly due to heavy use as we were told by one of the App Inventor technicians at MIT.

In spite of all the challenges, however, as a prototyping tool App Inventor showed its worth and we decided on using it within the second-run of the course and semester projects as well.

Evaluation of the Didactical Planning and Learning Achieved

From a didactical point of view bringing in App Inventor as a prototyping tool in a user-centred design project has allowed the students to focus better on the design parts and first and foremost the user involvement. In our experience, the results of spending less time on implementing prototypes are that the students are able to do a lot more iterations and because of that they gain a much better understanding of how to involve the users and how to ensure high usability and user experience in interactive products. From the students' evaluation of the course we did receive a lot of complaints about the timing of the introduction of App Inventor. They stated that they would like us to introduce it much earlier in the course in order for them to start learning the specifics and gaining experience through the development of example programs.

Within the HCI-course, through which the students were supposed to pick up the theoretical methods for their project, it was definitely a challenge to include App Inventor lessons and simultaneously plan the activities of this course to fit exactly with the proceeding of the projects, and although the students seemed quite willing to search for the answers themselves we decided upon changing the curriculum as described below.

SECOND-RUN COURSE CURRICULUM

When starting the planning of the second-run of the course, we decided on keeping the original learning objectives for the course, as these were general enough not to be affected by the changes we wanted to do:

The new course plan is presented below:

The main changes made to the course plan compared to the first-run of the course are the inclusion of App Inventor lessons at the very first lesson as well as lesson 10. Besides those data gathering, data analysis and evaluation was placed within the first five lessons as well. This was done in order to dress our students much better for the initial user contact within their projects as well as providing them with the theory on how to evaluate their prototypes much earlier. In short, they were introduced to what it means to do user-centred design before they learnt the specifics of interaction design, such as cognitive aspects, social and emotional interaction and learning about all the different interface possibilities.

Also, we changed the exercises within the course to be a continuous mini-project split into

three portfolio exercises, where the students would be able to practise some of the specifics of their semester project using primarily each other as users, and also using App Inventor for the more advanced digital prototypes.

In order to give the students some extra time to work on their portfolio-exercises, two lesson slots were included, which would also be used for helping them with App Inventor-specific challenges.

As an addition to the course plan we also offered the students an App Inventor workshop in the middle of October, trying to bridge the large span between the first and the tenth lesson.

SELECT SECOND-RUN DISCOVERIES AND REFLECTIONS

This section describes the findings that have recently taken place during the second run of this course. At the time of writing this chapter, the students were just in between the 2nd and 3rd iteration phase of their semester project – coming from simple prototypes and starting implementing their first digital prototypes in App Inventor. In the mid-term evaluation of the course we received complaints about having to use App Inventor as a prototyping tool. The stated reasons for the complaints were quite similar to those we received in the last run, although some were actually now complaining about App Inventor being too hard to learn how to use properly. With the second run of this course, we had now put more effort into introducing App Inventor earlier in the course, so that the students would have a chance to get to know the programming environment and try implementing small example programs before starting out on their own prototypes. The consequences of this early acquaintance apparently were that the students now to some degree realised App Inventor's similarity to a textual programming language and they were facing the challenges of programming in general. This discovery comes earlier than in the last run, and we thus expect the

Table 2.

Week	#	Lesson
36	1	Introduction to the course: What is interaction design? Introducing App Inventor.
37	2	The interaction design process and data gathering.
38	3	Data analysis and establishing requirements.
39	4	Design, Prototyping and Construction.
40	5	Evaluating results.
41	6	Cognitive aspects
43	7	Work on portfolio exercise
44	8	Social and emotional interaction
45	9	Interfaces
46	10	More App Inventor
47	11	Work on portfolio exercise
48	12	Course résumé and exam preparation.

students to take App Inventor more seriously this time, not considering it only a children's programming language tool.

One of the other changes we did during this run was to ask the students to design and implement the interface and the basic navigation in their app first in App Inventor, before implementing the more behavioral parts. Most students succeeded in doing this quite rapidly, although some had problems getting the appearance of the interface just right. Setting up the interface and implementing the navigation does not require heavy use of the blocks editor. It only requires setting up some relevant actions, like switching screens in the event of e.g. a button being pressed. This task strengthened the students' focus on the user-interactive parts, and actually provided them with yet another prototype to test. We believe that this will provide a more solid ground for the students to implement their behavioural parts and hopefully make them accomplish at least the same results as our students did at the end of the last run of the course.

Another improvement compared to the last run was that we discovered a way for the students to split up their applications into their individual screens with a tool named "MergeTool". This tool allows the students within the groups to work individually on different parts of the project and even do individual evaluations with the users and merge the different parts when preparing to evaluate the entire app. This possibility was missed very much during the last run, as it resulted in only one or two persons doing most of the implementation, and as a result the rest of the group had to wait until everything was working until they could evaluate with the users.

FIRST-RUN AND SECOND-RUN COMPARISON

Within this section we compare the solutions to the discovered challenges we stated in the section "Benefits and challenges of running a HCI-course at first semester of an engineering education". As written previously the design of this course and the semester project has been an iterative process, and the results presented above have helped us improving the course and the integration of App Inventor, although challenges still exist.

Integrating App Inventor Lessons into a HCI Course Curriculum

The integration of the App Inventor lessons have been quite a challenge, because the time that had to be set aside to teaching App Inventor had to be taken from the teaching of the interaction design theory. Compared to the first-run where all App Inventor lessons were planned as workshops outside the course plan, the second-run provide in-course lessons aligned with the rest of the curriculum.

From the programs delivered at the end of the projects it is actually hard to see any major difference in the complexity of the programs, and whether the students did benefit from more lessons on App Inventor during the 2nd run.

Aligning the Course Book Contents with the Multi-Iteration Projects

The alignment used in the 2nd run was well accepted, and made it much easier for the students to concentrate on the process first and implement that understanding in their projects before beginning on the more interaction-design specific issues. We have decided on keeping this course structure for the 3rd run.

Evaluating the Level of Knowledge Needed In Order For the Students to Develop Their Own App Inventor Programs

From our two runs, we clearly discovered that App Inventor as any other tool does have a learning curve. The low floor and high ceiling as stated by (Papert, 1993) is also existent in App Inventor, but from our experience and the evaluation results from our students the learning curve is quite flat at the beginning, but steepens quite a lot when you go from programming simple "hello world" programs to more complex programs as e.g. building a complex user interface, communicating with a web database, using lists to store data or sending data from screen to screen. App Inventor is a real c-style event-based programming language made into a graphical puzzle, and finding the right piece for the puzzle is in many cases just as difficult as using a textual programming language. Therefore, there is no doubt, that in order for the students to be able to do real programs with real behaviours and easy-to-use interfaces, they need a lot of experience and will benefit from many examples and exercises.

Identifying When Students Would Benefit From Going from Simple (Paper) Prototypes to Advanced (Digital) Prototypes

From our observations during both runs there is no doubt that those groups who did a lot of initial, simple prototypes did also much sooner obtain a clear idea about how the basics of their design should be. App Inventor does help the students build basic digital prototypes that can be introduced to the users earlier on, and even despite of its learning curve, the students in our experience seem more willing to experiment with the puzzle-blocks in App Inventor compared to e.g. a textual programming language. The constructionist approach has clear benefits here. From the users' point-of-view, there is no doubt that the early introduction of digital prototypes give them a better feel of, what this application is going to be like in the end, and while this could be dangerous because of the risk of the users stepping "out of the sandbox" and stopping contributing to the design with new ideas, the rather simplistic interfaces that the students built at the beginning of their projects still showed the users, that they were dealing with prototypes. We decided during the second run to let the students decide when to start using App Inventor instead of e.g. paper prototypes, and it seemed to work quite well, as their projects were quite different, and some actually needed to evaluate parts of their behavioural design with the users early in the project.

Identifying the Optimal or Minimum Amount of Development Iterations In Order For the Students to Understand the Importance of the Cyclic Design Process

As written above the students did a lot of sub-iterations within each of the three main iterations we specified in their project plan. During both runs of the course, most students achieved a good understanding of the importance of the iterative user-centered design process, which was apparent both through the examination of the projects as well as the succeeding course evaluation. A few groups were unfortunate to loose contact with their user group during the project, which severely influenced the outcome of their projects. This did however, help reinforcing the student's understanding of the importance of the user involvement. As of now, we do not have a measurement of the minimum amount of iterations necessary for the students to understand the importance of the process, and we are quite certain that this measurement is difficult to make. We do however recognize that with the current structuring of the course and with the use of App Inventor, our students do reach this understanding through several project iterations with the users.

Identifying Improved Learning Outcomes, In a New Course with No Comparison Possible

We have not yet done an objective comparison of our course with other HCI courses that do not use constructionist programming technologies. To that end the only comparison possible yet, is between the two course runs. This comparison was introduced in (Nielsen & Majgaard, 2013), and the final comparison will be published during 2014.

RECOMMENDATIONS

Recommendations for Constructionist Programming Tools

The different contructionism-inspired technologies presented in the background section all represent feasible solutions to the problem treated in this chapter, that is, getting the students to discover the value of doing HCI and user-centred design through multiple iterations of designing, prototyping and evaluating with the users. Each of them

could with relevant adjustment of the course plan and project description be implemented in a way similar to what we presented here.

Of the technologies we described, some of them are software-based, while others are physical real-world manipulatives, and we are now considering using these types of manipulatives for our 3rd run in order to build up experiences with the different technologies in the context of this course and to possibly compare and qualify more of them over time.

Recommendations for Course Curriculum

Including a contructionist programming technology in a HCI course curriculum has proven quite a challenge although the rewards are great. Our recommendations for others that would like to go down this path are to either plan the course to include enough lessons, which introduces and exemplifies this technology on the sideline of the traditional HCI theory. It is important to let the students still experiment with simple paper prototypes and present those to the user, before they start introducing the constructionism-based digital prototypes. Right now we are considering changing the programming course that runs in parallel with the HCI course and the semester project, in order to let that course include the introduction to e.g. App Inventor or any of the other constructionist tools we describe here.

FUTURE RESEARCH DIRECTIONS

Future research within what has been described in this chapter may include further optimization of the way the constructionist programming tools are integrated into the course and project and efforts to discover the effects of the "low floor, high ceiling" that these tools promise. Our students are still facing quite steep learning curves with these tools, but in our opinion the increased levels of fast experimentation and feedback make up for this with regards to the speed at which the students are able to acquire the necessary skills to overcome these curves. We would, however, like to investigate this further and compare the different tools to identify the common and individual challenges in overcoming these learning curves.

CONCLUSION

Using a constructionist programming tool such as App Inventor as a prototyping tool for first-semester engineering students has definite benefits with regards to the students' learning. The main benefit is that App Inventor takes the focus away from some of the tedious parts of programming, allowing the students to implement even advanced functionalities within a shorter time and with less frustrations than with a standard textual programming language. As a consequence the students are able to spend more time on the design and the user involvement and thereby do a lot more project iterations which gives them a profound experience in the user-centred design process. Another benefit of using App Inventor is that it still looks sufficiently similar to a real programming language (variables, functions, control structures) so that the students have been able to draw parallels to their programming courses, and actually learn a lot about the basics of programming through working with App Inventor. Most of the programming tools and technologies presented in the background section are still in their early stages of development, and during the students' projects we have had quite a few complaints about errors in App Inventor that would halt the students' projects for a while until fixed. Installing App Inventor on our own local server solved some of these problems.

From the project supervision hours and the project examination it was clear that the main part of the student groups did an excellent work of involving the users and making both paper- and App Inventor prototypes to validate these. Not all students understood either the iterative process or the benefits of involving users from the beginning of the project, but this was learned over the project period, and as a consequence we received a lot of well-tested and highly usable prototypes at the end of the first semester.

We used App Inventor again during the second run of this course, and further improved the structuring of the course, the inclusion of App Inventor in the course and project and the distribution of implementing and evaluating the prototype applications within the project groups.

We consider these constructionism programming tools a valuable addition to the teaching of e.g. HCI, and we suggest that further research keep investigating how to integrate them the best way possible with regards to the students' learning.

REFERENCES

Akker, J. V. D., Gravemeijer, K., McKenney, S., & Nieveen, N. (2006). *Educational Design Research*. New York, NY: Routledge.

App. Inventor. (2012). Retrieved November 2nd, 2013, from http://appinventor.mit.edu

Arduino. (2013). Retrieved November 2nd, 2013, from http://arduino.cc

Bateson, G. (2000). *Steps to an Ecology of Mind: Collected Essays in Anthropology, Psychiatry, Evolution, and Epistemology*. Chicago, IL: University of Chicago Press.

Caspersen, M. E., & Christensen, H. B. (2000). *Here, there and everywhere - on the recurring use of turtle graphics in CS1*. Paper presented at the Australasian conference on Computing Education. Melbourne, Australia.

Dewey, J. (2008). *Democracy and Education: An Introduction to the Philosophy of Education*. Radford, VA: Wilder Publications.

Grover, S., & Pea, R. (2013). Using a discourse-intensive pedagogy and android's app. inventor for introducing computational concepts to middle school students. In *Proceedings of the 44th ACM technical symposium on Computer science education* (pp. 723-728). Denver, CO: ACM Press.

Lahart, J. (2009, November 13). Tinkering Makes Comeback Amid Crisis. *The Wall Street Journal.* Retrieved from http://online.wsj.com/news/articles/SB125798004542744219

Lifelong Kindergarten Group. M. M. L. (2003). *Scratch.* Retrieved November 2nd, 2013, from http://scratch.mit.edu

Majgaard, G. (2012a). Brug af interaktive klodser i ingeniørundervisningen. [Using interactive blocks in engineering education]. *MONA: Matematik og Naturfagsdidaktik,* (4), 24-40.

Majgaard, G. (2012b). Design af computerspil i undervisningen: fra indfødt spilverdenen til reflekteret designer. *Læring og Medier (LOM), 5*(9).

Majgaard, G., Misfeldt, M., & Nielsen, J. (2011). How design-based research, action research and interaction design contributes to the development of designs for learning. *Designs for Learning, 4*(2), 8–21.

Maloney, J., Burd, L., Kafai, Y., Rusk, N., Silverman, B., & Resnick, M. (2004). Scratch: A Sneak Preview. In *Proceedings of the Second International Conference on Creating, Connecting and Collaborating through Computing* (pp. 104-109). Washington, DC: IEEE Computer Society.

Maloney, J., Resnick, M., Rusk, N., Silverman, B., & Eastmond, E. (2010). The scratch programming language and environment. *ACM Transactions on Computing Education, 10*(4), 16. doi:10.1145/1868358.1868363

Nielsen, J., Jessen, C., & Bærendsen, N. K. (2008). RoboMusicKids – Music Education with Robotic Building Blocks. In *Proceedings of the 2nd IEEE International Conference on Digital Game and Intelligent Toy Enhanced Learning* (DIGITEL) (pp. 149-156). Banff, Canada: IEEE Press.

Nielsen, J., & Lund, H. H. (2003). Spiking neural building block robot with Hebbian learning. In *Proceedings of the IEEE/RSJ International Conference on the Intelligent Robots and Systems* (IROS 2003) (pp. 1363 - 1369). Las Vegas, NV: IEEE Press.

Nielsen, J., & Lund, H. H. (2008). Modular robotics as a tool for education and entertainment. *Computers in Human Behavior, 24*(2), 234–248. doi:10.1016/j.chb.2007.01.011

Nielsen, J., & Majgaard, G. (2013). Self-Assessment and Reflection in a 1st Semester Course for Software Engineering Students. In *Proceedings of the IADIS International Conference on Cognition and Exploratory Learning in the Digital Age* (CELDA 2013) (pp. 150-158). Forth Worth, TX: IADIS Press.

Papert, S. (1993). *Mindstorms: Children, computers, and powerful ideas.* Cambridge, MA: Da Capo Press.

Resnick, M. (1996). StarLogo: an environment for decentralized modeling and decentralized thinking. In *Proceedings of the Conference Companion on Human Factors in Computing Systems* (pp. 11-12). Vancouver, Canada: ACM Press.

Resnick, M., Maloney, J., Monroy-Hernández, A., Rusk, N., Eastmond, E., Brennan, K., & Kafai, Y. (2009). Scratch: programming for all. *Communications of the ACM, 52*(11), 60–67. doi:10.1145/1592761.1592779

Resnick, M., Martin, F., Berg, R., Borovoy, R., Colella, V., Kramer, K., & Silverman, B. (1998). Digital manipulatives: new toys to think with. In *Proceedings of the SIGCHI conference on Human factors in computing systems* (pp. 281-287). Los Angeles, CA: ACM Press.

Rogers, Y., Sharp, H., & Preece, J. (2011). *Interaction Design: Beyond Human-Computer Interaction* (3rd ed.). Hoboken, NJ: John Wiley and Sons, Ltd.

Sabelli, N. (1987). *Constructionism: A New Opportunity for Elementary Science Education.* DRL Division of Research on Learning in Formal and Informal Settings. Retrieved from http://nsf.gov/awardsearch/showAward?AWD_ID=8751190

Schön, D. A. (1983). *The Reflective Practitioner: How Professionals Think in Action.* London, UK: Maraca Temple Smith.

Sharples, M., McAndrew, P., Weller, M., Ferguson, R., FitzGerald, E., Hirst, T., & Gaved, M. (2013). *Maker Culture: Learning by making, Innovating Pedagogy* (pp. 33–36). London, UK: The Open University Press.

Wolber, D. (2011). App. inventor and real-world motivation. In *Proceedings of the 42nd ACM technical symposium on Computer science education* (pp. 601-606). Dallas, TX: ACM Press.

ADDITIONAL READING

Akker, J. V. d., Gravemeijer, K., McKenney, S., & Nieveen, N. (2006). *Educational Design Research.* New York, NY: Routledge.

Bateson, G. (2000). *Steps to an Ecology of Mind: Collected Essays in Anthropology, Psychiatry, Evolution, and Epistemology.* Chicago, IL: University of Chicago Press.

Dewey, J. (2008). *Democracy and Education: An Introduction to the Philosophy of Education.* Radford, VA: Wilder Publications.

Rogers, Y., Sharp, H., & Preece, J. (2011). *Interaction Design: Beyond Human-Computer Interaction* (3rd ed.). Hoboken, NJ: John Wiley and Sons, Ltd.

Schön, D. A. (1983). *The Reflective Practitioner: How Professionals Think in Action.* London, UK: Maraca Temple Smith.

KEY TERMS AND DEFINITIONS

Constructionism: Seymour Papert defined constructionism in a proposal to the National Science Foundation entitled Constructionism: A New Opportunity for Elementary Science Education as follows: "The word constructionism is a mnemonic for two aspects of the theory of science education underlying this project. From constructivist theories of psychology we take a view of learning as a reconstruction rather than as a transmission of knowledge. Then we extend the idea of manipulative materials to the idea that learning is most effective when part of an activity the learner experiences as constructing is a meaningful product." (Sabelli, 2008).

Constructionist Tools: We define these as tools for learning adhering to Seymour Paperts concept of constructionism. Constructionist tools are building blocks (visual or physical) that are easy to learn how to use (low floor) while still allowing people to be creative and build advanced systems (high ceiling).

Design-Based Research: The Design-based research method supports digital educational research and allows for strong retrospective analysis of educational designs. The empirical data is based on class discussions and semester project documentation.

Learning by Doing: Dewey (2008) introduced the ideas of experimental learning, which takes place outside the classroom, and he is famous for the expression, "learning by doing".

Maker Culture: Learning by Making - There has been a recent renewed interest in learning through making, focused on the social construction of artefacts. While this might appear to echo earlier formal apprenticeship models of learning, the emerging 'maker culture' emphasises informal, networked, peer-led, and shared learning motivated by fun and self-fulfilment (Sharpes et al., 2013).

Reflections on Actions: Reflection on action is the retrospective reflection where the student focusses on how to optimise the design process and how to improve the product. The student tries to answer questions like: how can we optimise the design process? How can we make a similar product better the next time? The concept of reflection on action is inspired by Schön (1983).

Semester Project: At our institution (The Engineering Faculty, University of Southern Denmark) this is classified as a student project often conducted in groups of 4-6 students, which contains theoretical and practical elements of all courses taught that semester.

Chapter 5
Website Interaction between a Football Club and its Supporters:
The Case of Sporting Clube de Portugal

João Silva
University of Lisbon, Portugal

Pedro Isaías
Universidade Aberta (Portuguese Open University), Portugal

ABSTRACT

Football teams can explore the benefits of Websites and increase their popularity through the creation of a well-designed Website that will attract users. The fact that football is the leading sport in most countries constitutes an advantage, as it becomes an appealing subject for Internet navigation. This chapter explores the type of relationship that the supporters of Sporting Clube de Portugal have with the football team on the club's official Website. This objective demands an analysis of the characteristics that a Website is required to have in order to attract and engage its intended users. Through a survey conducted via different social media and email communication, this study asked Sporting Clube de Portugal's supporters about their engagement with the Website. In addition, this chapter presents the features that users consider to be most important in a football club Website.

INTRODUCTION

The Internet has an assorted range of users with different interests and requirements. "In order to arrange for high-quality websites, we need to consider the HCI aspects of the phenomena, which require knowledge about the users, their prior experience, expectations and needs" (Sørum,

Andersen, & Vatrapu, 2012, p. 698). The definition of a good website depends on the person doing the evaluation. The effectiveness and user-friendliness of a website are not guarantees of its success among internet users (Sørum et al., 2012). The increased competition between companies that focus entirely on a particular business activity drives companies to expand to several points of

DOI: 10.4018/978-1-4666-6228-5.ch005

the globe in search of other markets. A company that focuses on the customer should take into account the type of needs that each client has. It is important to understand their consumption patterns and levels of satisfaction, so it can guarantee customer retention and loyalty.

According to Miranda, Chamorro, Valero, and Maestre (2010), the number of Internet users has grown significantly over the last few years, having reached approximately 1.04 billion, which represents 16% of the world's population. Hence, the creation of a website has become essential to the dissemination of news about companies and their products to various parts of the globe. The website should reflect the image that the company is trying to project and it should be one that the users will remember and want to return to (Cox, & Dale, 2002). Football and the Internet have shown early signs of a prosperous marriage (Miranda et al., 2010). Technology has become settled deep within football fandom (The Social Issues Research Centre, 2008). They allow the company to publicize its business, and, if they reflect a good company image, they are a way to achieve success. In light of the power of the Internet and the popularity of football, the creation of an effective and user-friendly website, offering various services and products, is a valuable asset. Through their websites, football clubs would be able to reach both the local and the international supporters. On the one hand, the website is useful for the supporters who are local to the club, in the sense that it provides digital and immediate access to the club's services, products and news. On the other hand, via the website, national supporters who live abroad and foreign supporters in general can be in contact with the club and know more about what it offers, despite being geographically distant.

This chapter intends to explore the link between football and the Internet, by providing an outline of the Internet's current situation and an analysis of how football can benefit from its power. This chapter is divided as follows: the first section pres-

ents a review of the literature, which reveals the demand for football and the kind of media the fans use to check news. This review analyses current academic literature regarding football teams and their websites to determine what the supporters use to keep up to date about the team's news and where they purchase the club's products. In the next section, this chapter analyses what features should be present on a quality website and on a football club website, and finally it determines the type of relationship that exists between football and the Internet. In the third section, the methodology is presented and the hypotheses are formulated. There is also a description of the research approach, the sample, and the tests performed. In the fourth section, the results are analyzed, and finally conclusions are drawn.

FOOTBALL AND ITS SCOPE

Football is not only a social phenomenon but also big business: large amounts of money circulate; there is a multiplicity of stakeholder groups that are interconnected worldwide; and the clubs have changed from simple sports teams to international entertainment companies, especially the highly competitive teams that try to obtain the best business strategies (Dolles, & Söderman, 2005). The media contribute, in many ways, to the expansion of football. The next section explains how media and other kinds of communication methods disseminate news about football. To start with television, cable and satellite television have contributed to engagement between fans and sports, providing debates via text, phone or email (Cleland, 2011). Sports fans can now be informed about sports 24 hours a day, anywhere.

There are some clubs which have their internal media, i.e. media sources that the clubs control, such as the match day program and the official club website (Cleland, 2011). Although there have been advances in the relationship between 'new' media and football, many football fans still prefer to gather news and information from traditional sources (Cleland, 2011). Local radio continues to play an active role in providing commentary on matches and a phone line for supporters to call and discuss particular clubs (Cleland, 2011). Local newspapers have developed parts of their football section for supporters writing in and becoming involved in discussing their club (Cleland, 2011). Although 'traditional' sources remain an important part of modern football, it should be noted that one of the clear reasons behind the rapidly changing media–fan relationship is a result of the Internet (Cleland, 2011). Supporter dialogue has not only developed the relationship between the specific media source and the supporters but also aided supporters to feel that the club is 'theirs', which can be noted in clubs which encourage supporters to engage in dialogue through the available internal channels (Cleland, 2011). Football stadiums, especially those of the top clubs, are equipped with the most sophisticated technology (Dolles, & Söderman, 2005).

To reach their international supporters, the biggest clubs use various strategies, such as arranging games in remote locations or offering ticket packages for sale on the website of the club (Dolles, & Söderman, 2005). Dolles and Söderman (2005) use Manchester United as an example. Manchester United (an English League football team) has the objective of creating global sponsorship to seek alliances that will encourage and reward investment in the club to the mutual advantage of both parties. According to Dolles and Söderman (2005), the bigger the influence of the brand, in both the local market and the sports arena, the bigger the potential revenue for the team.

Internet and Website Quality

With the coming of the Internet, people are spending more and more time on the Web, gaining more information from the Web unconsciously (Ho, Kuo, & Lin, 2012). According to Loiacono, Watson, and Goodhue (2002), the website should present a consistent image, which corresponds to the real image of the company and what it demands to the user.

The evaluation of a website's quality entails many viewpoints and approaches. It can be seen from the point of view of content, user-friendliness, technical aspects or the experience of the user. Web interactivity is one of the elements that are receiving a great deal of attention from the research community. There are studies that prove that users value the interactive nature of websites and prefer to use those rather than websites that have no interactivity. Also, with the inreased of use of interactive websites, users have become more likely to choose them (Al-Shamaileh and Sutcliffe, 2013).

Isaías and Coelho (2013) analyzed the 36 most frequently visited Portuguese e-commerce websites in 2010, and observed that Web 2.0 tools have a set of varied characteristics that all together create a global tool; this research allowed them to discover which Web 2.0 tools are most used by Portuguese online retailers. Isaías, Miranda, and Pífano (2009) observed that, with Web 2.0 tools, users can create information themselves, using more efficient components with better features and possibilities.

Sousa and Voss (2012) in 'The impacts of e-service quality on customer behavior in multi-channel e-services' argued that e-service quality dimensions may affect how customers use multiple channels. They associated information availability with information quality; pursuit of efficiency with ease of use; risk with privacy/security; and convenience and waiting time with satisfaction.

Parasuraman, Zeithaml, and Malhotra (2005) created a multiple-item scale for assessing electronic service quality consisting of four dimensions: efficiency in navigation; satisfaction; system availability; and privacy. They observed that efficiency and satisfaction were the most critical dimensions of website service quality. Lee, Goh, Chua, and Ang's work (2010) showed that perceived quality factors of the Internet, such as information discovery, entertainment, information quality, socialisation and relationship maintenance, significantly predicted the intended and actual use of Internet applications. Cox and Dale (2002) in their study examined various key quality factors in website design and use. Those were: clarity of purpose, design, accessibility and speed, content, customer service. After consideration, Cox and Dale (2002) grouped these factors into four categories: ease of use; customer confidence; online resources; and relationship services.

According to Parasuraman, Zeithaml, and Berry (1994), the SERVQUAL scale was developed in an attempt to measure how consumers perceive the quality of a service. This scale comprises five dimensions: tangibles, reliability, responsiveness, assurance and empathy. Trocchia and Janda (2003) suggested that consumers perceive online service quality to consist of five dimensions:

- Performance, which includes the elements of reliability and responsiveness in SERVQUAL
- Access, which emerged as a characteristic unique to Internet service quality for customers who live in distant places
- Security, which resembles the SERVQUAL dimension of assurance and reliability
- Sensation, which corresponds to SERVQUAL'S tangibles and empathy dimensions
- Information, a characteristic unique to Internet service quality, and customers regarded information credibility and quantity.

Loiacono et al. (2002) started from four general categories of website quality, and proposed the use of the WebQual instrument to measure consumers' perceptions of website service quality using twelve dimensions. The four categories were: ease of use, usefulness, entertainment and complementary relationship. These were subdivided thus: usefulness included the information's fitness for the

task, interaction, trust, response time, ease of use and intuitiveness; entertainment included visual appeal and flow; and complementary relationship included consistent image, business processes, and substitutability, which is related to the capacity of the website to conduct all the business processes without the need to use other means.

Li, Tan, and Xie. (2002) examined web-based service quality using a modified SERVQUAL scale which defined quality as the extent to which services based on the web technology help the effective and efficient online communication, purchase and distribution of products/services. This definition of quality included six dimensions: responsiveness of the website; competence; quality of information; empathy; web assistance; and call-back systems.

Kriemadis, Kotsovos, and Kartakoullis (2009) provided a better understanding of how the Internet is used in the football sector. They described the online environment, how customers should be served and how the website should be designed. According to Gehrke and Turban (1999), the website should include: page-loading speed, which includes simple and meaningful graphics; business content; navigation efficiency; security; and marketing/customer focus.

Chen and Dibb (2010) developed a conceptual framework about consumer trust in a retail context. This framework paid attention to important features of website quality, including website usability; security/privacy of customer's information; speed of download; website information quality; and aesthetic aspects.

They found that usability, security and privacy, and quality of information about the products presented on the website have a positive and significant impact on trust.

Smith and Smith (2012) initially selected only e-retailers and other online service providers that hosted secure websites. A website is relatively secure if it uses encryption technology to transfer information. Smith and Smith (2012) mentioned that fraud could be avoided if customers created accounts with essential information.

Websites for Football Clubs

Cleland (2011) stated that there have been few attempts by clubs to establish meaningful links or dialogue with supporters through the official website, even though supporters have opportunities to engage with the official website on its message board service and to contact the club personally (as cited in Beech, Chadwick, & Tapp, 2000).

The design of the website needs to be viewed primarily as a business task, as suggested in previous research, not a technical task (Kriemadis et al., 2009). Kriemadis et al. (2009) compared two football clubs' websites (Manchester United and Liverpool FC) and they observed that the website designs were appropriate to the needs of the club and focused on supporting business goals.

Miranda et al. (2010), in evaluating football club websites, selected four broad categories as the basis for a quality website: accessibility; speed of download; navigability; and site content.

However, football clubs need to be aware about the regional differences in the demographic patterns of Internet use. Crolley (2008) considered that Spanish clubs need to be aware of the demographic profile of their fan base and the risks of alienating some fans if the Internet were to be used as their exclusive communication tool.

According to Crolley (2008), most football clubs are only in a position to develop their Internet sites if they can make a business case to do so, because keeping a website up to date and ensuring its information is reliable involves costs for the club, and they need to ensure that the site generates revenue.

Hur, Ko, and Claussen (2011) developed a Sport Website Acceptance Model (SWAM), which proposed that beliefs about sports websites influenced the intention to use websites. This model incorporates four key variables based on the Technology Acceptance Model (TAM):

- Perceived ease of use: the belief that using a particular system will not require a big effort
- Perceived usefulness: defined by Davis (1989) and Davis, Bagozzi, and Warshaw (1989) as the probability that a user utilizing one application system will get better results within an organizational context
- Perceived enjoyment: the perception that the use of the website brings inherent entertainment and fun to the user (Hur et al., 2011, as cited by Davis, Bagozzi, & Warshaw, 1992; Eighmey & McCord, 1998; Hur et al., 2011, as cited by Jarvenpaa & Todd, 1997; Moon & Kim, 2001)
- Perceived trustworthiness: defined by Belanger, Hiller and Smith (2002) as the perception of confidence in the electronic commerce marketer's reliability and integrity.

Kriemadis et al. (2009), when they compared Manchester United and Liverpool's websites, observed how customers were served in both online environments. They concluded that both websites provided options to users if they had any questions or needed assistance.

Football and Internet: Relationship with Football Fans through the Football Club Website

Nowadays, fans interact on the fan club site, where forums serve as a good organizational tool by which leaders can coordinate the fan club's activities, from songs and chants to trips to away games; the sites also become a place where fans share their love and their feelings about the game (The Social Issues Research Centre, 2008). This process allows fans with online capabilities to access up-to-date information through the official club website, with Cleland (2011) suggesting that this can only aid the club–fan relationship (as cited in Turner, 1999).

According to Miranda et al. (2010), people' loyalty to one team should not be confused with loyalty to the team's official website, because there are authoritative and comprehensive websites provided by newspapers, TV channels and others, including "unofficial" fan websites, that provide alternatives for users to turn to. Fans prefer updated and reliable news to be presented on the club website, instead of content for commercial purposes.

Crolley (2008) took the example of Villarreal Club de Futbol's website, where the President used a statement to greet the visitors to its website. This president admitted that that the club website will be the club's future communication channel and recognized the globalizing potential of the Internet to reach all football fans around the world.

Yang (2011) argued that fans would be more attracted to the club if the club offered interactive marketing, using information systems that transform fans into club partners by designing fans' products, pricing match tickets, improving customer services and so on.

Crolley (2008) observed that all the Spanish football clubs' websites use Castilian, the official language in Spain. However, there are other websites that use regional languages to communicate with their fans because the club is closely identified with its local community. There are also clubs that use an English version: those that are or expect to be playing in the European competitions, or other clubs that, despite not playing in the European competitions, use English to attract international people. To these factors, Hur et al. (2011) added the fans' sports involvement and psychological commitment to a team as constraints that may affect behavioral intentions in the context of sports website consumption.

According to Hur et al. (2011), identifying the individual's level of involvement in sport could be a key element in understanding sports information search behavior. Hur et al. (2011) considered that the level of involvement in sports serves as a starting point that may influence other

constructs within the Sport Website Acceptance Model (SWAM). Based in a sports perspective, Mahony, Madrigal, and Howard (2000) developed the 'psychological commitment to team' (PCT) scale, which provides researchers with a reliable and valid tool for measuring loyalty or the strength of fans' commitment to a particular sports team. They considered that the scale is relatively short, easy to administer, and easy to adjust to different team sports at different competition levels, and it could allow marketers to evaluate loyalty toward their team more effectively and to be better prepared for their future.

Briefly, a quality website with a business perspective should contain the following features presented in Table 1.

METHODOLOGY

Chen and Dibb (2010) developed a conceptual framework about consumer trust in a retail context. They found that usability, security and privacy, and quality of information about the products presented on the website have a positive and significant impact on trust. Speed of download, quality of information about the services and aesthetic aspects do not have a great impact on consumers' trust in a website.

Parasuraman et al. (2005) stated that consumers' perceptions of service quality can affect consumer loyalty and behavioral intentions. They observed that efficiency and satisfaction are the most critical dimensions of website service quality. Taking this into account, the following hypothesis is presented: H1: The survey shows which features and sub-features users find most important.

Despite the effort to reach all kinds of fans, for example by offering packages for sale on the website of the club to allow supporters to watch the games (Dolles and Söderman, 2005), according to Cleland (2011) many football fans still prefer to gather news and information from traditional sources, such as local evening newspapers and

Table 1. Features of a website

Features' Categories	Features	Authors
Quality of Information	Information availability	Sousa & Voss, 2012
	Products and price details, Information about the services	Chen & Dibb, 2010
	Information quality	Lee et al., 2010; Li, Tan, and Xie, 2002
	Online resources	Cox and Dale, 2002
	Fit-to-Task information	Loiacono et al., 2002
	Business content	Gehrke and Turban, 1999
	Responsiveness to provide precise information	Li, Tan, and Xie, 2002
	Information credibility and quantity	Trocchia & Janda, 2003
Ease of Use	Pursuit of efficiency	Sousa & Voss, 2012
	Information discovery	Lee et al., 2010
	Accessibility	Trocchia & Janda, 2003
	Navigation efficiency	Gehrke and Turban, 1999
	Website usability and familiarity	Chen & Dibb, 2010
	Interaction, informational fitness for purpose, ease of understanding and intuitiveness	Loiacono et al., 2002
	Efficiency	Parasuraman et al., 2005
Security and Privacy	Customer confidence	Cox and Dale, 2002
	Assurance and reliability	Parasuraman et al., 1994
	Security/privacy usability	Trocchia & Janda, 2003; Gehrke and Turban, 1999; Smith and Smith, 2012; Sousa & Voss, 2012
	Trust	Chen & Dibb, 2010; Loiacono et al., 2002
	Risk	Chen & Dibb, 2010; Sousa & Voss, 2012
	Fraud	Smith and Smith, 2012
	Performance	Trocchia & Janda, 2003
	Competence	Li, Tan, and Xie, 2002
Processing Speed	Convenience and waiting time	Sousa & Voss, 2012
	Customer confidence in terms of speed	Cox and Dale, 2002
	Page-loading speed	Gehrke and Turban, 1999
	Performance and system availability	Trocchia & Janda, 2003; Parasuraman et al., 2005
	Speed of download	Chen & Dibb, 2010
Aesthetic	Visual appeal, innovativeness and flow	Loiacono et al., 2002
	Simple and meaningful graphics and animation and/or multimedia plug-ins	Gehrke and Turban, 1999
	Socialisation and relationship maintenance	Lee et al., 2010

continued on following page

Table 1. Continued

Features' Categories	Features	Authors
Relationship with the User	Waiting time associated with satisfaction	Sousa & Voss, 2012
	e-loyalty: Behavioural intentions	Sousa & Voss, 2012; Parasuraman et al., 2005
	Relationship services	Cox and Dale, 2002
	Empathy	Parasuraman et al., 1994; Li et al., 2002
	Sensation, Access	Trocchia & Janda, 2003
	Web assistance and call-back systems	Li et al., 2002
	Marketing/Customer focus	Gehrke and Turban, 1999
	FAQs and customer support	Chen & Dibb, 2010; Gehrke and Turban, 1999
	Business processes, consistent image and substitutability	Loiacono et al., 2002
	Responsiveness	Li et al., 2002
	Fulfilment and privacy	Parasuraman et al., 2005

local radio. Based on these studies, the following hypothesis is presented: H2: The official website of Sporting Clube de Portugal is not the means of communication most utilized by users to find out about club news.

Taking the example of Manchester United, Dölles and Söderman (2005) observed that sponsorship brings value to the club. The bigger is the influence of the brand in both the local market and the sports arena, the bigger is the potential revenue for your team. However, these authors did not state if the Manchester United official website is used as a place where club's fans buy club products. According to this, the following hypothesis is presented: H3: The official website of Sporting Clube de Portugal is not the place most utilized by fans to buy the club's products.

Football club websites have a loyal fan base that they can rely upon. This loyalty should not be confused with loyalty to the team's official website because there are other media that fans can use to check news (Miranda et al., 2010). Crolley (2008) observed that many Spanish football clubs miss an opportunity to reinforce relationships with fans, give little emphasis to the sense of belonging of the fan base, and rarely reinforce their unique identity via their website.

Cleland (2011) observed there is a lack of interactive experience when compared to many unofficial websites. According to Kriemadis et al. (2009), the design of the website needs to be viewed primarily as a business task and needs to be appropriate to the needs of the club and to focus on supporting business goals. Based on these studies, the following hypothesis is presented: H4: The lack of regard for the feelings of the user when he/she visits the website explains why the feature 'relationship with user' is not the most important to be highlighted on the official website of Sporting Clube de Portugal.

Research Approach

The method chosen to collect the data was the questionnaire survey presented in Appendix A. This method has the advantage of collecting data faster and less expensively by using standardized questions; at the same time it ensures respondents' anonymity and the non-interference of the investigator at the time of data collection. It was designed using the tool *Google Docs*. This allows the questionnaire to be designed and completed over the Internet, generating, for this, an electronic address (link) associated with each questionnaire. The structure of the questionnaire is presented in Appendix A. The questionnaire was made available on the Internet between 5 August and 12 September 2013; the link was distributed by groups related to Sporting Clube de Portugal on Facebook, through blogs about the club, and by email to the post-graduation secretary of ISEG so it could be delivered to students. It obtained 157 answers; this number is considered valid for analysis. The tables in Appendix B present the sample characteristics. In order to illustrate the characteristics of the sample, descriptive statistics and the standard deviation of the variables are presented in Appendix C. To test the reliability of the sample, Cronbach's alpha test (Appendix D) was used to measure the internal consistency, where alpha measures the uniformity of the variables by correlating averages of all items. All the results show a high degree of reliability (>0.8). The Pearson correlation was used in order to measure the degree of linear correlation between all the variables (Appendix E).

ANALYSIS OF THE RESULTS

Data processing was done using Excel and SPSS. As can be seen from the results in the appendix all the hypotheses were confirmed. H1 was confirmed because users considered that there are some categories and features which are more important than others. The results showed that ´Quality of the information' was the category that users considered most important in relation to the club's official website, with an average of 4.64. Among the features, it was observed that, in the category 'Quality of the information', the feature 'Availability of the information' was considered the most important, with an average of 4.63. In the category 'Ease of use', 'Ease of understanding' was the feature that was considered the most important, with an average of 4.64. With respect to 'Security and privacy', the feature 'Prevention of risk and fraud' was considered the most important, with an average of 4.72. In relation to

'Processing speed', 'Efficiency of the system' was the most important feature from the point of view of the user, with an average of 4.58. In relation to 'Aesthetic appearance', the feature 'Visual aspect' was the most important, with an average of 4.44. It was also observed that, in the category 'Relationship with the user', 'Positive feeling' was the sub-feature considered the most important, with an average of 4.55.

It was found that only 17.14% of the sample in Table 2 used the club's official website for news. Of the 157 respondents, only 66 checked news of Sporting Clube de Portugal on the club's official website, confirming H2.

H3 was also confirmed. Only 18.45% of the sample in Table 3 (31 respondents out of 157) used the official website of Sporting Clube de Portugal to buy the club's products.

H4 was also confirmed, as can be seen in Table 4. Although the feature 'Relationship with the user' can be regarded as very important, users considered that 'Quality of the information' and 'Ease of use' are the most important features of a good website.

FUTURE RESEARCH DIRECTIONS

The growing importance of the role that websites play in the successful dissemination of products and services, combined with their increasing popularity among Internet users, places Web interaction at the centre of this subject. The imperativeness of developing high-quality websites applies across all areas of society. In this case, football was analysed from several perspectives (social, cultural, economic) because of its popularity in most countries. Nonetheless, this is an analysis that can be extended not only to other teams but also to other sports and subjects.

In the future, to make a further contribution to this subject, we suggest the following:

- Make a comparative analysis with the websites of other clubs that have had great success with their Internet presence.
- Make case studies of professional website development to indicate factors that could be improved.

From the results of this work, other clubs can obtain a useful tool and a good basis for comparison with their own website, and can make progress in some ways to improve their website and add new ideas. Next, we present some proposals:

- Clubs which have their own newspaper could provide an online version. This is one way for the users to use the club's website to check news.
- Taking into account that the feature 'Relationship with the user' is considered one of the least important features, clubs could use this fact when preparing a questionnaire about what aspects of the relationship with the user can be improved.
- Another way that was proposed to promote the relationship with the user is for users themselves to build a website for the club and submit their ideas to those responsible for the club.

Even in other kinds of businesses, companies can take advantage of this work. Knowing the power that football has in the world of the Internet, companies could use the techniques of marketing used in football to acquire new customers.

CONCLUSION

The results derived from the collection of data demonstrate that there are some factors that are not very important when interacting with the club's website. Namely, the respondents stated that they did not consider that the relationship with the user was a category that was very significant on the official website of Sporting Clube de Portugal when compared with other features.

Additionally, it became clear that, among all the features of 'Relationship with the user', 'Socialisation and relationship maintenance' is the one with the lowest average, which gives the idea that users do not consider that it is important for the website to give them a sense of interaction and a more intimate relationship. It was concluded that users prefer the website to be more informative and easy to navigate. Despite the preferences on the characteristics, it was observed that the official website of Sporting Clube de Portugal is not widely used for discovering news about the club.

The fact that users do not use the website in large numbers to buy Sporting Clube de Portugal products can be explained by the fact that 'Business processes' in the category 'Relationship with the user' is considered to be one of the least important sub-features in this website. The initial research questions were answered, because, as the results show, it was possible to observe which means of communication are used to refer to news of Sporting Clube de Portugal, where supporters buy club products, and what the relationship is between users and the club via the club's official website.

The interaction of users with the websites is determined by a variety of principles and factors, but one of the core concerns when a website is being developed is the users and their interests and objectives. A website which is user-oriented must engage with the user to understand his/her patterns and behaviour in order to accommodate them most effectively.

REFERENCES

Al-Shamaileh, O., & Sutcliffe, A. (2013). Website Interactivity and Repeated Exposure, what Influences User Experience? *Journal of Universal Computer Science, 19*(8), 1123–1139.

Beech, J., Chadwick, S., & Tapp, A. (2000). Towards a schema for football clubs seeking an effective presence on the internet. *European Journal for Sport Management, 7,* 30–50.

Belanger, F., Hiller, J. S., & Smith, W. J. (2002). Trustworthiness in electronic commerce: The role of privacy, security and site attributes. *The Journal of Strategic Information Systems, 11*(3-4), 245–270. doi:10.1016/S0963-8687(02)00018-5

Chen, J., & Dibb, S. (2010). Consumer Trust in the Online Retail Context: Exploring the Antecedents and Consequences. *Psychology and Marketing, 27*(4), 323–346. doi:10.1002/mar.20334

Cleland, J. (2011). The media and football supporters: A changing relationship. *Media Culture & Society, 33*(2), 299–315. doi:10.1177/0163443710393866

Cox, B., & Dale, G. (2002). Key quality factors in web site design and use: An examination. *International Journal of Quality & Reliability Management, 19*(7), 862–888. doi:10.1108/02656710210434784

Crolley, L. (2008). Using the Internet to strengthen its identity: the case of Spanish football. *Sport in Society: Cultures, Commerce, Media. Politics, 11*(6), 722–738.

Davis, F. D. (1989). Perceived usefulness, perceived ease of use and user acceptance of information technology. *Management Information Systems Quarterly, 13*(3), 319–340. doi:10.2307/249008

Davis, F. D., Bagozzi, R. P., & Warshaw, P. R. (1989). User acceptance of computer technology: A comparison of two theoretical models. *Management Science, 35*(8), 982–1003. doi:10.1287/mnsc.35.8.982

Davis, F. D., Bagozzi, R. P., & Warshaw, P. R. (1992). Extrinsic and intrinsic motivation to use computers in the workplace. *Journal of Applied Social Psychology, 22*(14), 1111–1132. doi:10.1111/j.1559-1816.1992.tb00945.x

Dolles, H., & Söderman, S. (2005). *Globalization of Sports - The Case of Professional Football and its International Management Challenges.* Retrieved December 10, 201, from http://dijtokyo.org/doc/WP05_1GlobalizationOfSportsProfessionalFootballDollesSoederman.pdf

Eighmey, J., & McCord, L. (1998). Adding value in the information age: uses and gratifications of sites on the World Wide Web: the World Wide Web presents new challenges for advertisers and consumers alike. *Journal of Business Research, 41*(3), 187–194. doi:10.1016/S0148-2963(97)00061-1

Gehkre, D., & Turban, E. (1999). Determinants of successful website design: relative importance and recommendations for effectiveness. In *Proceedings of the 32nd Hawaii International Conference on System Sciences.* Los Alamitos, CA: IEEE.

Green, R. (1999). Football information services: fanzines, Match of the Day and the modem. []. MCB UP Ltd.]. *Proceedings of Aslib, 51*(1), 20–29. doi:10.1108/EUM0000000006958

Hur, Y., Ko, Y. J., & Claussen, C. L. (2011). Acceptance of sports websites: A conceptual model. *International Journal of Sports Marketing & Sponsorship, 12*(3), 209–224.

Isaías, P., & Coelho, F. (2013). Web 2.0 Tools Adoption Model: A Study on Online Retailers. *International Journal of Information Communication Technologies and Human Development, 5*(3), 64–79. doi:10.4018/jicthd.2013070104

Isaías, P., Miranda, P., & Pífano, S. (2009). Critical Success Factors for Web 2.0 - A Reference Framework. In *Proceedings of the 3rd International Conference on Online Communities and Social Computing: Held as Part of HCI International 2009* (OCSC '09). Springer-Verlag.

Jarvenpaa, S. L., & Todd, P. A. (1997). Consumer reactions to electronic shopping on the World Wide Web. *International Journal of Electronic Commerce, 1*(2), 59–88.

Kriemadis, T., Kotsovos, A., & Kartakoullis, N. (2009). A Strategy for managing customer relations on the internet: Evidence from the football Sector. *Direct Marketing: An International Journal, 3*(4), 229–243.

Lee, C., Goh, D., Chua, A., & Ang, R. (2010). Indagator: Investigating perceived gratifications of an application that blends mobile content sharing with gameplay. *Journal of the American Society for Information Science and Technology, 61*(6), 1244–1257.

Li, Y. N., Tan, K. C., & Xie, M. (2002). Measuring Web-based service quality. *Total Quality Management, 13*(5), 685–700. doi:10.1080/0954412022000002072

Loiacono, E. T., Watson, R. T., & Goodhue, D. L. (2002). WebQual: A measure of Web site quality. In *Proceedings of 2002 Marketing Educators' Conference: Marketing Theory and Applications*. Academic Press.

Mahony, D. F., Madrigal, R., & Howard, D. R. (2000). Using the psychological commitment to team (PCT) scale to segment sport consumers based on loyalty. *Sport Marketing Quarterly, 9*(1), 15–25.

Miranda, F., J., Chamorro, A., Valero, V., & Maestre, J. (2010). Quantitative Assessment of Football Web Sites: An Empirical Study of the Best European Football Club. *J. Service Science & Management, 3*, 110–116.

Moon, J., & Kim, Y. (2001). Extending the TAM for a world wide web context. *Information & Management, 38*(4), 217–230. doi:10.1016/S0378-7206(00)00061-6

O'Brien, J. (2000). *Introduction to Information Systems* (9th ed.). New York: McGraw-Hill, Inc.

Parasuraman, A., Zeithaml, V. A., & Berry, L. L. (1994). Reassessment of expectations as a comparison standard in measuring service quality: Implications for further research. *Journal of Marketing, 6*(3), 173–183.

Parasuraman, A., Zeithaml, V. A., & Malhotra, A. (2005). E-S-Qual: A multiple- item scale for assessing electronic service quality. *Journal of Service Research, 7*(3), 213–233. doi:10.1177/1094670504271156

Smith, A. A., & Smith, A. D. (2012). CRM and identity theft issues associated with e-ticketing of sports and entertainment. *Electronic Government. International Journal (Toronto, Ont.), 9*(1), 1–26.

Social Issues Research Centre. (2008). Football Passions. *The Social Issues Research Centre, commissioned by Canon.* Retrieved December, 8 from, http://sirc.org/football/football_passions.pdf

Sousa, R., & Voss, C. (2012). The impacts of e-service quality on customer behaviour in multichannel e-services. *Total Quality Management, 23*(7), 789–806.

Trocchia, P., & Janda, S. (2003). How do consumers evaluate Internet retail service? *Journal of Services Marketing, 17*(3), 243–253. doi:10.1108/08876040310474800

Turner, P. (1999). Television and internet convergence: Implications for sport broadcasting. *Sport Marketing Quarterly, 8*(2), 43–49.

Yang, G. (2011). *A study of How Information Systems Facilitate Football Clubs.* (Ph.D. thesis). University of Boras, Boras, Sweden.

ADDITIONAL READING

Adamson, G., Jones, W., & Tapp, A. (2006). From CRM to FRM: Applying CRM in the football industry. *The Journal of Database Marketing & Customer Strategy Management, 13*(2), 156–172.

Atterer, R., Wnuk, M., & Schmidt, A. (2006, May). Knowing the user's every move: user activity tracking for website usability evaluation and implicit interaction. In *Proceedings of the 15th international conference on World Wide Web* (pp. 203-212). ACM.

Bailey, R. W. (1993). Performance vs. preference. *Human Factors and Ergonomics Society Annual Meeting Proceedings, 5,* 282–286.

Beech, J., Chadwick, S., & Tapp, A. (2000). Emerging trends in the use of the Internet–lessons from the football sector. *Qualitative Market Research: An International Journal, 3*(1), 38–46. doi:10.1108/13522750010310479

Butler, B., & Sagas, M. (2008). Making room in the lineup: Newspaper Web sites face growing competition for sports fans' attention. *International Journal of Sport Communication, 1*(1), 17–25.

Desbordes, M. (2007). *Marketing & Football: An International Perspective.* Oxford: Butterworth-Heinemann.

Duncan, S. (2007). Manchester United Football Club: Developing a Network Orchestration Model. *European Journal of Information Systems, 16*(5).

Gibbons, T., & Dixon, K. (2010). 'Surf's up!': A call to take English soccer fan interactions on the Internet more seriously. *Soccer & Society, 11*(5), 599–613. doi:10.1080/14660970.2010.497359

Heim, S. (2007). *The resonant interface: HCI foundations for interaction design.* London: Pearson Education, Inc.

Kellar, M., Hawkey, K., Inkpen, K., & Watters, C. (2008). Challenges of capturing natural web-based user behaviors. *International Journal of Human-Computer Interaction, 24*(4), 385–409. doi:10.1080/10447310801973739

Lindgaard, G., Fernandes, G., Dudek, C., & Brown, J. (2006). Attention web designers: You have 50 milliseconds to make a good first impression! *Behaviour & Information Technology, 25*(2), 115–126. doi:10.1080/01449290500330448

Mahlke, S. (2002). Factors influencing the experience of website usage. In CHI'02 extended abstracts on Human factors in computing systems (pp. 846-847). ACM. doi:doi:10.1145/506621.506628 doi:10.1145/506621.506628

Mulhern, F. (2009). Integrated marketing communications: From media channels to digital connectivity. *Journal of Marketing Communications, 15*(2/3), 85–101. doi:10.1080/13527260902757506

Nørgaard, M., & Hornbæk, K. (2009). Exploring the value of usability feedback formats. *International Journal of Human-Computer Interaction, 25,* 49–74. doi:10.1080/10447310802546708

Park, N., Kee, K. F., & Valenzuela, S. (2009). Being immersed in social networking environment: Facebook groups, uses and gratifications, and social outcomes. *Cyberpsychology & Behavior, 12*(6), 729–733. doi:10.1089/cpb.2009.0003 PMID:19619037

Phua, J. J. (2010). Sports fans and media use: Influence on sports fan identification and collective self-esteem. *International Journal of Sport Communication, 3*(2), 190–206.

Rahimizadeh, M., Sajadi, S. N., Goodarzi, M., & Ghamati, H. (2012). A comparison of online marketing and interaction with fans through official website of football clubs in Iran, Asia and Europe. *International Research Journal of Applied and Basic Sciences, 3*(5), 1065–1071.

Reichheld, E. F., & Schefter, P. (2000). E-loyalty: Your secret weapon on the web. *Harvard Business Review, 78*(4), 105–113.

Ruddock, A., Hutchins, B., & Rowe, D. (2010). Contradictions in media sport culture: The reinscription of football supporter traditions through online media. *European Journal of Cultural Studies, 13*(3), 323–339. doi:10.1177/1367549410363200

Snaprud, M., & Sawicka, A. (2007). Large scale web accessibility evaluation – a European perspective. In C. Stephanidis (Ed.), *Universal access in human–computer interaction: applications and services* (pp. 150–159). Lecture notes in computer science Berlin, Heidelberg: Springer. doi:10.1007/978-3-540-73283-9_18

Sundar, S. S. (2007). Social psychology of interactivity in human-website interaction. The Oxford handbook of Internet psychology, 89-104.

Tainsky, S., & Stodolska, M. (2010). Population migration and team loyalty in professional sports. *Social Science Quarterly, 91*(3), 801–815. doi:10.1111/j.1540-6237.2010.00720.x PMID:20645466

Toledano, M. (2010). Professional competition and cooperation in the digital age: A pilot study of New Zealand practitioners. *Public Relations Review, 36*(3), 230–237. doi:10.1016/j.pubrev.2010.04.009

Woo, C. W., An, S.-K., & Cho, S. H. (2008). Sports PR in message boards on Major League Baseball websites. *Public Relations Review, 34*(2), 169–175. doi:10.1016/j.pubrev.2008.03.009

Yoshida, M. (2009). Customer relationship management. *Sport marketing, 18*(2), 119.

KEY TERMS AND DEFINITIONS

E-Customer: A customer who is based on the Internet: an Internet user who searches for and purchases products or services online.

Football Fandom: This is an expression used to define the collective body of football supporters. It represents the generality of the existing groups and communities that are composed of people who share football as a common interest. These types of groups and communities often have their own culture and use a variety of media and social media resources to interact with each other.

Media: The array of traditional means of mass communication, such as radio, television and newspapers. Traditional media are unilateral in the sense that people will receive information from them, but they will not contribute their own views. The user has a passive role in this relationship.

Social Media: The multiplicity of web-based applications derived from Web 2.0's principles that are known for their ability to create interaction among their users, for example blogs, wikis and social networks. The information the user receives from social media is no longer unilateral; it is, rather, the product of user-generated content, the exchange of information among users and the general interaction between online users and content.

Sporting Clube de Portugal: Also known internationally as Sporting Lisbon – the title of a Portuguese club which embraces several types of sports, ranging from track and field to football. It is based in Lisbon, it has been in existence for over 100 years, and it has one of the most popular football teams in Portugal.

Web Interaction: The set of interactions that occur online between websites and Internet users. It includes all the reciprocal contributions and the influence that users and websites exert over each other in the pursuit of their respective objectives.

Website: A location on the World Wide Web with one or more web pages. Websites are usually a collection of information presented in several formats that can be dedicated to a particular subject, person or organization, or be a collection of information about several topics and people.

APPENDIX A: QUESTIONNAIRE

Basic Information

Gender?
   Male
   Female
   Age group?
   <20
   21-30
   31-40
   41-50
   >50

Media, Products and Services

This section aims to determine which is the medium used to check news and where consumers buy club products.
   What are the sources of communication you use to check the news about Sporting Clube de Portugal?
   Generalist newspapers
   Sports newspapers
   Radio
   TV
   Unofficial club websites
   Official website of the club
   If you usually buy Sporting Clube de Portugal products, where do you usually buy them?
   Sports shops (Sportzone, Decathlon)
   Internet sites (online stores, olx, fair cost, ebay)
   Official website of the club
   Do not buy

Features of the Official Website of Sporting Clube De Portugal

A website providing services to customers and selling products needs to have some characteristics that make it more attractive to visitors. The official website of Sporting provides news about the history and rules of the club, but also provides services and product sales, including ticket sales and club merchandise.
   With regard to the type of service that the official website of Sporting Clube de Portugal provides, the website should include the following features: quality of information; ease of use, security and privacy; speed of processing; aesthetic appearance; and relationship with the user. Next, assign the degree of importance of each feature.
   Quality of information?
   (1 – Minor importance; 6 - Most Importance)

1 2 3 4 5 6

Select a value in the range of 1 to 6.

Ease of use?

(1 - Minor importance; 6 - Most Importance)

1 2 3 4 5 6

Select a value in the range of 1 to 6.

Security and privacy?

(1 - Minor importance; 6 - Most Importance)

1 2 3 4 5 6

Select a value in the range of 1 to 6.

Processing speed?

(1 - Minor importance; 6 - Most Importance)

1 2 3 4 5 6

Select a value in the range of 1 to 6.

Aesthetic aspect?

(1 - Minor importance; 6 - Most Importance)

1 2 3 4 5 6

Select a value in the range of 1 to 6.

Relationship with the user?

(1 - Minor importance; 6 - Most Importance)

1 2 3 4 5 6

Select a value in the range of 1 to 6.

Quality of Information

This feature takes into account the following: the availability of information on the website; details of products and services; the usefulness of the content of the website; online resources, i.e. the ability of the website to inform users about products and services and the ability to provide accurate information. Next, assign the importance of each aspect:

Availability of information?

(1 - Minor importance; 6 - Most Importance)

1 2 3 4 5 6

Select a value in the range of 1 to 6.

Details of the products and services?

(1 - Minor importance; 6 - Most Importance)

1 2 3 4 5 6

Select a value in the range of 1 to 6.

Usefulness of content?

(1 - Minor importance; 6 - Most Importance)

1 2 3 4 5 6

Select a value in the range of 1 to 6.

Online resources?

(1 - Minor importance; 6 - Most Importance)

1 2 3 4 5 6
Select a value in the range of 1 to 6.
Ability to provide accurate information?
(1 - Minor importance; 6 - Most Importance)
1 2 3 4 5 6
Select a value in the range of 1 to 6.

Ease of Use

This feature takes into account the following aspects: the ability to access the website; information discovery on the website; interaction with the website; ease of understanding of the website; efficiency of navigation on the website. Next, assign the importance of each aspect:

Ability to access?
(1 - Minor importance, 6 - Most Importance)
1 2 3 4 5 6
Select a value in the range of 1 to 6.
Information discovery?
(1 - Minor importance, 6 - Most Importance)
1 2 3 4 5 6
Select a value in the range of 1 to 6.
Interaction?
(1 - Minor importance, 6 - Most Importance)
1 2 3 4 5 6
Select a value in the range of 1 to 6.
Ease of understanding?
(1 - Minor importance, 6 - Most Importance)
1 2 3 4 5 6
Select a value in the range of 1 to 6.
Efficiency of navigation?
(1 - Minor importance, 6 - Most Importance)
1 2 3 4 5 6
Select a value in the range of 1 to 6.

Security and Privacy

This feature takes into account the following aspects: user confidence in the website; secure website to provide services; risk and fraud prevention. Next, assign the importance of each aspect:

User confidence?
(1 - Minor importance; 6 - Most Importance)
1 2 3 4 5 6
Select a value in the range of 1 to 6.
Provision of services?
(1 - Minor importance; 6 - Most Importance)

1 2 3 4 5 6
Select a value in the range of 1 to 6.
Prevention of risk and fraud?
(1 - Minor importance; 6 - Most Importance)
1 2 3 4 5 6
Select a value in the range of 1 to 6.

Processing Speed of the Website

This feature takes into account the following aspects: convenience and waiting time; page loading speed; efficiency. Next, assign the importance of each aspect:

Convenience and waiting time?
(1 - Minor importance; 6 - Most Importance)
1 2 3 4 5 6
Select a value in the range of 1 to 6.
Upload speed?
(1 - Minor importance; 6 - Most Importance)
1 2 3 4 5 6
Select a value in the range of 1 to 6.
Efficiency of the system?
(1 - Minor importance; 6 - Most Importance)
1 2 3 4 5 6
Select a value in the range of 1 to 6.

Aesthetic Appearance

This feature takes into account the following aspects: visual aspect of the web site; innovation and flow; simple and meaningful graphs and animations. Next, assign the importance of each aspect:

Visual aspect?
(1 - Minor importance; 6 - Most Importance)
1 2 3 4 5 6
Select a value in the range of 1 to 6.
Innovation and flow?
(1 - Minor importance; 6 - Most Importance)
1 2 3 4 5 6
Select a value in the range of 1 to 6.
Simple and meaningful charts?
(1 - Minor importance; 6 - Most Importance)
1 2 3 4 5 6
Select a value in the range of 1 to 6.
Animations?
(1 - Minor importance; 6 - Most Importance)
Select a value in the range of 1 to 6.

Relationship with the User

This feature takes into account the following aspects: socialization and maintenance of the relationship; intention to remain loyal to the website; positive feeling in navigating the website; convenience and time delay associated with customer satisfaction; business processes; and FAQs and customer support. Next, assign the importance of each aspect:

Socialization and maintenance of the relationship?

(1 - Minor importance; 6 - Most Importance)

1 2 3 4 5 6

Select a value in the range of 1 to 6.

Intention to remain loyal to the website?

(1 - Minor importance; 6 - Most Importance)

1 2 3 4 5 6

Select a value in the range of 1 to 6.

Positive feeling in navigating the website?

(1 - Minor importance; 6 - Most Importance)

1 2 3 4 5 6

Select a value in the range of 1 to 6.

Convenience and time delay associated with customer satisfaction?

(1 - Minor importance; 6 - Most Importance)

1 2 3 4 5 6

Select a value in the range of 1 to 6.

Business processes?

(1 - Minor importance; 6 - Most Importance)

1 2 3 4 5 6

Select a value in the range of 1 to 6.

FAQ and customer support?

(1 - Minor importance; 6 - Most Importance)

1 2 3 4 5 6

Select a value in the range of 1 to 6.

APPENDIX B: TABLES OF THE SAMPLES

Table 2. Sample characteristics

Variable	Scale	Absolute Freq.	Relative Freq.
Sex	M	113	71.97%
	F	44	28.03%
	Total	157	
Age Group	20>	36	22.93%
	21-30	91	57.96%
	31-40	20	12.74%
	41-50	7	4.46%
	50>	3	1.91%
	Total	157	

Table 3. Media used to check news

What are the sources of communication you use to check news of Sporting?	Answers	Absolute Freq.	Relative Freq.
Generalist newspapers – GN	GN	23	5,97%
Sports newspapers – SN	SN	111	28,83%
Radio – R	R	25	6,49%
TV	TV	91	23,64%
Unofficial Websites of the Club – UWC	UWC	69	17,92%
Official Website of the Club - OWC	OWC	66	17,14%
	Total	385	

Table 4. Sites used to buy club products

If you usually buy products from Sporting, where do you usually buy them?	Answers	Absolute Freq.	Relative Freq.
Sports shops – SS	SS	46	27,38%
Internet sites - IS	IS	10	5,95%
Official Website of the club – OWC	OWC	31	18,45%
Do not buy - DB	DB	81	48,21%
	TOTAL	168	

APPENDIX C: TABLES OF DESCRIPTIVE STATISTICS

Table 5. Descriptive statistics of the features

Features	Quality of the Information	Ease of Use	Security and Privacy	Processing Speed	Aesthetic Appearance	Relationship with the Use
Average	4,636942675	4,535031847	4,49044586	4,312101911	4,23566879	4,292993631
Standard Error	0,105442639	0,10363658	0,110163655	0,10097253	0,105049753	0,097854306
Standard Deviation	1,321192479	1,29856263	1,380346642	1,265182176	1,315269629	1,226110938
Sample Variance	1,745549567	1,686264903	1,905356851	1,600685938	1,732565736	1,503348032
Minimum	1	1	1	1	1	1
Maximum	6	6	6	6	6	6
Sum	728	712	705	677	665	674
Count	157	157	157	157	157	157

Table 6. Descriptive statistics of the sub-features of 'Quality of the information'

Sub-Features	Availability of the Information	Details of the Products and Services	Usefulness of Content	Online Resources	Ability to Provide Accurate Information
Average	4,505955414	4,292993631	4,43949	4,21656051	4,630573
Standard Error	0,099245	0,091381483	0,089154	0,086825476	0,10155
Standard Deviation	1,243536285	1,145006699	1,117102	1,087920101	1,272423
Sample Variance	1,546382492	1,31104034	1,247918	1,183570145	1,619059
Minimum	1	1	1	1	1
Maxmum	6	6	6	6	6
Sum	708	674	697	662	727
Count	157	157	157	157	157

Table 7. Descriptive statistics of the sub-features of 'Ease of use'

Sub-Features	Ability to Access	Information Discovery	Interaction	Ease of Understanding	Efficiency of Navigation
Average	4,611464968	4,337579618	4,050955414	4,636942675	4,617834395
Standard Error	0,08975336	0,097139447	0,096820336	0,097809116	0,097968518
Standard Deviation	1,124606379	1,217153784	1,213155339	1225544705	1,227542009
Sample Variance	1,264739507	1,481463335	1,471745876	1,501959824	1,506859383
Minimum	1	1	1	1	1
Maxmum	6	6	6	6	6
Sum	724	681	636	728	725
Count	157	157	157	157	157

Table 8. Descriptive statistics of the sub-features of 'Security and privacy'

Sub-Features	User Confidence	Provision of Services	Prevention of Risk and Fraud	Ease of Understanding
Average	4,681528662	4,458598726	4,719745223	4,636942675
Standard Error	0,096922352	0,093688828	0,10912716	0,097809116
Standard Deviation	1,214433584	1,173917646	1,3673594	1225544705
Sample Variance	1,47484893	1,378082639	1,86967173	1,501959824
Minimum	1	1	1	1
Maxmum	6	6	6	6
Sum	735	700	741	728
Count	157	157	157	157

Table 9. Descriptive statistics of the sub-features of 'Speed of processing'

Sub-Features	Convenience and Waiting Time	Upload Speed	Efficiency of the System
Average	4,541401274	4,503184713	4,579617836
Standard Error	0,099192578	0,100414216	0,098629921
Standard Deviation	1,242879441	1,258938319	1,235829362
Sample Variance	1,544749306	1,58492569	1,527274212
Minimum	1	1	1
Maxmum	6	6	6
Sum	713	707	719
Count	157	157	157

Table 10. Descriptive statistics of the sub-features of 'Aesthetic appearance'

Sub-Features	Visual Aspect	Innovation and Flow	Simple and Meaningful Charts	Animations
Average	4,439490446	4,312101911	4,388535032	3,624203822
Standard Error	0,093622185	0,088472208	0,095910876	0,109343808
Standard Deviation	1,173082612	1,108553592	1,201759829	1,370073986
Sample Variance	1,376122816	1,228891066	1,444226686	1,877102727
Minimum	1	1	1	1
Maxmum	6	6	6	6
Sum	697	677	689	569
Count	157	157	157	157

Table 11. Descriptive statistics of the sub-features of 'Relationship with the user'

Sub-Features	Socialization and Maintenance of the Relationship	Behavioral Intentions of Loyalty	Positive Feelinf in Navigating the Website	Convenience and Time Delay Associated with Customer Satisfaction	Business Processes	FAQ and Customer Support
Average	4,197452229	4,363057325	4,547770701	4,420382166	4,140127389	4,369427
Standard Error	0,097928691	0,095271544	0,092793518	0,101083219	0,097099281	0113691
Standard Deviation	1,227042987	1,19374903	1,162699445	1,266569102	1,21665055	1,424541
Sample Variance	1,505634493	1,425036747	1,351869998	1,604197289	1,480238445	2,029316
Minimum	1	1	1	1	1	1
Maximum	6	6	6	6	6	6
Sum	659	685	714	694	650	686
Count	157	157	157	157	157	157

APPENDIX D: TABLES OF RELIABILITY STATISTICS

Figure 1. Reliability statistics of the features

Cronbach's alpha test	N of itens
0,901	6

Figure 2. Reliability statistics of the sub-features of 'Quality of the information'

Cronbach's alpha test	N of itens
0,905	5

Figure 3. Reliability statistics of the sub-features of 'Ease of use'

Cronbach's alpha test	N of itens
0,914	5

Figure 4. Reliability statistics of the sub-features of 'Security and privacy'

Cronbach's alpha test	N of itens
0,897	3

Figure 5. Reliability statistics of the sub-features of 'Speed of processing'

Cronbach's alpha test	N of itens
0,939	3

Figure 6. Reliability statistics of the sub-features of 'Aesthetic appearance'

Cronbach's alpha test	N of itens
0,86	4

Figure 7. Reliability statistics of the sub-features of 'Relationship with the user'

Cronbach's alpha test	N of itens
0,86	4

APPENDIX E: TABLES OF THE PEARSON CORRELATION

Table 12. Pearson correlation test between the features

Features		Quality of the information	Ease of Use	Security and Privacy	Speeding of Process	Aesthetic Appearance	Relationship with the user
Quality of the information	Pearson's Correlation Sig. (2 Tails) N	1 157	0,719 0 157	0,594 0 157	0,659 0 157	0,569 0 157	0,581 0 157
Ease of Use	Pearson's Correlation Sig. (2 Tails) N	0,719 0 157	1 157	0,579 0 157	0,69 0 157	0,578 0 157	0,614 0 157
Security and Privacy	Pearson's Correlation Sig. (2 Tails) N	0,594 0 157	0,579 0 157	1 157	0,602 0 157	0,483 0 157	0,524 0 157
Speeding of Process	Pearson's Correlation Sig. (2 Tails) N	0,659 0 157	0,69 0 157	0,602 0 157	1 157	0,571 0 157	0,631 0 157
Aesthetic Appearance	Pearson's Correlation Sig. (2 Tails) N	0,569 0 157	0,578 0 157	0,483 0 157	0,571 0 157	1 157	0,672 0 157
Relationship w/user	Pearson's Correlation Sig. (2 Tails) N	0,581 0 157	0,614 0 157	0,524 0 157	0,631 0 157	0,672 0 157	1 157

Table 13. Pearson correlation test between sub-features of 'Quality of the information'

Sub-Features		Availability of Information	Details of the products and services	Usefulness of content	Online Resources	Ability to provide accurate information
Availability of the information	Pearson's Correlation Sig. (2 Tails) N	1 157	0,633 0 157	0,618 0 157	0,534 0 157	0,667 0 157
Details of the products and services	Pearson's Correlation Sig. (2 Tails) N	0,633 0 157	1 157	0,696 0 157	0,721 0 157	0,682 0 157
Usefulness of content	Pearson's Correlation Sig. (2 Tails) N	0,618 0 157	0,696 0 157	1 157	0,665 0 157	0,742 0 157
Online Resources	Pearson's Correlation Sig. (2 Tails) N	0,534 0 157	0,721 0 157	0,665 0 157	1 157	0,646 0 157
Ability to provide accurate information	Pearson's Correlation Sig. (2 Tails) N	0,667 0 157	0,682 0 157	0,742 0 157	0,646 0 157	1 157

Table 14. Pearson correlation test between sub-features of 'Ease of use'

Sub-Features		Ability to access	Information discovery	Interaction	Ease of understanding	Efficiency of navigation
Ability to access	Pearson's Correlation Sig. (2 Tails) N	1 157	0,729 0 157	0,574 0 157	0,73 0 157	0,723 0 157
Information discovery	Pearson's Correlation Sig. (2 Tails) N	0,729 0 157	1 157	0,639 0 157	0,689 0 157	0,722 0 157
Interaction	Pearson's Correlation Sig. (2 Tails) N	0,574 0 157	0,639 0 157	1 157	0,642 0 157	0,599 0 157
Ease of understanding	Pearson's Correlation Sig. (2 Tails) N	0,73 0 157	0,689 0 157	0,642 0 157	1 157	0,772 0 157
Efficiency of navigation	Pearson's Correlation Sig. (2 Tails) N	0,723 0 157	0,722 0 157	0,599 0 157	0,772 0 157	1 157

Table 15. Pearson correlation test between sub-features of 'Security and privacy'

Sub-Features		User confidence	Provision of Services	Prevention of risk and fraud
User confidence	Pearson's Correlation Sig. (2 Tails) N	1 157	0,733 0 157	0,784 0 157
Provision of services	Pearson's Correlation Sig. (2 Tails) N	0,733 0 157	1 157	0,728 0 157
Prevention of risk and fraud	Pearson's Correlation Sig. (2 Tails) N	0,784 0 157	0,728 0 157	1 157

Table 16. Pearson correlation test between sub-features of 'Speed of processing'

Sub-Features		Convenience and waiting time	Upload Speed	Efficiency of the system
Convenience and waiting time	Pearson's Correlation Sig. (2 Tails) N	1 157	0,861 0 157	0,813 0 157
Upload Speed	Pearson's Correlation Sig. (2 Tails) N	0,861 0 157	1 157	0,833 0 157
Efficiency of the system	Pearson's Correlation Sig. (2 Tails) N	0,813 0 157	0,833 0 157	1 157

Table 17. Pearson correlation test between sub-features of 'Aesthetic appearance'

Sub-Features		Visual aspect	Innovation and flow	Simple and meaningful charts	Animations
Visual aspect	Pearson's Correlation Sig. (2 Tails) N	1 157	0,796 0 157	0,774 0 157	0,379 0 157
Innovation and flow	Pearson's Correlation Sig. (2 Tails) N	0,796 0 157	1 157	0,784 0 157	0,491 0 157
Simple and meaningful charts	Pearson's Correlation Sig. (2 Tails) N	0,774 0 157	0,784 0 157	1 157	0,521 0 157
Efficiency of the System	Pearson's Correlation Sig. (2 Tails) N	0,379 0 157	0,491 0 157	0,521 0 157	1 157
Animations	Pearson's Correlation Sig. (2 Tails) N	0,723 0 157	0,722 0 157	0,599 0 157	0,772 0 157

Table 18. Pearson correlation test between sub-features of 'Relationship with the user'

Sub-Features		Socialization and maintenance of the relationship	Behavioral intentions of loyalty	Positive feeling in navigating the web site	Convenience and time delay associated with customer satisfaction	Business processes	FAQ and customer support
Socialization and maintenance of the relationship	Pearson's Correlation	1	0,69	0,768	0,738	0,677	0,611
	Sig. (2 Tails)		0	0	0	0	0
	N	157	157	157	157	157	157
Behavioral intentions of loyalty	Pearson's Correlation	0,69	1	0,779	0,763	0,595	0,637
	Sig. (2 Tails)	0		0	0	0	0
	N	157	157	157	157	157	157
Positive feeling in navigating the web site	Pearson's Correlation	0,768	0,779	1	0,792	0,643	0,62
	Sig. (2 Tails)	0	0		0	0	0
	N	157	157	157	157	157	157
Convenience and time delay associated with customer satisfaction	Pearson's Correlation	0,738	0,763	0,792	1	0,698	0,713
	Sig. (2 Tails)	0	0	0		0	0
	N	157	157	157	157	157	157
Business processes	Pearson's Correlation	0,677	0,596	0,643	0,698	1	0,625
	Sig. (2 Tails)	0	0	0	0		0
	N	157	157	157	157	157	157
FAQ and customer support	Pearson's Correlation	0,611	0,637	0,62	0,713	0,625	1
	Sig. (2 Tails)	0	0	0	0	0	
	N	157	157	157	157	157	157

Section 2
Inclusion and Accessibility

Chapter 6
Including Dyslexic Users in the Early Design of the LITERACY Portal

Renate Motschnig
University of Vienna, Austria

Domink Hagelkruys
University of Vienna, Austria

Ján Struhár
University of Vienna, Austria

Kamila Balharová
Pedagogical and Psychological Counseling Center Brno, Czech Republic

ABSTRACT

Human-Centered Design requires end-user consideration and involvement in all steps of the human-computer interface design, but how can this be accomplished if the primary user group is users with special cognitive and affective needs? Would "classical" tools and techniques be sufficient or would they need to be adapted and complemented with special effort? This chapter shares the strategies the authors adopt and the experiences they are gradually gaining in including users with dyslexia in the design of the LITERACY Web-Portal. LITERACY is a project of the European Union aiming at improving social inclusion of youth and adults with dyslexia. The authors hope this case study provides insight on and gives courage for inclusion of end-users even though—or particularly because—they have special needs.

INTRODUCTION

In this chapter, we describe the strategies we applied and the experiences we gathered while designing a web-portal-interface for users with dyslexia by including dyslexic users in the early phases of the Human Centered Design process. We believe that end-user inclusion is a critical success factor because we are convinced that the acceptance of any software-tool hinges on the

DOI: 10.4018/978-1-4666-6228-5.ch006

degree to which we manage to meet the (special) needs of the primary target groups. Therefore the Human Centered Design process makes an optimal fit for the goals we are trying to achieve.

Before we were able to start including any users, we had to apply the initial steps of the Human Centered Design process. We began with analyzing the future users, by studying articles, looking at existing web-applications targeted at them, and personally talking to dyslexic persons we already were in contact with. Based on this information we extracted and described potential tasks that might be performed on the Literacy Portal. To achieve this we used three of the core elements of the HCD process: personas, context analysis and task analysis.

Regarding the strategy, we tried to contact people with dyslexia as soon as possible to get a feeling not only for their special needs but also for their special strengths. Initial contact with persons with dyslexia followed literature research and preparation of key questions such as to be knowledgeable partners in the dialogue, but otherwise as open as possible to learn from their life stories and experiences. Following this mindset, we considered it most helpful to engage in semi-structured interviews with dyslexic persons in various stages of life, and to gradually focus on some of their core issues that crystallized from the interviews such as finding work, using the internet, interacting in/with educational institutions, etc. Also very early in the process we asked dyslexic persons about the preferences for screen designs and what terms they found relevant or interesting to look for on the LITERACY portal.

Regarding our experience, we are going to point to issues worth specific consideration in order to share our experience with interested peers, thus make it reusable in the community of interface designers. In a nutshell, getting in contact with users with special needs may need special provisions, contacts with counseling centers, more time than talking to "ordinary" users, and an adaptation

of methods and/or tools and procedures to accommodate for the particular special needs.

This chapter is structured as follows: the next section discusses the background in which this research was conducted and provisions we are taking to maximize end-user inclusion in all aspects of the design process. Additionally we are going to mention related work and studies that influenced different aspects of our research design. The subsequent section describes our applied design strategies and how we included people with dyslexia into the design-process through individual direct and indirect means of end-user inclusion during the early stages of human centered design. The particular experiences of included dyslexic users will be highlighted throughout this section. The final sections summarize our work and experiences so far and give an outlook on further work. The contribution intends to confirm that the inclusion of end users in early stages of web-design is essential and that it should be done regardless of whether end-users have special needs or not. Furthermore, the article illustrates some concrete techniques and steps to include end-users with dyslexia and thus can serve as an example or inspiration on how to accomplish and exploit end-user inclusion for increased usability of a web-portal.

BACKGROUND AND RELATED WORK

As the British Dyslexia Association defined (BDA, 2013), "dyslexia is a specific learning difficulty that mainly affects the development of literacy and language related skills. It is likely to be present at birth and to be life-long in its effects. It is characterized by difficulties with phonological processing, rapid naming, working memory, processing speed, and the automatic development of skills that may not match up to an individual's other cognitive abilities." It often comes with other difficulties such as dyscalculia – numerical and math problems, dysgraphia and dysortographia – cognitive and motor writing difficulties, dyspraxia – coordination problems, and also attention deficit hyperactivity disorder (ADHD). These tend to be resistant to conventional teaching methods, but their effect can be mitigated by appropriately specific intervention, including the application of information technology and supportive counseling. Due to differences in languages and approaches of local bodies to defining and assessing dyslexia, it is hard to specify the prevalence of dyslexia in the population. Our experts suggest 10% and more, which would make more than 70 million people - in Europe only.

Human Centered Design (HCD) is a specific design approach, which sets the focus on the users of a product. The HCD-process is standardized (ISO 9241-210:2010) and follows the philosophy that a product can only be good if it suits the needs of the people who use it. The HCD-process is inclusive and iterative and therefore heavily relies on the inputs, comments and suggestions of target groups. Other than in the often used and easier to plan top-down (waterfall) approach, in which the users do not see the product before it is in an advanced stage, Human Centered Design already includes target groups in the early stages of the development. This early and constant inclusion makes it possible to take the requirements and needs of the users into account, thus enabling suitable design choices.

The context in which we apply HCD is the LITERACY project, a European-wide research endeavor funded by the European Commission in the area of ICT under the FP7 program. Its aim is to create an advanced online portal, which will aid both dyslexic youths and adults. The portal is destined to provide personalized e-learning programs, useful tools and methods for helping people with dyslexia to improve their abilities in reading and writing. It will also provide entry to an accessible online community of peers. A special-ized interface and Community Zone with programs and services will improve the skills of the users, drastically simplifying otherwise complicated tasks. This will be done by utilizing novel tools, which will be integrated with both existing and adapted ICT tools and hardware. Dyslexic users will be able to access this portal independently and receive real-time feedback on their progress.

The Human Centered Design process is a core element in creating this online portal, as it will allow us to fit the design of the portal to the specific needs of users with dyslexia.

There is a lot of quality work that influences different aspects of this article or discusses related topics. Certainly a source of information that was used throughout various design steps was the book "Interaction Design: Beyond Human-Computer Interaction" (Rogers et al, 2011). It offers a broad variety of topics that not only focus on design aspects but also describes interaction processes or cognitive aspects. Therefore it served as a handy lecture while setting up testing sessions for our special target groups. Another work that provided us with great insight and helpful tips on how to assess users with special needs is the book "Assessing Learners with Special Needs: An Applied Approach" (Overton, 2012). The information provided by Overton helped us set up tests and interpret their outcomes.

Another great source is Harold Thimbleby's article "Understanding User-Centred Design (UCD) for People with Special Needs" (Thimbleby, 2008), which offers valuable insights into the complex topic of Human-Centered Design in a special needs context. It served us as an initial stepping stone in our preparatory research phase.

Furthermore there are various works that describe projects or relevant topics, like interface design for people with dyslexia or special needs in general. Notably there is the article "Web Accessibility: Designing for dyslexia" (Bell, 2009), which focuses on web-accessibility and interface design for people with dyslexia. Additionally, there is the article "Multimedia Software Interface Design for Special-Needs Users" (Lányi, 2009), focusing on interface design for people with special needs in a more general way. The paper "Designing with users, How?" investigates user involvement tactics for effective inclusive design processes (Lee, 2008) and describes the inclusive design processes on a general level. These papers and articles, among others, were a great source for designing our web-portal, as they provided insights and valuable tips.

Lastly there exists also a lot of material generated by other special needs projects. The information we found while studying these other projects helped us to estimate the work necessary and identify potential problems. Notable examples are: "A mobile application concept to encourage independent mobility for blind and visually impaired students" (Liimatainen et al, 2012), "Under Watch and Ward at Night: Design and Evaluation of a Remote Monitoring System for Dementia Care" (Schikhof and Mulder, 2008) and the AGID-Project (http://agid-project.eu/), which creates web-based training for professionals on thee topics of ageing and intellectual disability by using a person-centered approach.

DESIGN STRATEGIES AND INCLUSION OF USERS

Strategies in the Design of the Literacy Portal

In our effort to create a successful online portal that suits the needs of its future users we decided to use certain methods and strategies that will support our ideas as well as the specific requirements of our target groups.

First of all we applied the Human Centered Design approach, which heavily includes users already in early design stages. Through this approach we learn about the specific needs and preferences of our users and therefore can eliminate potential problems before they surface. This itera-

tive process allows us to step by step decrease the cognitive load and enhance the user experience.

Apart from the actual screen design of the portal we also try to provide specific content for people with dyslexia. This not only includes theoretical input about dyslexia but also different ways to increase social inclusion of dyslexic youth and adults in the real world as well as in the virtual world. To achieve this goal we plan on using a variety of means, like tips, life stories, e-learning, training and ways for community building. These means will help people with dyslexia deal with problematic everyday situations, encourage them to work on their weaknesses, self-empower them and give them the possibility to get in contact with other people with dyslexia.

Furthermore we are focusing on a strength-based approach. We not only want to tell our users where they are weak and what they need to improve, we especially want to emphasize their strengths and encourage them to use them.

We want to transport this strength-based approach through Person-Centered Communication (Motschnig and Nykl, 2014) and appreciative inquiry (Barret and Fry, 2005) in all contacts and dialogues. This means that all communication between the portal and the users is done in a way that fits the needs of our target groups, makes navigation as easy as possible, reduces the cognitive load and leaves them with a feeling of appreciation and motivation. We want to facilitate transparency and personalization as well as make our users feel respect through inclusion and participation. Our plan for inclusion of users into the design of the online portal according to the HCD process will be achieved through different ways, which could be roughly classified into indirect and direct methods.

Indirect Inclusion

Indirect methods include a series of different steps in the design process. Firstly we researched, online as well as in specialist literature and relevant studies, the topic of dyslexia and users with special cognitive and affective needs, which gave us initial ideas and guidelines for the design. The bandwidth of sources and literature collected through this process is quite broad and extensive. It ranges from specialist websites, like the website of the British Dyslexia Association, over national organizations to papers and articles, like for example "What we know about dyslexia and Web Accessibility: A research review" (McCarth and Swierenga, 2009) to relevant expert literature like "Interacton Design: Beyond Human-Computer Interaction" (Rogers, Sharp and Preece, 2011). Parts of it can be found as sources of this article and in the "further reading" section. The life stories we read in the process of research provided a lot of insight and proved to be valuable in later tasks of the HCD, i.e. task analysis. Based on our research we created specific accessibility and design criteria to guide our further steps in the design of the online portal.

Additionally there are also the initial steps of the Human Centered Design: Personas, Task analysis and Context analysis.

Personas are a commonly used technique in Human Centered Design. They are fictional characters that represent real users during the design process. Their description is based on important user-groups and their specific characteristics, motivation and expectations. Personas were already used in many IT-projects and various adaptations for special needs applications and revisions of the concept itself were proposed, such as in the paper "Revisiting Personas: The Making-of for Special User Groups" (Moser et al, 2012), which describes a decision diagram for the creation of Personas for elderly and children. For our purpose we used a similar approach that influenced our data collection process. To create Personas we gathered information through online resources and literature as well as interviews with dyslexics and experts. In the end we identified ten different personas, which cover a wide range of users and include different types like students, parents or professionals. Based on these personas we chose and contacted users, which we wanted to get involved into the design process of the portal.

The Task analysis allows us to describe different use cases for users from their specific point of view. This is beneficial for the design process, because they describe what the users want to do and how the portal has to be designed to make it possible. By identifying major tasks that will potentially be done on the portal we get a better idea of how the interface should look like and how it should respond. The tasks we collected were stored in a database, in which they were organized in different categories and subcategories. Every task consists of a short description, an example, parameters for frequency and priority, ideas for implementations and comments from different reviewers. Furthermore every task is linked to one or several different personas. This provides a map of connections between different user groups and also helps identifying important design-goals.

The Context analysis represents a mixture of indirect and direct inclusion, as it is partly based on feedback from potential users and experts as well as research and the intended functionality of the portal. It showed that the Literacy Portal will be used in different environments and that the current state of mind of a user will have a huge impact on the reception of the information. We identified three important contexts: assessment, everyday life and work. Every one of these three contexts describes different usage conditions, which heavily affect the users in various ways and therefore result in shifting levels of cognitive load. The results of this analysis provide us with valuable information that has to be considered when designing the portal.

These initial steps allowed us to outline our target groups, set the main focus and identify potential problem areas.

Direct Inclusion

After we acquired knowledge about people with dyslexia and their challenges from indirect sources, we approached them directly. The further steps of the human-centered design process we chose were interviews, choosing from a set of screen designs and card-sorting. All of these activities were done with help of our colleagues in the Psychological and Pedagogical Counseling Center in Brno. They shortlisted a number of their current and past clients, then contacted them via email, personally or even through television and 30 out of 40 invited responded positively. After a small workshop in Brno that set a common vision of the direct inclusion, our colleagues also carried out interviews and participated on analysis of the results. The help of psychologists and special pedagogues was essential for reaching people with dyslexia, mainly because dyslexia is a sensitive matter, often concealed and not admitted. Our colleagues helped us pick people open to sharing, which is described in the following sub-sections.

Interviews and their evolution. The first mode of the end user inclusion was dialogue in the form of an interview. Our strategy was to apply appreciative inquiry: try to find the strengths of an interviewee, look for the conditions in which the strengths express themselves and search how to replicate these conditions. Adoption of Person-Centered Approach (Rogers and Roethlisberger, 1991; Motschnig and Nykl, 2011) including active listening (Rogers and Farson, 1957), resulted in creation of an atmosphere that was non-judgmental, empathic and open. Open also to the actual experience from the dialogue, so that we do not hold the findings from the preparatory research for rigid and directive constructs.

We started with one prototypical unstructured interview with N., a manager of technical support, formerly a teacher of informatics for pupils with special needs. In the search for strengths and motivations also the struggles and challenges he encounters came up and we collected a lot of information.

Then, based on this experience, we created a guide to interviewing, reviewed by doc. PhDr. Věra Vojtová, an associate professor of special pedagogy. This enabled scaling to a bigger number of interviews at the same time and supported data consistency. The guide summed up the strategy for interviewing, which consisted mainly of non-judgmental approach, active listening and non-directive questioning. Then it, gave an outline of topics (school life, work life, internet usage, hobbies) and examples of questions., as you can see in Appendix A.

Among the outcomes of the interviews was a collection of problems that adults with dyslexia encounter in their daily lives. They were related mainly to text in any form and medium. The top 12 problems as identified and reported by adults with dyslexia were that they:

- Read slowly
- Have difficulties reading small letters
- Get lost in text
- Do not understand what they read or have to focus too hard to understand
- Have problems moving to the next line
- Do not see numbers or other data in text
- Are unable to identify keywords in text thus evaluate it differently
- Detest the amount of text they have to read in their job
- Cannot focus deliberately
- Miss important information in emails
- Cannot write grammatically correct emails, yet these are requested by their employers
- Form sentences differently – these make sense to them, not to others

One example for all from a person working in a logistic firm, concerning misidentifying numbers in emails: "I sent a lorry to load the goods at a wrong hour. It could be forgiven once, but it kept happening. My boss had to let me go. I never told anyone about my dyslexia because I was afraid I would lose my job."

Moreover, we found out that majority of the respondents use internet daily because they need it either for work or study. They prefer sites relevant to their professions. Two thirds of the respondents use Facebook and more than a half have Google Chrome set as the default browser, the rest choosing Internet Explorer, Mozilla Firefox or Opera. Sitemap is welcome, too. Electronic diaries or schedulers and Skype came up in their lists of used tools only sporadically. Half of the respondents use office suites such as MS Office or Open Office, often criticizing the abundance of functions as unclear. Two respondents use Google Translator, 3 respondents are working with a text-to-speech tool and 2 adjust texts to their needs. Some did not know that an adjustment of a text could help them read.

The troubles that adults with dyslexia have when interacting with the internet are:

- Advertisement
- Too much text
- Low contrast
- Too many homepage sections
- Moving text
- Flashing text

Some of them described screen-readers and video tutorials as life-changers and told us about various tricks they developed over time. The importance of a loving and willing parent or teacher was stressed, too, and we heard how motivation from interests and hobbies can be transferred into reading.

Further experience motivated us to collect the most useful questions into a simple yes-no questionnaire, which was shared online among us and continuously expanded. (For the final version of the questionnaire, see Appendix B).

Moreover, through these interviews, we achieved what human-centered design requires - we stepped into the shoes of one with dyslexia and got to know and understand our end-user first-hand. (Norman, D. A., 2002)

As it can be seen in the evolution of the interview, we integrated the iterative nature of the Human Centered Design into the process itself, too. This might be helpful in cases such as our LITERACY project, when the end users have distinctly different, sometimes counter-intuitive

mental models. This was earlier presented to us by our experts in special pedagogy on the case of website background colour choice (choosing bright strong yellow over much subtler tones of yellow).

Extending interviews by screen design choice. By the time of having started interviewing, we created 5 screen designs. Each of them showed a different menu structure and three steps of going through it (the first screen, category choice and sub-category choice). Three of them, with the buttons in a grid, are based on suggestions of Dr. Gyarmathy, an expert on dyslexia, and supported by Dr. Beránek, an IT specialist, both members of our consortium. The fourth is a more recent book-flipping menu and the last one is a common vertical expanding menu, as briefly shown in the following figure:

As long as it was difficult to get in touch with our future end users and arrange meetings, we decided to join more activities of Human Centered Design together and on each interview meeting asked our interviewees to choose the screen design that is the most suitable for them. If they picked one, 2 points were assigned to it, and if they also picked a second choice it was assigned 1 point. Thus we were able to see how to proceed with the next prototypes. The results point to the vertical menu, which was chosen by the majority of the respondents. However, there is a difference between the genders. Whereas female participants strongly favored the vertical expanding menu (73%), the analysis of male participants shows an even outcome.

Although the vertical expanding menu is still the winner, the three button menus combined (34%) and the book-flipping menu (31%) are very close. A difference showed up between generations of users. Whereas respondents over the age 20 years preferred the vertical menu, the younger ones seem to be used to different styles of menu such as the Apple's coverflow or smartphone and tablet button menus.

Figure 1. The five different screen designs, each showing the menu with main categories

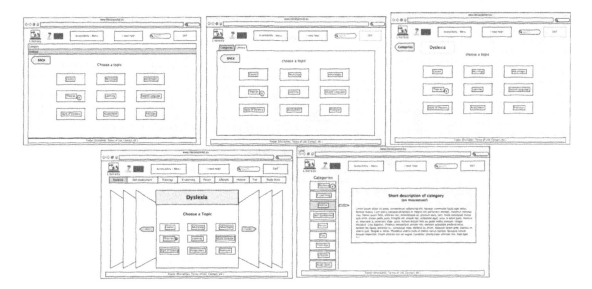

Extending interviews by card sorting. The next step in the design process of the LITERACY portal, also executed at the interview meetings described in previous sub-sections, was card-sorting. It is a simple activity which yields complex results. A broad offer of content and functions of our portal was assembled by our consortium and transcribed onto 60 paper cards. Our interviewees were told to go through them, ask for clarifications, create their own cards if necessary and then sort any chosen cards into their own menu structure. These results were photographed, noted in an Excel spreadsheet and analyzed by an application called xSort.

A cluster tree generated by xSort identified 8 main categories, which represent content and functions of our web portal. We also received clues about naming of the (sub)categories and learned that 60 cards is not too much for people with dyslexia as we feared. Quite on the contrary, they accepted the task with engagement and enjoyed the creative work. Similarly to the interviews, the card-sorting process was also iteratively improved, which is the fourth main learning we took from this activity.

Card-sorting also evaluated each function or piece of content planned for the portal. The re-

spondents were free to omit any cards they would not want on our portal. The top 20 chosen to stay were Tests (27 votes), Dyslexia, Learning methods (26), Signs of Dyslexia, Reading (25), E-learning, Contact, Games (24), Second Language, Memory, ADHD, Complex aids, Tutorial (23), Training, Forum, Theories, Learning, Study aids (22) and Tips (21 votes). Based on these choice sums, our professional partners were informed about which specific content and function they should focus on. More details about these improvements and results of our case study of card-sorting are published in (Motschnig et al., 2013).

Excursion to a class with dyslexic students. One of the opportunities for direct inclusion was a visit to a school in Budapest organized by our partners from the Hungarian Academy of Science. We and our colleagues (a team of 8 people) were taken to an English class at K-12 level of about 12 pupils between 17 and 19 years of age, each having a special need. After mutual introductions, when the pupils openly shared the challenges they face, we were given space for questions.

We asked mainly about their internet-usage habits and found out that they all use Facebook and can cope with it, but with variations. Some

Figure 2. Overall Screen design choice and gender preferences

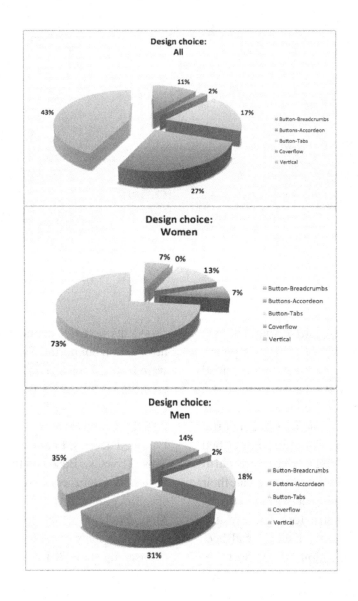

spent 5 minutes only to check agreements with friends, reading as little as possible, some browse for 5 hours. They hardly ever use discussion boards, reading in any form consumed too much of their energy.

Interestingly, one young lady was asked how it is for her to read transport schedules and responded that it would be better if it were pink. This shows the difference of the mental models that we, designers, have to bridge. Furthermore, most of the students were creative and motivated in other than textual ways and claimed that they like photographing, dance, music, fine arts and sports. Just as in the case of interviews, this encounter served as a way of understanding of daily life of people with dyslexia with focus on the internet usage.

Solutions and Recommendations

So far, carrying out preparatory research and applying methods of direct user-inclusion such as interviewing, prototyping and card-sorting have driven us to 4 main results.

First of all, we have reached a deeper level of understanding of people with dyslexia, our future end users. We have learned how differently they think, how this difference intertwines with their school-, work- and personal life and how they use internet. For example, inquiries into internet usage helped us realize that people with dyslexia mind long texts, prefer sans-serif fonts, and require consistency throughout a website. Implementing screen-reading is necessary and other tools and guides to using them are also welcome. Moreover, due to the variability of thinking styles and of manifestations of dyslexia, a high degree of personalization for a portal such as LITERACY seems to be critical. These and other findings not only support us in our design work and get us used to a different style of thinking, but also make us appreciate the potential that is in people with dyslexia. We feel motivated to help them develop this potential and a positive outlook on life. We therefore consider direct inclusion essential.

Secondly, we also collected specific ideas that will be implemented in the next phases of the design process of the LITERACY Portal. Together with our possible future users, we have chosen the vertical expanding menu as the most suitable menu style and we reorganized the content we will provide on the portal into 8 main categories, too. We also got some tips on naming of the (sub) categories, such as turning "Assistive technology" into "Helping tools".

Thirdly, we learned about the procedures of the HCD process in the case of users with special needs. Interviews evolved and a successful guide was created. Then we found out that 60 cards in the card-sorting procedure was an appropriate number and it was not necessary to develop a lighter version with fewer cards. With the willingness and coop-

erativeness of our interviewees on one hand and the appreciative and the person-centered approach on the other, these procedures went smoothly and all combined into one session took up to 2 hours per person (plus more time for preparation and then processing and analysis). However, some flexibility should be built-in each plan, whereas people with dyslexia vary in thinking and approach the questions and tasks they are given creatively. For example, our interview guide focuses rather on strategy of asking and suggests some topics, rather than providing a rigid structure of questions.

The final outcome of this phase of HCD in our project is that we have started to build a relationship between our future users and the LITERACY Portal. We hope that seeing that they are listened to and their ideas are implemented or at least seriously considered for the portal will make the adoption of the final product and spreading of the word among people with dyslexia more probable.

Our next steps again expect direct inclusion of individuals from our target group, preferring those who have already participated in the interviews so that we continue building the relationships and form a core group of first users.

In the second iteration of the menu choice, the user will be asked to pick either the vertical menu or the button menu, the top two menu styles. Two simple prototypes were built for this task, so that the tester can judge the menu style not only by its aesthetic appeal and assumptions, but also by its clarity and usability. These prototypes come both in online and offline version and the testing procedure is administered by professionals from the Psychological and pedagogical centre in Brno.

To ensure clear navigation, we are also testing the icons – an important non-textual cue. Taking all dyslexia-friendly practices into account, we created an online tool in which our respondents choose icons that speak to them most. This activity consists of three steps. First, our respondent fills an empty menu form by choosing one of 3-5 options for a specific menu item. Secondly, he or she chooses the best match for the terms "Settings" and "Login". In the third and last step, the respondent sees the whole homepage he or she set up and adjusts the size of the buttons. The whole activity and its length is captured and stored in a simple database and will provide valuable feedback both for the visual of the portal and for the design process.

After that, we plan an encompassing design step, namely task-based testing of a new clickable prototype derived from the results outlined in this paper, with the "thinking aloud" technique (the tester tells what he thinks and feels while performing any given task). A group dialogue or an informal focus group with some of the clients of the Pedagogical and psychological counseling center in Brno was also suggested by our colleagues at the center. Then we want to draw more users to the LITERACY Portal and get more feedback on it by organizing a contest, which will make use of the first running versions of the portal and take advantage of one of the strengths of people with dyslexia – creativity. After that, all of the feedback and results of the testing will be analyzed and they will again influence the following steps in our project, adhering to the iterative and inclusive nature of human-centered design and hopefully directing the LITERACY portal towards helping with the real everyday needs of people with dyslexia.

FUTURE RESEARCH DIRECTIONS

One of the outcomes of the LITERACY Project aims to be a "person-centered" portal, or, in other words, an online portal designed with focus on empathic understanding and acceptance of its end-user. Further research should specify a person-centered portal in more detail, inquire how the person-centered approach overlaps with human-centered design, how does a final product of such design process function and whether it promotes authenticity, inclusion and affective needs of its user.

Also, preparation of the LITERACY Portal's piloting in four different languages and two alphabets inspires to delve deeper into the language-specific strengths and weaknesses of ICT usage in case of people with dyslexia. Extension of the portal to Spanish and German mutation for more comprehensive research in this direction is envisioned, too.

CONCLUSION

This chapter illustrated various design decisions, techniques and steps of including dyslexic youth and adults in the early design stages of the LITERACY Portal, an interactive web-application that is intended to support the social inclusion of users who are struggling readers. Basically, we used two forms of end-user inclusion, an indirect one in which the design team studied the special cognitive and affective habits of dyslexic users from literature, web-resources and by talking to experts from pedagogy and psychology and a direct one in which users were asked about key aspects of the Portal. The latter employed procedures such as semi-structured interviews, screen design choice and card-sorting. The results and sample data gathered through these various means not only helped us get a better understanding of how an optimal interface for our specific user group should look like but also how our testing sessions have to be adapted to generate the best results. The findings of each individual design-step influenced subsequent ones and therefore helped us to create more suitable testing scenarios as well as estimate the limits of cognitive capabilities more closely or incorporate the creative tendencies of dyslexic users, which heavily influenced our design decisions, into our testing sessions. These gradual improvements were only possible thanks to the help of experts of various fields of expertise within the LITERACY-Consortium.

Our future design-steps will focus on direct inclusion in the form of icon testing, refined screen design choice, users' estimation of experience regarding the Portal's usability, and thinking-aloud based task testing.

So far, we have:

- deepened our understanding of a person with dyslexia,
- identified the most recurring difficulties people with dyslexia encounter online and collected ideas for next phases of portal design,
- learned about dyslexia-specific aspects of human centered design procedures,
- and started building relationships with our future users.

In this way, the portal has a higher chance of being accepted by its users, promoting inclusion of people with dyslexia and other reading difficulties and providing insights into human centered design and person-centered communication with people with special cognitive and affective needs.

REFERENCES

Balharová, K., Motschnig, R., Struhár, J., & Hagelkruys, D. (2013). A Case Study of Applying Card- sorting as an Initial Step in the Design of the LITERACY – Portal for People with Dyslexia. In *Proceedings of the Conference Universal Learning Design*. Brno, Czech Republic: Masaryk University.

Barret, F. J., & Fry, R. E. (2005). *Appreciative inquiry: a positive approach to building cooperative capacity*. Chagrin Falls.

Bell, L. (2009). *Web Accessibility: Designing for Dyslexia*. Retrieved October 15, 2013, from http://lindseybell.com/documents/bell_dyslexia.pdf

British Dyslexia Association. (2007). *Dyslexia Research Information*. Retrieved October 15, 2013, from http://www.bdadyslexia.org.uk/about-dyslexia/further-information/dyslexia-research-information-.html

ISO 9241. (2010). *Ergonomics of human-system interaction – Part 210: Human-centered design for interactive systems*. Geneva: ISO.

Lányi, C. S. (2009). Multimedia Software Interface Design for Special-Needs Users. In M. Khosrow-Pour (Ed.), *Encyclopedia of Information Science and Technology* (2nd ed., pp. 2761–2766). Hershey, PA: IGI Global.

Lee, Y., et al. (2008). Designing with users, how? Investigate users involvement tactics for effective inclusive design processes. In Design Thinking: New Challenges for Designers, Managers and Organizations. Cergy-Pointoise.

Liimatainen, J., Häkkinen, M., Nousiainen, T., Kankaanranta, M., & Neittaanmäki, P. (2012). A mobile application concept to encourage independent mobility for blind and visually impaired students. In *Proceedings of the 13th international conference on Computers Helping People with Special Needs*. Berlin: Springer Verlag.

McCarthy, J., & Swierenga, S. (2010). What we know about dyslexia and Web accessibility: A research review. *Universal Access in the Information Society*, *9*(2), 147–152. doi:10.1007/s10209-009-0160-5

Moser, C., Fuchsberger, V., Neureiter, L., Sellner, W., & Tscheligi, M. (2012). *Revisiting personas: the making-of for special user groups*. Paper presented at CHI '12. Austin, TX.

Motschnig, R., & Nykl, L. (2011). *Komunikace zaměřená na člověka: rozumět sobě i druhým*. Prague: Grada.

Motschnig, R., & Nykl, L. (2014). *Person-centred Communication Theory, Skills and Practice*. Maidenhead, UK: McGraw Hill.

Norman, D. A. (2002). *The design of everyday things*. New York: Basic Books.

Overton, T. (2012). *Assessing Learners with Special Needs: An applied approach*. Boston: Pearson Education.

Rogers, C. R., & Farson, R. E. (1957). Active Listening. In R. G. Newman, M. A. Danziger, & M. Cohen (Eds.), *Communication in Business Today*. Washington, DC: Heath and Company.

Rogers, C. R., & Roethlisberger, F. J. (1991). Barriers and Gateways to Communication. *Harvard Business Review*.

Rogers, Y., Sharp, H., & Preece, J. (2011). *Interaction Design: beyond human-computer interaction*. New York: Wiley.

Schikhof, Y., & Mulder, I. (2008). Under Watch and Ward at Night: Design and Evaluation of a Remote Monitoring System for Dementia Care. In *Proceedings of the 4th Symposium of the Workgroup Human-Computer Interaction and Usability Engineering of the Austrian Computer Society on HCI and Usability for Education and Work*. Berlin: Springer Verlag.

Thimbleby, H. W. (2008). Understanding User Centred Design (UCD) for People with Special Needs. In K. Miesenberger, J. Klaus, W. L. Zagler, & A. I. Karshmer (Eds.), *ICCHP*. Berlin: Springer Verlag. doi:10.1007/978-3-540-70540-6_1

ADDITIONAL READING

Edmondson, W. H. (2001). *A Taxonomical Approach to Special Needs Design in HCI* (pp. 909–913). New Orleans, USA: Universal Access in Human-Computer Interaction.

Goldsmith, S. (2007). *Universal Design*. Great Britain: Taylor & Francis.

Spencer, D. (2009). *Card Sorting: Designing Usable Categories*. Brooklyn, New York, USA: Rosenfeld Media.

KEY TERMS AND DEFINITIONS

Accessibility: Accessibility describes the extent to which persons with special needs or people who use assistive technologies can use a product, like for example software.

Card sorting: Card sorting is an interactive activity in which the participants choose cards from a set number of options with a specific goal in mind, like for example elements of a menu.

Dyslexia: Dyslexia can be characterized as a learning deficiency, which expresses itself in form of reading and writing difficulties.

Human-Centered-Design: Human-Centered-Design (HCD) is an iterative design approach that puts the focus on the users. A central part of HCD is the constant inclusion of end-users into the different steps of the design process.

IT for inclusion: IT for inclusion means the use of information technologies to support the social inclusion of specific user groups, such as users with special needs.

Personas: Personas are fictional characters that represent a certain user group. They comprise certain characteristics that are representative for this user group.

Screen design: Screen design includes all visual elements of an interface, including positioning of objects, color-schemes, fonts, styles, etc.

Social inclusion: Social inclusion depicts a form of inclusion that helps people to take part in social activities, like for example social media or different forms of communication.

Task analysis: Task analysis depicts the process of assessing and describing potential tasks that users need, have or want to perform with the product.

Usability: Usability describes the extent to which a product, like for example software, can be used to achieve specific goals in an effective, efficient, engaging, error tolerant and easy to learn way.

User analysis: User analysis is the process of assessing users of a product regarding a variety of different aspects, e.g. age, knowledge of the product, skill-level, etc.

APPENDIX A: INTERVIEWING

Strategy

- According to the appreciative inquiry – discover strengths, discover under which circumstances they prevail and how it would be possible to get into those circumstances more often
- According to the person centered approach – being open, trying to understand, empathize and no judging.
- Stating the purpose of the project – e.g. empowering struggling readers online, strengthening social inclusion, interest in their personal experience and us wanting them to become a part of the project
- Stating that the interviewee can ask for a pause whenever he feels like it and also the interview can be ended anytime.
- The interview is semi-structured, going around certain topics. If the interviewer feels that the natural flow of interview is going to a different topic, let it happen and go for it, but keep in the overall goal in mind and return to a topic if necessary
- Firstly, try to acquire uninfluenced ideas from the interviewee and only after that present ours, e.g. prototypes
- If the interviewer knows something more about the interviewee, adjust questions to that knowledge to make the flow of interview more interesting for him or her

Sample Questions

- What type of student were you? What did you study? What did you like at school? What tricks did you invent to make learning easier for you? What would you like to have at school so that it was more interesting for you and why? Were there any mentors you liked? What were they like?
- What do you like about your work-life? What do you do? Which activities do you like most? Could you take a few moments and name your strengths? What could you do to use them more? How do you imagine a better workplace?
- Do you use internet? How often? How does it help you? What kind of webpages do you prefer? Do you use social networks? How would you imagine an improved social network, e.g. Facebook? Do you use any other tools? Can you describe how do you use them? What tools would you like to have? How about you and speech recognition? And text-to-speech?
- Do you read? What kind of texts? Which ones do you read with passion? Who or what lead you to reading? Do you like to use any reading tools (text-to-speech, e-readers)? Could you imagine something that would make reading easier or more enjoyable?
- Do you have any particular hobbies? How do you usually motivate yourself? Note: In the first interview, the positive form of questions lead not only to discovery of various strengths, but many problems and issues as well. If the interviewer has a feeling that this is not happening, he or she can of course continue with questions on complications and problems as well.

APPENDIX B: AFTER-INTERVIEW QUESTIONNAIRE

I read slowly. Yes – No

I read small letters with difficulties. Yes – No

I get lost in text. Yes – No

I don't understand what I read. Yes – No – Partially (I can when I focus really hard)

It is hard for me to go to a next line in a text. Yes – No

I forget last letters, making it harder for me to understand. Yes – No

I forget or don't see numbers and other data in a text. Yes – No

Colouring numbers in a text helps. Yes – No

I cannot recognize keywords. Yes – No

I mind the amount of text I have to read in my job. Yes – No

Deliberate focus is a problem for me. Yes – No

I easily miss important information in an email. Yes – No

I don't process details when reading, even when they are important. Yes – No

I have to write grammatically correct emails at work. Yes – No

I have problems writing in proper grammar. Yes – No

I form sentences differently. Yes – No

Online, I mind:

Adverts. Yes – No

Too much text. Yes – No

Low contrast. Yes – No

Totally similar subpages (I get lost). Yes – No

Too many sections on the homepage. Yes – No

Moving text. Yes – No

Unclear text. Yes – No

Flashing text. Yes – No

Chapter 7
Designing with Vulnerable Children:
A Researcher's Perspective

Alma Leora Culén
University of Oslo, Norway

Anna Karpova
University of Oslo, Norway

ABSTRACT

In this chapter, the authors consider a researcher's perspective in projects involving design of assistive technologies for and with children who have moderate to severe limitations, such as cognitive impairments, impulse control issues, strongly reduced vision, or speech problems. The secondary objective is to introduce the concept of vulnerability in such complex design contexts, exploring it in relation to researchers, the user group, and other stakeholders. They argue that awareness of diverse risks can lead to a design process that reduces or even eliminates some of these risks, empowering both researchers and users in the process. The case used as a basis for discussion is that of an iPad app design for and with children in a special education class, and later, with children in occupational therapy.

INTRODUCTION

Many millions of children and students between ages of 6 and 17 have a condition, cognitive, motor or sensory, that impairs their ability to participate in a typical classroom environment (Hasselbring & Glaser, 2000). Technology has long been seen as having a potential to benefit children with special education needs. Children with special education needs are those who have challenges in learning due to cognitive, motor or sensorial disabilities.

Any technology that may support such children in increasing, maintaining, or improving functional capabilities is considered an *assistive technology* (AT). Assistive technologies are of enormous interest for schools with special education classes, where the technology is used to support children with special needs in maximizing their learning potential.

In spite of their real or perceived usefulness, assistive technologies are frequently abandoned (Phillips & Zhao, 1993; Riemer-Reiss & Wacker,

DOI: 10.4018/978-1-4666-6228-5.ch007

2000). The abandonment is often related to either inadequate design of ATs, or to users' perception of themselves in relation to their use. Adequate design of user interfaces is one of the key factors for both accessibility and adoption of assistive devices. It should also take into consideration users' self-perception. Users often feel stigmatized because of the visibility of technological assistance that they need. ATs can make their disability more obvious to others (Gasparini & Culén, 2012; Shinohara & Wobbrock, 2011) and negatively influence perception of the self. Thus, a good and adequate design of interfaces has a significant impact on integration of devices into children's daily lives, increasing chances for adoption of AT, better social integration and overall quality of life. The terms *design for all* and *inclusive design* refer to a design philosophy targeting the design of technology in ways that enable people with disabilities to use mainstream products and services without additional customization (Abascal & Nicolle, 2005; Goldsmith, 2012). Design for all is about ensuring that technology works for diverse people, towards increased social inclusion and equality. Mobile and personal technologies often follow design for all principles by providing for multimodal interactions, e.g. a voice-based interaction, in addition to a touch-based interaction. Further, a possibility for customization of interaction modes is enabled to a much higher degree than ever before by a wide choice of apps. At the same time, working with mobile devices makes special education children look and behave to a larger extent like typical peers, giving a significant appeal to these technologies. This appeal, in turn, may contribute to higher adoption rates of mobile and personal technologies as assistive technologies in education.

The appearance of tablets, in particular the iPad, on the market and their fast adoption by many schools worldwide, influenced also special education. The iPad was accepted as an adequate interface for many children with difficulties. It was also a mainstream, cool device, thus helping the self-image for those who could use it as assistive technology, e.g., students with dyslexia (Culén & Gasparini, 2012). Scholarly work, as well as mass media coverage, started reporting on cases where tablets were used to assist children with difficulties, e.g. (Gasparini & Culén, 2012; Hourcade, Bullock-Rest, & Hansen, 2012; McClanahan, Williams, Kennedy, & Tate, 2012; Seshadri, 2012). The iPad and other personal mobile devices, unlike more traditional 'desktop technologies', are considered to be easier to integrate into daily lives, also for those with severe limitations.

The primary objective of this chapter is to reflect on a researcher's perspective in projects involving design of assistive technology for and with children who have moderate to severe limitations, such as cognitive impairments, impulse control issues, strongly reduced vision, or speech problems. The case used as a basis for discussion is that of an iPad app design for and with children in a special education class, and later, with children in occupational therapy. The secondary objective is to introduce the concept of *vulnerability* in such complex design contexts, exploring it in relation to researchers, the user group and other stakeholders. We argue that awareness of diverse risks may lead to a design process that reduces or even eliminates some of them, empowering all involved parties in the process.

In the literature, vulnerable users are often described as people at risk because of their age, frailty, diagnosis or limited capacities, both physically and cognitively. Since the children in need of special education have limited capacities, and are thus at risk, the term vulnerable applies to them. Vulnerability is a current topic of discussion within the HCI community, e.g., CHI 2013 workshop on designing for and with vulnerable people (Vines et al., 2013), where the authors state: *By questioning how the HCI community typically defines people as vulnerable (or not) we hope to inspire alternative visions of technology where individuals are provided means to having a voice rather than being stigmatized as vulnerable or in need of assistance.* We participated in the above workshop with (Culén, van der Velden, & Karpova, 2013) and presented our initial results in (Karpova & Culén, 2013).

'Vulnerable' may not be the best choice of the term, since it may be perceived as stigmatizing in itself. It does, however, imply an identifiable set of risks. It may be possible to address some of these risks in a design process, by integrating their reduction or elimination into a set of design goals. Thus, the awareness of risks/vulnerabilities in a design situation may be helpful in designing better products for vulnerable people. Finally, it is important to say that we do not view the term 'vulnerable user' as pejorative. It is a term that may apply to all of us, since anyone may become a vulnerable user at some time, e.g., illness, temporary disability, or inability to adapt to a new situation in life.

We make a point in this chapter, that we, as researchers/designers, could also be considered as vulnerable when starting to work in a new situation, with new challenges. When designing with children in a special education class for the first time, we were limited by diverse factors such as the lack of expertise in working with children who have cognitive, motor or sensory impairments, the lack of well established guidelines on how to carry out a design process with such children, limited communication possibilities and need to rely on others to interpret children's speech and behaviour. Thus, from our point of view, by choosing the term 'vulnerable' we establish more equality between researchers and children than what is implied by alternative terms such as 'extreme', 'challenging' or 'special' users.

Designing for and with vulnerable children, thus, may provide additional challenges for researchers/designers, related to identifying both researcher's risks/vulnerabilities and those of users. However, these risks can also be seen as opportunities for HCI researchers to make a contribution to the research field and empower everyone involved (Brown, 2012). Researchers'

vulnerabilities may be reduced by, for example, joining forces with people who have in-depth knowledge of people with specific disabilities, finding adequate design methods, or adapting existing ones to the design context and users, finding ways to bridge the communication barriers, increasing empathy with vulnerable users' experience of the world, etc. Furthermore, there is a need for extra sensitivity in ethical conduct, as well as sensibility in interpretation of children's behaviors. In addition, awareness of users' vulnerabilities/risks may provide a basis for design that empowers users to a larger degree. For example, teachers often represent interests of their students with communication and cognition impairments in design processes. At the same time, teachers also have their own interest and desires for the outcome of the process. If these two interests are in conflict, the children may be at additional risk of not being represented adequately, and consequently, having to use the technology that was not designed with an understanding of their needs and abilities.

The disposition is structured as follows: in the next section, we provide a description of the context for our study and a very short research review of areas of relevance for this chapter. Further, we present our case, a design of an app for and with children in a special education class. In a subsequent section, we provide analysis and discussion, ending the chapter by presentation of the future work and the conclusion.

THE DESIGN CONTEXT AND THE BACKGROUND WORK

Ubiquitous (mobile and personal) technologies, as mentioned above, have the potential to aid students with special needs. Whether, and how, any of the potential that ubiquitous technologies hold for improvement of learning and learning practices is actualized can only be verified in real life educational settings. We were, thus, very pleased when an opportunity to research questions around the use of the iPad in a special education class presented itself. An elementary school purchased iPads and started to use them in teaching beginning in the spring semester of 2012. In addition to their use in a regular classroom, the school leadership was interested in the use of iPads in a special education class. Both the iPad and the game-based learning that it could facilitate were considered to be engaging and motivating for all students, including the students with special needs. The special education class at this school consisted of six boys aged 8-12, a main teacher, and two assistant teachers, one of whom was dedicated to a specific student requiring extra attention.

Several months into the project, just after the completion of the data gathering phase and concept development, during the summer holidays, the class was closed, and the children re-assigned to other schools. In (Karpova & Culén, 2013) we reported that students from the special education class and their teacher would participate in the final evaluation of the prototype. However, when the prototype was ready, the reality of the new situation, with students attending different schools, proved to be too complex, and we felt that the whole project was at risk. Fortunately, an occupational therapist helped us match, by age and disability, the children from the class with those in therapy with her, enabling us to evaluate the prototype developed. When further improvements were made to the prototype, an opportunity arose to test it with ten students in a special education class (not involving any of the children from the initial group). The change in the context implied the change in our methods and techniques, providing for a broader perspective involving multiple settings (McNaney et al., 2013). The sequence of events, though, also speaks of children's vulnerability as a group, as well as vulnerability of the project as a whole.

In preparation for the project, we have reviewed literature in areas as shown in Figure 1. The fields of occupational therapy, technology in education, assistive technology and design for and with children are all large, well-established research areas. Gamification and serious games are also fast growing areas of research. Therefore, we discuss only a small number of references that we have used actively in this work.

The acquisition and the use of educational technology have been problematic in the past. In (Bromley & Apple, 1998; Cuban, 1986, 2001), the authors point out that investments in technology for education are not done appropriately, the right questions are not asked when acquiring new technology, and the selected technology remains under-used (Cuban, 2001). Cuban supports his views by considering long-term patterns of technology use at schools (Cuban, 1986). The situation is even more complicated with assistive technologies, where additional factors play an important role e.g. the perception of the self and adoption of AT (Scherer & Federici, 2012), competence and knowledge on the side of providers of such technology and prohibitive costs (Berry & Ignash, 2003; Hasselbring & Glaser, 2000), and recommending AT for children with multiple disabilities (Desideri, Roentgen, Hoogerwerf, & de Witte, 2013).

One of the immediate appeals of tablets for educational purposes was the possibility to learn subjects through gamification (i.e. the use of game design elements in non-game contexts), using diverse apps tailored to specific learning goals. It has been shown that play and playful design, including gamification, have a huge effect on user motivation and engagement (Ferrara, 2012). Gamification has been adopted in many different arenas, e.g. health, business and education (Deterding, 2013; Domínguez et al., 2013). In (Deterding, 2013), the authors state that within a socio-cultural trend of ludification, there are at least three trajectories of importance for HCI: pervasive games, gamification and playful interaction. The authors also suggest the concept of gamefulness as complementary to playfulness in terms of design goals, user behaviors and experiences. In education, trying to

Figure 1. The red square represents the area of interest for this paper, and its relation to fields which impact this area

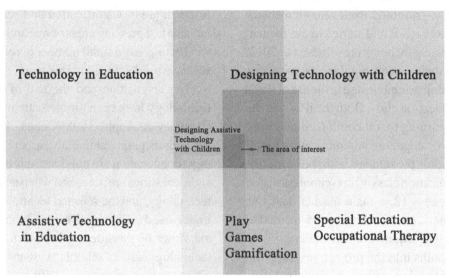

balance learning against one-sided perception of games as fun and entertaining, the educators are increasingly talking about "serious games", and gamefulness as ways of immersing students into complex problem-solving games that mimic real life situations, e.g. growing food in the desert, or solving environment and energy related problems (Westera, Nadolski, Hummel, & Wopereis, 2008).

Initially, our goal was to facilitate the use of apps already downloaded to children's iPads (the same apps that the rest of the school was using), as well as selected apps from the Apple app store such as Crazy Face ("Fun On Your iPad With Crazy Face," 2010) and Puppet Pals ("Puppet Pals HD," 2010) that support playful interactions, and observe students reactions to playful vs. gameful experiences, i.e. to open play without a goal and gamification for education purposes.

Playful and gameful interactions may be effective in engaging students with special needs in learning and development. However, we as researchers/designers within the field of interaction design are not experts in the area of special education. Thus, we used the literature to gain some understanding in this area. The book 'Play

in Occupational Therapy', (Parham & Fazio, 2007) helped to provide us with a working understanding of how play may be used in evaluating and treating children with disabilities. Chapters on accessing play through assistive technology and play in school-based occupational therapy were particularly relevant for our work.

Designing technology for and with children e.g. (Druin, 2009; Markopoulos, Read, MacFarlane, & Hoysniemi, 2008) is a challenging task. During the past two decades or so, multitudes of techniques have been developed and applied for designing technology with children, for children. Many of them are based on participatory design techniques e.g. (Culén, Bratteteig, Pandey, & Srivastava, 2013), and adapted to intergenerational design teams, see (Walsh, Foss, Yip, & Druin, 2013) for an overview.

Designing for and with children who have special needs is particularly challenging (Frauenberger, 2011; McNaney et al., 2013; Vines, 2013). For these children, the combination of power relationships, often reduced communication skills, the presence of additional stakeholders such as parents, teachers or caretakers, makes for a complex situation that needs to be handled with sensitivity, both methodological and ethical.

DESIGNING WITH VULNERABLE CHILDREN

The Pre-Design Phase

Prior to the first session with the class, informed consent forms were obtained from the parents. We carefully explained that children's participation was voluntary and that the children could withdraw from the study at any point, without any explanations. The objective of the study (originally, the use of the iPad and observation of how playful interactions influence learning, with the possibility of involvement in the design of an app) and activities the children would participate in were explained.

For our first meeting with the special education class, we wanted to create an engaging and friendly atmosphere through fun, simple games, which have worked well for us in the past. Thus, on our first visit to the class, we talked and played with the children, observed how they handled iPads on their own, and talked to their teachers. All of the boys were clearly excited about the change iPads brought into the classroom, and were very willing and eager to try new things.

The visit was followed by an hour-long interview with the main class teacher about specific issues and problems for each child, as well as how the class functions as a whole. The teacher was excited by the prospect of engaging the boys with the iPad in class, and trying game-based learning. Her hope was that all students, at the same time, could get involved in some school-related activity using iPads. One of the things we learned from the interview with the teacher was that, in spite of going to the same class for years, there was little sense of belonging to the class among the boys. Other information we received from the interview clarified, only to the extent needed in

order to plan further activities with the iPad in the class, the cognitive, social, sensory and physical development levels of students.

From these initial contacts with teachers and students in the class, we understood better the heterogeneity of the group. Some issues were similar in nature for all the children, e.g., concentration problems that all the children had to a varying degree. The others were very different e.g. speech problems vs. vision problems. It quickly became clear that this special education class could not use most of the installed apps. There were no apps that all of them could use at the same time, and in a manner similar to use in a typical classroom. The choices from the iTunes App Store were further limited by the fact that the children are not native English speakers. In fact, they were all children of immigrants, having as mother tongue a language different from the instruction language at school. Compounded with other issues the children had, this limitation was significant. Thus, it became clear rather fast that we would try to make an app together with students and their teachers. We had some experience with app co-design for the iPad, with children from a regular classroom (Culén & Gasparini, 2012).

The main teacher expressed her need related to the app design as 'something that the children could do with iPads that would be the same for all and, that supports learning'. The teacher further pointed out that it did not matter if it was an app for spelling, music, math or drawing. The underlying issue addressed here was a desire to create the sense of 'being a class'.

Based on our observations from the first meeting with students, and the interview with the main teacher, we chose to have individual skill assessment sessions, also to get to know each child as an individual. For these sessions, we selected, for each child, some apps from the App Store. The goal was to see the children play learning games and see what they could do, keeping the larger goal of making a common app in mind. Each session lasted about 20-30 minutes. Depending on the

Figure 2. The children trying existing apps for spelling, memory and creativity
Photo: Culén

child's physical and emotional condition, three to five apps were tried, see Figure 2. The child's interaction with the game, interest in it, amount of time spent on it and their ability to complete at least one round of the game were the parameters we considered.

The workshop outcomes were split into two categories:

1. Children's behavior
2. Children's academic skills

The findings in the first category showed that four boys had poor self-confidence and social awkwardness, three had large concentration issues, while all had concentration issues to a certain degree, five had problems with drawing and imagination, all had minor cognitive difficulties, three students had speech issues and poor vocabulary, one a severe visual issue and two impulse control issues. Furthermore, two students had poor fine-motor skills and had difficulties touching small objects on the screen. Every child had multiple limitations. This presented a huge challenge for us as designers, both in terms of the methodology and ethics. The latter had to do with questions such as whether our techniques were sensitive enough and if we had enough knowledge to interpret correctly children's behavior. The boys seemed happy to work with the iPad and try new things on the tablet. But when, for example, one boy left the iPad in the middle of the game and left the room, we were unsure of how to interpret this behavior. Did he not want to participate further, or was this part of the impulse control behavior? Another example is that of a student who switched fast between apps and showed them to us in a very quick succession. This could have been excitement or an expression of concentration problems. We relied on the teacher's interpretation of student's behavior. The teacher also had to interpret when we communicated with students with speech issues.

The findings in the second category, skills and needs in the learning arena, showed huge diversity among the children. Some had problems with the most basic math, others with reading and spelling, yet others with memory based games or music. Ultimately, we felt that a better direction would be to focus on value design (Iversen, Halskov, & Leong, 2010) and a more therapeutic approach, related to a common condition such as concentration difficulties or social isolation.

In order to understand the issues around concentration problems, we did a literature search on concentration disorders and technology. The work we chose to look in depth was the work of Klingberg (Klingberg et al., 2005) on exercising working memory, using gamification as an aid in the treatment of ADHD. In addition, we also considered the use of commercially available tools

Figure 3. a) A student testing the iPad based shopping scenario. b) Role-playing with money and beans. Photo: Karpova

such as Lumosity ("Lumosity Mobile," 2013) for improving the brain performance. Both were found to be inadequate for the children in this specific context. After a brainstorming session with the teacher, we finally landed on a design of an app that would focus on the behavior in common, everyday situations, such as shopping for food.

As a proof of concept, we conducted a workshop with children and the main class teacher. We used physical objects (coins with different denominations, coffee beans, etc.), as well as selected iPad apps for shopping, and role-played different purchasing scenarios. This was also done with each student individually, see Figure 3. The analysis of data from the workshop showed that this direction was promising; all children did get engaged and understood what they were doing. It was also possible to discuss their preferences for the future app. They were quite engaged in these decisions. For example, all the boys preferred either real images or good iconic representations for objects in the virtual store. Even if they could not do the math, they liked the idea being able to pay for merchandise. They preferred to play alone, but comparing scores with others was acceptable.

The concept for an app, which we hoped would be appropriate for the children involved, was thus starting to emerge. The preparations, the pre-design phase and the additional research we needed to do, took much longer time than anticipated and stretched from January until the end of the spring semester in June and the beginning of summer vacation. At the start of the project, the

school informed us that there was a possibility of closing the class and distributing the children to other schools with special education classes. This possibility became a reality at the start of the fall 2012 semester. The children started the year at six different schools. Both the main teacher and the children were interested in continued participation in the project. Contact with the main teacher was maintained throughout the summer. However, the logistics around participation and timing became much more complicated. We also needed additional skills and knowledge in order to tackle the problem better. Thus, we solicited help from an occupational therapist, first as a consultant and later to test our prototypes with some of her young patients with issues matched as much as possible to those in our user group.

Design and Prototyping Phases

Drawing on Gordon's game taxonomy, (Moggridge, 2007), we considered the gender, age and interests of the children we have worked with. We explored employment of both *padia* and *ludus*, padia representing playful actions and ludus representing the gameful ones (Caillois, 2001). Knowing that imagination was an issue for some of the children, we opted for gamification, thus providing for structure during the game. In addition, the possibility to achieve a set of specified goals and measure results was viewed as helpful for evaluation, both formative and summative.

Figure 4. A child testing the paper prototype of the game. The child could select a board and activity icons. New icons could be made as well
Photo: Karpova.

Next, several game scenarios were made and evaluated by three interaction designers. We had four scenarios that were worth considering further. In addition, three personas representing the six children were made, none of them representing a particular child (Moser, Fuchsberger, Neureiter, Sellner, & Tscheligi, 2012). This was done so that we could invite others to participate in a workshop where we role-played each scenario in order to determine what might work best. The role-playing was instrumental in gaining deeper understanding of the proposed scenarios and gamification concepts.

The concept chosen to work with further was a "board game" like app that could help teach children the appropriate behavior inside a store. The game included rules around behaviors related to choices of desired items, lack of those, amount of items desired and payment procedures. A child throws a die in order to move through a store or a shopping center on the board and pays at the finish line. Based on what field the child lands on after throwing the die, the child needs to move backward or forward. For example, if the field shows a screaming child or a child running in the store, both inappropriate behaviors in the context, the player has to jump some cells backward. On the other hand if the field shows walking next to parents or selecting a food to buy, the player

jumps some cells forward. Thus, by playing the game, a child is given an opportunity to learn commonly accepted behavior rules while shopping, see (Parham & Fazio, 2007, p.20). The first low fidelity prototype of the game was consequently made and tested with children, see Figure 4, with parental consent.

The testing of this low-fidelity prototype was carried out in the occupational therapy center with four children of similar age and with similar problems. This situation was also interesting as it provided an opportunity to further validate the concept with a similar user group outside the classroom context. The children were observed via Skype for about 10-15 minutes during their regular appointments with the therapist. The children had a tendency to forget the Skype entirely. Thus, we believe that we have also avoided some of the bias in favor of the prototype based on the children's desire to please us as researchers by giving the positive feedback.

We wanted to see whether our game was simple enough to be understandable. The relation between desirable behavior and moving forward on the board, or undesirable and moving backward, had to be clear.

The time spent on the game was important: could children concentrate long enough in order to finish the game? During sessions, the children

Figure 5. The children made additional icons. Sometimes they were clearly identifiable, such as the teddy, other times they were harder to identify, such as the tractor or the tomato
Photo: Karpova.

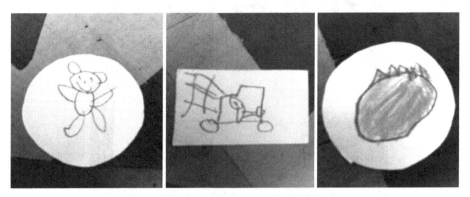

were asked to first choose the board and icons and then play the game. They were to choose the background and the shape of the play-fields (differing in the number of fields, providing for longer or shorter game-time), as well as a set of icons representing different activities in the store to be used during the game. The children placed the icons on the board. They were asked to draw any additional icons they would like to have in the game, see Figure 5 for some examples. After all chosen icons were placed on the board, a child was asked to play the game.

All of the children involved were enthusiastic and eager to participate in choosing the board shape, making icons and starting the game. Interest in playing the game was varying. One boy didn't want to play the game at all; he preferred to play only with the die. This child also did not understand the rules of the game. This was the most extreme case. Two of the children played the game. The fourth child obviously enjoyed playing the game. He asked to play several times during the session, and asked to play the game again during the next visit to the therapist. Overall, the response of the children to the game was positive. One child had problems carrying out the game due to cognitive issues; the others understood the game and were able to complete it. The feedback from the therapist was also important. The therapist thought that the game could have positive effect on the children and said that she would like to have a large analogue version on the floor of her office. She said that she could envision children using their bodies to move through the game. This could have further positive implications on her therapy sessions, as it would include the physical movement. The therapist was particularly pleased to hear children think aloud during the game.

The first prototype of the game was implemented on an android tablet, see Figure 6. The implementation was done in HTML5 and thus, could be easily adapted to run on any platform.

Formative Evaluation

The evaluation of the high fidelity prototype was done with children from the occupational therapy center. This time, the app was tested with two children. One of them was a participant in low-fidelity prototype testing, and the other was new to the game. The occupational therapist conducted these tests and one of the authors observed, without engagement. The evaluation lasted about 10-15 minutes for each child. During the session, the first participant played the game several times since he was already familiar with it. The second participant took some time to understand the rules first, but then successfully completed the game.

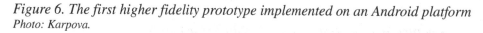

Figure 6. The first higher fidelity prototype implemented on an Android platform
Photo: Karpova.

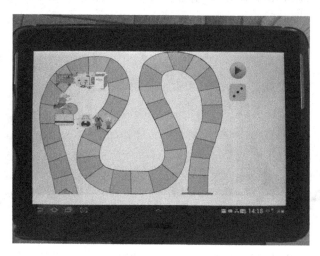

Both children seemed to enjoy playing the game and asked if they could play more next time. Since the first child was able to play the game several times during his session, we could tell that the game needed several levels of difficulty in order to keep the excitement. In addition, the technical performance of the game was not very smooth and needed improvement. The gaming pieces were sometimes hard to move. The response time needed to be faster in order to improve the overall user experience. Furthermore, the occupational therapist commented that it would be good to have more action icons, both positive and negative, because the boards have a relatively small number of fields and it was actually possible to play the game without landing on any icon. She also mentioned that the gaming piece should move automatically, or that the game should control children's movements so that children could not cheat – intentionally or not – by jumping over more cells than the die showed.

The overall impression of the game was positive for both the children and the occupational therapist. The therapist also commented that the combination of tablet technology and gamification has a large potential for her practice, as a good support tool during therapy sessions.

Re-Design and the Final Evaluation

In order to improve the performance of the game, the code was re-written several times, until the application ran smoothly on the iPad. The visual expression was also changed and icons redrawn; see Figure 7.

At present, the game has two levels, as shown in Figure 8. The first level of the game is set in a food store, the second in a toy store. The first level has fewer play-fields to traverse, and fewer icons.

During the game, a player scores points. After level completion, the player may choose one of the three prizes, at different prices. The child needs to know whether the number of points they made during playtime is sufficient for the prize of their choice. The game may then be re-played at the same level, played at the next level or exited.

This version of the prototype was evaluated with 15 children, based on its usability, enjoyment and behavior learning. For detailed results on each participant, see (Karpova, 2013). Five children were tested in the context of occupational therapy and 10 children at a boarding school for children with special needs. At school, the game was set up on laptops and computers, as the children were familiar with them.

Figure 7. The icons drawn by hand, but in a more realistic style
Photo: Karpova.

The two most important parameters for the usability were the ability of a child to learn how to control the game and the ability to understand the meaning of icons and consequently, take correct actions. Children were simply asked to play the game and were observed while doing so, see Figure 9. Some of the children, e.g. the child in Figure 9a), were not capable of touching the iPad on their own. In such cases, the therapist helped children to play the game.

The appropriateness of the emotional reaction of a child when landing on an icon representing the positive or the negative behavior was noted. If a child was confused because he/she had a problem understanding the behavior represented by an icon, this was recorded. The number of mistakes in moving on the board was noted. Enjoyment was evaluated by observation, as well as other evaluation methods, such as the use of Smiley. The Smiley evaluation was discarded, since the children always picked the widest smile, as they liked it the best. Making the connection between the quality of the game and the expression on the Smiley was too difficult.

The behavior learning was the hardest to evaluate, and this was done using short interviews with therapists, parents and a caretaker from the boarding school. We were interested in finding out if the children mentioned the game at home, school or therapy. The boarding school caretaker told us that the children were taken to the store for shopping. The group taken to the store had some children who had experience with the game and the some who did not. The children who had played the game observed the others and commented on their behavior. Both interview-analyses and children's behavior in the store indicate that the connection between real life and the game was established.

Figure 8. a) The new look of the game, here shown at level 2. b) After completion of level 1, three food items, with different price tags are shown. A child can get only those items for which they have enough points acquired during the game. c) At level 2, toys are possible prizes
Photo: Karpova.

Figure 9. a) A child needed help in order to play the game. b) and c) children playing the game on the iPad
Photo: Karpova

RESEARCHER'S CHALLENGES AND OPPORTUNITIES

The first challenge we met in this work had to do with how to *identify the needs* of the children. The teacher was very helpful and enthusiastic about the project. She was also very forward with her desire to engage the whole class in a common activity. But children's voices were silent. They did not show or express any need to do something with other children. When explicitly asked, they said that they preferred to play alone and that comparing results with others was OK. This does not imply that creating a more social context would not benefit the children. It simply shows that the children could not explicate what they need, while the teacher was quite forward and explicit with her needs.

The children, as mentioned, were interested in the iPad and clearly excited to have it in the class. Working with each child individually, we could identify apps that could support that child in his learning. So, the iPad indeed had a potential to help them with learning. Yet, we *made a decision* to follow the path of designing one app that could be used by all the children. Initially, because we thought that doing the same activity might be an incentive for increased communication among the boys, and, in turn, create a sense of being a group, a class. Later, we realized that this decision led to design of an app that could support children with wider set of limitations, similar in nature to those of students in the special

education class. However, the app worked best in individual therapy sessions, although it did show the potential to create some social interactions, as evidenced by the report on shopping experience with the children from the boarding school. How decisions such as this one are made is important for the HCI design practitioners when reflecting on the process and learning from it.

If we were *professional designers* instead of the *researchers/designers*, the process of designing the app would have been a much shorter one. If we were researchers only, then possibly, there would be no product at the end of this project at all. Being human computer interaction designers, we were somewhere in between. Thus, we feel, that here, too, there is an opportunity for defining closer what is a *human interaction designer's professional practice*. In a complex situation such as the one presented, this issue is of high relevance. We all know that the distribution and management of resources is fundamental. For example, as researchers, we could dedicate time (time as a resource) to this project, and increase our understanding of the context (knowledge as a resource), also from similar previous work, such as mentioned in the background section. For small research and development projects such as this one, financing may be an important issue. In the HCI literature, it is not customary to mention money, except in the acknowledgments, if the research received funding. However, in order to do the research and the design job properly, multidisciplinary teams (human resources) might be needed when working with vulnerable user groups. External competence may be found outside of research circles, e.g., an occupational therapist, or a professional designer. Good management of these and other resources, thus, we see as important in delivering good results. Lack of any of the above mentioned, in particular when working with vulnerable users (time, knowledge, human resources and others), may put the outcome of the project at risk and are thus, important factors to consider.

Further, values are also important to consider. Iversen et al. (Iversen, Halskov, & Leong, 2010) have considered re-kindling of values in participatory design, a discovery of what matters to all stakeholders.

In addition to values that emerge in design processes, there are also values, on the receiving end, for researchers/designers. Making an app and evaluating it is what we know how to do, but working with these specific children in a participatory setting and being able to reflect over our design and research practice, methods, ethical procedures, ways of engaging with children, was extraordinary and very valuable for us as both HCID researchers and practitioners.

It is however, difficult to label some of what we did. We did not exactly co-design with children, although we tried to do so. We certainly did not apply participatory design methodology, or a user-centered one. The best we can do is to say that we used a flexible, open, participatory approach. The processes felt familiar, yet they were different. Understanding these feelings of difference and familiarity, coupled with some help from a skilled occupational therapist, removed the initial vulnerability and left us truly enthusiastic about the opportunity to carry out this project to the end. Thus, creating teams with adequate skills worked well in our case. More case study descriptions from researcher's perspective, and reflections over the design practice, would potentially help others who are interested in working with vulnerable people.

The turning moment in the project was when the special education class children closed, and the project was in danger of being discontinued.

This, we learned, is not a rare occurrence when working with people with limitations. Others (caretakers, institutions, states) often have a strong power over them. Thus, being able to continue the work within the occupational therapy setting was truly a 'coup de grâce'. From this, we learned that turning challenges into opportunities might be a good skill to develop for any HCID practitioner working with vulnerable people.

The major ethical challenge has been how to ensure an ongoing consent from the children, in particular around interpreting their behavior. We found out that this was much easier in the occupational therapy sessions, than at school. At school, the authority of teachers was greater and the children did what was asked of them. In the therapy setting, we observed several instances where the children either did not want to play or played only once, thus showing a greater freedom in deciding for themselves. On the other hand, at school, we could spend more time in direct contact with children, while in occupational therapy sessions or at the boarding school, we were mostly passive observers. So, we can say that experiences from the two settings were very different. Direct contact with children was very important, but so was the knowledge gained during the therapy sessions. Working in both contexts is thus, ideal, and in line with (McNaney et al., 2013).

Teachman and Gibson (Teachman & Gibson, 2013) state that the quality of data gathered through interviews is always depending on the interviewer and adjunct to that, a good toolkit. We believe that the same goes for all other methods and techniques when working with vulnerable, special needs children. One needs good researcher/designer skills, good professional practices, sensibility and a more versatile, as well as, sensitive toolkit.

CONCLUSION AND FUTURE WORK

Working with vulnerable, special needs people in general, and children in particular, is challenging for researchers/designers. Diversity, nearly by the definition of a 'special need' is large, and every person, or a child, provides a unique set of challenges. Therefore, many researchers work with individuals who have similar disabilities, e.g., ADHD or dyslexia. In this chapter, however, we described a design process which involved a group of six children attending the same special education class, but with diverse and multiple issues. This heterogeneity significantly impacted the design process and its outcome, as well as the involvement of the children in the process.

We started from evaluation of children's capacity to use the iPad, and found that all the children could use the device – they knew how to turn it on and off, how to find apps, how to open them, regulate sound and similar. When it came to learning, the diversity in capacities was so great that instead of designing a learning app, we opted for gamification and a behavior modification app, which we hoped would help all involved children in their daily lives. The context for design and evaluation of the app changed several times, allowing us to gather data on how it could work in the context of school, occupational therapy or boarding school for children with special needs. Most importantly, since the class we started working with closed, and our research and design efforts moved within the framework of occupational therapy, we had the luxury to study how vulnerabilities, our own and those of our users and their situation, affected us as researchers/designers. We hope that we have argued well in favor of introducing vulnerability as a positive (or, at the very least, not pejorative) concept in HCI design with users with special needs.

We found that, when we became aware of our own lack of adequate knowledge about the children, we could turn that vulnerability into a power to act and ultimately create a different space for both design and research, learning a lot along the way. In our case, including the occupational therapist in the design process made this shift.

HCID practitioners have a unique opportunity to enrich lives of vulnerable children. Towards this goal, they should carefully consider their professional practices when working with vulnerable people, children in particular. This should include reflection on the practice itself, positioning the work on a continuum between design and research, including other professionals as part of the project team, considering distribution of resources at ones disposal (time, knowledge, human resources from other research fields and professional practices). In addition, the question of what happens to the high fidelity prototypes, which are the usual results from HCID, practice, little discussed in this chapter, is important to consider. In our case, the project has ended and, at this point, we do not know if that last push for the product to reach the market will be made. If one considers HCID also as a professional practice, then this type of decision-making needs to be part of the process from the start.

A multitude of issues are out there waiting to be better understood within HCID as a research field when working with vulnerability: who are really the vulnerable ones in a design process, what are the tools, techniques and methods that are best suited for work with vulnerable people, how to gain required knowledge most effectively, how to improve communication with people with cognitive and verbal limitations, how to better understand roles that caretakers, parents, therapists, medical professionals and others can play in lives of such people.

Thus, we consider finding out whether the use of the concept of vulnerability, and risk identification, can affect the outcome of HCID processes positively as a worthwhile goal for the future research. Results by Brown (Brown, 2012), a communication researcher, indicate that there is a power to be harnessed in vulnerability that increases a sense of empathy, understanding and communication. Our case points towards the same conclusion, but further research is needed.

ACKNOWLEDGMENT

First and foremost, we thank all of the amazing children for their participation in the study. Further, we thank the leadership of the school, and the teachers in the special education class, for the opportunity to work in the context of the special education class. Deep gratitude is also due to the two occupational therapists for supporting the project, sharing their knowledge and advice, and making room in their therapy sessions for evaluation of the prototype.

REFERENCES

Abascal, J., & Nicolle, C. (2005). Moving towards inclusive design guidelines for socially and ethically aware HCI. *Interacting with Computers, 17*(5), 484–505. doi:10.1016/j.intcom.2005.03.002

Berry, B. E., & Ignash, S. (2003). Assistive technology: Providing independence for individuals with disabilities. *Rehabilitation Nursing, 28*(1), 6–14. doi:10.1002/j.2048-7940.2003.tb01715.x PMID:12567816

Bromley, H., & Apple, M. W. (1998). *Education, technology, power educational computing as a social practice*. Albany, NY: State University of New York Press.

Brown, B. (2012). *The Power of Vulnerability: Teachings on Authenticity, Connection, & Courage*. Sounds True.

Caillois, R. (2001). *Man, Play, and Games*. University of Illinois Press.

Christopher Frauenberger, J. G. (2011). Designing Technology for Children with Special Needs - Bridging Perspectives through Participatory Design. *CoDesign: International Journal of Co-Creation in Design and the Arts, 7*, 1–28. doi:10.1080/15710882.2011.587013

Collins, A., & Halverson, R. (2009). *Rethinking education in the age of technology: the digital revolution and schooling in America*. New York: Teachers College Press.

Cuban, L. (1986). *Teachers and Machines: The Classroom Use of Technology Since 1920*. Teachers College Press.

Cuban, L. (2001). *Oversold and underused: computers in the classroom*. Harvard University Press.

Culén, A. L., Bratteteig, T., Pandey, S., & Srivastava, S. (2013). The Child-to-Child (C2C) Method: Participatory Design for, with and by Children in a Children's Museum. *IADIS International Journal on WWW/Internet, 11*(2), 92–113.

Culén, A. L., derVelden, M., & Karpova, A. (2013). Challenges in Designing Learning Apps for and with Vulnerable Children. In *Proceedings of CHI 2013 Workshop on Designing for and with Vulnerable People*. Paris, France: ACM.

Culén, A. L., & Gasparini, A. (2011). iPad: a new classroom technology? A report from two pilot studies. In Information Sciences and e-Society (pp. 199–208). University of Zagreb.

Culén, A. L., & Gasparini, A. (2012). Situated Techno-Cools: factors that contribute to making technology cool and the study case of iPad in education. *PsychNology Journal, 10*(2), 117–139.

Culén, A. L., & Gasparini, A. A. (2012). When is a Student-Centered, Technology Supported Learning a Success? *International Journal of Digital Information and Wireless Communications, 2*(3), 256–269.

Desideri, L., Roentgen, U., Hoogerwerf, E.-J., & de Witte, L. (2013). Recommending assistive technology (AT) for children with multiple disabilities: A systematic review and qualitative synthesis of models and instruments for AT professionals. *Technology and Disability, 25*(1), 3–13.

Deterding, S. (2013). Designing Gamification: Creating Gameful and Playful Experiences. In *Proceedings of CHI 2013*. ACM.

Domínguez, A., Saenz-de-Navarrete, J., de-Marcos, L., Fernández-Sanz, L., Pagés, C., & Martínez-Herráiz, J.-J. (2013). Gamifying learning experiences: Practical implications and outcomes. *Computers & Education, 63*, 380–392. doi:10.1016/j.compedu.2012.12.020

Druin, A. (2009). *Mobile Technology for Children: Designing for Interaction and Learning*. Morgan Kaufmann.

Fernández-López, Á., Rodríguez-Fórtiz, M. J., Rodríguez-Almendros, M. L., & Martínez-Segura, M. J. (2013). Mobile learning technology based on iOS devices to support students with special education needs. *Computers & Education, 61*, 77–90. doi:10.1016/j.compedu.2012.09.014

Ferrara, J. (2012). *Playful Design*. Rosenfeld Media.

Fun on Your iPad with Crazy Face. (2010). *AppAdvice*. Retrieved from http://appadvice.com/appnn/2010/03/fun-ipad-crazy-face

Gasparini, A. A., & Culén, A. L. (2012). Tablet PCs–An Assistive Technology for Students with Reading Difficulties? In *Proceedings of ACHI 2012, The Fifth International Conference on Advances in Computer-Human Interactions* (pp. 28–34). IARIA.

Goldsmith, S. (2012). *Universal Design*. Routledge.

Hasselbring, T. S., & Glaser, C. H. W. (2000). Use of Computer Technology to Help Students with Special Needs. *The Future of Children, 10*(2), 102–122. doi:10.2307/1602691 PMID:11255702

Hourcade, J. P., Bullock-Rest, N. E., & Hansen, T. E. (2012). Multitouch tablet applications and activities to enhance the social skills of children with autism spectrum disorders. *Personal and Ubiquitous Computing, 16*(2), 157–168. doi:10.1007/s00779-011-0383-3

Iversen, O. S., Halskov, K., & Leong, T. W. (2010). Rekindling values in participatory design. In *Proceedings of the 11th Biennial Participatory Design Conference* (pp. 91–100). New York, NY: ACM.

Karpova, A. (2013). *Heterogeneity in Technology Design for Children with Special Education Needs: Changing Perspective from a Group to an Individual*. (Master thesis). DUO, University of Oslo.

Karpova, A., & Culén, A. (2013). Challenges in Designing an App. for a Special Education Class. In *Proceedings of the IADIS International Conference on Interfaces and Human-Computer Interaction 2013* (pp. 95–102). IADIS.

Klingberg, T., Fernell, E., Olesen, P. J., Johnson, M., Gustafsson, P., & Dahlström, K. et al. (2005). Computerized training of working memory in children with ADHD - a randomized, controlled trial. *Journal of the American Academy of Child and Adolescent Psychiatry, 44*(2), 177–186. doi:10.1097/00004583-200502000-00010 PMID:15689731

Kukulska-Hulme, A., & Traxler, J. (2005). *Mobile learning: a handbook for educators and trainers*. Routledge.

Lumosity Mobile. (2013). *App. Store*. Retrieved from https://itunes.apple.com/us/app/lumosity-mobile/id577232024

Maor, D., Currie, J., & Drewry, R. (2011). The effectiveness of assistive technologies for children with special needs: a review of research-based studies. *European Journal of Special Needs Education, 26*(3), 283–298. doi:10.1080/08856 257.2011.593821

Markopoulos, P., Read, J. C., MacFarlane, S., & Hoysniemi, J. (2008). *Evaluating Children's Interactive Products: Principles and Practices for Interaction Designers*. Morgan Kaufmann.

McClanahan, B., Williams, K., Kennedy, E., & Tate, S. (2012). A Breakthrough for Josh: How Use of an iPad Facilitated Reading Improvement. *TechTrends, 56*(3), 20–28. doi:10.1007/s11528-012-0572-6

McNaney, R., Balaam, M., Marshall, K., Durrant, A., Read, J., & Good, J. … Abowd, G. (2013). Designing for and with children with special needs in multiple settings. In *Proceedings of the 12th International Conference on Interaction Design and Children* (pp. 603–605). New York, NY: ACM.

Moggridge, B. (2007). *Designing Interactions*. The MIT Press.

Moser, C., Fuchsberger, V., Neureiter, K., Sellner, W., & Tscheligi, M. (2012). Revisiting personas: the making-of for special user groups. In *Proceedings of CHI '12 Extended Abstracts on Human Factors in Computing Systems* (pp. 453–468). New York, NY: ACM.

Parham, L. D., & Fazio, L. S. (2007). *Play in Occupational Therapy for Children*. Mosby Elsevier.

Phillips, B., & Zhao, H. (1993). Predictors of Assistive Technology Abandonment. *Assistive Technology, 5*(1), 36–45. doi:10.1080/10400435.1993.10132205 PMID:10171664

Puppet Pals, H. D. (2010). *App. Store*. Retrieved from https://itunes.apple.com/ca/app/puppet-pals-hd/id342076546

Riemer-Reiss, M. L., & Wacker, R. R. (2000). Factors Associated with Assistive Technology Discontinuance among Individuals with Disabilities. *Journal of Rehabilitation, 66*(3), 44.

Scherer, M. J., & Federici, S. (2012). *Assistive Technology Assessment Handbook*. CRC Press.

Seshadri, S. (2012). iPad gives voice to kids with autism. *CNN*. Retrieved from http://www.cnn.com/2012/05/14/tech/gaming-gadgets/ipad-autism/index.html

Shinohara, K., & Wobbrock, J. O. (2011). In the shadow of misperception: assistive technology use and social interactions. In *Proceedings of the SIGCHI Conference on Human Factors in Computing Systems,* (pp. 705–714). ACM.

Teachman, G., & Gibson, B. E. (2013). Children and youth with disabilities: innovative methods for single qualitative interviews. *Qualitative Health Research, 23*(2), 264–274. doi:10.1177/1049732312468063 PMID:23208200

Vines, J. (2013). *Designing For- and With- Vulnerable People*. Retrieved from http://www.academia.edu/2989640/Designing_For-_and_With-_Vulnerable_People

Walsh, G., Foss, E., Yip, J., & Druin, A. (2013). FACIT PD: a framework for analysis and creation of intergenerational techniques for participatory design. In *Proceedings of the SIGCHI Conference on Human Factors in Computing Systems* (pp. 2893–2902). New York, NY: ACM.

Westera, W., Nadolski, R. J., Hummel, H. G., & Wopereis, I. G. (2008). Serious games for higher education: a framework for reducing design complexity. *Journal of Computer Assisted Learning, 24*(5), 420–432. doi:10.1111/j.1365-2729.2008.00279.x

KEY TERMS AND DEFINITIONS

Assistive Technology: Any technology that may support people, who have challenges due to cognitive, motor or sensorial disabilities, in increasing, maintaining, or improving functional capabilities.

Gameful Learning: Using games and game strategies to engage learners.

HCID Practice: The practice of designing interactive digital products, environments, or services, including resource management, reflection over choices of methods and techniques, decisions, evaluation and use of designed objects.

Heterogeneity in Design: A large diversity of issues and needs that need to be addressed when designing.

Ongoing Consent: Consent to users participation in design processes extending the consent obtained at the start of the study, usually in the written form, to oral agreement during every session with vulnerable users.

Participatory Approaches: Using methods and techniques in design processes requiring user participation, which inform the design process beyond a simple feedback.

Vulnerable Users: People who are at risk because of their age, frailty, diagnosis or limited capacities, both physically and cognitively, and who are users of digital technology.

Chapter 8
Supporting Accessible User Interfaces Using Web Services

Georgios Bouloukakis
Inria Paris-Rocquencourt, France

Ioannis Basdekis
Institute of Computer Science – Foundation for Research and Technology – Hellas (ICS-FORTH), Greece

Constantine Stephanidis
Institute of Computer Science – Foundation for Research and Technology – Hellas (ICS-FORTH), Greece & University of Crete, Greece

ABSTRACT

Web services are an emerging technology that has attracted much attention from both the research and the industry sectors in recent years. The exploitation of Web services as components in Web applications facilitates development and supports application interoperability, regardless of the programming language and platform used. However, existing Web services development standards do not take into account the fact that the provided content and the interactive functionality should be accessible to, and easily operable by, people with disabilities. This chapter presents a platform named myWebAccess, which provides a mechanism for the semi-automated "repair" of Web services' interaction characteristics in order to support the automatic generation of interface elements that conform to the de facto standard of the Web Content Accessibility Guidelines 2.0. myWebAccess enhances interaction quality for specific target user groups, including people with visual and motor disabilities, and supports the use of Web services on diverse platforms (e.g., mobile phones equipped with a browser). The Web developers can build their own design templates and the users of myWebAccess can create a personalized environment containing their favourite services. Thus, they can interact with them through interfaces appropriate to their specific individual characteristics.

DOI: 10.4018/978-1-4666-6228-5.ch008

INTRODUCTION

The number of World Wide Web users is growing steadily over the last decade, and its usage is permeating all aspects of daily life. The web has a great potential to improve the quality of life of citizens, by facilitating the provision of services in basic aspects such as employment, education, marketplace and health. Especially for citizens who face barriers in accessing physical services, the web, if utilized properly, offers one – and perhaps the only – alternative solution. These citizens include:

- People with disabilities, who constitute more than 10% of the world's population. About one billion of people face problems of physical access on a daily basis1.
- Aging people, whose number is increasing to the point where one in five people in the European Union is considered elderly2.
- Citizens with temporary inability to exploit some senses due to health problems.
- People with a low level of understanding and experience of technology.

The World Wide Web Consortium (W3C) has established the "Web Accessibility Initiative" (WAI-W3C), whose main objective is to provide solutions to Web Accessibility for people with visual, hearing, physical, cognitive and neurological disabilities. The results3 of this initiative include mainly technical guidelines such as the Web Content Accessibility Guidelines (WCAG), the Authoring Tool Accessibility Guidelines (ATAG), and the User Agent Accessibility Guidelines (UAAG). In addition, Mobile Web Best Practices provide generic instructions for building applications for mobile devices (Chuter & Yesilada, 2009). WCAG is the most renowned de facto standard, as it provides guidelines on how to create accessible interface and content elements in such a way that they can be read and manipulated by assistive technology solutions. Moreover, their

applicability it facilitates interoperability with new and emerging technology solutions (e.g., navigator with voice recognition for car drivers). It is worth pointing out that some of these guidelines are included in policies all over the world (e.g., the international standard ISO/IEC 40500:2012, which is exactly the same as the WCAG 2.0, is part of an EU proposal for a directive4). However, one major problem is that their application requires manual forethought, since existing development tools are not directly support compliant code (and outcome) generation.

Currently, the typical production of a web service (Alonso et al, 2003) as a function can be achieved through several development tools, greatly influencing the quality of the produced web content. In addition, interface and other content elements are integrated by the responsible development team or somehow inherited by the environment in use, so that every service acquires a similar look and feel presentation. However, a great advantage introduced by web services is the fact that their function can be reutilized and their input and output elements can be treated at other stages and by other development teams without having specific knowledge of how this web service operates, but only of the results it produces. Therefore, to support accessibility, web service core elements responsible for presentation issues must have an appropriate degree-of-freedom in order to:

- Support integrated and independent cooperation with assistive technologies (e.g., interoperability with screen readers, large keyboards, alternative pointing devices).
- Exhibit user interface which can adapt to users' preferences.
- Generate user-friendly auxiliary functionality (e.g., forms which can be filled out by using only the keyboard and quick access to areas of content).
- Upgrade with technological development (i.e., forward compatibility).

Figure 1. Meteorological weather forecast web service: image without equivalent alternative text to inform the user about the cloudy evening

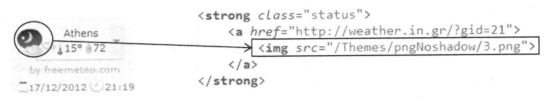

- Use and produce valid meta-language (e.g., HTML, XHTML).

Despite the proven usefulness of WCAG for web accessibility, it is common for web content manufacturers to ignore or overlook them, thus limiting the ability of disabled users to navigate to the information and services offered by a website. Thus, the aforementioned principles are far from being integrated, even to public web sites where legislation enforces them. Diachronically, studies reveal that web accessibility metrics are worsening worldwide [(Nomesa 2006), (Basdekis et al, 2010)]. Web services provide a standard form of communication between different software applications, which in turn support user's interaction through a GUI layout. They play a major role in providing content and services over the internet. The use of web services has been enhanced through standardization efforts which have resulted in interoperability specifications. However, the standards developed so far do not take into account the fact that the content and functionality that a web service offers should be accessible to people with disabilities.

For instance, the typical web service presented in Figure 1 is incorporated as a component to the www.in.gr website and provides the meteorological weather forecast for Athens. By inspecting the relevant "img" tag of the source code, it can be noted that there is no alternative description. Therefore, although it is easy for the "able-bodied" to understand the provided information, this infor-

mation is not available to a blind user interacting through a screen reader.

Aiming to fill in such accessibility gap, this paper contributes practically applicable solutions to ensure that web services have all the presentation characteristics required to render them accessible to people with disabilities. In the context of this work, by analyzing the standards for web services, the description of data was examined, in order to implement rules that indicate the "additional metadata". The final service should be enriched with such "additional metadata" in order to comply with accessibility guidelines when incorporating it into a web site.

The findings from the above analysis provided the specifications for the design and implementation of a system that is able to semi-automatically repair problematic web services, and offer them through a web application in a uniform and user-friendly manner compatible with assistive technology. In addition, this system automatically adapts content generated by third parties and provides it to various browser-equipped devices, using different personalization options for each end-user.

BACKGROUND

It is known that basically a web service is a software system designed to support interoperable machine-to-machine interaction over a network. It has an interface described in a machine-processable format (specifically WSDL). Other systems interact with a web service in a manner prescribed by its description using SOAP (Simple Object Access Protocol) or REST (REpresentational State Transfer) messages, typically conveyed using HTTP with an XML serialization in conjunction with other web-related standards.

Web services support application interoperability regardless of platform and programming language (Papazoglou, 2008). They use standards based on the XML language in order to describe the exchanged data with other applications, through the operation that has been invoked. Web services may offer a wide variety of information (e.g., theatre review articles, weather reports, credit checks, etc) in many forms (e.g., text, image, data tables, interactive forms, etc) to support a variety of devices (e.g., desktop, mobile, iTV, etc). In the future, some of the most interesting XML web services will - and maybe force to - support solutions for applications in order to overcome interoperability challenges of heterogeneous information systems. To support this argument, for example, healthcare applications are already copying with the problem of adaptation and interaction with existing systems in a constantly changing health environment because of the endless introduction of new devices. The enriched web services for those applications [(Barbarito et al, 2012), (Mykkanen et al, 2005)] will offer seamless and high quality care to the patients through a web application, especially to people with disabilities.

A study regarding the Return of Investment (ROI) of delivering e-accessibility (Brinck, 2008), made clear that achieving accessible designs should become more affordable over time, as awareness increases and more designer/developers receive appropriate training. However and despite this evidence, the majority of software vendors still seem reluctant to incorporate or have low awareness of e-accessibility benefits, and almost no awareness at all of the possible approaches that they can follow to achieve it. Moreover, even the "convinced" web developers who find themselves in the challenging position to (re)-produce a web service following accessibility requirements, have

limited knowledge about alternative approaches and issues that each solution involves in order to enhance the development processes (Basdekis et al., 2005). Unfortunately, methodologies, guidelines and supporting tools have - till now -failed to give practical guidance on supporting e-accessibility to inexperienced web service developers and providers. Inevitably, the notion of e-accessibility is generally undervalued in the web services domain, however sporadic efforts by the research community provide solutions to address this issue. Examples include an existing personalization system which contains as components the desired services of a user, as well as research efforts towards automatic content adaptation depending on the access device and the profile of the user. In particular, these efforts are:

- **Accessibility in the Web Services Domain:** To achieve the exploitation of web services by all users, including people with disabilities, (Giakoumis et al, 2011) proposed a tool for assessing the accessibility degree of a web service. By using this tool, it is possible to assess whether a SOAP or REST web service conforms to the WCAG. In particular, based on the presented functionality and due to the limited requirements of the WSDL (Web Service Definition Language) standard coupled with the common practice of developers that does not fully exploit the specifications during development, a SOAP type web service will rarely be assessed as fully accessible. Also, in the case of an input REST type web service, and due to the absence of a standard for this type (REST), the tool provides an interface through which a user is able to create a specification called WADL. The problem of this procedure is that the user puts significant effort with the risk not to define the necessary interaction metadata based on WCAG. Finally, the above tool provides only information about the accessibility degree of a web service, without proposing a solution to repair it. Furthermore, a system architecture based on services has been developed, which offers easier navigation in a city for motor impaired users. Based on the functionality of this system, it was noticed that the specifications which define the format of data in a WSDL are quite limited, especially in the case of annotating them with semantic information.

- **Personalized Interfaces:** An optimal environment for all internet users would be a web application that will collect all third party services which conform to WCAG 2.0 (Caldwell et al, 2008) in order to interact with assistive technology solutions. Additionally, the possibility of customizing the system for certain categories of users, including people with vision or motor impairment, would provide the necessary degree of personalization to achieve a friendly interface. There are many popular web applications that provide personalized interfaces with the favourite gadgets of each user as components (i.e., Netvibes, iGoogle, My Yahoo, WebWag and Gritwire). None of those applications uses third party services for their functionality, except some commercial services such as iGoogle, without conforming their interface to WCAG.

- **Automatic Adaptation of Content with Proxy as System:** Besides offering online applications that collect third party services, there are systems that use various methods to analyze a website in order to convert the extracted content to another format. These applications usually operate as a proxy by making an analysis of the web mark-up. Then, they reclassify the content while making some sort of corrections to continuously improve the accessibility. Examples of such systems are:
  - The BBC service named Betsie. By using this service, the BBC website content became easier to read for blind and color-blind users (Brown & Robinson, 2001).
  - The WebFACE tool (Alexandraki et al, 2004), through which extra features are added to enhance the accessibility. However, it is applied only to specific web page structures as the one of (Maeda et al, 2004).
  - A system for dynamically updating web pages to achieve a high contrast background-foreground, delete images and parts of the context that do not conform with WCAG 2.0 and offer an alternative navigation (Richards & Hanson, 2004).

All mentioned systems, by using some form of heuristic algorithms, parse the content and then adjust and rearrange it by using appropriate tags. The success of the final result depends on how the initial version of the website conforms to valid XHTML meta-language. In an effort to provide a different methodological approach, this book chapter is an extended version of the short paper (Bouloukakis et al, 2013), and introduces a platform named *myWebAccess*. The method involves an improved way to describe the metadata transferred via a web service, a repair mechanism to support e-accessibility requirements and finally the automatic generation of the appropriate web form for the delivery of the service.

MYWEBACCESS PLATFORM

There are several ways to describe the data transferred via a web service, such as the DTD5, XML Schema6, RSS7 and WSDL8. WSDL is an XML format for describing network services as a set of endpoints operating on messages containing either document-oriented or procedure-oriented information. The operations and messages are described at an abstract level, and subsequently are bounded to a concrete network protocol where each message has a specific structure for an endpoint (Papazoglou, 2008). In other words, the WSDL standard corresponds to a web service that specifies exactly the input/output and the necessary procedure to invoke it. The work reported in this book chapter utilizes the WSDL standard in order to improve content accessibility.

However, even in the case of using the WSDL specification, there are technical limitations. More specifically, developers in most cases fail to provide all the necessary information, since there are cases where WSDL does not cover exhaustively all situations, and as a result presented metadata are limited in order to conform to the specific provisions of the WCAG. An example is a web service which creates an image displaying the text given as input by the user. By using the WSDL specification, the input of the web services is represented by some parameters such as height (Integer), width (Integer), color (String) and text (String). In order to fill the above fields the WSDL standard does not completely determine the unit of measurement for the height of the image (pixel or inches). Also, there is no restriction on the font size of the image text. Finally, the color model (e.g., RGB, HSL, CMYK) that should be used is not clear. In order to support the provision of "correctly constructed" web services in practice, and make their usage easy and convenient by people with disabilities, the following should be provided:

- Possibility of adding of web services (add).
- Possibility of enriching parameters dealing with presentation or interaction elements (repair).
- Generation of the input and the outcome of the web service in a way that conforms to WCAG (adapt).

Thus, it seems necessary to create an information system able to scan the available functionality of a web service and include the related components. This system should provide a mechanism to add metadata in order to augment web services

with accessibility features. Additionally, the preferences stored in the user profile will further facilitate the interaction of end-users with the services and will provide easier access per user category (e.g., profiles for people with dyschromatopsia). At the same time, and in accordance with recent technological advances, any web service should be able to adapt to user device's capabilities.

In the context of this work, a platform called *myWebAccess* is proposed and implemented. The platform provides a mechanism for adding and semi-automatically "repairing" third-party web services, so that all the interaction elements can be determined and thus content generation complaint to WCAG 2.0 can be achieved.

Towards Ensuring Accessibility Characteristics in Web Services

Web services can be classified in two categories according to their interaction with the user. The first category includes web services that present information (outcome) without any user input, while the second requires implicitly or explicitly some input prior to the presentation of the outcome. For example, a weather forecast is a service of the second category that requires the name of the desired city through text input. Taking into account the interaction behavior of a user utilizing assistive technology, the input/outcome of such service should provide several technical features that enhance accessibility. More specifically, and besides adhering to WCAG 2.0:

- A convenient navigation mechanism need to be provided (e.g., extra features for motor impaired users).
- Balanced color contrast between foreground and background should be used increase text readability, with potential fluctuation of the font size.
- In the case of non-text context, an equivalent alternative text description should

Figure 2. Procedure to add accessibility features

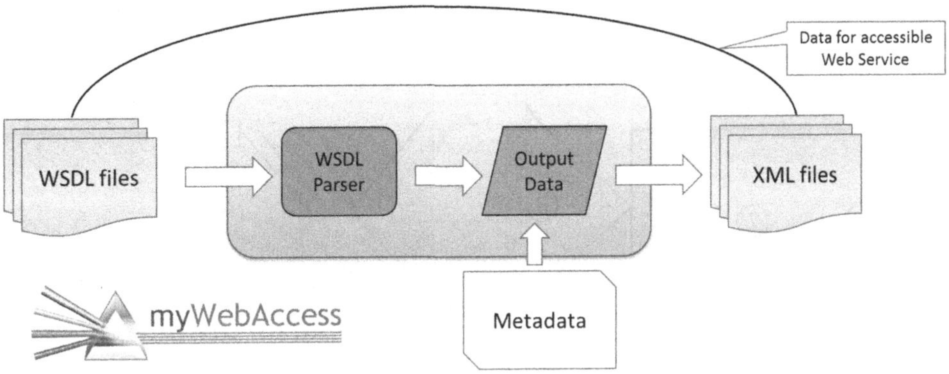

be provided for images, graphics and multimedia.

- Data tables must involve caption and summary tags.
- In the case of interactive forms, each "input" tag should have labels to be properly announced and navigational aids should speed up navigation between fields. In addition, a mechanism for validating user input should be provided for error prevention.
- Additional adaptation features can be triggered depending on the device used (e.g., width of a mobile screen).

Summarizing, the input/outcome of a web service should be suitably adapted to the specific preferences of the user and the technical capabilities of any screen in use. To improve the integration of a web service in an application, appropriate metadata characterizing the input/outcome elements should be present.

This additional information (metadata) should be provided somehow (e.g., by the manufacturer or at a later stage by a service administrator) in order to overcome limitations. In order to create a web service which will contain all the necessary interaction information to appropriately interact with the user, the implementation of the following steps was deemed necessary: (i) analysis of the WSDL file, (ii) separation of the parameters that needed the additional metadata, (iii) import of metadata for each parameter based on the WCAG and (iv) creation of an XML file that defines the additional metadata.

As depicted in Figure 2, the generated XML is directly linked to the originated WSDL, and both files will provide the necessary information for the exploitation of accessible web services. To evaluate the effect of the above procedure, the ideal scenario would be to analyze a web service and request suggestions from users experienced in web accessibility issues (Reich, 2009). These suggestions would indicate the additional metadata needed. Thus, an experienced web service administrator is needed to repair web services that contain poor or insufficient interaction metadata.

Platform Requirements to Import Web Services

One of the basic components of the platform is web services management and, more specifically, operations management, where operations can be added, edited and become available to the end-users. As already mentioned, in a web service, the information that is needed to perform an operation is defined in the WSDL file, which is an XML Schema (XSD) (Papazoglou, 2008) published on the web using a URL.

Figure 3. Process to import a web service to the myWebAccess platform

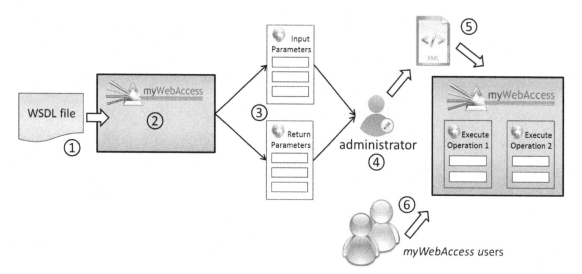

According to the steps described in Figure 2, the process followed for semi-automated repair of a web service and its functions is the following. The WSDL file is given as an input to a parser (step ① in Figure 3) that defines a variety of meta-data for each data type (i.e., input/output parameter) and correspond to a web service. Next, the additional metadata are analyzed9 (step ② in Figure 3) and presented to the system administrator by using a web interface that indicates the "gaps" that should be filled for each input/output parameter (step ③ in Figure 3). Next, the system generated or manually inserted metadata are stored in an XML file (step ④ in Figure 3). The WSDL and the additional metadata (XML file) are directly connected to each other, so that presentation elements conforming to the WCAG can be generated (step ⑤ in Figure 3). Finally, the end users are able to interact with services, since they are integrated with valid and compliant mark-up (step ⑥ in Figure 3). This process ensures the proper enrichment of the parameters prior to the publication and availability of the web service and its functions.

The exploitation of accessible web services as components in a web application has the following advantages:

- **Reuse:** Reduce manufacturing costs and availability [(Basdekis et al, 2005), (Clark, 2003)].
- **Multi-Device:** Easier adaptation of the presented information to various devices [(Basdekis et al, 2009), (Karampelas et al, 2009), and (Chiti & Leporini, 2012)].
- **Conformity with Standards:** Achievement of interoperability with assistive technology solutions.
- **Cost:** Lower upgrade costs accordance to the technological development (Sierkowski, 2002).

SUPPORT OF ACCESSIBLE AND MULTI-CHANNEL WEB INTERFACE GENERATION

The majority of web applications adopt a specific content structure during construction (Curtis, 2009). More specifically, according to common practice followed in recent years, there are four main areas (i.e., Header, Sidebar, Main content and Footer as shows the design template ① in Figure 4). Those areas usually have the same look & feel on

Figure 4. Various design templates for websites

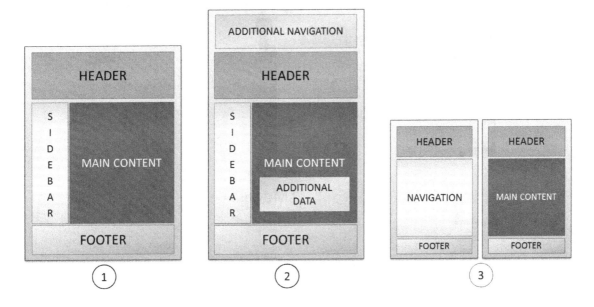

all pages of a website. Furthermore, this structure can easily reutilize different design templates. By setting specific content areas in advance, the initial structure (design template ① in Figure 4) can be enriched with additional navigation aids (design template ② in Figure 4), or in the case of a display on a mobile device, the initial structure can split into more pages for improved readability (design template ③ in Figure 4). In both cases, the developer has to ensure the proper adaptation of the main content that is updated frequently.

As mentioned earlier, web services can be treated in a web application as components where functionality is provided by third parties (Figure 5), resulting in easier adaptation to different design templates. Thus, appropriate mechanisms are necessary to present web services for different third parties in a unified presentation schema.

Figure 5. Web services as components to a website

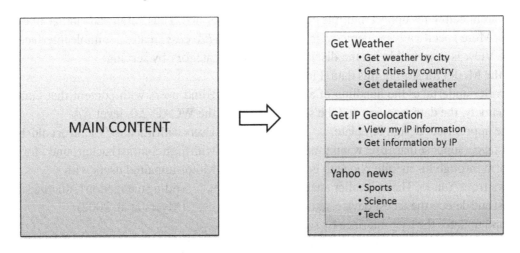

Figure 6. myWebAccess architecture

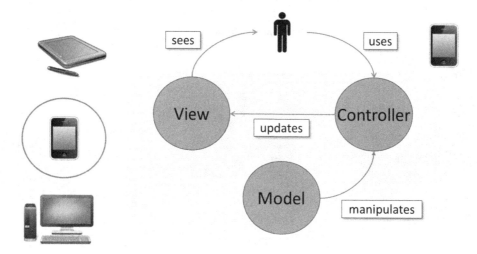

Platform Architecture

The purpose of most information systems is to retrieve data from a source and display it to the user. If the "user interface" and the "logic application" are connected to a single part/object of the application, then whenever the user requires a change in the user interface, the whole section containing the "logic" is modified too (Fielding, 2000).

The Model-View-Controller (MVC) architecture (Reenskaug, 2003) addresses this issue by separating the display of the data, the functionality of the application and the data storage. The *myWebAccess* platform has been built using the MVC architecture to support multiple design templates. More specifically, as depicted in Figure 6, the View is responsible for the display of data and the Model for storing this data. Finally, the Controller undertakes the handling of a user request, namely, the data recovery and the selection of the appropriate design template.

For instance, suppose that a user wants to access the platform through his mobile phone to get the latest news from Yahoo. The controller analyzes the request and detects the access device, retrieves the data and updates the user interface by select-

ing the appropriate design template. The same procedure is followed for a request from a tablet device, but a template for larger touch-screens is selected (Figure 6).

Adaptation of Services at Different Context of Use

After the insertion of a web service by the system administrator, the *myWebAccess* platform provides automatically generated content (step ⑤ in Figure 3) that is compliant to the WCAG 2.0 technical standards. This content is enriched with semantic information (if required), is adaptable to support specific interactions, and has the ability to invoke this service. Thus, taking advantage of the above, *myWebAccess* creates a suitable interface for each user category by serving:

1. Blind users with content that conforms to the WCAG 2.0, level AA.
2. Users with impaired vision or color blindness with high contrast background–foreground.
3. Motor impaired users with
   a. sliding navigation (Adams et al, 2007), (Myers et al, 2002).

Figure 7.Sliding navigation design template with a virtual keyboard

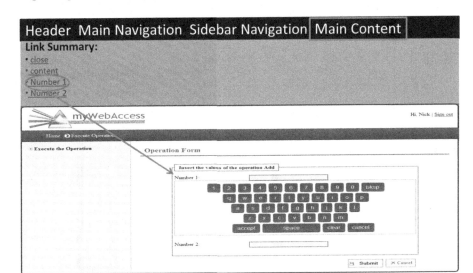

b. sliding navigation with a virtual keyboard (Norte & Lobo, 2007), (Zhai et al, 2000).

4. Supporting mobile devices.

The architecture of the *myWebAccess* platform provides the necessary degree of freedom to address the diversity of user requirements and devices, covering the different scenarios derived from the combination of these two factors. This is achieved through a library of alternative design templates and the classification of users into different profiles. For instance, in order to facilitate motor impaired users, the library contains a suitable design template and provides sliding navigation and a virtual keyboard [(Adams et al, 2007), (Norte & Lobo, 2007)], (Figure 7).

This enables the user to navigate the web page by using only one button. For example, in order to fill in the field named "Number 1", the sliding window contains the corresponding hyperlink and through it the virtual keyboard is displayed. Then, by using only two buttons (binary switches (Norte & Lobo, 2007)) the user can fill in the field. It is worth noting that without the repairing of services by the *myWebAccess* platform (Figure

3), the mark-up of the operation "add" would not be valid, and therefore it could not be invoked by using only two buttons.

Use by the Web Developer

Targeting facilitated extensibility of our solution, we provide a highly-optimized architecture, where each web service constitutes the common reusable part, giving the ability to the web developer for introducing a new design template. Therefore, a developer wishing to add a new service on the *myWebAccess* platform should play the system administrator's role in order to use the mechanism for adding third-party web services. Then, the already "repaired" services can be utilized as components to the existing design templates. There is the possibility to create the design template by following the specific content structure. In the *myWebAccess* platform, we build a specific content structure named "default-design-template". Thus, each developer is able to create the specific main areas (header, sidebar, main content and footer) with the desired presentation options that will be compliant to the WCAG 2.0 technical standards (due to the default design template).

Figure 8. Required time (min) for the completion of task

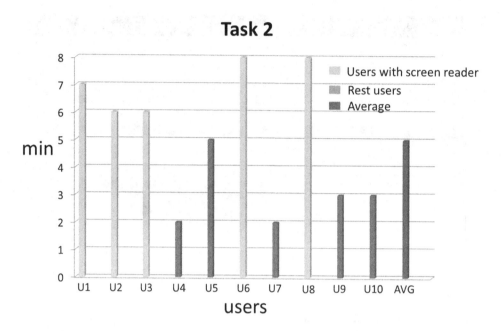

EVALUATION

This section describes the process and the results of the accessibility and usability assessment of the *myWebAccess* platform. Specifically, it is examined whether the proposed technical solution produces the desired results in accordance with the standards.

Evaluation Methodology

To assess the level of compliance of the services available to the end-user to WCAG 2.0, *myWebAccess* was tested using semi-automated accessibility testing tools. Three categories of web services were tested: (i) news feeds via RSS, (ii) meteorological weather forecast, and (iii) image generator. More specifically, proper display was checked on different browsers and devices, the usage of meta-language content was validated using the W3C validation tool10 and compliance with WCAG 2.0 was evaluated using the Web Accessibility Test (T.A.W.) tool11. Regarding the validation of

the used meta-language (XHTML), the generated web pages are constructed according to the W3C standards of XHTML and CSS. All the generated content complies with the accessibility guidelines WCAG 2.0 for all web pages of the *myWebAccess* platform. The results show that there were no problems observed, except for 30 notes.

These notes cannot be controlled by the tool and require the manual inspection of a specialist. For instance, a specialist has to check the description of the images and the page title that should be descriptive. Furthermore, the headers on each page, the labels and the forms should be well structured and quite descriptive. The combination of the selected colours and the degree of the contrast as well as the existence of alternative navigation on the website are all tested and were found to comply.

After making any adjustments arising from the results of the above-mentioned tests, the second step consisted of evaluating the usability with end users. In this context, a scenario of use was elaborated for evaluating the proper service performance, as well as the usability and usefulness of the service for each user category. This scenario contains three tasks for the selection, management and invocation of "repaired" services in the *myWebAccess* platform. Ten experts in the use of assistive technology were involved using profiles visual or motor impaired users. The scenario was executed in our laboratory using one computer to switch the profiles depending on the user.

All users completed the scenario within an acceptable period of time. The maximum time was 22 minutes. As depicted in the diagram of Figure 8, those using a screen reader were slower compared to the rest of the subjects and carried out tasks in two to four timeframes. This difference in performance was expected, since in this case the user is forced to listen to an important part of the content before understanding at which point that part is, while filling in data forms requires a special procedure. However, on the whole, everyone finished their task within reasonable timeframes.

The number of errors made by each user was also measured. Figure 9 illustrates in detail the number of errors that experienced users made

throughout the process. As expected, a high number of errors were observed in the category of users who use a screen reader. Especially in the case of the scenario simulating the behavior of a user with upper limb disability by using binary switches, a remarkable difference was noticed in the execution time compared to the rest of the users. The tasks performed by two users with prior experience in the use of these devices (binary switches). In this use case, an additional navigation with fast access hyperlinks (Sliding Navigation) was activated (Figure 7).

Figure 10 shows that, for each task usage scenario, the results of the execution time, between the user 1 and user 2, are similar. Compared to the rest of the users, the time is almost four times greater. This difference occurs due to the fact that the users were asked to fill data in forms using the virtual keyboard (with sequential selection of characters).

Summarizing, it appears that users who use assistive technology are able to achieve sufficient interoperability with the offered web services.

Figure 9. Number of errors for each user

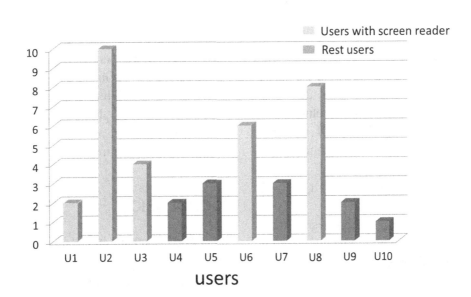

Figure 10. Time (min) for completing three tasks

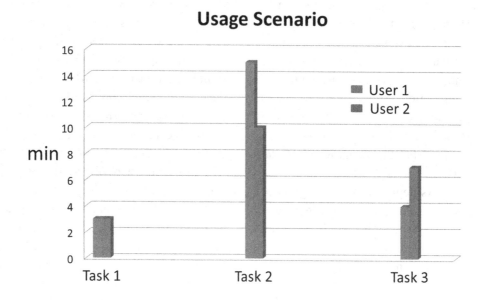

FUTURE RESEARCH DIRECTIONS

Following an extensive user-based evaluation the following extensions could be incorporated into the system in the future:

- Exporting to a script with XHTML valid mark-up by taking the metadata from the existing WSDL and XML files which have been created by the *myWebAccess* platform.
- Further exploitation of the Semantic Web (Berners-Lee et al, 2001), and Semantic Web Services (McIlraith et al, 2001) towards a more comprehensive solution that means transition from the WSDL standard, to a standard with semantic information (OWL-S12).
- The ability to exploit REST type web services.
- The creation of design templates for more use case environments covering specific disability, and modern devices (e.g. digital TV).

- The possibility to verify automatically WCAG's check point (concerning also the manual inspection of a specialist).
- Extend the platform to automatically repair one or more similar operations.
- Including the Accessible Rich Internet Applications Suite (WAI ARIA13) to improve the interaction via assistive technology (faster and easier).
- Evaluating the web services by using the "quality of service" and "quality of experience" in web services domain [(O'Sullivan et al, 2002), (Giakoumis et al, 2013)].
- Creating different registries of "repaired" services by leveraging QoS aspects (O'Sullivan et al, 2002) to support varied disability requirements.

CONCLUSION

The main idea behind the work presented in this book chapter is the exploitation of web services as components in a web interface in order to facilitate the development of accessible and multi-channel web interfaces. A technical process has been elaborated in order to enable accessibility characteristics in the web services domain. Leveraging on this process, the *myWebAccess* platform for repairing, enhancing and re-distributing web services accessible to people with disability has been developed. Moreover, the use of the platform has illustrated the adaptation of the repaired services in different context of use. Finally, the proposed approach has been evaluated by examining web services reusability and interoperability with assistive technology solutions.

REFERENCES

Adams, C., Collison, S., Budd, A., Boulton, M., & Clarke, A. (2007). *Web standards creativity: innovations in web design with XHTML, CSS, and DOM scripting* (Vol. 24). Friends of ED.

Alexandraki, C., Paramythis, A., Maou, N., & Stephanidis, C. (2004). Web accessibility through adaptation. *Computers Helping People with Special Needs*, 626-626.

Alonso, G., Casati, F., Kuno, H., & Machiraju, V. (2003). *Web services: concepts, architectures and applications*. Springer.

Barbarito, F., Pinciroli, F., Mason, J., Marceglia, S., Mazzola, L., & Bonacina, S. (2012). Implementing standards for the interoperability among healthcare providers in the public regionalized Healthcare Information System of the Lombardy Region. *Journal of Biomedical Informatics*. doi:10.1016/j.jbi.2012.01.006 PMID:22285983

Basdekis, I., Alexandraki, C., Mourouzis, A., & Stephanidis, C. (2005). Incorporating Accessibility in Web-Based Work Environments: Two Alternative Approaches and Issues Involved. In C. Stephanidis (Ed.), *Universal Access in HCI: Exploring New Dimensions of Diversity - Volume 8 of the Proceedings of the 11th International Conference on Human-Computer Interaction* (HCI International 2005). Las Vegas, NV: Lawrence Erlbaum Associates.

Basdekis, I., Karampelas, P., Doulgeraki, V., & Stephanidis, C. (2009). Designing Universally Accessible Networking Services for a Mobile Personal Assistant. In C. Stephanidis (Ed.), *Universal Access in Human-Computer Interaction - Intelligent and Ubiquitous Interaction Environments. – Volume 6 of the Proceedings of the 13th International Conference on Human-Computer Interaction* (HCI International 2009). San Diego, CA: Springer.

Basdekis, I., Klironomos, I., Metaxas, I., & Stephanidis, C. (2010). An overview of web accessibility in Greece: a comparative study 2004--2008. *Universal Access in the Information Society*, *9*(2), 185–190. doi:10.1007/s10209-009-0166-z

Berners-Lee, T., Hendler, J., & Lassila, O. et al. (2001). The semantic web. *Scientific American*, *284*(5), 28–37. doi:10.1038/scientificamerican0501-34

Bouloukakis, G., Basdekis, I., & Stephanidis, C. (2013). myWebAccess: A platform for repairing, enhancing and re-distributing Web Services accessible to people with disability. In *Proceedings of IADIS-International Conference on Interfaces and Human Computer Interaction*. IADIS.

Brinck, T. (2008). Return on Goodwill: Return on Investment for Accessibility. In S. Harper, & Y. Yesilada (Eds.), *Web Accessibility – A Foundation for Research* (pp. 385–414). Berlin: Springer.

Brown, S., & Robinson, P. (2001). A world wide web mediator for users with low vision. In *Proceedings of CHI'2001 Conference on Human Factors in Computing Systems Workshop*. ACM.

Caldwell, B., Cooper, M., Reid, L., & Vanderheiden, G. (2008). Web content accessibility guidelines 2.0. *W3C Recommendation, 11*.

Chiti, S., & Leporini, B. (2012). Accessibility of android-based mobile devices: a prototype to investigate interaction with blind users. In *Proceedings of the 13th international conference on Computers Helping People with Special Needs*. Linz, Austria: Academic Press.

Chuter, A., & Yesilada, Y. (2009). *Relationship Between Mobile Web Best Practices (MWBP) and Web Content Accessibility Guidelines (WCAG)*. Academic Press.

Clark, J. (2003). Building accessible websites Indianapolis: New Riders. Tech. rep., ISBN 0-7357-1150-x

Curtis, N. (2009). *Modular Web Design: Creating Reusable Components for User Experience Design*. New Riders Pub.

Fielding, R. (2000). *Architectural styles and the design of network-based software architectures*. (Ph.D. dissertation). University of California.

Giakoumis, D., Votis, K., & Tzovaras, D. (2013). Introducing web service accessibility assessment techniques through a unified quality of service context. *Service Oriented Computing and Applications*, 1–16.

Karampelas, P., Basdekis, I., & Stephanidis, C. (2009). Web User Interface Design Strategy: Designing for Device Independence. In C. Stephanidis, (Ed.), *Universal Access in Human-Computer Interaction - Addressing Diversity – Volume 5 of the Proceedings of the 13th International Conference on Human-Computer Interaction* (HCI International 2009). San Diego, CA: Springer.

Maeda, J., Fukuda, K., Takagi, H., & Asakawa, C. (2004). Web accessibility technology at the IBM Tokyo Research Laboratory. *IBM Journal of Research and Development*, 48(5-6), 735–749. doi:10.1147/rd.485.0735

McIlraith, S., Son, T., & Zeng, H. (2001). Semantic web services. *Intelligent Systems, IEEE*, 16(2), 46–53. doi:10.1109/5254.920599

Myers, B. A., Wobbrock, J. O., Yang, S., Yeung, B., Nichols, J., & Miller, R. (2002). Using handhelds to help people with motor impairments. In *Proceedings of the fifth international ACM conference on Assistive technologies* (pp. 89-96). New York, NY: ACM.

Mykkanen, J., Riekkinen, A., Laitinen, P., Karhunen, H., & Sormunen, M. (2005). Designing web services in health information systems: From process to application level. *Studies in Health Technology and Informatics*, 116, 515. PMID:16160309

Nomensa: United Nations global audit of web accessibility. (2006). Retrieved from http://www.un.org/esa/socdev/enable/documents/fnomensarep.pdf

Norte, S., & Lobo, F. (2007). A virtual logo keyboard for people with motor disabilities. *ACM SIGCSE Bulletin*, 39, 111–115. doi:10.1145/1269900.1268818

O'Sullivan, J., Edmond, D., & Ter Hofstede, A. (2002). What's in a Service? *Distributed and Parallel Databases*, 12(2), 117–133. doi:10.1023/A:1016547000822

Papazoglou, M. (2008). *Web services: principles and technology*. Addison-Wesley.

Reenskaug, T. (2003). *The Model-View-Controller (MVC) Its Past and Present Trygve Reenskaug*. University of Oslo.

Reich, K. (2009). eInclusion, eAccessibility and design for all issues in the context of European Computer-Based Assessment. *The Transition to Computer-Based Assessment, 68.*

Richards, J., & Hanson, V. (2004). Web accessibility: a broader view. In *Proceedings of the 13th international conference on World Wide Web* (pp. 72-79). Academic Press.

Sierkowski, B. (2002). Achieving web accessibility. In *Proceedings of the 30th Annual ACM SIGUCCS Conference on User Services* (pp. 288-291). ACM.

Zhai, S., Hunter, M., & Smith, B. A. (2000). The metropolis keyboard - an exploration of quantitative techniques for virtual keyboard design. In *Proceedings of the 13th Annual ACM Symposium on User Interface Software and Technology* (pp. 119-128). New York, NY: ACM.

ADDITIONAL READING

Abou-Zahra, S. (2012). WAI-ACT: web accessibility now. *Proceedings of the 21st international conference companion on World Wide Web* (pp. 215-218).

Abou-Zahra, S., & Henry, S. L. (2010). Exploring web accessibility solutions in developing regions as innovations for the benefit of all. *Proceedings of the 2010 International Cross Disciplinary Conference on Web Accessibility (W4A),* (pp. 5).

Aghdam, P. A., & Rafeh, R. (2013). Accessing Canvas Element in HTML5. *AWERProcedia Information Technology and Computer Science, 1.*

Atkinson, M. T., Bell, M. J., & Machin, C. H. (2012). Towards ubiquitous accessibility: capability-based profiles and adaptations, delivered via the semantic web. *Proceedings of the International Cross-Disciplinary Conference on Web Accessibility,* (pp. 14).

Bakalov, F., Meurs, M.-J., Konig-Ries, B., Sateli, B., Witte, R., Butler, G., et al. (2012). Empowering web portal users with personalized text mining services. *EMBnet. journal, 18*(B), pp--81.

Benslimane, D., Dustdar, S., & Sheth, A. (2008). Services mashups: The new generation of web applications. *Internet Computing, IEEE, 12*(5), 13–15. doi:10.1109/MIC.2008.110

Berger, S., McFaddin, S., Narayanaswami, C., & Raghunath, M. (2003). Web services on mobile devices-implementation and experience. *Mobile Computing Systems and Applications, 2003. Proceedings. Fifth IEEE Workshop on* (pp. 100-109).

Castanon, J., Maia, M., & Silva, M. (2012). The ambient intelligence for the sake of accessibility in residential projects: a proper study to the Brazilian scene. *Work: A Journal of Prevention. Assessment and Rehabilitation, 41,* 5686–5688.

Cavallaro, L., & Di Nitto, E. (2008). An approach to adapt service requests to actual service interfaces. *Proceedings of the 2008 international workshop on Software engineering for adaptive and self-managing systems* (pp. 129-136).

Cooper, M., Sloan, D., Kelly, B., & Lewthwaite, S. (2012). A challenge to web accessibility metrics and guidelines: putting people and processes first. *Proceedings of the International Cross-Disciplinary Conference on Web Accessibility,* (pp. 20).

de Santana, V. F., de Oliveira, R., Almeida, L. D., & Baranauskas, M. C. (2012). Web accessibility and people with dyslexia: a survey on techniques and guidelines. *Proceedings of the International Cross-Disciplinary Conference on Web Accessibility,* (pp. 35).

Fogli, D., Provenza, L. P., & Bernareggi, C. (n.d.). A universal design resource for rich Internet applications based on design patterns. *Universal Access in the Information Society,* 1-22.

Hoehl, J. (2012). Leveraging crowds and clouds: towards an intercommunity approach to improving web accessibility. *ACM SIGACCESS Accessibility and Computing*(102), 17-20.

Lai, P. P. (2011). Application of content adaptation in web accessibility for the blind. *Proceedings of the International Cross-Disciplinary Conference on Web Accessibility*, (pp. 6).

Lazar, J., Olalere, A., & Wentz, B. (2012). Investigating the accessibility and usability of job application Web sites for blind users. *Journal of Usability Studies*, 7(2), 68–87.

Lunn, D., & Harper, S. (2011). Improving the accessibility of dynamic web content for older users. *Proceedings of the International Cross-Disciplinary Conference on Web Accessibility*, (pp. 16).

Minifie, D., & Coady, Y. (2009). Getting mobile with mobile devices: Using the web to improve transit accessibility. *Proceedings of the 2009 International Cross-Disciplinary Conference on Web Accessibililty (W4A)* (pp. 123-126).

Mirri, S., Salomoni, P., & Prandi, C. (2011). Augment browsing and standard profiling for enhancing web accessibility. *Proceedings of the International Cross-Disciplinary Conference on Web Accessibility*, (pp. 5).

Paisios, N. (2012). *Mobile Accessibility Tools for the Visually Impaired*. Ph.D. dissertation, New York University.

Phillips, D., & Thompson, R. (2013). Limitations \& Advances in Mobile Web Application Development. *Enquiry-The ACES Journal of Undergraduate Research, 3*(1).

Rello, L. (2012). DysWebxia: a model to improve accessibility of the textual web for dyslexic users. *ACM SIGACCESS Accessibility and Computing*(102), 41-44.

Rello, L., & Baeza-Yates, R. (2012). Lexical quality as a measure for textual web accessibility. In *Computers Helping People with Special Needs* (pp. 404–408). Springer. doi:10.1007/978-3-642-31522-0_61

Salomoni, P., Mirri, S., Ferretti, S., & Roccetti, M. (2008). A multimedia broker to support accessible and mobile learning through learning objects adaptation. *ACM Transactions on Internet Technology, 8*(2), 4. doi:10.1145/1323651.1323655

Sathapornvajana, S., & Papasratorn, B. (2013). Effect of Culture, Age, and Language on Quality of Services and Adoption of IP Applications. *Wireless Personal Communications*, 1–9.

Sohaib, O., Hussain, W., ISMAILI, I., & BUKHARI, A. (2012). Exploring the Relationship between Web Usability and the Web Accessibility Guidelines. *Exploring the Relationship between Web Usability and the Web Accessibility Guidelines*. unpublished.

Sun, L. (2012). Web services for human interaction.

Trewin, S., Bellamy, R., Thomas, J., Brezin, J., Richards, J., Swart, C., et al. (2010). Designing for auditory web access: accessibility and cellphone users. *Proceedings of the 2010 International Cross Disciplinary Conference on Web Accessibility (W4A)*, (pp. 4).

Xu, H. (2013). *A Support System for Graphics for Visually Impaired People*. Ph.D. dissertation, The University of Western Ontario.

Zakraoui, J., & Zagler, W. (2012). A method for generating CSS to improve web accessibility for old users. In *Computers Helping People with Special Needs* (pp. 329–336). Springer. doi:10.1007/978-3-642-31522-0_50

KEY TERMS AND DEFINITIONS

Adaptation: Refers to a process, in which an interactive system (adaptive system) adapts its behaviour to individual users based on information acquired about its user(s) and its environment.

Design Template: Is a form of separation of presentation and content for web design in which the markup (i.e., HTML or XHTML) of a webpage contains the page's semantic content and structure.

myWebAccess: Is a platform which provides a mechanism for the semi-automated "repair" of web services' interaction characteristics in order to support the automatic generation of interface elements that conform to the de facto standard of the WCAG 2.0.

People with Disabilities: The term "disability" broadly describes an impairment in a person's ability to function, caused by changes in various subsystems of the body, or to mental health. The degree of disability may range from mild to moderate, severe, or profound. A person may also have multiple disabilities.

Standards: Is an established norm or requirement in regard to technical systems. It is usually a formal document that establishes uniform engineering or technical criteria, methods, processes and practices.

Web Accessibility: Refers to the inclusive practice of removing barriers that prevent access to websites by people with disabilities. When sites are correctly designed, developed and edited, all users have equal access to information and functionality.

Web Application: Is any application software that runs in a web browser or is created in a browser-supported programming language (such as the combination of JavaScript, HTML and CSS) and relies on a common web browser to render the application.

Web Developer: Is a programmer who specializes in, or is specifically engaged in, the development of World Wide Web applications, or distributed network applications that are run over HTTP from a web server to a web browser.

Web Interfaces: Refers to the interaction between a user and software running on a Web server. The user interface is the Web browser and the Web page it has downloaded and rendered.

Web Services: A software system designed to support interoperable machine-to-machine interaction over a network. It has an interface described in a machine-processable format (specifically WSDL). Other systems interact with the Web service in a manner prescribed by its description using SOAP messages, typically conveyed using HTTP with an XML serialization in conjunction with other Web-related standards.

ENDNOTES

1. http://www.disabled-world.com/disability/statistics
2. http://epp.eurostat.ec.europa.eu/portal/page/portal/eurostat/home
3. http://www.w3.org/standards/techs/accessibility#w3c_all
4. http://www.europarl.europa.eu/sides/getDoc.do?pubRef=-%2F%2FEP%2F%2FNONSGML%2BCOMPARL%2BPE-513.011%2B01%2BDOC%2BPDF%2BV0%2F%2FEN
5. http://www.w3.org/TR/xhtml1/dtds.html
6. http://www.w3.org/2003/09/xmlap/xml-schema-wg-charter.html
7. http://en.wikipedia.org/wiki/RSS
8. http://www.w3.org/TR/wsdl
9. http://www.urdalen.no/wsdl2php/index.php
10. http://validator.w3.org
11. http://www.tawdis.net
12. http://www.w3.org/Submission/OWL-S
13. http://www.w3.org/WAI/intro/aria

Section 3
Emerging Technologies

Chapter 9
The Impact of Enterprise 2.0 on SMEs

Diogo Antunes
University of Lisbon, Portugal

Pedro Isaías
Universidade Aberta(Portuguese Open University), Portugal

ABSTRACT

Enterprise 2.0 has been part of the business sector vocabulary for quite some time now. Web 2.0's revolutionary philosophy and applications have been absorbed by various areas of society. The success of the business sector benefits from a client-oriented approach, so when the benefits of a user-centric Web became evident, adopting it was the natural next step. Enterprise 2.0 presents advantages mainly in two areas: within organizations, as they enable communication through new dynamic methods of communication and interaction, in order to enhance efficiency and productivity; and between companies and customers, suppliers, and partners, as they increase both revenue and customer satisfaction and promote cooperation and co-creation to improve services or products. This chapter illustrates the reality of Small and Medium Enterprises' (SMEs) adoption of Web 2.0. An online questionnaire was developed to assess numerous SMEs in Portugal to understand if and how Web 2.0 implementation is taking place.

INTRODUCTION

The deep changes experienced in the global business environment, such as increased competition, globalization of markets and technological development, as well as the transformations experienced by information technology and management approaches, have led to a fundamental alteration of the way companies compete (Tapscott, 2006). Companies have been trying to adapt to the in-novations and shifts of conducting business and achieving competitiveness. The blooming of revenue and success is greatly dependent on the capacity that enterprises have to adjust and grow with change.

In the last years there has been a proliferation of new Web technologies that tend, among other things, to increase users' participation, to promote a more efficient organization of information, and to decentralize decision-making. Web 2.0 is a

DOI: 10.4018/978-1-4666-6228-5.ch009

platform that promotes a larger and better connection of people and increases new forms of collaboration (O'Reilly, 2005). The Social Web, as it is also called, has empowered users of all kinds of Information Technology (IT) proficiency to contribute with their own content and share their views with their peers. The 'boom' of Web 2.0 technologies (blogs, social networks and wikis) is felt, mostly, in personal use. However, there is an increasing propensity to use them in several areas of society, including the business arena. There are numerous reasons for the transference of social technology to business: the new generation of graduates has been, who has familiarity with these Web technologies, since the early stages are adapting them to their spheres of work (Bughin and Manyika, 2008; Marshall, 2008; Buytendijk, Cripe, Henson, & Pulverman, 2008); Web 2.0 has a demonstrated success in terms of client engagement; and inventiveness is causing businesses to experiment its different applications in order to identify the ways in which they can benefit from their potential (Almeida, 2012). This phenomenon has become known as Enterprise 2.0 (E2.0). E2.0 represents a potential opportunity for companies to reduce costs, boost revenue and productivity (Platt, 2007), increase innovation and realize new business opportunities (Manyika, Roberts, & Sprague, 2007).

E2.0 is an approach that is being applied more visibly in large companies, but it is also progressively being adopted by companies of smaller dimensions. According to the European Commission (2003), Small and Medium Enterprises (SMEs) stand for 99% of the entirety of European companies and represent a core resource of industrial ability, employability and modernization. This scenario also applies to Portugal. Widely recognized as the basis of the national economy, SMEs are also largely responsible for jobs creation (more than 2 million jobs) (INE, 2010). According to the National Institute of Statistics in Portugal, in 2008, SMEs absorbed 72.5% of employment in

Portugal and contributed to 58% of the national income - about 201,765 million euro (INE, 2010).

However, the competitive, dynamic and complex environment where SMEs interact has presented them with new challenges that make their survival in the market even more complicated (De Saulles, 2008). Given their meagre resources and limited capacity, E2.0 can be a springboard to promote cooperation and thus provide SMEs with new abilities (Blinn, Lindermann, Fäcks, & Nüttgens, 2010).

This chapter intends to evaluate the impact that Web 2.0 technologies have on SMEs, both within organizations and between companies and customers, suppliers and partners, through an empirical study based on questionnaires applied to Portuguese SMEs which have been distinguished with the status of "SME Excellence" awarded by IAPMEI (this Portuguese acronym stands for SMEs and Innovation Support Institute), in the years 2011 and 2012. This study aims to contribute to the already existing body of research on the implementation of Web 2.0 technologies in the business sector, by presenting a specific scenario of Portuguese SMEs. The results have no ambition of generalisation, but they do intend to lead to a deeper knowledge of how different circumstances and national realities can impact on how these technologies are perceived and applied. More than generalist literature, SMEs need research that is specific and that can facilitate the adoption of E2.0 to respond to the competitiveness challenges of actual market environment.

ENTERPRISE 2.0

There are numerous Web 2.0 technologies that can be deployed for business reasons. Each of the different tools has their peculiar value and contribution. Wikis, for example, are seen as a quick and inexpensive way of sharing and aggregating business knowledge in one area (AIIM, 2008a; Marshall, 2008). Wikipedia is the most popular wiki, with more than 10 million articles. Blogs, can be useful for companies to spread their messages without intermediaries (Serrano and Torres, 2010), to increase the collaboration and participation of employees in projects, to present innovative concepts, and to encourage feedback (Marshall, 2008). Additionally, according to Gordeyeva (2010), through Microblogs people focus on "What are you working on?" instead of the traditional "What are you doing?", which can improve the sharing of information, collaboration and communication (both inside and outside the company). As said by Marshall (2008), Really Simple Syndication (RSS) can be used on companies' portals to inform knowledge workers of newly published blogs. This mix of technologies can be a powerful tool to attract more readers and promote more feedback between employees. Social bookmarking as a categorization system can reflect the information structures and associations that people actually use, which could lead to easier identification of patterns and processes of knowledge related to work within an enterprise (employees could use it to keep track of useful Internet pages consulted) (McAfee, 2006). Podcasts' digital format improves collaboration and the sharing of knowledge between enterprises' employees, since it allows people to download, send and receive media files by e-mail (Köhler-Krün, 2009). Mash-ups allow, for instance, a real estate site combining online maps with a property advertising service, as a way to provide a unified resource for locating homes for sale (Bughin, 2008). There has been an investment in the development of social networks, as illustrated by IBM. IBM has invested in Fringe, an internal network, which has evolved from a basic web employee directory to a social network with several stimulating features, such as profiles, links to resumes, skills, tagging, testimonials and user groups (Marshal, 2008).

The use of Web 2.0 technologies in business is evident mainly in two scenarios (Platt, 2007; Kim et al., 2009): within organizations, in order to enhance efficiency and productivity; and between companies and customers, suppliers and partners, with the aim of increasing revenue, and customer satisfaction, and promoting co-creation with customers, suppliers and partners. In most companies, E2.0 implementation intends to facilitate the increase of the access to knowledge, the exchange of information and the promotion of collaboration and communication (AIIM, 2008a; Bughin, 2008). Web 2.0 technologies have thus boosted the role of information and knowledge in organizational processes, which may lead to the achievement of competitive advantages. E2.0 has therefore transformed the working universe of companies. According to Platt (2007), Web 2.0 tools have a greater impact on business areas that are developed through an interface with customers, such as customer service, sales or CRM. In marketing, the use of blogs and wikis not only promotes interaction with customers but also provides new ways to attract potential customers.

More specifically, Web 2.0 can be used in business scenarios to:

- **Create growth:** Web 2.0 tools are used to attract new customers quickly and include their dynamic inputs directly in the business (Hinchcliffe, 2010).
- **Improve efficiency and productivity:** Web 2.0 technologies allow users to access structured and unstructured information within the organization in a single search (Epicor, 2008); they also enable companies to distribute more work through specialists, free agents, and talent networks, which can improve processes within a company since "the best person for a task may be a free agent in India or an employee of a small company in Italy" (Manyika et al., 2007).
- **Harness knowledge through collaboration:** Web 2.0 tools promote collaboration, foster communication and improve the sharing of information, which leads to improvements in productivity and helps to solve business problems (Epicor, 2008).

- **Transform the customer relationship to generate revenue:** the creation of customer community relationships, mainly in activities such as product development and customer service, will generate better outcomes and lower costs (Hinchcliffe, 2010). "Engaging with brands in the creation process gives customers a sense of collaboration and can increase loyalty. At the same time, involving clients will provide the company with more information on what their needs are, which will potentially increase consumer satisfaction" (Isaías, Pífano & Miranda, 2011).

- **Encourage innovation:** Web 2.0 tools can enable companies to outsource innovation to business partners and customers who can reduce their costs and put enhanced products faster on the market (co-creation). For example, Threadless is a successful online clothing store whose success is directly related to its business strategy. They ask people to present new designs for T-shirts that can be voted on by everyone. Winners receive store credits and money prizes (Manyika et al., 2007).

- **Incorporate new business models and sources of revenue:** strategies like the one above (Threadless) lead to the participation of thousands of individuals which conduct to having less costs on research and advertising (Manyika et al., 2007).

- **Drive operational costs down:** E2.0 tools reduce the costs of creating, researching and sharing knowledge and upgrading and maintaining applications, among other costs (Epicor, 2008; Hinchcliffe, 2010).

Some studies have shown that, despite the growing popularity of Web 2.0 tools implementation in the business sector, among SMEs, their adoption is still restricted. E2.0 seems to be thriving more proficiently in large companies and SMEs should harness its potential to better benefit from its advantages (Consoli, 2011).

The implementation of E2.0 is organic, i.e. Web 2.0 technologies are driven by employees familiar with these technologies (Newman and Thomas, 2009). However, Köhler-Krün (2009) believes that successful E2.0 implementation requires commitment. According to the author (Köhler-Krün, 2009), the first rule that a CEO must respect in implementing E2.0 in a company is to be assured that he and his collaborators really comprehend the complexity of E2.0 and especially the company's business culture and technological strategy. In this context, Köhler-Krün (2009) emphasizes the value of education for all companies' key players as well the importance of an open organizational culture. Unlike those with hierarchical structures, in companies whose organizational structure is flexible, communication and collaboration are fostered and the spread of technology is faster, which makes E2.0 implementation easier.

In order to potentiate the impact of implementing social technology on a company's organizational culture, managers should enable access to information and technologies, build a culture of participatory management, and give constant feedback (Buytendijk et al., 2008). Moreover, this implementation becomes easier with the participation of leaders and the actual integration of these technologies in business management (Jedd, 2008). Leaders have the responsibility to motivate and to encourage employees to facilitate the voluntary use of these technologies (Manyika et al., 2007; McAfee, 2006). It is also essential that organizations develop clear strategies that allow employees to focus on business objectives. The strategy must therefore incorporate the goals and methods of the business and should enable the use of E2.0 technologies as well as the identification of critical success factors (AT & T, 2009; Köhler-Krün, 2009).

SMES AND WEB 2.0

Despite the recognized value of social technology in terms of customer service and the maximization of information collection, the dominant belief seems to be that web 2.0 has no business pertinence for SMEs. Also, the perceived associated risks with the implementation of E2.0 inside SMEs, such as abusive use and legal grey areas, constitute a strong deterrent of adoption (Blinn, Lindermann, Fäcks & Nüttgens, 2012).

The fierce competition of markets represents a central challenge for SMEs. In order to address this growing concern, cooperation has been regarded and defended as an effective strategy to enhance the competitive capacity of individual SMEs. The interactivity and collaboration that characterise Web 2.0 makes it an important tool for SMEs (Peris, Sperling, Blinn, Nüttgens, & Gehrke, 2011). "With regard to their restricted resources, SMEs are facing a limited capacity for innovation to compete with new challenges in a complex and dynamic competitive environment. Given this context, SMEs need to increasingly cooperate to generate innovations on an extended resource base" (Lindermann, Valcárcel, Schaarschmidt & von Kortzfleisch, 2009). The peculiar entrepreneurial structure of SMEs usually means that innovation is the product of the initiative of few employees. The entirety of the staff is not included in the creation of new strategies. Also, the management of SMEs, and their immediate subordinates, seem to have insufficient information on the advantages of Web 2.0 tools and collaboration in general (Mañas, Hamburg & Hall, 2011).

However, to boost competitive advantage, these technologies should be integrated in the company's business strategy (Levy, Powell, & Yetton, 2001). Many of these companies are often structured in a patriarchal way, where business initiatives are determined by one or two individuals, instead of involving the employees (Blinn et al., 2010). Since there are few SMEs that have an IT department, the adoption of these technologies, in a large proportion of them, is a result of the interest and knowledge (often limited) of the owners rather than being strategically planned (Levy et al., 2001; Blinn et al., 2010).

The development and implementation of information technologies in general inside SMEs is very challenging, namely due to their heterogeneity in terms of size. SMEs can range from enterprises with hundreds of employees to companies with barely a dozen staff members. Some companies will have an IT department that is capable of developing and managing software and applications and some others will have only one person that has to manage all IT aspects. This disparity impedes the development of specific software for SMEs' use (De Saulles, 2008). This makes Web 2.0's flexibility an advantage, as it can adapt easily to the several technical needs of the different SMEs.

SMEs have the advantage of being dynamic entities, but in terms of IT most of them do not have a department solely dedicated to it. The IT decisions and innovations are mainly at the owner's discretion. Although inside SMEs the internet is a widespread tool the employment of Web 2.0 technologies is still scarce (Blinn et al., 2012). Kim, Lee and Lee (2013) conducted a study, using information from the webpages of the top 50 SMEs to work for in the USA in 2009 and 50 other randomly selected SMEs, to assess Web 2.0 implementation. In their research the authors concluded that despite of the fact that the majority of the SMEs had, to a certain level, incorporated E2.0 practices into their business routine, the other companies that were studied still had a long way to go until successful implementation. They argued that the SMEs that fell short of the use of Web 2.0 applications and tools need to intensify their determination and investment in these technologies in order to enhance performance, to improve their relation with customers and to guarantee their competitiveness (Kim, Lee & Lee, 2013).

METHODS

In order to assess the impact and extension of Web 2.0 technologies implementation in SME's in Portugal, this study defined its population based on an award given by IAPMEI, entitled "SME Excellence". This award recognises SMEs, from various sectors of activity, for their active involvement in the creation of employment, their investment in the development of their local area and for their predominance in terms of quality of their outcomes and high levels of competitiveness, and also for their, above the national average, ratios of financial stability and profitability. The status that this award attributes lasts for a year (IAPMEI, S.D.). The working sample for this study was composed by 438 companies, from a population of 1481 companies that were awarded with the "SME Excellence" status, between 2010 and 2011. This sample was created using the simple stratified method, to ensure that the selected companies were representative of the population. Stratification allows a research to uncover a population characteristics by selecting a subset of it (Fernandes, Kamienski et al. 2008). This subset was constituted by roughly four "SME Excellence" companies from each year (2011 and 2012), each business sector and each district of Mainland Portugal and in Azores and Madeira. An online questionnaire was then developed and sent to these 438 companies during one month in 2012. The questionnaire was comprised of questions relating to the respondents' personal data, the characteristics of each company, the participants' personal use of Web 2.0 technologies and the employment of the E2.0 practices in the organization. The questionnaire was distributed online, in its final and improved version, after a pilot with one of the companies.

ANALYSIS AND DISCUSSION OF RESULTS

The results of the empirical research were based on 99 valid questionnaires. The majority of the respondents were aged 31 to 54 years old. Only 26% were aged less than 30 years old (of whom 16% were over 25 years old). The survey was completed mostly by men (70.7%) and as for the positions held by the respondents, one-third of the questionnaires were answered by CEOs and at least 20% by employees in managerial positions. With regard to their industries, more than two-thirds of the respondents were in organizations that performed tertiary activities (31.3% commerce, 30.3% services, 5.1% tourism and 1% transport). A large proportion of the companies represented in the study (about 64%) employ between 10 and 49 employees. Only 9% of the companies have less than 10 employees. This array of respondents allowed different perspectives to come to light.

In terms of personal usage of Web 2.0 technologies, the results show that the use of e-mail is still prevalent to Web 2.0 technologies. While the data confirms that technologies such as instant messaging (IM) and blogs have been playing an increasingly important role in the personal sphere, it also shows that application such as wikis and podcasts have indicating levels of initial adoption.

At the level of enterprise communication, the results highlight the dominance of traditional channels like e-mail (about 67% of respondents use it intensively), telephone/mobile phone (on average 47% actively use these devices), and personal contact (approximately 50% of organizations emphasize personal contact). In communications with employees and customers, the enterprise portal use registered a regular to intensive score (between levels 4 and 6) by 30% of the companies. In contrast, the new Web 2.0 technologies are poorly used by companies for communicating with their stakeholders (employees, customers and suppliers). More than three-quarters of respondents

Table 1. Rates of technology use in the organization work environment

Score	Blogs	Wikis	RSS	Mashups	Podcast	S. Voting	S. Bookmarking	Virtual worlds	Web/Video Conferencing	Professional Networks	Social Networks	Chat Rooms	Micro-blogs	Youtube & similar	Microsoft SharePoint	Internal Portal	Intranet
0	60%	60%	61%	74%	72%	73%	72%	81%	38%	43%	36%	54%	62%	47%	44%	38%	21%
1	17%	11%	13%	7%	8%	8%	9%	10%	6%	9%	8%	16%	14%	11%	9%	3%	3%
2	8%	9%	6%	5%	6%	3%	3%	3%	4%	5%	12%	6%	8%	9%	10%	7%	5%
3	6%	6%	7%	7%	10%	8%	10%	2%	13%	13%	17%	12%	8%	13%	8%	8%	10%
4	4%	7%	7%	3%	2%	5%	3%	2%	13%	14%	10%	5%	2%	12%	7%	7%	11%
5	4%	2%	3%	2%	1%	2%	2%	1%	14%	8%	10%	2%	3%	5%	6%	9%	14%
6	0%	4%	2%	1%	0%	0%	0%	0%	10%	6%	5%	4%	2%	0%	14%	26%	35%
N/R	1%	1%	1%	1%	1%	1%	1%	1%	1%	1%	1%	1%	1%	2%	1%	1%	0%

stated that blogs, wikis and podcasts are not used for communication purposes.

As for the other organizational practices, Table 1 illustrates that the data reveals a strong disparity between the use of internal portals and intranet, 42% and 61% respectively, and the use of other technologies, in which the average of use (regular to intensive) is about 14%. Technologies such as Web/video conferencing were regularly or intensively employed by 37% of respondents; professional networks like LinkedIn were regularly or intensively used by 28%; Microsoft SharePoint had a regular to intensive use by 27%; and social networks were regularly to intensively used by 25% of the participants. Table 1 uses a score of 0 to 6 where 0 is "not used" and 6 is "intensively used", to measure the adoption of certain technologies inside enterprises.

The low use of technologies such as wikis, podcasts and blogs can be explained by the fact that 41% of the CEOs represented in the study do not have a clear idea of what is E2.0 or its benefits. Only 10% of CEOs have established E2.0 practices and merely 3% of them use (regularly or intensively) wikis and podcasts. There is not a single CEO that publishes blogs. Another reason for the limited use of these new technologies may be the percentage of respondents (73.5%) who are more than 31 years old (38% are 40 years old or more). The results show that among respondents aged between 31 and 40 years the (regular to intensive) use of podcasts (12%) and wikis (9%) and the publication of blogs (6%) is quite low. The data show even lower values among respondents who are more than 40 years old. However, the personal practices of young people (between 18 and 30) may indicate that the future of these technologies within companies can be exciting. More than 40% of them read blogs (regularly to intensively), 12% publish blogs (regularly to intensively), and almost 30% use wikis (regularly to intensively). About 32% of the respondents revealed that they do not have a clear idea about E2.0 technologies or the benefits that might result from their use, and almost two-fifths of the survey's participants said they are slightly familiar with these technologies but do not have enough information to take advantage of them (18.4%) or are simply not doing so (20.4%) despite knowing the inherent benefits of their implementation.

Table 2. E2.0 implementation level inside SMEs

Implementation Level	Percentage
I don't have a clear idea of what E2.0 is	32%
I'm slightly familiar with the concepts but I don't have enough information to make an informed decision	19%
We know the impact of E2.0 implementation but we are not taking advantage of it	20%
We have already started to spread E2.0 practices	20%
E2.0 practices are established and we are taking advantage of them	9%
Total	100%

However, more than 20% of organizations have been spreading these practices among employees and 9% of represented companies are already benefiting from E2.0 practices as Table 2 shows.

One of the realities that this study wanted to capture was the relationship between personal use and organizational use of these technologies. This analysis focused on wikis because their use in this study was greater than the production of blogs and the use of podcasts. Despite the low values, the survey's participants who had higher levels of personal use of wikis (from levels 4 to 6) were also those who used them more in the work sphere.

The analysis of levels of E2.0 implementation by sector of activity make these results clear, since two-thirds of companies with fewer than 10 employees are involved in the commercial sector, where 39% of study participants claim not to have a clear idea of what E2.0 is and only 3% confirm that they are already benefiting from E2.0 practices. In fact, besides the commercial sector, only companies from the service sector are taking advantage of E2.0 practices (23%). The service sector is divided into 70% small companies, 23% medium and 7% micro-companies. Despite the low rate of E2.0 implementation, reasonable percentages of companies in the remaining sectors have E2.0 practices spread among employees (between 15% and 30%).

When the relationship between the use of Web 2.0 technologies and company size is analysed, the data shows that (regular to intensive) use of these technologies is low but similar in small and medium enterprises. The biggest differences occur in the utilization of RSS (higher in small companies) and Web/video conferencing (higher in medium enterprises, perhaps because of the great difficulty in bringing together stakeholders). In micro-enterprises, use rates of these technologies are zero or near zero, except for the intranet. In fact the internal portal and intranet technologies are used by companies with more than 10 and fewer than 250 employees, with regular to intensive use rates between (44% and 63%).

The questionnaire also investigated the use of Web 2.0 technologies by specific departments. In order to get a more realistic analysis of E2.0 adoption by different departments, the data were examined not by taking the total number of responses but by subtracting the responses "not existing" (N/E) from the total number of responses. The data analysis detected that the marketing and communication departments have the highest levels of regular to intensive use. In a similar level, but with less use, is the department of information technology (IT). Another interesting fact is the very low percentage of non-use of these technologies in all departments.

However, when the analysis focuses only on companies whose E2.0 practices are established, the results confirm that R&D departments (67%) together with the IT (78%) and communication (71%) divisions have the highest levels of intensive use. When the regular to high (levels 4 and 5) use of Web 2.0 technologies is included, the data

Figure 1. E2.0 Implementation: Key players in companies that are taking advantage of it

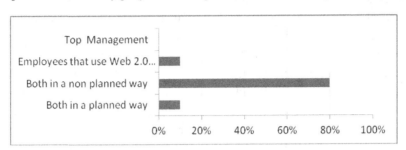

shows that all other departments have extremely high levels of adoption. According to the AIIM Study (2008a), this may indicate the beginning of a true "penetration of Enterprise 2.0". The analysis also highlighted that nearly 30% of respondents considered that the role of top management was essential to the introduction of these new technologies in their enterprises, and 23% considered that it was mainly the employees who contributed to the adoption of Web 2.0 technologies within organizations. On the other hand, half of the survey's participants (49%) gave the credit of success to the joint effort of top management and employees, whether planned (29%) or not (20%).

Nevertheless a specific analysis limited to those involved in companies that already benefit from E2.0 practices highlights the importance of an implementation which is incorporated in the company's business strategy and which takes advantage of the joint effort of top management and employees (Figure 1).

According to the survey's participants, besides the reasons already presented, the low integration of Web 2.0 technologies in organizations is also due to the concern of the administration with the possibility of wasting employees' time as well as the difficulty of adapting the E2.0 practices to the corporate culture of the organization. The costs that these technologies can incur and the insufficient tangible results are also obstacles to the success of E2.0 implementation.

Despite these difficulties, numerous advantages of E2.0 practices were demonstrated. About

half of the respondents highlighted results such as increased access to knowledge, improved knowledge sharing and cost reduction in phone calls. Other benefits were also repeatedly mentioned, such as the improvement of individual performance, an increase in employee satisfaction, the reduction of travel costs, the maximization of efficiency in marketing and in the relationship with customers, the attraction of new customers, and an improvement in proactivity and reciprocity in the relationship between employees.

However, 33% of the survey's participants said they had obtained no results/clear benefits. Bearing in mind that over 70% of respondents did not take advantage of E2.0 practices, this result cannot be surprising. In a specific analysis of organizations that recognize E2.0 implementation, positive results increased exponentially. Despite the poor rate of E2.0 implementation in SMEs, 79% of the survey's participants confirmed that their organizations recently had been focusing on these technologies, and more than 92% (a percentage that rises to 100% in companies that have established E2.0 practices) were sure that the impact was positive. Finally, another reason which may indicate that the future use of these technologies in SMEs is promising was the percentage (83%) of the study's participants who were satisfied or very satisfied with the introduction of E2.0 (a percentage that rises to 100% in companies that have established E2.0 practices).

In short, although the rate of E2.0 implementation in SMEs is still low, the results were not disappointing. The data showed that blogs, wikis, RSS and podcast are achieving a considerable degree of early implementation. Inside enterprises' departments, there are records of a high level of propagation of E2.0. The commitment to E2.0 was confirmed by the 29% of respondents who assured that, in their companies, the adoption of Web 2.0 technology accounted for the business strategies and places and harnesses the work of both staff members and high level management. The same percentage of people (29%) stated that their institutions had already taken the adequate steps to disseminate E2.0 practices. About 79% of the participants revealed the recent efforts of their organisations in focusing on the Social Web. With regard to their level of satisfaction and E2.0 positive effects, the numbers were overwhelmingly high. Over 92% of the respondents classified E2.0's impact as positive. Also, 83% of the participants claimed that were satisfied or very satisfied regarding E2.0. This number was even higher when only the answers of the participants whose companies were already employing the precepts of E2.0, were considered. Exactly 100% of them claimed to be satisfied or very satisfied.

SME 2.0: MOVING FORWARD

The peculiarities of SME's structure and organization make them a potential beneficiary of Web 2.0 technologies. The social technology is far from its earlier stages of polemic. Although some might still question its benefits outside the social and personal arena, now there are specific case studies that show that Web 2.0 can be a powerful ally in business.

The disparity of the results of the questionnaire that was developed in this paper demonstrates that there is still a lack of knowledge not only about Web 2.0 technologies, but about the way they work and their value to ease the day to day of managing a SME. It seems that the most important step now, that there is much more information about

the subject, is to analyse what technologies best suit a specific SME and how to develop proficient methods of harnessing them.

Web 2.0 technologies must be disseminated to all employees and should aim to create a "network enterprise" that encourages suppliers and customers to participate (Bughin, 2009). There are both technical and organizational demands for the successful application of Web 2.0 (Blinn et al., 2012). "Using web 2.0 applications within SMEs implies consequently breaking down innovation processes to employees' level and thus systematically opening up a heterogeneous and broader knowledge base to idea generation" (Lindermann, Valcárcel, Schaarschmidt, & von Kortzfleisch, 2009). The hierarchical structure of SMEs would have to shift to embrace this new culture of inclusive participation. Communities of practice are a good example of how to apply Web 2.0 to SMEs. The scarcity of resources and the customary financial difficulties can benefit from a more qualified and skilled staff. E-learning 2.0 communities of practice are a resource that facilitates tranining in a consistent and frequent manner, by allowing people to share insights, concerns and expertise. This is the type of resource that SMEs could employ because it is flexible and easy to access. It is a valuable instrument to drive change inside SMEs and it is an opportunity to enhance their business practices and ensure their integration in markets at an European level (Hamburg, Engert, & Anke, 2007).

One important element of the implementation of Web 2.0 inside enterprises is the role of the Web Community Manager. This job entails the management of web based communities and should ideally be occcupied by a member of staff of the enterprise itself. The employees are in the best position to fully understand the business routine, its services and products and also the customers. Although an external service provider can be used in the beginning, this is really the type of position best occupied by someone from the inside (Consoli, 2011).

The use of Web 2.0 tools by SMEs employees' in their private lives can be a contributing factor for the use of E2.0 inside SMEs. The staff members familiarity and self-assurance in using Web 2.0 applications and services for personal reasons can enhance their availability and willingness to use them for professional purposes and thus facilitate their implementattion in SMEs (Blinn, et al., 2012).

The successful implementation of Web 2.0 tools within SMEs enhances advantages at many levels, namely in terms of marketing, customer service and internal communication and collaboration. Web 2.0 constitutes a competitive advantage in product creation and promotion, as it allows companies to create communities with shared interests and active participation in the development of new products and in their publicity. This facilitates the process of product creation as well as enhances the relation between the companies and their customers. Also, internally it means more collaboration among employee as well as an increased interaction, and it allows the flow of information to be shared and augmented (Mañas, Hamburg & Hall, 2011).

CONCLUSION

Despite the size of the sample used in this study, the results reveal an early, but fast-moving stage in the adoption of E2 technologies (39% of respondents had a vague familiarity with the concept of E2.0, whereas about 30% said that they already use these technologies in organizational practices). This will ensure a competitive advantage to those who implement these new technologies strategically into their business.

The age factor and the CEOs' unawareness of these technologies, such as mash-ups, wikis and podcasts, are the main reasons for their low use. The data show that the social practices of Millennials (people between 18 and 30 years old), familiarized since early with new technologies, may indicate a "sunny" future for these tools within

companies. These results were highlighted because of the correlation between personal use and social use of Web 2.0 technologies, but especially because they reinforce the role of employees in the introduction of these technologies in organizations. The hierarchical structures of many SMEs (characterized by a rigid corporate culture), the difficulty of measuring results from E2.0 practices and the fear that these technologies would waste employees' time have been obstacles to a greater rate of E2.0 implementation in SMEs.

On the other hand, E2.0 practices have already had a positive impact on business dynamics, particularly on internal ones. Web 2.0 technologies are enabling a greater access to knowledge and increasing the sharing of ideas, which leads to better individual performance and improvement in employee satisfaction. Externally these technologies have been contributing to the maximization of the efficiency of marketing and have been developing the relationship with customers as well as attracting new ones.

It is also important to keep in mind that the correct form of E2.0 implementation and its success in SMEs will, naturally, vary according to a wide range of factors such as the company's size and type of activity and the sector in which it operates. The successful adoption of Web 2.0 technologies inside enterprises, is, hence, intrinsically connected with the knowledge of SMEs' peculiar characteristics and needs.

This chapter presented a specific scenario of Web 2.0 technologies that involved the elite Portuguese SMEs and as such it cannot be generalised to other countries or specific realities, but it provided an important depiction of what is the reality of Web 2.0 implementation in a particular situation. More than generalisations, the study of SMEs' Web 2.0 implementation, needs to be focusing on real scenarios, whether they are national, regional or global. It is the collection of data from specific SMEs experience that will ultimately create the theoretical and empirical evidence required to help the people in command of SMEs to create the conditions to implement them or decide not to, but by an enlightened choice and not because they are afraid of using them or do not know how. Although these results are particular to the Portuguese case and Portuguese elite SMEs, the results help to depict the current and real application of the concept of E2.0. Also, they are a stepping stone for further and more in-depth research on the subject and the questions they raise open way to other forms of empirical research and different investigative approaches.

REFERENCES

AIIM. (2008a). *What is Enterprise 2.0?* Retrieved December 1, 2013, from http://www.aiim.org/What-is-Enterprise2.0-E2.0.aspx

AIIM. (2008b). Enterprise 2.0 Technologies Critical to Business Success. *International Journal of Micrographics & Optical Technology, 26*(1/2), 6.

Almeida, F. (2012). Web 2.0 Technologies and Social Networking Security Fears in Enterprises. *International Journal of Advanced Computer Science and Applications, 3*(2). AT&T. (2009). *Speeding the Adoption of Enterprise 2.0.* Retrieved November 21, 2013 from http://blog.earlystrategies.com/wp-content/uploads/2010/02/Speeding-the-Adoption-of_Enterprise-2-0.pdf

Blinn, N., Lindermann, K., Fäcks, M., & Nüttgens, M. (2010). Web 2.0 in SME networks - A Design Science Approach Considering Multi-Perspective Requirements. *Journal of Information Science & Technology, 7*(1), 3–21.

Blinn, N., Lindermann, N., Fäcks, K., & Nüttgens, M. (2012). Web 2.0 artifacts in SME-networks– A qualitative approach towards an integrative conceptualization considering organizational and technical perspectives. In Proceedings of Software Engineering (Workshops) (pp. 273-284). Academic Press.

Bughin, J. (2008a). The Rise of Enterprise 2.0. *Journal of Direct. Data and Digital Marketing Practice, 9*(3), 251–259. doi:10.1057/palgrave.dddmp.4350100

Bughin, J. (2009). How companies are Benefiting from Web 2.0: McKinsey Global Survey Results. *The McKinsey Quarterly,* 4.

Bughin, J., & Manyika, J. (2008). Building the Web 2.0 Enterprise: McKinsey Global Survey Results. *The McKinsey Quarterly,* 10.

Buytendijk, F., Cripe, B., Henson, R., & Pulverman, K. (2008). *Business Management in the Age of Enterprise 2.0: Why Business Model 1.0 Will Obsolete You.* Redwood Shores, CA: Oracle Corporation.

Consoli, D. (2011). *The web community manager in SMEs: a key figure to implement a model of Enterprise 2.0. itAIS 2011.* Paper presented at the VIII Conference of the Italian Chapter of AIS Information Systems: a crossroads for Organization, Management, Accounting and Engineering Viale Pola 12. Roma, Italy.

De Saulles, M. (2008). Never Too Small to Join the Party. *Information World Review, 249,* 10–12.

Epicor. (2008). *Bringing Web 2.0 to the Enterprise: Leveraging Social Computing Technologies for ERP Applications.* Epicor White Paper. Irvine, CA: Epicor.

European Commission. (2003). The new SME Definition – User guide and model declaration. *Enterprise and Industry Publication.* Retrieved November 30, 2013, from http://ec.europa.eu/enterprise/policies/sme/files/sme_definition/sme_user_guide_en.pdf

Fernandes, S., Kamienski, C., Kelner, J., Mariz, D., & Sadok, D. (2008). A stratified traffic sampling methodology for seeing the big picture. *Computer Networks, 52*(14), 2677–2689. doi:10.1016/j.comnet.2008.05.011

Gordeyeva, I. (2010). *Enterprise 2.0: theoretical foundations of social media tools influence on knowledge sharing practices in organizations.* (Master's thesis). University of Twente.

Hamburg, I., Engert, S., & Anke, P. (2007). Communities of Practice and Web 2.0 to support learning in SMEs. In Proceeding of RoEduNet. RoEduNet.

Hinchcliffe, D. (2010). Why all the fuss about Web 2.0. *Infonomics, 24*(1), 26–31.

INE. (2010), *Estudos sobre Estatísticas Estruturais das Empresas -2008.* [Internet] <http://www.ine.pt/xportal/xmain?xpid=INE&xpgid=ine_publicacoes&PUBLICACOESpub_boui=87680294&PUBLICACOEStema=55579&PUBLICACOESmodo=2>

Isaías, P., Pífano, S., & Miranda, P. (2011). Social Network Sites: Modeling the New Business-Customer Relationship. In *Social Networking and Community Behavior Modeling: Qualitative and Quantitative Measures.* Hershey, PA: IGI Global. doi:10.4018/978-1-61350-444-4.ch014

Jedd, M. (2008). Enterprise 2.0. *AIIM E-Doc Magazine, 22*(1), 26–29.

Kim, D. J., Yue, K.-B., Hall, S. P., & Gates, T. (2009). Global Diffusion of the Internet XV: Web 2.0 Technologies, Principles, and Applications: A Conceptual Framework from Technology Push and Demand Pull Perspective. *Communications of the Association for Information Systems,* (24): 657–672.

Kim, H. D., Lee, I., & Lee, C. K. (2013). Building Web 2.0 enterprises: A study of small and medium enterprises in the United States. *International Small Business Journal, 31*(2), 156–174. doi:10.1177/0266242611409785

Köhler-Krün, H. (2009). Best Practices for Implementing E2.0. *Infonomics, 23*(4), 40–45.

Levy, M. (2007). Web 2.0 Implications on Knowledge Management. *Journal of Knowledge Management, 13*(1), 120–134. doi:10.1108/13673270910931215

Levy, M., & Powell, P. (2005). *Strategies for Growth in SMEs: The Role of Information and Information Systems.* Butterworth-Heinemann.

Levy, M., Powell, P., & Yetton, P. (2001). SMEs: Aligning IS and the Strategic Context. *Journal of Information Technology, 16*(3), 133–144. doi:10.1080/02683960110063672

Lindermann, N., Valcárcel, S., Schaarschmidt, M., & von Kortzfleisch, H. (2009). SME 2.0: Roadmap towards Web 2.0-Based Open Innovation in SME-Networks–A Case Study Based Research Framework. In Information Systems–Creativity and Innovation in Small and Medium-Sized Enterprises (pp. 28-41). Springer.

Lomas, C. (2005). *7 Things you should know about Social Bookmarking.* Educause Learning Initiative.

Mañas, M. Hamburg, & Hall, T. (2011). Learning to use Web 2.0 and net collaborative practices in SMEs. In *Proceedings of International Conference on Life Long Learning for Competitiveness, Employability and Social Inclusion.* Craiova, Romania: Academic Press.

Manyika, J., Roberts, R., & Sprague, K. (2007). Eight Business Technology Trends to Watch. *The McKinsey Quarterly, 1*, 60–71.

Marshall, K. (2008). *Utilizing Web 2.0 Technology to Enhance Enterprise Knowledge Management.* Retrieved November 2, from, http://pt.scribd.com/doc/8644735/Utilizing-Web20-Technology-to-Enhance-Enterprise-Knowledge-Management

McAfee, A. (2006). Enterprise 2.0: The Dawn of Emergent Collaboration. *MIT Sloan Management Review, 47*(3), 21–28.

Newman, A., & Thomas, J. (2008). *Enterprise 2.0 Implementation*. McGraw-Hill Osborne Media.

O'Reilly, T. (2005). What Is Web 2.0? *O'Reilly Network*. Retrieved November 4, from http://oreilly.com/web2/archive/what-is-web20

Peris, M., Sperling, A., Blinn, N., Nüttgens, M., & Gehrke, N. (2011). *Participatory Design of Web 2.0 Applications in SME Networks*. Paper presented at the 24th Bled eConference eFuture: Creating Solutions for the Individual, Organisations and Society. Bled, Slovenia

Platt, M. (2007). Web 2.0 in Enterprise. *The Architecture Journal, 12*.

Serrano, N., & Torres, J. M. (2010). Web 2.0 for Practitioners. *IEEE Software, 27*(3), 11–15. doi:10.1109/MS.2010.84

Tapscott, D. (2006). *Winning with Enterprise 2.0: IT&CA research program*. New Paradigm Learning Corporation. Retrieved from http://newparadigm.com/media/Winning_with_the_Enterprise_2.0.pdf

Weyant, L., & Gardner, C. (2010). Web 2.0 Application usages: Implications for Management Education. *Journal of Business. Society & Government, 2*(2), 67–78.

ADDITIONAL READING

Alvarez, I., Cilleruelo, E., Zamanillo, I., & Zarrabeitia, E. (2012). Knowledge management practices in SME. Case study in Basque Country SME. In (Eds.) Prado, J., García, J., Comesaña J., & Fernández, A., *Industrial Engineering: Overcoming the Crisis. Book of Full Papers of the 6th International Conference on Industrial Engineering and Industrial Management*, Universidad de Vigo edn, Vigo, pp. 555-562.

Borges, B. (2009). *Marketing 2.0: Bridging The Gap Between Seller And Buyer Through Social Media Marketing*. Tucson, Arizona: Wheatmark.

Chan, K. W., Yim, C. K., Simon, S. K., & Lam, S. S. K. (2010). Is Customer Participation in Value Creation a Double-Edged Sword? Evidence from Professional Financial Services Across Cultures. *Journal of Marketing, 74*(3). doi:10.1509/jmkg.74.3.48

Cunningham, J. (2010). New workers, new workplace? Getting the balance right. *Strategic Direction, 26*(1), 5–6. doi:10.1108/02580541011009725

DiMicco, J. M., Geyer, W., Millen, D. R., Dugan, C., & Brownholtz, B. (2009). People Sensemaking and Relationship Building on an Enterprise Social Network Site. *HICSS '09: 42nd Hawaii International Conference on System Sciences,* 1-10

Engert, S., Hamburg, I., & Terstriep, J. (2011). Promoting online education for new working environments in companies. In U. Demiray, & S. Sever (Eds.), *Marketing online education programs: frameworks for promotion and communication*. Hershey, PA: Information Science Reference.

European Commission, Directorate General INFSO (2010), *Summary of the outcome of previous consultations in the area of ICT for governance and policy modelling*. Position Paper, mimeograph, 2010.

Fleck, M., Von Kaenel, A., & Meckel, M. (2010). Web 2.0 concepts, social software and business models. In I. Lee (Ed.), *Encyclopedia of E-Business Development and Management in the Global Economy* (pp. 1215–1224). Business Science Reference. doi:10.4018/978-1-61520-611-7.ch119

Gagliardi, D. (2011). Next Generation Entrepreneur: How Web 2.0 Technologies Creep into SMEs. *eChallenges e-2011 Conference Proceedings*, IIMC International Information Management Corporation, 2011

Hall, T., & Hamburg, I. (2009). Learning in social networks and Web 2.0 in SMEs' continuing vocational education. *International Journal of Web Based Communities, 5*(4), 593–607. doi:10.1504/IJWBC.2009.028092

Hodgkinson, S. (2007). *Does your enterprise need Web 2.0?* Ovum PLC Report.

Li, C., & Bernoff, J. (2008). *Groundswell: Winning in a World Transformed by Social Technologies.* Boston, Massachusetts: Harvard Business Press.

Li, Y., Lin, C., & Lai, C. (2010). Identifying influential reviewers for word-of-mouth marketing. *Electron. Commer. Rec. App, 9*(4), 294–304. doi:10.1016/j.elerap.2010.02.004

Mannonen, P., & Runonen, M. (2008). SMEs in social media. Paper presented at the *NordiCHI'08 Workshop - How Can HCI Improve Social Media Development?* Lund, Sweden, October

McAfee, A. (2009). *Enterprise 2.0: New Collaborative Tools for Your Organization's Toughest Challenges.* Harvard Business Press.

Miller, N. J., Bresser, T., & Malshe, A. (2007). Strategic networking among small businesses in small US communities. *International Small Business Journal, 25*(6), 631–665. doi:10.1177/0266242607082525

Qualman, E. (2009). *Socialnomics: How Social Media Transforms the Way We Live and Do Business.* Hoboken, New Jersey: John Wiley & Sons, Inc.

Ritchie, R. L., & Brindley, C. S. (2005). ICT adoption by SMEs: Implications for relationships and management. *New Technology, Work and Employment, 20*(3), 205–217. doi:10.1111/j.1468-005X.2005.00154.x

Rowley, J., Teahan, B., & Leeming, E. (2007). Customer community and co-creation: A case study. *Marketing Intelligence & Planning, 25*(2), 136–146. doi:10.1108/02634500710737924

Scoble, R., & Israel, S. (2006). *Naked Conversations: How Blogs Are Changing The Way Businesses Talk With Customers.* Hoboken, New Jersey: John Wiley & Sons, Inc.

Scott, D. M. (2010). *The New Rules of Marketing and PR: How to Use Social Media, Blogs, News Releases, Online Video, and Viral Marketing to Reach Buyers Directly* (2nd ed.). Hoboken, New Jersey: John Wiley & Sons, Inc.

Scullin, S. S., Fjermestad, J., & Romano, N. C. (2004). E-relationships marketing: Changes in traditional marketing as the outcome of eCRM. *Journal of Enterprise Information Management, 17*, 410–415. doi:10.1108/17410390410566698

Simpson, M., & Docherty, A. (2004). E-commerce adoption support and advice for UK SMEs. *Journal of Small Business and Enterprise Development, 11*(3), 315–328. doi:10.1108/14626000410551573

Stocker, A., Dosinger, G., Us Saeed, A., & Wagner, C. (2007). The three pillars of 'Corporate Web 2.0': A model for definition. *Proceedings of I-Media'07 and I-Semantics'07*, Graz, Austria, September.

Vascellaro, J. E. (2007, August 28). Social Networking Goes Professional: Doctors, Salesmen, Executives Turn to New Sites to Consult, Commiserate With Peers, Weeding Out Impostors. *Wall Street Journal*, Washington, D.C.

Wang, M. (2009). Integrating organizational, social and individual perspectives in Web 2.0-based workplace learning. *Information Systems Frontiers.*

Zhan, J., Loh, H. T., & Liu, Y. (2009). Gather customer concerns from online product reviews - A text summarization approach. *Expert Systems with Applications, 36*(2), 2107–2115. doi:10.1016/j.eswa.2007.12.039

KEY TERMS AND DEFINITIONS

Business Strategy: Concerns the approaches and means that companies employ to attain their objective. It is similar to a business plan for the long-term.

Enterprise 2.0: Refers to the use of Web 2.0 technologies, tools and principles in enterprises.

Small and Medium Enterprises: Small and Medium Enterprises (SMEs) is the denomination of companies that have smaller dimensions. The standards vary from country to country, despite a general definition. This title can be given according to number of employees, revenue and other criteria.

SME 2.0: It derives from the term E2.0, but in this case it is related solely to the use of Web 2.0 inside Small and Medium enterprises.

Social Technologies: Can also be referred to as collaborative technologies and include all the applications, features and tools that allow users to create, edit and share content online, usually in numerous formats.

Web 2.0: Also known as Social Web or Collaborative Web, consists in a set of revolutionary, user-centred principles of interaction, collaboration, user content and openness; and the entirety of technologies and tools that derive from and support them.

Chapter 10
Visual IHME:
Co–Designing Meaningful Places for Sustainability

Marketta Niemelä
*VTT Technical Research Centre of Finland,
Finland*

Antti Tammela
*VTT Technical Research Centre of Finland,
Finland*

Tuomo Kivinen
*VTT Technical Research Centre of Finland,
Finland*

Veikko Ikonen
*VTT Technical Research Centre of Finland,
Finland*

Minna Kulju
*VTT Technical Research Centre of Finland,
Finland*

Heidi Korhonen
*VTT Technical Research Centre of Finland,
Finland*

ABSTRACT

In the context of human-driven design and environmental sustainability, the authors have developed a computer-based platform concept for studying and co-designing places (i.e. socially meaningful locations). The Visual IHME platform provides a photo-based, interactive spherical panorama environment with a set of co-creative interaction tools such as discussion boards, questionnaires, and polls on-screen. All creative content can be pinned to specific spatial spots on the image. In a preliminary end-user evaluation of the concept demonstration, the authors found that the participants valued the co-design platform, though many doubted the role of this kind of social technology in terms of real impact on issues that are important to people. They discuss how co-design platforms like Visual IHME can have an impact on environmental sustainability and the evolving role of human-computer interaction research and design in addressing sustainability problems.

DOI: 10.4018/978-1-4666-6228-5.ch010

INTRODUCTION

Human-driven design builds on understanding people and deploying this knowledge in design. From this background, we have developed a computer-based platform concept, Visual IHME, for studying and co-designing places, i.e. understanding, co-creating and sharing meanings bound to or growing from specific locations. The second part of the platform name comes from Finnish: IHME is an acronym for 'IHmislähtöiset MEnetelmät' (human-driven methods). This reflects our aim to develop and apply technology from a deeply human point of view. In the end, our aim is to study how this kind of human-computer interaction application could work for environmental sustainability – as a persuasive technology yet taking seriously the criticism and constructive suggestions raised by a number of researchers (e.g. DiSalvo & al., 2010; Dourish, 2010; Brynjarsdóttir & al., 2012; Mankoff, 2012). In this article, we describe the platform as a concept demonstration and discuss the theoretical backgrounds to why and how co-design could support sustainable behaviour.

Co-design refers to a collective and creative design approach in which people who are not trained in design create together with designers and researchers (Sanders & Stappers, 2008). In the last decade, a number of different computer-based collaborative platforms have emerged that could be applied to co-designing places. For instance, there are platforms that build on abstract communicative features of social media (e.g. IdeaMarket in Holtzblatt & Tierney, 2011; Owela in Näkki & Antikainen, 2008; Kaasinen & al., 2012), and those that, similarly to Visual IHME, aim to provide users specifically with location-based co-design. Some platforms are based on map portrayals (e.g. Urban Mediator in Botero & Saad-Sulonen, 2008) or represent the environment as virtual reality (e.g. StringCVE in Moloney & Amor, 2003). Some focus on creating meaning by enabling users to share, comment on and re-mix their experiences with rich multimedia elements (but in abstract social space only) (e.g. SparkInfo

in Hwang & Holtzman, 2012). Yet another way to co-design places would be augmented reality, which allows virtual objects to be positioned 'on' real environments (e.g. Oksman & al., 2012).

When trying to understand and design a *place* with meaning, experiences and personal attachment and not just mere *space* as a physical and geometrical opportunity (for a deeper analysis, see Harrison & Dourish, 1996; Dourish 2006), we need to focus on supporting the social meaning-making that makes spaces places. It is for this purpose that we have developed Visual IHME, a platform that aims to awaken and encourage people's associations and stories attached to locations by showing a realistic image of the location (unlike map- or VR-based tools) and letting people concretely pin their acts of co-creation to any spot in the place that is meaningful to them (unlike social media tools): a building, a park, or an event that took place in the park. Visual IHME co-design can also be done fully remotely with any computing device with an Internet connection and browser (unlike augmented reality, which requires a mobile device with a camera).

Our hypothesis is that realistic, photo-based platforms such as Visual IHME allow studying, understanding and designing of places and related experiences and social meanings in a usable and rich manner that promotes sustainability.

We start this article by reviewing recent work on human-computer interaction (HCI) for sustainability and the resulting insights into the question of how more sustainable behaviour could be achieved with the help of information and communication technologies, and interaction design. We then present the Visual IHME platform concept with its co-design features and the technical implementation of the current demonstration. We proceed to presenting the results of a preliminary end-user evaluation we have carried out to study the user experience and perceived usefulness of the platform. Finally, we discuss how to apply the platform as an interactive, persuasive technology for sustainability.

SUSTAINABLE HUMAN-COMPUTER INTERACTION

There has been growing interest among HCI researchers and designers in promoting sustainability with interaction design in the last few years. A number of workshops, articles and special issue journals have been published.

The Relationship between Sustainability and HCI Design

In regard to sustainability, the role and responsibility of HCI as a field and as individual practitioners can be seen as twofold: first, HCI can address sustainability in design, and second, HCI can promote sustainability through design (Mankoff & al., 2007). *Sustainability in design* is related to how to take account of sustainability as part of the material design of products. This domain includes issues such as energy use, device re-use, reduction and waste, and enabling sharing of devices or energy resources.

Sustainability through design is about supporting sustainable lifestyles and decision-making through the design of technology. Information technologies can form an effective channel for intervention in the everyday decisions and mind-sets of people and thus cause a behavioural shift towards sustainability (Mankoff & al., 2007). Interactive technologies can have an impact at the level of individuals, groups or society. At the individual level, interactive technologies could make abstract environmental data more concrete and thus usable for making behavioural decisions. At group level, HCI could promote the design of systems and interactions that involve groups of people, e.g. to support public deliberation and decision-making around sustainability. One example is car-pooling systems. A longer-term, societal-level goal for interactive technologies would be to support cultural change and development of networks and social movements for sustainability.

Mankoff et al. (2007) appear to suggest that environmental sustainability can be seen as a multifaceted and fruitful point of view, albeit still 'extra' to the core of HCI. Blevis (2007) takes a stricter stance: sustainability can and should be a central focus of interaction design. This perspective is called *Sustainable Interaction Design* (SID). According to Blevis, design should denote and account for its effects on the environment and sustainable behaviours by assessing particular interaction design cases in terms of forms of use, reuse and disposal. For instance, designers should consider whether the design makes use of recycled physical materials or provides for their future recycling, and whether the design allows sharing of physical materials by many people for maximal use.

Can HCI Produce Sustainability?

As design cases and applications of sustainable HCI have emerged, researchers have started to review and critically investigate the results in the field. DiSalvo et al. (2010) provide an empirical analysis of how sustainable HCI has so far defined itself as a research field. They have identified established genres, key unrecognised intellectual differences and emerging issues in the field. They base their observations on a corpus of 83 programmatic statements and articles on the topic.

According to their analysis, the major theme in the sustainable HCI literature is *persuasive technology* (about 45% of the corpus), which refers to systems that attempt to convince users to behave in a more sustainable way. Another main topic is *ambient awareness* (approx. 25% of the corpus), which, as a theme, is close to persuasive technology, making users aware of some aspect of the sustainability of their behaviour or qualities of the environment associated with issues of sustainability. The aim of the papers on *sustainable interaction design* (approx. 10%) is to fundamentally rethink the methods of HCI in order to address sustainability. One way to achieve this is to focus on material effects such as resource wastage and pollution as a result of design. *Formative user studies* (approx. 15%) focus on understanding how users think about and approach sustainability as a first step of new design. Users are seen as embedded in social and cultural systems that greatly impact their choices and attitudes to sustainable behaviour. Yet another genre is *pervasive and participatory sensing* (approx. 22%), which uses sensors to monitor and report on usually adverse environmental conditions. The implicit goal is to use the data to change the conditions. In HCI, the data are often collected by non-expert individuals; for instance, data about road surface conditions is collected by enthusiastic cyclists who know and ride different routes.

In their review, DiSalvo et al. (2010) recognise that there are some ambiguous presumptions and aims in HCI for sustainability. A main inconsistency is that HCI itself supports a wasteful rapid obsolescence cycle of IT products. Another issue is related to the user, who can be given contradictory roles in sustainable HCI. According to some papers, it is user behaviour that is causing environmental problems and that behaviour therefore needs to change, whilst other articles see users more as an opportunity for change. Another controversial issue is that some researchers see that the well-known HCI method packages map poorly to sustainability because they do not recognise the complexity of the sustainability problem or because the evaluation of long-term and systemic effects is not properly dealt with in HCI. Research and design in HCI are not well linked to political and societal discussion, although this discussion greatly impacts on our conceptions of sustainability (e.g. which behaviour is sustainable and which is not) as well as opportunities that we see and are able to implement for sustainability. Several researchers argue for a need to design systems to support political activism and thus to be able to connect HCI to the political level.

Overall, sustainable HCI research should move on to extend its early, already established, results to new, uncovered fields such as how to address collectives and regional and national contexts in addition to individual consumers, or how HCI can help users to become experts on sustainability on their own terms (DiSalvo & al., 2010). HCI should also draw on the broader literature of sustainability, which is highly interdisciplinary in nature.

Brynjarsdóttir et al. (2012) provide a further critical analysis on persuasive technologies, the main genre in sustainable HCI (DiSalvo & al., 2010). Based on persuasive sustainability research from 2009-2011, the researchers have analysed the framing of persuasion within sustainable HCI and its impact, as well as the future needs for sustainable HCI. According to their results, the framing of persuasive sustainability has failed, and that has led to the failure of persuasive technologies in regard to improving sustainability. For instance, persuasive technologies focus on impact on a scale that is too small, such as changes in individual consumption and aiming for incremental change instead of systemic change. Persuasive technologies also tend to put the user in the role of non-expert, whilst designers manifest the expertise on sustainability. This is not necessarily the case, especially when it comes to opportunities of sustainable behaviour in the user's daily life.

Suggestions for Remediation of Sustainable HCI

Three suggestions can be considered to overcome the shortcomings of persuasive sustainability (Brynjarsdóttir & al., 2012). First, the understanding of persuasion should be broadened: persuasion is a process for shaping people's beliefs and actions, a rhetoric act rather than a coercion technique. Second, users should be included in the design process. Participatory design can maintain or increase the sense of agency in users and make the designs closer to the definition of sustainability that users enact in daily life, thus leading to more acceptable, satisfying and effective designs. Third, social relationships and realities beyond the individual should be taken into account. Persuasive sustainability should also consider community, political and infrastructural involvement.

Furthermore, Brynjarsdóttir et al. (2012) suggest that HCI should consider alternative approaches that could be taken by encouraging users to reflect on what it actually means to be sustainable, instead of sustainability being prescribed for them by the designer. The focus should also be shifted from individual behaviour (e.g. home energy consumption) to broader sociocultural practices that make the context of the behaviour.

Other researchers are in line with these findings. For instance, Mankoff (2012) points out that current HCI for sustainability focuses on issues that are too 'small', e.g. reducing energy use at home. Indirect impact may work better. HCI should contribute to science, education, politics and mobilisation of people to collaborate for sustainability. What is needed is locally grounded, socially focused solutions and attempts to decentralise, increase sharing and encourage environmentality. Dourish (2010) examines HCI for sustainability in the context of ecological politics and the political economy of environmentalism and suggests that HCI needs to take the question of scales more seriously. He suggests that HCI should work not on "connecting people *to* their actions and their consequences" but on "connecting people *through* their actions and their consequences" (2010, p. 7). This approach would enable individual users to identify others with similar thinking and join groups to pursue sustainability in their own ways.

Summarising the insight above, it seems that in order to promote sustainable behaviour in the field of HCI, we first need not to forget the complexity of the problem of sustainability. It is an issue of the individual user's behaviour as well as sociocultural practices and opportunities that societal and political decisions afford individuals to take in their daily life. To overcome this, in part at least, users need to be involved in design: they are the experts in the way sociocultural reality is manifested in their everyday activities. The users need to be given tools for reflection and meaning to make sustainability for themselves.

Our proposed solution here is to design tools and interaction for collaborating and coming together around design. Co-design is a process in which people examine and create together within a given theme (Sanders & Stappers, 2008). The results of co-design are based on a shared understanding growing during the process as participants approach the theme together but all from their own personal viewpoints. ICT and interactive technology for co-design sounds like an interesting option, since supporting co-design appears to be in line with the suggestions made above (Brynjarsdóttir & al., 2012; DiSalvo & al., 2010; Dourish, 2010; Mankoff, 2012). Visual IHME is a platform concept that seeks to encourage co-design for sustainability.

VISUAL IHME CO-DESIGN PLATFORM AND CONCEPT

The Visual IHME platform for co-designing places has been developed in two phases. Originally, the platform was built as a virtual travel application demonstrator for a travel agency (Ikonen & al., 2010). The virtual travel application enabled users to move virtually in a panoramic environment projected on a big screen, receive detailed information from various services or other points of interests related to the location, leave comments or guidance for the other travellers or service providers and receive online or recorded video guidance related to the specific location.

Later, we developed the application to provide better support for co-ideating and research purposes. We have integrated different co-design features, familiar from social media, into the panorama of Visual IHME. Simultaneously, based on our attempts to understand the psychology of sustainable behaviour (as part of our human-driven design approach), we have elaborated on the idea that the platform as an enabler for shared meaning-making related to places could also lead to increased sustainability by making the place more meaningful and thus valued by the users. To encourage joint meaning-making, Visual IHME should include a variety of co-design features to attract different people from different backgrounds to participate.

The current demonstration of Visual IHME includes an image of a real space as a spherical panorama picture that can be shown on a website on any ICT device (desktop computer, tablet or mobile device). The platform thus allows participation regardless of the user's location or time, as long as the user has access to the Internet. For user involvement, the platform includes several interactive co-design features, e.g. discussion. These functionalities allow the users to share and reflect on their experience and desires in regard to the place. Visual IHME thus works as a platform for users to: 1) contribute to the design of a place, 2) share experiences, associations and ideas in regard to the place, and 3) grow a shared understanding and meaning of the place.

Co-Design Platform Concept Demonstration

The end-user interface of the Visual IHME demonstration shows a 'window' to a spherical panorama picture that covers an environment in all directions from the point the picture is taken. The window can be turned around with a mouse, or a finger if a touch screen is used. The user can move from one panorama picture to another by clicking on an arrow button (Figure 1 bottom left). Sound can be added to the panorama to increase realism. Other types of files such as images, photographs and texts can also be attached to the panorama picture.

The current set of co-design features includes comment/discussion boards (either pinned to a location or positioned beside the image) with 'thumb up/down' voting, questionnaires and polls.

In the current demonstration system, any user can start a new discussion topic, but only users with editor rights can create questionnaires. The gathered data are stored in a database in the Visual IHME software. The data can be exported and analysed in Microsoft Excel format. Future needs concern developing more co-design features, an elaborated user right system and analysis tools to handle the collected data.

Technical Implementation of the Demonstration

The Visual IHME demonstration runs on a server that is connected to suitable client devices through a secured Internet connection. The basic components of the Visual IHME system are 1) a file system for the panorama image files, 2) a database for user, scene and panorama data, 3) software for viewing the images on the server and 4) clients, which can be any device supporting Flash or HTML5 (Figure 2).

Visual IHME runs on an Apache 2 HTTP server on the Ubuntu operating system. In addition to the basic HTTP server software, PHP5, SSL and SQLite modules have to be installed and configured. SSL is used for securing the communication between the user and the server as the conducted research may include confidential data as well as securing the users' demographic data and passwords.

The web pages are implemented using HTML5 and JavaScript with Ajax calls to PHP scripts for updating the data without refreshing the pages. All the data, except the photos, are currently saved in a SQLite database (soon to be replaced with MongoDB for its capability to handle more data) for easy access and manipulation. The photos are saved as files in the server's file system and the database only has references to them. A jQuery JavaScript library is also used for manipulation, event handling and animation throughout the pages.

Figure 1. Screen shot of the Visual IHME end-user interface

The viewing of the interactive panoramas is handled by krpano Viewer, which is a high-performance viewer for panoramic images and is available for both HTML5 and Flash. The links, hotspots, topics and extra content on top of the panoramas are all dynamically added with scripts.

A new environment is added to the platform with four steps. The first step is to take the photos that make up the spherical panorama used as backgrounds for the scenes. This can be done with a DSLR camera with a wide-angle lens mounted on a panoramic head and a tripod. The photos are taken using manual mode with a locked aperture, white balance and exposure and saved in RAW format to enable good post-processing capabilities. The second step is to process and save the images in the correct format for panorama stitching software.

In the third step, the processed images are fed into the stitching software, which outputs a spherical panorama. Currently, Autopano Giga from Kolor is used for image stitching as it yields the best final results. In the fourth step the stitched spherical panorama has to be split into parts for

Figure 2. Basic technical components of Visual IHME

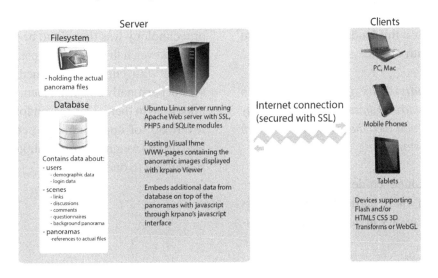

viewing in web browsers. This is handled by krpano Tools, which has ready-made droplets for converting spherical panoramas into cubical ones. Krpano Tools outputs the necessary pieces (left, front, right, back, up and down) for uploading to the Visual IHME server. After the panorama has been uploaded to the server, it is available for use in co-design.

Preliminary User Evaluation

We have carried out a small-scale end-user evaluation of the Visual IHME demonstration with ten individual adult volunteers of different ages (seven female, three male). The evaluation was initially to test the user experience of the co-design platform and to gather information about the perceived usefulness of the co-design features and the platform concept itself.

In the evaluation, each participant was first given a brief demonstration of the platform on a tablet computer: how the interaction took place and how to use the co-design features. After the demonstration and hands-on testing, the participant filled in a questionnaire about her/his user experience, further expectations and development ideas for the platform. The participant was also interviewed briefly to deepen and clarify her/his answers.

Visual IHME received positive feedback from all of the participants. Nine of the participants said that they would use this kind of tool to share and develop ideas with others.

Like-minded individuals gather together to exchange and share opinions. Somebody may come up with a good idea that is useful. Through networks things start going.

The most valued co-design features were 'thumb up/down' (8/10 participants thought this function was necessary in the interface), discus-sions (7/10), ability to create new discussion topics (6/10) and questionnaires (6/10) (Figure 3).

In general, the participants thought the role of the platform was to support the collection of ideas from citizens or consumers and elaborating on them together with designers. This kind of co-design tool would even increase social equality because it would enable more people to engage in the design, taking into account that the tool itself requires certain technical facilities and skills.

Everyone has the opportunity to participate equally in the design and make his voice heard, although not everyone necessarily has the technical equipment to enable this.

We received some ideas of how and where Visual IHME could be applied when, for instance, designing land use, traffic or telecommunications networks, and designing for equality and accessibility (e.g. accessibility in a city for disabled inhabitants as one stakeholder group in the co-design process).

We also probed the importance of social media and user involvement in service and technology development for the participants with a few questions (Fig. 4). The participants found social media and the Internet to be useful tools to involve users in design and development, especially when developing new services or technology. In general, involving users in the development of new services or technology was thought to be important.

However, half of the participants had a conception that with (current) social media services, they are not personally able to influence issues that are important to them. One reason for this may be an 'overload' of opportunities to comment, which leads to less weighted participation and comments. According to one participant,

Figure 3. Perceived usefulness of the co-design features available in Visual IHME at the time of the evaluation. The number indicates how many participants (of the ten) found the selected feature useful

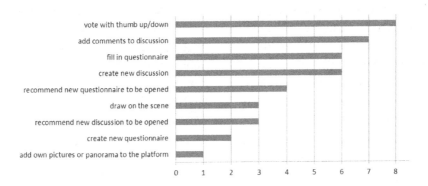

When you need to be commenting all the time, you just throw ideas about and never concentrate on anything.

In line with Dourish (2010), we take the participants' expressed doubt about making a difference through social media as a hint that better tools and methods are needed. Even in the modern world penetrated with communication technologies and possibilities for involvement, there is still plenty of space to develop virtual or technology-mediated platforms that can truly attract and empower people to effectively focus their efforts on influencing the conditions in which they live.

DISCUSSION

Visual IHME as a Tool for Promoting Sustainable Behaviour

The attempts to promote sustainability by means of HCI, especially with applications of persuasive technology, have encountered criticism for downscaling and even misunderstanding the efforts that are required to have a real impact on environmental sustainability (Brynjarsdóttir & al., 2012; DiSalvo & al., 2010; Dourish, 2010; Mankoff, 2012). Why would our co-design platform Visual IHME do better in this case?

Figure 4. Responses concerning the meaning of social media and user involvement in service and technology development. The bars indicate the average of responses on a scale of 1 (Completely disagree) to 4 (Completely agree)

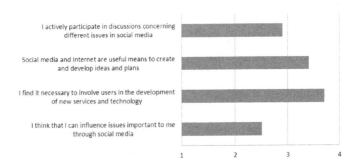

Our argumentation is based on findings from environmental psychology and thinking that the 'value' and 'meaning' people give to things make them care more about them and, thus, behave in a more sustainable way in regard to those things. For instance, Oehlberg et al. (2007) have argued for "sustainability through meaning": products surrounded by rich stories can become more meaningful to their owners and thus more likely to be retained beyond their initial use. Thus, more sustainable behaviour can be fostered through the creation of meaning attached to consumer goods. Increased meaning around products, achieved through stories, will encourage consumers to develop deeper connections with their material possessions, resulting in increased instrumental materialism and more sustainable behaviour as they consume fewer but more meaningful objects. In line with this, other researchers (e.g. Blevis, 2007; Jung & al., 2011) have discussed the "heirloom status", an immaterial quality of certain goods that makes them appealing to the owners for long-term preservation.

If goods can have this kind of sustainability-promoting appeal from shared stories and meanings, can a place have that too? Apparently it can: the more history, shared stories and identity of the community a place has, especially with positive emotional content, the more difficult it is to rebuild it. The stories for a place need not be existing ones but can be created in a co-design process. Co-design is a process of meaning-making. As Sanders and Stappers (2008) put it, "we are moving from the design of categories of 'products' to designing for people's purposes". Co-design is expressing, sharing and collectively creating those purposes – things in which people find value and meaning.

In short, we claim that the photo-real, interactive, explorable image of an environment in Visual IHME can, in the location-based co-design process that the platform supports, become a focus or centre of the participants' purposes and meanings. The environment can thus become meaningful and even emotionally attached, which would be a step towards sustainability.

Visual IHME enables more than just the socio-psychological process of place-centred meaning-making however. Real promotion of sustainability requires action by collectives and thus we should focus "not on connecting people *to* their actions and their consequences, but on connecting people *through* their actions and their consequences" (Dourish, 2010, 7, italics original). Sustainability is not an issue of consumer behaviour alone, nor is it an issue of the designer's decisions alone. Sustainability requires communication and negotiation between different stakeholder groups around the place. Visual IHME with its space-related, interactive co-design tools can provide a common, easy-to-use platform to carry this communication and negotiation for co-created value between the stakeholder groups. In this way, the platform can also allow designers to understand better the impacts of their design decisions.

Making Visual IHME a tool to promote sustainability still requires much more development. The current co-design features do not allow good sharing and co-development of rich stories about and around a place, nor talking about developing heirloom status. More elaborated co-design features need to be built, such as attracting opportunities to 'share your story', such as tasks and visualisations that could mediate the psychological and social meanings of the place to the users.

The Evolving Role of HCI for Sustainability

A critical point we still want to discuss here is the embedded "belief of technology" in HCI for sustainability. DiSalvo et al. (2010) phrased the problem in the following way (italics original):

[Researchers raise] serious issues about how belief in technology as a neutral solution itself may be implicated in the problems of sustainability. However, a move away from an emphasis on

technology design, or even from research aimed primarily at informing such design, presents challenges to HCI as a field — if technology is not the point, then what becomes the work of sustainable H'C'I? (p. 1981)

We believe that with Visual IHME, we have partly succeeded in answering this question. We see that to have an impact on complex, social and networked issues such as sustainability, HCI should develop from an approach of "design for interaction *with* computer" towards "design for interaction *on* computer". This means that HCI should aim to study the possibilities of ICT for interaction and overcome its limitations, whether the interaction is between individuals, at the level of society or in a political context. This would require widening of the HCI design concept of 'task' or 'goal': an individual's goal when using Facebook, for instance, is not to 'like' the status updates she finds likable but to show her existence to her peer group, build her identity, appear friendly to some friends or show interest in or encourage some actors.

Another way to address the problem of HCI for sustainability is to put technology at the centre of sustainability design. For example, Whitehouse and Patrignani (2013) introduce a concept of *slow tech* that borrows its contents from the slow food movement. Slow tech refers to good, fair and clean ICT – technology designed around human beings that focuses on equality, equity, and social and employment conditions, and takes the entire life cycle of the technology from design and development to use and recycling into consideration. Thus, the technology itself, and HCI accordingly, becomes a partial solution to the sustainability challenge. A major difficulty of this approach may be in ensuring that the technology really is sustainable to the core. The production chains and networks underlying ICT products may be extremely complex and difficult to trace.

In the future, we will see Visual IHME and similar co-design tools as a natural and even necessary part of the design of places to enable user involvement, idea sharing and social meaning-making, all important in design. Taking inspiration from the genre classification of persuasive technologies (DiSalvo & al., 2010), Visual IHME could also be used as a tool for 'formative user studies' to understand user-driven sustainability of places (what people see as sustainable in a place). Visual IHME could also serves as a platform for 'participatory sensing' as it provides interactive tools for users to collect location-related information, e.g. about the subjective experience of the aesthetics of a place. More importantly, however, right now Visual IHME represents a persuasive technology, but, in the other meaning of persuasion, it denotes a rhetoric act (cf. the section *Suggestions for remediation of sustainable HCI*; for a deeper discussion, see Brynjarsdóttir & al., 2012). Visual IHME is a statement in itself that user involvement and collaborative methods in designing places is important, and sustainability can be approached indirectly in this way.

CONCLUSION

Our intention is to develop Visual IHME into a tool for sharing and co-creating meanings, experiences and personal bonds that make spaces into places. Our ultimate focus with Visual IHME is sustainability through design (Mankoff, 2007), in terms of environmental well-being. Faced with the global challenges related to the ecology and climate, we are not alone in the battle, as there are many sustainability-promoting activities in the HCI field (see, for example, the comprehensive review of DiSalvo & al., 2010). ICT-based co-design tools have great potential to address sustainability as they utilise as well as extend social interaction and reality. After all, sustainability is first and foremost a social and cultural challenge. The role of technology and HCI is then to support the social and cultural change towards solutions.

ACKNOWLEDGMENT

This chapter was made possible by SHAPE (Shaping Markets for Sustainability), a joint research project coordinated by VTT and carried out by VTT, MTT, the University of Helsinki, Aalto University and Demos Helsinki. SHAPE is funded by Tekes (the Finnish Funding Agency for Technology and Innovation), the research organisations and participating companies.

REFERENCES

Blevis, E. (2007). Sustainable interaction design: invention & disposal, renewal & reuse. In *Proceedings of the SIGCHI Conference on Human Factors in Computing Systems* (pp. 503-512). New York, NY: ACM.

Botero, A., & Saad-Sulonen, J. (2008). Co-designing for new city-citizen interaction possibilities: Weaving prototypes and interventions in the design and development of Urban Mediator. In *Proceedings of Participatory Design Conference 2008* (pp. 266-269). Bloomington, IN: Academic Press.

Brynjarsdóttir, H., Håkansson, M., Pierce, J., Baumer, E., DiSalvo, C., & Sengers, P. (2012). Sustainability unpersuaded: how persuasion narrows our vision of sustainability. In *Proceedings of the SIGCHI Conference on Human Factors in Computing Systems* (pp. 947-956). New York, NY: ACM.

DiSalvo, C., Sengers, P., & Brynjarsdóttir, H. (2010). Mapping the landscape of sustainable HCI. In *Proceedings of the SIGCHI Conference on Human Factors in Computing Systems* (pp. 1975-1984). New York, NY: ACM.

Dourish, P. (2006). Re-space-ing place: place and space ten years on. In *Proceedings of the 2006 20th anniversary conference on Computer supported cooperative work* (pp. 299-308). New York, NY: ACM.

Dourish, P. (2010). HCI and environmental sustainability: the politics of design and the design of politics. In *Proceedings of the 8th ACM Conference on Designing Interactive Systems* (pp. 1-10).). New York, NY: ACM.

Harrison, S., & Dourish, P. (1996). Re-place-ing space: the roles of space and place in collaborative systems. In *Proceedings of the 1996 ACM conference on Computer supported cooperative work* (pp. 67-76). New York, NY: ACM.

Holtzblatt, L., & Tierney, M. L. (2011). Measuring the effectiveness of social media on an innovation process. In *Extended Abstracts on Human Factors in Computing Systems* (CHI '11) (pp. 697-712). New York, NY: ACM.

Hwang, J. Y., & Holtzman, H. (2012). SparkInfo: designing a social space for co-creation of audiovisual elements and multimedia comments. In *Extended Abstracts on Human Factors in Computing Systems* (CHI '12) (pp. 1559-1564). New York, NY: ACM.

Ikonen, V., Hakulinen, J., Kivinen, T., Aloja, M., Hokkanen, L., Ruutikainen, P., et al. (2010). IHME = Miracle - Make, Imagine and Research Applications for Computerised Living Environments. In *Proceedings of the 14th International Academic MindTrek Conference: Envisioning Future Media Environments* (pp. 3-6). New York, NY: ACM.

Jung, H., Bardzell, S., Blevis, E., Pierce, J., & Stolterman, E. (2011). How deep is your love: deep narratives of ensoulment and heirloom status. *International Journal of Design*, 5(1), 59–71.

Kaasinen, E., Koskela-Huotari, K., Ikonen, V., Niemelä, M., & Näkki, P. (2012). Three approaches to co-creating services with users. In *Proceedings 4th International Conference on Applied Human Factors and Ergonomics (AHFE)*. Stoughton, WI: USA Publishing.

Mankoff, J. (2012). HCI and sustainability: a tale of two motivations. *Interactions (New York, N.Y.)*, *19*(3), 16–19. doi:10.1145/2168931.2168937

Mankoff, J. C., Blevis, E., Borning, A., Friedman, B., Fussell, S. R., Hasbrouck, J., et al. (2007). Environmental sustainability and interaction. In *Proceedings of CHI EA '07 CHI '07 Extended Abstracts on Human Factors in Computing Systems* (pp. 2121-2124). New York, NY: ACM.

Moloney, J., & Amor, R. (2003). StringCVE: Advances in a game engine-based collaborative virtual environment for architectural design. In *Proceedings of 2nd conference on Construction Applications of Virtual Reality* (pp. 24-26). Academic Press.

Näkki, P., & Antikainen, M. (2008). Online tools for co-design: user involvement through the innovation process. In A. Karahasanovic & A. Følstad, (Eds.), The NordiCHI 2008 Workshops: New Approaches to Requirements Elicitation & How Can HCI Improve Social Media Development? (pp. 92-97). Trondheim: Tapir akademisk forlag.

Oehlberg, L., Aipperspach, R., & Jeffery, S. R. (2007). *Sustainability through meaning: providing information to promote meaningful products*. Paper presented at Ubicomp 2007. Innsbruck, Austria.

Oksman, V., Siltanen, S., & Ainasoja, M. (2012). User participation in co-creative services: developing virtual and augmented reality tools for do-it-yourself home design. In *Proceeding of the 16th International Academic MindTrek Conference* (pp. 229-230). New York, NY: ACM.

Sanders, E., & Stappers, P. J. (2008). Co-creation and the new landscapes of design. *CoDesign: International Journal of CoCreation in Design and the Arts*, *4*(1), 5–18. doi:10.1080/15710880701875068

Whitehouse, D., & Patrignani, N. (2013). From slow food to slow tech: a reflection paper. In *Proceedings of the IADIS International conferences: Interfaces and Human Computer Interaction 2013*. IADIS.

ADDITIONAL READING

Axelrod, L. J., & Lehman, D. R. (1993). Responding to environmental concerns: What factors guide individual action? *Journal of Environmental Psychology*, *13*, 149–159. doi:10.1016/S0272-4944(05)80147-1

Bechtel, R. B., & Churchman, A. (Eds.). (2002). *Handbook of environmental psychology*. New York: Wiley.

Bradwell, P., & Marr, S. (2008). *Making the most of collaboration: an international survey of public service co-design*. London: Demos.

Braund, P., & Schwittay, A. (2006). The Missing Piece: Human Driven Design and Research in ICT and Development. In *Proceedings of the International Conference on Information and Communications Technologies and Development* (pp. 2-10).

Buur, J., & Larsen, H. (2010). The quality of conversations in participatory innovation. *CoDesign: International Journal of CoCreation in Design and the Arts*, *6*(3), 121–138. doi:10.1080/15710 882.2010.533185

Friedrich, P. (2013). *Web-based co-design: Social media tools to enhance user-centred design and innovation processes*. Doctoral dissertation. VTT Science 34. Kuopio, Finland: Kopijyvä Oy. http://www.vtt.fi/inf/pdf/science/2013/S34.pdf

Grönroos, C. (2011). Value co-creation in service logic. A critical analysis. *Marketing Theory*, *11*(3), 279–301. doi:10.1177/1470593111408177

Hallnäs, L., & Redström, J. (2001). Slow Technology: Designing for Reflection. *Personal and Ubiquitous Computing, 5*(3), 201–212. doi:10.1007/PL00000019

Kals, E., & Mays, J. (2002). Sustainable development and emotions. In P. Schmuck, & P. W. Schultz (Eds.), *Psychology of sustainable development* (pp. 97–122). Dordrecht, Netherlands: Kluwer Academic. doi:10.1007/978-1-4615-0995-0_6

Kyle, G. T., Graefe, A. R., & Manning, R. E. (2004). Effects of place attachment on users' perceptions of social and environmental conditions in a natural setting. *Journal of Environmental Psychology, 24*, 213–225. doi:10.1016/j.jenvp.2003.12.006

Leikas, J. (2009). *Life-Based Design - A holistic approach to designing human-technology interaction*. Doctoral Dissertation. VTT Publications 726. Helsinki, Finland: Edita Prima Oy. http://www.vtt.fi/inf/pdf/publications/2009/P726.pdf

Mattelmäki, T., Brandt, E., & Vaajakallio, K. (2011). On Designing open ended interpretations for collaborative exploration. *CoDesign Journal, 7*(2), 79–93. doi:10.1080/15710882.2011.609891

Mattelmäki, T., & Sleeswijk Visser, F. (2011). Lost In Co-X: Interpretations Of Co-Design And Co-Creation. In *Proceedings of the 4th World Conference on Design Research*, Delft, the Netherlands.

McKenzie-Mohr, D. (2000). Fostering sustainable behavior through community-based social marketing. *The American Psychologist, 55*, 531–537. doi:10.1037/0003-066X.55.5.531 PMID:10842434

Olli, E., Grendstad, G., & Wollebaek, D. (2001). Correlates of environmental behaviors: Bringing back social context. *Environment and Behavior, 33*, 181–208. doi:10.1177/00139160121972945

Patrignani, N., & Whitehouse, D. (2013). *Slow Tech: Towards Good, Clean and Fair ICT*. Paper presented at ETHICOMP 2013, Kolding, Denmark, 12-14 June 2013.

Prahalad, C. K., & Ramaswamy, V. (2004). Co-creation Experiences: The New Practice in Value Creation. *Journal of Interactive Marketing, 18*(3), 5–14. doi:10.1002/dir.20015

Saariluoma, P., Heinilä, J., Kuisma, E., Leikas, J., Vilpponen, H., & Ylikauppila, M. (2013). Designing technology for positive solitude. *Modern Behavioral Science, 1*(1).

Sanders, E. B.-N., Brandt, E., & Binder, T. (2010). A framework for organizing the tools and techniques of participatory design. In *Proceedings of the 11th Biennial Participatory Design Conference* (pp. 195-198). New York, NY, USA: ACM.

Stedman, R. (2002). Toward a social psychology of place: Predicting behavior from place-based cognitions, attitude, and identity. *Environment and Behavior, 34*, 561–581. doi:10.1177/0013916502034005001

Vanattenhoven, J., & Jans, G. (2007). Enhancing Social Interaction and User Participation in the Development of Social Applications. Paper presented in the workshop Supporting non-professional users in the new media landscape, *Conference on Human Factors in Computing Systems*, April 28 – May 3, 2007. San Jose, USA.

Vaske, J. J., & Kobrin, K. C. (2001). Place attachment and environmentally responsible behavior. *The Journal of Environmental Education, 32*(4), 16–21. doi:10.1080/00958960109598658

Von Schomberg, R. (Ed.). (2011). *Towards Responsible Research and Innovation in the Information and Communication Technologies and Security Technologies Fields*, European Commission, Directorate General for Research and Innovation. Luxembourg: Publication Office of the European Union. http://ec.europa.eu/research/science-society/document_library/pdf_06/mep-rapport-2011_en.pdf

Whitehouse, D., Hilty, L., Patrignani, N., & van Lieshout, M. (2011). *Social Accountability and Sustainability in the Information Society: Perspectives on Long-term Responsibility*, Notizie di Politeia - Rivista di Etica e Scelte Pubbliche, Anno XXVII, n.104.

Winter, D. D., & Koger, S. M. (2004). *The psychology of environmental problems* (2nd ed.). Mahwah, NJ: Lawrence Erlbaum Associates.

KEY TERMS AND DEFINITIONS

Co-Design: A process in which people investigate and create together within a given theme. Co-design aims to create conditions such that the participants in the process are able to ideate and share existing and new meanings about the topical issues under design.

Co-Design Platform: A technology or application that allows the users to interact with each other by digital means and to create, share and elaborate on ideas and thoughts together.

Human-Driven Design (HDD): A holistic approach to design that is based on understanding human beings and their individual needs and behaviours in social and cultural contexts. HDD is based on human-related sciences, the most important being psychology and sociology.

Persuasive Technology: Technology that is designed to change the attitudes or behaviours of the users through persuasion and social influence.

Spherical Panorama: An image that shows the view as if the viewer were in the centre of it. The viewer can look around, up and down. Panoramas are created using special photographic equipment or software.

Sustainable HCI, HCI for Sustainability: A branch of HCI that promotes sustainability (mainly) in environmental terms in interaction design. Sustainable HCI considers, e.g., how to make user behaviour more environmentally friendly and how to reduce the material effects in the production, use and disposal of ICT.

Chapter 11
Teaching Design of Emerging Embodied Technologies

Gunver Majgaard
University of Southern Denmark, Denmark

ABSTRACT

How does design of emerging embodied technologies enrich the HCI learning processes? The authors introduce a model for embodied interaction and use it in the development of a painting app for children based on the motion sensor Asus Xtion Pro (similar to Kinect). The development of the app was part of a HCI course for engineering students. The motion sensor was interesting as a design tool, because it appealed to full body interaction. The development exemplified and unfolded the embodied elements: multiple modalities, physical, bodily, social, and symbolic interaction in a situated environment. Subsequently, the authors introduce a physical-digital toolbox, illustrating the span of parameters within the model for embodied interaction: robot technology, tangibles, wearables, interactive surroundings, and bigger objects.

INTRODUCTION

In this article, we explore how having a body affects interaction design (Pfeifer, 2007). Last autumn, my fifth semester engineering students used the motion sensing input device, *Asus Xtion Pro* (similar to *Microsoft's Kinect*), for the design of embodied interaction tools for children. The platform was interesting as a design tool, because it appealed to full body interaction. In addition, it appealed to innovative and creative development projects (Borenstein, 2012).

The design was part of a course in physical-digital interaction design, where the students explored other interactive platforms than PCs and tablets. The students developed a painting application, where at the end, users painted in ten different colours by waving one of their hands.

Basically, we have several categories of physical-digital interactive devices for embodied interaction: Robots and Robot Technology, Touch and Tangibles, Interactive Wearables, Interactive Surroundings, and Bigger Objects. Interactive Surroundings are Sensor Networks, such as cam-

DOI: 10.4018/978-1-4666-6228-5.ch011

era tracking, hands-free speech recognition and motion sensor devices, such as Microsoft Kinect or Asus Xtion Pro.

For many years, it has been our desire to develop effective and easy to use handsfree user interfaces. Kinect was the first on the market and was launched in November 2010. It sold 8 million units in the first 60 days and entered the Guinness World Records as the fastest selling consumer electronic device in history (Melgar, 2012).

In this study, we want to investigate the relationship between emerging technologies, embodied and natural interaction, and learning activities. Our teaching and learning approaches are based on participatory, exploratory and reflective learning. The students are to participate actively in all the phases of the design: initial field study, prototyping and testing. This contrasts HCI courses focusing on theoretical studies and analyses of other people's designs. This participatory and reflective learning philosophy is supported theoretically by Schön (1983), Papert, (1993) and Bateson (2000). The students basically learn, while they are exploring and designing new prototypes. In the classroom and in project work, the students reflect on their design ideas, concepts, programming, target groups, test results and academic knowledge. Active participation and reflection is the core of learning (Bateson, 2000; Wenger, 1998). The overall question explored in this paper is:

How does a design of emerging embodied technologies, such as Asus Xtion Pro, enrich the HCI learning processes in Engineering Education?

First, we discuss enriched learning processes in an embodied context and relate this to kinaesthetic, auditory and visual modalities. Then we introduce the concept of embodied interaction, as a combination of multiple modalities, physical, symbolic and social interaction, in a situated environment. As an illustration of this, we describe the students' development of the painting prototype and the user test. In order to focus on the Asus Xtion as an educational tool in the HCI course, we discuss how the students' learning unfolded.

The HCI learning loops are illustrated, focusing on the interplay between the students and children in real-life situations. The course is evaluated and the learning activities are pinned down. This is followed by a section on the physical-digital toolbox, which supports embodied interaction. The various categories of physical-digital platforms are: Robot technology, Touch and Tangibles, Interactive Wearables, Interactive Surroundings, and Bigger Objects. Finally, we summarize and conclude.

The research method used in this study is based on Design-based Research and Action Research (Majgaard, 2011; van den Akker 2006; Lewin, 1946). Design-based Research is a branch of educational research that uses the iterative design of educational interventions to exemplify and develop theories of learning. Action Research brings a change in the behaviour of the target group into focus and allows emerging goals. Experiments and critical reflections are at the core of this research method, allowing learning from and through practice. The interventions took place in the target group's natural surroundings e.g. in the classroom.

APPROACHES: EMBODIED INTERACTION AND LEARNING

This study focuses on how embodied technologies theoretically may enrich learning processes. But first we need to describe what we mean by embodied interaction.

The Embodied Interaction Model

The rise of embedded computers helps us move around in the world, do household tasks and automates processes in industry. It also affects the way we learn, teach, experience and explore the world. Both the increase of computational power and embedded computing, provide new ways of interacting. Basically our computers become more and more physical-digital interactive and we use our bodies in the interaction. Smartphones and tablets allow interaction with a high level of graphical abstraction combined with diverse physical-digital participation. Research in Human-Computer Interaction (HCI) has begun to explore these new ways of interacting. Dourish defines this new type of interaction below:

Embodied interaction is interaction with computer systems that occupy our world, a world of physical and social reality, and that exploit this fact in how they interact with us (Dourish, 2004, p. 3).

Dourish describes embodied interaction as a mixture of a physical, social and symbolic reality, see the figure below. The interaction takes place in the physical world and perhaps partly in the virtual world, e.g. a child connects tangible interactive blocks, which symbolically represent music instruments. Secondly, the interaction takes place in a social context. Thirdly, the interaction also has certain modalities e.g. auditory, visual and/or kinaesthetic. The modalities can also be broken up into Gardner's multiple intelligences: musical - rhythmic, visual - spatial, verbal - linguistic, logical - mathematical, bodily - kinaesthetic, interpersonal, intrapersonal, and naturalistic (Gardner, 1983). The aspects of embodied interaction are summarised in the figure below.

Embodied interaction is of a physical nature and unfolds between humans and physical-digital tools. The physical-digital tool, such as the motion sensor, communicates through certain modalities within its context. The modalities relate to all the human senses e.g. visual and kinaesthetic. In the context humans interact physically, socially and symbolically. The interaction is situated in time and space and takes place "here and now".

Modalities and Learning Processes

Embodied interaction supports multimodal learning processes. As mentioned above, there are basically three major sensory learning modalities: auditory, visual and kinaesthetic. Gardner adds several modalities and characterise them as the multiple intelligences (Gardner, 1983). The multiple intelligences are: musical - rhythmic, visual - spatial, verbal - linguistic, logical - mathematical, bodily - kinaesthetic, interpersonal, intrapersonal, and naturalistic. Each of them represents a relatively independent form of information processing. Among them, bodily-kinaesthetic intelligence, which describes one's ability to control body movements, gestures, and the capacity to handle, objects skilfully. Gardner's philosophy is that each student has one or more strengths in their way of learning – some students are primarily verbal; others are primarily kinaesthetic or visual. Consequently, the teacher has to provide learning materials that support different ways of learning. In other words the learning material should support several intelligences at once. A study shows that children at the age of five learn phonetic rules, while tracing words with an index finger, while pronouncing it and looking at it (Hsu, 2011). This multi-sensory or multi intelligence approach seems to be effective in establishing the connection between visual and auditory representations. The physical-digital motion sensor supports the bodily – kinaesthetic intelligence. Most application will involve the visual and/or auditory modalities as well. This makes motion sensors, such a Kinect and Asus suited as platforms for multimodal educational tools.

Hsu analysed in 2011 the potentials of the motion sensor Kinect as an educational tool (Hsu, 2011). The motion sensor is a physical-digital tool. She recommends the tool as support to kinaesthetic pedagogical practices, to benefit learners with strong bodily kinaesthetic intelligence. The interactivity facilitated by Kinect applications, covers kinaesthetic and visual sensory modalities. Of technical constraints Hsu mentions that calibration takes time.

In summary, multimodal learning processes accommodate the learners' different ways of learning. Embodied interactive technology supports several learning modalities and several of Gardner's intelligences.

Situatedness

The interaction is situated and takes place in the "here and now" environment. Situatedness is introduced by Brooks (1991) who addresses a more engineering and robotics related approach to embodied interaction research.

Embodied interaction incorporates a wider range of human skills and abilities. The physical-digital tools are accessible and integrated in our everyday lives, such as smartphones or GPS-systems. They reduce complexity of specific interactions.

Embodiment is very much in focus in the world of artificial intelligence and robotics. Modern robots understand the world though sensors positioned in the right places. And a robot adapts to its surroundings through sensors and effectors. Pfeifer (2007) stresses that intelligence requires a body. He believes that the body enables cognition and thinking. There are two cornerstones in modern robotics: embodiment and situatedness. Embodiment refers to the intelligent and physical-digital body:

Embodiment: The robots have bodies and experience the world directly - their actions are part of a dynamic with the world, and the actions have immediate feedback on the robots' own sensations(Brooks, 1991).

When an interactive system integrates sensors, effectors and a control system, it is able to sense changes in the souroundings and react accordingly. The system is embodied, when it reacts dynamically to changes in the world e.g. the Endomondo App senses my running route using its GPS sensor. Endomondo reacts by showing graphics and speaking to me about my speed. Brooks and Pfeifter have a robotic-physiological

approach to embodied interaction, focusing on artificial intelligence, grasping physical objects, arrangements of sensors and material properties for the digital agents. The digital agent is another word for robot. They research on the design of the digital agent; how to shape its body, and the embodied interaction with the dynamic environment. Embodiement relates to the physical proporties and physical interaction in Pfeifers and Brooks perspective. They don't describe the surroundings as social, and they don't link embodiment to something social. In contrast Dourish links embodiment to social aspects, such as incorporating social understandings into the design of interaction (Dourish, 2004:16). An understanding of the social world and incorporation of this understanding into the embodied interaction design processes. First we need to explore the concept of situatedness. Situatedness refers to the"here and now" communication between system and user. Books defines it as:

Situatedness refers to how the interactive robot is situated in the world and how it reacts to the "here" and "now" of the environment that directly influences the behavior of the system (Brooks, 1991).

Brooks focuses here on the dynamics between the robot and the environment, and on how the robot's actions have an impact on its own sensations. Embodied interaction is closely related to both embodiment and situatedness.

Embodied interaction requires a supportive interface. This interface consists of sensors, which are able to sense "here and now" changes in the dynamic surroundings. The interface must in order to communicate meaningfully, be able to process and interpret its sensations and react accordingly. Being situated is a way for the system to understand the surroundings or context. The specific sensors bring attention to specific parts of the context. In the old days before the 1990's, robots weren't situated, they just executed their program without regard to the surrounding environment (Brooks,

Figure 2. (a) IR Projected light on a blank surface; (b) 3D image based on IR information

1991). The old industrial robots couldn't see or feel their surroundings, and they could harm humans in their near proximity. This meant that humans and robots couldn't work in the same physical area. When robots became more situated, robots and humans could begin to interact more directly. Situatedness forms the basis for the research field of Human Robotic Interaction.

EMBODIED INTERACTION IN THE DEVELOPMENT OF A PAINTING APP

Contexts and modalities of embodied interaction are illustrated in the development of the painting application.

The Physical-Digital Tool: The motion sensor in this case is Asus Xtion similar to the Kinect. The motion device is for Windows PCs. Asus Xtion Pro (no RGB camera) and Xtion Pro Live (RGB camera) were released in 2012. The Asus Xtion Pro sees the world in 3D. It is based on an infrared camera that enabled users to control and interact with the computer without touching a game controller. The interaction takes place through a natural interaction, using body and hand gestures.

Asus Xtion makes use of an infrared camera for recording the movements of the user, and the recordings are based on variations in depth. The camera has two lenses: one lens projecting an infrared grid, see the figure 2(a) above; the second

lens captures and creates a 3D image, see figure 1(b). The closer, the object is to the IR camera, the whiter the image is. The Asus Xtion connects by USB to a PC (Christensen et al, 2013).

The software development kit is called OPEN NI (2013), and it offers methods for skeleton tracking, hand-point tracking, and gesture recognition. The programming was done in the programming environment *Processing* and was based on simple Java-like syntax (Borenstein, 2012; Melgar, 2012).

The Asus competes with the Kinect, Wii Remote and Eye Toy. Recently, a new motion sensor called Leap Motion has appeared on the market and it is for hand gestured computer interaction (Leap Motion, 2013). This new device senses hands and fingers and follows their every move. It lets them move in all directions in the space between you and your computer screen (Leap Motion, 2013).

Bob Heddle Director of Kinect for Windows announces that Microsoft will deliver a new generation of Kinect for Windows sensors next year (Kinect for windows blog, 2013). Some of the key capabilities of the new Kinect sensor will most likely include: Higher fidelity, expanded field of view, improved skeletal tracking and new active infrared (IR). Especially, the improved skeletal tracking will promote future innovative physiotherapeutic training applications and other applications.

Related Work on Using the Motion Sensor as Educational Tool: Villaroman et al (2011)

Figure 1. Embodied interaction model

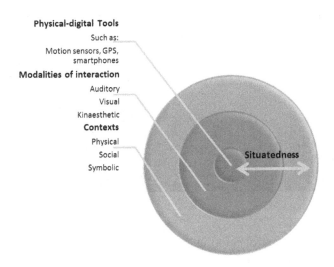

present examples of Kinect-assisted teaching, used to achieve some of the learning goals in Human Computer Interaction (HCI) courses. The motion sensor device introduces a natural form of interaction (Melgar, 2012; Villaroman et al, 2011). Exploration of this type of interaction in HCI courses can become very instructive. Kinect or Asus Xtion can provide activities that aid the study of natural user interaction which would otherwise be unavailable. Villaroman et al suggest learning activities such as: (1) "Study how cognitive principles, affordance, and feedback should influence the design of Kinect controlled interfaces in desktop computers;" (2) "Design and implementation for a specific application domain – such as web browsing;" (3) "As an emerging technology, exploring how Kinect or Asus Xtion can help advance the field of gesture-based, natural user interaction;" (4) "Test and analyse whether usability and user-experience requirements can be met with the current capabilities of the Kinect-enabled user interfaces." Villaroman et al believe that students, who have gone through an undergraduate advanced programming course in C/C++, will find it relatively easy to develop applications directly from the project libraries.

The Development Process: The students in our case were fifth semester students from the engineering programme, *Learning and Experience Technology. Learning and Experience Technology* is a 3 plus 2 years IT Engineering Program. The overall learning goal of the course was to design interactive tools for play and learning. The designs should be based on other media than traditional PCs. Each student did an individual programming assignment and participated in team-oriented project work. As a part of the project work, the students conducted field observations of the target group and they also tested the interactive prototype on the target group. In order to get started on the technological platform, the students read and did exercises from the book, *Arduino and Kinect Projects* by Melgar and Diez (2012).

The painting application was the result of the project work. The graphical part of the interactive painting prototype was divided into two equal parts, see the figure below. The left side showed the user's painting and the right side showed the representation of the infrared 3D image. An invisible colour pencil was attached to one hand. The pencil was displaced from the centre of the palm to the fingertips. This worked intuitively correct. The registration of the user's hand was done by

Figure 3. Testing the interactive drawing prototype (the star is subsequently made more colourful)

waving in front of the camera. To control painting functions, an Arduino board with three buttons was used: (1) One switched cyclically between 10 different colours; (2) The second deleted everything that was painted on the screen; (3) The third switched between five different pencils.

The test was conducted in the students' classroom. The testers were four school children from the third grade, who were about 9 years old, see the figure above. The summary of the test is based on quotes from the students' test log and the oral examination: "the children were excited about the test and the program...". "They tried to paint Harry Potter, stars, dogs etc., and they learned quickly how to use the programme", wrote the students. The programme had some bugs, e.g. the hand recognition deadlocked. The students wrote: "When the program went into a deadlock, the children helped each other and restarted the programme." The students observed that the children took their own playing activity into the testing process: "They took turns to paint and they started to dance and sing, while they were waiting. They could see their own IR image, while they danced and this made it more interesting". After the test, the students made a short interview. They asked the children what they liked about the programme, and what could be done differently. They got the following suggestions: use the feet as a pencil instead of hands; draw on top of another picture; eraser; undo button; more colour options; insert

squares, circles, triangles, etc. The children found it annoying that they had to wave so much to start drawing, and they found the infrared camera was more fun than a normal camera. And they would like the students to develop structured gaming elements, e.g. a competition to draw a human or an animal and receive points.

Finally, the students participated in the student conference (SIDeR, 2013), where they presented the painting application (Christensen et al, 2013) and won an EU funded award of excellence for designing for vulnerable generations - children and elderly (Device, 2013). Another group presented an installation called Chimecloud also based on Kinect technology (Jepsen, 2013; Chimecloud, 2013). Wind chimes are often made by metallic tubes and are to be played by the wind. This Chimecloud installation was to be played, by bodies moving below the chimes. The Kinect sensors detected how fast a person walked by and transformed this into acoustical feedback. Sticks connected to the servo motors pushed the pipes all depended of input from the Kinect sensors. More users could collaborate in playing the chimes. The installation was developed in collaboration between Chalmers University and the municipality of Lundby, and was exhibited in Backaplan Kulturhus. This installation presented the rich potentials in combining aesthetic installations, art and embodied interactivity.

Figure 4. Embodied Interaction using the painting application

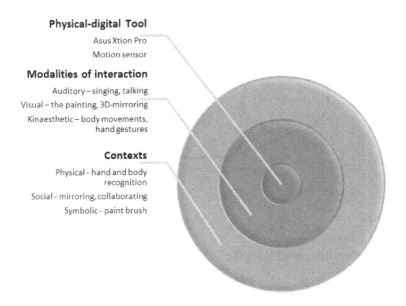

Physical-digital Tool
Asus Xtion Pro
Motion sensor

Modalities of interaction
Auditory – singing, talking
Visual – the painting, 3D-mirroring
Kinaesthetic – body movements, hand gestures

Contexts
Physical - hand and body recognition
Social - mirroring, collaborating
Symbolic - paint brush

DISCUSSION: EMBODIED INTERACTION AND THE HCI LEARNING LOOP

The discussion focuses on how embodied interaction is implemented in the Painting application. We discuss how the students learn, while they are designing and testing their application. And we call this particular way of learning for the HCI Learning Loop. Finally we evaluate the course and look at upcoming ideas.

The Embodied Interaction Model Applied on the Painting App

Does the painting application really support all aspects of embodied interaction? The Painting App viewed in an embodied interaction perspective, see the figure below.

The children interacted physically, using their hands as paintbrushes. The hand symbolised a paintbrush and worked like one, when the children were interacting with the system. The painting app reacted instantly, when the children waved their hands. This exemplifies that the system is situated and reacts to "here and now" sensations. The painting app supported the children's social interaction, because more than one could interact with the system e.g. one child could change colours, while another one was painting. The children could also see each other's 3D reflections on the projector, this also mirrored their social interaction. The physical, symbolic, social and situated aspects of embodied interaction are supported by the designed painting application. The children also used the three major learning modalities. The auditory modality came into play, while the children discussed how to use the painting app and while they sang. There was no audio output from the Painting app – so the audio modality is debatable. The visual sensory modality came into play, when the system mirrored their bodily movements and visualised their hand drawings. The mirroring of their bodies and body movements, also describe a special interaction between the children and the system. The children also communicated with each other, by watching each other in the painting app mirror.

Figure 5. HCI learning loops

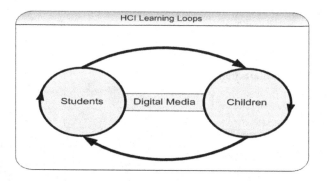

HCI Learning Loop

How did the students learn while developing the system?

Figure 5 illustrates the students' and children's learning loops. First, the students' learning process took place during the iterative design process, illustrated in the left cycle. The cycle on the right side, illustrates the children's playful learning process. The cycles are learning loops of action and reflections (Schön, 1983). The digital media were developed and understood in interplay between students and children. The media constituted a community of practice (Wenger, 1998). Secondly, the students learned, while they watched the media in use. The arrows between the students' and children's learning cycles, illustrate the dialogue, instructions and feedback that took place. Additionally, we reflected on the embodied interaction in the classroom. We discussed the platform potentials in games, rehabilitation, as a hands free web browser etc. We evaluated the design process and the students testing experiences. This type of reflection is retrospective and is a way of optimising design processes. It is also a way to combine theoretical knowledge on embodied interaction and real life experiences.

All the students managed individually programming the device, one of the students made a traditional ping pong game, another combined a music video and the user's body as a skeleton; a third painted circles, and a fourth used the hand as a computer mouse.

The project work resulted in a painting application prototype. The users used their hands for painting and they painted in different colours and used pencils in different sizes. The prototype was tested by four school children from the third grade. The students got a lot of useful feedback from the testers. The feedback fell into three categories: (1) *Usability issues* such as deadlock situations and the hand recognition problem. (2) *Creative ideas* e.g. painting using feet instead of hands. (3) *Unexpected playful use.* The children danced and sang, while they were taking turns. If the painting application was to be developed further, there are promising possibilities for full-body interaction, participatory interaction, and creative interaction.

Altogether, the figure above illustrates learning processes in real-life situations.

Evaluation of the Course and Future Teaching

The students were fifth semester students, and they had been programming since their first semester. The students combined Arduino and Asus technology. They programmed their application from the Arduino programming environment Processing. Processing is a complete and thorough development environment, which makes the development processes smoother for the students. It was relatively easy for the students to develop interactive prototypes, using the additional OpenNI middleware for programming the Asus Xtion. Altogether, it was a very successful experience, to use the Asus in HCI teaching. This is also supported by Villaroman et al (2011). There were some limitations, e.g. it was sometimes difficult, to make the system recognise the hand in the initial phase.

The learning philosophy was based on active participation; experimentation and reflection. The students participated actively in all the phases of design: initial field studies, prototyping, and testing. This contrasts HCI courses, focusing on theoretical studies and analysis of others designs. The learning activities covered: Design using emerging technologies; User testing and experimenting on various conditions that could increase usability; Identification of ways a Kinect sensor could assist users with certain disabilities; Analysis of usability and affordance. The students learned while they iteratively designed and tested. Furthermore they learned from retrospective analysis of the design process. The learning process can be described as cycles of action and reflections.

Overall, the motion device, Asus Xtion, enriched the HCI learning processes in the classroom.

The students learning activities included:

- Design using emerging technologies.
- User testing and experimenting on various conditions that could increase usability.
- Identification of ways a Kinect sensor can assist users with certain disabilities.
- Analysis of usability and affordance.
- Some of the students explored the sensors advantages and disadvantages, as a web-browsing tool.

A new generation of fifth semester students are now exploring the Asus Xtion Pro. This year, they are developing a mannequin for a fictive clothing store in town. The idea is to mirror bodily movements, from people watching the mannequin. The mannequin is to be built in Plexiglas and the limbs are to be cut out of Plexiglas and connected to the servo motors. The students are currently working on the servo motors and the Kinect separately. The first prototype will be mirroring an arm.

PERSPECTIVES: THE PHYSICAL-DIGITAL TOOLBOX FOR EMBODIED INTERACTION

In this section, we put focus on the physical-digital tools. We zoom into the left box: Physical-digital Tools in the embodied interaction model. See the figure below:

There are several categories of interfaces for physical-digital interaction. This paper introduces multiple characteristic types: Humanoids and robot technology; Handheld Interaction so-called Tangibles; Interactive Wearable's; Interactive Surroundings and Bigger Objects. In actual applications, the platforms might be integrated. The painting app is an example of the category Interactive Surroundings. Below we introduce the toolbox for exploring emerging embodied technologies in HCI teaching.

Robot Technology and Humanoids

Humanoids and robot technology are in a broad sense technology, which senses the surroundings and react according to a programmed algorithm. The robot consists of sensors, such as touch or motion sensors. In addition, it consists of effectors such as: light diodes, sound or servomotors. Drivers and software, controls the robot. LEGO Mindstorm is the most well-known robotic kit in Denmark. It is widely use in schools and universities for applied sciences.

At the moment I am part of a research project, where robots are introduced in primary and secondary schools (Fremtek, 2013; Majgaard, 2014). The robots, we are using are the so-called NAO from Aldebaran (Aldebaran-robotic, 2013), see the figure below. The NAO is a programmable,

Figure 6. Embodied interaction – focus on physical-digital tools

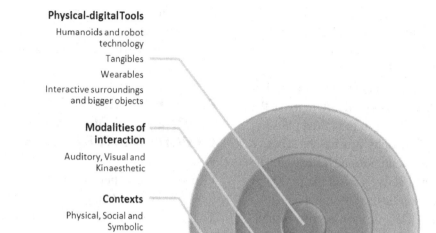

Physical-digital Tools

Humanoids and robot technology

Tangibles

Wearables

Interactive surroundings and bigger objects

Modalities of interaction

Auditory, Visual and Kinaesthetic

Contexts

Physical, Social and Symbolic

58 cm tall humanoid robot with the following key components: electric motors, LED lights, cameras, microphones, tactile sensors, and pressure sensors, CPU, battery and much more. The robot is programmable in both drag and drop language for programming novices. More low level programming in python or C++ is available for experienced programmers. In our research, school

Figure 7. NAO robot (Aldebaran-robotic, 2013)

children are using the robots in the classroom. Below is a picture of the NAO. The educational goals cover programming, potentials of humanoids, mathematics, physics, storytelling and so on.

The NAO can be programmed to walk, dance, recognise faces or objects, avoid objects, transform text messages into audio and much more. The programmed NAO robot is situated and reacts immediately, if for example a known face appears in front of it.

The NAO is developed as an educational tool. It is used in schools and universities for programming, understanding of technology, automation, physics, and mathematics (Aldebaran-robotic, 2013).

The embodied interaction covers all the major sensory modalities. The robot provides auditory feedback. If programmed properly, it can recognise your face and e.g. say "Hello Harry". The robot can visualise a geometric form, by walking by it. The users can in a special mode, program the robot by moving its body parts. This supports the kinaesthetic modality. The humanoid supports the modalities differently, depending on whether it is in programming or executable mode (Majgaard, 2014).

Handheld Devices: Tangibles

Handheld tangibles are devices such as smartphones or modular cubes. A smartphone supports embodied interaction, e.g. when I touch the camera app icon on my smartphone. The touch sensor detects precisely the position of my touch and opens the camera app. The physical interaction with the display and symbolic interaction with the app, produces the embodied interaction in this example.

As ideal types, it has been customary to distinguish between screen-based interaction on the one hand and the purely physical interaction with interactive tangibles, e.g. cubes, on the other (Majgaard, 2011; Sharp, 2007; Dourish, 2004). Screen-based media is known from PCs, tablets and smartphones. Tablets may e.g. be iPads. Screen-based media's classic strength is in their use of abstract visual and auditory symbols, and their support in learning processes. Interactive blocks can provide a more tangible physical form of symbolic information and support more intuitive, bodily, and embodied learning processes. However, the tendency is that the two types of media are merging. Traditional screen-based media now contain multiple sensors and become more bodily in their interactions, and interactive blocks or cubes are being equipped with screens.

Our computers are becoming more and more physical. Smartphones and tablets allow for interaction with a high level of abstraction and graphical interactive participation. Furthermore, they offer new forms of interaction in terms of touch and pressure sensitive displays. Additionally, there will often be a compass, GPS and 3D accelerometer, for detecting where and how it is situated in the world. It is for example the 3D accelerometer that senses your tablets/iPads position and causes

change in orientation of the display. And it is the same group of sensors in the smartphone, which count the number of steps we take, or record our running route. Thus, it suddenly becomes possible, to integrate body and movement in the interaction. This is done without sacrificing the visual abstract possibilities. For example, we do not just count the number of steps or specific GPS coordinates - we get the route shown on maps and view statistics about how our speed have varied through the run. Approximately, half of the Danes have smartphones, and one in five of them would rather throw out their television than their smartphone (Media Watch, 2012). Families and Kindergartens in Denmark show a great interest in tablets. They are bigger than the smartphones, this means more than one user can look and collaborate. Currently many experiments are going on involving IPads in Danish kindergartens and schools, in order to support the children in their development and learning processes

The intelligence can also be distributed between several modular tangible devices. A lot of development and research have been done in modular tangibles over the last ten years (Lund, H. et al, 2007; Majgaard, 2011; Majgaard, Misfeldt & Nielsen, 2010; Nielsen, et al, 2008; Piper & Ishii, 2002) The devices are able to interact with each other and the people around them. See the figure below:

The Sifteo cubes are interactive cubes for playing and learning. They are an example of modular tangibles. Sifteo merges interactive blocks and screen-based interfaces, and each block has a small display of 128 x 128 pixels. This is enough to dynamically perform small animations and display pictures, letters, numbers and other symbols. Each Sifteo package consists of 3-6 Sifteo blocks. Each block is clickable, contains a colour display, a number of motion sensors and a rechargeable battery. Each block is just under 4 x 4 cm. The blocks are connected wirelessly to a computer via a USB radio link. Sifteo applications are executed from a special Sifteo-runner program

Figure 8. Tangible Sifteo cubes (www.sifteo.com)

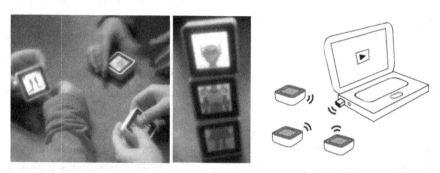

on your computer. It is possible without programming experience, to develop simple variations of Sifteo Creativity Kit. On the above figure are the Sifteo cubes and a sketch of how they are linked wirelessly to the computer. The children interact while connecting, shaking, tossing, and turning the cubes. The children can also collaborate with each other, while interacting with the cubes.

My students have been developing new software for the cubes, in order to explore new ways of interacting (Majgaard, 2012). We wanted the students to try out other, more natural user interfaces such as robotics, interactive blocks and Kinect. We wanted our students to experience embodied interaction, and to develop systems which focused on movement, spaciousness, motor skills and physicalities in general. Our intention is for our students to master both the development of graphical and physical interfaces. The students analyse and explore the applicability of these interfaces, and in a design process assess when to use physical and/or graphic-based interfaces. They can hopefully therefore in practice understand and utilize these media comparative strengths.

Basically the interactive cubes support embodied interaction. This embodied interacting Sifteos are more natural, varied and direct than the indirect manipulation of the graphical user interface (GUI) via a mouse. The users' get physical and bodily experiences, while they operate the system.

Interaction with interactive cubes is physical, and the cubes represent something other than their physical form. The tangibles support both physical-digital and symbolic interaction. This is particularly true for Sifteo cubes, which represent symbols in the terms of graphics, animations, letters or numbers. Even interactive cubes without a graphical interface often refer to something else. In another example a pink cube symbolises a particular musical instrument, but physically it just looks like an overgrown dice (Majgaard, 2012). The symbolic expression adds a meaning into the interaction. Dourish describes the link between physical and symbolic interaction as:

Tangible computing is of interest precisely because it is not purely physical. It is a physical realization of a symbolic reality, and the symbolic reality is, often, the world being manipulated. (Dourish, 2004, p. 207)

Tangible computing relies on symbolic interaction instead of eliminating it. From a design perspective, the physical and symbolic expression needs to complement each other. The embodied interaction connects both the physical-digital and the symbolic interaction.

The embodied interaction covers all the major sensory modalities. The cubes can provide auditory feedback. Each cube has an interactive display, and the visualisations can change, when the cubes are touched or connected in new combinations. They are kinaesthetic, because the children can touch and connect the physical artefacts.

Figure 9. The wearable shoe sole

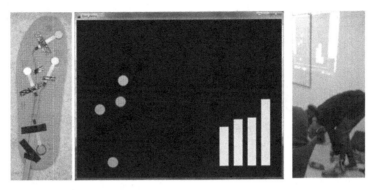

Embodiment in Wearables and Body Area Networks

Wearables address the technology you might wear such as Google glasses, smart phones, GPS watches, heart rate monitors, interactive clothes, accelerometers etc.

Body Area Networks are currently mostly being used as part of rehabilitation and fitness training. For instance, you can monitor your pulse as a part of a spinning class. Or you can put touch sensors in your running shoes, to measure walking or running style. A very popular application is the Endomondo running app. You attach a smartphone on your arm and start Endomondo. The program then tracks you by using GPS, while being linked to Google Maps. During the exercise, you dynamically get feedback on speed and distance. Another growing area is design of interactive clothes, shoes, and accessories. People can place interactive modules on their clothes, such as programmable light diodes (Melgar, 2012).

In research on engineering and rehabilitation a lot of experiments are done based Body Area Network. For instance systems performing real-time analysis of data, collected from sensors placed on the body. This provides guidance and feedback to the user, and can generate warnings based on the user's state, level of activity, and environmental conditions. In addition, all recorded information can be wirelessly send to medical servers and in-tegrated into the user's electronic medical records (Jovanov et al, 2005 and 2009; Choquette, 2008).

I have been involved in a project, where engineers and physiotherapists developed an interactive shoe sole (WTR, 2013). The shoe sole were to be placed in the shoe, and four pressure sensors monitored how the users walk was executed. The system gave dynamically visual feedback on their walking, see the figure below. The prototype was developed using the electronic kit Arduino (Arduino, 2013).

In our case the interactive shoe sole basically supported visual and kinaesthetic modalities. The users' physical behaviour was interpreted visually. The users interacted symbolically and explored their walking stiles by watching the symbolic interpretation on the screen.

Interactive Surroundings and Bigger Intelligent Objects

Interactive Surroundings are sensor networks, gesture-based interfaces, and bigger intelligent objects in our surroundings. This technology can be integrated in the environment, e.g. as part of the room or furniture. Some of the technologies are not in direct physical contact with the body and requires a more controlled and limited environment. Examples are Microsoft Kinect and Camera tracking and hands-free speech recognition. One of the most popular Kinect applications is Dance

Figure 10. The interactive playground

Central – combining game play and physical activity. The Asus Xtion Pro case introduced later in this article, is similar to the Kinect.

Some years ago, I was involved in the analysis of an interactive playground called ICON by playground producer KOMPAN A/S (Majgaard, G., & Jessen, C., 2009; Kompan, 2013). The playground is an example of a bigger intelligent object. It was a combination between an outdoor playground and a digital game. This playground combined playing, physical climbing, pushing pressure sensors and physical-digital gaming.

The aim of the digitization of the play equipment in ICON was to initiate physical play among the digital native children, who grow up with digital games as one of their favorite toys. We wanted the children to use their body, to become more physically active. Video game research has shown that children learn new digital games by using tricks and skills, they used in other digital games. They are learning a new kind of literacy (Gee, 2003), and because more and more children are experts in digital games, it seems natural, and even necessary to use this expertise in outdoor games, to promote physical play among children.

The children both used the playground for analogue and digital activities. Analogue activities are traditional play e.g. climbing or hide and seek. Digital activities are e.g. video games or digital games on the climbing rack. See the figure below:

The digital playground used various games to challenge the children, to play physically. The playground was divided into three areas, offering different game options.

The first area was a digital top called the Digital Supernova, which was circular and about 6 meter in diameter (above figure to the left). One or more children could participate by making the top turn. In the center was a game console, which invited the children to play different games. A moving arrow was displayed, and the children had to turn the top according to the arrow. The children could also decide to ignore the game console and use the top in the traditional analog manner.

In the middle was a climbing rack the so-called Digital Galaxy. It was about 7 meter in length, 3 meter in breath and 2.5 meter in height and consisted mostly of galvanized steel. In all junctions were programmable light diode buttons. The diodes were e.g. red, green, blue, white, or yellow. In front of the climbing rack was a game console, which could be activated, when a child rocked the seesaw in front of the console. One of the digital games was the Colour-race, and when the game was executed five of the light buttons, became active and lighted up each in different colours. The players would choose a colour each and then chase and touch their colour as fast as possible. When they touched the diode buttons, the light randomly "moved" to another button in the climbing rack. The child, who had touched 10

Figure 11. Various categories of physical-digital interfaces

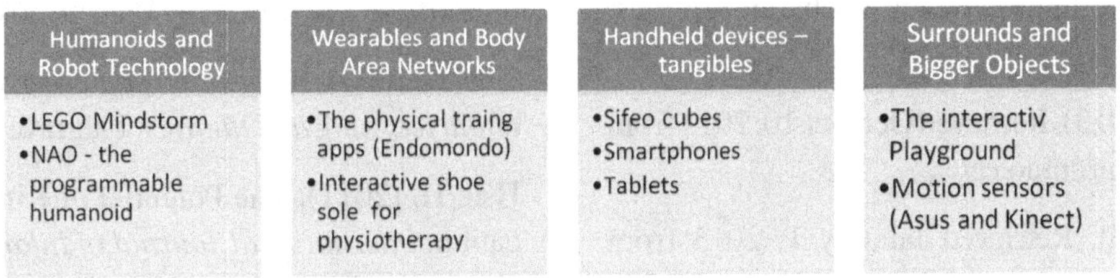

Humanoids and Robot Technology	Wearables and Body Area Networks	Handheld devices – tangibles	Surrounds and Bigger Objects
• LEGO Mindstorm • NAO - the programmable humanoid	• The physical traing apps (Endomondo) • Interactive shoe sole for physiotherapy	• Sifeo cubes • Smartphones • Tablets	• The interactiv Playground • Motion sensors (Asus and Kinect)

buttons first, was the winner. The digital games could be played by one or more children. The Digital Galaxy was also used traditionally for climbing, exploring, balancing, training and so on. The digital playground is an example of a bigger intelligent embodied object.

The learning modalities in this case cover auditory, visual and kinesthetic. The playground plays a kind of game-music, when the digital games are activated. The light diodes changes colours, while the children are playing. And the children use their bodies to climb and reach the buttons. The light diodes symbolise the specific game-pieces.

Overview of the Embodied Toolbox

Below is an overview of the various digital interfaces, which support embodied interaction, see the figure below:

The toolbox is a work in progress, and we haven't yet found a fully adequate toolbox model.

SUMMARY AND CONCLUSION

Enrichment in learning processes support new and multiple ways of participation. In the embodied field, we basically focus on the three major sensory modalities: auditory, visual and kinaesthetic.

Embodied interaction integrates multiple sensory modalities, physical, symbolic, social, and digital interaction. Embodied technologies make it easy for the designers, to bridge modalities. The multisensory and multimodal approach supports enrichment in learning processes. The feedback of the embodied system is situated and based on "here and now" sensations.

We unfolded the embodied interaction model, using a motion sensor in the development of a painting application. The motion sensor, Asus Xtion, was promising for exploratory design of gesture-based and full-body interaction. The available software package made it possible for the students to design interactive prototypes. In the beginning, they had all kinds of practical installation problems, but soon they were all up and running. In our study we experienced a minor delay in the initial hand recognition routines.

In the second part of the article, we introduced the embodied toolbox: Robot technology, Touch and Tangibles, Interactive Wearables, Interactive Surroundings, and Bigger Objects. The toolbox can be used as inspiration for future research and teaching in the field of embodied interaction. Question for future research: How can embodied technology support and bridge modalities in learning processes? – And how do specific technologies bridge modalities?

REFERENCES

Akker, J. V. d., Gravemeijer, K., McKenney, S., & Nieveen, N. (2006). *Educational Design Research*. Routledge.

Aldebaran-robotics. (2013). Retrieved October 10, 2013 from http://www.aldebaran-robotics.com/en/

Arduino. (2013). Retrieved October 10, 2013 from http://www.arduino.cc/

Asus. (2013). Retrieved January 1, 2013 from http://www.asus.com/Multimedia/Xtion_PRO/

Bateson, G. (2000). *Steps to an Ecology of Mind: Collected Essays in Anthropology, Psychiatry, Evolution, and Epistemology.* Chicago Press.

Borenstein, G. (2012). *Making Things See. 3D vision with Kinect, Processing, Arduino, and MakerBot.* Maker Media, Inc.

Brooks, R. A. (1991). New Approaches to Robotics. *Science*, (253): 1227–1232. doi:10.1126/science.253.5025.1227 PMID:17831441

Chimecloud. (2013). Retrieved October 14, 2013 from http://vimeo.com/53239679

Choquette, S. et al. (2008). Accelerometer-based wireless body area network to estimate intensity of therapy in post-acute rehabilitation. *Journal of Neuroengineering and Rehabilitation*, 5, 20. doi:10.1186/1743-0003-5-20 PMID:18764954

Christensen, K., Monsen, E., Hansen, J. V., Andersen, M., & Safiri, S. (2013). Physical-digital Interaction Design for Children. In *Proceeding of the 9th Student Interaction Design Research (SIDeR 2013)*. Aarhus.

Device. (2013). Retrieved October 10, 2013 from http://www.deviceproject.eu/modules/news/article.php?storyid=6

Dourish, P. (2004). *Where the Action Is: The Foundation of Embodied Interaction.* The MIT Press.

Fremtek. (2013). Retrieved October 10, 2013 from http://www.insero.dk/Uddannelse/projekter-og-aktiviteter/Fremtek

Gardner, H. (1983). *Frames of Mind: The Theory of Multiple Intelligences.* Basic Books.

Gee, J. (2003). *What video games have to teach us about learning and literacy.* Palgrave Macmillan.

Hsu, H. (2011). The Potential of Kinect in Education. *International Journal of Information and Education Technology*, 1(5).

Jepsen, A., Dondana, M., & Reiter, L. (2013). Chimecloud - An Evocative, Responsive Sound Installation. In *Proceeding of the 9th Student Interaction Design Research (SIDeR 2013)*. Aarhus.

Jovanov, E. et al. (2005). A wireless body area network of intelligent motion sensors for computer assisted physical rehabilitation. *Journal of Neuroengineering and Rehabilitation*. doi:10.1186/1743-0003-2-6 PMID:15740621

Jovanov, E., et al. (2009). Avatar – a Multi-sensory System for Real Time Body Position Monitoring. In *Proceedings of IEEE Eng Med Biol Soc*. IEEE. doi: 10.1109/IEMBS.2009.5334774

Kinect for Windows Blog. (2013). Retrieved October 10, 2013 from http://blogs.msdn.com/b/kinectforwindows/archive/2013/05/23/the-new-generation-kinect-for-windows-sensor-is-coming-next-year.aspx

Kompan. (2013). Retrieved October 10, 2013 from http://icon.kompan.com/ retrieved 2013-10-10

Leap Motion. (2013). Retrieved October 10, 2013 from https://www.leapmotion.com/

Lewin, K. (1946). Action research and minority problems. *The Journal of Social Issues*, 2(4), 34–46. doi:10.1111/j.1540-4560.1946.tb02295.x

Lund, H., Pedersen, M., & Beck, R. (2007). Modular Robotic Tiles – Experiments for Children with Autism. *Artificial Life and Robotics*, 13, 394–400. doi:10.1007/s10015-008-0623-4

Majgaard, G. (2009). The Playground in the Classroom – Fractions and Robot Technology. In Proceedings of Cognition and Exploratory Learning in Digital Age (pp. 10-17). International Association for Development, IADIS.

Majgaard, G. (2011). *Learning Processes and Robotic Systems. Design of Educational Tools using Robots as Media and Children as Co-designers.* (PhD dissertation). University of Southern Denmark.

Majgaard, G. (2012). Brug af interaktive klodser i ingeniørundervisningen. [Use of interactive blocks in Engineering education]. *MONA: Matematik og Naturfagsdidaktik,* (4), 24-40.

Majgaard, G. (2014). Initial Phases of Design-based Research into the Educational Potentials of NAO-Robots. In *Proceedings of Human Robotic Interaction Conference HRI'14.* Bielefeld, Germany: ACM.

Majgaard, G., & Jessen, C. (2009). Playtesting the Digital Playground. In *Proceedings of the International Conference on games and Entertainment Technologies 2009* (pp. 87-92). International Association for Development, IADIS.

Majgaard, G., Misfeldt, M., & Nielsen, J. (2010). Robot Technology and Numbers in the classroom. In *Proceedings of Cognition and Exploratory Learning in Digital Age* (pp. 231–234). IADIS.

Majgaard, G., Misfeldt, M., & Nielsen, J. (2011). *How Design-based Research, Action Research and Interaction Design Contributes to the Development of Designs for Learning.* Designs for Learning.

Mediawatch. (2012). Retrieved July 9, 2012 from http://mediawatch.dk/artikel/smartphones-styrker-kommercielt-mediepotentiale

Melgar, E. R., & Diez, C. C. (2012). *Arduino and Kinect Projects: Design, Build, Blow Their Minds.* Apress. doi:10.1007/978-1-4302-4168-3

Nielsen, J., Jessen, C., & Bærendsen, N. K. (2008). RoboMusicKids – Music Education with Robotic Building Blocks. In *Proceedings of the 2nd IEEE International Conference on Digital Game and Intelligent Toy Enhanced Learning (DIGITEL)* (pp. 149-156). IEEE.

OPEN NI. (2013). Retrieved January 20, 2013 from http://www.openni.org/

Papert, S. (1993). *Mindstorms Children, Computers, and Powerful Ideas.* Basic Books.

Pfeifer, R., & Bongard, J. (2007). *How the body shapes the way we think.* MIT Press.

Piper, B., & Ishii, H. (2002). PegBlocks: A Learning Aid for the Elementary Classroom. In *Proceedings Extended Abstracts of Conference on Human Factors in Computing Systems (CHI '02).* Minneapolis, MN: ACM.

Rogers, Y., Sharp, H., & Preece, J. (2011). *Interaction Design: beyond human-computer interaction* (3rd ed.). John Wiley & Sons.

Schön, D. (1983). The Reflective Practitioner, How Professionals Think. In *Action.* Basic Books.

Scratch2kinect. (2013). Retrieved September 20, 2013 from http://scratch.saorog.com/

Scratch and Kinect. (2013). Retrieved September 20, 2013 from http://scratched.media.mit.edu/discussions/teaching-scratch/scratch-kinect

Sharp, H. et al. (2007). *Interaction Design: Beyond Human-Computer Interaction.* John Wiley & Sons Ltd.

SIDeR. (2013). Retrieved October 10, 2013 from http://sider2013.au.dk/

Villaroman, N., et al. (2011). Teaching Natural User Interaction Using OpenNI and the Microsoft Kinect Sensor. In *Proceedings of SIGITE'11.* West Point, NY: ACM.

Wenger, E. (1998). *Communities of Practice: Learning, Meaning, and Identity*. Cambridge University Press. doi:10.1017/CBO9780511803932

WTR. (2013). Retrieved October 10, 2013 from http://www.welfaretech.dk/aktiviteter/wtr-efter-uddannelse/

KEY TERMS AND DEFINITIONS

Contexts: Embodied interaction takes place in a given environment. Dourish (2004) describes the context a mixture of a physical, social and symbolic reality. The interaction takes place in the physical world and perhaps partly in the virtual world, e.g. a child connects tangible interactive blocks, which symbolically represent music instruments. The social context covers the social norms and expectations.

Embodied Interaction: Embodied interaction is of a physical nature and unfolds between humans and physical-digital tools. Embodied interaction combines multiple modalities of interaction: physical, symbolic and social interaction, in a situated environment.

Embodied Technologies: Embodied technology is based on interactive technology where we use our bodies in the interaction. Smartphones, robots, wearables, tangibles and cars are examples of embodied technology. Embodied technologies can also be described as physical-digital tools.

Modalities of Interaction: Embodied interaction has certain modalities e.g. auditory, visual and/or kinaesthetic. The modalities can also be broken up into Gardner's multiple intelligences: musical - rhythmic, visual - spatial, verbal - linguistic, logical - mathematical, bodily - kinaesthetic, interpersonal, intrapersonal, and naturalistic (Gardner, 1983). Meaningful embodied interaction often covers more than one modality.

Situatedness: Situatedness refers to how the embodied technology is situated in the world and how it reacts to the "here" and "now" of the environment that directly influences the behaviour of the system (Brooks, 1991). Situatedness is a prerequisite for interaction. Interaction can't become meaningful without immediate feedback.

Tangibles: Tangibles are handheld interactive tools e.g. smartphones or interactive blocks.

Wearables: Wearables are sensors and effectors placed on the body or in clothing. Wearables are also named as Body Area Networks.

Section 4
Mobile and Ubiquitous Computing

Chapter 12
Augmented Reality Interfaces for Smart Objects in Ubiquitous Computing Environments

A. W. W. Yew
National University of Singapore, Singapore

S. K. Ong
National University of Singapore, Singapore

A. Y. C. Nee
National University of Singapore, Singapore

ABSTRACT

It is the goal of ubiquitous computing (UbiComp) to hide computers from the users. Instead, everyday objects embedded with computer processing capability become smart objects that act as interfaces to computer software. A challenge with this new paradigm of computing is to create natural and obvious ways for people to interact with objects and receive output from the computer software that these objects serve as interfaces to. In this chapter, a solution is proposed whereby virtual user interfaces are added to smart objects. These virtual interfaces are viewed in augmented reality through personal viewing devices which also allow people to interact directly with them. The implementation of UbiComp environments and personal viewing devices is described in order to illustrate the use of current technology in creating user-friendly UbiComp environments.

INTRODUCTION

Ubiquitous computing (UbiComp) refers to a paradigm of computing wherein computing can take place anywhere and everywhere. It was the vision of the man who coined the term "ubiquitous computing", Mark Weiser, that computer hardware would disappear into the natural environment, with seemingly everyday objects taking the place of computers so that "people will simply use them unconsciously to accomplish everyday tasks" (Weiser, 1991).

A subtle impact of UbiComp can be seen with the emergence of smart buildings and smart cit-

DOI: 10.4018/978-1-4666-6228-5.ch012

ies. To save cost and energy and provide a more comfortable environment, sensor networks and distributed computing systems built into modern shopping malls and office complexes allow for optimized and automated lighting and temperature control; this is with the help of occupancy tracking and ambient lighting and temperature sensing and forecasting ("Occupying Yourself", 2010; "LonWorks®-based Office Building", n.d.).

UbiComp has begun to manifest in recent years in a literal sense. With embedded computer systems, smartphones and mobile devices, computers are practically everywhere. The pervasiveness of wireless internet and thus access to cloud computing allows for traditional computer tasks, e.g., checking e-mail, writing a document, and even playing games, to be done anywhere. There are also numerous smartphone "apps", which are lightweight computer applications that support people in practically any conceivable way.

UbiComp can achieve its full potential if apps are built into the environment and the physical objects within the environment. This way, location-based services can be provided to people without them having to be aware of apps which have to be downloaded to their mobile device. The challenge lies in presenting such environment-embedded services to the people in the environment and the ways they can interact with these services.

This chapter presents a framework for implementing UbiComp environments that allows for virtual graphical user interfaces to be added to objects in the environment. These objects are imbued with computing and networking capabilities, and are thus known as smart objects. Using augmented reality (AR) technology, every smart object is given a virtual user interface that is augmented onto the user's view of the physical environment, which can be seen through a personal viewing device. This means that the user does not have to shift his focus away from the environment while still being able to access rich interactivity and complex functionality of the environment. The end result is a person being able to walk into an environment and immediately see the objects that

are providing services and functionality beyond their physical capability.

The rest of the chapter is structured as follows. First, other solutions to the issues that have been discussed are explored. The proposed framework is described, followed by details on the ways to create smart objects and their individual user interfaces, as well different personal viewing devices that can be developed to provide intuitive and natural interaction with smart objects. Finally, future research directions are discussed.

BACKGROUND

In the traditional computing model, a graphical user interface provides the awareness of the functionality of the software through helpful tooltips and contextually relevant iconic buttons; these are the means for interaction with the software through interaction elements like buttons and sliders, and the primary means of system output is via a computer screen. In UbiComp, the environment and the objects therein make up the computing platform, which means radically different implementations of user interfaces are required.

A novel kind of user interface is tangible user interfaces (TUIs) which are made up of physical objects that are directly and intuitively manipulated in order to interact with a computer-aided task. Some TUIs are designed as application-specific systems where the modes of interaction with the physical elements correspond to the functionality of the system (Lee, Hong, & Johnson, 2006; Nagel, Heidmann, Condotta, & Duval, 2010). There is also a generic approach in TUI implementation in which physical objects are converted to standard interface devices, e.g., buttons, sliders and pointers, to interact with a UbiComp environment, as demonstrated in the iStuff framework (Ballagas, Ringel, Stone, & Borchers, 2003). With this generic approach, applications and system output are abstracted from the TUI so that any kinds of applications can be developed to work with the interaction objects. Short of labeling every interactive object, the TUI approach does not provide the awareness of functionality to the users. This means that the UbiComp environments utilizing TUIs require that users are familiar with the environments.

A different approach is the use of interactive surfaces. The traditional desktop computing model shifts focus and attention away from the environment. Therefore, interactive surfaces, which are essentially multi-touch computer displays, are more natural for users because interactive surfaces can be placed on practically any surface with multi-touch providing intuitive user interaction. Some interactive surfaces also track proximal physical objects and output visual feedback according to users' interactions with the objects, which makes it a kind of TUI as well (Wilson, 2005). Since interactive surfaces allow for the display of virtual graphics and media, functionality awareness cues can be provided easily. The problem with using interactive surfaces is the high cost of implementing such an environment.

AR brings an added dimension to UbiComp. AR refers to a perception of the physical world augmented with computer-generated information like graphics and sound that are registered to actual physical locations in the environment. AR systems started to appear in the 1990's. In 1992, a see-through head-mounted display device implemented by researchers led by Caudell at Boeing was reported which could overlay diagrams on real-world objects during aircraft manufacturing operations (Caudell & Mizell, 1992). A system of "virtual fixtures" developed by Rosenberg was also reported in 1992 which improved the performance of tele-operated tasks by augmenting the operator's vision with a view of the remote environment, having an exoskeleton to restrict the operator's motion thus providing a haptic fixture, and sound overlaid on the operator's view of the remote environment to aid in the perception of the haptic fixture (Rosenberg, 1992). AR application development and research was made widely accessible with the release of ARToolKit ("How Does ARToolKit", n.d.) in

1999. The ARToolKit platform works by searching for square planar markers called fiducial markers with known patterns to obtain their 3D pose in the camera image (Kato & Billinghurst, 1999) and renders 3D computer graphics based on the pose of the markers so that virtual objects appear to be sitting on the markers in the physical space. AR has been applied in numerous domains, such as manufacturing (Nee, Ong, Chryssolouris, & Mourtzis, 2012), navigation, tourism, medical applications, and entertainment (Krevelen & Poelman, 2010). AR fulfills the tenets of UbiComp quite well because firstly, the display of information registered to physical locations does not shift focus away from the natural environment, and secondly, the physical environment and its objects are a part of the system.

Most research works applying AR in UbiComp focus on using AR as a contextual visualization tool of digital information in a UbiComp environment (Schmalstieg & Reitmayr, 2005; Li, Chen, & Xiahou, 2009) rather than as an interaction tool in a UbiComp environment. However, AR has tremendous potential in complex object-centric interaction. AR technology can add complex interaction options to simple objects and enable them to be used as output devices at the same time. Furthermore, advancements in mobile computing have made it possible for smartphones and mobile devices to perform the environmental tracking computations that are required to render graphics in AR, thus making the cost of implementing AR systems economical.

FRAMEWORK FOR UBICOMP ENVIRONMENTS

Architecture

The UbiComp environment proposed by the authors in this research essentially consists of smart objects with individual virtual user interfaces that appear to overlap with their physical structure when seen through a personal viewing

Figure 1. Architecture of the augmented reality ubiquitous computing environment framework

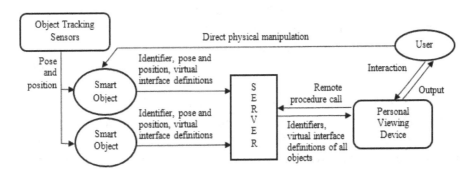

device. Each smart object behaves independently and defines its own user interface, making the overall functionality of the UbiComp environment modular. As personal viewing devices are basically thin clients with no prior knowledge of the smart objects and the environment, a server and a network infrastructure are needed in order to communicate the information to personal viewing devices. Personal viewing devices must also be able to track their location and orientation within the environment so as to be able to achieve the effect of the virtual user interfaces overlaying with their corresponding smart objects. If the smart objects move, object tracking sensors will also be required. These elements of the framework, summarized in Figure 1, will be detailed in the sub-sections that follow.

Smart Objects

Physical objects are the front-end interfaces of the ubiquitous computing environment to the end users. Networking components and a microprocessor are attached to each object, together with any sensors and electrical components that are needed to fulfill their functionality, thus turning them into smart objects. The underlying computing functions programmed into an object's microprocessor are exposed to the end users as interaction options.

It is possible to trigger each interaction option of an object through some physical manipulation of the object, such as tilting it to a certain angle or moving it at a certain speed, provided sensors that can detect such states are associated with the smart object. Interaction options might also be filtered or adapted to their underlying behavior based on other conditions, such as the time of day, location of the object, temperature of the environment, etc., to provide a contextually aware set of interactions to the users. However, simple objects with limited possible ways to be manipulated will have limited interaction options that can be triggered. AR can alleviate this problem by augmenting virtual interface controls on an object which the users can interact with so as to trigger interaction options via remote procedure calls (RPCs).

Smart objects can also act as output devices for information from the UbiComp environment. The output can be via physical components, such as LEDs and speakers. However, this may become too costly for simple smart objects or there may not even be enough space to attach the requisite hardware. In this case, AR is used to overcome these physical limitations by enabling output via augmented virtual graphics.

Tracking and Registration

In order for personal viewing devices to render augmented graphics correctly, knowledge of their own transformation, i.e., position and orientation, within a coordinate system that maps the environment is required as well as knowledge of the transformations of smart objects in the same map. Tracking and registration refers to the process of tracking the transformations of objects and physical landmarks in the environment so that augmented virtual graphics can be displayed to appear fixed at specific physical locations in the environment.

There are many possible methods of environment tracking. Optical tracking, where a camera making use of computer vision algorithms recognizes features or objects in the environment and computes its transformation relative to these objects, is commonly used because it is cost-effective and precise. There are several different optical tracking approaches. The most basic is the tracking of fiducial markers ("How Does ARToolKit", n.d.) which requires the markers to be placed in the environment. Markerless tracking methods like planar feature tracking (Wagner, Reitmayr, Mulloni, Drummond, & Schmalstieg, 2008) and 3D feature tracking (Klein & Murray, 2007) track features in the environment directly instead of markers, and are more desirable for the reduced need for environmental preparation.

Mapping the landmarks in the environment is not a difficult task. A simultaneous localization and mapping algorithm can automatically map targets tracked by a device by referring to mapped targets (Lim & Lee, 2009). In such a mapping process, the only user intervention needed is to define the landmarks that mark the origin of the map, specify the size of the landmarks if different sized landmarks are used, and walk around the environment pointing the viewing device at landmarks to map them.

If smart objects in the environment are not at fixed positions and orientations, they will need to be tracked as well. Objects can be tracked by sensors or cameras in the environment using the same optical and non-optical methods that were mentioned previously. Separating the tracking of objects from the tracking of the environment allows for a single universal tracking method to be used by all personal viewing devices entering UbiComp spaces while a mixture of any tracking

methods can be used on the objects that they are suitable for.

SMART OBJECT CREATION

The creation of smart objects takes place in two main steps. First, the behavior of the smart object is programmed into a microprocessor that is attached to the object along with a networking device, such as a wireless communication transceiver, and the relevant sensors and other electrical components. Next, the virtual elements of the augmented smart object interface are modeled in 3D and their input and output methods are defined. All the data is stored on memory that is attached to the smart object, and is shared with the personal viewing devices via the server.

Virtual Interface Creation

The 3D model of the virtual interface of a smart object plays a crucial role in providing complex object-centric interaction methods with the object and is stored in a 3D assets file with the smart object. The 3D assets file includes the usual mesh data, such as vertices, normals, and material properties, and the personal viewing devices required in order to render the virtual interface. In addition, the definitions for the interface element, including the RPCs that it triggers, must be added to the 3D assets file. The interface element definitions determine the ways with which the element is interacted, e.g., whether the user simply has to touch it to activate it or whether it involves some other actions, and the data that is passed to the RPC of the object.

The interface element definitions are included with the 3D model data, and registered to individual 3D objects in the model. That is to say, a 3D model of a virtual interface is made up of multiple simpler 3D objects, each of which defines one particular interface element. These definitions can be added to existing 3D asset file formats, such as COLLADA ("COLLADA 1.4 Specification", n.d.). In this way, smart object creators will be able to use any 3D modeling software to create and export the virtual interface elements as separate 3D objects, after which a plugin or standalone software can be used to define specific 3D objects as interface elements.

Interface Element Definition Schema

An XML-based schema for the definition of interface elements in a COLLADA file is provided in Table 1. This schema also represents the data structures that are maintained in viewing devices in order to display the virtual interfaces. Note that the top level tag in the schema, "Interface", is a sub-element of the "Node" element, which is used to define a specific 3D object in the scene, of the COLLADA schema. It is assumed that one node contains one 3D object. The schema allows for three types of user interactions to be used with the interface elements, touch, drag, and rotate. The touch gesture allows an interface element to function like a button, while the drag and rotate gestures allow an element to function like a slider and knob respectively. Other XML tags in the schema define the RPC triggered by each interaction, the input value of the RPC, and the appearance of the interface element in response to certain events.

Under the "Input" tag, the tags for each of the three user input gestures are defined. Each gesture tag has an "id" attribute which uniquely identifies the set of definitions for it. Each gesture tag defines the input value for the interaction option which is named in the "RPC" attribute. The input value can be explicitly defined using the "Value" tag. The "type" attribute specifies the data type of the value, i.e., string, integer, floating-point, etc. The input value may also be interpolated from the position or rotation angle of the 3D model of the interface element from its origin, with the minimum and maximum input values as well as the minimum and maximum 3D positions or rotation angles defined as attributes. The input value can also be explicitly defined for a certain range of 3D positions or rotation angles of the interface element. Personal viewing devices can render the interface element in the correct position or angle as the user drags or rotates it, and use the minimum and maximum position or rotation angles to stop the change in the interface element when the limits have been reached.

The definitions under the "Output" tag are for elements that are used as output devices. There are four events that can cause the element to produce some forms of output. The first event is a non-event defined by the "Static" tag. The "Static" tag has two possible graphical outputs. The first is a color overlay which can have different degrees of translucency based on the alpha value of the color attribute, and the second is a string of text which will be textured onto the element using the texture coordinates defined in the COLLADA file for that 3D object and a texture generated by the personal viewing device. The other three events are for the three user input gestures occurring on the element. These may result in a color overlay or text output on the element, or a translation, rotation, or scaling of the element. Using the attributes for each of the "Translate", "Rotate", and "Scale" tags, the movement of the element can be smoothly animated by transforming it by the desired amount over a specified duration. The "stay" attribute is used to indicate whether the element should remain in the final state after the duration of the animation or return to its original state.

Possible Interface Elements

There is a high degree of flexibility with which virtual interfaces for smart objects can be implemented. In a COLLADA file, each node can have multiple "Interface" tags as the "id" attribute allows interface elements to be uniquely identified. The same applies for each gesture event. This allows different interfaces to be used at different times and gives smart objects access to

Table 1. Schema for virtual interface element definitions

Tag	Attribute	Data
Interface	Id, visibility	
Input		
Touch	Id, RPC, RPC description	
Value	Type	Input value to RPC
Drag	Id, RPC, RPC description	
Interpolate	Type, minimum value, maximum value, minimum position, maximum position	
Range	Type, minimum position, maximum position	Input value to RPC
Rotate	Id, RPC, RPC description	
Interpolate	Type, minimum angle, maximum angle, minimum value, maximum value, axis of rotation	
Range	Type, minimum angle, maximum angle, axis of rotation	Input value to RPC
Output		
Static	Id	
Overlay	Color (RGBA)	
Text	Font, color (RGBA)	Text to be displayed
Translate	Duration, displacement, stay	
Rotate	Duration, angular displacement, axis of rotation, stay	
Scale	Duration, scale amount, stay	
Touch	Id	
Overlay	Color (RGBA)	
Text	Font, color (RGBA)	Text to be displayed
Translate	Duration, displacement, stay	
Rotate	Duration, angular displacement, axis of rotation, stay	
Scale	Duration, scale amount, stay	
Drag	Id	
Overlay	Color (RGBA)	
Text	Font, color (RGBA)	Text to be displayed
Translate	Duration, displacement, stay	
Rotate	Duration, angular displacement, axis of rotation, stay	
Scale	Duration, scale amount, stay	
Rotate	Id	
Overlay	Color (RGBA)	
Text	Font, color (RGBA)	Text to be displayed
Translate	Duration, displacement, stay	
Rotate	Duration, angular displacement, axis of rotation, stay	
Scale	Duration, scale amount, stay	

their properties to modify them. This is useful for implementing context-aware user interfaces that change in response to different user or environmental conditions.

An "Interface" tag has a "visibility" attribute that can indicate to the personal viewing device to make the 3D model of the interface invisible. This is useful for using physical parts of the object as interface elements, and for allowing physical parts to occlude virtual parts. In addition, each interface element can have more than one "Input" and "Output" tag, allowing multiple interaction and output methods with a single element.

The animation tags, i.e., "Translate", "Rotate", and "Scale", can serve as information output to users. For example, touching a button that responds by expanding can be used to indicate an increase in some values, such as an increase in the temperature of the object. The animation tags can also be used as visual feedback to indicate that a user's interaction with a specific interface element has been picked up by the system, similar to the vibration of a smartphone when a button on the touch-screen is touched. The "stay" attribute of the animation tags is useful to indicate the current state of a smart object. An example is a virtual flip switch, which is in the down position if a smart object is in an inactive state and up position when it is switched on. The "Input" property of the flip switch will send an RPC to the smart object to activate it while the "Output" property is used to animate the rotation of the flip switch downwards and make it remain there. The smart object will then send a message to change the down state of the switch to a "Static" property while the "angular displacement" attribute of the "Touch" event will be changed to an upwards rotation of the switch.

A mixture of different input and output gestures and their attributes can result in many different kinds of interface elements. Figure 2 shows two input element types, namely, button and knob, and two output element types, namely, overlay and text, augmented on a simple coffee mug. The mug has a temperature sensor and microcontroller attached at the bottom. The user sets a threshold temperature for the coffee using a virtual knob on the side of the coffee mug and the threshold value is stored in the microcontroller. While the temperature is above the threshold value, the microcontroller activates the color overlay interface element of the mug to shade it red, indicating that the coffee is still too hot. When it drops below the threshold temperature, the color attribute of the overlay is changed to green. The virtual interface also displays the duration that the coffee has been brewing for which is monitored and updated by the microcontroller.

SMARTPHONE AS A PERSONAL VIEWING DEVICE

If an UbiComp environment were to be implemented today for use by the general public, the most viable device for use as personal viewing devices in terms of cost and ease of use would be the users' own smartphones. Any average smartphone by today's standards is theoretically sufficiently equipped to serve as a personal viewing device as long as it has an embedded camera. An Android app was created to demonstrate the use of a smartphone as a personal viewing device and tested on a Samsung Galaxy S2 device.

Tracking

An AR view can be accomplished on a smartphone by using the embedded camera to recognize and track features in the environment. The app uses the OpenCV open source computer vision library ("OpenCV", n.d.) to aid in implementing a natural planar feature tracking algorithm. A map of the planar features of the environment, having been pre-created, is transferred to the app over Wi-Fi from the server in the environment. The map contains information to describe each set of planar features (Rublee, Rabaud, Konolige, & Bradski, 2011), so that the app can recognize them, and the transformation of the planar feature set. The transformations and user interface definitions of

Figure 2. A coffee mug (a) augmented with a virtual interface, (b) with temperature shading turned on using the square button, (c) shaded green after the coffee temperature falls below the threshold, (d) shaded red again after the threshold is lowered using knob

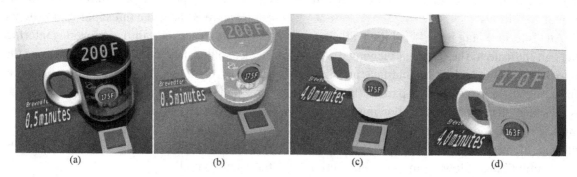

smart objects in the environment are also transferred from the server. The virtual interfaces are rendered on a video feed of the smartphone camera to achieve the AR view.

Interaction

Interaction with the user interface elements is achieved through the touch-screen. The selection of 3D objects on the touch-screen is similar to using a mouse for picking 3D objects on a monitor, for which there are several well-established methods. Once a user interface element is selected, the user can perform a drag or rotate gesture on it if the element accepts such input. Otherwise, a touch operation is performed once the user's finger leaves contact with the screen. Interactions with each element will result in the corresponding RPC being sent to the smart object via the server. Figure 3 depicts the three operations performed through the smartphone app on three different interface elements.

WEARABLE SYSTEM AS A PERSONAL VIEWING DEVICE

Wearable computers have begun to gain traction in recent times and are really where the future of AR lies. While the smartphone approach requires that the user to hold and interact with the mobile device, a lightweight wearable system using a head-mounted display that augments the full view of the wearer allows the wearer to walk around unencumbered and hands-free while being able to view the augmented UbiComp environment. Unfortunately, a lightweight and low-cost wearable system is unavailable thus far, though a number of companies are working on it. Nevertheless, a prototype system was created so as to illustrate its potential to make an AR UbiComp environment extremely useful and user-friendly.

The prototype system works on the Windows platform and comprises a laptop which outputs video to a head-mounted display which has a mounted camera (Figure 4). Similar to the smartphone system, the camera tracks its transformation by recognizing planar features in the environment and the AR view is achieved by rendering the virtual interfaces over the camera feed as the background.

Interaction is achieved through bare-hand interaction and gesture recognition. To achieve this, a sequence of image processing operations using the OpenCV library is performed on the camera video to detect a hand in the camera view and determine the gesture that the hand is making.

Hand Detection

To detect the hand, the colors of the pixels are analyzed to determine skin-colored pixels. A

Figure 3. Interaction with virtual interface elements through a smartphone

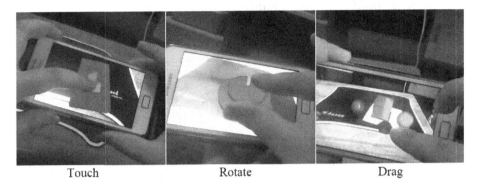

Touch   Rotate   Drag

black and white image is produced where pixels determined to be skin color are set to white and everything else black. Contour analysis is then performed on the black and white image to determine no more than one region as the most probable region to be a hand based on its size and shape. The contour of this region is further analyzed to detect individual fingers.

Fingers are detected by obtaining the convex hull of the hand contour and finding its "convexity defects", which are regions within the convex hull that are not within the hand contour. Only convexity defects of a minimum depth indicate the presence of a finger (Figure 5a). Individual fingers are classified as either a "pointer finger", of which there can only be one, or an "additional finger". If there is only one convexity defect of

sufficient depth, there is only one finger that is automatically classified as a pointer.

It is also important to obtain the screen coordinates of the tip of each finger for the later step of gesture detection. The tip of the pointer finger is defined as the furthest contour point from the centroid of the contour (Figure 5b). The tip of an additional finger is the second furthest contour point, and that of a second additional finger is the third furthest contour point, and so on.

Gesture Recognition and Interaction

The possible gestures that can be used to interact with the virtual user interface elements in the wearable system are click, drag, and rotate, which correspond to touch, drag, and rotate in the smartphone system. The click gesture is reminiscent

Figure 4. The prototype wearable system

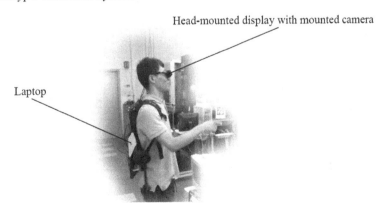

Head-mounted display with mounted camera

Laptop

Figure 5. (a) Convexity defect of sufficient depth indicates presence of finger. (b) Fingertip is the furthest contour point from the centroid of the hand contour

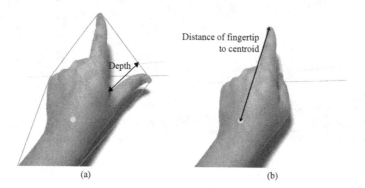

of using the pointer finger to press a switch or button. The drag gesture resembles the pointer finger holding down a button and dragging it in one direction. The rotate gesture involves the pointer finger and another finger, most appropriately the thumb, rotating as if they are turning a knob. These are gestures that most people would be familiar with from their experience with using smartphones. Figure 6 shows these gestures being used to interact with virtual interface elements.

The click gesture consists of four stages (top row of Figure 7). The first stage is the initialization stage, wherein the hand must remain in the same position and pose for a fixed duration, e.g., one second. The dot on the finger shows the position of

the fingertip and the dot on the hand indicates the position of the centroid of the hand contour. The circles around the two dots indicate the regions that these two points must remain within during the initialization stage. If the initialization is successful, the circles turn from orange to green. Otherwise, the initialization is restarted. The second stage occurs after the initialization stage. The user can start performing a click action at any time during this stage. The system continues monitoring the fingertip and the centre of mass during this stage. If the hand centroid moves out of the circle, the gesture is cancelled and the initialization stage is activated again. If the user bends his finger such that the fingertip goes out of the circle around the

Figure 6. Interaction with virtual interface elements through a wearable system

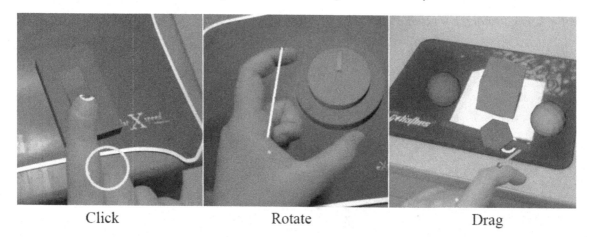

Click   Rotate   Drag

fingertip and the distance between the fingertip and the centroid decreases, the system interprets this as a finger pressing action and the third stage is activated. A yellow dot indicates the original position of the fingertip before the pressing action started. During this third stage, as long as the centroid stays within the circle, the click gesture is active. If the click gesture is still active and the fingertip returns inside the circle, the click gesture is completed. This is indicated by the yellow dot turning red momentarily before the initialization stage restarts. On completion of the click gesture, the screen coordinates of the yellow/red dot, i.e., the screen coordinates of the fingertip when the click gesture first started, is obtained and used to determine the object or element that has been clicked on.

The stages of the drag gesture are shown in the middle row of Figure 7. The first stage is the same initialization stage as for the click gesture. After initialization, when the user bends his finger downwards, this is still considered part of a click gesture. The click gesture turns into a drag gesture in the third stage, when the user moves his entire hand until the centroid leaves the circle, which marks the region within which the centroid was originally located when the click gesture started. At this point, the click gesture is turned into a drag gesture. The drag distance is indicated by a line joining the start-point of the drag gesture and the current position of the fingertip. During this stage, the distance dragged is continuously monitored and used as interaction input. The small circle near the fingertip shows where the finger must return to in order to complete the drag gesture (the finger release stage). This circle translates by following the translation of the centroid. After the finger release, the drag gesture ends and the initialization stage is restarted.

The rotate gesture (bottom row of Figure 7) starts with the same initialization stage as in the click and drag gestures. The appearance of a second finger triggers the start of a rotate gesture. A line is displayed to illustrate the rotation action as the user performs it. As the line rotates from its previous orientation, the rotation angle is monitored and used as interaction input. The rotate gesture ends when the second finger disappears, i.e., the user retracts his finger back into the palm.

Occlusion of Virtual Elements by the Hand

As the AR view is achieved by overlaying virtual elements on the camera feed, every virtual element will appear on top of everything in the physical environment including the user's hands. However, to maintain a perception of depth and thus the immersiveness of the UbiComp environment, the user's hand should occlude virtual elements (Figure 8). This also makes it easier to interact with virtual elements because the user is able to see where he is pointing. This of course assumes that the hand is always nearer to the user than the virtual elements. However, this is a reasonable assumption because of the unlikelihood of a virtual element being between the user's face and hand.

Making the user's hand appear to occlude virtual elements involves manipulating the graphics rendering pipeline. After the camera feed is drawn as the background of the screen, a depth mask is created from a black and white image of the user's hand in order to set the depth value of the pixels belonging to the hand to a minimum value (these pixels of minimum depth represent objects that are nearest to the graphics rendering engine's virtual camera). When the virtual elements are drawn, the graphics rendering engine performs a depth test, which means that any virtual element that occupies the same pixels as the hand pixels will fail the depth test and not be drawn.

SYSTEM EVALUATION

The smartphone and wearable viewing device prototypes were used to evaluate AR user interfaces and their interaction methods in a user study. A

Figure 7. Hand gestures detected by the wearable system

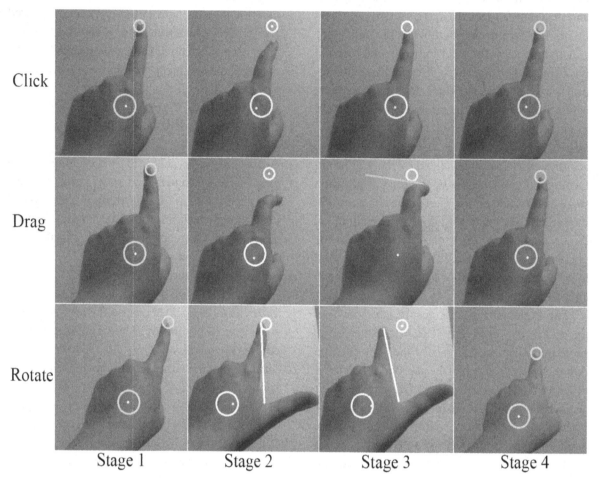

video player was created on a desktop computer with an AR user interface containing a button to play/pause the video, a knob to adjust the volume, and a slider to seek a particular time in the video. The user study consisted of 15 people of ages between 7 and 68. All but four of them own and use a smartphone or tablet device with the typical touch gestures used in the Android and iOS systems (pinch, rotate, swipe, etc.). The users were asked play and pause, adjust the volume, and seek specific positions in a video played on the video player using the AR user interface through each of the two prototype viewing devices. They were also asked to perform the same operations on a television using its remote control. Their feedback was obtained through an interview. In the interview, they were asked for the good and bad aspects of their experience in using the AR video player and to compare it with their use of the television. They were also asked to comment on their experience of using AR interfaces compared to physical controls on a device and 2D interfaces on touchscreens in general. The feedback for interaction with AR interfaces through the smartphone and wearable system is collated and summarized in Tables 2 and 3 respectively, along with the demographic of the users who raised or agreed with a particular comment, while that for interaction through AR interfaces compared to physical controls and 2D interfaces is given in Table 4.

Figure 8. Occlusion of virtual elements by the user's hand

The feedback shows that the main problem with the smartphone system is that the screen is small. The advantage of the wearable system over the smartphone is that it is hands-free and allows for full field of vision augmentation. However, the major problems are its ergonomics and the quality of the video display. The feedback regarding AR user interfaces indicated that they are successful in providing visual cues and feedback but effecting interactions with them through either the smartphone or wearable system still needs to be improved.

FUTURE RESEARCH DIRECTIONS

The user study shows that the improvements that need to be made are with respect to the implementation of the personal viewing devices. Personal viewing devices combine tracking, display and natural interaction technologies. Many of the technologies have ongoing research issues that limit their practical use and acceptance on a large scale. Further research is warranted in these areas in order to realize a highly immersive and user-friendly UbiComp environment.

Tracking Technology

There are a great number of different tracking technologies which have differing advantages and disadvantages. While optical approaches are often low-cost and precise, they are not perfectly robust to lighting conditions and noise, which often results in slight jittering of the virtual elements and occasional loss of tracking. Furthermore, these algorithms have a large computational requirement that contributes greatly to the system latency and drains mobile battery life.

Table 2. Feedback from user study on the use of a smartphone as a viewing device

Comment	User Profile
The gestures that are used to control the AR interface are intuitive because they are largely the same as the default touch-screen gestures.	All smartphone users
Using the smartphone to control a video player is more convenient than using a physical remote control because my phone is usually kept by my side.	10 out of the 15 users, all of whom are smartphone users
The gestures are easy to become familiar with.	All non-smartphone users
Performing the rotate operation takes a little getting used to because of the two-step process of first touching the interface element with one finger and then using two fingers to rotate.	All users
The screen is small, making it difficult to see and select interface elements accurately.	All users

Non-optical approaches for environmental tracking, like magnetic ("3D Guidance trak-STAR", n.d.) and ultrasonic (Newman, Ingram, & Hopper, 2001) tracking, are precise but expensive and require external hardware that also limits the range of use. Sensor-based tracking with GPS, electronic compass, and accelerometers is becoming more economical with the lowering cost of sensors and do not require environmental preparation. However, accuracy is to the order of several metres, which is much worse than the other methods.

Many researchers have started to turn to hybrid tracking methods to combine the advantages of different tracking approaches and overcome their disadvantages (Waechter et al., 2010; Schall, Mulloni, & Reitmayr, 2010; Kurz & Himane, 2011).

Another idea is to develop specialized hardware that greatly optimizes the computer processing for AR and reduces battery consumption, and this is something that the AR technology company Metaio has been working on ("Metaio brings world's", 2013).

Display Technology

Apart from the large size and weight of currently available hardware, there are fundamental problems with wearable systems which are quite well-documented (Rolland, Holloway, & Fuchs, 1995), chief among which is system latency. With video see-through head-mounted displays, where the user's perception of the real environment is through a video feed, there is a slight lag between

Table 3. Feedback from user study on the use of the wearable system as a viewing device

Comment	User Profile
The augmentation of the full field of vision makes the AR interface seem to blend into the physical environment better.	12 out of the 15 users
The wearable system allows the hands to remain free which makes it much faster and more convenient to interact with the AR interface.	All users
The wearable system is too troublesome and uncomfortable to wear.	All users
Watching a video through another video (the head-mounted display) degrades the experience of watching the video greatly.	All users
Though the graphical hints help, the gestures still take a lot of getting used to because of the multiple steps needed to effect a gesture detection.	All users
Once gotten used to the gestures, they seem quite intuitive and thus easy to remember.	All smartphone users and two non-smartphone users

Table 4. Feedback from user study on interaction through AR user interfaces

Comment	User Profile
The purpose and interaction method of the AR interface elements are obvious because of their appearance.	13 out of the 15 users
The animations help reinforce the feeling that the interactions have been effected, so there is less tendency to repeatedly press a button unlike the scenario of using a physical remote control.	9 out of the 15 users
The rendering of the AR user interface upon the object that it controls helps to reduce confusion by making it clear which device the user interface is for.	13 out of the 15 users

what goes on in reality and when it is reflected in the video feed. This affects human reaction time to events in real life, reduces the confidence of the wearer in moving through a busy environment, and makes the experience more uncomfortable than immersive.

With optical see-through devices, which give the user a direct view of the real environment through transparent lenses, the issue of system latency is mitigated but can still be perceptible because virtual elements may not align correctly with real objects if there is lag and large relative movements between the user and the objects. Furthermore, a calibrated optical see-through device once worn by the user cannot be shifted relative to the user's eyes lest the user be required to perform calibration again. Without re-calibration, any small shift may translate to a large misalignment of the virtual elements on the real objects.

There are quite a few companies working on cheaper and lighter head-mounted displays and with increasing mobile computational power, which may greatly reduce the issue of system latency to imperceptible levels one day. There are more advanced technologies being developed, such as virtual retinal displays (Silverman, Schowengerdt, Kelly, & Seibel, 2003) and contact lens displays (Lingley et al., 2011), both of which produce images directly onto the eye and would thus greatly simplify the calibration requirements. The challenge, though, is not just to discover new display technologies but to explore ways of integrating new and novel display technologies with other UbiComp-enabling technologies.

Natural Interaction Methods

Natural interaction is a movement away from the traditional human-computer interaction devices, like the keyboard and mouse, to methods that seem more intuitive and easy to use by people. A good example that most people are now familiar with is touch-screen and stylus interaction on smartphones and tablets. However, this requires the user to hold the device and cannot be considered completely natural.

Many researchers are working on hand gesture recognition to enable natural interaction with computer software because it is possible to use non-contact sensors for these systems, which frees up the user's hands. Hand gesture recognition based on a single standard camera (Černeková, Malerczyk, Nikolaidis, & Pitas, 2008; Xu, Gu, Tao, & Wu, 2009) is a well-researched topic because of the potentially low-cost systems that can be made. However, similar to optical-based tracking, the variation of results due to adverse lighting conditions and noise still cannot be eliminated. More specialized hardware like depth cameras and ultrasonic sensors are becoming common and have opened the way for the development of more robust and precise hand gesture interaction methods (Kalgaonkar & Raj, 2009; Ren, Yuan, Meng, & Zhang, 2013).

Apart from hand gestures and hand manipulation, other modalities can be exploited for natural interaction. An example is voice recognition, which is a relatively established technology though issues like the handling of new words and the recognition of confusable words remain difficult challenges for voice recognition interfaces (Huang, Baker, & Reddy, 2014). There are also less explicit forms of natural interaction, such as facial expression detection (Cerezo et al., 2007; Anand et al., 2012), gaze tracking (Bulling & Gellersen, 2010; Zsolt & Levente, 2010), and activity detection (Aggarwal & Ryoo, 2011). Sensor fusion is a common technique in both UbiComp and natural interaction, and hence continued research in this direction would likely lead to more intelligent and robust methods of interaction.

CONCLUSION

A framework for creating UbiComp environments, where the interaction with smart objects and system output through smart objects is enhanced through AR has been presented. Under this framework, the creation of smart objects is relatively simple, involving the attachment of networking hardware and a microprocessor at minimum, and the creation of a virtual model of the smart object with virtual interaction and output elements. The schema for defining virtual interaction and output elements is based on COLLADA and can potentially be implemented with other existing 3D asset file formats. This paves the way for plugins for popular 3D modeling software and standalone tools to be developed for modeling the virtual aspects of smart objects.

With the flexibility of having any kind of underlying behavior, smart objects with complex functionality can be interacted with under this framework through direct manipulation of virtual 3D objects, dynamically changing to suit the user's context. The smart object virtual interface schema allows many different kinds of virtual elements to be created and interacted with in different ways, and this allows for the seamless mixture of physical and virtual parts of a smart object. The framework also enables the abstraction of smart object functionality from actual interaction and output methods so that there is flexibility in the use of different kinds of personal viewing devices. The implementation of two such devices was described to showcase the short term solution of using smartphones and the more desirable approach for the future of using wearable systems.

A user study conducted to evaluate an AR user interface based on this framework shows that this approach can be accepted provided improvements are made on the technologies related to tracking, display and interaction. Hopefully with further development in these areas, the proposed system will be able to achieve its full potential.

With widespread adoption, companies and hobbyists alike will be able to create smart objects that are useful and accessible to everyone in a wide variety of environments, like homes, schools, offices, hospitals, shopping malls, etc, and for a wide variety of tasks and purposes. The authors' vision is that with this framework, traditional computer hardware will disappear, and computer software will be embedded in objects so that people will simply use them unconsciously to accomplish everyday tasks.

REFERENCES

3D. *Guidance trakSTAR*. (n.d.). Retrieved October 2, 2013 from http://www.ascension-tech.com/medical/trakSTAR.php

Aggarwal, J. K., & Ryoo, M. S. (2011). Human Activity Analysis: A Review. *ACM Computing Surveys*, *43*(3), 16. doi:10.1145/1922649.1922653

Anand, B., Navathe, B. B., Velusamy, S., Kannan, H., Sharma, A., & Gopalakrishnan, V. (2012). Article. In *Proceedings of 2012 IEEE Consumer Communications and Networking Conference* (pp. 255 – 259). Washington, DC: IEEE Computer Society.

Ballagas, R., Ringel, M., Stone, M., & Borchers, J. (2003). iStuff: A Physical User Interface Toolkit for Ubiquitous Computing Environments. In *Proceedings of SIGCHI Conference on Human Factors in Computing Systems* (pp. 537 – 544). New York, NY: ACM.

Bulling, A., & Gellersen, H. (2010). Toward Mobile Eye-Based Human-Computer Interaction. *IEEE Pervasive Computing / IEEE Computer Society [and] IEEE Communications Society*, 9(4), 8–12. doi:10.1109/MPRV.2010.86

Caudell, T., & Mizell, D. (1992). Augmented reality: an application of heads-up display technology to manual manufacturing processes. In *Proceedings of the Twenty-Fifth Hawaii International Conference on System Sciences* (Vol. 2, pp. 659 - 669). Washington, DC: IEEE Computer Society.

Cerezo, E., Hupont, I., Manresa-Yee, C., Varona, J., Baldassarri, S., Perales, F. J., & Seron, F. J. (2007). Real-Time Facial Expression Recognition for Natural Interaction. *Lecture Notes in Computer Science*, 4478(1), 40–47. doi:10.1007/978-3-540-72849-8_6

Černeková, Z., & Malerczyk, C. Nikolaidis, N., & Pitas, I. (2008). Single Camera Pointing Gesture Recognition for Interaction in Edutainment Applications. In *Proceedings of the 24th Spring Conference on Computer Graphics* (pp. 121 – 125). New York, NY: ACM.

COLLADA 1.4 Specification Reference Card. (n.d.). Retrieved April 11, 2013 from http://www.khronos.org/developers/view_online/12577249

How Does ARToolkit Work? (n.d.). Retrieved October 10, 2013 from http://www.hitl.washington.edu/artoolkit/documentation/userarwork.htm

Huang, X., Baker, J., & Reddy, R. (2014). A Historical Perspective of Speech Recognition. *Communications of the ACM*, 57(1), 94–103. doi:10.1145/2500887

Kalgaonkar, K., & Raj, B. (2009). One-handed Gesture Recognition using Ultrasonic Doppler Sonar. In *Proceedings of the 2009 IEEE International Conference on Acoustics, Speech and Signal Processing* (pp. 1889–1892). Washington, DC: IEEE Computer Society.

Kato, H., & Billinghurst, M. (1999). Marker Tracking and HMD Calibration for a Video-based Augmented Reality Conferencing System. In *Proceedings of 2nd IEEE and ACM International Workshop on Augmented Reality* (pp. 85 - 94). Washington, DC: IEEE Computer Society.

Klein, G., & Murray, D. (2007). Parallel Tracking and Mapping for Small AR Workspaces. In *Proceedings of the 6th IEEE and ACM International Symposium on Mixed and Augmented Reality* (pp. 225 – 234). Washington, DC: IEEE Computer Society.

Kurz, D., & Himane, S. (2011). Inertial-sensor Aligned Visual Feature Descriptors. In *Proceedings of the 2011 IEEE Conference on Computer Vision and Pattern Recognition* (pp. 161 –166). Washington, DC: IEEE Computer Society.

Lee, E. S., Hong, S., & Johnson, B. R. (2006). Context Aware Paper-Based Review Instrument: A Tangible User Interface for Architecture Design Review. In G.A. Luhan (Ed.), *Proceedings of the 25th Annual Conference of the Association for Computer-Aided Design in Architecture* (pp. 317 –327). Louisville, KY: Association for Computer-Aided Design in Architecture.

Li, X., Chen, D., & Xiahou, S. (2009). Ubiquitous Augmented Reality System. In *Proceedings of Second International Symposium on Knowledge Acquisition and Modeling* (pp. 91 – 94). Washington, DC: IEEE Computer Society.

Lim, H., & Lee, Y. S. (2009). Real-Time Single Camera SLAM Using Fiducial Markers. In *Proceedings of ICCAS-SICE International Joint Conference 2009* (pp. 177 – 182). Washington, DC: IEEE Computer Society.

Lingley, A.R., Ali, M., Liao, Y., Mirjalili, R., & Klonner, M., Sopanen, …Parviz, B.A. (2011). A Single-pixel Wireless Contact Lens Display. *Journal of Micromechanics and Microengineering, 21*(12), 1–8. doi:10.1088/0960-1317/21/12/125014

LonWorks®-based Office Building Cuts HVAC, Lighting Costs 80%. (n.d.). Retrieved October 2, 2013 from http://www.echelon.com/customers/smart-buildings/bob.htm

Metaio Brings World's First Augmented Reality Accelerated Chipset to Market, Signs Agreement with ST-Ericsson to Integrate Future Mobile Platforms. (2013). Retrieved October 10, 2013 from http://www.metaio.com/press/press-release/2013/metaio-brings-worlds-first-augmented-reality-accelerated-chipset-to-market-signs-agreement-with-st-ericsson-to-integrate-future-mobile-platforms/

Nagel, T., Heidmann, F., Condotta, M., & Duval, E. (2010). Venice Unfolding: A Tangible User Interface for Exploring Faceted Data in a Geographical Context. In *Proceedings of the 6th Nordic Conference on Human-Computer Interaction: Extending Boundaries* (pp. 743–746). New York, NY: ACM.

Nee, A.Y.C., Ong, S.K., Chryssolouris, G., & Mourtzis, D. (2012). Augmented Reality Applications in Design and Manufacturing. *CIRP Annals – Manufacturing Technology, 61*(2), 657–679.

Newman, J., Ingram, D., & Hopper, A. (2001). Augmented Reality in a Wide Area Sentient Environment. In *Proceedings of the 2nd IEEE and ACM International Symposium on Augmented Reality* (pp. 77–86). Washington, DC: IEEE Computer Society.

Occupying Yourself with Energy and Occupancy. (2010). Retrieved October 2, 2013 from http://www.automatedbuildings.com/news/aug10/articles/sinopoli1/100728121202sinopoli.htm

OpenCV (Open Source Computer Vision). (n.d.). Retrieved October 2, 2013 from http://opencv.org/

Ren, Z., Yuan, J., Meng, J., & Zhang, Z. (2013). Robust Part-Based Hand Gesture Recognition Using Kinect Sensor. *IEEE Transactions on Multimedia, 15*(5), 1110–1120. doi:10.1109/TMM.2013.2246148

Rolland, J.P., Holloway, R.L., & Fuchs, H. (1995). A Comparison of Optical and Video See-through Head-mounted Displays. In H. Das (Ed.), *SPIE Proceedings Volume 2351, Telemanipulator and Telepresence Technologies* (pp. 293–309). SPIE.

Rosenberg, L. (1992). *The Use of Virtual Fixtures as Perceptual Overlays to Enhance Operator Performance in Remote Environments.* Dayton, OH: Wright-Patterson Air Force Base.

Rublee, E., Rabaud, V., Konolige, K., & Bradski, G. (2011). ORB: An Efficient Alternative to SIFT or SURF. In *Proceedings of the 2011 IEEE International Conference on Computer Vision* (pp. 2564–2571). Washington, DC: IEEE Computer Society.

Schall, G., Mulloni, A., & Reitmayr, G. (2010). North-centred Orientation Tracking on Mobile Phones. In *Proceedings of the 9th IEEE International Symposium on Mixed and Augmented Reality* (pp. 267–268). Washington, DC: IEEE Computer Society.

Schmalstieg, D., & Reitmayr, G. (2005). The World as a User Interface: Augmented Reality for Ubiquitous Computing. In G. Gartner, W. Cartwright, & M. P. Peterson (Eds.), *Location Based Services and TeleCartography* (pp. 369–391). Berlin: Springer-Verlag.

Silverman, N. L., Schowengerdt, B. T., Kelly, J. P., & Seibel, E. J. (2003). 58.5L: Late-News Paper: Engineering a Retinal Scanning Laser Display with Integrated Accommodative Depth Cues. *SID Symposium Digest of Technical Papers, 34*(1), 1538-1541.

van Krevelen, D. W. F., & Poelman, R. (2010). A Survey of Augmented Reality Technologies, Applications and Limitations. *The International Journal of Virtual Reality*, *9*(2), 1–20.

Waechter, C., Huber, M., Keitler, P., Schlegel, M., Klinker, G., & Pustka, D. (2010). A Multi-sensor Platform for Wide-area Tracking. In *Proceedings of the 9th IEEE International Symposium on Mixed and Augmented Reality* (pp. 275 –276). Washington, DC: IEEE Computer Society.

Wagner, D., Reitmayr, G., Mulloni, A., Drummond, T., & Schmalstieg, D. (2008). Pose Tracking from Natural Features on Mobile Phones. In *Proceedings of the 7th IEEE/ACM International Symposium on Mixed and Augmented Reality* (pp. 125 – 134). Washington, DC: IEEE Computer Society.

Weiser, M. (1991). The Computer for the 21st Century. *Scientific American*, *265*(3), 94–104. doi:10.1038/scientificamerican0991-94

Wilson, A. D. (2005). PlayAnywhere: A Compact Interactive Tabletop Projection-vision System. In *Proceedings of the 18th Annual ACM Symposium on User Interface Software and Technology* (pp. 83 – 92). New York, NY: ACM.

Xu, Y., Gu, J., Tao, Z., & Wu, D. (2009). Bare Hand Gesture Recognition with a Single Color Camera. In *Proceedings of the 2nd International Congress on Image and Signal Processing* (pp. 1 – 4). Academic Press.

Zsolt, J., & Levente, H. (2010). Improving Human-Computer Interaction by Gaze Tracking. In *Proceedings of the 3rd International Conference on Cognitive Infocommunications* (pp. 155 – 160). Washington, DC: IEEE Computer Society.

ADDITIONAL READING

Abowd, G. D., & Mynatt, E. D. (2000). Charting Past, Present, and Future Research in Ubiquitous Computing. *ACM Transactions on Computer-Human Interaction*, *7*(1), 29–58. doi:10.1145/344949.344988

Amft, O., & Lukowicz, P. (2009). From Backpacks to Smartphones: Past, Present, and Future of Wearable Computers. *Pervasive Computing*, *8*(3), 8–13. doi:10.1109/MPRV.2009.44

Azuma, R. (1997). A Survey of Augmented Reality. *Presence (Cambridge, Mass.)*, *6*(4), 355–385.

Azuma, R., Baillot, Y., Behringer, R., Feiner, S., Julier, S., & MacIntyre, B. (2001). Recent Advances in Augmented Reality. *IEEE Computer Graphics and Applications*, *21*(6), 34–47. doi:10.1109/38.963459

Barakonyi, I., & Schmalstieg, D. (2008). Augmented Reality Agents for User Interface Adaptation. *Computer Animation and Virtual Worlds*, *19*(1), 23–35. doi:10.1002/cav.220

Bell, G., & Dourish, P. (2007). Yesterday's Tomorrows: Notes on Ubiquitous Computing's Dominant Vision. *Personal and Ubiquitous Computing*, *11*(2), 133–143. doi:10.1007/s00779-006-0071-x

Billinghurst, M., Kato, H., & Myojin, S. (2009). Advanced Interaction Techniques for Augmented Reality Applications. In R. Shumaker (Ed.), *Virtual and Mixed Reality* (pp. 13–22). Berlin: Springer-Verlag. doi:10.1007/978-3-642-02771-0_2

Boyer, E. W., Smelson, D., Fletcher, R., Ziedonis, D., & Picard, R. W. (2010). Wireless Technologies, Ubiquitous Computing and Mobile Health: Application to Drug Abuse Treatment and Compliance with HIV Therapies. *Journal of Medical Toxicology; Official Journal of the American College of Medical Toxicology*, *6*(2), 212–216. doi:10.1007/s13181-010-0080-z PMID:20623215

Carmigniani, J., Furht, B., Anisetti, M., Ceravolo, P., Damiani, E., & Ivkovic, M. (2011). Augmented Reality Technologies, Systems and Applications. *Multimedia Tools and Applications, 51*(1), 341–377. doi:10.1007/s11042-010-0660-6

Fjeld, M. (2003). Introduction: Augmented Reality-Usability and Collaborative Aspects. *International Journal of Human-Computer Interaction, 16*(3), 387–393. doi:10.1207/S15327590IJHC1603_1

Garcia-Macias, J. A., Alvarez-Lozano, J., Estrada-Martinez, P., & Aviles-Lopez, E. (2011). Browsing the Internet of Things with Sentient Visors. *Computer, 44*(5), 46–52. doi:10.1109/MC.2011.128

Jones, B. R., Sodhi, R., Campbell, R. H., Garnett, G., & Bailey, B. P. (2010). Build Your World and Play In It: Interacting with Surface Particles on Complex Objects. In *Proceedings of the 9th IEEE International Symposium on Mixed and Augmented Reality 2010* (pp. 165 – 174). Washington, DC: IEEE Computer Society.

Karray, F., Alemzadeh, M., Saleh, J. A., & Arab, M. N. (2008). Human-Computer Interaction: Overview on the State of the Art. *International Journal on Smart Sensing and Intelligent Systems, 1*(1), 137–159.

Milgram, P., & Kishino, F. (1994). A Taxonomy of Mixed Reality Visual Displays. *IEICE Transactions on Information Systems. E (Norwalk, Conn.), 77-D*(12), 1321–1329.

Petersen, N., & Stricker, D. (2009). Continuous Natural User Interface: Reducing the Gap Between Real and Digital World. In *Proceedings of the 8th IEEE International Symposium on Mixed and Augmented Reality 2009* (pp. 23 – 26). Washington, DC: IEEE Computer Society.

Porta, M. (2002). Vision-based User Interfaces: Methods and Applications. *International Journal of Human-Computer Studies, 57*(1), 27–73. doi:10.1006/ijhc.2002.1012

Rekimoto, J., & Nagao, K. (1995). The World Through the Computer: Computer Augmented Interaction with Real World Environment. In *Proceedings of the 8th Annual Symposium on User Interface and Software Technology* (pp. 29 – 36). New York, NY: ACM.

Resatsch, F. (2010). Human Computer Interaction and Technology Acceptance. In *Ubiquitous Computing* (pp. 47–85). Germany: Gabler-Verlag. doi:10.1007/978-3-8349-8683-2_3

Spataru, C., & Gillott, M. (2011). The Use of Intelligent Systems for Monitoring Energy Use and Occupancy in Existing Homes. *Intelligent Buildings International, 3*(1), 24–31. doi:10.3763/inbi.2010.0006

Telkenaroglu, C., & Capin, T. (2013). Dual-Finger 3D Interaction Techniques for Mobile Devices. *Personal and Ubiquitous Computing, 17*(7), 1551–1572. doi:10.1007/s00779-012-0594-2

Thomas, B. H. (2012). Have We Achieved the Ultimate Wearable Computer? In *Proceedings of the 16th International Symposium on Wearable Computers* (104 – 107). Washington, DC: IEEE Computer Society.

Weiser, M. (1993). Some Computer Science Issues in Ubiquitous Computing. *Communications of the ACM, 36*(7), 75–84. doi:10.1145/159544.159617

Weiser, M., & Brown, J. S. (1997). The Coming of Age of Calm Technology. In P. J. Denning, & R. M. Metcalfe (Eds.), *Beyond Calculation* (pp. 75–85). New York, NY: Copernicus. doi:10.1007/978-1-4612-0685-9_6

Zhou, F., Duh, H. B.-L., & Billinghurst, M. (2008). Trends in Augmented Reality Tracking, Interaction and Display: A Review of Ten Years of ISMAR. In *Proceedings of the 7th IEEE/ACM International Symposium on Mixed and Augmented Reality 2008* (pp. 193 – 202). Washington, DC: IEEE Computer Society.

KEY TERMS AND DEFINITIONS

Augmented Reality: A perception of a reality that consists of the real environment with computer generated sensory input added into it; abbreviated to AR in this chapter.

Gesture Recognition: A kind of natural interaction where a user's physical actions are recognized by a computer system, usually in order to activate a computer function.

Human-Computer Interaction: The two-way interaction between computers and human users.

Natural Interaction: Human-computer interaction methods and interfaces that are intuitive to the user and do not involve having to learn how to use specific devices and software.

Smart Objects: Normal everyday objects that have computational and networking capability embedded within them.

Ubiquitous Computing: A paradigm of computing in which computers are everywhere but the hardware is hidden; abbreviated to UbiComp in this chapter.

User Interface: A collection of elements that a user perceives and controls in order to interact with computer software.

Chapter 13
A Study of Mobile Guide Applications in Wayfinding Context

Yu-Horng Chen
University of Taipei, Taiwan

Yih-Shyuan Chen
St. John's University, Taiwan

ABSTRACT

This chapter investigates the research projects and prototypes related to currently available mobile applications used in wayfinding and navigation. The advancement in small-screen devices, mobile computing and modelling counterpart, location awareness techniques, and wireless technologies have improved screen resolutions and provided technical solutions for delivering textual, 2D, and 3D information to a mobile device. After investigating small-screen representations and the related navigation content and mobile interface design from the previous cases, two suggestions are presented in this chapter in order to enhance the design for future mobile wayfinding systems: 1) pseudo-3D representations and 2) personalised and on-demand services.

INTRODUCTION

In a contemporary world information is available from a variety of sources, and a wide range of digital environments now provide us with information on many levels and via many routes. (Brown, 2010, p.44)

As the improvement of digital media and network technologies, receiving a wide range of information has been involved in our daily life. Moreover,

a mobile device is one of the commonly used equipments for accessing emails, Internet and a variety of online sources. The advance of mobile processing power, network communications and related mobile development kit have increased the applications of hand-held devices in different fields in recent years. one of the examples is the virtual visit of artistic works delivers to mobile computers (Belinky *et al.*, 2012). The essential knowledge and information can also be presented in palmtop systems, e.g. instructions for health

DOI: 10.4018/978-1-4666-6228-5.ch013

care, exercise advice and real-time navigation for fire or emergency escaping (Buttussi *et al.*, 2006). Moreover, the integration of mobile maps and GIS information could provide location-based information for navigation and wayfinding use (Realinho *et al.*, 2011; Pospischil *et al.*, 2002).

The research conducted by Brown *et al.* (2001 & 2005) points out the possibility of delivering city information in a variety of forms and different platforms. In addition, two key issues have been indicated in their works: one is the types of representation in a small-screen device and the other one is the way of operating and viewing the system. Conventionally, a keyboard and a mouse are the general input devices that individuals use to input data and operate a program in order to interact with the device. Some alternative means are applied to manage the missions mentioned previously, such as the bicycle (Knight & Brown, 1999), tangible blocks (Abdelmohsen & Do, 2007) and a Wayfinding kiosk with interactive touch screen maps (WAYFINDER, 2013). The development of novel and alternative input interfaces have increased the means to operate a system, as well as have changed the way of interaction among users, devices and the environment.

The main representation used in a mobile guide design could be different from one research project to another. Some cases apply 2D maps to design the application, for example Cyberguide (Abowd *et al.*, 1997) and CityInMyPocket (Depuydt *et al.*, 2006), while some prototypes take 3D models as the main representation, e.g. m-LOMA (Nurminen, 2006). In addition, there are also some projects devoted to examine the alternative or novel techniques in order to increase the speed of rendering, and to provide a better and easy-to-understand visualisation for users. As various projects have employed particular representational techniques and input facilities, this study intends to collect the available research projects which concern with the small-screen representation and standalone mobile guide design. Moreover, the investigation focuses on the purpose, key representation, information content

and interface design involved in individual cases in order to recognise and acknowledge the benefit of each representational technique and the related issues about wayfinding and navigation.

Given the above, the present study aims to investigate the following key issues:

1. Studying currently available mobile representations and modelling techniques.
2. Considering the designs of mobile and small-screen user interface for developing navigation systems.
3. Evaluating the understanding of each particular representations and illustrations by a wide audience.

WAYFINDING AND PERCEPTION

In the following sections, the background knowledge of the essential elements required for designing an effective mobile guide is presented and then the designs of the mobile guide, as well as the related research projects are discussed.

Wayfinding

This section presents the conceptual framework for the present research based on two areas of literature. The first area of the literature involves individuals' wayfinding behaviour and spatial knowledge concerning the design of hand-held walking guides. The other area of the literature focuses on individuals' visual perceptions which may influence personal feelings about distance and sense of space.

Wayfinding and navigation are a purposive behaviour between travellers and the surroundings (Allen, 1999). In addition, wayfinding performance involves various direction and shape identification, decision making and interactions between the environment and individuals in order to reach a destination. As the definition indicated by Golledge (1999, p.6), wayfinding is 'the process of determining and following a path or route between an origin and a destination'. Moreover, Passini (1984, p.153) pointed out that this behaviour is 'a person's ability, both cognitive and behavioural, to reach spatial destinations and refer to one's static relation to space as well as the dynamics involved in his/her purposeful mobility'.

In the case of finding a particular route or a tourist attraction involving in a wayfinding context, individuals may apply their experiences and knowledge to reach the target. As the experience and knowledge could help them to identify the surroundings and decide their next moves, it would be beneficial to study the key factors involved in the environment that could help in individuals' wayfinding and navigation processes. However, wayfinding activities consist of complex observation, identification, determination and modification, as discussed previously. Therefore, a certain assistant, such as maps, brochures or digital guides, with the essential elements which are useful to recognise a signage, path and landmark may provide better references for wayfinding and navigation.

Spatial Knowledge

Constructing spatial knowledge including objects identifications and interactions with the environment has been studied by a number of researchers (Piaget & Inhelder, 1967; Lynch, 1960, Siegel & White, 1975). In addition, these investigations have pointed out the stage of learning spatial relationship and identifying the distance between an observer and an object. Siegel and White (1975) suggest that there are a range of key elements or processes in terms of memorising the environment and learning how to interact with the world. The designs of a city map and a navigation system benefit from these studies in not only designing the information for recognising directions and locations, but also in refining the instructions given for wayfinding and navigation.

A spatial problem-solving process takes place continuingly while wayfinding and navigation in an urban area. A range of spatial information and messages encompass the surroundings offer individuals a number of cues and hints for locating themselves and identifying directions. The term – spatial information (Downs & Stea, 1973) or environmental information (Passini, 1992) have been specified for describing the key factors which are spread around the spaces and have the potential of recognising locations and directions. Moreover, the representations of a place or an area are constructed by accumulating the spatial cues and organising them in a systematic way.

The research conducted by Siegel and White (1975) indicates that Landmark-Route-Survey (LRS) model is the fundamental process of constructing individuals' knowledge of the spaces. In order to develop a person's spatial knowledge, the first step is to recognise landmarks – the most significant or distinct buildings in the surroundings – followed by connecting these landmarks together with various routes and paths. Finally, a comprehensive mental representation of the environment can be build up for the future navigation use.

Lynch (1960) specifies five categories – path, edge, landmark, node and district in his well-known book 'The Image of The City'. According to Lynch's research, the participants' mental images of the environment can be derived from their daily experiences and activities in the cities. These fundamental factors are considered to be the most essential features which can be memorised by individuals and form the mental representations of the spatial relationships in the real-world.

In Lynch's book (1960), the spatial information is categorised into five key elements. Additionally, the research presented by Siegel and White (1975) provides the step-by-step learning process in terms of constructing individuals' spatial knowledge by memorising and utilising the essential environmental features. The outcome has been widely applied to generating various walking instructions and developing navigation systems in order to support orientation and wayfinding.

Perception

When it comes to visual perceptions and the associated aspects, David Marr indicates three specific principles including primal sketch, 2.5D sketch and 3D sketch (Eysenck & Keane, 2005) in terms of constructing a mental image of an object and producing a 3D representation in individuals' perceptual systems.

1. **Primal Sketch:** The outline and border of an object is perceived as standing out from the background or the other elements around this object.
2. **2.5D Sketch:** The information including depth, shading and texture of an object are given in an observer centred viewpoints to increase the feelings of perspectives without viewing the back and invisible parts of the object.
3. **3D Sketch:** An object can be observed in various viewpoints in order to perceive the details of an object three-dimensionally from different angles.

The feelings of the distance and the depth are one of the key information for determining figure and background from the real-world setting. The spatial information for locating objects and estimating distance is an important cue to help people in judging the distance between two objects or the distance between an object and the viewer in order to construct 3D perception. In addition, linear perspectives (Durand, 2002), size and shape constancy (Parkin, 2000) are the most important spatial knowledge in terms of identifying the distance in depth.

1. Linear perspectives are useful for estimating distance and identifying depth information. The example is observing rails. When stand-

ing in front of the rails, the lines get closer and closer as the vision of sight goes farther.
2. The second cue is size constantly which provides an intuitive way to recognise and identify the depth impression when comparing two objects or items. For example, two cars appear to be the same size whether one car is close to the viewer or driving away from the viewer.
3. The third cue is shape constancy. Parkin (2000) points out that individuals can always remember the typical shape of an object even when the shape does not appear to be the same. For instance, when standing in front of a building and looking up to its roof, the top of the building seems smaller than its bottom. Although the shapes of the building are different in a person's eyes, its outline stays rectangular in one's perceptions.

Mobile Representation

When it comes to designing a mobile navigation guide, a wide range of information and representations which have the potential to help users in wayfinding have been added to the systems. In addition, some prototypes may be designed to enclose all kinds of available components in order to provide as much as information for users. In order to guide users, some designs may apply a number of key contents that provide the most important routes, landmarks, attractions and so on. According to the research conducted by Kray *et al.* (2003), the information which is commonly used for designing a mobile guide is identified as follows: texts, spoken instructions, 2D routes, 2D maps and pseudo realistic representations. Furthermore, the other elements – photographs and 3D models – which can be added to the list are discussed in Chittaro and Burigat (2005) and Nurminen's studies (2006).

It is evident that individual technique and representation have their benefits and weakness. For example, textual information could provide background knowledge and descriptions about a place, a building or an event; spoken instructions could be used in a certain context while viewing the screen of a mobile guide under the bright sunlight; routes and maps could offer not only directional information, but also present a greater image about an area and the surroundings for individuals. In some of the prototype designs, these techniques are placed together in order to provide a comprehensive picture of the target area to users. Nevertheless, some research projects are devoted to investigate the novel or alternative means which could offer understandable and reliable wayfinding information with less resource demand under the limitations of mobile devices.

One of the studies investigates the effectiveness of 3D models and 2D graphics in a mobile walking context (Rakkolainen & Vainio, 2001). It is found that 3D representation is useful in real world recognition when comparing with 2D graphics. Laakso's study (2002) indicates that 2D and 3D representations could be helpful for users in different ways. 2D maps are easier to be understood and the speed of visualisation is faster when comparing with 3D representations. However, 3D models are useful in recognising real world buildings and scenes.

The applications of 2D and 3D content have been used in many research projects, but little research takes pseudo realistic representation into consideration. The term 'pseudo realistic representation' is applied 2D elements and images to building up a 3D scene. Some studies named this technique as pseudo-3D representations (Brown 2006; Brown 2010; Chen, 2009). A number of city maps and brochures have used these techniques in their layout, for example Liverpool NAViGator and London Walking Map. In addition, the use of pseudo-3D representation in a mobile application can be divided into two ways: 1) those enclose whole area, landmarks and all available information; 2) those contain the most important attractions, buildings and city information.

DEVELOPMENT IN MOBILE GUIDES

There are various mobile navigation systems that have been developed for research projects and become more and more widespread at commercial levels. Computer Aided Architectural Design (CAAD) and the advancement of mobile and modelling technologies provide the essential component to deliver a wide range of textural and graphic information in different level-of-detail to a mobile user. The cases collected in this study focus on the particular features as follows: the representations and interfaces which are designed for mobile devices and standalone systems in the scenarios of city navigation.

Some of the previous developments, such as Cyberguide (Abowd *et al.*, 1997) and CityInMy-Pocket (Depuydt *et al.*, 2006), investigate the use of 2D maps and the on-location information in order to provide location-aware services. Some of the projects apply 3D visualisations in order to build up a realistic model with a close to real-life feeling to users, for example m-LOMA (Nurminen, 2006). Some cases focus on developing a system through a combination of various resources and information for enhancing the effectiveness of wayfinding and navigation aids, such as LOCUS (Mountain & Liarokapis, 2007). Furthermore, the later design in Liverpool employs pseudo-3D techniques to design the prototype. These achievements have shown the possibility of designing a mobile guide with a wide range of representations and techniques in order to deliver customised, understandable and recognisable wayfinding and navigation content to users.

The coming sections illustrate the applications of 2D graphics, 3D representations and the other currently available visualisations in the prototype design of mobile navigation systems. Moreover, the discussions and examinations involved in the following cases are considered to shape the main idea of this study.

2D Representation

Conventionally, maps have been used as one of the main representations in terms of wayfinding and navigation scenarios. A map can offer symbolic images of the reality of the space and the features, details of the real-world. In addition, these messages can provide the essential spatial information for building up individual knowledge of the surroundings. Therefore, a range of research (Depuydt *et al.*, 2006; Kramer *et al.*, 2005) and commercial systems (Garmin; TomTom; Navi-King) have adopted these features to develop their navigation applications.

In order to emphasise the most important wayfinding and navigation factors, a number of suggestions have been indicated in the research conducted by Reichenbacher (2004). This study specifies various techniques to design maps, for example, using colours, transparency and animation to emphasise the most important objects, as well as highlighting outlines, augmenting contrast and increasing level-of-detail of key elements. In addition, applying abstracting representation, interactive elements, and the functionality, such as zoom and tooltips, to design mobile guides are pointed out by Heidmann *et al.* (2003) and Nagi (2004). Moreover, the design of map-based mobile wayfinding systems could be categorised into three features: 1) 'refining map visualisation', 2) 'supporting additional services' and 3) 'adding applications to different circumstances' (Chen, 2009, p.33).

The design of Cyberguide is one of the earliest studies which applies maps and 2D elements as the main representations to mobile navigation systems (Abowd *et al.*, 1997). This project endeavours to develop an indoor and outdoor mobile navigation guide. The recommendations indicated by Lynch (1960), Siegel and White (1975) are used to generate the main representations, for example landmarks, routes (paths) and districts. In addition, the techniques identified by Reichenbacher (2004) are applied to highlight the most important

landmarks, nodes, edges and districts in various colours and textures. The functions which are placed at the bottom of the screen offer the basic ways to browse the maps with different level of details and to find a particular place.

A number of additional services, such as personal travel diaries, location-aware information, interaction among the neighbouring users and servers are added to the prototype (see Figure 1). These features are designed to offer personalised information and to record individuals' preference. Moreover, the functions also increase the interactions between different users, as well as the interaction between one user and the surroundings in order to retrieve more wayfinding and navigation details from different source types.

The CityInMyPocket is one of the examples of using maps as the main representation (Depuydt *et al.*, 2006). An interactive sightseeing tour in the city of Mechelen is available in this prototype. The tour provides 2D maps, photographs and the related textural information as navigation aids (see Figure 2). Furthermore, the points of interest (PoIs), attractions and the location-related services which are located in the target area are highlighted in numbers and the particular symbols, e.g. a restaurant is represented by a 'fork and knife' icon, as well as a car park is represented by the 'P' symbol.

The suggestions, such as abstract representation and interactive elements, carried out by Heidmann *et al.* (2003) and Nagi (2004) are applied to fulfil the design of the prototype. In addition, three additional customised modules, Thematic Information, Travel Planning and Help are offered to support the users with particular requirements. For example, the users may want to have a cultural tour or take part in a social event in the local area by using the module of Thematic Information. Moreover, the individuals may plan their own routes or journey by using the function of Travel Planning. Finally, the users may require further information and instructions from the

Figure 1. The interface of Cyberguide (Adapted from Abowd et al., 1997, p.426)

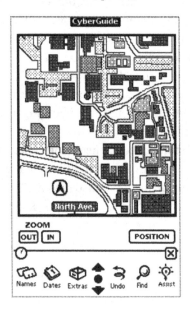

Tourist Information Centre (TIC) by choosing the module of Help.

The project, Local Location Assistant (LoL@), was developed in 2000 and encloses a number of multimedia assistants and location information about the city, Vienna (Pospischil *et al.*, 2002). In order to provide better representations of the local area, the points of interest (PoIs), landmarks, position-based services, an abstract map is offered. A number of navigation tools are placed in the same screen with the map for supporting the individuals in a wayfinding scenario.

The prototype integrates a wide range of customised functionality in order to provide a personal preference tour and location-based navigation (see Figure 3). The functionality is consistent in the results which are indicated by Heidmann *et al.* (2003) and Nagi's (2004) studies. Furthermore, additional services, for example spoken instructions and video clips are added to its later version. However, GPS information is required in order to provide accurate positioning information and the related location-based services.

3D Representation

Laakso *et al.* (2003) specifies that 2D mapping can be delivered to devices faster than 3D content. However, 3D graphics have the potential to help users in terms of recognising the real-world scenes and buildings. In addition, Chiatto and Burgat (2005) indicate that the integration of 3D graphics and geographic content can offer users a real-life view in position and simplify wayfinding and navigation processes. The use of perspective views and 3D representations has been applied to design location-based information and the associated services for mobile users. The idea of using 3D visualisation for recognising the real-world scenes is consistent with the results concluded by Rakkolainen & Vainio (2001) and Laakso (2002).

A one-year study – m-LOMA project (Nurminen, 2006) – aims to build up a full-scale 3D models in mobile devices (see Figure 4). The system is designed to render 3D models on portable devices in real-time. In order to reduce the time which is spent on rendering 3D representations, the the technique of avoiding the rendering of

Figure 2. The interface of CityInMyPocket (Adapted from Depuydt et al., 2006, p.28)

Figure 3. A screenshot of LoL@ (Adapted from Pospischil et al., 2002, p.146)

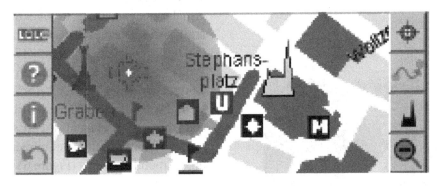

unimportant structures is applied to design this prototype. However, the details of routes, directions and additional information are not included in this prototype. The positioning service is required with the purpose of providing accurate location information to the users.

AR

The development of the LOCUS project (Mountain & Liarokapis, 2007) examines the potential of using 3D representations in the previous works. Moreover, an additional navigation service with integrated augmented reality (AR) in hand-held systems is developed in the later prototype (see Figure 5). The AR interface contains virtual directional content, real-world scenes and textural instructions in order to provide location-based information.

The most important directional and location information is selected to design its system. Therefore, the photographs of landmarks, buildings and crossroads are taken from the real-world scenes which are superimposed by directional and textural content. In addition, the directional information could offer the subsequent steps and moves to the next locations and the texts could provide the distance between two places or the descriptions of current positions. The design of step-by-step instructions, the use of location information as

well as the key navigation elements are consistent with the key elements which is useful to develop spatial knowledge and generate the image of a city indicated by Lynch (1960) and Siegel and White (1975).

Simulated 3D

As discussed in the previous sections, some of the tourist maps and brochures have applied 2D elements and features to simulate a real-world

Figure 4. A screenshot of m-LOMA (Adapted from Nurminen, 2006, p.15)

Figure 5. The interface of LOCUS (Adapted from Mountain & Liarokapis, 2007, p.3)

Figure 5. The interface of LOCUS (Adapted from Mountain & Liarokapis, 2007, p.3)

scene and 3D views in order to help in wayfinding and navigation activities. A pseudo-3D graphic is one of the alternative techniques which is different from the other representations discussed previously. The technique of pseudo-3D content applies 2D elements, such as lines and frames, to simulate a close to 3D perception. The use of this kind of graphics draws attention to the most distinctive characteristics and figures of landmarks and structures of the environment in order to facilitate the processes of identifying and recognising the surroundings.

Base on this idea, one of the projects – City in the Palm of Your Hand – conducted by Computer Aided Architectural Design Research Unit (CAADRU) in University of Liverpool has developed a series of mobile navigation systems. The initial development is derived from the design of an online tour of Liverpool. The tour is available at http://www.liverpoolarchitecture.com/tours/index.php.

With the aim to design a portable and effective version, two key factors are considered: 1) a small and optimised file size which can be delivered to mobile computers wiredly or wirelessly in a short time; 2) an information enriched database with

architectural details of the city. Moreover, the visualisations and navigation aids used in the guide are derived from the results which are specified in the studies conducted by Lynch (1960), Siegel and White (1975) and Reichenbacher (2004). Thus, a prototype which is named ArchiTours (Knight *et al.*, 2007) is designed for working in desktops and laptops environment (Figure 6 left).

A revision of ArchiTours, particularly for working on mobile systems (Figure 6 right), has been launched in order to rearrange the information for viewing in limited screen sizes. The pseudo-3D representations, 2D mapping, photographs and textural content are available in this interface. These representations provide more services and city information than the previous prototype for users in identifying their positions and retrieving more wayfinding content.

Later Design of Liverpool Example

The early works of ArchiTours and its modified format for small-screen devices have applied the representations to a larger screen size. Moreover, the larger screen size which is mentioned here is compared to the traditional mobile devices' and Symbian systems' screen sizes. Therefore, the subsequent developments that integrate the results and experience derived from the previous research and deliver the prototype to an iPhone (Figure 7) are launched in order to design an appropriate representation and interface for iPhone users. Moreover, the ongoing project may further develop the format which can be operated in Android environment.

Google Maps

Google Maps is one of the digital map services with a number of useful traffic and location information which are available online for retrieving in various devices, such as desktops, laptops, smartphones and ubiquitous devices. The design of Google Maps offers road-based and direction-

Figure 6. ArchiTours (left) and its mobile version (right) (Adapted from Chen, 2009, p.125 & 131)

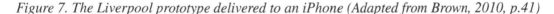

based route planner which is useful to plan and manage wayfinding activities. In recent years, one of the particular navigation aids is added to Google Maps which offers step-by-step wayfinding directions together with spoken instructions in order to assist mobile device users to arrange and plan their journey. However, the maps may not work correctly without the connections of WiFi, network connections and GPS services.

The representation used in Google Maps, as shown in Figure 8, is a closed to pseudo-3D graphics. The shapes of individual route and path are formed as 3D perspective view. Moreover, it also provides turn-by-turn navigation to support wayfinding activities in every crossroad or deci-

Figure 7. The Liverpool prototype delivered to an iPhone (Adapted from Brown, 2010, p.41)

Figure 8. The navigation mode in Google Maps (Adapted from Google Maps, 2013)

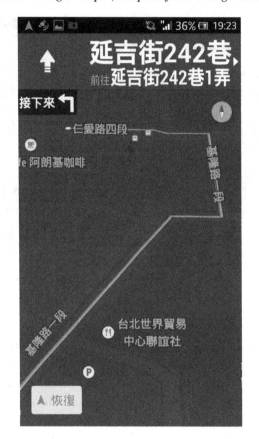

sion point. These particular features are as similar as the technique which is used in the design of LOCUS project and Liverpool example.

The highlighted starting points, destinations and the paths between them are consistent with the ideas pointed out by Lynch (1960) and Siegel and White (1975). The applications of the interactive elements and the additional functionality, such as zoom, satellite view, traffic, photos and weather offered in Google Maps are helpful to the users for retrieving more details about their current positions and investigating location information with different types of visualisations. In addition, the studies conducted by Heidmann *et al.* (2003), Nagi (2004) and Chen (2009) have specified the potential of offering these services.

METHODOLOGY

In order to collect the appropriate research projects for further investigation, this study browsed through a number of books, journal articles and research papers via online sources and web search engines with mixed use of the following keywords: small-screen, mobile, guide, walking, interface, computing, representation, visualisation, augmented reality, 3D maps, location awareness and so forth. The cases collected in this study are the projects which have been published in book chapters, journal articles, conference proceedings and so on. However, Google Maps is involved in this investigation due to the following reasons: 1) it is one of the built-in mobile applications in most of currently available smartphones and mobile devices; 2) it can be operated in different

Table 1. A comparison of different representations used in the cases

Research Projects	Representations			
	Maps	Photos	VRML	Pseudo-3D
CityInMyPocket	√	√		
Cyberguide	√			
LoL@	√	√		
m-LOMA*			√	
LOCUS		√		
ArchiTours		√		√
Google Maps	√			√**

* this is a prototype with 3D VRML models only

** the particular representation is not fully applied to the design

operating systems (i.e. Android and iOS); 3) it provides open API which is helpful for developing additional value-added services, and these services can be superimposed with its current navigation aids.

There are seven projects which are described and analysed in detail in the previous sections. In addition, the key elements and the unique techniques used in these projects are categorised in Table 1. Finally, the discussions and analysis are conducted according to the mobile limitations, representations, and interface design applied to individual case in the following sections.

DISCUSSIONS

The examination of currently available prototypes and studies is divided into three aspects: mobile limitations, representations and interface design in order to investigate the difference among these projects.

Mobile Limitations

Conventionally, a digital navigation guide is designed available for rendering and operating models and database on desktops and laptops. However, a problem occurred while utilising the guide in a hand-held device due to the small screen size cannot present legible details without zooming-in and -out the representations. Moreover, the speed of mobile computing and wireless connections may not deliver accurate or clear representations to individuals straight away. Thus, parallel to the browser problem, Brown *et al.* (2006) point out the important issues, such as the arrangement of graphical, textual and the related services which should be considered in developing a mobile map or guide. Therefore, the available representations and information content should be wisely selected and organised in order to deliver the essential content in a short time.

Representations

Although 2D mapping, 3D modelling and the integration of real-world scenes and virtual signs have been applied to develop portable navigation systems, the use of pseudo-3D representation is only available in the design of some city maps and prototype designs. The application of pseudo-3D graphics could be one of the alternative techniques for designing a mobile guide under the restrictions of mobile devices (Brown *et al.*, 2006; Knight *et al.*, 2007; Knight *et al.*, 2008; Chen, 2009). Furthermore, this particular representation can not only provide essential wayfinding assistant and navigation aids, but also be visualised and delivered to mobile devices within an acceptable time while comparing to rendering a full-3D model.

Interface Design

This study aims to investigate mobile navigation systems which are used in standalone mode and their interface designs. Therefore, connections to the Internet or wireless network are not available at all times. Also, the interactions and communications between the server and the clients are not the focus of this study. Some of the research projects place the functions at both sides of the screen, e.g. LoL@ (Pospischil *et al.*, 2002) and ArchiTours (Knight *et al.*, 2007), while some cases lay the functions at the bottom of the prototype, e.g. Cyberguide (Abowd *et al.*, 1997) and City-InMyPocket (Depuydt *et al.*, 2006). However, the case, Google Maps, offers a particular means by hiding the functions automatically at the side of the screen in order to represent more navigation content and on-location information in the limited screen size.

As discussed above, individual project has applied particular techniques to design its particular mobile guide, from 2D graphics, 3D models, AR to pseudo-3D representations. These cases apply only one technique to illustrate or highlight the surroundings, landmarks and points of interest (PoIs). However, the study conducted by Brown (2010) indicates that the functionality and effectiveness of mobile guides could be enhanced by attaching layers of information. Moreover, textual content, route information, graphic representation and the related wayfinding details are considered to be of equal importance in order to offer comprehensive background knowledge of the environment to users. Therefore, the organisation of different wayfinding information, representations and available functionality in a limited screen has been one of the most important issues while designing mobile navigation systems.

CONCLUSION

After the investigation of the previous prototypes and research projects, three suggestions are concluded:

Pseudo-3D Representation

The study discusses a number of digital representations used in different research projects which concern a number of overlapping fields and examine the prototypes of various mobile city guides. As the advance of digital media and the related technologies, the data and representations could be added to a mobile guide design by adding layers of information (Brown, 2010). Peudo-3D representations could be one of the techniques for visualising city information and for delivering the information to mobile devices in a short time. In order to extend the design of the guide based on pseudo-3D visualisations and increase the usability and applicability of the system. Further research including the implementation of the representations used in parallel small-screen context (such as Android and iOS), and the studies of user experience are worthy of study.

Personalised and On-Demand Design

The mobile computing, functions and storage have been improved due to the rapid advance of mobile technologies. However, individuals' requirements and preference in wayfinding and navigation are different from one another. The designs discussed in the previous sections have considered 2D, 3D and the other related representations in order to fulfil users' wayfinding requirements. Therefore, a system with various visualisations and functions which could be selected and viewed (e.g. Google Maps) for different users and under different conditions may be one of the ways to design a mobile guide. In addition, the study concerns the arrangement of different representations and functions in a limited screen, as well as the user experiences and preferences of using mobile interfaces is worth further investigation.

Future Development

As the discussions indicated above, this study investigates the unique mobile guide designs and provides one of the early examples to several researches in the related fields. In addition, there are two main points that were acknowledged for further investigations.

Knight and Brown (1999) have applied a portable exercise bike as a medium to ride with architectural models. Later study conducted by Brown (2010) specifies another touchable and interactive interface (an exhibition stand in the Liverpool Pavilion) in Shanghai Expo, in August 2010. The interactions between users and digital model interfaces encompass the related implementations which are different from our experiences of using desktops or the other immersive interactions. In terms of adding interesting features and reducing the difficulties of using mobile interfaces, there are various issues worthy of study while developing an easy-to-operate user interface.

In order to enhance the use of pseudo-3D or the other representations and consider location awareness and on-site services in wayfinding context, positioning systems (2D barcode and RFID) can be added to the design of mobile guides. One of the related studies (Saeed, 2008) has pointed out the capability of using 2D barcode and RFID in wayfinding context. As the employ of such applications, the accuracy of location content can be improved, as well as the up-to-date information and real-time references about the surroundings can be delivered to mobile users.

REFERENCES

Abdelmohsen, S. M., & Do, E. Y.-L. (2007). *TangiCAD: Tangible Interface for Manipulating Architectural 3D Models.* Paper presented at the 10th International Conference on Computer Aided Architectural Design Research in Asia (CAADRIA). Nanjing, China.

Abowd, G. D., Atkeson, C. G., Hong, J., Long, S., Kooper, R., & Pinkerton, M. (1997). Cyberguide: a mobile context-aware tour guide. *Wireless Networks*, *3*(5), 421–433. doi:10.1023/A:1019194325861

Allen, G. L. (1999). Spatial abilities, cognitive maps, and wayfinding: Bases for individual differences in spatial cognition and behavior. In R. G. Golledge (Ed.), *Wayfinding behavior: Cognitive maps and other spatial processes* (pp. 46–80). Baltimore, MD: Johns Hopkins University Press.

Belinky, I., Lanir, J., & Kuflik, T. (2012). Using handheld devices and situated displays for collaborative planning of a museum visit. In *Proceedings of the 2012 International Symposium on Pervasive Displays*. Academic Press.

Brown, A. (2010). The Digital City. In A. Brown (Ed.), *Urban design futures – better city, better life* (pp. 31–48). Liverpool, UK: Liverpool School of Architecture Press.

Brown, A., Knight, M., Chen, Y.-H., & Saeed, G. (2006). *City information delivered to Mobile Digital devices - Reflection on contemporary potentials and problems*. Paper presented at the 24th eCAADe Conference. Volos, Greece.

Brown, A., Knight, M., & Winchester, M. (2005). *Representation and Delivery of City Models*. Paper presented at the 10th International Conference on Computer Aided Architectural Design Research in Asia (CAADRIA). New Dehli, India.

Brown, A. G. P., & Knight, M. W. (2001). *NAVR-gate: Gateways to architectural virtual reality - A review and thought on future directions*. Paper presented at the 6th International Conference on Computer Aided Architectural Design Research in Asia (CAADRIA). Sydney, Australia.

Buttussi, F., Chittaro, L., & Nadalutti, D. (2006). Bringing mobile guides and fitness activities together: a solution based on an embodied virtual trainer. In *Proceedings of the 8th conference on Human-computer interaction with mobile devices and services*, (pp. 29-36). Academic Press.

Chen, Y. H. (2009). *Navigation Using Portable Digital Architectural Guides*. (Unpublished Ph.D. Thesis). University of Liverpool, Liverpool, UK.

Chittaro, L., & Burigat, S. (2005). Augmenting audio messages with visual directions in mobile guides: an evaluation of three approaches. In *Proceedings of the 7th international conference on Human computer interaction with mobile devices & services*, (pp. 107-114). Academic Press.

Depuydt, S., Vanattenhoven, J., & Engelen, J. (2006). CityInMyPocket: Digital Walking Guides. [ELPUB.]. *Proceedings of, ELPUB2006*, 17–26.

Downs, R. M., & Stea, D. (1973). Theory. In R. M. Downs, & D. Stea (Eds.), *Image and Environment* (pp. 1–13). Chicago: Aldine Press.

Durand, F. (2002). Limitations of the medium and pictorial techniques. In *Perceptual and Artistic Principles for Effective Computer Depiction, Course Notes for ACM SIGGRAPH 2002*, (pp. 27-45). ACM. Retrieved from http://people.csail.mit.edu/fredo/SIG02_ArtScience/

Eysenck, M. W., & Keane, M. T. (2005). *Cognitive psychology: a student's handbook* (5th ed.). New York: Psychology Press.

Golledge, R. G. (1999). *Wayfinding behavior: cognitive mapping and other spatial processes*. Baltimore, MD: The Johns Hopkins University Press.

Google Maps. (2013), Retrieved November 22, 2013, from https://maps.google.com.tw/

Heidmann, F., Hermann, F., & Peissner, M. (2003). Interactive Maps on Mobile, Location-Based Systems: Design Solutions and Usability Testing. In *Proceedings of the 21st International Cartographic Conference*, (pp. 1299-1306). Academic Press.

Knight, M., & Brown, A. (1999). *Working in Virtual Environments through appropriate Physical Interfaces*. Paper presented at the 17th eCAADe Conference. Liverpool, UK.

Knight, M., Chen, Y.-H., Winchester, M., & Brown, A. (2008). *Perception, Placement and Wayfinding Applied to Mobile Architectural Guides*. Paper presented at the 26th eCAADe Conference. Antwerp, Belgium.

Knight, M., Saeed, G., Chen, Y.-H., & Brown, A. (2007). *Remote Location in an Urban Digital Model*. Paper presented at the 25th eCAADe Conference. Frankfurt, Germany.

Kramer, R., Modsching, M., & Hagen, K. T. (2005). Development and evaluation of a context-driven, mobile tourist guide. *International Journal of Pervasive Computing and Communications*, 3(4), 378–399. doi:10.1108/17427370710863121

Kray, C., Elting, C., Laakso, K., & Coors, V. (2003). Presenting route instructions on mobile devices. In *Proceedings of the 8th international conference on Intelligent user interfaces*, (pp. 117-124). Academic Press.

Laakso, K. (2002). *Evaluating the use of navigable three-dimensional maps in mobile devices*. (Unpublished master dissertation). University of Helsinki, Helsinki, Finland.

Laakso, K., Gjesdal, O., & Sulebak, J. R. (2003). Tourist information and navigation support by using 3D maps displayed on mobile devices. In *Proceedings of the Mobile HCI Workshop on HCI in Mobile Guides*, (pp. 34-39). HCI.

Lynch, K. (1960). *The image of the city*. Cambridge, MA: MIT Press.

Mapping London. (2013). Retrieved November 22, 2013, from http://mappinglondon.co.uk/2012/tfl-why-not-walk-it-maps/

Mountain, D., & Liarokapis, F. (2007). Mixed reality (MR) interfaces for mobile information systems. *Aslib Proceedings*, *59*, 422–436. doi:10.1108/00012530710817618

Nagi, R. S. (2004). *Cartographic visualization for mobile applications*. (Unpublished master dissertation). The International Institute for Geo-Information Science and Earth Observation, Enschede, The Netherlands.

Nurminen, A. (2006). m-LOMA - a mobile 3D city map. In Proceedings of Web3D 2006 (pp. 7-18). New York: ACM Press.

Parkin, A. J. (2000). *Essential cognitive psychology*. London: Psychology Press.

Passini, R. (1984). Spatial representation: a wayfinding perspective. *Journal of Environmental Psychology*, *4*(2), 153–164. doi:10.1016/S0272-4944(84)80031-6

Passini, R. (1992). *Wayfinding in architecture* (2nd ed.). New York: Van Nostrand Reinhold.

Piaget, J., & Inhelder, B. (1967). *The child's conception of space*. London: Routledge & Kegan Paul.

Pospischil, G., Umlauft, M., & Michlmayr, E. (2002). Designing LoL@, a Mobile Tourist Guide for UMTS. In F. Paternò (Ed.), *Mobile HCI* (pp. 140–154). HCI. doi:10.1007/3-540-45756-9_12

Rakkolainen, I., & Vainio, T. (2001). A 3D City Info for mobile users. *Computers & Graphics*, *25*, 619–625. doi:10.1016/S0097-8493(01)00090-5

Realinho, V., Romão, T., Birra, F., & Dias, A. E. (2011). Building mobile context-aware applications for leisure and entertainment. In *Proceedings of the 8th International Conference on Advances in Computer Entertainment Technology*. Academic Press.

Reichenbacher, T. (2004). *Mobile Cartography - Adaptive Visualisation of Geographic Information on Mobile Devices*. (Unpublished Ph.D. Dissertation). Technischen Universität München, München, Germany.

Saeed, G. (2008). *Pedestrian Real-Time Locatiuon and Routing Information Delivered to Mobile Digital Architectural Guides*. (Unpublished Ph.D. Thesis). University of Liverpool, Liverpool, UK.

Siegel, A. W., & White, S. H. (1975). The development of spatial representations of large-scale environments. In H. W. Reese (Ed.), *Advances in Child Development and Behavior* (Vol. 10). New York: Academic Press. doi:10.1016/S0065-2407(08)60007-5

WAYFINDER. (2013). Retrieved November 22, 2013, from http://www.academia.edu/180289/TangiCAD_Tangible_Interface_for_Manipulating_Architectural_3D_Models

KEY TERMS AND DEFINITIONS

2D Barcode: A 2D barcode looks like a 2D symbol or tag which can be read by using barcode readers or particular optical scanners and cameras. A 2D barcode can be used to store the information, for example URLs, price and numbers, relating to the goods or objects to which it is attached. The information could be retrieved by browsing the code via a mobile device or a web browser. QR-code is known as one type of 2D barcode which could provide URL (Hyper Text Transfer Protocol), email address, contact details, SMS (Systems Management Server) information and so forth.

Augmented Reality (AR): Augmented Reality is one kind of virtual reality. This technique generates a virtual environment which helps to superimpose the real-world scenes and virtual elements or virtual views in order to provide additional information to the viewers.

Computer Aided Architectural Design (CAAD): An application, software or technique which could help architects and architectural companies to design and complete a project.

Computer Aided Architectural Design Research Unit (CAADRU): CAADRU is one of the research units in School of Architecture, University of Liverpool.

Point(s) of Interest (POI): POI is a particular location, attraction or landmark. In addition, a visitor may be interested in planning a tour to it, learning more details about its history and enjoying the atmosphere.

Pseudo-3D: It is a technique by applying 2D graphical elements and representations to simulate a 3D perception. A number of video games have used this kind of visualisation to construct 3D scenes.

Radio Frequency Identification (RFID): RFID is an electronic tag or label for storing information and can be used to track objects and record travel history which is similar to the feature of 2D barcode. However, RFID tags can be read in a short distance and can be placed inside an object which is different from the use of a 2D barcode.

Section 5
User Experience

Chapter 14

The Impact of Perceived Visual Complexity, Gender, and Cognitive Style on Children's Aesthetic Preferences for Learning Web Pages

Hsiu-Feng Wang
National Chiayi University, Taiwan

Ching-Chih Liao
Ming Chuan University, Taiwan

Pei-Yu Wang
National Chiayi University, Taiwan

Yu-Yin Lin
National Chiayi University, Taiwan

ABSTRACT

This chapter examines children's aesthetic preferences for learning Web pages designed for them. It applies Berlyne's theory of aesthetic preference to these Web pages: a theory that suggests that people prefer a medium level of stimuli to a low or high level of stimuli. The experiment employs a 3 x 2 x 2 between-subject design; it explores perceived visual complexity, gender, cognitive style, and aesthetic preference. A total of 120 children (60 boys and 60 girls) aged between 11 to 12 years-old take part in the experiment. The children are asked to rate learning Web pages of different levels of perceived visual complexity for aesthetic preference. These Web pages have been created by the authors. The results of the experiment show that overall the children prefer Web pages that display a medium level of perceived visual complexity to those that display a high or low level of perceived visual complexity. Thus, the results support Berlyne's theory. However, when aesthetic preference is analysed with respect to gender, it is found that different levels of perceived visual complexity have an impact on boys' aesthetic preferences but not girls'. In other words, Berylne's theory is only partly supported. Likewise, Berylne's theory is only partly supported when aesthetic preference is analysed with respect to cognitive style. Here, imagers prefer a high level of perceived visual complexity and verbalisers prefer a medium level of perceived visual complexity. This chapter should be of interest to anyone who designs learning Web pages for children.

DOI: 10.4018/978-1-4666-6228-5.ch014

1. INTRODUCTION

Many children's educational establishments have learning web-pages. In order for these web-pages to be useful they need to be informative; they also need to be usable and attractive. However, while much research has been conducted into the usability of web-pages (e.g. Hart, Chaparro & Halcomb, 2008; Haak, Jong & Schellens, 2007; Battleson, Booth & Weintrop, 2001), little has been conducted into their aesthetics. This area deserves more exploration as aesthetics impacts on many areas of HCI including usability, overall impression and users' experiences (Tuch, Bargas-Avila & Opwis, 2010). Furthermore, and perhaps more importantly as far as children's learning web-pages are concerned, aesthetics impacts on children's learning motivation: children are more motivated by web-pages with good aesthetics than web-pages with poor aesthetics (Zain, Tey & Goy, 2007).

Research into aesthetics that has been conducted includes studies into first impressions (Lindgaard, Fernandes, Dudek, & Brown, 2006; Tuch, Presslaber, Stocklin, Opwisa, & Bargas-Avila, 2012), the importance of aesthetics with respect to mode of use (Schaik & Ling, 2009) and the affect of colour on emotions (Cyr, Head & Larios, 2010). Research has also been conducted into users' preferences with regard to perceived visual complexity in web-pages; however, most of this work has involved adults (see Michailidou, Harper, & Bechhofer, 2008; Pandir & Knight, 2006; Tuch, Bargas-Avila, & Opwis, 2010). As such, little is known as to whether perceived visual complexity impacts on children's aesthetic preferences of web-pages or whether gender or cognitive style plays a role.

An increasing number of organisations that create web-pages for children design them with children (e.g. Children's International Library; see Hutchinson, Bederson & Druin, 2006). However, unfortunately, many do not. Indeed, Nielsen (2010) states that much website design for children

is based "purely on folklore" or, at best, with "insights gleaned when designers observe their own children". Certainly, the authors have found this to be the case in Taiwan where websites are frequently developed on extremely tight budgets. However, while the authors do not want to discourage companies that can afford to undertake user research from doing so, better results would be undeniably be obtained if those designers who do not have the funds to conduct research based their decisions on information attained through empirical research.

2. BACKGROUND OF STUDY

2.1 Aesthetic Preference, Perceived Visual Complexity and Berylne's Theory

Many factors influence people's aesthetic preferences for web-pages including typography, pictures, sound and perceived visual complexity (Reinecke et al., 2013; Thorlacius, 2007); of these aspects, many researchers argue that perceived visual complexity may have the biggest impact (see Reinecke et al., 2013 for references). While no agreed definition of perceived visual complexity exists with relation to web-pages (Harper, Michailidou & Stevens, 2009), a number of researchers refer to Heaps and Handel's (1999) definition; this states that perceived visual complexity is "the degree of difficulty in providing a description of an image". One researcher who cites this quotation and has carried out much research into perceived visual complexity is Michailidou (2008). In her work, she describes web-pages that are dense and contain a high number of diverse elements as having a high level of perceived visual complexity and web-pages that are sparse and contain a low number of diverse elements as having a low level of perceived visual complexity (Michailidou, 2005). The authors of this chapter use this distinction in this chapter.

2.1.1 Participants

A total of 120 participants (60 boys and 60 girls) were randomly selected for the experiment. They were all 6th grade students at a primary school in Taichung, Taiwan. The participants were aged between 11 and 12 years (M=11.61, SD=.45); they all received computer lessons at least once a week and often played computer games and browsed the Internet at home. No participants reported known reading difficulties (they all had normal or corrected-to-normal vision). After completing the experiment, each participant received a small toy for his/her participation.

2.1.2 Equipment

The experiment used Intel Core i3 based desktop PC computers with 19-in LED screens. The screens were set to a resolution of 1280 × 1024 pixels. Mice and keyboards were also used. The computer screens were viewed at an approximate distance of 55 cm. Each participant had his/her own computer.

2.2 Materials

The following paragraphs explain the materials used in the experiment. To ease reading the issues of text, perceived visual complexity and links have been discussed separately.

2.2.1 Text

The text used in the experiment was Traditional Chinese. It told of 'The Legend of Amis': a well-known Taiwanese fable. The text was adapted from a 3rd grade elementary school text book. It was shown to each participant on three web-pages. Participants could move between the web-pages by clicking on-screen arrow buttons. The text was shown on three web-pages rather than one as children dislike scrolling and lengthy-looking articles (Nielsen, 2000). The text contained 450 words (approximately 150 words per page) and was written in 14-point.

2.2.2 Perceived Visual Complexity

Three sets of web-pages were created for the experiment. They had different levels of perceived visual complexity (high, medium and low). Geissler et al.'s (2006) paper on perceived visual complexity guided their creation. The web-pages with a high level of perceived visual complexity had more colours, more links and more images than the web-pages with a medium level of perceived visual complexity. The web-pages with a low level of perceived visual complexity were mainly text: they had the least number of colours, the fewest links and, unlike the other web-pages, no images (see Figure 1).

2.2.3 Links

Each web-page contained text links. These links, when clicked, either took a reader to the 'The Concise Chinese Dictionary' online (http://dict. concised.moe.edu.tw/), where an explanation of the linked word was given, or opened a pop-up that explained the linked word using an image. The level of perceived visual complexity used in the pop-ups reflected the level of perceived visual complexity used in the web-pages they were associated with (see Figure 2 for examples).

The text links were all words that the authors either thought were likely to be unfamiliar to children or particularly relevant to the text.

Initial studies in experimental aesthetics resulted in a number of theories, one of which was Berylne's psychobiological theory of aesthetics (Berlyne, 1971). This theory proposed that aesthetic preference is related to a stimulus' arousal potential and that medium levels of arousal are preferred to low and high levels. Berlyne argued that arousal potential was a function of a number of different 'collative variables' (Berlyne, 1971,

Figure 1. Three web-pages used in the experiment each showing a different level of perceived visual complexity

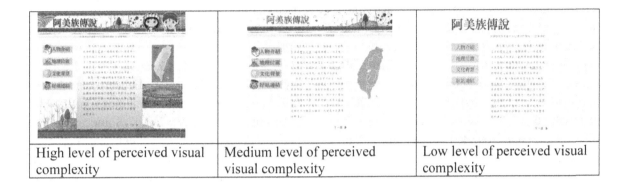

High level of perceived visual complexity	Medium level of perceived visual complexity	Low level of perceived visual complexity

p.141), one of which was perceived visual complexity.

Since Berlyne formulated his theory, a number of researchers have explored perceived visual complexity, mostly with adults, in relation to aesthetic preference. Some of these experiments have supported Berylne's theory (e.g. Geissler et al., 2006; Kaplan et al., 1972; Wang & Bowerman, 2012) while others have not (e.g. Michailidou et al., 2008; Pandir & Knight, 2006; Tuch et al., 2009). This suggests that using previous research to predict children's preferences with respect to perceived visual complexity in learning web-pages would be unwise. It also suggests that the topics of aesthetic preference and perceived visual complexity would benefit from more exploration.

2.3 Gender Differences

Research has revealed differences between the way males and females relate to the Internet. Males have been found to be less concerned about security, more satisfied with their interaction experiences and less loyal to online stores that offer them an enjoyable experience than females; they have also been found to trust online information less (Cyr, Hassanein, Head & Ivanov, 2007; Garbarino & Strahilevitz, 2004; Simon, 2001). Differences

Figure 2. Images with different levels of perceived visual complexity used in the pop-ups

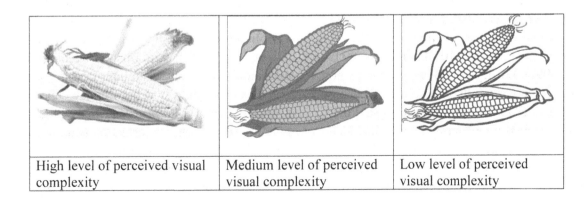

High level of perceived visual complexity	Medium level of perceived visual complexity	Low level of perceived visual complexity

have also been found in way males and females prefer information to be displayed online. Males have been found to prefer websites that have many pictures and little text whereas females have been found to prefer the opposite (Simon, 2001); males have also been found to prefer websites that display content asymmetrically than symmetrically whereas females have been found to have no preference (Tuch et al., 2010). Furthermore, it has been found that when creating websites, females prefer to use more rounded shapes and colours than men (Moss, Gunn & Heller, 2006).

However, while research has revealed gender differences with respect to the Internet, much of this research relates to adults. Presently, little is known about how gender affects children's perceptions of web-pages. Clearly, more research in this area would assist designers who make web-pages directed at boys or girls.

2.4 Cognitive Style

2.4.1 Definition and Relationship to Learning Style

Cognitive style has been a key concept in educational and psychological research for many decades (e.g. Paivio, 1971, Riding & Calvey, 1981; Riding & Watts, 1997). This has resulted in numerous models for cognitive style (e.g. Gullo, 1998; McKenna, 1984) and researchers using the term 'cognitive style' differently (Curry, 2002; Peterson, Rayner & Armstrong, 2009; Plass et al., 1998). Some researchers use it interchangeably with other terms such as 'learning style' and 'learning preference', while others do not (see Mayer & Massa, 2003; Perdikaris, 2011; Valley, 1997). Hartley (1998) is one author who afforded cognitive style its own meaning. Drawing on Reber's (1995) definition, which stated that cognitive style is the preferred manner in which an individual perceives, remembers and thinks, Hartley described cognitive style as the way in which an individual normally approaches cogni-

tive tasks. As such, he maintained that cognitive style was distinct from people's ability to learn or their approach to learning. This is the definition used in this chapter.

Many researchers claim that cognitive style is, in fact, a component of learning style (e.g. Cassidy, 2004; Riding & Cheema, 1991). Learning style is described Steward, Felicetti, and Kuehn (1996), as the "educational conditions under which a student is most likely to learn". Some researchers argue that individuals alter their learning styles to fit their instructor's style of teaching and what is being taught (e.g. Cornett, 1983). However, the central tenet of learning-styles instruction is that learning is most effective when instruction is tailored to the student's learning style (Grasha, 1996; Pashler et al., 2008).

2.4.2 The Verbal-Imagery Dimension

Paivio (1971) maintained that the mind uses two systems to process and recall information: a verbal system and an image system. He argued that while these two systems generally interact, they can also work independently. However, he explained that when they work independently, information is not retained nor recalled as easily. Several researchers have built on Paivio's work. Riding (1991), for example, has developed a test for cognitive style called Cognitive Style Analysis. The test measures two dimensions, one of which is the verbal-imagery dimension. According to many researchers (e.g. Riding & Buckle, 1990), students learn more effectively if information is delivered to them in the format that matches their cognitive style. In other words, students who are superior at working with verbal information (verbalisers) learn more effectively when information is presented as text, while students who are superior at working with visual material (imagers) learn more effectively when information is presented as pictures. Other researchers who have explored the verbal-imagery dimension include Peterson, Deary, and Austin (2003) and Richardson (1977).

The researchers used the Style Of Processing, which was developed by Childers, Houston, and Heckler (1985). (It was an improved version of the Verbal-Imagery Cognitive Styles test and the Visualizer Verbalizer Questionnaire). Research into the verbal-imagery dimension is important to the design of learning web-pages as one of the advantages of electronic information is that it can be tailored to a learner's cognitive style (Rezaei & Katz, 2004).

2.5 Measurement Tools

In the experiment a questionnaire was used to collect information from participants. The questionnaire, which was written in Chinese, had three parts. The first part collected information on cognitive style and measured individual preferences for information processing. To do this, it used 22 questions (which were modified slightly so the children could understand them more easily) taken from a questionnaire called the Style Of Processing (see Childers et al., 1985). Each question had four possible answers: always false, usually false, usually true, and always true. These answers were attributed scores of 1 to 4 respectively. By adding a participant's scores together, it was possible to establish whether he/she was a verbaliser or a visualiser. A high score indicated that he/she was a verbaliser and a low score indicated that he/she was a visualiser. The internal consistency and construct validity for the Style Of Processing questionnaire have been demonstrated by Childers et al., 1985 and Heckler, Childers & Houston, 1993. The internal consistency has been found to be $\alpha= .86$ (Childers et al., 1985).

The second part of the questionnaire used questions based on those developed by Lavie and Tractinsky (2004). It employed Likert scales, ranging from 1 (very strongly disagree) to 7 (very strongly agree), to capture levels of agreement with statements about the web-pages' aesthetics. Three different factors were explored: classical aesthetics, expressive aesthetics and pleasure.

The statements on classical aesthetics explored pleasantness, clarity, beauty and symmetry. For example, one statement read: "I feel these web-pages are well ordered". Cronbach's α indicated that the scales used for these statements were reliable ($\alpha= .778$). The statements on expressive aesthetics explored originality, creativity, fascinating design and sophistication. For example, one statement read: "I feel these web-pages are creative". Cronbach's α indicated that the scales used for these statements were reliable ($\alpha= .837$). The statements on pleasure explored joy, pleasure, gratification, satisfaction and relaxation. For example, one statement read: "I feel these web-pages are pleasant". Cronbach's α indicated that the scales used for these statements were reliable ($\alpha= .704$).

The final part of the questionnaire collected demographic information. This included information on gender, age, level of education, reasons for using computers, and time spent using computers each week.

2.6 Procedure

The study was carried out in a computer lab with groups of 20 participants in 18 sessions. Each session commenced with a practice trial to ensure that the participants could use their equipment properly and knew what to do. The trial involved participants viewing one set of three web-pages, and answering two multiple choice questions about it. The questions, which were displayed onscreen, were simple. For example, one read: 'How many aboriginal tribes are mentioned in the text?'. The questions were asked solely to encourage the participants to look carefully at their screens (the answers were not examined by the experimenters). To answer the questions, the participants needed to click checkboxes. The participants were instructed that they should click a button labelled 'Done' once they had answered both questions. During the trial (and the experiment) each participant worked alone.

Once the practice trial had been completed, the experiment begun. In the experiment every time the 'Done' button was clicked a new set of web-pages and a new set of questions were shown. In total, each participant saw three sets of web-pages and answered three sets of questions. Each participant saw web-pages of the same level of perceived visual complexity (high, medium or low). The sets of web-pages and their respective questions were shown in a random order for each participant.

After everyone had seen their one set of web-pages, the questionnaire was handed out. All the children filled out the questionnaire at the same time and each question was explained by the experimenter.

3. THE STUDY

The study aimed to explore the relationship between aesthetic preference, perceived visual complexity, gender and cognitive style with respect to children and learning web-pages. In doing so, it tested Berlyne's theory of aesthetic preference: a theory that maintains that people prefer a medium level of stimuli to high or low level of stimuli.

3.1 Research Questions

The study was guided by four research questions. All the questions related to children and web-pages designed for them; they were:

1. Does perceived visual complexity impact on aesthetic preference?
2. Does gender impact on aesthetic preference?
3. Does cognitive style impact on aesthetic preference?
4. Is there any interaction between perceived visual complexity, gender and cognitive style with respect to aesthetic preference?

3.2 Method

3.2.1 Experimental Design

The experiment used three independent variables, one variable had three conditions and the others had two (3x2x2). The independent variable that had three conditions was perceived visual complexity. The conditions were: a high level of perceived visual complexity, a medium level of perceived visual complexity and a low level of perceived visual complexity. The other two independent variables were gender and cognitive style: gender's conditions were male and female, and cognitive style's conditions were verbal and imagery. The dependent variable was aesthetic preference. It had three factors: classical aesthetics, expressive aesthetics and pleasure (See Table 1). The design of the experiment was between-subject.

4. RESULTS

The data was examined with respect to overall aesthetic preference and the three aesthetic factors (classical aesthetics, expressive aesthetics and pleasure). Three-way analysis of variance (3-way ANOVA) was carried out to evaluate the effect of perceived visual complexity, participants' gender and cognitive style in terms of differences in mean scores. Scheffé post-hoc comparisons were used to test for differences between the different levels of perceived visual complexity in relation to participants' gender and cognitive style. For all statistical tests an alpha level of .05 was used.

4.1 Overall Aesthetic Preference

4.1.1 Perceived Visual Complexity

The mean and standard deviation for the ratings of aesthetic preference are illustrated in Table 2. The results showed that a main effect for the different levels of perceived visual complexity was

Table 1. The independent variables and dependent variables used in this experiment

Independent Variables		Dependent Variables	
Perceived Visual Complexity	High level	Aesthetic Preference	Classical aesthetics
	Medium level		
	Low level		Expressive aesthetics
Gender	Male		Pleasure
	Female		
Cognitive style	Verbal		
	Imagery		

significant, $F(2, 108) = 19.151, p=.000, \eta^2=.262$. The participants preferred the web-pages that had a medium level of perceived visual complexity the most, followed by the web-pages that had a high level of perceived visual complexity, then the web-pages that had a low level of perceived visual complexity.

Multiple comparisons showed that the ratings for aesthetic preference for the web-pages that had a medium level of perceived visual complexity were significantly higher than the web-pages that had a low level of perceived visual complexity ($p=.000$). Moreover, the ratings for aesthetic preference for the web-pages that had a high level of perceived visual complexity were significantly higher than the web-pages that had a low level of perceived visual complexity ($p=.000$). However, no difference was found between the ratings for the web-pages that had a high level of perceived visual complexity and the web-pages that had a medium level of perceived visual complexity ($p=.779$).

4.1.2 Gender and Cognitive Style

Analyses of variance showed that overall aesthetic preference ratings made by imagers were higher than verbalisers, $F(1, 108) = 17.164, p=.000,$

Table 2. Means and standard deviations for aesthetic preference, children's gender and cognitive style with respect to different levels of perceived visual complexity

	Overall aesthetic		Classical aesthetic		Expressive aesthetic		Pleasure	
	M	SD	M	SD	M	SD	M	SD
Visual Complexity								
High	4.74	.73	4.64	.56	4.54	1.38	5.03	.98
Medium	4.83	.52	4.49	.64	4.84	1.07	5.16	1.04
Low	4.09	.66	3.83	.56	4.06	1.48	4.39	1.00
Gender								
Boys	4.56	.76	4.36	.71	4.33	1.40	5.00	1.07
Girls	4.55	.67	4.28	.66	4.64	1.29	4.72	1.03
Cognitive Style								
Verbal	4.34	.76	4.23	.64	4.20	1.48	4.57	1.16
Imagery	4.77	.60	4.40	.72	4.77	1.14	5.15	.86

Figure 3. Interaction plot. Overall and classical aesthetic preference ratings for gender and different levels of perceived visual complexity (1 = highly dislike; 7= highly like)

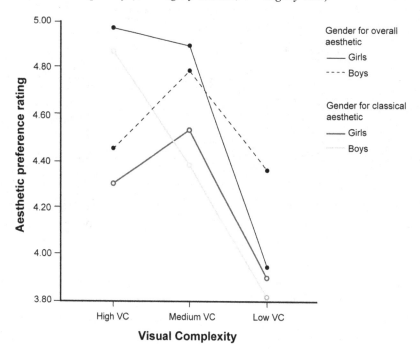

η^2=.137. However, no differences were found between the aesthetic preference ratings for boys and girls.

4.1.3 Interactions

There was a significant interaction between gender and the different levels of perceived visual complexity on overall aesthetic preference, $F(2, 108)$ =6.780, p=.002, η^2=.112. This interaction is illustrated in Figure 3. Boys' aesthetic preferences for the three different levels of perceived visual complexity were significantly different, $F(2, 57)$ =23.440, p=.000, η^2=.451.

The means and standard deviations for the overall aesthetic preference ratings for the two genders are shown in Table 3. Looking at the genders separately, boys preferred web-pages that had a high level of perceived visual complexity significantly more than web-pages that had a low level of perceived visual complexity (p=.000). They also preferred web-pages that had a me-

dium level of perceived visual complexity more than web-pages that had a low level of perceived visual complexity (p=.000). However, they did not have a preference between web-pages that had a high level of perceived visual complexity and web-pages that had a medium level of perceived visual complexity; the difference was insignificant (p=.913).

Girls did not have a preference for any of the levels of perceived visual complexity, $F(2, 57)$ =2.233, p=.117, η^2=.073. In other words, in relation to overall aesthetic preference, different levels of perceived visual complexity had an impact for boys but not for girls.

4.2 Classical Aesthetics

4.2.1 Perceived Visual Complexity

The ratings for different levels of perceived visual complexity had an effect on children's classical aesthetic preference ratings, $F(2, 108)$ =23.776,

Table 3. The means and standard deviations for overall aesthetic preference with respect to gender

Visual Complexity	Boys		Girls	
	M	SD	M	SD
High	4.96	.68	4.52	.72
Medium	4.88	.48	4.78	.56
Low	3.85	.55	4.34	.67

$p=.000, \eta^2=.306$. The web-pages that had a high level of perceived visual complexity received the highest classical aesthetic preference ratings, followed by the web-pages that had a medium level of perceived visual complexity, then the web-pages that had a low level of perceived visual complexity.

Multiple comparisons showed that the web-pages that had a high level of perceived visual complexity received significantly higher classical aesthetic preference ratings than the web-pages that had a low level of perceived visual complexity ($p=.000$). Moreover, the differences between the web-pages that had a medium level of perceived visual complexity were significantly higher than the web-pages that had a low level of perceived visual complexity ($p=.000$). However, no difference was found between the web-pages that had a high level of perceived visual complexity and the web-pages that had a medium level of perceived visual complexity ($p=.494$).

4.2.2 Gender and Cognitive Style

There was no difference between the classical aesthetic preference ratings for children of different cognitive style, $F(1, 108)=2.739, p=.101, \eta^2=.025$. In addition, there was no difference between the classical aesthetic preference ratings for boys and girls, $F(1, 108)=.658, p=.419, \eta^2=.006$.

4.2.3 Interactions

An interaction between gender and the different levels of perceived visual complexity had a significant effect on classical aesthetic preference, $F(2,$

$108) = 5.403, p=.006, \eta^2=.091$. This interaction is illustrated in Figure 3. The differences between levels of perceived visual complexity were significant for both genders. Boys preferred a high level of perceived visual complexity, followed by a medium level of perceived visual complexity while girls preferred a medium level of perceived visual complexity, followed by a high level of perceived visual complexity.

4.3 Expressive Aesthetics

4.3.1 Perceived Visual Complexity

The results showed that a main effect for the different levels of perceived visual complexity with respect to expressive aesthetics was significant, $F(2, 108)=4.434, p=.014, \eta^2=.076$. The web-pages that had a medium level of perceived visual complexity received the highest expressive aesthetic preference ratings, followed by the web-pages that had a high level of perceived visual complexity, then the web-pages that had a low level of perceived visual complexity.

Multiple comparisons showed that the web-pages that had a medium level of perceived visual complexity received significantly higher expressive aesthetic preference ratings than the web-pages that had a low level of perceived visual complexity ($p=.015$). However, no difference was found either between the web-pages that had a high level of perceived visual complexity and the web-pages that had a medium level of perceived visual complexity ($p=.528$) or the web-pages that had a high level of perceived visual complexity and the web-pages that had a low level of perceived visual complexity ($p =.196$).

4.3.2 Gender and Cognitive Ctyle

There was no difference between the expressive preference ratings for boys and girls, $F (1, 108) =2.035$, $p=.157$, $\eta^2=.018$. However, expressive aesthetic preference ratings made by imagers were higher than those made by verbalisers, $F (1, 108) =6.875$, $p=.010$, $\eta^2=.060$.

4.3.3 Interactions

The results showed two two-way interactive effects. The first was a significant interaction between gender and the different levels of perceived visual complexity with respect to expressive aesthetic preference, $F (2, 108) =9.369$, $p=.000$, $\eta^2=.148$. This interaction is illustrated in Figure 4. Boys preferred a medium level of perceived visual complexity, followed by a high level of perceived visual complexity. Girls preferred a low level of perceived visual complexity, followed by a medium level of perceived visual complexity; however this difference was not significant.

The result indicated that boys' expressive aesthetic preference increased as perceived visual complexity increased.

The second significant interaction was between children's cognitive style and the different levels of perceived visual complexity with respect to expressive aesthetic preference, $F (2, 108)=4.501$, $p=.013$, $\eta^2=.077$. This interaction is illustrated in Figure 5. The expressive aesthetic preference ratings of verbalisers with respect to the three different levels of perceived visual complexity were significantly different, $F (2, 57) =6.779$, $p=.002$, $\eta^2=.192$.

The result showed that participants gave the highest expressive aesthetic preference ratings to the web-pages that had the medium level of perceived visual complexity and the lowest expressive aesthetic preference ratings to the web-pages that

had a low level of perceived visual complexity. This was done regardless of cognitive style.

The means and standard deviations of overall aesthetic preference for the two cognitive styles are shown in Table 4. Looking at cognitive style separately, verbalisers preferred a medium level of perceived visual complexity significantly more than a low level of perceived visual complexity ($p=.002$). However, no significant difference was found between the ratings they gave to web-pages that had a high level of perceived visual complexity and the ratings they gave to web-pages that had a medium level of perceived visual complexity ($p=.298$). Nor was a significant difference found between the ratings they gave to a high level of perceived visual complexity and the ratings they gave to a low level of perceived visual complexity ($p=.120$).

For imagers, there was no significant difference between the different levels of perceived visual complexity, $F (2, 57) =.024$, $p=.976$, $\eta^2=.001$. In other words, with respect to expressive aesthetic preference, different levels of perceived visual complexity had impact for verbalisers but not for imagers.

4.4 Pleasure

4.4.1 Perceived Visual Complexity

The results showed that a main effect for the different levels of perceived visual complexity with respect to pleasure was significant, $F (2, 108) =7.501$, $p=.001$, $\eta^2=.122$. The participants rated the web-pages that had a medium level of perceived visual complexity the highest, followed by the web-pages that had a high level of perceived visual complexity, then the web-pages that had a low level of perceived visual complexity.

Multiple comparisons showed that the pleasure ratings for the web-pages that had a medium level of perceived visual complexity were significantly higher than the web-pages that had a low level of perceived visual complexity ($p=.002$). Moreover,

Figure 4. Interaction plot. Expressive aesthetic preference ratings for gender and different levels of perceived visual complexity (1 = highly dislike; 7= highly like)

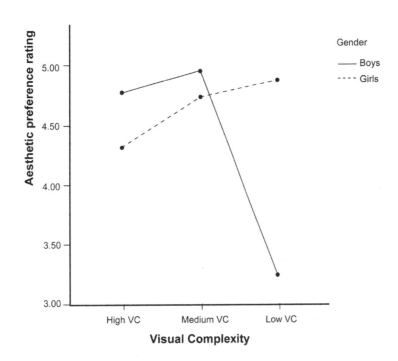

the pleasure ratings for the web-pages that had a high level of perceived visual complexity were significantly higher than the web-pages that had a low level of perceived visual complexity (p =.013). However, no difference was found between the ratings for the web-pages that had a high level of perceived visual complexity and the web-pages that had a medium level of perceived visual complexity (p =.840).

4.4.2 Gender and Cognitive Style

A significant difference was found in the pleasure ratings of visualisers and imagers, F (1, 108) =11.283, p=.001, η^2=.095. The pleasure ratings given by imagers were higher than the pleasure ratings given by verbalisers. However, there was no significant difference between the pleasure ratings given by boys and girls, F (1, 108) =2.622, p=.108, η^2=.024.

4.4.3 Interactions

The results showed a significant interaction between cognitive style and the different levels of perceived visual complexity with respect to pleasure, F (2, 108) =3.240, p=.043, η^2=.057. This interaction is illustrated in Figure 5. The differences between the different levels of perceived visual complexity for both imagers and verbalisers were significant. Moreover, the pleasure ratings for imagers and verbalisers were different for different levels of perceived visual complexity. Imagers preferred a medium level of perceived visual complexity, followed by a high level of perceived visual complexity whereas verbalisers preferred a high level of perceived visual complexity followed by a medium level of perceived visual complexity.

Figure 5. Interaction plot. Pleasure and expressive aesthetic preference ratings for cognitive style and the different levels of perceived visual complexity (1 = highly dislike; 7= highly like)

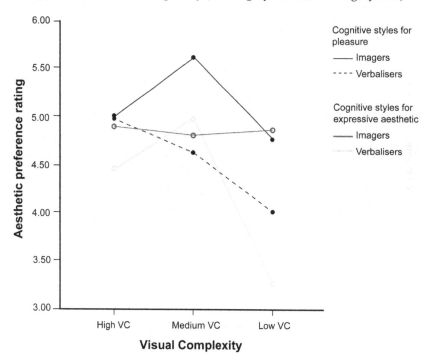

5. DISCUSSION

The experiment examined the influence of three variables—perceived visual complexity, gender, and cognitive style—on children's aesthetic preferences for learning web-pages. It also tested Berlyne's theory of aesthetic preference: a theory claims that people prefer a medium level of stimuli to a high or low level of stimuli.

5.1 Perceived Visual Complexity

Analysis of the data indicated that perceived visual complexity had an impact on aesthetic preference. Overall, children preferred web-pages that had a medium levels of perceived visual complexity. This finding supported Berlyne's theory. However, a more in depth analysis of the data revealed that children preferred web-pages that had a medium level of perceived visual complexity with respect to expressive aesthetics and pleasure, but web-pages that had a high level of perceived visual complexity with respect to classical aesthetics.

5.2 Cognitive Style

Analysis showed that cognitive style had an impact on aesthetic preference ratings for overall aesthetics, expressive aesthetics and pleasure, but not for classical aesthetics. Generally, imagers provided higher aesthetic preference ratings to the web-pages shown than verbalisers. Looking at the data in more detail, it was found that imagers preferred the web-pages that had a high level of perceived visual complexity most, followed by those that had a medium level of perceived complexity, then those that had a low level of perceived complexity. Verbalisers, on the other hand, preferred the web-pages that had a medium level of perceived visual complexity most, followed by those that had a high level of perceived visual complexity

Table 4. The means and standard deviations for overall aesthetic preference with respect to cognitive style

Visual Complexity	Verbalisers		Imagers	
	M	**SD**	**M**	**SD**
High	4.28	1.56	4.81	1.15
Medium	4.95	1.24	4.74	.87
Low	3.37	1.24	4.75	1.41

then those that had a low level of perceived visual complexity.

5.3 Gender Differences

The results showed that with respect to overall aesthetic preference ratings, girls preferred web-pages that had a medium level of perceived visual complexity to those that had a high or low level; boys, on the other hand, preferred web-pages that had a high level of perceived visual complexity. Thus, in this case, Berlyne's theory was supported only for girls. This finding is comparable to that of Tuch et al. (2010) who discovered that men and women did not judge aesthetic balance in web-pages the same. The researchers found that men preferred vertically symmetrical web-pages to vertically asymmetrical web-pages while women showed no preference between the two.

5.4 Aesthetic Preference

The results showed that girls had a more favourable impression of classical aesthetics than boys; and boys, unlike girls, preferred high levels of perceived complexity. These differences are likely to be of interest to anyone developing gender specific learning materials for children. Indeed, mobile technologies now allow children to access web-pages on their own (see Read & Druin, 2009); it is thus increasingly important for educators to create web-pages that appeal to users as well as educate.

6. CONCLUSION

This experiment clearly identified that perceived visual complexity has a significant impact on children's aesthetic preferences towards learning web-pages created for them. The children in the experiment found web-pages with a medium level of perceived visual complexity more aesthetically appealing than web-pages with a high or a low level of perceived visual complexity. The results showed that differences existed between the children who had different cognitive styles. Children who were verbalisers showed greater aesthetic preference to the web-pages shown than children who were imagers. Differences were also found with respect to gender: girls preferred classical aesthetic more than boys. These findings should be taken into consideration by educators, instructional designers and web designers when creating learning web-pages for children.

This experiment had a number of limitations. First, the experiment only involved children's learning web-pages. As such, further research is necessary before applying the findings to other children's web-pages. Second, it was conducted with Taiwanese children who were 11 to 12 years old, all of whom were either Grade 5 or Grade 6 students. Caution, therefore, is advised before generalising the results to other populations (e.g. to children of other nationalities, age groups and grade levels).

ACKNOWLEDGMENT

This experiment was kindly supported by a grant from the National Science Council of Taiwan (Contract number: NSC 101-2410-H-415-039).

REFERENCES

Battleson, B., Booth, A., & Weintrop, J. (2001). Usability testing of an academic library web site: a case study. Journal of Academic Librarianship, 237, 188–198. doi:10.1016/S0099-1333(01)00180-X

Berlyne, D. E. (1971). Aesthetics and psychobiology. New York: Appleton Century Crofts Publishing.

Cassidy, S. (2004). Learning styles: an overview of theories models and measures. Educational Psychology, 24(4), 419–444. doi:10.1080/0144341042000228834

Childers, T. L., Houston, M. J., & Heckler, S. E. (1985). Measurement of individual differences in visual versus verbal information processing. The Journal of Consumer Research, 12, 125–134. doi:10.1086/208501

Cornett, C. E. (1983). What you should know about teaching and learning styles. Bloomington, IN: Phi Delta Kappa Educational Foundation.

Curry, L. (2002). Individual Differences in Cognitive Style, Learning Style and Instructional Preference in Medical Education. In G. Norman, C. Van der Vleuten & D. Newble (Eds.), International Handbook of Research in Medical Education, (vol. 7, pp. 263-276). Academic Press.

Cyr, D., Hassanein, K., Head, M., & Ivanov, A. (2007). The role of social presence in establishing loyalty in e-Service environments. Interacting with Computers, 19, 43–56. doi:10.1016/j.intcom.2006.07.010

Cyr, D., Head, M., & Larios, H. (2010). Colour appeal in website design within and across cultures: A multi-method evaluation. International Journal of Human-Computer Studies, 68(1-2), 1–21. doi:10.1016/j.ijhcs.2009.08.005

Garbarino, E., & Strahilevitz, M. (2004). Gender differences in the perceived risk of buying online and the effects of receiving a site recommendation. Journal of Business Research, 57(7), 768–775. doi:10.1016/S0148-2963(02)00363-6

Geissler, G. L., Zinkhan, M. Z., & Watson, R. T. (2006). The influence of website complexity on consumer attention, attitudes, and purchase intent. Journal of Advertising, 35(2), 69–80. doi:10.1080/00913367.2006.10639232

Grasha, A. F. (1996). Teaching with style: A practical guide to enhancing learning by understanding teaching and learning styles. Pittsburgh, PA: Alliance Publishers.

Gullo, B. (1998). An investigation of cognitive tempo and its effects on evaluating kindergarten children's academic and social competencies. Early Child Development and Care, 34, 201–215. doi:10.1080/0300443880340115

Haak, van den, M.J., Jong, de, M.D.T., & Schellens, P.J. (2007). Evaluation of a Municipal Website: three variants of the think-aloud method compared. *Technical Communication, 54*(1), 58-71.

Harper, S., Michailidou, E., & Stevens, R. (2009). Toward a definition of visual complexity as an implicit measure of cognitive load. ACM Transactions on Applied Perception, 6(2), 1–10. doi:10.1145/1498700.1498704

Hart, T. A., Chaparro, B. S., & Halcomb, C. G. (2008). Evaluating websites for older adults: adherence to 'senior-friendly' guidelines and end-user performance. Behaviour & Information Technology, 27(3), 191–199. doi:10.1080/01449290600802031

Hartley, J. (1998). Learning and Studying: A research perspective. London: Routledge. doi:10.4324/9780203270189

Heaps, C., & Handel, C. H. (1999). Similarity and features of natural textures. Journal of Experimental Psychology. Human Perception and Performance, 25, 299–320. doi:10.1037/0096-1523.25.2.299

Heckler, S. E., Childers, T. L., & Houston, M. J. (1993). On the Construct Validity of the SOP Scale. Journal of Mental Imagery, 17(3-4), 119–132.

Hutchinson, H. B., Bederson, B. B., & Druin, A. (2006). The evolution of the International Children's Digital Library searching and browsing interface. In *Proceedings of the 2006 Conference on Interaction Design and Children*. Academic Press.

Kaplan, S., Kaplan, R., & Wendt, S. (1972). Rated preference and complexity for natural and urban visual material. Perception & Psychophysics, 12, 354–356. doi:10.3758/BF03207221

Lavie, T., & Tractinsky, N. (2004). Assessing dimensions of perceived visual aesthetics of web sites. International Journal of Human-Computer Studies, 60, 269–298. doi:10.1016/j.ijhcs.2003.09.002

Lindgaard, G., Fernandes, G., Dudek, C., & Brown, J. (2006). Attention web designers: You have 50 milliseconds to make a good first impression! Behaviour & Information Technology, 25(2), 115–126. doi:10.1080/01449290500330448

Mayer, R. E., & Massa, L. J. (2003). Three facets of visual and verbal learners: Cognitive ability, cognitive style and learning preference. Journal of Educational Psychology, 95, 833–846. doi:10.1037/0022-0663.95.4.833

McKenna, F. P. (1984). Measures of field-dependence: cognitive style or cognitive ability? Journal of Sociology & Social Psychology, 47, 593–603.

Michailidou, E. (2005). *Metrics of visual complexity*. (Master's thesis). School of Computer Science, Faculty of Science and Engineering, University of Manchester, Manchester, UK.

Michailidou, E. (2008). Determining users' perception of web page visual complexity and aesthetic characteristics (HCW technical report). Manchester, UK: University of Manchester.

Michailidou, E., Harper, S., & Bechhofer, S. (2008). Visual complexity and aesthetic perception of web pages. In *Proceedings of the 26th annual ACM international conference on Design of communication* (pp. 215-224). ACM.

Moss, G., Gunn, R., & Heller, J. (2006). Some men like it black, some women like it pink: Consumer implications of differences in male and female website design. Journal of Consumer Behaviour, 5(4), 328–341. doi:10.1002/cb.184

Nielsen, J. (2000). Designing web usability: The practice of simplicity. Indianapolis, IN: New Riders.

Nielsen, J. (2010). *Children's websites: Usability issues in designing for kids*. Retrieved from http://www.nngroup.com/articles/childrens-websites-usability-issues/

Paivio, A. (1971). Imagery and verbal processes. New York: Holt, Rinehart & Winston.

Pandir, M., & Knight, J. (2006). Homepage aesthetics: The search for preference factors and the challenges of subjectivity. Interacting with Computers, 18(6), 1351–1370. doi:10.1016/j.intcom.2006.03.007

Pashler, H., McDaniel, M., Rohrer, D., & Bjork, R. (2008). Learning styles: Concepts and evidence. Psychological Science in the Public Interest, 9(3), 105–119.

Perdikaris, S. C. (2011). Using the Cognitive Styles to Explain an Anomaly in the Hierarchy of the van Hiele Levels. Journal of Mathematical Sciences & Mathematics Education, 6(2), 35–43.

Peterson, E., Rayner, S., & Armstrong, S. (2009). The psychology of cognitive style and learning styles: is there really a future? Learning and Individual Differences Journal, 19(4), 518–523. doi:10.1016/j.lindif.2009.06.003

Plass, J. L., Chun, D. M., Mayer, R. E., & Leutner, D. (1998). Supporting visual and verbal learning preferences in a second-language multimedia learning environment. Journal of Educational Psychology, 90, 25–36. doi:10.1037/0022-0663.90.1.25

Read, J., & Druin, A. (2009). Design for the future. In A. Druin (Ed.), Mobile Technology for Children: Designing for Interaction and Learning. New York: Morgan Kaufmann. doi:10.1016/B978-0-12-374900-0.00016-8

Reber, A. S. (1995). The Penguin Dictionary of Psychology. London: Penguin.

Reinecke, K., Yeh, T., Miratrix, L., Mardiko, R., & Zhao, Y. Liu, J., & Gajos, K.Z. (2013). Predicting users' first impressions of website aesthetics with a quantification of perceived visual complexity and colourfulness. In *Proceedings of the SIGCHI Conference on Human Factors in Computing Systems*. ACM.

Rezaei, A. R., & Katz, L. (2004). Evaluation of the reliability and validity of the cognitive styles analysis. Personality and Individual Differences, 36(6), 1317–1327. doi:10.1016/S0191-8869(03)00219-8

Richardson, A. (1977). Verbalizer-Visualizer: A cognitive style dimension. Journal of Mental Imagery, 1, 109–126.

Riding, R. J., & Buckle, C. F. (1990). Learning Styles and Training Performance. Sheffield: Training Agency.

Riding, R. J., & Calvey, I. (1981). The assessment of verbal-imagery learning styles and their effect on the recall of concrete and abstract prose passages by eleven year old children. The British Journal of Psychology, 72, 59–64. doi:10.1111/j.2044-8295.1981.tb02161.x

Riding, R. J., & Cheema, I. (1991). Cognitive styles-An overview and integration. Educational Psychology, 11(3&4), 193–215. doi:10.1080/0144341910110301

Riding, R. J., & Watts, S. (1997). The effect of cognitive style on the preferred format of instructional material. Educational Psychology, 17, 179–183. doi:10.1080/0144341970170113

Riding, R. J. (1991). Cognitive styles analysis. Birmingham, UK: Learning & Training Technology.

Schaik, P., & Ling, J. (2009). The role of context in perceptions of the aesthetics of web pages over time. Journal of Human-Computer Studies, 67, 79–89. doi:10.1016/j.ijhcs.2008.09.012

Simon, S. J. (2001). The impact of culture and gender on web sites: An empirical study. The Data Base for Advances in Information Systems, 32(1), 18–37. doi:10.1145/506740.506744

Steward, K., Felicetti, L., & Kuehn, S. (1996). The attitudes of business majors toward the teaching of business ethics. Journal of Business Ethics, 15(8), 913–918. doi:10.1007/BF00381859

Thorlacius, L. (2007). The role of aesthetics in web design. Nordicom Review, 28(1), 63–76.

Tuch, A. N., Bargas-Avila, J. A., & Opwis, K. (2009). Visual complexity of websites: Effects on users' experience, physiology, performance, and memory. International Journal of Human-Computer Studies, 67(9), 703–715. doi:10.1016/j.ijhcs.2009.04.002

Tuch, A. N., Bargas-Avila, J. A., & Opwis, K. (2010). Symmetry and aesthetics in website design: It's a man's business. Computers in Human Behavior, 26, 1831–1837. doi:10.1016/j.chb.2010.07.016

Tuch, A. N., Presslaber, E. E., Stocklin, M., Opwis, K., & Bargas-Avila, J. (2012). The role of visual complexity and prototypicality regarding first impression of websites: Working towards understanding aesthetic judgments. International Journal of Human-Computer Studies, 70, 794–811. doi:10.1016/j.ijhcs.2012.06.003

Valley, K. (1997). Learning styles and courseware design. Association for Learning Technology Journal, 5(2), 42–51. doi:10.1080/0968776970050205

Wang, H. F., & Bowerman, C. J. (2012). The Impact of Perceived Visual Complexity on Children's Websites in Relation to Classical and Expressive Aesthetics. In P. K. Blashki (Ed.), *IADIS International Conference IADIS Interfaces and Human Computer Interaction 2012* (pp. 269-273). Lisbon: Inderscience Publishers.

Zain, J. M., Tey, M., & Goy, Y. (2007). Does aesthetics of web page interface matters to Mandarin learning? International Journal of Computer Science and Network Security, 7(8), 43–51.

KEY TERMS AND DEFINITIONS

Aesthetic Preference: Aesthetic preference refers to someone's predilection towards a particular aesthetic over another.

Berlyne's Experimental Theory: Berlyne's experimental theory suggests that an inverted-U shaped relationship exists between the preference for a stimuli and its arousal potential. Berlyne proposed that complexity, hedonic value and novelty affect arousal potential.

Classical Aesthetics: Classical aesthetics relates to design that is both clear, clean and orderly. It often employs standard usability principles such as symmetry.

Cognitive Style: Cognitive style is the way an individual normally approaches a cognitive task.

Expressive Aesthetics: Expressive aesthetics relates to design that is creative, visually rich and original.

Imagers: Imagers are people who are superior at working with visual material. They learn more effectively when information is presented as pictures.

Verbalisers: Verbalisers are people who are superior at working with verbal information. They learn more effectively when information is presented as text.

Chapter 15
Intermedia and Transmedia User Experience with Multi-Touch Apps

Huberta Kritzenberger
Stuttgart Media University, Germany

ABSTRACT

In the Web of devices, information and services are designed for multi-device use. As each device has its specific characteristics, inter-device adjustments and adaptations result in inconsistent inter-device (system) models. They are perceived by users on visual and functional experience layers as well as on information architecture and prevent users from building transparent mental models. Evidence from case studies reveals the nature of cognitive information processing in this situation of rich user experience. Consistency design rules seem to be insufficient to overcome the rich user experience problems, as users' exploration of inconsistencies lead to interaction problems. In consequence, a systemic intermedia perspective is needed. This is explored in this chapter.

INTRODUCTION

Within the emergent web of devices (W3C), many web-based services (content and functions) are available for multiple interaction devices. In human-computer interaction literature, these systems, platforms or applications are either referred to as multi-device systems, multi-device environments, multiple user interfaces (MUI) (Denis & Karsenty, 2004) or cross-media systems (Segerståhl, 2008).

Calvary et al. (2003) already stated that many multi-device environments allow users utilizing variable devices (e.g. desktop PC, multi-touch tablet, smart phone etc.) in order to do the same task within variable contexts of use or combine several devices for one task (transmedia processes). Each device has its specific characteristics, e.g. interface conventions (Kurkovsky, 2009), modalities, and variable contexts of use. Therefore, web-based services need to be transferred, configured, and adapted across different devices for multi-device use.

Levin (2014) pointed to multiple-device environments as a design challenge, because their usage is not yet fully understood. The main

DOI: 10.4018/978-1-4666-6228-5.ch015

design approaches for multi-device environments are consistent design approaches (Levin, 2014). According to Denis and Karsenty (2004), they aim at inter-device consistency, which seems to satisfy claims on ergonomic design principles of consistency (DIN EN ISO 9241-110:2008-09). Therefore, these approaches port the same content and features across devices in a like manner, and attempt to replicate the desktop experience onto the mobile device. Some adjustments or adaptations are made to accommodate specific device characteristics (Levin, 2014).

Responsive web design, as it is understood by Marcotte (2011), is a consistent design approach, which ports content and features across devices (desktop PC, tablet, smart phone) in a like manner with some necessary adjustments to the characteristics of each device (Nielsen & Budiu, 2013). Levin (2014) emphasized that the resulting inconsistencies mainly address form factor, screen size, interaction model (touch, key or voice), and sensor data (GPS etc.). Many adaptations are visually, e.g. screen layouts or grids, but can also involve other experience layers like information architecture or functionality.

In view of the consistency principle, there is an inherent problem for the design of multiple-device environments. Because each device has its specific characteristics, e.g. screen size, interaction models etc., inconsistencies are inevitable and consistent in multi-device environments cannot mean identical. Differences between devices cause adjustments and adaptations to the respective characteristics of each device. Furthermore, Segerståhl (2008) emphasized that sometimes heterogeneity and functionality in the case of cross-media services may even add value for their use.

Available design principles are insufficient. Wäljas, Segerståhl, Väänänen-Vainio-Mattila and Oinas-Kukkonen (2010) claim inter-device consistency with respect to core-functionality and common look and feel (visual language) and Levin (2014) considers consistent information architecture across devices to be important. However, these recommendations are not precise enough, and to some extent even not realizable, as, sometimes, it is the case for relationships hold between larger displays like the desktop and smaller displays like the smart phone (see case two in the case studies). Anyway, inconsistencies are inevitable, because of specific device characteristics.

However, from the user's point of view, inconsistencies cause insecurity, as they do not support mental model formation during the interaction process. Little is known on rich user experience in multi-device environments. To get evidence, we studied inter-device consistency from the user's point of view. According DIN EN ISO Standards (DIN EN ISO 9241-210:2011-01) the concept of user experience covers the user's perceptions and responses during use of a system or service. This includes all emotions, beliefs, preferences, physical and psychological responses, behaviors and accomplishments to occur before, during and after use. The user perceives the presentation, functionality, system performance, context of use and so on, and these perceptions are central to the user's information processing during interaction. Therefore, the user's cognitive perceptual and information processing during the interaction process was one aspect of user experience, which was studied with news apps on multi-touch tablets in two case studies.

A common psychological model for describing the user's information processing in human-computer interaction is the cognitive concept of mental model, which has a long tradition in cognitive science and engineering psychology (Gentner & Stevens, 1983; Wilson & Rutherford, 1989). The concept of mental model helps to understand the complex user experience with multi-device systems, and, as in our case studies, to understand especially the user experience with inter-device consistency. Schmitt, Cassens, Kindsmüller and Herczeg (2011) described different concepts of the meaning of mental models. The most helpful one seems to be the meaning of a mental model as a kind of working model, which is permanently updated during the interaction process. User's understanding of the system behavior according to their mental model can be studied with thinking aloud and observation during the interaction, which is combined with subsequent data and discourse analysis. This combination of research methods gives evidence on the user's perceptions and cognitive information processing procedures during the interaction process.

In this paper, two case studies with inter-device consistency in multi-display environments are reported, in which the user's mental model was studied. The two cases are reference models for variable concept realization of inter-device consistency. The study revealed usability problems in both cases and raised questions for further research.

The system model of case one resembles a printed newspaper, and, on the perceptual level, it seems as no adaptations to device characteristics were done in the system model. In case two, we examined a journal as example of a multi-device system with a complementary system model. In this case, there was a core of functions, look and feel, as well as information architecture with necessary adaptations done for each device. So, there was, at least to some extent, a relatively high level of consistency achieved by responsive design procedures. The results, reported here, from this case study, show, that adjustments and adaptations for inter-device use are not immediately transparent to the user. The case study results give evidence for the user's understanding and cognitive information processing of some aspects of inter-devices consistency.

As tracking of mental models with thinking aloud and observation methods does not cover emotional aspects of user experience, further research for the case study one was done with the standardized questionnaire (AttrakDiff) designed by Hassenzahl, Burmester and Koller (2003). Based on a psychological model, represented in word pairs, according to Hassenzahl (2008, 2010), this questionnaire allows to get insight into the user's emotional reactions to the multi-device

environment. Therefore, this questionnaire study covers emotion as an important further component of user experience.

CONCEPTUAL AND MENTAL MODELS IN THE CONTEXT OF MULTI-DEVICE ENVORONMENTS

Users form mental models during interaction with interactive systems. These dynamically built models have explanatory and predictive power during interaction. According to Norman (1983), it is necessary that the designer's conceptual model and the user's mental model are compatible. As the designer's conceptual model determines the system model, the user is confronted with this model during the interaction process. Incompatible models will lead to interaction problems.

This conceptual framework of mental models helps to reveal the user's perception and information processing during the interaction process. With reference to responsive web design, this framework helps to identify how users experience adjustments and adaptations made for multi-device interaction. It also helps to understand how inter-device consistency and inter-device inconsistency will be perceived and processed in the user's mental model. The designer's conceptual model, which is a concrete realization of the concept of inter-device consistency, determines the system model and shapes the interface. It should initially be understood by the user and should be compatible with the user's understanding in his/her mental model. Users experience the intermedia differences. That is, they experience the differences, adjustments and adaptations caused by the characteristics of each device. The term intermedia refers to these differences between media.

User's Mental Models

From Norman (1983), we know, that users generate internal models of the objects they interact with.

Figure 1. Conceptual and mental models

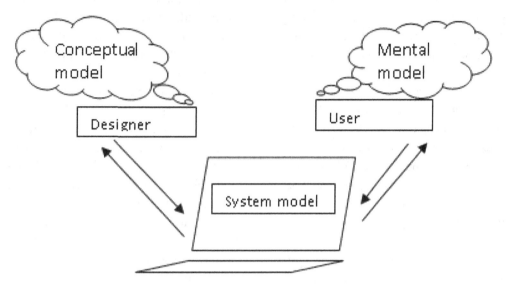

These mental models are progressively constructed during interaction. They include observations, assumptions, pieces of external information, and structures from long-term memory (like schemes).

According to Norman (1983), these mental models have explanatory and predictive power for understanding and planning the interaction. From their mental models, users are able to generate descriptions of the system they are working with. This includes its purpose, its form, and its working mechanism. From their mental models, users can also explain the interaction with the system and its functions. Furthermore, their mental models allow users to deduce explanations of the functioning of the observed system states and anticipate the system's future behavior (Rouse & Morris, 1986). The process of mental model formation is dynamic, where prior knowledge (e.g. schemes) as well as perceptions during the interaction process and system reactions are also included.

Norman (1983) further states that not only the users form internal mental models of the devices they interact with, but also the designer has a model on what the system should look like, and this designer's conceptual model shape the application and the user interface. Since the

conceptual model building for information and services that are provided on user interfaces of different platforms is rather complex, it will be explained in the following sections.

Intermedia Mental Models

With the development of smart phones and multi-touch tablets in the recent years, it became common use to provide the same information and services for use on different devices. Depending on the situation of use, the users switch from device to device and even combine these devices to get access to information and services. Switching between various devices to complete a task is called transmedia, where the task completion is distributed over devices.

There are two general strategies for information and service providers to offer information and services for multi-device environments. One approach is to design the application exclusively for each device (for example native apps on multi-touch tablets). Another approach is to use web browser interface and adapt the central web-based service as a specific version for each device (desktop, multi-touch tablet, smart phone).

Marcotte (2011) proposed a technical solution for this approach with the responsive design strategy as a method to utilize web-based services from one database on multiple displays in multi-device environments.

In the case of producing distinct applications, the way and style of the information and service provided differ completely. This is inconvenient for information and service providers, because additional work has to be done to design und run these distinct models. Nylander, Bylund and Waern (2005) argue that providers have to do development and maintenance work separately and run danger of consistency problems. From the provider's point of view, responsive web design tries to overcome these problems. Only one basis of information and services is provided, which is adjusted and adapted according to the characteristics of the respective device. Responsive web design technology enables automation of the necessary adaptations in order to optimize information and service delivery for use on the respective device and its capabilities of user interaction and presentation.

The native application approach and the responsive web design approach differ with respect to the system model. Native applications utilize a separate system model for each device, whereas, responsive web design utilizes a common model, which is adjusted and adapted to the respective device characteristics. From the user's perspective, the use of native apps means that the way and style of the information and service differ completely from the desktop version. Users are faced with a specific system model provided by the native app. When users switch from one device to another one, they are faced with different system models, e.g. with the system model of the desktop, and with the system model of the native app. The users have to deal with these different models in order to complete their tasks. If the two models are completely different, the user might be forced to complete the same task in different ways, depending on the use of the one device or the other device. In the responsive design case, however, the user is confronted with the adjustments and adaptations done within one system model and he/she will have problems to recognize them immediately, because they are not necessarily transparent.

For responsive web design two general strategies, as understood by Kadlec (2012) are available: progressive enhancement (starting with designing for the smallest device) and graceful degradation (starting with designing for the biggest device).

In Figure 2, the responsive design strategy of automatically adapting content and services to devices is illustrated. This adaptation process reacts to the specific characteristics of each device (e.g. display size, gesture use etc.). In consequence, the system models will differ from device to device to some extent. Responsive design tries to flexibly adapt information and service delivery to the characteristics of the respective device. This solves at least some size and architectural problems. However, it is often regarded, that especially on the smaller devices, the users can only be provided with less information and services. It is harder to give the users an overview, as huge amounts of information need to be organized, and this often results in an unusable and non-transparent information architecture. Therefore, often the amount of information and services provided on the different platforms is also adapted and differs by the way. In order to meet the needs of mobile use in a better way, the strategy of mobile first (to start design with the smaller devices) has been proposed by Kadlec (2012) and Wroblewski (2010).

This design strategy tries to overcome the problems of graceful degradation. Graceful degradation conceptually starts with the mostly rather elaborated and complex web version and reduces it for mobile use on the mobile devices. The smaller the device is, the more problems are induced to design. Design reacts to this situational frame with reductions of information and services. Progressive enhancement realizes the philosophy of mobile first, which means to start with the smallest display and the respective use situation

Figure 2. Conceptual multi-device design models: progressive enhancement and graceful degradation

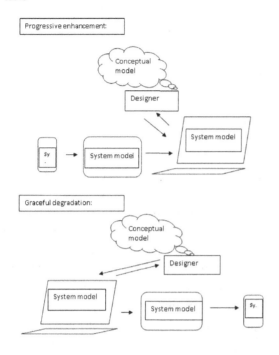

with the necessary information and services. Then the information and services are progressively enriched for the characteristics and use situations of the other devices.

The fact, that information and services are provided on different devices, creates a new situation to the system model. Each of the devices will have its own system model, which has to be formed in the designer's conceptual model and understood and inferred by the user's mental model building during the use process. As there are different characteristics for each device, there will be changes in the way, how information and services are offered on each of the media platforms. In other words, there is an intermedia relationship between these devices, which is solved either by native design or by responsive web design. This relationship should be illustrated by Figure 3:

The model illustrates that designer and user are not only confronted with one system model but – if they have to design or use these devices

– with three system models. There are relations between these models, which can be regarded as a kind of intermedia relationship. How exactly is this intermedia relationship shaped? It depends on the design model (either native or responsive). Both responsive design strategies result in changes in the user interface and more or less changes in the available information and services. The reduction of information and services available on the different devices will only work if task analysis will be carefully done on user needs in intermedia use processes. We suppose that the intermedia relationship further complicates the user's mental model formation during the interaction process.

Transmedia Use Processes and Transmedia Mental Models

The intermedia relationship between devices is one aspect in model formation for interaction. Another aspect is the use process of devices for task completion. Task completion may sometimes be distributed over various devices. This distribution means that users do part of their task on one device, and switch to another device for other subtasks or for completing the task not entirely done on the one device. Reasons for the switching may be, for example, that the user changes his/her location or that a certain device better fits for that task. We refer to this kind of context as transmedia use processes.

If people switch between devices, another problem may arise. If they are used to do procedures in a certain way on the one device, they will port their expectations on the task solution process as it is on the other device. These expectations may, for example, concern available functions or the steps for task solving. Figure 4 illustrates this process in terms of mental model building.

Conceptual design models shape the user's interaction and the user's experience with the multi-device environment, as we observed in our case studies with the mobile app. As a consequence of this transfer, mobile web apps often

Figure 3. Intermedia conceptual and mental models

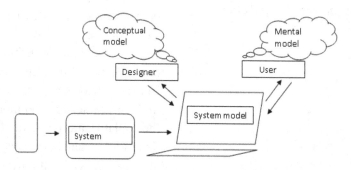

provide the same or similar features as do their counterparts from desktop, but these features are often misleading for the user in the mental model formation process, which takes place during interaction. As stated by Schmitt et al. (2011), mental models are understood as a construction of the user's working memory, and therefore, we must assume that mental models are progressively constructed during interaction. They will include the user's assumptions derived from observations and from prior knowledge. Design concepts and other design features highly influence mental models. Inadequate conceptual models and inconsistencies of these models confuse the user's mental model as in the two cases reported in this paper will be shown for the use of an inadequate conceptual design model and an inconsistent models for news app. The design model causes the instantiation of schemes from prior knowledge. Subsequently, the situation is framed accordingly and any per-

ceptional cues from the interface are interpreted within this cognitive framework.

On the other side, according to Herczeg (2005), appropriate design and system models will support the mental model formation process, whereas inappropriate design and system models will complicate it and result in interaction problems. This may occur, for example, if the system model is not adequate to the task or if the conceptual design model is not compatible with the user's mental model. Complications for user's mental model formation may also occur if the user interface is not compatible with the user's expectations. In inter-device interaction, users have expectations derived from prior interaction with other system models on other devices. These experiences will intensively influence the interaction with the current device. Expectations cause that structures from long-term memory will be instantiated, and subsequently the users plan and try to understand

Figure 4. Transmedia use process and transmedia conceptual and mental models

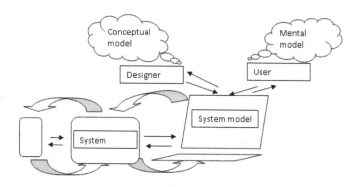

the interaction process with respect to the knowledge of these structures. The models and expectations may be misleading, if the system model of the current system is not compatible with the user experiences derived from prior knowledge.

This problem of users having prior experience and knowledge, which they bring along to the current system they work with, mainly occurs when web browser, multi-touch tablet, and smart phone are used as alternatives to get access to information and services. Often these different devices are used in transmedia use processes, where people switch between the devices according to the current situation and the context of use.

EMPIRICAL EVIDENCE FOR INTERMEDIA USER EXPERIENCE

The research reported here is part of a research agenda on examining intermedia (adaptations and differences of system models in multi-device environments) and transmedia (distributed tasks to be complete using different devices) interaction processes. The focus of the cases, presented in this chapter, is on the question, how user will experience the inter-device consistencies and inconsistencies. In the following sections, results on user's mental model building in intermedia situations are reported.

The research question was how the intermedia transformation of a conceptual design model from one device to another device influences user experience. We did two case studies where the users (10 persons, age 25-30 years in each of the two case studies) had to solve typical newspaper reading tasks. As argued by Benbasat, Goldstein and Mead (1987) explanatory case studies are adequate to answer how and why questions, which are typical for an incomplete and preliminary understanding of the problem and its context.

In the explanatory case study, we observed how potential users accomplish tasks, and use available functions in typical newspaper reading

situations. The insights from the inquiry can inform both system design and further investigation. We monitored the user behavior in the scenario-based user testing situations and recorded user's thinking aloud in our user experience lab. After observation, qualitative data analyses on the transcriptions of thinking aloud protocols and video protocols was done. Additionally, users completed the AttrakDiff questionnaire after the scenario-based testing. The thinking aloud data allow insight into the process of mental model formation during the interaction process, and the additional questionnaire data show the user's emotional states.

Intermedia Design and User's Mental Model Building

The focus of the case study, reported here, was on the horizontal usability of the multi-device newspaper.

According to Denis and Karsenty (2004), horizontal usability focus on transitions between the devices. In each of the two case studies, there were inter-device inconsistencies in the system model, concerning the perceptional, lexical, syntactic and semantic layers.

However, in case one (FAZ) inter-device inconsistencies were hardly to recognize for the user, because the on the perceptual level, the look and feel was that of a newspaper. The same model was available also for the desktop PC, which, however, was not subject to this study. That is, the newspaper looks much the same on all devices. However, the consistency is mainly a perceptual consistency. From the thinking aloud protocols we learnt about users mental model formation. As the perceptual model looks like a printed newspaper, it was not necessary to let the user work on the other device, because the transfer of the system model was quite obvious and was actually realized immediately.

In case two inter-device adaptations have been done in the system model. At least the adaptations on the perceptual level were directly visible for the

Figure 5. iPad App of "Frankfurter Allgemeine Zeitung." The design imitates the print layout

user. It were the typical adaptations which were caused by responsive web design procedures, like the column layout.

Case 1: Frankfurter Allgemeine Zeitung (FAZ)

The research reported here, was done with news apps available at multi-touch tablets. In our case, it was the news app of the "Frankfurter Allgemeine Zeitung" (FAZ). The system model for this app was derived from the print version of newspaper and maintains appearance and layout of the print version (see Figure 5). The design of the print newspaper is mainly kept for the reasons of branding. The transformation of the print model got some adaptations from one medium (the print medium) to another medium (the iPad). In the migration process transformations were done, of course, for example with respect to available functions to interact with the newspaper. However, these transformations are not immediately perceptible for the user.

Although some necessary adaptations according to iPad characteristics have been done, the characteristics of the print medium are still dominant and the newspaper as presented on the iPad resembles a printed newspaper. Therefore, there is at least the perceptual consistency.

According to the designer's conceptual model, the design of the front page of the iPad version of the „Frankfurter Allgemeine Zeitung" imitates the newspaper's print layout. Confronted with the print layout version of the Frankfurter Allgemeine Zeitung on the iPad, many users first supposed to use a .pdf, which is an electronic print version equivalent to the print newspaper. Those users explicitly relied on their supposition of using a .pdf, which, however, they regarded as not being optimized for iPad use.

As mentioned above and according to Norman (1983), people form internal models of the objects they interact with, which have explanatory and predictive power for understanding and planning interaction. The case study gave evidence for this way of the user's cognitive information processing. The users analyzed mainly the perceptual cues on the user interface, which made them recognize a .pdf and this meant them to interact with an electronic print version of the newspaper. They inferred from the perceptual level of consistency to other levels of consistency, e.g. to the syntactic level. On the perceptual level the user thought to recognize genre elements, in the sense of Halliday (2002), of a newspaper. In consequence, the relevant scheme from their long-term memory was retrieved and framed the further interaction process with respect to the perceived .pdf.

There was evidence for user's interpreting the semiotic contexts they were presented from the print layout. Starting from the recognition that the layout of the iPad version of the "Frankfurter Allgemeine Zeitung" imitates exactly the print layout, they made further conclusions for framing the whole the interaction situation. Consequently, they supposed to face the semiotic sign system of the print paper version. Therefore, they immediately started using it intuitively as they would use a .pdf document.

For example, when a user was asked to complete a task of viewing one article closer and subsequently putting this article on the memory list, he/she tried to find a certain button (star button) and this reaction and also subsequent reaction showed that the user did understand the .pdf concept as a concept of a "static picture". This user reaction shows that his/her mental model of working with a .pdf does prevent him/her from thinking about and figuring out the actual conceptual model behind the system model. As a consequence of the .pdf-framing of the situation according to the activated scheme, the user did not find, but not even really look for the function. As he/she is permanently working on cognitive assimilations for the instantiated frame, which is a scheme of working with a .pdf (printed newspaper), he/she was unable to search for a relevant function for solving the task, although this function would have been available for use in the current situation. This example illustrates the assimilation effect of frames and shows, if a schematic knowledge structure is activated, all incoming information will be interpreted and framed to fit into the scheme. Even the attention of the user is focused on scheme-relevant and scheme-consistent information, whereas other information will not be recognized. As long as the user in the situation is working on scheme assimilation within the irrelevant scheme, she will not be able to form an appropriate mental model for her current interaction process.

Furthermore, of course, the scheme of .pdf will not be sufficient for the user to explain all aspects of the interaction. The users in our case study were familiar with other iPad applications and with the gestures applied there. With other words, the users were aware, that necessary adjustments and adaptions to the interaction and presentation model of the device must have been done by the designers. Therefore, the user tried also to explore, which adaptations to the device have been done. Some users tried to combine the .pdf model with an, at least from their points of view, appropriate model known from prior interaction experience with the iPad. Users were engaged in exploration and in some cases, it was mostly by chance, that they applied gestures and caused the intended system reactions. However, in these cases, the user did not know why, as these users were not able to form a mental model on what is the relation between their action and the app's reaction.

In the case study it was observed that one of the users only applied gestures, which he/she is familiar with, from interaction with the iOS photo album. In the photo album there are static pictures and this characteristics seemed relevant to him/her for the interaction with a – from her point of view – static .pdf. Consequently, he/she tried to get the article view only by these gestures which work in the iOS photo album.

Although, the user recognized elements from the iPad interface and tried to integrate them into interaction planning, it is in so far still compatible with the initial framing of the newspaper as both interaction elements share the feature of being static. From the user's point of view, this feature seems to be adequate to be assimilated to the .pdf-scheme. This example shows that, although the user finds and applies functions provided by the iPad (iOS), he/she still frames the interaction with her previously activated scheme of the print newspaper .pdf-model.

There are further examples of the user's scheme assimilation. In another task, the user should read an article in the view mode of the iPad. The user opens the article view (which is a function provided by the iPad). The article view is different now from the newspaper view because the picture, which is part of the article, is missing here and the user wonders why. As the user is working on scheme assimilation in her mental model of the iPad news app, he/she is astonished, because he/she can't infer the meaning of the system's reaction from his/her mental model.

In the case study, there are still other examples, which show the user's assimilation strategy with his/her mental model building. Users articulated several thoughts for their evaluation, e.g. the ty-

pography is too small or the user's expectations were disappointed because .pdf was not felt as being adequate for an iPad use. Users tried to turn pages and wanted to apply page numbers as orientation marker. Those, who thought to interact with a .pdf, tried to scroll down or to scroll vertical because they supposed to find more text there. This seems to be a consequent action, which they could infer from the conceptual model in thought, as they were in search for more text.

These cases of user reactions revealed that the users interpreted the cues of the genre, which was triggered by the visual perception of newspaper, and tried to apply them in the interaction process with the tablet app, but without success. The users' interaction problems in this situation resulted from the instantiation of a not relevant scheme or frame, which was nevertheless triggered by the user's interpretation of the perceptual cues of the system model.

The scheme instantiation and scheme assimilation can be done with any prior knowledge of the user. In other case studies with other news apps, which kept a browser model of the PC (e.g. with responsive design), the user instantiated his/her web browser model when he/she recognized cues from the interface that led him/her to assume that the interaction works similar to interacting with a web browser. Those users, who analyzed a web browser model (in tests with other design models for news apps), instantiated their scheme of a web browser and interpreted the interaction with the iPad within this frame. Those users wanted to double click on the elements they wanted to select and gave reasons for their intended behaviors with behaviors they were uses from Web Browser of their PCs.

Case 2: Complementary Devices

Complementary devices share a zone of data and functions, but one or more of the devices provide access to data or functions that are not available on the other devices. As example for this design model, we did user testing with the marketing journal "W&V" (www.wuv.de). Two interesting aspects from the case study with this journal are reported here.

There is a widget "top aktuell" ("Current Affairs"), which is in the desktop device on the left side of the display. It is presented there in the context of other similar elements, among them also commercials. The placement of the element and its context of presentation prevented users from recognizing its function. From cues like position and layout, they framed its functional use as commercial.

When users switched to the responsive web application at their smart phone device, where the layout of the journal was adjusted to one column, they, however, draw attention to this "top aktuell"-widget. The common visual adjustment, which has a standard multi-column page layout on the desktop, and a single column on the smart phone, changes user experience. Closer examination of the user behavior shows, that the adjustment of column layout to the smart phone is not only a visual adjustment, changing the look and feel, but a substantial change in information architecture, as far as the user's point of view is concerned. In this case, the user perceived elements of the layout not only as look and feel elements, but as functional elements in the sense of genre, where even the placement on the layout carries some semiotic information.

User interface elements, like buttons and images, often change size, position, and interaction mode, when they are presented on different devices. This kind of perceptual modifications are inevitable in inter-device design (transmedia) design. They are due to the characteristics of each device, and, therefore, cannot fulfil the claim to inter-device consistency. They are inevitable and result in a kind of inter-device inconsistency. The case study examples show, that some of these inconsistencies influence user experience and user behavior.

There was another example in case two, for this kind of adjustment. On the desktop application of "W&V", there was a drop down menu available, which was appreciated by users, who wanted to get an overview of the application. Switching from the desktop application to the multi-touch tablet application during the test session, the users wanted to further use this function, which they knew from the desktop. However, the procedure to activate it, was different now, because of the gesture-based interaction paradigm, which is specific to the multi-touch tablet environment. The way of activating this function with touch gesture on the tablet was not recognized by many users in the test situation. The activation should be done by interacting with a small icon, which is inadequate for tablet use. This seemed to be an attempt by the design model to stay in the design philosophy of menus, which did not really fit into the multi-touch philosophy. Furthermore, when switching to the smart phone, the users had to give up completely the menu navigation and search for replacement strategies, which was to scroll up and down the long single column. However, they did not feel it to be an adequate compensation.

The interaction situations, reported from this case study, show that inter-device consistency is not possible in detail. Inter-device inconsistencies may concern user interface elements on the perceptual, syntactic or semantic layer. Each device has specific characteristics, which need adjustments and adaptations to presentation and interaction capabilities of the other device. If users switch between devices, they are faced with this changes. As demonstrated by the examples in the case two, it is often syntactic and semantic consistencies, which are not kept, even by small, but inevitable, adjustments. The adjustments for inter-device interaction make a difference in user experience and user behavior. They are even a barrier, for example, if the same operations to attain a given goal are not available, even if the adaptations are intended as added value in the system model.

The situations reported from both of the case studies showed intermedia relationship between the devices, and how users make intermedia experience during interaction. This is a kind of rich user experience, where knowledge structures from prior knowledge and the resulting expectations strongly influence the mental model building process. Expectations are raised by prior knowledge structures, which are either built from prior experience with the application on another device or from other knowledge sources, like domain knowledge, as in case one, where domain knowledge on newspaper structure is activated, and subsequently combined with other relevant information of the actual perception of the current situation.

The examples of user behavior and user information processing illustrate, that consistency cannot mean identical. However, they also illustrate that attempts to consistent design need not really be successful with respect to the user's mental model formation. The adjustments and adaptations are always within the characteristics of the device and the examples illustrate that the characteristics are specific, and, therefore, the claim to consistency leads to the mixture of two design philosophies, which do not go well together. In both case studies, users sometimes had problems to combine the two system models, when switching from one device to the other device. The adjustments and adaptations to the characteristics are not standardized, and, therefore, the users had to explore the combinations.

The Influence of Prior Knowledge on User's Expectations and Mental Model Building

Some of the user comments in case study one reveal, that the user was misled by the designer's conceptual model. On the perceptual level, a conceptual model of a print paper was suggested. In consequence, the users activate a scheme on how to work with an electronic print. In other cases, if the conceptual design model would be a web browser on the desktop PC, then the users would activate their respective knowledge from the long-term memory, on how web browsers work. As the models belong to devices, which they have experience with, they have interaction knowledge structured organized as schemes within their long-term memory. Users refer to these long-term memory structures when they recognize cues in order to use the activated knowledge structure for their mental model building process during interaction with the actual platform (which was in our case the iPad).

It was obvious in the case study, that many users believed that they worked with a .pdf of the print version. This reaction was due to cues on the perceptual level, which were interpreted by the users. These cues were typical elements of newspaper organization and newspaper look and feel. User's prior knowledge was domain knowledge on newspaper genres. A good theoretical model for understanding this kind and nature of user's prior knowledge of newspaper format is the functional linguistic concept of genre, as introduced by Halliday (2002). According to genre theory, a document's total meaning is constructed out of a combination of text, layout, graphics, images, and probably other elements, which work together as a semiotic sign system. In this context, one must regard newspaper design as semiotic structure of the newspaper, as stated by Bateman, Delin and Henschel (2007) and Ihlström and Lundberg (2004). Decoding of its meaning helps the user to recognize organizational structure and to locate content within it, without the need for long searching procedures. Layout elements like typography, visual structuring into columns, and dividing content into categories contribute to the semiotic sign system. As already found by Ihlström and Lundberg (2004), the elements of the sign system enable the reader or user to shape models of understanding the genre and form a framework of familiarity. Without giving further information, the user is able to interpret the given signs and make sense of them, as explained by semiotic theory.

However, additionally to genre, there is an interactive system, and therefore, the user inferred further that print in electronic version must be a .pdf, which does not fit into the genre model. The problem of genre interpretation became further evident when the users wanted to go from the front page (Figure 5) to a single article in order to read it. Unfortunately, the print newspaper genre, which is provided as an interaction model, is only able to offer content and form within its sign system, but has no cues on how to activate any function on the iPad. Therefore, the users were not able to use it as metaphor for the interaction process in order to infer any ways how to interact with the newspaper beyond the pdf-like page turning.

The special case of genre instantiation, as it is in our case one, can be generalized to scheme instantiation in general. As cognitive knowledge structures, schemes direct human cognition and information processing. A scheme contains generalized objects and concepts of implicit knowledge. As such, schemes allow people to summarize their knowledge to reasonable structures and sequences, which can be used in information processing processes to understand and frame the actual situation. If relevant cues are found in the situation, the respective schemes are instantiated from long-term memory and used in the working memory to manage recurring situations. After it was activated, it supplies the information processing system with the necessary data to understand and plan situational adequate actions. Schemes work top down, that is, they act as filters for incoming information, and can help the user to infer and fill information gaps by the slots contained in the scheme.

In the one case, the user's scheme for newspaper and for electronic paper use was instantiated. It contained information, which was used in the mental model building process for interpretation of the incoming data of the actual situation, where the system model was interpreted as a .pdf. In the other case, the users found cues on the user interface that made them activate their scheme on using the newspaper on a web browser, and, therefore, interactions were framed within this conceptual model.

As soon as scheme is activated, all incoming information (objects, functions etc.) of the actual situational context (in our case studies of the functionality of the iPad) is in the process of assimilation interpreted from the point of view of the instantiated scheme. After activation, the scheme delivers necessary data for situational relevant actions. New data can be processed more effectively, complexity is reduced, and occurring events get a reasonable interpretation and context. The instantiated scheme directs the user's recognition and attention only to scheme-consistent information. This filter function of schemes help the cognitive system to ease the burden of thinking about recurrent events. Exactly this mechanism causes problems in mental model building during the actual interaction, as it misleads the interpretation of actual system features in the interaction process. Therefore, the user is unable to work on a correct mental model as he/she further mixes up, and experiences conflicts of concepts as framed in her transmedia mental model. This transmedia model further causes interaction problems as the characteristics of the actual platform (e.g. iOS-function on the iPad) will hardly be separated from the instantiated scheme. Schemes and their assimilation mechanism direct interaction. Only in surprising situations, there are not schemes, but controlled and conscious cognition directing the interaction, however, this could not be observed in our studies.

There are further implications of this mental model building process for transmedia situations in general.

In general, schemes are long-term memory structures, which were formed from user's prior experiences. When they are instantiated in the process of mental model building during interaction, they are a source of generating expectations. The activation of their prior knowledge causes interaction problems and prevent users from constructing appropriate mental models of the media platform and user interface they are actually working with. In human factors, it is an important quality criteria to meet user's expectations by design (DIN EN ISO 9241-110:2008-09). The claim to design consistent is an important criteria concerning the user's expectations. Furthermore, there should be inter-system consistency. Inconsistent system models prevent users from building a stable, correct and transparent mental model.

The problem of rich user experience with inter-device consistency is, that users have various sources of information for mental model formation. Users have information from prior knowledge structures (like domain models), they have knowledge structures on similar system models from the application as it is organized on the other device they know, and they get information on the system model of the device, they are currently interacting with. If user have prior knowledge of a similar system model (of the information and service on other devices), the danger will be, that users will instantiate this prior knowledge structure and will try to explain the interaction from this structure. However, the users are not aware of the adjustments and adaptations. In consequence, they will have to explore these inter-device differences. That is, the instantiation of prior knowledge structures will lead to interaction problems, because in cases of adjustments and adaptations of the system model, the user's view on these adaptations will be dominated by the instantiated knowledge structures. This is an inherent problem for inter-device consistency as discussed in the previous chapters.

In interaction situations where users are confronted with inter-device consistency, they will activate prior knowledge. From cognitive psychology, we know, that these knowledge structures are very stable, because of scheme assimilation procedures. People try to use the prior knowledge structures and try to explain the situation from this

structures as long as possible. Only if there are surprising situations, people switch to controlled and conscious cognition. However, this kind of surprising situations will be rare in situations with inter-device consistency.

The Emotional Component of Intermedia User Experience: Attractiveness

As already mentioned in previous sections of this paper, user experience has a pragmatic component and an emotional component. The pragmatic component for inter-device consistency was analyzed in the previous section in terms of user's cognitive information processing. In this section some results on the analysis of the emotional component of user experience is given.

Emotions assess events, influence reactions, and also influence cognitive information processing (Hamker, 2003). As a method to measure the emotional component of user interaction, we employed the AttrakDiff questionnaire from Hassenzahl et al. (2003) for case study one. Based on the model of emotional design from Norman (2005), the questionnaire takes measures on different aspects of attractiveness. Attractiveness is understood as the global ranking of a system according to the user's perceived quality (which is rated from the user's personal point of view on the basis of word pairs suggested by the questionnaire). AttrakDiff differs two user experience elements, which are the perceived usability (not necessarily identical with objective usability, which would otherwise be measured in a usability test), and the hedonic qualities of the device. The overall emotional reaction of the user, as reported by the questionnaire, is the device's attractiveness to him/her.

The results of the AttrakDiff show that the attractiveness rate is about an average of 1 (not very high, but also not bad). Perceived usability and the hedonic quality of identification contribute much to it. The perceived usability is rather high rated,

Figure 6. Average values of AttrakDiff questionnaire on attractiveness of "Frankfurter Allgemeine Zeitung (FAZ - case 1). It differs perceived usability (PQ) and hedonic qualities (HQ-I: hedonic quality identification; HQ-S: hedonic quality stimulation) and gives and overall rating for attractiveness (ATT)

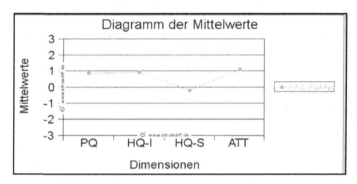

compared to the reality of usability problems users actually faced in the test sessions. The reason might be, that users built their mental model from prior knowledge structures, and, therefore, they had the impression to understand the system model. However, their mental model building, actually, was rather misleading in non-consistent interaction situations. Sometimes, they thought to have solved the task with their mental model, but it was objectively not true. Nevertheless, they did not know that the task was not really solved in many cases. However, according to their knowledge structures (schemes), they had explanations for their presumption of being on an adequate task-solving way. That they utilized an inadequate model to explain interaction, was not realized by them, and, therefore, this might explain why users gave a good rate for perceived usability.

Furthermore, the relatively low rating for stimulation, as in our case studies, is also an interesting fact. The system model makes the user believe to do well known activities, that is, reading a newspaper. However, the user utilizes a device with high multi-media potential and novel interaction modes. But these device characteristics are well hidden behind the system model, which the user can actually perceive. Some users even articulated their disappointment, when faced with the misleading system model.

FUTURE RESEARCH DIRECTIONS

The web of devices, which allows distribution and adaptation of information and services over various devices, is understood as intermedia environment. As each device has its own characteristics, adaptations to the respective interface are inevitable. There are relations between these devices, which have an equivalent in the user's mental model building process. With responsive web design, we have a technical solution to solve the inter-device problem. Definitely, the adaptations alter the system model as identical system models are not possible, because of the specific device characteristics. However, the rich user experience with the resulting inter-device inconsistencies is hardly understood. And, therefore, helpful and more detailed design rules are needed, which take into consideration the rich user experience with inter-device interaction.

In general, the problem, we are faced here, is an intermedia problem, spoken in terms of media science. As for other intermedia relationships, e.g. for fiction presented in book or presented as film, media science tries to describe systematic relationships. Such a kind of systematic description of interrelationships would also be necessary for multi-device interaction. The resulting interrelations between devices and their consequences for mental model building have to be further studied. It is especially interesting in the context of the claim of designing consistent (DIN EN ISO 9241-110:2008-09). The question is, what consistency could mean in multi-device environments and how the variety of meanings of consistency might influence user experience in positive or negative manners.

Intermedia research is not restricted to responsive design cases in multi-device web environments. There are other cases of intermedia design in human-computer interaction. Examples are certain kinds of serious games, where genre elements of computer games are transferred to serious games in game-based learning environments like adventures. Kritzenberger (2012) found that in the user's mental model building processes the respective game genre is instantiated as a framework for understanding and interpreting the situation. The problem there is a similar one. The user recognizes cues from the interface, which he/she interprets within the activated knowledge frame. However, adaptions to the interface and to other situational and contextual features (like learning model or domain model) were done. As these adaptations vary the system model compared to the instantiated knowledge for mental model building. As there are many elements, which do not fit for assimilation into the framing knowledge structures, the users do not accept these games.

CONCLUSION

Consistent design approaches to multi-device environments seem to satisfy claims on the ergonomic principle of consistency. These approaches port content and features across devices in a like manner and attempt to replicate similar system models on each device. Users are supposed to benefit from consistent design approaches, because they would not need to switch between different system models.

In fact, consistent design approaches can only provide inter-device consistency to some extent, e.g. keeping a core functionality, look and feel, and information architecture. Some adjustments and adaptations to devices are inevitable to meet specific device characteristics. In every case, no matter if the adaptations are more or less, they alter system models.

Although, in some cases the inter-device inconsistencies seem to be small, they influence the user's mental model building. Inter-device consistent environments have similarities and have differences. They may be on perceptual, lexical, syntactic or semantic level. The problem for the user experience is, that users are neither aware of the scope nor the level of alternations. From the user's perspective, it is often not transparent, what the similarities and what the differences in the system models of the devices in multi-device environments are, and, therefore, users have to explore the system, and this causes interaction problems. Systemic interrelations between the system models are not defined, but could probably help users to understand alternations in inter-device interaction.

When users interact in multi-device environments, they refer to prior knowledge structures, if they identify cues, which cause instantiation of these knowledge structures. Prior knowledge structures may also refer to other devices, which users are familiar with. Consequently, the subsequent interaction process is guided by assimilation processes, which lead to incorrect mental models and to interaction problems, because solid mental models of the system, the user is working with, would be needed to understand and plan the interaction.

Schemes, as organizing cognitive knowledge structures, normally help people – and also users in interaction situations – to frame the situation and to act adequately. However, this mechanism is only helpful, if the instantiated schemes are really adequate.

If – like in our case study – an inadequate scheme is triggered and instantiated, users run into interaction problems. Then the user's elaboration of his/her mental model needs extensive exploration procedures in order to evaluate hypothesis and integrate the evaluation results into the mental model.

No matter, if an adequate or an inadequate scheme was instantiated, assimilation procedures are guiding the user's information processing and acting. The problem cannot be solved by consistent design alone, because in intermedia contexts, inconsistencies between the devices are often inevitable because of the specific characteristics of the devices. Therefore, it might be advisable for design, also to think about how to control mental model building processes and prevent them from assimilation to non-adequate schemes. From psychology we know that persons only in surprising situations switch from scheme association to controlled and conscious cognition. Therefore, user experience research should consider to integrate cognitive information processing and emotional and motivational issues to get better results for the design of intermedia and transmedia interaction processes.

The findings are relevant for responsive design also. If responsive design transfers not only content but also sign systems, which are recognized by the users, there is the danger that the sign system may not be adequate to support the formation of the user's mental model on the platform which the design model was ported to. In this case of rich user experience, the user will have problems to infer further interaction from the actual mental model and, therefore, run into interaction problems.

Our results of transmedia mental models help to understand the wider range of problems that occur when information and services are provided on multi-device environments. The results give reason to think carefully about design and system models when information and services are provided in multi-device environments.

REFERENCES

Bateman, J., Delin, J., & Henschel, R. (2007). Mapping the Multimodal Genres of Traditional and Electronic Papers. In T. Royce, & W. Bowcher (Eds.), *New Directions in the Analysis of Multimodal Discourse* (pp. 147–172). Lawrence Erlbaum Associates.

Benbasat, I., Goldstein, D., & Mead, M. (1987). The Case Research Strategy in Studies of Information Systems. *Management Information Systems Quarterly*, *11*(3), 369–386. doi:10.2307/248684

Calvary, G., Coutez, J., Thevenin, D., Limbourg, Q., Bouillon, L., & Vanderdonckt, J. (2003). A unifying reference framework for multi-target user interfaces. *Interacting with Computers*, *15*, 289–308. doi:10.1016/S0953-5438(03)00010-9

Denis, C., & Karsenty, L. (2004). Inter-usability of multi-device systems – a conceptual framework. In A. Seffah, & H. Javahery (Eds.), *Multiple User Interfaces: Cross-Platform Applications and Context-Aware Interfaces* (pp. 373–386). Chichester, UK: John Wiley & Sons, Ltd.

DIN EN ISO 9241-110:2008-09. (2006). *Ergonomie der Mensch-System-Interaktion - Teil 110: Grundsätze der Dialoggestaltung* (ISO 9241-110:2006). Deutsche Fassung EN ISO 9241-110:2006.

DIN EN ISO 9241-210:2011-01. (2010). *Ergonomie der Mensch-System-Interaktion - Teil 210: Prozess zur Gestaltung gebrauchstauglicher interaktiver Systeme* (ISO 9241-210:2010). Deutsche Fassung EN ISO 9241-210:2010.

Gentner, D., & Stevens, A. L. (1983). *Mental Models*. Hillsdale, NJ: Lawrence Erlbaum Associates.

Halliday, M. A. K. (2002). *Linguistic studies of text and discourse*. London: Continuum International Publishing.

Hamker, A. (2003). *Emotion und ästhetische Erfahrung. Internationale Hochschulschriften* (Vol. 407). Münster: Waxmann Verlag.

Hassenzahl, M. (2008). User Experience (UX), Towards an Experiential Perspective on Product Quality. In *Proceedings from IHM'08: The 20th International Conference of the Association Francophone D'Interaction Homme Machine* (pp. 11-15). New York, NY: ACM Press.

Hassenzahl, M. (2010). Experience Design: Technology for All the Right Reasons. *Synthesis Lectures on Human-Centered Informatics, 3*(1), 1–95. doi:10.2200/S00261ED1V01Y201003HCI008

Hassenzahl, M., Burmester, M., & Koller, F. (2003). AttrakDiff: Ein Fragebogen zur Messung wahrgenommener hedonischer und pragmatischer Qualität. In G. Szwillus, & J. Ziegler (Eds.), *Mensch & Computer 2003: Interaktion in Bewegung* (pp. 78–82). München: Oldenbourg. doi:10.1007/978-3-322-80058-9_19

Herczeg, M. (2005). *Software-Ergonomie*. München: Oldenbourg.

Ihlström, C., & Lundberg, J. (2004). A genre perspective on online newspaper front page design. *Journal of Web Engineering, 3*(1), 50–74.

Kadlec, T. (2012). *Implementing Responsive Web Design: Building Sites for Anywhere, Everywhere Web (Voices that Matter)*. Berkeley, CA: New Riders.

Kritzenberger, H. (2012). Understanding Player Experience in Educational Games. In T. Amiel & B. Wilson (Eds.), *Proceedings of World Conference on Educational Multimedia, Hypermedia and Telecommunications 2012* (pp. 1329-1335). Chesapeake, VA: AACE.

Kurkovsky, S. (2009). *Multimodality in Mobile Computing and Mobile Devices: Methods for Adaptable Usability*. Hershey, PA: IGI Global. doi:10.4018/978-1-60566-978-6

Levin, M. (2014). *Designing Multi-Device Experience*. Retrieved from amazon.com

Marcotte, E. (2011). Responsive Webdesign. New York, NY: A Book Apart.

Nielsen, J., & Budiu, R. (2013). *Mobile Usability*. Berkeley, CA: New Riders Press.

Norman, D. (2005). *Emotional Design: Why We Love or Hate Everyday Things*. New York, NY: Basic Books.

Norman, D. A. (1983). Some Observations on Mental Models. In D. Gentner, & A. L. Stevens (Eds.), *Mental Models* (pp. 7–14). Hillsdale, NJ: Lawrence Erlbaum Associates.

Nylander, S., Bylund, M., & Waern, A. (2005). Ubiquitous service access through adapted user interfaces on multiple devices. *Journal Personal and Ubiquitous Computing, 9*(3), 123–133. doi:10.1007/s00779-004-0317-4

Rouse, W. B., & Morris, N. (1986). On looking into the black box: Prospects and limits in the search for mental models. *Psychological Bulletin, 100*(3), 349–363. doi:10.1037/0033-2909.100.3.349

Schmitt, F., Cassens, J., Kindsmüller, M. C., & Herczeg, M. (2011). Mental Models of Ambient Systems: A Modual Research Framework. In M. Beigl, H. Christiansen, T.R. Roth-Berghofer, K. R. Coventry, A. Kofod-Petersen, & H.R. Schmidtke (Eds.), *Proceedings from CONTEXT 2011: Modeling and Using Context: The Seventh International and Interdisciplinary Conference* (pp. 278-291). Berlin: Springer.

Väänänan-Vainio-Mattila, K., & Oinas-Kukkonen, H. (2010). Cross-Platform Service User Experience: A Field Study and an Initial Framework. In *Proceedings from MobileHCI'10: The 12th International Conference on Human Computer Interaction with Mobile Devices and Services* (pp. 219-228). New York, NY: ACM.

Wilson, J. R., & Rutherford, A. (1989). Mental models: theory and application in human factors. *Human Factors, 31*(6), 617–634.

Wroblewski, L. (2012). *Mobile First*. Paris: Éditions Eyrolles.

KEY TERMS AND DEFINITIONS

Conceptual Model: The term refers to the model which the designer develops during the design process. They are derived from systematic analysis and research and contain information on the user's task, his/her preferences, properties, behavior and other relevant information to form a system model during the interaction process.

Inter-Device Consistency: It means coherency and unity of elements and functions on the user interface of different devices, concerning their appearance and their behavior.

Intermedia: Generally, the term means the relationship between different media and focus on the different characteristics of these media, which cause different design condition and variations in media products. Here, the term is used for the fact that different device characteristics cause differences for the user interface design.

Mental Model: During the interaction with an interactive system, users develop internal representations of these systems and devices. A mental model is construct of the human working memory, which directs the interaction and is permanently updated during the interaction process.

Multi-Device Environments: With emergent mobile technologies, interactive systems are no longer restricted to a single platform. They allow users to migrate applications from one device to another. Therefore, users may access services, content and functions to complete certain tasks using a network of mobile and non-mobile devices (e.g. PC, multi-touch tablet, smart phone) in varying use contexts.

Responsive Web Design: Responsive web design is a technical and design approach to adapt the web site automatically to the user interface. As the size and the resolution of different devices (like PC, multi-touch tablet and smart phone) are different, the graphic layout needs to be adapted to the display size. Responsive web design is a technical design approach to do these adapta-

tions to interface characteristics automatically. Necessary adaptations and adjustments may affect orders and representation of any interface elements, such as text layout, positions and size of graphics, information architecture, and input modalities. Content and service providers create only one version of the web site and the adaptations is done by media queries.

Scheme: The term belongs to cognitive psychology, where it is understood as a cognitive framework for organization and storage of knowledge in long-term memory. They are formed during interaction with a person's environment and are retrieved from long-term memory in order to be applied to interpret similar situations where they frame the actual cognition of the situational features. Inadequate schemes, which do not really fit the situation may also prevent the person from a proper understanding.

Transmedia: Generally, the term is used concerning phenomena that are distributed over different media. The term is mostly used in the context of transmedia storytelling, where it means that parts of a story are distributed and emerge in different media. In this chapter, it is used for the distribution of task-completion over different devices, where each device is understood as one medium and where different contexts of media use apply. Users start part of a task on one device, e.g. on the PC, and continue this task on a mobile, when they are on their way. This requires a certain kind of continuity between the tasks as they are represented on the different devices.

User Experience: User experience concerns the user's perceptions and reactions to an interactive system, which arise before, during and after system use. It comprises all his/her psychological, emotional and physical reactions. These reactions are regarded as reactions to the system's properties and qualities, like design, functions, and performance. The user's prior experience and the user's expectation may also influence user experience.

Chapter 16
Length Perceptual Characteristics on Raised–Dot Slippages

Yoshihiko Nomura
Mie University, Japan

Kazuki Iwabu
Mie University, Japan

ABSTRACT

If line-shape information was physically presented by virtue of some kind of mechanical interface, man-machine communication would be enhanced in the sense of multi-modal interactions. In order for such interactions to be available with ease, they should be realized as simple, small, and cheap devices even though suffering from a bit of performance decrease. Thus, the authors have studied a mouse-like computer-human mechanical interface. The idea is that slippage stimuli on a fingerpad would be effective enough to provide users a piece of motion information, and that the mechanism for slippage can be embodied in mouse interfaces. Here, to enhance the slippage perceptual performance, raised-dots were considered to be useful, and thus, a series of psychophysical experiments were carried out by using raised-dot planes with the period of 1.5, 3.1, 12.5, 30, and 50 mm, together with a without-dot flat plane. It was confirmed that the perceptual lengths were well formulated by a power law: they were proportional to the power of both speed and length. The exponential constants with the length factor were a little less than 1 corresponding to the ideal linear relationship. While the ones with the speed factor were in negative, nearly 0 corresponding to the ideal undisturbed relationship. Then, it was found that the pathway length perceptual accuracies for the raised-dot planes were much superior to that for the flat plane from the viewpoint of (1) length-related perceptual length contractions, (2) speed-induced perceptual length contractions, and (3) perceptual length random errors. This is shown in this chapter.

DOI: 10.4018/978-1-4666-6228-5.ch016

INTRODUCTION

Cutaneous sensation on finger pad is one of essential functions in hand-contact-based haptic sense to perceive objects' physical properties such as shapes and surface roughness. Introducing raised-dot, the authors have studied some sliding length perceptual characteristics on fingerpad in the passive touch framework: the raised-dot pathway was expected to be effective for presenting physical line segments, which can be applied to computer-human interfaces.

Thus, the raised dots are expected to contribute for a new physical-line presenting computer-human interface. Paying notice to the sliding-raised dots with a specific period of interval lengths, the authors have studied cutaneous sensation characteristics on fingerpads in the passive touch scheme (Nomura, Yoshihiko et al. 2013). In the paper, subjects were informed that they should perceive dot slippage based on either a dot-counting scheme with long dot periods or a speed-based scheme in short periods. Although the dot-counting scheme showed better linearity than the other speed-perceptual scheme, that suffers a sampling error because the countable dot numbers were confined to natural numbers. To avoid the sampling errors in the dot-counting scheme for the long dot periods, the latter speed-based scheme was expected to be an alternative to the dot-counting scheme even for the long dot periods as well as the short dot periods.

Thus, in this paper, the authors focused their attention on the speed-based sliding length perceptual scheme not only in a short period but also in a long period.

There have been some studies on mouse type tactile interfaces. Akamatsu and MacKenzie (1996) might first present a tactile-slip displaying mouse-interface: the mouse had a function of presenting 2D slip, the amount of which was limited within a small length. Kyung, Choi, Kwon, and Son (2004) proposed a multi-functional mouse: it reflected 1 DOF grabbing force as well as 2 DOF translation force, and pin array tactile patterns. Kuchenbecker, Provancher, Niemeyer, and Cutkosky (2004) also proposed a haptic device that integrates contact location feedback with grounded point-force display where a roller type of slip display was combined with a haptic device, PHANTOM. Minamizawa, Prattichizzo, and Tachi (2010) also presented a similar concept of a haptic device that integrates kinesthetic feedback to the arm and tactile feedback to the finger. Tsagarakis, Horne, and Caldwell (2005) proposed a genius slip/stretch feedback device that used a V configuration of frustum cones: the device provided sensations of lateral motion (direction and velocity) in arbitrary directions onto the user's fingertips in the form of producing a vector sum. It was reported that subjects were able to discriminate angle changes of 15 degrees with the correct answer rate of about 70%. Webstar, Todd, Lawton, and Allison (2005) proposed another genius 2 degree of freedom (DOF) tactile device: it reproduced the sensations of sliding contact through the rotation of a ball positioned on the user's fingertip. In their device, values relating to just noticeable differences (JNDs) with directions were given as 20–25°. Gleeso, Horschel, and Provancher (2010) proposed another fingertip-mounted tactile interface: it reflected a tangential skin displacement feedback.

Here, note that existing mouse-applied slip displays have employed non-bumpy and smooth surfaces. Therefore, the introduction of raised dots allows us to carry out some feasibility studies. Based on the findings described in this paper, the authors develop raised-dot-based mouse interfaces as described in the final section.

BACKGROUND

The cutaneous sensation-based perceptual characteristics have been studied from various viewpoints. For example, slip length perceptual characteristics of moving flat surface were studied as follows. Under the active touch condition, Hollins and Goble (1988) reported a formula of perceived-lengths, which represented velocity-and-duration dependence. Focusing on the duration time, Armstrong and Marks (1999) suggested that the radial–tangential anisotropy in the length perception can be explained by temporal differences in exploratory movements. The passive length perception scheme has also been studied. For example, Terada, Kumazaki, Miyata, and Ito (2006) found a complimentary characteristic between the cutaneous and proprioceptive sensations and proposed some formulas representing velocity-and-length dependences. Tiest, Vander Hoff, and Kapagesers (2011) reported that the cutaneous-only condition was inferior to a proprioceptive-only-condition. In the cutaneous-combined proprioceptive condition, the cutaneous sensation contributes a little to the proprioceptive one. Introducing another aspect of movement direction, Najib, Nomura, Sakamoto, and Iwabu (2012) have also presented some formulas for the velocity-&-duration dependence on the length perception.

Raised dots have been used for Braille of dotted letters and for tactile-graphics since they are distinctive and informative stimuli for representing spatial configurations (Shimizu, 1982) (Jansson & Pedersen, 2005) (Wall & Brewster, 2006) (Pietrzak, Pecci, & Martin, 2006) (Tahir, Bailly, Lecolinet, & Mouret, 2008) (Garcia-Hernandez, Tsagarakis, & Caldwell, 2011) (Okamoto, Konyo, & Tadokoro, 2011). As a similar stimulus to the raised dots, gratings on fingerpad can be utilized, and have been studied by Morley, Goodwin, and Darian-Smith (1983), Lawrence, Kitada, Klatzky, and Lederman (2007), Lederman (1983), Cascio, and Sathian (2001), and Bensmaia, Craig, Yoshioka, and Johnson (2006). The perceptual characteristics with the grating stimuli would principally provide some useful information, but most of the works focused on roughness perception, and we cannot get useful enough information for slip perception as in this chapter.

Although there were a few researches for sensing raised-dots, the papers took up the perception of single site vibration (Lederman, 1991), (Wang, Turner, & Hewitt, 2006), (Deco, Scarano, & Soto-Faraco, 2007), (Pongrac, 2008).

LENGTH PERCEPTUAL CHARACTERISTICS ON RAISED DOT SLIPPAGES

Problem was Extended from Speed to Length

There were also some studies on moving-raised-dot stimuli as in this work. Salada, Vishton, Colgate, and Frankel (2004) developed a dot-slip-employing proprioceptive interface, and reported that dot-slips little contribute slippage perception. Dépeault1, Meftah, and Chapman (2008) reported that the speed scaling performance was much improved in the dot pattern than in the flat plane, but they didn't consider the effect of speed on the length perception.

Experimental Method

Apparatus: Figure 1 shows an experimental apparatus. It consisted of a linear actuator (IAI-ICSA series) and a thin steel cover plate. The linear actuator drove an end effector in the 550 mm range within the speed of 300 mm/s. A pedestal was attached to the end effector, and, furthermore, a piece of specimen was adhered to the top surface of the pedestal. The gap between the steel cover plate and the specimen surface was set at 3 mm. A hole opened at the steel cover plate. Subjects inserted their index finger through the hole, and put their fingerpad on the surface of the specimen. A linear scale was put on the linear actuator as a reference: the linear scale was composed of 5 mm period ticks from 5 to 550 mm where, nearby the ticks, number codes are written one by one.

Figure 1. Schematic view of experimental setup: Linear actuator (IAI-ICSA series) was mounted on the top of a desk actuated a specimen within the 550mm range. A Specimen was attached at the top of the linear actuator. Above the specimen, a cover plate with a hole was attached

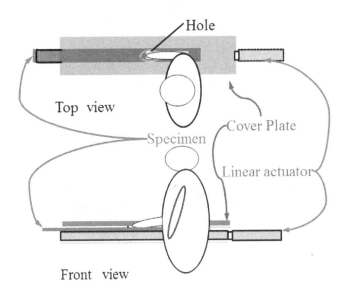

Specimens: We introduced six kinds of specimens. A specimen was flat plane, and was referred as "Flat plane" in this paper. The remaining five specimens had raised dots that were aligned in straight on the flat surface of the specimen: the periods were 1.5, 3.1, 12.5, 30, and 50 mm, and they were referred as "1.5mm-dot" and so on. The specimens were set in parallel with the direction of the linear actuator stroke. Here note that the five kinds of periods had some mean the 12.5, 30 and 50 mm period raised dots permit us to perceive each of the sliding dots one-by-one. While the 1.5, 3.1 mm period raised dots don't enable us one-by-one way perception, but only permit us to perceive the sliding motion of clustered dots. The difference in stimulating patterns would result in the change of the perceptual characteristic. The raised dots were 1.5 mm in diameter and 0.4 mm in height (see Figure 2). All the specimens are made of a lapping film (#2000, grain size of 9μm, 3M Corp.).

Subjects: Nine male subjects aged 22 to 57 years, voluntarily participated in the experiment.

The authors obtained informed consent from our participants for using the data in anonymous ways.

Procedures: Neither twisting one's body at the waist nor twisting one's head at the neck, a subject was seated on a chair, and faced the front. Setting one's elbow flexion angle at about 90°, the subject forearm was set parallel to the table base, and was also set parallel to the direction in the sagittal plane. A white noise sound was applied to the subjects via headphones for masking any sound cues and for avoiding any side effects on the spatial perception. After the subject puts their finger pad on the specimen, in an arbitrary waiting time, the specimen started to move, and stopped at one of the given points: the linear actuator drove the specimens with a rectangular velocity pattern. The line lengths being presented were 50, 70, 100, 141, 200, 282, 400, and 550 mm. The speed was set at 25, 35, 70, 100, 141, 200, 282, 300 mm/s. These experimental conditions were determined based on human perceptual limitations. The combinations of the 8 kinds of lengths and the 8 kinds of speeds made 64 line

Figure 2. Specimen (Upper 2/3 part shows a top view. Lower 1/3 part shows a front view.): On the specimens, raised dots were configured, aligning in a straight line. (1) In the cases of the 12.5, 30, and 50 mm dot periods, we can notice one-by-one way coming dot. It can be said an isolated dot mode. While (2) In the other cases of the 1.5 and 3.1mm dot period, multiple dots contact on fingerpad at a time, and we should perceive the dot set movements. It can be said a united dot mode. Both were compared with a flat plane taken as a standard

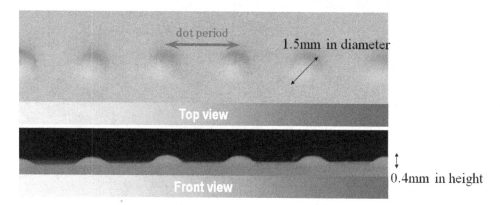

segment patterns, and the patterns were presented in pseudo random orders. It took about 4 hours for the whole experiment per subject.

Task: During experiments, the subject was instructed to relax, and to focus on perceiving the presented linear sliding lengths via one's index fingerpad. They were asked to answer the perceived length by the following way. After opening their eyes, they looked at the reference linear scale, and phonated a number code.

Experimental Results with the Perceived Pathway Lengths

The actual lengths being taken as a parameter, Figure 3 shows the experimental results with the sliding speed dependences of the perceived pathway lengths for the six kinds of specimens. In Figure 3, we can see a speed-caused length-foreshortening effect. Especially, in the case of the flat plane, the effect was markedly larger.

In order to make it clear the ill effects, i.e., the perceptual-length nonlinearity and a less dynamic range among the lengths, the perceptual and actual length relationships are shown as in

Figure 4. The speeds of 35 mm/s and 300 mm/s are taken as representatives of slow and fast sliding conditions. Figure 4 (a) and (b) is plotted by linear scale. These mean that length-related perceptual characteristics were represented by convex functions: the longer length resulted in the larger foreshortening effect. We can also see that the perceptual length nonlinearity was especially salient in the flat plane in comparison with those in the other dotted planes. While plotting the same data as Figure 4 (a) and (b) on logarithmic coordinates in both the horizontal and vertical axes, we got Figure 4 (c) and (d). In the logarithmic plot, slopes of straight lines represent exponential coefficients. Furthermore, the closer to 45° the slope is, the higher the linearity is. Putting it the other way, the more far from 45° the slope is, the more increased the nonlinearity is. From Figure 4 (c) and (d), we can see the non-linearity were represented by a power function.

Discussion (Statistical Analyses)

For the perceived length, l_{perc}, we assumed a model as a power function with the actual length L and

Figure 3. Perceived lengths for each of the actual lengths of 50 to 550 mm (The symbol represents the mean of the perceived lengths, and the error bar represents the standard error of those)

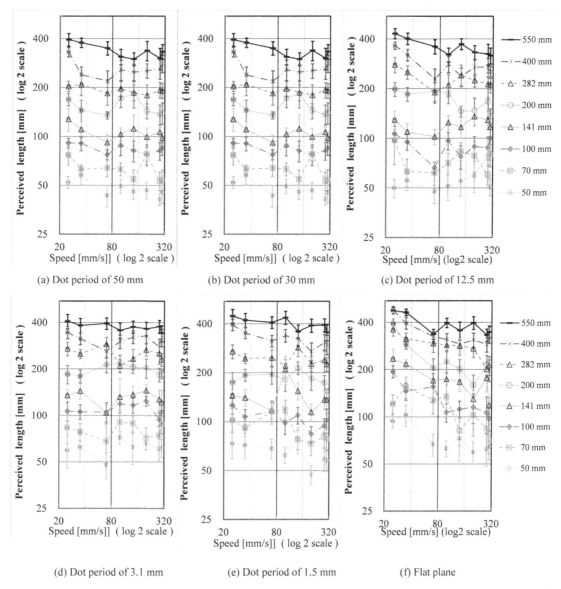

(a) Dot period of 50 mm   (b) Dot period of 30 mm   (c) Dot period of 12.5 mm

(d) Dot period of 3.1 mm   (e) Dot period of 1.5 mm   (f) Flat plane

the velocity V, that is, the model length, l_{model}, for the perceived length, would be given by

$$l_{model} = \alpha \, V^{\beta V} L^{\beta L} \qquad (1)$$

The authors examined the experimental results by using the model. The speed-caused length-foreshortening effect and the length-related non-linearity can be expressed by parameters β_V and β_L, respectively: the former effect is represented by the negative value of β_V, and the latter, by the value of less than 1 of β_L. The estimated parameter values and the standard errors of the estimated parameter are shown in Figure 5, and the values together with one-tailed t-test results are shown in Table 1.

First of all, the authors carried out statistical tests. Let's confirm the effectiveness of the

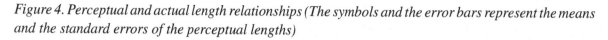

Figure 4. Perceptual and actual length relationships (The symbols and the error bars represent the means and the standard errors of the perceptual lengths)

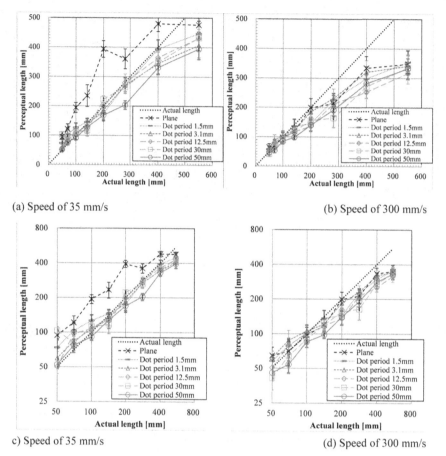

(a) Speed of 35 mm/s   (b) Speed of 300 mm/s

c) Speed of 35 mm/s   (d) Speed of 300 mm/s

estimates. The *t*-test statistics to evaluate the effectiveness of the estimates are given by the ratio of the estimated value against the standard deviation of the estimated value, and are also shown in the Table 1. Since all the *t*-test statistic were much larger than the critical values even with a probability of 0.1%, all the estimates concluded to be effective.

Then, let's consider some characteristics of the estimated parameter value.

- As a whole, the smaller the dot period was, the more similar to the flat plane the estimated values are. It means that the high spatial frequency resulted in the flat plane-like stimuli. It is very interesting that the

higher spatial frequency dot approached to the zero spatial frequency of the flat plane.

- The β_v values in the dotted planes were relatively closer to zero than that of -0.23 in the flat plane, which confirmed that the speed-caused length foreshortening effect was less in the dotted plane than in the simple plane as described in the former section. The authors furthermore carried out statistical two-tailed *t*-tests. As a result, the authors found significant differences between the flat plane and the other dotted planes with a significant level of 0.1% for the $\ln\alpha$-pairs and for the β_v-pairs.

- While, the β_L values in the dotted planes were relatively closer to 1 than that of 0.75

Figure 5. Estimated parameter values

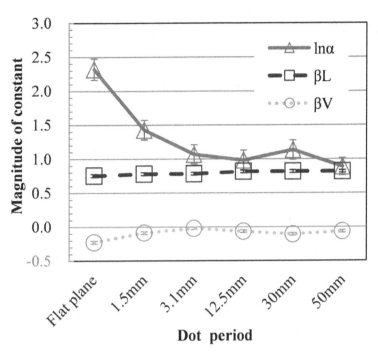

in the flat plane. Carrying out statistical two-tailed *t*-tests, the authors found significant differences in the pairs between the flat plane and the 12.5, 30, and 50mm dotted planes with a significant level of 5%. Correspond to the single dot contact mode.

- As a whole, there was little difference between the single dot contact mode and the multiple dot contact mode, compared with the flat plane.

Similar to this work, the authors had carried out a former work of the raised-dot experiment (Nomura, Najib, Iwabu, & Sakamoto, 2013). Figure 6 shows a comparison between this work of the 3.1 mm dot period and the former work of the 2.5 mm dot period. In both cases, the multiple dot speed perception mode was considered to be applied in both cases. Therefore, both should do agree with each other, but they would not, especially in the high speed condition. Actually, the authors got the estimates of $\ln\alpha=1.9$, $\beta_V=-0.11$,

$\beta_L=0.62$ in the former work. These estimates had differed from those in this paper shown in Table 1. Both the length-related nonlinearity and the speed-caused length foreshortening effect were decreased in this work. The difference might have originated from the difference of an experimental condition: (1) the moved lengths in the former paper ranged from 20.1 to 140.7 mm, while those in this paper much widely ranged from 50 to 550 mm, (2) the speed in the former paper ranged from 25 to 200 mm/s, while those in this paper much widely ranged from 25 to 300 mm/s. The larger dynamic range in the length and the speed might resulted in the suppression of decrease ranging from the shortest length to the middle length. The effect of the variation of the estimates from the viewpoint of the moved length and speed range should be further examined.

Furthermore, Figure 7 shows a comparison between this work of the 30 mm dot period and the former work of the 20.1 mm dot period. For the large dot period, the linearity in this work was

Table 1. Estimated parameter values and their test statistics

Dot Period	Estimated Values			Standard Errors			Test Statistics			Critical Values		
	$\ln\alpha$	β_V	β_L	σ_{lnd}	$\sigma_{\beta V}$	$\sigma_{\beta L}$	$\tau_{ln\alpha}$	$\tau_{\beta V}$	$\tau_{\beta L}$	$T_{0.05}$	$T_{0.01}$	$T_{0.001}$
Flat Plane	2.3	-0.23	0.75	0.16	0.02	0.02	14.8	-10.6	32	2.0	2.6	3.3
1.5mm	1.4	-0.09	0.78	0.14	0.02	0.02	9.9	-4.4	36	2.0	2.6	3.3
3.1mm	1.1	-0.02	0.78	0.14	0.02	0.02	7.7	-1.0	38	2.0	2.6	3.3
12.5mm	1.0	-0.06	0.82	0.15	0.02	0.02	6.6	-3.1	37	2.0	2.6	3.3
30mm	1.1	-0.10	0.82	0.14	0.02	0.02	7.9	-5.3	38	2.0	2.6	3.3
50mm	0.9	-0.06	0.82	0.13	0.02	0.02	7.0	-3.7	43	2.0	2.6	3.3

much inferior to that of the former work, especially in the low speed condition. (With it rebound effect, the speed-caused length foreshortening effect was much worse in the former work than that in this work.) The difference of the performance in the low speed condition was worthy of consideration, and was assumed as follows. In this work of 30 mm period, the subjects were instructed to perceive the sliding lengths by employing a speed-based length perception scheme. While, in the former work of 20.1 mm period, the subjects must not employ a speed-based length perception scheme, and, if possible, may perceive the sliding lengths by employing a dot-counting-based length perception scheme. The dot-counting-based length perception scheme was able to apply in the lower speed conditions. As a result, since the dot-counting scheme is very powerful in length perceptions, the former work of 20.1 mm dot period showed better performance than this work of 30 mm dot period.

Finally, the authors have examined random errors, σ_{lperc}^2: they were given by the variances of

Figure 6. Comparison between this work of the3.1 mm dot period and the former work of the 2.5 mm dot period (Nomura, Najib, Iwabu, & Sakamoto, 2013) (a) This work (Dot period of 3.1 mm, by the multiple dot speed perception mode) (b) Former work (Dot period of 2.5 mm, by the multiple dot speed perception mode)

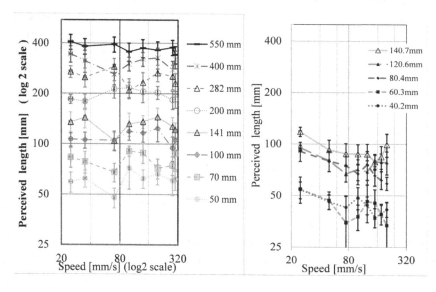

Figure 7. Comparison between this work of the 30 mm dot period and the former work of the 20.1 mm dot period (Nomura, Najib, Iwabu, & Sakamoto, 2013) (a) This work (Dot period of 30 mm, by the single dot speed perception mode) (b) Former work (Dot period of 20.1 mm, by a dot-counting mode)

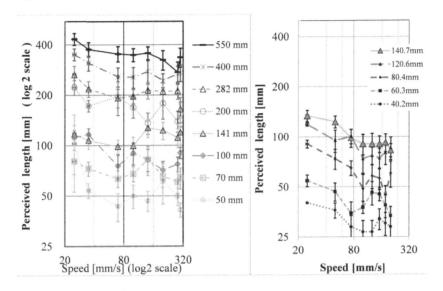

the ratios between the perceptual lengths l_{perc} and the modelled lengths l_{model} for each of the planes. The random errors, σ_{lperc}^{2} are shown in Figure8, together with the results of one-tailed F-tests. It can be told from the viewpoint of random errors that, as a whole, the dotted planes were superior to the flat plane, and, furthermore, the multiple dot contact mode of the 50 mm dot plane was best among the superior dotted planes.

Discussion (Comparison with Existing Works)

In this section, the above explained perceptual models with the raised dots were compared with the existing two haptic length perceptual models. One is Terada model (Terada, Kumazaki, Miyata, & Ito, 2006) that was formulated for flat plane surfaces. The model is similar to the Najib model (Najib, Nomura, Sakamoto, & Iwabu, 2012). In Figure 9 (a), in logarithm scale both in the horizontal

Figure 8. Random errors, σ_{lperc}^{2}: variances of the ratio between the perceived length l_{perc} and the modelled length l_{model} (NS: p>0.05, *: p<0.05, **: p<0.01, ***: p<0.001))

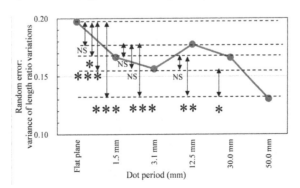

Figure 9. Comparison with some of existing works (a) The 50 mm period model to Terada's one (b) The 50 mm period dot model to Hollins' one

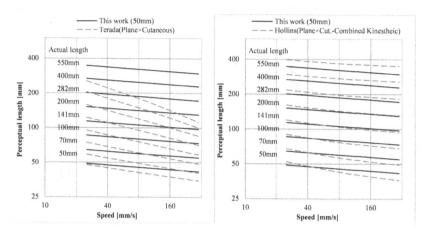

and vertical axes, the model-calculated perceived lengths by this work of the 30 mm period dot plane are shown by the solid lines together with the broken lines calculated by the Terada model. Thanks to the dots, this work shows markedly better performance than the Terada model from the viewpoints of the speed caused the foreshortening effect and the perceptual-length-linearity although

both the models by this work and by Terada were based on the cutaneous sensation only.

The authors compared with the other perceptual length model by (Hollins & Goble, 1988). In Figure 9 (b), the model-calculated perceived lengths by this work of the 30 mm period dot plane are shown by the solid lines together with the Hollins model shown by the broken lines. Here note that Hollins' work did utilize a kinesthetic sensation

Figure 10. A prototype of a tactile mouse for presenting physical-lines (under-development). The wheel was 65 mm in diameter, and was able to be rotated with respect to orthogonal two axes by a couple of servomotors. One servomotor was connected to the other base-fixed servomotor via a swivel joint. This mechanism made the wheel possible to rotate in 2DOF. Touching the wheel surface on their fingerpad through a hole (12.8 mm diameter) of a polyester film (100μ thick), subjects were able to perceive specific slippages. (a) General view (b) Rotating wheel, on the surface of which raised dots are formed

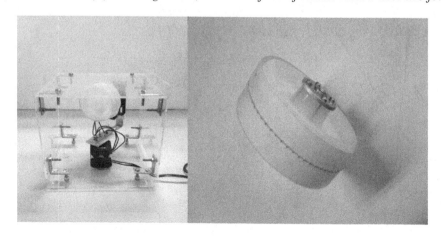

Figure 11. A practical model of a tactile mouse for presenting physical-lines. Although the trial product made shown in Figure 10 was very large in size, it was difficult to use as a mouse interface. In the future, the authors will embed the much smaller size of the wheel into a mouse interface as active wheel mouse. This model is also under-development.(a) Top view of a mouse (b) Side view of rotating disc with raised dots (c) Rotating disc without raised dots

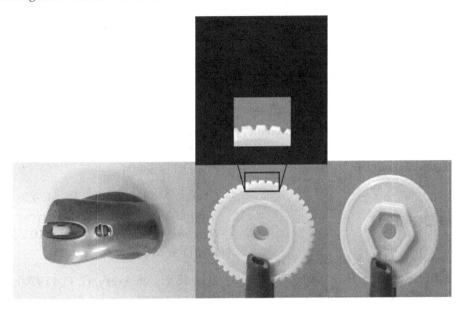

that is very powerful cue for length perceptions. Contrary to the Hollins work, this work did not utilize a kinesthetic sensation, but a cutaneous sensation only. Nevertheless, this work showed so good performance: specifically, the speed caused foreshortening effect was a little worse, while the perceptual-length-linearity was so good as the Hollins' work.

CONCLUSION

Introducing raised dots, the authors have studied sliding pathway perceptual characteristics via index fingerpad cutaneous sensation in the passive-touch framework. Dot periods of 1.5, 3.1, 12.5, 30, and 50 mm planes were taken as representatives of dotted planes, and their perceptual performances were compared to that for a flat plane where the 12.5, 30, and 50 mm dot periods corresponded

to the single dot contact mode, 1.5, 3.1 mm dot periods did the multiple dot contact mode.

1. The authors formulated a model for the perceived length as a power function of actual lengths and velocities for the dotted planes together with a flat plane

2. Comparing the dotted planes with the flat plane, both the contact modes showed significantly better performances from the viewpoints of the perceptual length linearity, the speed-caused contraction effect, and the random errors.

3. The dotted plane showed such a high performance as that of Hollins work where not only the cutaneous sensation, but also the proprioceptive sensation was employed, while the cutaneous sensation being much inferior to the proprioceptive one was just employed in this work.

FUTURE RESEARCH DIRECTIONS

Thus, the raised dots are expected to contribute for a new physical-line presenting computer-human interface. In the future, based on the results of this paper, the authors are directed to develop fingerpad-based computer-human interfaces as a physical-line presenting device by using a new type of effective cue, i.e., the raised dots. For example, by forming raised dots on actively rotating wheel surface, and by embedding the wheel into a mouse interface, it is expected to make up novel active mouse interfaces (see Figure 10, a prototype and Figure 11, a practical model.).

ACKNOWLEDGMENT

This work was supported by KAKENHI (Grant-in-Aid for Scientific Research (B), No. 21300307) from Japan Society for the Promotion of Science (JSPS).

REFERENCES

Akamatsu, M., & MacKenzie, I. S. (1996). Movement characteristics using a mouse with tactile and force feedback. *International Journal of Human-Computer Studies*, *45*(4), 483–493. doi:10.1006/ijhc.1996.0063

Armstrong, L., & Marks, L. E. (1999). Haptic perception of linear extent. *Perception & Psychophysics*, *61*(6), 1211–1226. doi:10.3758/BF03207624 PMID:10497438

Armstrong, L., & Marks, L. E. (1999). Haptic perception of linear extent. *Perception & Psychophysics*, *61*(6), 1211–1226. doi:10.3758/BF03207624 PMID:10497438

Bach-y-Rita, P. (1972). *Brain mechanisms in sensory substitution*. Academic Press.

Bensmaia, S. J., Craig, J. C., Yoshioka, T., & Johnson, K. O. (2006). SA1 and RA afferent responses to static and vibrating gratings. *Journal of Neurophysiology*, *95*(3), 1771–1782. doi:10.1152/jn.00877.2005 PMID:16236779

Blumenfeld, W. (1936). The relationship between the optical and haptic construction of space. *Acta Psychologica*, *2*, 125–174. doi:10.1016/S0001-6918(37)90011-8

Cascio, C. J., & Sathian, K. (2001). Temporal cues contribute to tactile perception of roughness. *The Journal of Neuroscience*, *21*(14), 5289–5296. PMID:11438604

Cheng, M. F. (1968). Tactile-kinesthetic perception of length. *The American Journal of Psychology*, *81*(1), 74–82. doi:10.2307/1420809 PMID:5661568

Day, R. H., & Avery, G. C. (1970). Absence of the horizontal-vertical illusion in haptic space. *Journal of Experimental Psychology*, *83*(1), 172–173. doi:10.1037/h0028514 PMID:5436478

Day, R. H., Wong, T. S., & Brooks, C. I. (1971). Radial and tangential movement directions as determinants of the haptic illusion in an L figure. *Journal of Experimental Psychology*, *90*(2), 19–22. doi:10.1037/h0030155 PMID:5541561

Deco, G., Scarano, L., & Soto-Faraco, S. (2007). Weber's Law in Decision Making: Integrating Behavioral Data in Humans with a Neurophysiological Model. *The Journal of Neuroscience*, *27*(42), 11192–11200. doi:10.1523/JNEUROSCI.1072-07.2007 PMID:17942714

Dépeault1, A., Meftah, El-Mehdi, & Chapman, C. E. (2008). Tactile Speed Scaling: Contributions of Time & Space. *Journal of Neurophysiology*, *99*, 1422-1434.

Deregowski, J., & Ellis, H. D. (1972). Effect of stimulus orientation upon haptic perception of the horizontal-vertical illusion. *Journal of Experimental Psychology, 95*(1), 14–19. doi:10.1037/h0033264 PMID:5070280

Faineteau, H., Gentaz, E., & Viviani, P. (2003). The kinaesthetic perception of Euclidean distance: a study of the detour effect. *Experimental Brain Research, Springer, 152*(2), 166–172. doi:10.1007/s00221-003-1526-1 PMID:12898094

Garcia-Hernandez, N., Tsagarakis, N. G., & Caldwell, D. G. (2011). Feeling through tactile displays: a study on the effect of the array density and size on the discrimination of tactile patterns. *IEEE Transactions on Haptics, 4*(2), 100–110. doi:10.1109/TOH.2010.59

Gibson, J. J. (1962). Observations on active touch. *Psychological Review, 69*(6), 477–491. doi:10.1037/h0046962 PMID:13947730

Gleeso, B. T., Horschel, S. K., & Provancher, W. R. (2010). Design of a fingertip-mounted tactile display with tangential skin displacement feedback. *IEEE Transactions on Haptics, 3*(4), 297–301. doi:10.1109/TOH.2010.8

Haggard, P., Newman, C., Blundell, J., & Andrew, H. (2000). The perceived position of the hand in space. *Perception & Psychophysics, 68*(2), 363–377. doi:10.3758/BF03205556 PMID:10723215

Hollins, M., & Goble, A. K. (1988). Perception of the length of voluntary movements. *Somatosensory & Motor Research, 5*(4), 335–348. doi:10.3109/07367228809144635 PMID:3381043

Hollins, M., & Goble, A. K. (1988). Perception of the length of voluntary movements. *Somatosensory & Motor Research, 5*(4), 335–348. doi:10.3109/07367228809144635 PMID:3381043

Jansson, G., & Pedersen, P. (2005). Obtaining geographical information from a virtual map with a haptic mouse. In *Proceedings of XXII International Cartographic Conference.* Academic Press.

KGS Corp. (n.d.). Retrieved from http://www.kgs-jpn.co.jp/

Kuchenbecker, K. J., Provancher, W. R., Niemeyer, G., & Cutkosky, M. R. (2004). Haptic display of contact location. In *Proceedings of the 12th International Symposium on Haptic Interfaces for Virtual Environment and Teleoperator Systems (HAPTICS'04),* (pp. 40-47). HAPTICS.

Kyung, K.-U., Choi, H., Kwon, D. S., & Son, S. W. (2004). Interactive mouse systems providing haptic feedback during the exploration in virtual environment. In *Proceedings of Computer and Information Sciences-ISCIS 2004.* Springer. doi:10.1007/978-3-540-30182-0_15

Lawrence, M. A., Kitada, R., Klatzky, R. L., & Lederman, S. J. (2007). Haptic roughness perception of linear gratings via bare finger or rigid probe. *Perception, 36,* 547–557. doi:10.1068/p5746 PMID:17564201

Lechelt, E. C., & Verenka, A. (1980). Spatial anisotropy in intramodal and cross-modal judgments of stimulus orientation: The stability of the oblique effect. *Perception, 9*(5), 581–589. doi:10.1068/p090581 PMID:7443398

Lederman, S. J. (1983). Tactual roughness perception: Spatial and temporal determinants. *Canadian Journal of Psychology, 37*(4), 498–511. doi:10.1037/h0080750

Lederman, S. J. (1991). *Skin and Touch.* Academic Press.

Lederman, S. J., Klatzky, R. L., & Barber, P. O. (1985). Spatial and movement-based heuristics for encoding pattern information through touch. *Journal of Experimental Psychology. General, 114*(1), 33–49. doi:10.1037/0096-3445.114.1.33 PMID:3156945

Loomis, J. M. (1974). Tactile letter recognition under different modes of stimulus presentation. *Perception & Psychophysics, 16*(2), 401–408. doi:10.3758/BF03203960

Magee & Kennedy. (1980). Exploring pictures tactually. *Nature, 283*, 287–288. doi:10.1038/283287a0

Marchetti, F. M., & Lederman, S. J. (1983). The haptic radial-tangential effect: Two tests of "Wong's moments-of-inertia" hypothesis. *Bulletin of the Psychonomic Society, 21*, 43–46. doi:10.3758/BF03329950

Minamizawa, K., Prattichizzo, D., & Tachi, S. (2010). Simplified design of haptic display by extending one-point kinesthetic feedback to multipoint tactile feedback. In *Proceedings of 2010 IEEE Haptics Symposium*, (pp. 257-260). IEEE.

Morley, J. W., Goodwin, A. W., & Darian-Smith, I. (1983). Tactile discrimination of gratings. *Experimental Brain Research, 49*(2), 291–299. doi:10.1007/BF00238588 PMID:6832261

Najib, S. M., Nomura, Y., Sakamoto, R., & Iwabu, K. (2012). A Study on the duration and speed sensibility via fingerpad cutaneous sensations. *Procedia Engineering, 41*, 1268–1276. doi:10.1016/j.proeng.2012.07.310

Najib, S. M., Nomura, Y., Sakamoto, R., & Iwabu, K. (2012). A Study on the duration and speed sensibility via finger-pad cutaneous sensations. *Procedia Engineering, 41*, 1268–1276. doi:10.1016/j.proeng.2012.07.310

Nomura, Y., Najib, S. M., Iwabu, K., & Sakamoto, R. (2013). Sliding raised-dots perceptual characteristics: speed perception or dot count. In *Proc. ACHI 2013*, (pp. 303-308). ACHI.

Nomura, Y., Najib, S. M., Iwabu, K., & Sakamoto, R. (2013). Sliding raised-dots perceptual characteristics: speed perception or dot count. In *Proc. ACHI 2013*, (pp. 303-308). ACHI.

Nomura, Y., Najib, S. M., & Sakamoto, R. (2013). Hand-motion perception by four haptic modes: Active/passive and with/without fingerpad cutaneous sensation. *Journal of Advanced Mechanical Design, Systems and Manufacturing, 7*(4), 560–575. doi:10.1299/jamdsm.7.560

Okamoto, S., Konyo, M., & Tadokoro, S. (2011). Vibrotactile stimuli applied to finger pads as biases for perceived inertial and viscous loads. *IEEE Transactions on Haptics, 4*(4), 307–315. doi:10.1109/TOH.2011.16

Pietrzak, T., Pecci, I., & Martin, B. (2006). Static and dynamic tactile directional cues experiments with VTPlayer mouse. [Eurohaptics.]. *Proceedings of Eurohaptics, 2006*, 63–68.

Pongrac, H. (2008). Vibrotactile perception: examining the coding of vibrations and the just noticeable difference under various conditions. *Multimedia Systems, 13*, 297–307. doi:10.1007/s00530-007-0105-x

Salada, M., Vishton, P., Colgate, J. E., & Frankel, E. (2004). Two experiments on the perception of slip at the fingertip. In *Proceedings 12th International Symposium on Haptic Interfaces for Virtual Environment and Teleoperator Systems*, (pp. 146-153). Academic Press.

Schwartz, A. S., Perrey, A. J., & Azulay, A. (1975). Further analysis of active and passive touch in pattern discrimination. *Bulletin of the Psychonomic Society, 6*(1), 7–9. doi:10.3758/BF03333128

Sensable. (n.d.). Retrieved from http://www.sensegraphics.com/index.php

Shimizu, Y. (1982). Temporal effect on tactile letter recognition by a tracing mode. *Perceptual and Motor Skills*, 55(2), 343–349. doi:10.2466/pms.1982.55.2.343 PMID:7155729

Tahir, M., Bailly, G., & Lecolinet, E. (2008). Exploring the impulsion and vibration effects of tactile patterns. In *Proceedings of the 22nd British HCI Group Annual Conference on People and Computers: Culture, Creativity* []. HCI.]. *Interaction*, 2, 237–240.

Tahir, M., Bailly, G., Lecolinet, E., & Mouret, G. (2008). TactiMote: a tactile remote control for navigating in long lists. In *Proceedings of the 10th international conference on Multimodal interfaces*, (pp. 285-288). Academic Press.

Terada, K., Kumazaki, A., Miyata, D., & Ito, A. (2006). Haptic Length Display Based on Cutaneous-Proprioceptive, Integration. *Journal of Robotics and Mechatronics*, 18(4), 489–498.

Terada, K., Kumazaki, A., Miyata, D., & Ito, A. (2006). Haptic length display based on cutaneous-proprioceptive integration. *Journal of Robotics and Mechatronics*, 18(4), 489–498.

Tiest, W. M. B. vander Hoff, L.M.A., & Kappers, A.M.L. (2011). Cutaneous and kinaesthetic perception of traversed distance. In *Proceedings of the World Haptics Conference* (pp. 593-597). IEEE.

Tiest, W. M. B., van der Hoff, L. M. A., & Kappers, A. M. L. (2011). Cutaneous and kinaesthetic perception of traversed distance. In *Proceedings of the World Haptics Conference* (pp. 593-597). IEEE.

Tsagarakis, N. G., Horne, T., & Caldwell, D. G. (2005). Slip aesthesis: a portable 2D slip/skin stretch display for the fingertip. In *Proceedings of First Joint Eurohaptics Conference, 2005 and Symposium on Haptic Interfaces for Virtual Environment and Teleoperator Systems, 2005: World Hap-tics 2005*, (pp. 214 -219). Haptics.

Vega-Bermudez, F., Johnson, K. O., & Hsiao, S. S. (1991). Human tactile pattern recognition: active versus passive touch, velocity effects, and patterns of confusion. *Journal of Neurophysiology. Am Physiological Soc.*, 65(3), 531–546.

Wall, S. A., & Brewster, S. (2006). Sensory substitution using tactile pin arrays: Human factors, technology and applications. *Signal Processing*, 86(12), 3674–3695. doi:10.1016/j.sigpro.2006.02.048

Wang, Y., Turner, M. J., & Hewitt, W. T. (2006). Creating a novel multiple frequency based vibration built upon human perception analysis. In *Proceedings of the 41st United Kingdom Group Meeting on Human Responses to Vibration*, (pp. 1-12). Academic Press.

Webstar, R. J. III, Todd, E. M., Lawton, N. V., & Allison, M. O. (2005). A novel two-dimensional tactile slip display: design, kinematics and perceptual experiments. *ACM Transactions on Applied Perception*, 2(2), 150–165. doi:10.1145/1060581.1060588

Whitsel, B. L., Franzen, O., Dreyer, D. A., Hollins, M., Young, M., Essick, G. K., & Wong, C. (1986). Dependence of subjective traverse length on velocity of moving tactile stimuli. *Somatosensory & Motor Research*, 3(3), 185–196. doi:10.3109/07367228609144583 PMID:3749661

Wydoodt, P., Gentaz, E., & Streri, A. (2006). Role of force cues in the haptic estimations of a virtual length. *Experimental Brain Research*, *171*, 481–489. doi:10.1007/s00221-005-0295-4 PMID:16369791

KEY TERMS AND DEFINITIONS

Cutaneous Sensation: Cutaneous sensation is a generic name of warmth, cold, contact, pain sensations, and others arose by stimulation of sensory organs in the skin. In this section, the slippage sensation on fingerpad was examined.

Length Perception: It means the length perception of the specimen slippage on fingerpad by the use of cutaneous sensations. Accepting continuously-provided slippage-stimuli, and increase the slippages cumulatively, the subject is considered to be able to perceive the slippage length.

Raised Dots: Raised dots are ordinarily convex-shaped small-bump-dots as in this section, and have been used as tactile marker as in Braille and tactile graphics for blind or low vision people. Touching patterns of raised dots on fingerpads, users get character and graphical information.

Random Error: Random errors are statistical fluctuations in the measured and perceived data due to the precision limitations of the measurement device and perceptual sensation, respectively.

Speed Perception: It means the speed perception of the specimen slippage on the subject fingerpad by the use of his/her cutaneous sensations: driven by a linear actuator, the specimen slid on the subject fingerpad, and provided slippage sensation to the subject.

Systematic Error: Systematic errors are biases in measurement and perception, and are reproducible inaccuracies that are consistently in the same conditions. In this section, they were also referred to as factor effects.

APPENDIX

General View of Haptic Length Perception

The haptic technology described in this chapter is referred to with graphical information representations. As for the graphical information representations, there have been various researches and systems with alternative technologies for visually impaired persons. For examples, Dot View (KGS Corp.) would be a representative device for displaying two-dimensional dot patterns: their devices are able to represent 24×32 or 32×48 dot array. Different from the parallel representations like Dot View, line drawing patterns can be expressed by haptic devices such as PHANTOM (Sensable): two/three dimensional patterns might be represented by trajectories of arm end positions. The kinds of haptic devices have an advantage that they can afford to provide a guidance function to users by taking user's hand along with some routes. The kind of use is considered to be beneficial for visually impaired persons.

The theme of this chapter is with slippage perceptions. Since the slippages can be regarded as line segments, the results can be said to be one of the fundamental issues with respect to the latter framework of line drawing presentations. Now, let's overlook the brief history of the haptic length perceptions. Paying attention to two kinds of important factors, i.e., a user's initiative factor and a sensation factor, haptic perceptual characteristics are explained in the following sections.

Sensation Factor: Cutaneous, Proprioceptive, Cutaneous-Combined Proprioceptive

Related to haptic contacts, the perceptual process can also be categorized from sensation factors. Representative sensations include cutaneous sensations on fingerpads (where an index fingerpad is most commonly used) and such proprioceptive senses as joint rotation and kinematic/force related to muscle expansions and contractions. For the two sensations, the following three modes can be considered:
1. Cutaneous-combined proprioceptive sensation, referred to as "Cu".
2. Cutaneous-combined proprioceptive sensation, referred to as "Co".
3. Without-cutaneous proprioceptive-only sensation, referred to as "Pr".

User's Initiative Factor: Active Touch and Passive Touch

The words, the active touch and the passive touch generally mean some kinds of haptic perceptual frameworks utilizing kinesthetic sensations and/or the cutaneous sensations. Both the touch frameworks were matter of concerns, and they have been examined from various viewpoints. As for the pattern recognition, comparative studies of perceptual performance between the active touch and the passive touch. Although some of them reported that the passive touch shows no inferiority to the active touch (Schwartz, 1975), many of them reported that the active touch was superior to the passive touch (Gibson,1962), (Bach-y-Rita1972). For, further analysis of active and passive touch in pattern discrimination, see Schwartz, Perrey and Azulay (1975).

Table 2. Classification of haptic perception modes for lines in 2D space

Physical quantity to be perceived	Employed information (Temporal response)	Sense		Physical condition		Subject's initiative in exploration		
		Major division	Minor division	Surface	External force		Mode	Index
Line direction	Static edge direction / Moving direction at the tracing point	Cutaneous	Touch + pressure	Physical stimulus	Irrelevance	Passive	CuPa	1
		Proprioceptive (joint and muscle)	2D force	Irrelevance	Tractional force	Passive	PrPa	2
					Force free	Active	PrAc	3
		Combined	Combined	Plane	Tractional force	Passive	CoPa	4
					Force free	Active	CoAc	5
				Physical stimulus	No external force	Active	CoAc	6
Line length traced from start to end points	Integration of dynamically varying tracing velocity	Cutaneous	Slip (2D velocity)	Plane	Irrelevance	Passive	CuPa	7
				Raised dots	Irrelevance	Passive	CuPa	8
		Proprioceptive (joint rotation and muscle expansion and contraction)	2D kinesthetic (position) and 2D force (acceleration)	Irrelevance	Fully tractional force	Passive	PrPa	9
					Assistive tractional force	Passive	PrPa	10
					No external force	Active	PrAc	11
					Resistant flowback force	Active	PrAc	12
		Combined	Combined	Plane	Fully tractional force	Passive	CoPa	13
				Physical stimulus	No external force	Active	CoAc	14
Euclidean distance between the start and end points	Static placements at both the points	Proprioceptive (joint rotation and muscle expansion and contraction)	2D kinesthetic position	Irrelevance	Fully tractional force towards both end points	Passive	PrPa	15
				Raised points	No external force	Active	PrAc	16

Physical stimulus: Raised dot, Raised edge, Raised figure, Slot, Ditch, Rod

Tractional force: the force working in the traveling direction

Resistant force: the force working in the opposite direction of the traveling direction

Force free: the reaction force perpendicular to the travelling direction works only in the case of deviating from predetermined route

CuPa: cutaneous passive

PrPa: proprioceptive passive

CoPa: combined passive

PrAc: proprioceptive active

CoAc: combined active

On the other hand, as in the above described pattern recognition tasks, for representing line stroke patterns with the haptic devices, two kinds of force feedback controllers can be considered from a viewpoint that either human or haptic-device takes initiative to the other in the kinesthetic motion activation.

Table 3. Classification of haptic perception modes for lines in 2D space

	1936	1970	1971	1974	1980	1983	1985	1986	1988	1991	1999	2000	2003	2006	2006	2011	2013	This work
Index																		
1																		
2																	O	
3																	O	
4																	O	
5																	O	
6	Thread			Rod														
7								Brush was swept						O	O			O
8																		O
9														O	O	O	O	
10														O				
11														×				
12														O			O	
13										Embossed				O	O		O	
14		Slot	Raised edge	Vibrotactile dots		Rod	Raised dot		Rod	Embossed	Raised lines or solid blocks		Ditch				O	
15												O						
16					O							O						

1936 Blumenfeld, W.
1970 Day, R.H. & Avery, G.C.
1971 Day, R. H., Wong, T. S., & Brooks, C. I.
1974 Loomis, J. M.
1980 Lechelt, E. C. & Verenka, A.
1983 Marchetti, F. M. &Lederman, S. J.
1985 Lederman, S. J., Klatzky, R. L. & Barber, P. O.
1986 Whitsel, B. L., Franzen, O., Dreyer, D. A., Hollins, M., Young, M., Essick, G. K., & Wong, C.
1988 Hollins, M. & Goble, A. K.
1991 Vega-Bermudez, F., Johnson, K. O. & Hsiao, S. S.
1999 Armstrong, L. & Marks, L. E.
2000 Haggard, P., Newman, C., Blundell, J., & Andrew, H.
2003 Faineteau, H., Gentaz, E., & Viviani, P.
2006 Wydoodt, P., Gentaz, E., & Streri, A.
2006 Terada, K., Kumazaki, A., Miyata, D., & Ito, A.
2011 Tiest, W.M.B., van der Hoff, L.M.A., & Kappers, A.M.L.
2013 Nomura, Y., Najib, S. M., Iwabu, K., & Sakamoto, R.

1.   Passive kinesthetic perception, referred to as "Pa": haptic-devices take initiative to humans, where the humans passively accept haptic stimuli exerted from the haptic devices.

2.   Active kinesthetic perception, referred to as "Ac": humans try to exploit to get stimulative information, and humans, vice versa, take initiative.

Thus, taking account that Pr is unconditionally employed in the active mode, and, therefore, the combination of Cu and Ac is not necessary to consider, we can classify haptic perceptions into five modes:
1. CuPa (cutaneous passive)
2. PrPa (proprioceptive passive)
3. CoPa (combined passive)
4. PrAc (proprioceptive active)
5. CoAc (combined active)

Overview of the Five Modes: CuPa, PrPa, CoPa, PrAc, CoAc

Next, let's make a survey on the five modes. Since it was not popular to use precisely controllable electric-powered actuators in the early years, line segment perception experiments were carried out by subjects' voluntary touch-and-slide movements along with presented physical objects: subjects themselves moved their hands to exploit the line segment lengths and directions of the object. Thus, these works can be regarded as physical-object-based combined active (CoAc) where the physically line segments were made of such as threads (Blumenfeld 1937), raised edge (Day, Wong, & Brooks, 1971), slots (Day & Avery, 1970), edges (Day, Wong, & Brooks, 1971), rods (Lechelt & Verenka,1980) (Marchetti &Lederman, 1983) (Hollins & Goble, 1988), raised dots (Lederman, Klatzky, & Barber, 1985), embossed ditch (Vega-Bermudez, Johnson, & Hsiao, 1991) (Lochlan & Kennedy, 1980), and raised lines and solid blocks (Faineteau, Gentaz, & Viviani, 2003).

Here, assuming that the line segments are straight, the values to be perceived are the lengths and directions of the line segments. Consequently, the line segment perception characteristics can be dissolved into length and direction perception characteristics.

Let's review some representative results on the length perception characteristics. One of the most important characteristics is the length-related contraction effect and the speed-caused length foreshortening effect (Whitsel, Franzen, Dreyer, Hollins, Young, Essick, & Wong, 1986) (Hollins & Goble, 1988).

Perceived location distortions were related to the object position relative to the subject's body centered coordinates. The anisotropies of the foreshortening effect were reported by various papers: they were related to the directional difference against the frontal parallel plane (Cheng, 1968)(Day & Avery 1970)(Day, Wong, & Brooks, 1971). They reported that the anisotropies were given a reason that there is a mass difference between the hand movements in the radial and tangential directions. However, other researchers denied the reason (Marchetti, &Lederman, 1983). Taking into account of the horizontal-vertical illusion, Deregowski and Ellis (1972) explained the effect of stimulus orientation upon haptic perception. Raised-dots were introduced to enhance the perceptual characteristics, and two frameworks of the speed perception and the dot count were examined (Nomura, Najib., Iwabu, & Sakamoto, 2013). The work was continued in the work of this chapter.

As for a reason of the length-related contraction effect, the importance of duration times consumed for explorations (Armstrong & Marks, 1999). The characteristic would be legitimate because of the simple fact that the duration times are proportional to lengths under an iso-velocity condition. Relating to the duration time issue, there were some papers with the detour-related lengthening effect (Faineteau, Gentaz, & Viviani, 2003) (Lederman, Klatzky, & Barber, 1985). Recently, the length perceptual errors were related to the sum of the duration-time perceptual errors and moving velocity perceptual errors (Najib, Nomura, Sakamoto, & Iwabu, 2012).

Let's move on to review some representative results on the direction perception characteristics. Errors in the decision of parallelism will increase as the presented lines come near to a subject's body (Blumenfeld, 1936). An oblique effect was reported (Lechelt & Verenka, 1980). Haggard, Newman, Blundell, & Andrew (2000) reported that the direction perceptual errors in the passive touch was worsen to 4.9 degrees from that of 3.4degree in the active touch.

In these years, objects to be explored via haptic sensations can be virtually represented by positional feedback and even by force feedback, thanks to the development of robotic technologies as in this chapter. Some interesting results with the line length perceptions were reported by using Phantom: the lengths were overestimated in PrPa (proprioceptive passive) and, contrary to this, they were underestimated in PrAc (proprioceptive active). In the same year, another interesting characteristic was found by Terada, Kumazaki, Miyata, & Ito (2006): they reported that the speed caused length foreshortening effects were smaller than those reported by Whitsel, Franzen, Dreyer, Hollins, Young, Essick, and Wong (1986), and Hollins and Goble (1988). Furthermore, they examined on the perceptual characteristics in CoPa (combined passive), and the sensory fusion of the cutaneous and proprioceptive sensations was given by the maximum operator (Terada, Kumazaki Miyata, & Ito, 2006). Recently, nevertheless the experimental conditions were restricted in a specific length of 10 cm, length perceptual characteristics for all the three passive modes, i.e., CoPa, PrPa, and CuPa were compared: the perceptual errors for the three modes were found to be CuPa>PrPa≒CoPa, and CuPa was much the worst among them, and Pr sensation was dominant over Cu sensation (Tiest & Kappers, 2011).

Wydoodt, Gentaz, and Streri (2006) did interesting work on Ac and Pa touches, and investigated how force cues induce bias effects in haptic length perception using the haptic device, PHANTOM. They introduced four force-disturbed conditions together with an ordinary condition called the force-free condition: in the force-free condition, the line segment lengths were actively explored by subjects without disruptions. For the force-disturbed conditions, they made (a) two types of opposite-force-impressed conditions (elastic and viscous resistant) and (b) two types of forward-force-impressed conditions (partial and full traction). The force-free and the full-traction condition correspond to the active and the passive condition in this work. They reported an interesting length contraction/expansion effect with systematic errors. Length expansion occurred with the opposite-force-impressed conditions, and length contraction occurred with the forward-force-impressed condition, in contrast to the force-free condition where neither contraction nor expansion occurred. Since only 10 cm of virtual rod length was employed, the length variations of the presented lines were inadequate to quantitatively model the bias effects in their experiments. (Wydoodt, Gentaz, & Streri, 2006).

In 2013, by using the haptic device, i.e., PHANTOM, the four modes, i.e., CuPa, PrPa, CoAc and CoPa mode, were comprehensively studied (Nomura, Najib, & Sakamoto, 2013).

As for the moved distance perceptions, they found the followings.

1. Among the four modes, CoAc mode was a little bit more proactive than the others from the viewpoints of both systematic and random errors, that is, CoAc mode showed the largest sensibility.

2. They established the presented and perceived line length relationships as a power model.

3. They also determined factor effects of the sensation, the initiative, and the directional factors.

As for the moved directional perception, they found the followings.

1. The subjects perceived the moving directions by another trigonometric systematic error with $1.5°$ amplitude and $8.2°$ bias in the clockwise direction.

2. The subjects perceived the moving directions with random error of $15°$ by standard deviation.

To summarize, based on CoAc mode, human length perceptual characteristics were intensively studied before 2000. Since then, positional-control-based mechanical actuators were introduced, and Pa mode-based line segment perceptual characteristics, that is, CuPa, PrPa, and CoPa modes were eventually examined although experimental conditions were restricted in narrow factors and a few levels. Recently, force feedback devices were only available by low costs in the market, we finally acquire an ability to examine the machine-based, not human-volunteered, Ac mode.

Compilation of References

3D. *Guidance trakSTAR*. (n.d.). Retrieved October 2, 2013 from http://www.ascension-tech.com/medical/trakSTAR.php

Abascal, J., & Nicolle, C. (2005). Moving towards inclusive design guidelines for socially and ethically aware HCI. *Interacting with Computers, 17*(5), 484–505. doi:10.1016/j.intcom.2005.03.002

Abdelmohsen, S. M., & Do, E. Y.-L. (2007). *TangiCAD: Tangible Interface for Manipulating Architectural 3D Models*. Paper presented at the 10th International Conference on Computer Aided Architectural Design Research in Asia (CAADRIA). Nanjing, China.

Abowd, G. D., Atkeson, C. G., Hong, J., Long, S., Kooper, R., & Pinkerton, M. (1997). Cyberguide: a mobile context-aware tour guide. *Wireless Networks, 3*(5), 421–433. doi:10.1023/A:1019194325861

Adams, C., Collison, S., Budd, A., Boulton, M., & Clarke, A. (2007). *Web standards creativity: innovations in web design with XHTML, CSS, and DOM scripting* (Vol. 24). Friends of ED.

Ae Project. (2013). *Ae - Aprendizado Eletrônico Environment*. Retrieved October 20, 2013, from http://tidia-ae.iv.org.br/

Aggarwal, J. K., & Ryoo, M. S. (2011). Human Activity Analysis: A Review. *ACM Computing Surveys, 43*(3), 16. doi:10.1145/1922649.1922653

AIIM. (2008a). *What is Enterprise 2.0?* Retrieved December 1, 2013, from http://www.aiim.org/What-is-Enterprise2.0-E2.0.aspx

AIIM. (2008b). Enterprise 2.0 Technologies Critical to Business Success. *International Journal of Micrographics & Optical Technology, 26*(1/2), 6.

Aiken, C., et al. (2012). Shaking up earth science: Visual and auditory representation of earthquake interactions. In *Proceedings of the 18th International Conference on Auditory Display*. Atlanta, GA: Georgia Institute of Technology Publishing.

Akamatsu, M., & MacKenzie, I. S. (1996). Movement characteristics using a mouse with tactile and force feedback. *International Journal of Human-Computer Studies, 45*(4), 483–493. doi:10.1006/ijhc.1996.0063

Akker, J. V. D., Gravemeijer, K., McKenney, S., & Nieveen, N. (2006). *Educational Design Research*. New York, NY: Routledge.

Aldebaran-robotics. (2013). Retrieved October 10, 2013 from http://www.aldebaran-robotics.com/en/

Alexandraki, C., Paramythis, A., Maou, N., & Stephanidis, C. (2004). Web accessibility through adaptation. *Computers Helping People with Special Needs*, 626-626.

Allen, G. L. (1999). Spatial abilities, cognitive maps, and wayfinding: Bases for individual differences in spatial cognition and behavior. In R. G. Golledge (Ed.), *Wayfinding behavior: Cognitive maps and other spatial processes* (pp. 46–80). Baltimore, MD: Johns Hopkins University Press.

Allport, F. H. (1924). *Social Psyshology*. Boston: Houghton Mifflin.

Almeida, F. (2012). Web 2.0 Technologies and Social Networking Security Fears in Enterprises. *International Journal of Advanced Computer Science and Applications, 3*(2). AT&T. (2009). *Speeding the Adoption of Enterprise 2.0*. Retrieved November 21, 2013 from http://blog.earlystrategies.com/wp-content/uploads/2010/02/Speeding-the-Adoption-of_Enterprise-2-0.pdf

Alonso, G., Casati, F., Kuno, H., & Machiraju, V. (2003). *Web services: concepts, architectures and applications.* Springer.

Al-Shamaileh, O., & Sutcliffe, A. (2013). Website Interactivity and Repeated Exposure, what Influences User Experience? *Journal of Universal Computer Science, 19*(8), 1123–1139.

Alty, J., & McCartney, C. (1991). *Design of a Multi-Media Presentation System For A Process Control Environment.* Paper presented at the Eurographics Multimedia Workshop, Session 8: Systems. Stockholm, Sweden.

Anand, B., Navathe, B. B., Velusamy, S., Kannan, H., Sharma, A., & Gopalakrishnan, V. (2012). Article. In *Proceedings of 2012 IEEE Consumer Communications and Networking Conference* (pp. 255–259). Washington, DC: IEEE Computer Society.

App. Inventor. (2012). Retrieved November 2nd, 2013, from http://appinventor.mit.edu

Arduino. (2013). Retrieved October 10, 2013 from http://www.arduino.cc/

Armstrong, L., & Marks, L. E. (1999). Haptic perception of linear extent. *Perception & Psychophysics, 61*(6), 1211–1226. doi:10.3758/BF03207624 PMID:10497438

Asus. (2013). Retrieved January 1, 2013 from http://www.asus.com/Multimedia/Xtion_PRO/

Bach-y-Rita, P. (1972). *Brain mechanisms in sensory substitution.* Academic Press.

Balharová, K., Motschnig, R., Struhár, J., & Hagelkruys, D. (2013). A Case Study of Applying Card-sorting as an Initial Step in the Design of the LITERACY – Portal for People with Dyslexia. In *Proceedings of the Conference Universal Learning Design.* Brno, Czech Republic: Masaryk University.

Ballagas, R., Ringel, M., Stone, M., & Borchers, J. (2003). iStuff: A Physical User Interface Toolkit for Ubiquitous Computing Environments. In *Proceedings of SIGCHI Conference on Human Factors in Computing Systems* (pp. 537–544). New York, NY: ACM.

Bangalore, S., & Johnston, M. (n.d.). Robust Understanding in Multimodal Interaction. *Computational Linguistic, 35*(3), 345-397.

Barbarito, F., Pinciroli, F., Mason, J., Marceglia, S., Mazzola, L., & Bonacina, S. (2012). Implementing standards for the interoperability among healthcare providers in the public regionalized Healthcare Information System of the Lombardy Region. *Journal of Biomedical Informatics.* doi:10.1016/j.jbi.2012.01.006 PMID:22285983

Baron, R. S. (1986). Distraction-conflict theory: Progress and problems. *Advances in Experimental Social Psychology, 19*, 1–40. doi:10.1016/S0065-2601(08)60211-7

Barret, F. J., & Fry, R. E. (2005). *Appreciative inquiry: a positive approach to building cooperative capacity.* Chagrin Falls.

Basdekis, I., Alexandraki, C., Mourouzis, A., & Stephanidis, C. (2005). Incorporating Accessibility in Web-Based Work Environments: Two Alternative Approaches and Issues Involved. In C. Stephanidis (Ed.), *Universal Access in HCI: Exploring New Dimensions of Diversity - Volume 8 of the Proceedings of the 11th International Conference on Human-Computer Interaction* (HCI International 2005). Las Vegas, NV: Lawrence Erlbaum Associates.

Basdekis, I., Karampelas, P., Doulgeraki, V., & Stephanidis, C. (2009). Designing Universally Accessible Networking Services for a Mobile Personal Assistant. In C. Stephanidis (Ed.), *Universal Access in Human-Computer Interaction - Intelligent and Ubiquitous Interaction Environments. – Volume 6 of the Proceedings of the 13th International Conference on Human-Computer Interaction* (HCI International 2009). San Diego, CA: Springer.

Basdekis, I., Klironomos, I., Metaxas, I., & Stephanidis, C. (2010). An overview of web accessibility in Greece: a comparative study 2004--2008. *Universal Access in the Information Society, 9*(2), 185–190. doi:10.1007/s10209-009-0166-z

Bateman, J., Delin, J., & Henschel, R. (2007). Mapping the Multimodal Genres of Traditional and Electronic Papers. In T. Royce, & W. Bowcher (Eds.), *New Directions in the Analysis of Multimodal Discourse* (pp. 147–172). Lawrence Erlbaum Associates.

Bateson, G. (2000). *Steps to an Ecology of Mind: Collected Essays in Anthropology, Psychiatry, Evolution, and Epistemology.* Chicago, IL: University of Chicago Press.

Battleson, B., Booth, A., & Weintrop, J. (2001). Usability testing of an academic library web site: a case study. Journal of Academic Librarianship, 237, 188–198. doi:10.1016/S0099-1333(01)00180-X

Baumeister, R. F. (1982). A selfpresentational view of social phenomena. *Psychological Bulletin, 91*, 3–26. doi:10.1037/0033-2909.91.1.3

Bearden, W. O., & Etzel, M. J. (1982). Reference group influence on product and brand purchase decisions. *The Journal of Consumer Research, 9*(2), 183–194. doi:10.1086/208911

Bearman, N. (2011). Using sound to represent uncertainty in future climate projections for the United Kingdom. In *Proceedings of the 17th International Conference on Auditory Display*. Budapest, Hungary: Academic Press.

Beder, D. M., Silva, A. C., Otsuka, J. L., Silva, C. G., & Rocha, H. V. (2007). A Case Study of the Development of e-Learning Systems Following a Component-based Layered Architecture. In *Proceedings of the 7th IEEE International Conference on Advanced Learning Technologies*, (pp. 21-25). Los Alamitos, CA: IEEE Computer Society. doi: 10.1109/ICALT.2007.4

Beech, J., Chadwick, S., & Tapp, A. (2000). Towards a schema for football clubs seeking an effective presence on the internet. *European Journal for Sport Management, 7*, 30–50.

Belanger, F., Hiller, J. S., & Smith, W. J. (2002). Trustworthiness in electronic commerce: the role of privacy, security and site attributes. *The Journal of Strategic Information Systems, 11*, 245–270. doi:10.1016/S0963-8687(02)00018-5

Belinky, I., Lanir, J., & Kuflik, T. (2012). Using handheld devices and situated displays for collaborative planning of a museum visit. In *Proceedings of the 2012 International Symposium on Pervasive Displays*. Academic Press.

Bell, L. (2009). *Web Accessibility: Designing for Dyslexia*. Retrieved October 15, 2013, from http://lindseybell.com/documents/bell_dyslexia.pdf

Benbasat, I., Goldstein, D., & Mead, M. (1987). The Case Research Strategy in Studies of Information Systems. *Management Information Systems Quarterly, 11*(3), 369–386. doi:10.2307/248684

Benford, S., & Giannachi, G. (2012). Interaction as Performance. *Interaction, 19*(3), 38–43. doi:10.1145/2168931.2168941

Bensmaia, S. J., Craig, J. C., Yoshioka, T., & Johnson, K. O. (2006). SA1 and RA afferent responses to static and vibrating gratings. *Journal of Neurophysiology, 95*(3), 1771–1782. doi:10.1152/jn.00877.2005 PMID:16236779

Berjon, R., Leithead, T., Navara, E. D., O'Connor, E., & Pfeiffer, S. (2012). *HTML5 - A vocabulary and associated APIs for HTML and XHTML W3C Candidate Recommendation*. Retrieved March 25, 2013, from http://www.w3.org/TR/html5/

Berlyne, D. E. (1971). Aesthetics and psychobiology. New York: Appleton Century Crofts Publishing.

Berners-Lee, T., Hendler, J., & Lassila, O. et al. (2001). The semantic web. *Scientific American, 284*(5), 28–37. doi:10.1038/scientificamerican0501-34

Bernsen, N. O. (2008). Multimodality Theory. In D. Tzovaras (Ed.), *Multimodal user Interfaces: From signal to interaction* (pp. 5–28). Berlin: Springer. doi:10.1007/978-3-540-78345-9_2

Berry, B. E., & Ignash, S. (2003). Assistive technology: Providing independence for individuals with disabilities. *Rehabilitation Nursing, 28*(1), 6–14. doi:10.1002/j.2048-7940.2003.tb01715.x PMID:12567816

Bersen, N. O., & Dykjær, L. (2010). *Multimodal Usability*. London: Springer-Verlag. doi:10.1007/978-1-84882-553-6

Blascovich, J., Mendes, W. B., Hunter, S. B., & Salomon, K. (1999). Social facilitation as challenge and threat. *Journal of Personality and Social Psychology, 77*(1), 68–77. doi:10.1037/0022-3514.77.1.68 PMID:10434409

Blevis, E. (2007). Sustainable interaction design: invention & disposal, renewal & reuse. In *Proceedings of the SIGCHI Conference on Human Factors in Computing Systems* (pp. 503-512). New York, NY: ACM.

Blinn, N., Lindermann, N., Fäcks, K., & Nüttgens, M. (2012). Web 2.0 artifacts in SME-networks–A qualitative approach towards an integrative conceptualization considering organizational and technical perspectives. In Proceedings of Software Engineering (Workshops) (pp. 273-284). Academic Press.

Blinn, N., Lindermann, K., Fäcks, M., & Nüttgens, M. (2010). Web 2.0 in SME networks - A Design Science Approach Considering Multi-Perspective Requirements. *Journal of Information Science & Technology, 7*(1), 3–21.

Blumenfeld, W. (1936). The relationship between the optical and haptic construction of space. *Acta Psychologica, 2*, 125–174. doi:10.1016/S0001-6918(37)90011-8

Bond, C. F. (1982). Social facilitation: A self-presentational view. *Journal of Personality and Social Psychology, 42*(6), 1042–1050. doi:10.1037/0022-3514.42.6.1042

Borenstein, G. (2012). *Making Things See. 3D vision with Kinect, Processing, Arduino, and MakerBot*. Maker Media, Inc.

Botero, A., & Saad-Sulonen, J. (2008). Co-designing for new city-citizen interaction possibilities: Weaving prototypes and interventions in the design and development of Urban Mediator. In *Proceedings of Participatory Design Conference 2008* (pp. 266-269). Bloomington, IN: Academic Press.

Bouloukakis, G., Basdekis, I., & Stephanidis, C. (2013). myWebAccess: A platform for repairing, enhancing and re-distributing Web Services accessible to people with disability. In *Proceedings of IADIS-International Conference on Interfaces and Human Computer Interaction*. IADIS.

Bregman, A. S. (1990). *Auditory Scene Analysis: The Perceptual Organization of Sound*. Cambridge, MA: MIT Press.

Brignull, H., & Rogers, Y. (2003). Enticing People to Interact with Large Public Displays in Public Spaces. [INTERACT.]. *Proceedings of INTERACT, 03*, 17–24.

Brinck, T. (2008). Return on Goodwill: Return on Investment for Accessibility. In S. Harper, & Y. Yesilada (Eds.), *Web Accessibility – A Foundation for Research* (pp. 385–414). Berlin: Springer.

British Dyslexia Association. (2007). *Dyslexia Research Information*. Retrieved October 15, 2013, from http://www.bdadyslexia.org.uk/about-dyslexia/further-information/dyslexia-research-information-.html

Bromley, H., & Apple, M. W. (1998). *Education, technology, power educational computing as a social practice*. Albany, NY: State University of New York Press.

Brooks, R. A. (1991). New Approaches to Robotics. *Science*, (253): 1227–1232. doi:10.1126/science.253.5025.1227 PMID:17831441

Brown, A. G. P., & Knight, M. W. (2001). *NAVRgate: Gateways to architectural virtual reality - A review and thought on future directions*. Paper presented at the 6th International Conference on Computer Aided Architectural Design Research in Asia (CAADRIA). Sydney, Australia.

Brown, A., Knight, M., & Winchester, M. (2005). *Representation and Delivery of City Models*. Paper presented at the 10th International Conference on Computer Aided Architectural Design Research in Asia (CAADRIA). New Dehli, India.

Brown, A., Knight, M., Chen, Y.-H., & Saeed, G. (2006). *City information delivered to Mobile Digital devices - Reflection on contemporary potentials and problems*. Paper presented at the 24th eCAADe Conference. Volos, Greece.

Brown, S., & Robinson, P. (2001). A world wide web mediator for users with low vision. In *Proceedings of CHI'2001 Conference on Human Factors in Computing Systems Workshop*. ACM.

Brown, A. (2010). The Digital City. In A. Brown (Ed.), *Urbandesignfutures – better city, better life* (pp. 31–48). Liverpool, UK: Liverpool School of Architecture Press.

Brown, B. (2012). *The Power of Vulnerability: Teachings on Authenticity, Connection, & Courage*. Sounds True.

Brynjarsdóttir, H., Håkansson, M., Pierce, J., Baumer, E., DiSalvo, C., & Sengers, P. (2012). Sustainability unpersuaded: how persuasion narrows our vision of sustainability. In *Proceedings of the SIGCHI Conference on Human Factors in Computing Systems* (pp. 947-956). New York, NY: ACM.

Bughin, J. (2008a). The Rise of Enterprise 2.0. *Journal of Direct. Data and Digital Marketing Practice*, 9(3), 251–259. doi:10.1057/palgrave.dddmp.4350100

Bughin, J. (2009). How companies are Benefiting from Web 2.0: McKinsey Global Survey Results. *The McKinsey Quarterly*, 4.

Bughin, J., & Manyika, J. (2008). Building the Web 2.0 Enterprise: McKinsey Global Survey Results. *The McKinsey Quarterly*, 10.

Bulling, A., & Gellersen, H. (2010). Toward Mobile Eye-Based Human-Computer Interaction. *IEEE Pervasive Computing/IEEE Computer Society [and] IEEE Communications Society*, 9(4), 8–12. doi:10.1109/MPRV.2010.86

Buttussi, F., Chittaro, L., & Nadalutti, D. (2006). Bringing mobile guides and fitness activities together: a solution based on an embodied virtual trainer. In *Proceedings of the 8th conference on Human-computer interaction with mobile devices and services*, (pp. 29-36). Academic Press.

Buytendijk, F., Cripe, B., Henson, R., & Pulverman, K. (2008). *Business Management in the Age of Enterprise 2.0: Why Business Model 1.0 Will Obsolete You*. Redwood Shores, CA: Oracle Corporation.

Caillois, R. (2001). *Man, Play, and Games*. University of Illinois Press.

Caldwell, B., Cooper, M., Reid, L., & Vanderheiden, G. (2008). Web content accessibility guidelines 2.0. *W3C Recommendation, 11*.

Calvary, G., Coutez, J., Thevenin, D., Limbourg, Q., Bouillon, L., & Vanderdonckt, J. (2003). A unifying reference framework for multi-target user interfaces. *Interacting with Computers*, 15, 289–308. doi:10.1016/S0953-5438(03)00010-9

Cascio, C. J., & Sathian, K. (2001). Temporal cues contribute to tactile perception of roughness. *The Journal of Neuroscience*, 21(14), 5289–5296. PMID:11438604

Caspersen, M. E., & Christensen, H. B. (2000). *Here, there and everywhere - on the recurring use of turtle graphics in CS1*. Paper presented at the Australasian conference on Computing Education. Melbourne, Australia.

Cassidy, S. (2004). Learning styles: an overview of theories models and measures. Educational Psychology, 24(4), 419–444. doi:10.1080/0144341042000228834 doi:10.1080/0144341042000228834

Caudell, T., & Mizell, D. (1992). Augmented reality: an application of heads-up display technology to manual manufacturing processes. In *Proceedings of the Twenty-Fifth Hawaii International Conference on System Sciences* (Vol. 2, pp. 659 - 669). Washington, DC: IEEE Computer Society.

Cerezo, E., Hupont, I., Manresa-Yee, C., Varona, J., Baldassarri, S., Perales, F. J., & Seron, F. J. (2007). Real-Time Facial Expression Recognition for Natural Interaction. *Lecture Notes in Computer Science*, 4478(1), 40–47. doi:10.1007/978-3-540-72849-8_6

Černeková, Z., & Malerczyk, C. Nikolaidis, N., & Pitas, I. (2008). Single Camera Pointing Gesture Recognition for Interaction in Edutainment Applications. In *Proceedings of the 24th Spring Conference on Computer Graphics* (pp. 121 – 125). New York, NY: ACM.

Chamorro-Koc, M. (2007). *Experience, Context-of-Use and the Design of Product Usability*. (Doctoral dissertation). Queensland University of Technology.

Chee, Y., Franke, K., Froumentin, M., Madhvanath, S., Magaña, J., & Pakosz, G. ... Yaeger, L. (2011). *Ink Markup Language (InkML) W3C Recommendation*. Retrieved October 20, 2013, from http://www.w3.org/TR/InkML

Chen, Y. H. (2010). *Navigation Using Portable Digital Architectural Guides*. (Unpublished Ph.D. Thesis). University of Liverpool, Liverpool, UK.

Cheng, M. F. (1968). Tactile-kinesthetic perception of length. *The American Journal of Psychology*, 81(1), 74–82. doi:10.2307/1420809 PMID:5661568

Chen, J., & Dibb, S. (2010). Consumer Trust in the Online Retail Context: Exploring the Antecedents and Consequences. *Psychology and Marketing*, 27(4), 323–346. doi:10.1002/mar.20334

Childers, T. L., Houston, M. J., & Heckler, S. E. (1985). Measurement of individual differences in visual versus verbal information processing. The Journal of Consumer Research, 12, 125–134. doi:10.1086/208501

Chimecloud. (2013). Retrieved October 14, 2013 from http://vimeo.com/53239679

Chiti, S., & Leporini, B. (2012). Accessibility of android-based mobile devices: a prototype to investigate interaction with blind users. In *Proceedings of the 13th international conference on Computers Helping People with Special Needs*. Linz, Austria: Academic Press.

Chittaro, L., & Burigat, S. (2005). Augmenting audio messages with visual directions in mobile guides: an evaluation of three approaches. In *Proceedings of the 7th international conference on Human computer interaction with mobile devices & services*, (pp. 107-114). Academic Press.

Choquette, S. et al. (2008). Accelerometer-based wireless body area network to estimate intensity of therapy in post-acute rehabilitation. *Journal of Neuroengineering and Rehabilitation*, *5*, 20. doi:10.1186/1743-0003-5-20 PMID:18764954

Christensen, K., Monsen, E., Hansen, J. V., Andersen, M., & Safiri, S. (2013). Physical-digital Interaction Design for Children. In *Proceeding of the 9th Student Interaction Design Research (SIDeR 2013)*. Aarhus.

Christopher Frauenberger, J. G. (2011). Designing Technology for Children with Special Needs - Bridging Perspectives through Participatory Design. *CoDesign: International Journal of CoCreation in Design and the Arts*, *7*, 1–28. doi:10.1080/15710882.2011.587013

Chuter, A., & Yesilada, Y. (2009). *Relationship Between Mobile Web Best Practices (MWBP) and Web Content Accessibility Guidelines (WCAG)*. Academic Press.

Clark, J. (2003). Building accessible websites Indianapolis: New Riders. Tech. rep., ISBN 0-7357-1150-x

Cleland, J. (2011). The media and football supporters: a changing relationship. *Media Culture & Society*, *33*(2). doi:10.1177/0163443710393866

COLLADA 1.4 Specification Reference Card. (n.d.). Retrieved April 11, 2013 from http://www.khronos.org/developers/view_online/12577249

Collins, A., & Halverson, R. (2009). *Rethinking education in the age of technology: the digital revolution and schooling in America*. New York: Teachers College Press.

Community, S. A. K. A. I. (2013). *Sakai Project | collaboration and learning - for educators by educators.* Retrieved October 20, 2013, from http://sakaiproject.org

Consoli, D. (2011). *The web community manager in SMEs: a key figure to implement a model of Enterprise 2.0. itAIS 2011.* Paper presented at the VIII Conference of the Italian Chapter of AIS Information Systems: a crossroads for Organization, Management, Accounting and Engineering Viale Pola 12. Roma, Italy.

Cooper, G. (1991). Context and Its Representation. *Interacting with Computers*, *3*, 243–252. doi:10.1016/0953-5438(91)90015-T

Cornett, C. E. (1983). What you should know about teaching and learning styles. Bloomington, IN: Phi Delta Kappa Educational Foundation.

Cottrell, N. B. (1972). Social facilitation. In C. G. McClintock (Ed.), *Experimental Social Psychology* (pp. 185–236). New York: Holt.

Cottrell, N. B., Wack, D. L., Sekerak, G. J., & Rittle, R. H. (1968). Social facilitation of dominant responses by the presence of an audience and the mere presence of others. *Journal of Personality and Social Psychology*, *9*, 245–250. doi:10.1037/h0025902 PMID:5666972

Cox, B., & Dale, G. (2002). Key quality factors in web site design and use: an examination. *International Journal of Quality & Reliability Management*, *19*, 862–888. doi:10.1108/02656710210434784

Crolley, L. (2008). Using the Internet to strengthen its identity: the case of Spanish football. *Sport in Society: Cultures, Commerce, Media. Politics*, *11*(6), 722–738.

Crystal, A., & Ellington, B. (2004). Task analysis and human-computer interaction: approaches, techniques, and levels of analysis. In *Proceedings of the Tenth Americas Conference on Information Systems*, (pp. 391-397). New York: Association for Information Systems.

Cuban, L. (1986). *Teachers and Machines: The Classroom Use of Technology Since 1920*. Teachers College Press.

Cuban, L. (2001). *Oversold and underused: computers in the classroom*. Harvard University Press.

Culén, A. L., & Gasparini, A. (2011). iPad: a new classroom technology? A report from two pilot studies. In Information Sciences and e-Society (pp. 199–208). University of Zagreb.

Culén, A. L., Bratteteig, T., Pandey, S., & Srivastava, S. (2013). The Child-to-Child (C2C) Method: Participatory Design for, with and by Children in a Children's Museum. *IADIS International Journal on WWW/Internet, 11*(2), 92–113.

Culén, A. L., derVelden, M., & Karpova, A. (2013). Challenges in Designing Learning Apps for and with Vulnerable Children. In *Proceedings of CHI 2013 Workshop on Designing for and with Vulnerable People*. Paris, France: ACM.

Culén, A. L., & Gasparini, A. (2012). Situated Techno-Cools: factors that contribute to making technology cool and the study case of iPad in education. *PsychNology Journal, 10*(2), 117–139.

Culén, A. L., & Gasparini, A. A. (2012). When is a Student-Centered, Technology Supported Learning a Success? *International Journal of Digital Information and Wireless Communications, 2*(3), 256–269.

Curry, L. (2002). Individual Differences in Cognitive Style, Learning Style and Instructional Preference in Medical Education. In G. Norman, C. Van der Vleuten & D. Newble (Eds.), International Handbook of Research in Medical Education, (vol. 7, pp. 263-276). Academic Press.

Curtis, N. (2009). *Modular Web Design: Creating Reusable Components for User Experience Design*. New Riders Pub.

Cyr, D., Hassanein, K., Head, M., & Ivanov, A. (2007). The role of social presence in establishing loyalty in e-Service environments. Interacting with Computers, 19, 43–56. doi:10.1016/j.intcom.2006.07.010

Cyr, D., Head, M., & Larios, H. (2010). Colour appeal in website design within and across cultures: A multi-method evaluation. International Journal of Human-Computer Studies, 68(1-2), 1–21. doi:10.1016/j.ijhcs.2009.08.005

Da Silva, A. C., & da Rocha, H. V. (2013). InkBlog: A Pen-Based Blog Tool for e-Learning Environments. *Issues in Informing Science and Information Technology, 10*, 121–135.

Dashiell, J. F. (1930). An Experimental Analysis of Some Group Effects. *Journal of Abnormal and Social Psychology, 25*(2), 190–199. doi:10.1037/h0075144

Davis, F. D. (1989). Perceived usefulness, perceived ease of use and user acceptance of information technology. *Management Information Systems Quarterly, 13*(3), 319–340. doi:10.2307/249008

Davis, F. D., Bagozzi, R. P., & Warshaw, P. R. (1989). User acceptance of computer technology: a comparison of two theoretical models. *Management Science, 35*(8), 982–1003. doi:10.1287/mnsc.35.8.982

Davis, F. D., Bagozzi, R. P., & Warshaw, P. R. (1992). Extrinsic and intrinsic motivation to use computers in the workplace. *Journal of Applied Social Psychology, 22*, 1111–1132. doi:10.1111/j.1559-1816.1992.tb00945.x

Day, R. H., & Avery, G. C. (1970). Absence of the horizontal-vertical illusion in haptic space. *Journal of Experimental Psychology, 83*(1), 172–173. doi:10.1037/h0028514 PMID:5436478

Day, R. H., Wong, T. S., & Brooks, C. I. (1971). Radial and tangential movement directions as determinants of the haptic illusion in an L figure. *Journal of Experimental Psychology, 90*(2), 19–22. doi:10.1037/h0030155 PMID:5541561

De Saulles, M. (2008). Never Too Small to Join the Party. *Information World Review, 249*, 10–12.

Deco, G., Scarano, L., & Soto-Faraco, S. (2007). Weber's Law in Decision Making: Integrating Behavioral Data in Humans with a Neurophysiological Model. *The Journal of Neuroscience, 27*(42), 11192–11200. doi:10.1523/JNEUROSCI.1072-07.2007 PMID:17942714

Denis, C., & Karsenty, L. (2004). Inter-usability of multi-device systems – a conceptual framework. In A. Seffah, & H. Javahery (Eds.), *Multiple User Interfaces: Cross-Platform Applications and Context-Aware Interfaces* (pp. 373–386). Chichester, UK: John Wiley & Sons, Ltd.

Dépeault1, A., Meftah, El-Mehdi, & Chapman, C. E. (2008). Tactile Speed Scaling: Contributions of Time & Space. *Journal of Neurophysiology, 99*, 1422-1434.

Depuydt, S., Vanattenhoven, J., & Engelen, J. (2006). CityInMyPocket: Digital Walking Guides.[ELPUB.]. *Proceedings of, ELPUB2006*, 17–26.

Deregowski, J., & Ellis, H. D. (1972). Effect of stimulus orientation upon haptic perception of the horizontal-vertical illusion. *Journal of Experimental Psychology*, *95*(1), 14–19. doi:10.1037/h0033264 PMID:5070280

Desideri, L., Roentgen, U., Hoogerwerf, E.-J., & de Witte, L. (2013). Recommending assistive technology (AT) for children with multiple disabilities: A systematic review and qualitative synthesis of models and instruments for AT professionals. *Technology and Disability*, *25*(1), 3–13.

Desmet, P. M. A., & Hekkert, P. (2007). Framework of Product Experience. *International Journal of Design*, *1*(1), 57–66.

Deterding, S. (2013). Designing Gamification: Creating Gameful and Playful Experiences. In *Proceedings of CHI 2013*. ACM.

Device. (2013). Retrieved October 10, 2013 from http://www.deviceproject.eu/modules/news/article.php?storyid=6

Dewey, J. (2008). *Democracy and Education: An Introduction to the Philosophy of Education*. Radford, VA: Wilder Publications.

Diener, E. (1979). Deindividuation, Self-awareness and Disinhibition. *Journal of Personality and Social Psychology*, *37*(7), 1160–1171. doi:10.1037/0022-3514.37.7.1160

DIN EN ISO 9241-110:2008-09. (2006). *Ergonomie der Mensch-System-Interaktion - Teil 110: Grundsätze der Dialoggestaltung* (ISO 9241-110:2006). Deutsche Fassung EN ISO 9241-110:2006.

DIN EN ISO 9241-210:2011-01. (2010). *Ergonomie der Mensch-System-Interaktion - Teil 210: Prozess zur Gestaltung gebrauchstauglicher interaktiver Systeme* (ISO 9241-210:2010). Deutsche Fassung EN ISO 9241-210:2010.

DiSalvo, C., Sengers, P., & Brynjarsdóttir, H. (2010). Mapping the landscape of sustainable HCI. In *Proceedings of the SIGCHI Conference on Human Factors in Computing Systems* (pp.1975-1984). New York, NY: ACM.

Dolles, H., & Söderman, S. (2005). *Globalization of Sports - The Case of Professional Football and its International Management Challenges*. Retrieved December 10, 201, from http://dijtokyo.org/doc/WP05_1GlobalizationOfSportsProfessionalFootballDollesSoederman.pdf

Domínguez, A., Saenz-de-Navarrete, J., de-Marcos, L., Fernández-Sanz, L., Pagés, C., & Martínez-Herráiz, J.-J. (2013). Gamifying learning experiences: Practical implications and outcomes. *Computers & Education*, *63*, 380–392. doi:10.1016/j.compedu.2012.12.020

Dourish, P. (2006). Re-space-ing place: place and space ten years on. In *Proceedings of the 2006 20th anniversary conference on Computer supported cooperative work* (pp. 299-308). New York, NY: ACM.

Dourish, P. (2010). HCI and environmental sustainability: the politics of design and the design of politics. In *Proceedings of the 8th ACM Conference on Designing Interactive Systems* (pp. 1-10).). New York, NY: ACM.

Dourish, P. (2004). What We Talk About When We Talk About Context. *Personal and Ubiquitous Computing*, *8*(1), 19–30. doi:10.1007/s00779-003-0253-8

Dourish, P. (2004). *Where the Action Is: The Foundation of Embodied Interaction*. The MIT Press.

Downs, R. M., & Stea, D. (1973). Theory. In R. M. Downs, & D. Stea (Eds.), *Image and Environment* (pp. 1–13). Chicago: Aldine Press.

Druin, A. (2009). *Mobile Technology for Children: Designing for Interaction and Learning*. Morgan Kaufmann.

Dumas, B., Lalanne, D., & Oviatt, S. (2009). Multimodal Interfaces: A Survey of Principles, Models and Frameworks. In *Human-Machine Interaction* (pp. 3–26). Berlin, Germany: Springer. doi:10.1007/978-3-642-00437-7_1

Durand, F. (2002). Limitations of the medium and pictorial techniques. In *Perceptual and Artistic Principles for Effective Computer Depiction, Course Notes for ACM SIGGRAPH 2002*, (pp. 27-45). ACM. Retrieved from http://people.csail.mit.edu/fredo/SIG02_ArtScience/

Eighmey, J., & McCord, L. (1998). Adding value in the information age: uses and gratifications of sites on the World Wide Web: the World Wide Web presents new challenges for advertisers and consumers alike. *Journal of Business Research*, *41*(3), 187–194. doi:10.1016/S0148-2963(97)00061-1

Epicor. (2008). *Bringing Web 2.0 to the Enterprise: Leveraging Social Computing Technologies for ERP Applications*. Epicor White Paper. Irvine, CA: Epicor.

European Commission. (2003). The new SME Definition – User guide and model declaration. *Enterprise and Industry Publication*. Retrieved November 30, 2013, from http://ec.europa.eu/enterprise/policies/sme/files/sme_definition/sme_user_guide_en.pdf

Eysenck, M. W., & Keane, M. T. (2005). *Cognitive psychology: a student's handbook* (5th ed.). New York: Psychology Press.

Faineteau, H., Gentaz, E., & Viviani, P. (2003). The kinaesthetic perception of Euclidean distance: a study of the detour effect. *Experimental Brain Research, Springer*, *152*(2), 166–172. doi:10.1007/s00221-003-1526-1 PMID:12898094

Fernandes, S., Kamienski, C., Kelner, J., Mariz, D., & Sadok, D. (2008). A stratified traffic sampling methodology for seeing the big picture. *Computer Networks*, *52*(14), 2677–2689. doi:10.1016/j.comnet.2008.05.011

Fernández-López, Á., Rodríguez-Fórtiz, M. J., Rodríguez-Almendros, M. L., & Martínez-Segura, M. J. (2013). Mobile learning technology based on iOS devices to support students with special education needs. *Computers & Education*, *61*, 77–90. doi:10.1016/j.compedu.2012.09.014

Ferrara, J. (2012). *Playful Design*. Rosenfeld Media.

Festinger, L., Pepitone, A., & Newcomb, T. (1952). Some consequences of deindividuation in a group. *Journal of Abnormal and Social Psychology*, *47*, 382–389. doi:10.1037/h0057906 PMID:14937978

Fielding, R. (2000). *Architectural styles and the design of network-based software architectures*. (Ph.D. dissertation). University of California.

Flowers, J. H. et al. (1996). Desktop Data Sonification: Comments on Flowers et al. *ACM Transactions on Applied Perception*, *2*(4), 473–476. doi:10.1145/1101530.1101545

Frauenberger, C. (2009). *Auditory Display Design*. (Unpublished PhD Thesis). Queen Mary University of London, London, UK.

Fremtek. (2013). Retrieved October 10, 2013 from http://www.insero.dk/Uddannelse/projekter-og-aktiviteter/Fremtek

Fun on Your iPad with Crazy Face. (2010). *AppAdvice*. Retrieved from http://appadvice.com/appnn/2010/03/fun-ipad-crazy-face

Garbarino, E., & Strahilevitz, M. (2004). Gender differences in the perceived risk of buying online and the effects of receiving a site recommendation. Journal of Business Research, 57(7), 768–775. doi:10.1016/S0148-2963(02)00363-6

Garcia-Hernandez, N., Tsagarakis, N. G., & Caldwell, D. G. (2011). Feeling through tactile displays: a study on the effect of the array density and size on the discrimination of tactile patterns. *IEEE Transactions on Haptics*, *4*(2), 100–110. doi:10.1109/TOH.2010.59

Gardner, H. (1983). *Frames of Mind: The Theory of Multiple Intelligences*. Basic Books.

Gasparini, A. A., & Culén, A. L. (2012). Tablet PCs–An Assistive Technology for Students with Reading Difficulties? In *Proceedings of ACHI 2012, The Fifth International Conference on Advances in Computer-Human Interactions* (pp. 28–34). IARIA.

Gee, J. (2003). *What video games have to teach us about learning and literacy*. Palgrave Macmillan.

Gehkre, D., & Turban, E. (1999). Determinants of successful website design: relative importance and recommendations for effectiveness. In *Proceedings of the 32nd Hawaii International Conference on System Sciences*. Los Alamitos, CA: IEEE.

Geissler, G. L., Zinkhan, M. Z., & Watson, R. T. (2006). The influence of website complexity on consumer attention, attitudes, and purchase intent. Journal of Advertising, 35(2), 69–80. doi:10.1080/00913367.2006.10639232

Gentner, D., & Stevens, A. L. (1983). *Mental Models.* Hillsdale, NJ: Lawrence Erlbaum Associates.

Giakoumis, D., Votis, K., & Tzovaras, D. (2013). Introducing web service accessibility assessment techniques through a unified quality of service context. *Service Oriented Computing and Applications,* 1–16.

Gibson, J. J. (1962). Observations on active touch. *Psychological Review, 69*(6), 477–491. doi:10.1037/h0046962 PMID:13947730

Gleeso, B. T., Horschel, S. K., & Provancher, W. R. (2010). Design of a fingertip-mounted tactile display with tangential skin displacement feedback. *IEEE Transactions on Haptics, 3*(4), 297–301. doi:10.1109/TOH.2010.8

Goldsmith, S. (2012). *Universal Design.* Routledge.

Golledge, R. G. (1999). *Wayfinding behavior: cognitive mapping and other spatial processes.* Baltimore, MD: The Johns Hopkins University Press.

Google Maps. (2013), Retrieved November 22, 2013, from https://maps.google.com.tw/

Gordeyeva, I. (2010). *Enterprise 2.0: theoretical foundations of social media tools influence on knowledge sharing practices in organizations.* (Master's thesis). University of Twente.

Grasha, A. F. (1996). Teaching with style: A practical guide to enhancing learning by understanding teaching and learning styles. Pittsburgh, PA: Alliance Publishers.

Green, R. (1999). Football information services: fanzines, Match of the Day and the modem.[]. MCB UP Ltd.]. *Proceedings of Aslib, 51,* 20–29. doi:10.1108/EUM0000000006958

Grover, S., & Pea, R. (2013). Using a discourse-intensive pedagogy and android's app. inventor for introducing computational concepts to middle school students. In *Proceedings of the 44th ACM technical symposium on Computer science education* (pp. 723-728). Denver, CO: ACM Press.

Gruenstein, A., McGraw, I., & Badr, I. (2008). The WAMI Toolkit for Developing, Deploying, and Evaluating Web-Accessible Multimodal Interfaces. In *Proceedings of 10th International Conference on Multimodal Interfaces* (pp. 141-148). New York, NY: ACM. doi:10.1145/1452392.1452420

Guerin, B., & Innes, J. M. (1984). Explanations of Social Facilitation: A Review. *Current Psychology (New Brunswick, N.J.), 3*(2), 32–52. doi:10.1007/BF02686548

Gullo, B. (1998). An investigation of cognitive tempo and its effects on evaluating kindergarten children's academic and social competencies. Early Child Development and Care, 34, 201–215. doi:10.1080/0300443880340115

Haak, van den, M.J., Jong, de, M.D.T., & Schellens, P.J. (2007). Evaluation of a Municipal Website: three variants of the think-aloud method compared. *Technical Communication, 54*(1), 58-71.

Haggard, P., Newman, C., Blundell, J., & Andrew, H. (2000). The perceived position of the hand in space. *Perception & Psychophysics, 68*(2), 363–377. doi:10.3758/BF03205556 PMID:10723215

Halim, Z., et al. (2006). Sonification: A Novel Approach towards Data mining. In *Proceedings of IEEE International Conference on Emerging Technologies.* Peshawar, Pakistan: IEEE.

Halliday, M. A. K. (2002). *Linguistic studies of text and discourse.* London: Continuum International Publishing.

Hamburg, I., Engert, S., & Anke, P. (2007). Communities of Practice and Web 2.0 to support learning in SMEs. In Proceeding of RoEduNet. RoEduNet.

Hamker, A. (2003). *Emotion und ästhetische Erfahrung. Internationale Hochschulschriften* (Vol. 407). Münster: Waxmann Verlag.

Harper, S., Michailidou, E., & Stevens, R. (2009). Toward a definition of visual complexity as an implicit measure of cognitive load. ACM Transactions on Applied Perception, 6(2), 1–10. doi:10.1145/1498700.1498704

Harrison, S., & Dourish, P. (1996). Re-place-ing space: the roles of space and place in collaborative systems. In *Proceedings of the 1996 ACM conference on Computer supported cooperative work* (pp. 67-76). New York, NY: ACM.

Hart, T. A., Chaparro, B. S., & Halcomb, C. G. (2008). Evaluating websites for older adults: adherence to 'senior-friendly' guidelines and end-user performance. Behaviour & Information Technology, 27(3), 191–199. doi:10.1080/01449290600802031

Hartley, J. (1998). Learning and Studying: A research perspective. London: Routledge. doi:10.4324/9780203270189

Hasselbring, T. S., & Glaser, C. H. W. (2000). Use of Computer Technology to Help Students with Special Needs. *The Future of Children, 10*(2), 102–122. doi:10.2307/1602691 PMID:11255702

Hassenzahl, M. (2008). User Experience (UX), Towards an Experiential Perspective on Product Quality. In *Proceedings from IHM'08: The 20th International Conference of the Association Francophone D'Interaction Homme Machine* (pp. 11-15). New York, NY: ACM Press.

Hassenzahl, M. (2010). Experience Design: Technology for All the Right Reasons. *Synthesis Lectures on Human-Centered Informatics, 3*(1), 1–95. doi:10.2200/S00261ED1V01Y201003HCI008

Hassenzahl, M., Burmester, M., & Koller, F. (2003). AttrakDiff: Ein Fragebogen zur Messung wahrgenommener hedonischer und pragmatischer Qualität. In G. Szwillus, & J. Ziegler (Eds.), *Mensch & Computer 2003: Interaktion in Bewegung* (pp. 78–82). München: Oldenbourg. doi:10.1007/978-3-322-80058-9_19

Hassenzahl, M., & Tractinsky, N. (2006). User Experience - A Research Agenda. *Behaviour & Information Technology, 25*(2), 91–97. doi:10.1080/01449290500330331

Hayes, B. (2008). Gartner's Seven IT Grand Challenges. *Communications of the ACM, 51*(7), 10.

Heaps, C., & Handel, C. H. (1999). Similarity and features of natural textures. Journal of Experimental Psychology. Human Perception and Performance, 25, 299–320. doi:10.1037/0096-1523.25.2.299

Heckler, S. E., Childers, T. L., & Houston, M. J. (1993). On the Construct Validity of the SOP Scale. Journal of Mental Imagery, 17(3-4), 119–132.

Heidmann, F., Hermann, F., & Peissner, M. (2003). Interactive Maps on Mobile, Location-Based Systems: Design Solutions and Usability Testing. In *Proceedings of the 21st International Cartographic Conference*, (pp. 1299-1306). Academic Press.

Hekkert, P., & Van Dijk, M. (2001). Designing from Context: Foundations of the VIP Approach and Two Applications. In P. Lloyd & H. Christiaans (Eds.), *Designing in Context: Proceedings of Design Thinking Research Symposium*. Delft, The Netherlands: DUP Science.

Henchy, T., & Glass, D. C. (1968). Evaluation apprehension and the social facilitation of dominant and subordinate responses. *Journal of Personality and Social Psychology, 10*(4), 446–454. doi:10.1037/h0026814 PMID:5708047

Herczeg, M. (2005). *Software-Ergonomie*. München: Oldenbourg.

Hermann, T., et al. (2002). Sonifications for EEG data analysis. In *Proceedings of the 8th International Conference on Auditory Display*, (pp. 37-41). Kyoto, Japan: The International Community for Auditory Display.

Hermann, T. et al. (2011). *The Sonification Handbook*. Berlin: Logos Publishing.

Hinchcliffe, D. (2010). Why all the fuss about Web 2.0. *Infonomics, 24*(1), 26–31.

Hollins, M., & Goble, A. K. (1988). Perception of the length of voluntary movements. *Somatosensory & Motor Research, 5*(4), 335–348. doi:10.3109/07367228809144635 PMID:3381043

Holtzblatt, L., & Tierney, M. L. (2011). Measuring the effectiveness of social media on an innovation process. In *Extended Abstracts on Human Factors in Computing Systems* (CHI '11) (pp. 697-712). New York, NY: ACM.

Hourcade, J. P., Bullock-Rest, N. E., & Hansen, T. E. (2012). Multitouch tablet applications and activities to enhance the social skills of children with autism spectrum disorders. *Personal and Ubiquitous Computing, 16*(2), 157–168. doi:10.1007/s00779-011-0383-3

How Does ARToolkit Work ? (n.d.). Retrieved October 10, 2013 from http://www.hitl.washington.edu/artoolkit/documentation/userarwork.htm

Hsu, H. (2011). The Potential of Kinect in Education. *International Journal of Information and Education Technology, 1*(5).

Huang, X., Baker, J., & Reddy, R. (2014). A Historical Perspective of Speech Recognition. *Communications of the ACM, 57*(1), 94–103. doi:10.1145/2500887

Hur, Y., Ko, Y. J., & Claussen, C. L. (2011). Acceptance of sports websites: a conceptual model. *International Journal of Sports Marketing & Sponsorship, 12*(3), 209–224.

Hutchinson, H. B., Bederson, B. B., & Druin, A. (2006). The evolution of the International Children's Digital Library searching and browsing interface. In *Proceedings of the 2006 Conference on Interaction Design and Children*. Academic Press.

Hwang, J. Y., & Holtzman, H. (2012). SparkInfo: designing a social space for co-creation of audiovisual elements and multimedia comments. In *Extended Abstracts on Human Factors in Computing Systems* (CHI '12) (pp. 1559-1564). New York, NY: ACM.

Ideum. (2013). *GestureML*. Retrieved October 20, 2013, from http://www.gestureml.org/

Ihlström, C., & Lundberg, J. (2004). A genre perspective on online newspaper front page design. *Journal of Web Engineering, 3*(1), 50–74.

Ikonen, V., Hakulinen, J., Kivinen, T., Aloja, M., Hokkanen, L., Ruutikainen, P., et al. (2010). IHME = Miracle - Make, Imagine and Research Applications for Computerised Living Environments. In *Proceedings of the 14th International Academic MindTrek Conference: Envisioning Future Media Environments* (pp. 3-6). New York, NY: ACM.

Isaías, P., Miranda, P., & Pífano, S. (2009). Critical Success Factors for Web 2.0 - A Reference Framework. In *Proceedings of the 3rd International Conference on Online Communities and Social Computing: Held as Part of HCI International 2009* (OCSC '09). Springer-Verlag.

Isaías, P., & Coelho, F. (2013). Web 2.0 Tools Adoption Model: A Study on Online Retailers. *International Journal of Information Communication Technologies and Human Development*. doi:10.4018/jicthd.2013070104

Isaías, P., Pífano, S., & Miranda, P. (2011). Social Network Sites: Modeling the New Business-Customer Relationship. In *Social Networking and Community Behavior Modeling: Qualitative and Quantitative Measures*. Hershey, PA: IGI Global. doi:10.4018/978-1-61350-444-4.ch014

ISO. Moser, C., Fuchsberger, V., Neureiter, L., Sellner, W., & Tscheligi, M. (2012). *Revisiting personas: the making-of for special user groups*. Paper presented at CHI '12. Austin, TX.

Iversen, O. S., Halskov, K., & Leong, T. W. (2010). Re-kindling values in participatory design. In *Proceedings of the 11th Biennial Participatory Design Conference* (pp. 91–100). New York, NY: ACM.

Jansson, G., & Pedersen, P. (2005). Obtaining geographical information from a virtual map with a haptic mouse. In *Proceedings of XXII International Cartographic Conference*. Academic Press.

Jarvenpaa, S. L., & Todd, P. A. (1997). Consumer reactions to electronic shopping on the World Wide Web. *International Journal of Electronic Commerce, 1*(2), 59–88.

Jedd, M. (2008). Enterprise 2.0. *AIIM E-Doc Magazine, 22*(1), 26–29.

Jepsen, A., Dondana, M., & Reiter, L. (2013). Chime-cloud - An Evocative, Responsive Sound Installation. In *Proceeding of the 9th Student Interaction Design Research (SIDeR 2013)*. Aarhus.

Jordan, P. W. (1999). Pleasure with Products: Human Factors for Body, Mind and Soul. In W. S. Green, & P. W. Jordan (Eds.), *Human Factors in Product Design: Current Practice and Future Trends* (pp. 206–217). London: Taylor and Francis.

Jordan, P. W. (2000). *Designing Pleasurable Products*. London: Taylor and Francis.

Jovanov, E., et al. (2009). Avatar – a Multi-sensory System for Real Time Body Position Monitoring. In *Proceedings of IEEE Eng Med Biol Soc*. IEEE. doi: 10.1109/IEMBS.2009.5334774

Jovanov, E. et al. (2005). A wireless body area network of intelligent motion sensors for computer assisted physical rehabilitation. *Journal of Neuroengineering and Rehabilitation*. doi:10.1186/1743-0003-2-6 PMID:15740621

Jung, H., Bardzell, S., Blevis, E., Pierce, J., & Stolterman, E. (2011). How deep is your love: deep narratives of ensoulment and heirloom status. *International Journal of Design*, 5(1), 59–71.

Kaasinen, E., Koskela-Huotari, K., Ikonen, V., Niemelä, M., & Näkki, P. (2012). Three approaches to co-creating services with users. In *Proceedings 4th International Conference on Applied Human Factors and Ergonomics (AHFE)*. Stoughton, WI: USA Publishing.

Kadlec, T. (2012). *Implementing Responsive Web Design: Building Sites for Anywhere, Everywhere Web (Voices that Matter)*. Berkeley, CA: New Riders.

Kalgaonkar, K., & Raj, B. (2009). One-handed Gesture Recognition using Ultrasonic Doppler Sonar. In *Proceedings of the 2009 IEEE International Conference on Acoustics, Speech and Signal Processing* (pp. 1889–1892). Washington, DC: IEEE Computer Society.

Kaplan, S., Kaplan, R., & Wendt, S. (1972). Rated preference and complexity for natural and urban visual material. Perception & Psychophysics, 12, 354–356. doi:10.3758/BF03207221

Karampelas, P., Basdekis, I., & Stephanidis, C. (2009). Web User Interface Design Strategy: Designing for Device Independence. In C. Stephanidis, (Ed.), *Universal Access in Human-Computer Interaction - Addressing Diversity – Volume 5 of the Proceedings of the 13th International Conference on Human-Computer Interaction* (HCI International 2009). San Diego, CA: Springer.

Karat, C., et al. (1992). Comparison of empirical testing and walkthrough methods in user interface evaluation. In *Proceedings of CHI92 Human Factors in Computing Systems*, (pp. 397-404). New York: ACM Publishing.

Karpova, A. (2013). *Heterogeneity in Technology Design for Children with Special Education Needs: Changing Perspective from a Group to an Individual*. (Master thesis). DUO, University of Oslo.

Karpova, A., & Culén, A. (2013). Challenges in Designing an App. for a Special Education Class. In *Proceedings of the IADIS International Conference on Interfaces and Human-Computer Interaction 2013* (pp. 95–102). IADIS.

Karpov, A., Carbini, S., Ronzhin, A., & Viallet, J. E. (2008). Two SIMILAR Different Speech and Gestures Multimodal Interfaces. In D. Tzovaras (Ed.), *Multimodal user Interfaces: From signal to interaction* (pp. 155–184). Berlin: Springer. doi:10.1007/978-3-540-78345-9_7

Kato, H., & Billinghurst, M. (1999). Marker Tracking and HMD Calibration for a Video-based Augmented Reality Conferencing System. In *Proceedings of 2nd IEEE and ACM International Workshop on Augmented Reality* (pp. 85 - 94). Washington, DC: IEEE Computer Society.

Kazman, R., & Bass, L. (1994). *Toward Deriving Software Architectures From Quality Attributes* (Technical Report, CMU/SEI-94-TR-10). Software Engineering Institute, Carnegie Mellon University. Retrieved October 20, 2013 from http://www.sei.cmu.edu/reports/94tr010.pdf

KGS Corp. (n.d.). Retrieved from http://www.kgs-jpn.co.jp/

Kim, D. J., Yue, K.-B., Hall, S. P., & Gates, T. (2009). Global Diffusion of the Internet XV: Web 2.0 Technologies, Principles, and Applications: A Conceptual Framework from Technology Push and Demand Pull Perspective. *Communications of the Association for Information Systems*, (24): 657–672.

Kim, H. D., Lee, I., & Lee, C. K. (2013). Building Web 2.0 enterprises: A study of small and medium enterprises in the United States. *International Small Business Journal*, 31(2), 156–174. doi:10.1177/0266242611409785

Kinect for Windows Blog. (2013). Retrieved October 10, 2013 from http://blogs.msdn.com/b/kinectforwindows/archive/2013/05/23/the-new-generation-kinect-for-windows-sensor-is-coming-next-year.aspx

Klein, G., & Murray, D. (2007). Parallel Tracking and Mapping for Small AR Workspaces. In *Proceedings of the 6th IEEE and ACM International Symposium on Mixed and Augmented Reality* (pp. 225 – 234). Washington, DC: IEEE Computer Society.

Klingberg, T., Fernell, E., Olesen, P. J., Johnson, M., Gustafsson, P., & Dahlström, K. et al. (2005). Computerized training of working memory in children with ADHD - a randomized, controlled trial. *Journal of the American Academy of Child and Adolescent Psychiatry, 44*(2), 177–186. doi:10.1097/00004583-200502000-00010 PMID:15689731

Knight, M., & Brown, A. (1999). *Working in Virtual Environments through appropriate Physical Interfaces*. Paper presented at the 17th eCAADe Conference. Liverpool, UK.

Knight, M., Chen, Y.-H., Winchester, M., & Brown, A. (2008). *Perception, Placement and Wayfinding Applied to Mobile Architectural Guides*. Paper presented at the 26th eCAADe Conference. Antwerp, Belgium.

Knight, M., Saeed, G., Chen, Y.-H., & Brown, A. (2007). *Remote Location in an Urban Digital Model*. Paper presented at the 25th eCAADe Conference. Frankfurt, Germany.

Köhler-Krün, H. (2009). Best Practices for Implementing E2.0. *Infonomics, 23*(4), 40–45.

Kompan. (2013). Retrieved October 10, 2013 from http://icon.kompan.com/ retrieved 2013-10-10

Kramer, G. et al. (1999). *The sonification report: Status of the field and research agenda (Technical report)*. National Science Foundation.

Kramer, R., Modsching, M., & Hagen, K. T. (2005). Development and evaluation of a context-driven, mobile tourist guide. *International Journal of Pervasive Computing and Communications, 3*(4), 378–399. doi:10.1108/17427370710863121

Kray, C., Elting, C., Laakso, K., & Coors, V. (2003). Presenting route instructions on mobile devices. In *Proceedings of the 8th international conference on Intelligent user interfaces*, (pp. 117-124). Academic Press.

Kriemadis, T., Kotsovos, A., & Kartakoullis, N. (2009). A Strategy for managing customer relations on the internet: evidence from the football Sector. *Direct Marketing: An International Journal, 3*(4), 229–243. doi:10.1108/17505930911000847

Kritzenberger, H. (2012). Understanding Player Experience in Educational Games. In T. Amiel & B. Wilson (Eds.), *Proceedings of World Conference on Educational Multimedia, Hypermedia and Telecommunications 2012* (pp. 1329-1335). Chesapeake, VA: AACE.

Kuchenbecker, K. J., Provancher, W. R., Niemeyer, G., & Cutkosky, M. R. (2004). Haptic display of contact location. In *Proceedings of the 12th International Symposium on Haptic Interfaces for Virtual Environment and Teleoperator Systems (HAPTICS '04)*, (pp. 40-47). HAPTICS.

Kugler, L. (n.d.). Goodbye, Computer Mouse. *Communications of the ACM, 51*(9), 56.

Kukulska-Hulme, A., & Traxler, J. (2005). *Mobile learning: a handbook for educators and trainers*. Routledge.

Kurkovsky, S. (2009). *Multimodality in Mobile Computing and Mobile Devices: Methods for Adaptable Usability*. Hershey, PA: IGI Global. doi:10.4018/978-1-60566-978-6

Kurz, D., & Himane, S. (2011). Inertial-sensor Aligned Visual Feature Descriptors. In *Proceedings of the 2011 IEEE Conference on Computer Vision and Pattern Recognition* (pp. 161 –166). Washington, DC: IEEE Computer Society.

Kyung, K.-U., Choi, H., Kwon, D. S., & Son, S. W. (2004). Interactive mouse systems providing haptic feedback during the exploration in virtual environment. In *Proceedings of Computer and Information Sciences-ISCIS 2004*. Springer. doi:10.1007/978-3-540-30182-0_15

Laakso, K. (2002). *Evaluating the use of navigable three-dimensional maps in mobile devices*. (Unpublished master dissertation). University of Helsinki, Helsinki, Finland.

Laakso, K., Gjesdal, O., & Sulebak, J. R. (2003). Tourist information and navigation support by using 3D maps displayed on mobile devices. In *Proceedings of the Mobile HCI Workshop on HCI in Mobile Guides*, (pp. 34-39). HCI.

Lahart, J. (2009, November 13). Tinkering Makes Comeback Amid Crisis. *The Wall Street Journal*. Retrieved from http://online.wsj.com/news/articles/SB125798004542744219

Lalanne, D., Nigay, L., Palanque, P., Robinson, P., Vanderdonckt, J., & Ladry, J. (2009). Fusion Engine for Multimodal Input: A Survey. In *Proceedings of the 11th International Conference on Multimodal Interfaces* (pp. 153-160). Cambridge, MA: ACM. doi:10.1145/1647314.1647343

Lányi, C. S. (2009). Multimedia Software Interface Design for Special-Needs Users. In M. Khosrow-Pour (Ed.), *Encyclopedia of Information Science and Technology* (2nd ed., pp. 2761–2766). Hershey, PA: IGI Global.

Larson, A. (2013). *Should You Build a Multimodal Interface for Your Web Site?* Retrieved October 20, 2013, from http://www.informit.com/articles/article.aspx?p=29024

Latané, B. (1981). The psychology of social impact. *The American Psychologist*, 36(4), 343–356. doi:10.1037/0003-066X.36.4.343

Latané, B., & Darley, J. M. (1970). *The unresponsive bystander: Why doesn't he help?* New York: Appleton-Century-Crofts.

Lavie, T., & Tractinsky, N. (2004). Assessing dimensions of perceived visual aesthetics of web sites. International Journal of Human-Computer Studies, 60, 269–298. doi:10.1016/j.ijhcs.2003.09.002

Lawrence, M. A., Kitada, R., Klatzky, R. L., & Lederman, S. J. (2007). Haptic roughness perception of linear gratings via bare finger or rigid probe. *Perception*, 36, 547–557. doi:10.1068/p5746 PMID:17564201

Le Bon, G. (1895). *The Crowd: A Study of the Popular Mind*. Retrieved from http://etext.virginia.edu/toc/modeng/public/BonCrow.html

Leap Motion. (2013). Retrieved October 10, 2013 from https://www.leapmotion.com/

Lechelt, E. C., & Verenka, A. (1980). Spatial anisotropy in intramodal and cross-modal judgments of stimulus orientation: The stability of the oblique effect. *Perception*, 9(5), 581–589. doi:10.1068/p090581 PMID:7443398

Lederman, S. J. (1983). Tactual roughness perception: Spatial and temporal determinants. *Canadian Journal of Psychology*, 37(4), 498–511. doi:10.1037/h0080750

Lederman, S. J. (1991). *Skin and Touch*. Academic Press.

Lederman, S. J., Klatzky, R. L., & Barber, P. O. (1985). Spatial and movement-based heuristics for encoding pattern information through touch. *Journal of Experimental Psychology. General*, 114(1), 33–49. doi:10.1037/0096-3445.114.1.33 PMID:3156945

Lee, E. S., Hong, S., & Johnson, B. R. (2006). Context Aware Paper-Based Review Instrument: A Tangible User Interface for Architecture Design Review. In G.A. Luhan (Ed.), *Proceedings of the 25th Annual Conference of the Association for Computer-Aided Design in Architecture* (pp. 317 – 327). Louisville, KY: Association for Computer-Aided Design in Architecture.

Lee, Y., et al. (2008). Designing with users, how? Investigate users involvement tactics for effective inclusive design processes. In Design Thinking: New Challenges for Designers, Managers and Organizations. Cergy-Pointoise.

Lee, C., Goh, D., Chua, A., & Ang, R. (2010). Indagator: Investigating perceived gratifications of an application that blends mobile content sharing with gameplay. *Journal of the American Society for Information Science and Technology*, 61(6), 1244–1257.

Levin, M. (2014). *Designing Multi-Device Experience*. Retrieved from amazon.com

Levy, M. (2007). Web 2.0 Implications on Knowledge Management. *Journal of Knowledge Management*, 13(1), 120–134. doi:10.1108/13673270910931215

Levy, M., & Powell, P. (2005). *Strategies for Growth in SMEs: The Role of Information and Information Systems*. Butterworth-Heinemann.

Levy, M., Powell, P., & Yetton, P. (2001). SMEs: Aligning IS and the Strategic Context. *Journal of Information Technology*, 16(3), 133–144. doi:10.1080/02683960110063672

Lewin, K. (1946). Action research and minority problems. *The Journal of Social Issues*, 2(4), 34–46. doi:10.1111/j.1540-4560.1946.tb02295.x

Li, X., Chen, D., & Xiahou, S. (2009). Ubiquitous Augmented Reality System. In *Proceedings of Second International Symposium on Knowledge Acquisition and Modeling* (pp. 91 – 94). Washington, DC: IEEE Computer Society.

Lifelong Kindergarten Group. M. M. L. (2003). *Scratch*. Retrieved November 2nd, 2013, from http://scratch.mit.edu

Liimatainen, J., Häkkinen, M., Nousiainen, T., Kankaanranta, M., & Neittaanmäki, P. (2012). A mobile application concept to encourage independent mobility for blind and visually impaired students. In *Proceedings of the 13th international conference on Computers Helping People with Special Needs*. Berlin: Springer Verlag.

Lim, H., & Lee, Y. S. (2009). Real-Time Single Camera SLAM Using Fiducial Markers. In *Proceedings of ICCAS-SICE International Joint Conference 2009* (pp. 177 – 182). Washington, DC: IEEE Computer Society.

Lindermann, N., Valcárcel, S., Schaarschmidt, M., & von Kortzfleisch, H. (2009). SME 2.0: Roadmap towards Web 2.0-Based Open Innovation in SME-Networks–A Case Study Based Research Framework. In Information Systems–Creativity and Innovation in Small and Medium-Sized Enterprises (pp. 28-41). Springer.

Lindgaard, G., Fernandes, G., Dudek, C., & Brown, J. (2006). Attention web designers: You have 50 milliseconds to make a good first impression! Behaviour & Information Technology, 25(2), 115–126. doi:10.1080/01449290500330448

Lingley, A. R., Ali, M., Liao, Y., Mirjalili, R., & Klonner, M., Sopanen, …Parviz, B.A. (2011). A Single-pixel Wireless Contact Lens Display. *Journal of Micromechanics and Microengineering*, 21(12), 1–8. doi:10.1088/0960-1317/21/12/125014

Li, Y. N., Tan, K. C., & Xie, M. (2002). Measuring Web-based service quality. *Total Quality Management*, 13(5), 685–700. doi:10.1080/0954412022000002072

Loiacono, E. T., Watson, R. T., & Goodhue, D. L. (2002). WebQual: A measure of Web site quality. In *Proceedings of 2002 Marketing Educators' Conference: Marketing Theory and Applications*. Academic Press.

Lomas, C. (2005). *7 Things you should know about Social Bookmarking*. Educause Learning Initiative.

LonWorks®-based Office Building Cuts HVAC, Lighting Costs 80 %. (n.d.). Retrieved October 2, 2013 from http://www.echelon.com/customers/smart-buildings/bob.htm

Loomis, J. M. (1974). Tactile letter recognition under different modes of stimulus presentation. *Perception & Psychophysics*, 16(2), 401–408. doi:10.3758/BF03203960

Lumosity Mobile. (2013). *App. Store*. Retrieved from https://itunes.apple.com/us/app/lumosity-mobile/id577232024

Lund, H., Pedersen, M., & Beck, R. (2007). Modular Robotic Tiles – Experiments for Children with Autism. *Artificial Life and Robotics*, 13, 394–400. doi:10.1007/s10015-008-0623-4

Lynch, K. (1960). *The image of the city*. Cambridge, MA: MIT Press.

Maeda, J., Fukuda, K., Takagi, H., & Asakawa, C. (2004). Web accessibility technology at the IBM Tokyo Research Laboratory. *IBM Journal of Research and Development*, 48(5-6), 735–749. doi:10.1147/rd.485.0735

Magee & Kennedy. (1980). Exploring pictures tactually. *Nature*, 283, 287–288. doi:10.1038/283287a0

Maguire, M. C. (1999). A review of user-interface design guidelines for public information kiosk systems. *International Journal of Human-Computer Studies*, 50(3), 263–286. doi:10.1006/ijhc.1998.0243

Mahony, D. F., Madrigal, R., & Howard, D. R. (2000). Using the psychological commitment to team (PCT) scale to segment sport consumers based on loyalty. *Sport Marketing Quarterly*, 9(1), 15–25.

Majgaard, G. (2009). The Playground in the Classroom – Fractions and Robot Technology. In Proceedings of Cognition and Exploratory Learning in Digital Age (pp. 10-17). International Association for Development, IADIS.

Majgaard, G. (2011). *Learning Processes and Robotic Systems. Design of Educational Tools using Robots as Media and Children as Co-designers*. (PhD dissertation). University of Southern Denmark.

Majgaard, G. (2012a). Brug af interaktive klodser i ingeniørundervisningen. [Using interactive blocks in engineering education]. *MONA: Matematik og Naturfagsdidaktik*, (4), 24-40.

Majgaard, G. (2012b). Design af computerspil i undervisningen: fra indfødt spilverdenen til reflekteret designer. *Læring og Medier (LOM)*, 5(9).

Majgaard, G. (2014). Initial Phases of Design-based Research into the Educational Potentials of NAO-Robots. In *Proceedings of Human Robotic Interaction Conference HRI'14*. Bielefeld, Germany: ACM.

Majgaard, G., & Jessen, C. (2009). Playtesting the Digital Playground. In *Proceedings of the International Conference on games and Entertainment Technologies 2009* (pp. 87-92). International Association for Development, IADIS.

Majgaard, G., Misfeldt, M., & Nielsen, J. (2010). Robot Tech nology and Numbers in the classroom. In *Proceedings of Cognition and Exploratory Learning in Digital Age* (pp. 231–234). IADIS.

Majgaard, G., Misfeldt, M., & Nielsen, J. (2011). *How Design-based Research, Action Research and Interaction Design Contributes to the Development of Designs for Learning*. Designs for Learning.

Maloney, J., Burd, L., Kafai, Y., Rusk, N., Silverman, B., & Resnick, M. (2004). Scratch: A Sneak Preview. In *Proceedings of the Second International Conference on Creating, Connecting and Collaborating through Computing* (pp. 104-109). Washington, DC: IEEE Computer Society.

Maloney, J., Resnick, M., Rusk, N., Silverman, B., & Eastmond, E. (2010). The scratch programming language and environment. *ACM Transactions on Computing Education*, *10*(4), 16. doi:10.1145/1868358.1868363

Mañas, M. Hamburg, & Hall, T. (2011). Learning to use Web 2.0 and net collaborative practices in SMEs. In *Proceedings of International Conference on Life Long Learning for Competitiveness, Employability and Social Inclusion*. Craiova, Romania: Academic Press.

Mankoff, J. C., Blevis, E., Borning, A., Friedman, B., Fussell, S. R., Hasbrouck, J., et al. (2007). Environmental sustainability and interaction. In *Proceedings of CHI EA '07 CHI '07 Extended Abstracts on Human Factors in Computing Systems* (pp. 2121-2124). New York, NY: ACM.

Mankoff, J. (2012). HCI and sustainability: a tale of two motivations. *Interactions (New York, N.Y.)*, *19*(3), 16–19. doi:10.1145/2168931.2168937

Manyika, J., Roberts, R., & Sprague, K. (2007). Eight Business Technology Trends to Watch. *The McKinsey Quarterly*, *1*, 60–71.

Maor, D., Currie, J., & Drewry, R. (2011). The effectiveness of assistive technologies for children with special needs: a review of research-based studies. *European Journal of Special Needs Education*, *26*(3), 283–298. doi:10.1080/08856257.2011.593821

Mapping London. (2013). Retrieved November 22, 2013, from http://mappinglondon.co.uk/2012/tfl-why-not-walk-it-maps/

Marchetti, F. M., & Lederman, S. J. (1983). The haptic radial-tangential effect: Two tests of "Wong's moments-of-inertia" hypothesis. *Bulletin of the Psychonomic Society*, *21*, 43–46. doi:10.3758/BF03329950

Marcotte, E. (2011). Responsive Webdesign. New York, NY: A Book Apart.

Markopoulos, P., Read, J. C., MacFarlane, S., & Hoysniemi, J. (2008). *Evaluating Children's Interactive Products: Principles and Practices for Interaction Designers*. Morgan Kaufmann.

Marshall, K. (2008). *Utilizing Web 2.0 Technology to Enhance Enterprise Knowledge Management*. Retrieved November 2, from, http://pt.scribd.com/doc/8644735/Utilizing-Web20-Technology-to-Enhance-Enterprise-Knowledge-Management

Mayer, R. E., & Massa, L. J. (2003). Three facets of visual and verbal learners: Cognitive ability, cognitive style and learning preference. Journal of Educational Psychology, 95, 833–846. doi:10.1037/0022-0663.95.4.833

Mayes, T. (1992). The 'M' Word: Multimedia interfaces and their role in interactive learning systems. In Multimedia Interface Design in Education (pp. 1-22). Berlin, German: Springer-Verlag.

Mayring, P. (2010). *Qualitative Inhaltsanalyse*. Beltz Publishing.

McAfee, A. (2006). Enterprise 2.0: The Dawn of Emergent Collaboration. *MIT Sloan Management Review*, *47*(3), 21–28.

McCarthy, J., & Swierenga, S. (2010). What we know about dyslexia and Web accessibility: a research review. *Universal Access in the Information Society*, *9*(2), 147–152. doi:10.1007/s10209-009-0160-5

McClanahan, B., Williams, K., Kennedy, E., & Tate, S. (2012). A Breakthrough for Josh: How Use of an iPad Facilitated Reading Improvement. *TechTrends*, *56*(3), 20–28. doi:10.1007/s11528-012-0572-6

McCobb, G. (2013). *The W3C Multimodal Architecture, Part 2: the XML specification stack*. Retrieved October 20, 2013, from http://www.ibm.com/developerwo rks/web/library/wa-multimodarch2/index.html

McIlraith, S., Son, T., & Zeng, H. (2001). Semantic web services. *Intelligent Systems, IEEE*, *16*(2), 46–53. doi:10.1109/5254.920599

McKenna, F. P. (1984). Measures of field-dependence: cognitive style or cognitive ability? Journal of Sociology & Social Psychology, 47, 593–603.

McNaney, R., Balaam, M., Marshall, K., Durrant, A., Read, J., & Good, J. ... Abowd, G. (2013). Designing for and with children with special needs in multiple settings. In *Proceedings of the 12th International Conference on Interaction Design and Children* (pp. 603–605). New York, NY: ACM.

Mediawatch. (2012). Retrieved July 9, 2012 from http://mediawatch.dk/artikel/smartphones-styrker-kommer-cielt-mediepotentiale

Melgar, E. R., & Diez, C. C. (2012). *Arduino and Kinect Projects: Design, Build, Blow Their Minds*. Apress. doi:10.1007/978-1-4302-4168-3

Metaio Brings World's First Augmented Reality Accelerated Chipset to Market, Signs Agreement with ST-Ericsson to Integrate Future Mobile Platforms. (2013). Retrieved October 10, 2013 from http://www.metaio.com/press/press-release/2013/metaio-brings-worlds-first-augmented-reality-accelerated-chipset-to-market-signs-agreement-with-st-ericsson-to-integrate-future-mobile-platforms/

Michailidou, E. (2005). *Metrics of visual complexity*. (Master's thesis). School of Computer Science, Faculty of Science and Engineering, University of Manchester, Manchester, UK.

Michailidou, E. (2008). Determining users' perception of web page visual complexity and aesthetic characteristics (HCW technical report). Manchester, UK: University of Manchester.

Michailidou, E., Harper, S., & Bechhofer, S. (2008). Visual complexity and aesthetic perception of web pages. In *Proceedings of the 26th annual ACM international conference on Design of communication* (pp. 215-224). ACM.

Minamizawa, K., Prattichizzo, D., & Tachi, S. (2010). Simplified design of haptic display by extending one-point kinesthetic feedback to multipoint tactile feedback. In *Proceedings of 2010 IEEE Haptics Symposium*, (pp. 257-260). IEEE.

Miranda, F., J., Chamorro, A., Valero, V., & Maestre, J. (2010). Quantitative Assessment of Football Web Sites: An Empirical Study of the Best European Football Club. *J. Service Science & Management*, *3*, 110–116. doi:10.4236/jssm.2010.31014

Moggridge, B. (2007). *Designing Interactions*. The MIT Press.

Moloney, J., & Amor, R. (2003). StringCVE: Advances in a game engine-based collaborative virtual environment for architectural design. In *Proceedings of 2nd conference on Construction Applications of Virtual Reality* (pp. 24-26). Academic Press.

Moodle Community. (2013). *Moodle.org: Open-source community-based tools for learning*. Retrieved October 20, 2013, from http://www.moodle.org

Moon, J., & Kim, Y. (2001). Extending the TAM for a world wide web context. *Information & Management*, *38*, 217–230. doi:10.1016/S0378-7206(00)00061-6

Morley, J. W., Goodwin, A. W., & Darian-Smith, I. (1983). Tactile discrimination of gratings. *Experimental Brain Research*, *49*(2), 291–299. doi:10.1007/BF00238588 PMID:6832261

Moser, C., Fuchsberger, V., Neureiter, K., Sellner, W., & Tscheligi, M. (2012). Revisiting personas: the making-of for special user groups. In *Proceedings of CHI '12 Extended Abstracts on Human Factors in Computing Systems* (pp. 453–468). New York, NY: ACM.

Moss, G., Gunn, R., & Heller, J. (2006). Some men like it black, some women like it pink: Consumer implications of differences in male and female website design. *Journal of Consumer Behaviour, 5*(4), 328–341. doi:10.1002/cb.184

Motschnig, R., & Nykl, L. (2011). *Komunikace zaměřená na člověka: rozumět sobě i druhým.* Prague: Grada.

Motschnig, R., & Nykl, L. (2014). *Person-centred Communication Theory, Skills and Practice.* Maidenhead, UK: McGraw Hill.

Mountain, D., & Liarokapis, F. (2007). Mixed reality (MR) interfaces for mobile information systems. *Aslib Proceedings, 59*, 422–436. doi:10.1108/00012530710817618

Myers, B. A., Wobbrock, J. O., Yang, S., Yeung, B., Nichols, J., & Miller, R. (2002). Using handhelds to help people with motor impairments. In *Proceedings of the fifth international ACM conference on Assistive technologies* (pp. 89-96). New York, NY: ACM.

Mykkanen, J., Riekkinen, A., Laitinen, P., Karhunen, H., & Sormunen, M. (2005). Designing web services in health information systems: From process to application level. *Studies in Health Technology and Informatics, 116,* 515. PMID:16160309

Nagel, T., Heidmann, F., Condotta, M., & Duval, E. (2010). Venice Unfolding: A Tangible User Interface for Exploring Faceted Data in a Geographical Context. In *Proceedings of the 6th Nordic Conference on Human-Computer Interaction: Extending Boundaries* (pp. 743 – 746). New York, NY: ACM.

Nagi, R. S. (2004). *Cartographic visualization for mobile applications.* (Unpublished master dissertation). The International Institute for Geo-Information Science and Earth Observation, Enschede, The Netherlands.

Najib, S. M., Nomura, Y., Sakamoto, R., & Iwabu, K. (2012). A Study on the duration and speed sensibility via fingerpad cutaneous sensations. *Procedia Engineering, 41,* 1268–1276. doi:10.1016/j.proeng.2012.07.310

Näkki, P., & Antikainen, M. (2008). Online tools for co-design: user involvement through the innovation process. In A. Karahasanovic & A. Følstad, (Eds.), The NordiCHI 2008 Workshops: New Approaches to Requirements Elicitation & How Can HCI Improve Social Media Development? (pp. 92-97). Trondheim: Tapir akademisk forlag.

Nee, A.Y.C., Ong, S.K., Chryssolouris, G., & Mourtzis, D. (2012). Augmented Reality Applications in Design and Manufacturing. *CIRP Annals – Manufacturing Technology, 61*(2), 657 – 679.

Newman, J., Ingram, D., & Hopper, A. (2001). Augmented Reality in a Wide Area Sentient Environment. In *Proceedings of the 2nd IEEE and ACM International Symposium on Augmented Reality* (pp. 77 – 86). Washington, DC: IEEE Computer Society.

Newman, A., & Thomas, J. (2008). *Enterprise 2.0 Implementation.* McGraw-Hill Osborne Media.

Nielsen, J. (2000). Designing web usability: The practice of simplicity. Indianapolis, IN: New Riders.

Nielsen, J. (2010). *Children's websites: Usability issues in designing for kids.* Retrieved from http://www.nngroup.com/articles/childrens-websites-usability-issues/

Nielsen, J., & Lund, H. H. (2003). Spiking neural building block robot with Hebbian learning. In *Proceedings of the IEEE/RSJ International Conference on the Intelligent Robots and Systems* (IROS 2003) (pp. 1363 - 1369). Las Vegas, NV: IEEE Press.

Nielsen, J., & Majgaard, G. (2013). Self-Assessment and Reflection in a 1st Semester Course for Software Engineering Students. In *Proceedings of the IADIS International Conference on Cognition and Exploratory Learning in the Digital Age* (CELDA 2013) (pp. 150-158). Forth Worth, TX: IADIS Press.

Nielsen, J., Jessen, C., & Bærendsen, N. K. (2008). RoboMusicKids – Music Education with Robotic Building Blocks. In *Proceedings of the 2nd IEEE International Conference on Digital Game and Intelligent Toy Enhanced Learning (DIGITEL)* (pp. 149-156). IEEE.

Nielsen, J., & Budiu, R. (2013). *Mobile Usability.* Berkeley, CA: New Riders Press.

Nielsen, J., & Lund, H. H. (2008). Modular robotics as a tool for education and entertainment. *Computers in Human Behavior, 24*(2), 234–248. doi:10.1016/j.chb.2007.01.011

Nigay, L., & Coutaz, J. (1995). A Generic Plataform for Addressing the Multimodal Challenge. In *Proceedings of the 13th Conference On Human Factors in Computing Systems* (pp. 98-105). New York, NY: ACM Press / Addison-Wesley Publishing Co.

Nomensa: United Nations global audit of web accessibility. (2006). Retrieved from http://www.un.org/esa/socdev/enable/documents/fnomensarep.pdf

Nomura, Y., Najib, S. M., Iwabu, K., & Sakamoto, R. (2013). Sliding raised-dots perceptual characteristics: speed perception or dot count. In *Proc. ACHI 2013*, (pp. 303-308). ACHI.

Nomura, Y., Najib, S. M., & Sakamoto, R. (2013). Hand-motion perception by four haptic modes: Active/passive and with/without fingerpad cutaneous sensation. *Journal of Advanced Mechanical Design, Systems and Manufacturing*, 7(4), 560–575. doi:10.1299/jamdsm.7.560

Norman, D. (2005). *Emotional Design: Why We Love or Hate Everyday Things*. New York, NY: Basic Books.

Norman, D. A. (1983). Some Observations on Mental Models. In D. Gentner, & A. L. Stevens (Eds.), *Mental Models* (pp. 7–14). Hillsdale, NJ: Lawrence Erlbaum Associates.

Norman, D. A. (2002). *The design of everyday things*. New York: Basic Books.

Norte, S., & Lobo, F. (2007). A virtual logo keyboard for people with motor disabilities. *ACM SIGCSE Bulletin*, 39, 111–115. doi:10.1145/1269900.1268818

Nurminen, A. (2006). m-LOMA - a mobile 3D city map. In Proceedings of Web3D 2006 (pp. 7-18). New York: ACM Press.

Nylander, S., Bylund, M., & Waern, A. (2005). Ubiquitous service access through adapted user interfaces on multiple devices. *Journal Personal and Ubiquitous Computing*, 9(3), 123–133. doi:10.1007/s00779-004-0317-4

O'Brien, J. (2000). *Introduction to Information Systems* (9th ed.). New York: McGraw-Hill, Inc.

Occupying Yourself with Energy and Occupancy. (2010). Retrieved October 2, 2013 from http://www.automatedbuildings.com/news/aug10/articles/sinopoli1/100728121202sinopoli.htm

Oehlberg, L., Aipperspach, R., & Jeffery, S. R. (2007). *Sustainability through meaning: providing information to promote meaningful products*. Paper presented at Ubicomp 2007. Innsbruck, Austria.

Okamoto, S., Konyo, M., & Tadokoro, S. (2011). Vibro-tactile stimuli applied to finger pads as biases for perceived inertial and viscous loads. *IEEE Transactions on Haptics*, 4(4), 307–315. doi:10.1109/TOH.2011.16

Oksman, V., Siltanen, S., & Ainasoja, M. (2012). User participation in co-creative services: developing virtual and augmented reality tools for do-it-yourself home design. In *Proceeding of the 16th International Academic MindTrek Conference* (pp. 229-230). New York, NY: ACM.

OPEN NI. (2013). Retrieved January 20, 2013 from http://www.openni.org/

OpenCV (Open Source Computer Vision). (n.d.). Retrieved October 2, 2013 from http://opencv.org/

O'Reilly, T. (2005). What Is Web 2.0? *O'Reilly Network*. Retrieved November 4, from http://oreilly.com/web2/archive/what-is-web20

O'Sullivan, J., Edmond, D., & Ter Hofstede, A. (2002). What's in a Service? *Distributed and Parallel Databases*, 12(2), 117–133. doi:10.1023/A:1016547000822

Overton, T. (2012). *Assessing Learners with Special Needs: An applied approach*. Boston: Pearson Education.

Oviatt, S. (2002). Multimodal Interfaces. In A. Sears, & J. Jacko (Eds.), *Handbook of Human-Computer Interaction: Fundamentals, Evolving Technologies and Emerging Applications* (pp. 413–432). Lawrence Erlbaum.

Oviatt, S. (2003). Advances in Robust Multimodal Interface Design. *IEEE Computer Graphics and Applications*, 23(55), 62–68. doi:10.1109/MCG.2003.1231179

Paivio, A. (1971). Imagery and verbal processes. New York: Holt, Rinehart & Winston.

Pandir, M., & Knight, J. (2006). Homepage aesthetics: The search for preference factors and the challenges of subjectivity. Interacting with Computers, 18(6), 1351–1370. doi:10.1016/j.intcom.2006.03.007

Papazoglou, M. (2008). *Web services: principles and technology*. Addison-Wesley.

Papert, S. (1993). *Mindstorms Children, Computers, and Powerful Ideas*. Basic Books.

Parasuraman, A., Zeithaml, V. A., & Berry, L. L. (1994). Reassessment of expectations as a comparison standard in measuring service quality: implications for further research. *Journal of Marketing*, *6*(3), 173–183.

Parasuraman, A., Zeithaml, V. A., & Malhotra, A. (2005). E-S-Qual: A multiple- item scale for assessing electronic service quality. *Journal of Service Research*, *7*, 213–233. doi:10.1177/1094670504271156

Parham, L. D., & Fazio, L. S. (2007). *Play in Occupational Therapy for Children*. Mosby Elsevier.

Parkin, A. J. (2000). *Essential cognitive psychology*. London: Psychology Press.

Pashler, H., McDaniel, M., Rohrer, D., & Bjork, R. (2008). Learning styles: Concepts and evidence. Psychological Science in the Public Interest, 9(3), 105–119.

Passini, R. (1984). Spatial representation: a wayfinding perspective. *Journal of Environmental Psychology*, *4*(2), 153–164. doi:10.1016/S0272-4944(84)80031-6

Passini, R. (1992). *Wayfinding in architecture* (2nd ed.). New York: Van Nostrand Reinhold.

Perdikaris, S. C. (2011). Using the Cognitive Styles to Explain an Anomaly in the Hierarchy of the van Hiele Levels. Journal of Mathematical Sciences & Mathematics Education, 6(2), 35–43.

Peris, M., Sperling, A., Blinn, N., Nüttgens, M., & Gehrke, N. (2011). *Participatory Design of Web 2.0 Applications in SME Networks*. Paper presented at the 24th Bled eConference ́eFuture: Creating Solutions for the Individual, Organisations and Society. Bled, Slovenia

Peterson, E., Rayner, S., & Armstrong, S. (2009). The psychology of cognitive style and learning styles: is there really a future? Learning and Individual Differences Journal, 19(4), 518–523. doi:10.1016/j.lindif.2009.06.003

Pfeifer, R., & Bongard, J. (2007). *How the body shapes the way we think*. MIT Press.

Phillips, B., & Zhao, H. (1993). Predictors of Assistive Technology Abandonment. *Assistive Technology*, *5*(1), 36–45. doi:10.1080/10400435.1993.10132205 PMID:10171664

Piaget, J., & Inhelder, B. (1967). *The child's conception of space*. London: Routledge & Kegan Paul.

Pietrzak, T., Pecci, I., & Martin, B. (2006). Static and dynamic tactile directional cues experiments with VT-Player mouse.[Eurohaptics.]. *Proceedings of Eurohaptics*, *2006*, 63–68.

Piper, B., & Ishii, H. (2002). PegBlocks: A Learning Aid for the Elementary Classroom. In *Proceedings Extended Abstracts of Conference on Human Factors in Computing Systems* (CHI '02). Minneapolis, MN: ACM.

Plass, J. L., Chun, D. M., Mayer, R. E., & Leutner, D. (1998). Supporting visual and verbal learning preferences in a second-language multimedia learning environment. Journal of Educational Psychology, 90, 25–36. doi:10.1037/0022-0663.90.1.25 doi:10.1037/0022-0663.90.1.25

Platt, M. (2007). Web 2.0 in Enterprise. *The Architecture Journal, 12*.

Polli, A. (2004). Atmospherics/Weather works: A multi-channel storm sonification project. In *Proceedings of the 10th International Conference on Auditory Display*. Sydney, Australia: Georgian Institute of Technology.

Pongrac, H. (2008). Vibrotactile perception: examining the coding of vibrations and the just noticeable difference under various conditions. *Multimedia Systems*, *13*, 297–307. doi:10.1007/s00530-007-0105-x

Pospischil, G., Umlauft, M., & Michlmayr, E. (2002). Designing LoL@, a Mobile Tourist Guide for UMTS. In F. Paternò (Ed.), *Mobile HCI* (pp. 140–154). HCI. doi:10.1007/3-540-45756-9_12

Preece, J., Rogers, Y., Sharp, H., Benyon, D., Holland, S., & Carey, T. (n.d.). *Human-Computer Interaction: Methods for User-Centred Design*. Addison-Wesley.

Puppet Pals, H. D. (2010). *App. Store*. Retrieved from https://itunes.apple.com/ca/app/puppet-pals-hd/id342076546

Rakkolainen, I., & Vainio, T. (2001). A 3D City Info for mobile users. *Computers & Graphics, 25*, 619–625. doi:10.1016/S0097-8493(01)00090-5

Rashotte, L. (2007). Social Influence. In G. Ritzer (Ed.), *The Blackwell Encyclopedia of Sociology*. Retrieved from http://www.blackwellreference.com/subscriber/tocnode. html?id=g9781405124331_chunk_g978140512433125_ ss1-154

Ratner, R. K., & Kahn, B. E. (2002). The impact of private versus public consumption on variety-seeking behaviour. *The Journal of Consumer Research, 29*, 246–257. doi:10.1086/341574

Read, J., & Druin, A. (2009). Design for the future. In A. Druin (Ed.), Mobile Technology for Children: Designing for Interaction and Learning. New York: Morgan Kaufmann. doi:10.1016/B978-0-12-374900-0.00016-8

Realinho, V., Romão, T., Birra, F., & Dias, A. E. (2011). Building mobile context-aware applications for leisure and entertainment. In *Proceedings of the 8th International Conference on Advances in Computer Entertainment Technology*. Academic Press.

Reber, A. S. (1995). The Penguin Dictionary of Psychology. London: Penguin.

Reenskaug, T. (2003). *The Model-View-Controller (MVC) Its Past and Present Trygve Reenskaug*. University of Oslo.

Reich, K. (2009). eInclusion, eAccessibility and design for all issues in the context of European Computer-Based Assessment. *The Transition to Computer-Based Assessment, 68*.

Reichenbacher, T. (2004). *Mobile Cartography - Adaptive Visualisation of Geographic Information on Mobile Devices*. (Unpublished Ph.D. Dissertation). Technischen Universität München, München, Germany.

Reinecke, K., Yeh, T., Miratrix, L., Mardiko, R., & Zhao, Y. Liu, J., & Gajos, K.Z. (2013). Predicting users' first impressions of website aesthetics with a quantification of perceived visual complexity and colourfulness. In *Proceedings of the SIGCHI Conference on Human Factors in Computing Systems*. ACM.

Ren, Z., Yuan, J., Meng, J., & Zhang, Z. (2013). Robust Part-Based Hand Gesture Recognition Using Kinect Sensor. *IEEE Transactions on Multimedia, 15*(5), 1110–1120. doi:10.1109/TMM.2013.2246148

Resnick, M. (1996). StarLogo: an environment for decentralized modeling and decentralized thinking. In *Proceedings of the Conference Companion on Human Factors in Computing Systems* (pp. 11-12). Vancouver, Canada: ACM Press.

Resnick, M., Martin, F., Berg, R., Borovoy, R., Colella, V., Kramer, K., & Silverman, B. (1998). Digital manipulatives: new toys to think with. In *Proceedings of the SIGCHI conference on Human factors in computing systems* (pp. 281-287). Los Angeles, CA: ACM Press.

Resnick, M., Maloney, J., Monroy-Hernández, A., Rusk, N., Eastmond, E., Brennan, K., & Kafai, Y. (2009). Scratch: programming for all. *Communications of the ACM, 52*(11), 60–67. doi:10.1145/1592761.1592779

Rezaei, A. R., & Katz, L. (2004). Evaluation of the reliability and validity of the cognitive styles analysis. Personality and Individual Differences, 36(6), 1317–1327. doi:10.1016/S0191-8869(03)00219-8

Richards, J., & Hanson, V. (2004). Web accessibility: a broader view. In *Proceedings of the 13th international conference on World Wide Web* (pp. 72-79). Academic Press.

Richardson, A. (1977). Verbalizer-Visualizer: A cognitive style dimension. Journal of Mental Imagery, 1, 109–126.

Riding, R. J. (1991). Cognitive styles analysis. Birmingham, UK: Learning & Training Technology.

Riding, R. J., & Buckle, C. F. (1990). Learning Styles and Training Performance. Sheffield: Training Agency.

Riding, R. J., & Calvey, I. (1981). The assessment of verbal-imagery learning styles and their effect on the recall of concrete and abstract prose passages by eleven year old children. The British Journal of Psychology, 72, 59–64. doi:10.1111/j.2044-8295.1981.tb02161.x

Riding, R. J., & Cheema, I. (1991). Cognitive styles-An overview and integration. Educational Psychology, 11(3&4), 193–215. doi:10.1080/0144341910110301

Riding, R. J., & Watts, S. (1997). The effect of cognitive style on the preferred format of instructional material. Educational Psychology, 17, 179–183. doi:10.1080/0144341970170113

Riemer-Reiss, M. L., & Wacker, R. R. (2000). Factors Associated with Assistive Technology Discontinuance among Individuals with Disabilities. *Journal of Rehabilitation, 66*(3), 44.

Rogers, C. R., & Roethlisberger, F. J. (1991). Barriers and Gateways to Communication. *Harvard Business Review.* ISO 9241. (2010). *Ergonomics of human-system interaction – Part 210: Human-centered design for interactive systems.* Geneva.

Rogers, C. R., & Farson, R. E. (1957). Active Listening. In R. G. Newman, M. A. Danziger, & M. Cohen (Eds.), *Communication in Business Today.* Washington, DC: Heath and Company.

Rogers, Y., Sharp, H., & Preece, J. (2011). *Interaction Design: Beyond Human-Computer Interaction* (3rd ed.). Hoboken, NJ: John Wiley and Sons, Ltd.

Rolland, J. P., Holloway, R. L., & Fuchs, H. (1995). A Comparison of Optical and Video See-through Head-mounted Displays. In H. Das (Ed.), *SPIE Proceedings Volume 2351, Telemanipulator and Telepresence Technologies* (pp. 293 – 309). SPIE.

Rosenberg, L. (1992). *The Use of Virtual Fixtures as Perceptual Overlays to Enhance Operator Performance in Remote Environments.* Dayton, OH: Wright-Patterson Air Force Base.

Rouse, W. B., & Morris, N. (1986). On looking into the black box: Prospects and limits in the search for mental models. *Psychological Bulletin, 100*(3), 349–363. doi:10.1037/0033-2909.100.3.349

Rublee, E., Rabaud, V., Konolige, K., & Bradski, G. (2011). ORB: An Efficient Alternative to SIFT or SURF. In *Proceedings of the 2011 IEEE International Conference on Computer Vision* (pp. 2564 – 2571). Washington, DC: IEEE Computer Society.

Sabelli, N. (1987). *Constructionism: A New Opportunity for Elementary Science Education.* DRL Division of Research on Learning in Formal and Informal Settings. Retrieved from http://nsf.gov/awardsearch/showAward?AWD_ID=8751190

Saeed, G. (2009). *Pedestrian Real-Time Locatiuon and Routing Information Delivered to Mobile Digital Architectural Guides.* (Unpublished Ph.D. Thesis). University of Liverpool, Liverpool, UK.

Salada, M., Vishton, P., Colgate, J. E., & Frankel, E. (2004). Two experiments on the perception of slip at the fingertip. In *Proceedings 12th International Symposium on Haptic Interfaces for Virtual Environment and Teleoperator Systems,* (pp. 146-153). Academic Press.

Sanders, E., & Stappers, P. J. (2008). Co-creation and the new landscapes of design. *CoDesign: International Journal of CoCreation in Design and the Arts, 4*(1), 5–18. doi:10.1080/15710880701875068

Sanders, G. S., & Baron, R. S. (1975). The motivating effects of distraction on task performance. *Journal of Personality and Social Psychology, 32*(6), 956–963. doi:10.1037/0022-3514.32.6.956

Sanders, G. S., Baron, R. S., & Moore, D. L. (1978). Distraction and social comparison as mediators of social facilitation effects. *Journal of Experimental Social Psychology, 14,* 291–303. doi:10.1016/0022-1031(78)90017-3

Schaik, P., & Ling, J. (2009). The role of context in perceptions of the aesthetics of web pages over time. Journal of Human-Computer Studies, 67, 79–89. doi:10.1016/j.ijhcs.2008.09.012

Schall, G., Mulloni, A., & Reitmayr, G. (2010). North-centred Orientation Tracking on Mobile Phones. In *Proceedings of the 9th IEEE International Symposium on Mixed and Augmented Reality* (pp. 267–268). Washington, DC: IEEE Computer Society.

Scherer, M. J., & Federici, S. (2012). *Assistive Technology Assessment Handbook.* CRC Press.

Schifferstein, H. N. J., & Hekkert, P. (Eds.). (2008). *Product Experience.* Amsterdam: Elsevier.

Schikhof, Y., & Mulder, I. (2008). Under Watch and Ward at Night: Design and Evaluation of a Remote Monitoring System for Dementia Care. In *Proceedings of the 4th Symposium of the Workgroup Human-Computer Interaction and Usability Engineering of the Austrian Computer Society on HCI and Usability for Education and Work*. Berlin: Springer Verlag.

Schmalstieg, D., & Reitmayr, G. (2005). The World as a User Interface: Augmented Reality for Ubiquitous Computing. In G. Gartner, W. Cartwright, & M. P. Peterson (Eds.), *Location Based Services and TeleCartography* (pp. 369–391). Berlin: Springer-Verlag.

Schmitt, F., Cassens, J., Kindsmüller, M. C., & Herczeg, M. (2011). Mental Models of Ambient Systems: A Modual Research Framework. In M. Beigl, H. Christiansen, T.R. Roth-Berghofer, K. R. Coventry, A. Kofod-Petersen, & H.R. Schmidtke (Eds.), *Proceedings from CONTEXT 2011: Modeling and Using Context: The Seventh International and Interdisciplinary Conference* (pp. 278-291). Berlin: Springer.

Schön, D. A. (1983). *The Reflective Practitioner: How Professionals Think in Action*. London, UK: Maraca Temple Smith.

Schwartz, A. S., Perrey, A. J., & Azulay, A. (1975). Further analysis of active and passive touch in pattern discrimination. *Bulletin of the Psychonomic Society, 6*(1), 7–9. doi:10.3758/BF03333128

Scratch and Kinect. (2013). Retrieved September 20, 2013 from http://scratched.media.mit.edu/discussions/teaching-scratch/scratch-kinect

Scratch2kinect. (2013). Retrieved September 20, 2013 from http://scratch.saorog.com/

Sensable. (n.d.). Retrieved from http://www.sensegraphics.com/index.php

Serrano, N., & Torres, J. M. (2010). Web 2.0 for Practitioners. *IEEE Software, 27*(3), 11–15. doi:10.1109/MS.2010.84

Seshadri, S. (2012). iPad gives voice to kids with autism. *CNN*. Retrieved from http://www.cnn.com/2012/05/14/tech/gaming-gadgets/ipad-autism/index.html

Sharples, M., McAndrew, P., Weller, M., Ferguson, R., FitzGerald, E., Hirst, T., & Gaved, M. (2013). *Maker Culture: Learning by making, Innovating Pedagogy* (pp. 33–36). London, UK: The Open University Press.

Shaw, M., & Garlan, D. (1996). *Software Architecture: Perspectives on an Emerging Discipline*. Upper Saddle River, NJ: Prentice Hall.

Shimizu, Y. (1982). Temporal effect on tactile letter recognition by a tracing mode. *Perceptual and Motor Skills, 55*(2), 343–349. doi:10.2466/pms.1982.55.2.343 PMID:7155729

Shinohara, K., & Wobbrock, J. O. (2011). In the shadow of misperception: assistive technology use and social interactions. In *Proceedings of the SIGCHI Conference on Human Factors in Computing Systems,* (pp. 705–714). ACM.

Shneiderman, B. (2002). *Leonardo's Laptop: Human Needs and the New Computing Technologies*. Cambridge, MA: MIT Press.

SIDeR. (2013). Retrieved October 10, 2013 from http://sider2013.au.dk/

Siegel, A. W., & White, S. H. (1975). The development of spatial representations of large-scale environments. In H. W. Reese (Ed.), *Advances in Child Development and Behavior* (Vol. 10). New York: Academic Press. doi:10.1016/S0065-2407(08)60007-5

Sierkowski, B. (2002). Achieving web accessibility. In *Proceedings of the 30th Annual ACM SIGUCCS Conference on User Services* (pp. 288-291). ACM.

Silverman, N. L., Schowengerdt, B. T., Kelly, J. P., & Seibel, E. J. (2003). 58.5L: Late-News Paper: Engineering a Retinal Scanning Laser Display with Integrated Accommodative Depth Cues. *SID Symposium Digest of Technical Papers, 34*(1), 1538 - 1541.

Simon, S. J. (2001). The impact of culture and gender on web sites: An empirical study. The Data Base for Advances in Information Systems, 32(1), 18–37. doi:10.1145/506740.506744

Smith, A. A., & Smith, A. D. (2012). CRM and identity theft issues associated with e-ticketing of sports and entertainment. *Electronic Government. International Journal (Toronto, Ont.)*, *9*(1), 1–26.

Social Issues Research Centre. (2008). Football Passions. *The Social Issues Research Centre, commissioned by Canon*. Retrieved December, 8 from, http://sirc.org/football/football_passions.pdf

Sørum, H., Andersen, K. N., & Vatrapu, R. (2012). Public websites and human–computer interaction: an empirical study of measurement of website quality and user satisfaction. *Behaviour & Information Technology*, *31*(7), 697–706. doi:10.1080/0144929X.2011.577191

Sousa, R., & Voss, C. (2012). The impacts of e-service quality on customer behaviour in multi-channel e-services. *Total Quality Management*, *23*(7), 789–806. doi:10.1080/14783363.2012.661139

Steward, K., Felicetti, L., & Kuehn, S. (1996). The attitudes of business majors toward the teaching of business ethics. Journal of Business Ethics, 15(8), 913–918. doi:10.1007/BF00381859 doi:10.1007/BF00381859

Strauss, B. (2002). Social Facilitation in Motor Tasks: A Review of Research and Theory. *Psychology of Sport and Exercise*, *3*(3), 237–256. doi:10.1016/S1469-0292(01)00019-X

Suchman, L. A. (1987). *Plans and Situated Actions: The Problem of Human-Machine Communications*. Cambridge, UK: Cambridge University Press.

Tahir, M., Bailly, G., Lecolinet, E., & Mouret, G. (2008). TactiMote: a tactile remote control for navigating in long lists. In *Proceedings of the 10th international conference on Multimodal interfaces*, (pp. 285-288). Academic Press.

Tahir, M., Bailly, G., & Lecolinet, E. (2008). Exploring the impulsion and vibration effects of tactile patterns. In *Proceedings of the 22nd British HCI Group Annual Conference on People and Computers: Culture, Creativity*[]. HCI.]. *Interaction*, *2*, 237–240.

Tapscott, D. (2006). *Winning with Enterprise 2.0: IT&CA research program*. New Paradigm Learning Corporation. Retrieved from http://newparadigm.com/media/Winning_with_the_Enterprise_2.0.pdf

Teachman, G., & Gibson, B. E. (2013). Children and youth with disabilities: innovative methods for single qualitative interviews. *Qualitative Health Research*, *23*(2), 264–274. doi:10.1177/1049732312468063 PMID:23208200

Teiche, A., Rai, A. K., Yanc, C., Moore, C., Solms, D., & Çetin, G. … Sandler, S. (2009). *Multitouch Technologies*. Retrieved October 20, 2013, from http://nuicode.com/attachments/download/115/Multi-Touch_Technologies_v1.01.pdf

TelEduc Project. (2013). *TelEduc. Ensino a Distância*. Retrieved October 20, 2013 from http://www.teleduc.org.br

Terada, K., Kumazaki, A., Miyata, D., & Ito, A. (2006). Haptic Length Display Based on Cutaneous-Proprioceptive, Integration. *Journal of Robotics and Mechatronics*, *18*(4), 489–498.

Thimbleby, H. W. (2008). Understanding User Centred Design (UCD) for People with Special Needs. In K. Miesenberger, J. Klaus, W. L. Zagler, & A. I. Karshmer (Eds.), *ICCHP*. Berlin: Springer Verlag. doi:10.1007/978-3-540-70540-6_1

Thorlacius, L. (2007). The role of aesthetics in web design. Nordicom Review, 28(1), 63–76.

Tiest, W. M. B., van der Hoff, L. M. A., & Kappers, A. M. L. (2011). Cutaneous and kinaesthetic perception of traversed distance. In *Proceedings of the World Haptics Conference* (pp. 593-597). IEEE.

Triplett, N. (1898). The Dynamogenic Factors in Pacemaking and Competition. *American Journal of Technology*, *9*, 507–533.

Trocchia, P., & Janda, S. (2003). How do consumers evaluate Internet retail service? *Journal of Services Marketing*, *17*(3), 243–253. doi:10.1108/08876040310474800

Tsagarakis, N. G., Horne, T., & Caldwell, D. G. (2005). Slip aesthesis: a portable 2D slip/skin stretch display for the fingertip. In *Proceedings of First Joint Eurohaptics Conference, 2005 and Symposium on Haptic Interfaces for Virtual Environment and Teleoperator Systems, 2005: World Hap-tics 2005*, (pp. 214 -219). Haptics.

Tuch, A. N., Bargas-Avila, J. A., & Opwis, K. (2009). Visual complexity of websites: Effects on users' experience, physiology, performance, and memory. International Journal of Human-Computer Studies, 67(9), 703–715. doi:10.1016/j.ijhcs.2009.04.002

Tuch, A. N., Bargas-Avila, J. A., & Opwis, K. (2010). Symmetry and aesthetics in website design: It's a man's business. Computers in Human Behavior, 26, 1831–1837. doi:10.1016/j.chb.2010.07.016

Tuch, A. N., Presslaber, E. E., Stocklin, M., Opwis, K., & Bargas-Avila, J. (2012). The role of visual complexity and prototypicality regarding first impression of websites: Working towards understanding aesthetic judgments. International Journal of Human-Computer Studies, 70, 794–811. doi:10.1016/j.ijhcs.2012.06.003

Turner, P. (1999). Television and internet convergence: implications for sport broadcasting. *Sport Marketing Quarterly, 8*(2), 43–49.

Väänänan-Vainio-Mattila, K., & Oinas-Kukkonen, H. (2010). Cross-Platform Service User Experience: A Field Study and an Initial Framework. In *Proceedings from MobileHCI'10: The 12th International Conference on Human Computer Interaction with Mobile Devices and Services* (pp. 219-228). New York, NY: ACM.

Valley, K. (1997). Learning styles and courseware design. Association for Learning Technology Journal, 5(2), 42–51. doi:10.1080/0968776970050205

van Krevelen, D. W. F., & Poelman, R. (2010). A Survey of Augmented Reality Technologies, Applications and Limitations. *The International Journal of Virtual Reality, 9*(2), 1–20.

VandenBos, G., Knapp, S., & Doe, J. (2001). Role of reference elements in the selection of resources by psychology undergraduates. *Journal of Bibliographic Research, 5*, 117–123.

Vastenburg, M. H., Romero Herrera, N., Van Bel, D., & Desmet, P. M. A. (2011). PMRI: Development of a Pictorial Mood Reporting Instrument. In *Proceedings of the 2011 annual conference extended abstracts on Human factors in computing systems,* (pp. 2155-2160). Academic Press.

Vega-Bermudez, F., Johnson, K. O., & Hsiao, S. S. (1991). Human tactile pattern recognition: active versus passive touch, velocity effects, and patterns of confusion. *Journal of Neurophysiology. Am Physiological Soc., 65*(3), 531–546.

Villaroman, N., et al. (2011). Teaching Natural User Interaction Using OpenNI and the Microsoft Kinect Sensor. In *Proceedings of SIGITE'11.* West Point, NY: ACM.

Vines, J. (2013). *Designing For- and With- Vulnerable People.* Retrieved from http://www.academia.edu/2989640/Designing_For-_and_With-_Vulnerable_People

Vogt, K., & Höldrich, R. (2010). A metaphoric sonification method - towards the acoustic standard model of particle physics. In *Proceedings of the 16th International Conference on Auditory Display.* Washington, DC: International Community for Auditory Display Publishing.

Vogt, K., et al. (2008). Exploration of 4d-data spaces. Sonification of lattice QCD. In *Proceedings of the 14th International Conference on Auditory Display.* Paris, France: International Community for Auditory Display Publishing.

W3C. (2013). *Multimodal Architecture and Interfaces.* Retrieved October 20, 2013 from http://www.w3.org/TR/2012/REC-mmi-arch-20121025/

Waechter, C., Huber, M., Keitler, P., Schlegel, M., Klinker, G., & Pustka, D. (2010). A Multi-sensor Platform for Wide-area Tracking. In *Proceedings of the 9th IEEE International Symposium on Mixed and Augmented Reality* (pp. 275–276). Washington, DC: IEEE Computer Society.

Wagner, D., Reitmayr, G., Mulloni, A., Drummond, T., & Schmalstieg, D. (2008). Pose Tracking from Natural Features on Mobile Phones. In *Proceedings of the 7th IEEE/ACM International Symposium on Mixed and Augmented Reality* (pp. 125 – 134). Washington, DC: IEEE Computer Society.

Wall, S. A., & Brewster, S. (2006). Sensory substitution using tactile pin arrays: Human factors, technology and applications. *Signal Processing, 86*(12), 3674–3695. doi:10.1016/j.sigpro.2006.02.048

Walsh, G., Foss, E., Yip, J., & Druin, A. (2013). FACIT PD: a framework for analysis and creation of intergenerational techniques for participatory design. In *Proceedings of the SIGCHI Conference on Human Factors in Computing Systems* (pp. 2893–2902). New York, NY: ACM.

Wang, H. F., & Bowerman, C. J. (2012). The Impact of Perceived Visual Complexity on Children's Websites in Relation to Classical and Expressive Aesthetics. In P. K. Blashki (Ed.), *IADIS International Conference IADIS Interfaces and Human Computer Interaction 2012* (pp. 269-273). Lisbon: Inderscience Publishers.

Wang, Y., Turner, M. J., & Hewitt, W. T. (2006). Creating a novel multiple frequency based vibration built upon human perception analysis. In *Proceedings of the 41st United Kingdom Group Meeting on Human Responses to Vibration*, (pp. 1-12). Academic Press.

WAYFINDER. (2013). Retrieved November 22, 2013, from http://www.academia.edu/180289/TangiCAD_Tangible_Interface_for_Manipulating_Architectural_3D_Models

Webstar, R. J. III, Todd, E. M., Lawton, N. V., & Allison, M. O. (2005). A novel two-dimensional tactile slip display: design, kinematics and perceptual experiments. *ACM Transactions on Applied Perception, 2*(2), 150–165. doi:10.1145/1060581.1060588

Weiser, M. (1991). The Computer for the 21st Century. *Scientific American, 265*(3), 94–104. doi:10.1038/scientificamerican0991-94

Wenger, E. (1998). *Communities of Practice: Learning, Meaning, and Identity*. Cambridge University Press. doi:10.1017/CBO9780511803932

Westera, W., Nadolski, R. J., Hummel, H. G., & Wopereis, I. G. (2008). Serious games for higher education: a framework for reducing design complexity. *Journal of Computer Assisted Learning, 24*(5), 420–432. doi:10.1111/j.1365-2729.2008.00279.x

Weyant, L., & Gardner, C. (2010). Web 2.0 Application usages: Implications for Management Education. *Journal of Business. Society & Government, 2*(2), 67–78.

Whitehouse, D., & Patrignani, N. (2013). From slow food to slow tech: a reflection paper. In *Proceedings of the IADIS International conferences: Interfaces and Human Computer Interaction 2013*. IADIS.

Whitsel, B. L., Franzen, O., Dreyer, D. A., Hollins, M., Young, M., Essick, G. K., & Wong, C. (1986). Dependence of subjective traverse length on velocity of moving tactile stimuli. *Somatosensory & Motor Research, 3*(3), 185–196. doi:10.3109/07367228609144583 PMID:3749661

Wilson, A. D. (2005). Play Anywhere: A Compact Interactive Tabletop Projection-vision System. In *Proceedings of the 18th Annual ACM Symposium on User Interface Software and Technology* (pp. 83 – 92). New York, NY: ACM.

Wilson, J. R., & Rutherford, A. (1989). Mental models: theory and application in human factors. *Human Factors, 31*(6), 617–634.

Wolber, D. (2011). App. inventor and real-world motivation. In *Proceedings of the 42nd ACM technical symposium on Computer science education* (pp. 601-606). Dallas, TX: ACM Press.

Wroblewski, L. (2012). *Mobile First*. Paris: Éditions Eyrolles.

WTR. (2013). Retrieved October 10, 2013 from http://www.welfaretech.dk/aktiviteter/wtr-efteruddannelse/

Wydoodt, P., Gentaz, E., & Streri, A. (2006). Role of force cues in the haptic estimations of a virtual length. *Experimental Brain Research, 171*, 481–489. doi:10.1007/s00221-005-0295-4 PMID:16369791

Xu, Y., Gu, J., Tao, Z., & Wu, D. (2009). Bare Hand Gesture Recognition with a Single Color Camera. In *Proceedings of the 2nd International Congress on Image and Signal Processing* (pp. 1 – 4). Academic Press.

Yang, G. (2011). *A study of How Information Systems Facilitate Football Clubs.* (Ph.D. thesis). University of Boras, Boras, Sweden.

Zain, J. M., Tey, M., & Goy, Y. (2007). Does aesthetics of web page interface matters to Mandarin learning? International Journal of Computer Science and Network Security, 7(8), 43–51.

Zajonc, R. B. (1980). Compresence. In R. B. Paulus (Ed.), *Psychology of group influences* (pp. 35–60). Hillsdale, NJ: Erlbaum.

Zajonc, R. B. (1980). Social Facilitation. *Science, 149*, 269–274. doi:10.1126/science.149.3681.269 PMID:14300526

Zhai, S., Hunter, M., & Smith, B. A. (2000). The metropolis keyboard - an exploration of quantitative techniques for virtual keyboard design. In *Proceedings of the 13th Annual ACM Symposium on User Interface Software and Technology* (pp. 119-128). New York, NY: ACM.

Zhu, Z., Nakata, C., Sivakumar, K., & Grewal, D. (2007). Self-service technology effectiveness: the role of design featuresand individual traits. *Journal of the Academy of Marketing Science, 35*(4), 492–506. doi:10.1007/s11747-007-0019-3

Zimbardo, P. G. (1969). The human choice: Individuation, reason, and order versus deindividuation, impulse, and chaos. *Nebraska Symposium on Motivation. Nebraska Symposium on Motivation, 17*, 237–307.

Zsolt, J., & Levente, H. (2010). Improving Human-Computer Interaction by Gaze Tracking. In *Proceedings of the 3rd International Conference on Cognitive Infocommunications* (pp. 155 – 160). Washington, DC: IEEE Computer Society.

About the Contributors

Pedro Isaías is an associate professor at the Universidade Aberta (Portuguese Open University) in Lisbon, Portugal, responsible for several courses and director of the master degree program in Electronic Commerce and Internet since its start in 2003. He holds a PhD in Information Management (in the speciality of information and decision systems) from the New University of Lisbon. Author of several books, book chapters, papers, and research reports, all in the information systems area, he has headed several conferences and workshops within the mentioned area. He has also been responsible for the scientific coordination of several EU funded research projects. He is also member of the editorial board of several journals and program committee member of several conferences and workshops. At the moment, he conducts research activity related to Information Systems in general, E-Learning, E-Commerce, and WWW related areas.

Katherine Blashki, with a recognised background in the Communication, Arts, and Information Technology faculties at numerous universities including Monash and Deakin Universities in Australia and Noroff University College in Norway, Professor (Dr) Katherine Blashki is also acknowledged for her extensive experience in the creative industries sector with a focus on game-based learning, creating narrative, and systems development. Previously Head of School of Multimedia Systems, Faculty of Information Technology at Monash University, Chair of New Media Technologies, a collaboration between the Faculties of Arts, and Science and Technology, both at Deakin University, and Director of Research and Education at AFTRS, Katherine now consults with aspiring higher education institutions across the world. With a demonstrated commitment to encouraging industry innovation, her research and writing credits include more than 110 papers and journals together with participation in community, industry, and international consultancies in communication, IT, and the creative industries. Katherine is currently Program Chair for the IADIS Games and Entertainment Technologies and Human Computer Interfaces conferences, held since 2005, and a past Board member for Film Victoria based in Australia.

* * *

Diogo Antunes completed his sociology degree at Oporto University in 2009 and finished his masters degree in Corporate Science at Lisbon Technical University in 2011. He began his professional career in 2010 as a consultant, responsible for managing several university challenges in Portugal, Spain, and Brazil. In 2011, he moved to Deloitte Portugal. Mainly focused on Telecommunications, Construction, Energy and Public Sector industries, he has integrated project teams for major companies in Portugal and Angola.

Kamila Balharová has been working at the Elementary School Táborská in Prague. She has a doctorate in special pedagogy from the Charles University in Prague. She has been teaching students with dyslexia and other learning disabilities since 1998. She has created Websites for students with dyslexia as well as for their teachers. She is a regular lecturer at conferences aimed at teaching students with dyslexia and other learning disabilities and an author of papers on that topic. She is an official lecturer of Ministry of Education. She is a member of the Czech Dyslexia Association and a member of an expert group at National Office of Education. She also participates in EC project Literacy.

Ioannis Basdekis is a collaborating Researcher at the Institute of Computer Science of the Foundation for Research and Technology – Hellas. Since 2003, he leads the eAccessibility monitoring activity of the Hellenic Web, and he is responsible for the implementation of several accessible eServices. Currently, he serves on the advisory technical committee on e-government of Hellenic Ministry of Administrative Reform and e-Governance. He holds a PhD in Electronic Engineering from University of KENT, and both a M.Sc in Computer Science and a B.Sc in Applied Mathematics from National and Kapodistrian University of Athens. His research interests include eAccessibility, universal access, adaptive and intelligent interfaces. His publications can be found at http://www.researchgate.net/profile/Ioannis_Basdekis/publications/.

Georgios Bouloukakis is a Ph.D. student at Inria (Paris – Rocquencourt center), in the ARLES project-team since October 2013. Before starting his PhD, he was an Expert Development Engineer in the same institute, working on CHOReOS European Project. Before joining Inria, he was a Student Research Assistant at the Institute of Computer Science of the Foundation for Research and Technology – Hellas (ICS-FORTH) since November 2010. His current research focuses on middleware, distributed systems, software engineering, and the future Internet. He holds a M.S. degree in Computer Science from the University of Crete and a B.S. degree in Telecommunications Science from the University of Peloponnese.

Yih-Shyuan Chen was born in Taiwan in 1981. She has received her B.A. degree in Taipei Municipal Teacher's College, Taiwan (2003), her M.A. degree in Information and Communication Technologies from the University of Birmingham, UK (2005), and her Ph.D. degree in School of Education from the University of Birmingham, UK (2010). Currently, she is an Assistant Professor at the Department of Digital Literature and Arts at St. John's University and one of the Secretaries of Taiwan Association of Digital Media Design (TADMD). She is teaching undergraduate students Computer Graphics, Animation, e-Publishing, Image Processing, and e-Learning. Her research interests include technology acceptance, computer users' intention and behaviour, interface design, digital learning, and ICT leadership.

Yu-Horng Chen was born in Taiwan in 1979. He has received his B.Sc. degree in Graphic Design Communications from Chinese Culture University, Taiwan (2001), his M.Des. degree (with distinction) in Media Space Design from Ming Chuan University, Taiwan (2004), and his Ph.D. degree in School of Architecture from the University of Liverpool, UK (2010). Currently, he is an Assistant Professor at the Department of Learning and Materials Design, University of Taipei and the Secretary General of Taiwan Association of Digital Media Design (TADMD). He is teaching Design Basics, Colour Scheme, Computer Graphics and e-Publishing to Undergraduate students and Contemporary Curriculum and Instruction

Issues to Post Graduate students. His research interests include Computer-Aided Architectural Design (CAAD), Human-Computer Interaction (HCI), mobile navigation, and individual difference in perception.

Alma Leora Culén is an Associate Professor at the Institute of Informatics, University of Oslo. For the past 11 years, she worked in the fields of human-computer interaction and interaction design, teaching these subjects at both undergraduate and graduate levels. As a researcher, Alma is interested in the design of digital products and services. Her research has included interaction design for and with children, elderly and young adults. Her research has been implemented in diverse projects (e.g., the design of exhibits for Oslo Children's museum, design of cool technology for young chronically ill patients, and design of smart and personal technologies for elderly).

Çiğdem Erbuğ is an Associate Professor of Department of Industrial Design at Middle East Technical University (METU), Ankara, Turkey. She teaches ergonomics for designers and User Experience Research. She is also the founder and director of UTEST, Product Usability Unit and Automative design testing laboratory. She works together with design and manufacturing firms on the assessment of product expression and user experience. She has an experience on design information systems. She conducts research on interaction design, user experience and smart products.

Visda Goudarzi is currently a PhD candidate in Sonification and Audio Engineering at Institute of Electronic Music and Acoustics in Graz, Austria. Her research interests are in Human Computer Interaction (HCI), Auditory Interfaces, Sonic Interaction Design, and Data Sonification. She has a MA in Music, Science, and Technology from CCRMA (Center for Computer Research in Music and Acoustics) at Stanford University and a MSc. in Computer Science from Vienna University of Technology. Besides research, she curates concert series at IEM, and teaches Live Electronics and Sonification.

Aslı Günay is a PhD candidate and research assistant in Department of Industrial Design at Middle East Technical University (METU), Ankara, Turkey. She is also a researcher in product usability unit and she has experiences in data collection, qualitative and quantitative data analysis process. Her research interest falls into two different idiosyncratic products in a broad sense: public and personal products. Until now, she has focused on diverse types of self-service kiosks and social context's effects during people's interactions with self-service kiosks. Recently, she conducts research about personal systems, especially for healthcare. It is of vigor to address diverse dimensions involved in user experience in those distinct public and personal products.

Dominik Hagelkruys is a research assistant and doctoral student at the University of Vienna. He studied IT and history at the University of Vienna and the Institutionen för data- och systemvetenskap, DSV (Department of Computer and Systems Sciences) in Stockholm. He wrote his Masters Thesis in the area of accessibility and is a teacher of computer science at secondary level. His research interests lie in the areas of accessibility, usability, Human-Computer Interaction, eLearning, Web-technologies, and input devices.

Paul Hekkert is full professor of form theory, and head of the Industrial Design department, Delft University of Technology. Paul conducts research on the ways products impact human experience and behavior, and leads the international project UMA (Unified Model of Aesthetics). Paul has published articles dealing with product experience and aesthetics in major international journals and is co-editor of *Product Experience* (2008). He also published *Vision in Design: A Guidebook for Innovators* (2011), a book that describes an approach to design and innovation. Paul is co-founder and chairman of the Design and Emotion society and chairman of the executive board of CRISP, a national collaborative research initiative for and with the Dutch creative industries.

Natalia Romero Herrera works as an Assistant Professor in the Industrial Design Engineering Faculty at Delft University of Technology. She is an experience UX/HCI researcher who dedicates her research and education time to develop knowledge and teach about living labs methodologies in the context of home and work situations. In her research Natalia addresses issues related to participant's motivation, situated measurement tools, and sampling of experiences in long-term and large-scale studies. Her main application area relates to the design of innovative technologies to support sustainable wellbeing and sustainable energy practices around daily life activities. Her research focuses on the assessment of user experience in the complexity of real life settings, with the aim to develop a research approach that involves subjective and objective measurement tools as well as situated design interventions of high ecological validity and sensitiveness to time dynamics.

Veikko Ikonen (M.A., Design Anthropologist) is working as a Research Team Leader for the Human-Driven Design and System Dynamics team. Mr. Ikonen is focused on human-driven design of future technologies, applications, and services. His research interests include ethical issues (including privacy and security) and recently the development of Responsible Research and Innovation approach both for academia and industry. Ikonen has taken part to the several ITEA and EU projects, where user involvement and ethical issues for the product or application development has been in the central role: Mimosa, Nomadic Media, Minami, and Guardian Angels. Recently, Ikonen has been leading work packages and tasks in several EU projects focusing on the dimensions of responsibility in the technological development (ETICA, GREAT, and Responsible Industry).

Kazuki Iwabu is a graduate student in the Dept. of Mechanical Eng. Grad. School of Eng. at Mie University. Iwabu was given his Bachelor Degree and Master Degree at Mie University in 2012 and in 2014, respectively. His research interests lie in the area of human haptic perceptual characteristics, especially those by the integrated senses of both the tactile and kinesthetic senses.

Anna Karpova earned her bachelor degree at the University of Oslo, in Digital Media. She received her master degree in 2013, in Informatics: Design, Use, and Interaction program at the same university. Her master thesis, "From a Group to an Individual: Influence of Heterogeneity of Disabilities among Children with Special Education Needs on Design Processes," was supervised by Associate Professor Alma Leora Culén. Anna's passion, from long before she started on the interaction design track, was work with children with special needs. She has written several academic articles presented at different Human-Computer Interaction conferences. She is currently working for Accenture.

Tuomo Kivinen is a senior software developer at Leadin Software Oy. He previously worked as a research scientist at VTT, Technical Research Centre of Finland until summer 2013. He is an experienced

Human-Technology Interaction researcher used to carrying out field-evaluations, interviews and lab tests in a number of projects mainly related with media and mobile services. He has also implemented various prototypes demonstrating future applications and designs. Since his research career, Tuomo has focused on developing consumer and industrial systems and services. He is educated in Human-Computer Interaction, HCI, (M.Sc. 2008) at the University of Tampere.

Heidi Korhonen works as a Senior Scientist at VTT Technical Research Centre of Finland. She is the consortium leader in the research project SHAPE (Shaping Markets for Sustainability). Her research focus is on innovation management and business development. Her current research interests cover sustainable business, business ecosystems development, service business, open innovation, co-development, systems thinking, and customer and stakeholder orientation. She has published her research widely in international peer-reviewed journals, books, and conferences. She is currently finishing her Doctoral Dissertation in Industrial Management at Aalto University. The topic of her dissertation is the implementation of customer orientation in industrial service business development.

Huberta Kritzenberger is Professor for Human-Computer Interaction, Multimedia Communication and E-Learning at the Stuttgart Media University since 2002. She holds a PhD in Information Science from the University of Regensburg (Germany) and worked in numerous academic (Universities of Regensburg and Luebeck, Germany) and industrial research and development projects on human-computer interaction. In the faculty of electronic media of the Stuttgart Media University, she teaches courses on design and evaluation of interactive media. Her research interest is in user experience (UX) with human-computer systems and interactive media. Her current research focus is on rich UX in cross-media systems (e.g. multi-device environments, serious games, and transmedia systems).

Minna Kulju is a research scientist at VTT, Technical Research Centre of Finland. Her primary research areas are in conducting user studies for collecting data related to the usability, user experience, and user acceptance of new technologies, applications, and services in different areas. Her expertise covers Human-Driven Design and Human-Technology Interaction. She has carried out a number of interviews, user studies from lab tests to field evaluations, and also benchmarking studies. She has worked in many projects which cover multiple different areas like industry, media platforms, consumer services, and also healthcare services.

Ching-Chih Liao is a senior lecture in the Department of Graphic Design at Ming Chuan University, Taiwan. She studied for a bachelor's degree in Graphic Communication in the Department of Graphic Design at Ming Chuan University, Taiwan. She then completed a Master's Degree at National Taiwan University of Science and Technology, Taiwan. Before starting her academic career she worked for a graphic design consultancy in the areas of advertising, book design and Web design. Her research interests include typography, information design and layout design.

Yu-Yin Lin is a MA student in the Department of e-Learning Design and Management, at National Chiayi University, Taiwan. She received her bachelor's degree in Information Technology and Management from Shih Chien University, Taiwan. She has worked in industry for various design-related companies and is interested in enhancing learning experiences through the application of information technology.

Gunver Majgaard (PhD) is Associate Professor at The Maersk McKinney Moller Institute, University of Southern Denmark. She has background in electrical engineering and has been teaching at the Technical Faculty at University of Southern Denmark since 2001. She has taught courses in game design, fundamental of game programming, learning theory, design of educational tool, etc. Over the years, Gunver has become more and more interested in how technology can enrich learning processes in formal education. Her research interests are technology in education, design of digital educational tools; participatory design processes; learning processes; didactical design; program and curriculum development. She has developed the engineering program Learning and Experience Technology.

Renate Motschnig is professor at the Faculty of Computer Science at the University of Vienna and head of the Computer Science Didactics and Learning Research Center. She received her Dipl.-Ing. degree in Computer Science (Informatik) in 1982 and her Dr. techn. in Computer Science in 1988, both (with honors) from the Vienna University of technology. She has repeatedly been a visiting professor at the Computer Science Department of the University of Toronto, Canada. In 1995/96, she was on the faculty of the Computer Science Department of the RWTH-Aachen, Germany. Currently, Prof. Motschnig teaches and coordinates the modules Project Management, Human-Computer Interaction and Psychology, Communication, and Advanced eLearning Technologies. Since 2005, she has been teaching interdisciplinary courses in the field of communication, qualitative research in media-pedagogy, human-computer interactions & psychology and technology-enhanced learning.

A. Y. C. Nee is professor in the Department of Mechanical Engineering, National University of Singapore since 1989. He received his PhD and DEng from UMIST. His research interest is in CAD of tool, die, fixture and process planning, augmented reality, sustainable manufacturing. He is a Fellow of CIRP and SME, both elected in 1990. He served as the President of CIRP (2012). Currently, he is Editor-in-Chief of the Springer's *International Journal of Advanced Manufacturing Technology*, as well as editorial boards of some 20 international journals. He has published over 500 refereed journal and conference papers, with Google Scholar citation >7000 and H-Index of 44. He also has 12 edited and authored books. He holds honorary professorship from Tianjin University, NUAA, BUAA, Shanghai and HUST. He has received many awards and is a Fellow of the Academy of Engineering of Singapore.

Jacob Nielsen (PhD) is a Post-Doc at the Maersk McKinney Moller Institute, University of Southern Denmark. His research area lies within the fields of Embodied Artificial Intelligence, Interaction Design (HRI/HCI) and Modular Robotics. He received his masters in computer systems engineering degree in 2002 with the thesis titled "Intelligent Bricks" and his PhD in 2009 with the thesis titled: "User-Configurable Modular Robotics: Design and Use." His research focus is on modularizing technologies in order to make them accessible to non-experts. This modularization is very much inspired by the constructionism term coined by Seymour Papert and in parallel to the constructionist tools described within his chapter.

Marketta Niemelä is a senior scientist at VTT Technical Research Centre of Finland. Her research focus is on human-driven design and co-design of emerging ICTs. Her current research interests cover RRI (Responsible Research and Innovation) and service robotics, and how to engage people in development of new technologies and in design for sustainability. She has been involved in several EU projects carrying out user involvement and research on ethical issues (e.g. Mimosa, Minami, GREAT). Her experience in user studies covers lab tests, field studies and several-year living labs. She is educated in psychology (Ps.M.) and had her doctoral dissertation of Human-Computer Interaction in information systems and computer science in University of Jyväskylä, Finland, 2003.

Yoshihiko Nomura is a Professor in the Dept. of Mechanical Eng. Grad. School of Eng. at Mie University where he has been a faculty member since 1997. During the period, he had also served as an Executive Vice President in Educational Development from 2007 to 2011. Nomura was given his Bachelor Degree and Master Degree at Nagoya University in 1976 and in 1978, and was given his Dr. Degree Eng. at Tokyo Institute of Technology in 1987. His research interests lie in the area of mechatronics and their application to intelligent robots, ranging from theory to design to implementation. In recent years, he has focused on the application to welfare engineering, e-learning, and man-machine interfaces with a focus on cognitive science with human haptic perceptual characteristics, especially those by the integrated senses of both the tactile and kinesthetic senses.

Soh Khim Ong is an Associate Professor in the Mechanical Engineering Department at the National University of Singapore. Her research interests are virtual and augmented reality applications in manufacturing and assistive technology and parallel kinematic manipulators. She has published 2 books and over 300 international refereed journal and conference papers. SK Ong received the 2004 Outstanding Young Manufacturing Engineer Award from US Society of Manufacturing Engineers. She is a recipient of the 2004 Singapore Youth Award for the Science and Technology Category, and the 2013 Medal of Commendation, where she is the first female technology recipient for both awards. In 2006, S. K. Ong was awarded The Outstanding Young Person of Singapore Award for the Science and Technology Category. She was awarded the 2009 Emerging Leaders Award in Academia by the US Society for Women Engineers. In 2012, she was elected a fellow of CIRP, The International Academy for Production Engineering.

Heloísa Vieira da Rocha is Professor in Institute of Computing (IC) and researcher at the Nucleus of Informatics Applied on Education (NIED) of State University of Campinas (UNICAMP). She lectured in the areas of artificial intelligence, human-computer interaction, and informatics applied on education at both undergraduate and postgraduate levels. Her main topic of interest is the junction of the Information Technologies in Education and Human-Computer Interfaces areas. She was the coordinator of the e-Labora lab in the TIDIA-Ae project, funded by FAPESP from 2004 until 2009, to develop an e-learning environment to the advanced Internet. She is involved with e-learning environments development and use since 1997 coordinating the development of the TelEduc project, the first Brazilian open-source e-learning environment.

André Constantino da Silva teaches on Federal Institute of São Paulo (IFSP), Campus Hortolândia, since 2012, lecturing about logic programming, object-oriented programming, software analysis and design, and Human-Computer Interaction in undergraduate courses. His topics of interest include e-Learning, m-Learning, mobility, multimodalities, educational software, and educational games development. He studied about multimodality and e-learning environments in his doctoral thesis in Institute of Computing (IC) of State University of Campinas (UNICAMP). His master dissertation was about how Software Engineering patterns and Human-Computer patterns can be applied to integrated multidisciplinary development teams. Between 2005 until 2008, he worked as a researcher in the FAPESP-funded TIDIA-Ae project to develop an e-learning environment to the advanced Internet. In this project, it was possible to get experience about development of e-learning environment and distance and blended courses. In 2010, he worked as tutor in undergraduate distance courses of SEAD/UFSCar using the Moodle platform.

João Silva has a degree in Sports Management and a master degree in Management of Information Systems. He has further qualifications in stock market and financial products analysis. He is interested in the area of Sports and has developed research in Web site analysis and assessment and how to improve Sports site both in terms of efficiency as well as for visitors.

Constantine Stephanidis, Professor at the Department of Computer Science of the University of Crete, is the Director of the Institute of Computer Science of the Foundation for Research and Technology – Hellas (ICS-FORTH), Founder and Head of its Human-Computer Interaction (HCI) Laboratory, and Founder and Head of its Ambient Intelligence (AmI) Programme. He is the Founder and Editor-in-Chief of the Springer international journal *Universal Access in the Information Society*. He is the Editor of the books *User Interfaces for All: Concepts, Methods and Tools* published by Lawrence Erlbaum Associates (2001) and *The Universal Access Handbook* published by CRC Press Taylor & Francis Group (2009). He has published more than 500 articles in scientific archival journals, proceedings of international conferences and workshops related to the fields of his expertise. In 2010, Prof. Stephanidis was elected member of the Informatics Section of the Academia Europaea, the European Academy of Humanities, Letters, and Sciences. Since March 2014, he is member of the National Council for Research and Technology.

Ján Struhár is a research assistant and a doctoral student at the University of Vienna. He is focused on human-centered design for the LITERACY Portal. His main interests are person-centered communication, education, and learning; human-computer interaction; and the not-so-unrelated field of marketing. He studied Service Science, Management, and Engineering at the Faculty of Informatics of Masaryk University in Brno and his thesis was about inbound marketing in higher education. Ján is currently also a volunteering Business IT Club coordinator and a Communication and Soft-skills course tutor.

Antti Tammela is a senior scientist at VTT, Technical Research Centre of Finland. His research focus is on human-driven design and co-design innovations and concepts. His current research interests cover RRI (Responsible Research and Innovation) and healthcare studies. His expertise cover interactive quality and quantitative user study methods, service concepts, sustainability and different co-creation methods. He has carried out a number of user studies from lab tests to many years living labs. He has worked in many projects which cover different areas like industry, media platforms, consumer services and also health care services. He is educated in technology (Lic. Sc.) and education (M.A.).

Hsiu-Feng Wang is an assistant professor in the Department of e-Learning Design and Management at National Chiayi University, Taiwan. She studied for a bachelor's degree in Graphic Communication in the Department of Graphic Design at Ming Chuan University, Taiwan. She then completed a Master's Degree at Middlesex University, UK, before reading for her PhD in the Department of Typography and Graphic Communication at Reading University, UK. She is interested in graphic icon design, information design, the legibility of Traditional Chinese writing and user-centred design. Her current research is concerned with how design variables influence the effectiveness of online teaching materials for children.

Pei-Yu Wang is an assistant professor in the department of e-learning design and management, National Chiayi University, Taiwan. Pei-Yu studied for the bachelor's degree in National Chengchi University, Taiwan, and she double majored in Education and Management Information System. She then got a Master's Degree at Graduate Institute in Information and Computer Education, National Taiwan Normal University. In 2010, she completed her PhD in the Department of Curriculum and Instruction at the University of Taxes at Austin, US. She has conducted studies in instructional systems and multimedia design for more than ten years. Currently she focuses studies on e-book design and production.

Andrew Yew Weiwen is a Ph.D candidate in the Augmented Reality and Assistive Technology Lab in the Department of Mechanical Engineering, National University of Singapore. He received a B.Eng. degree in Mechanical Engineering, with a minor in Computer Science, from the National University of Singapore in July 2009. In his research in mobile augmented reality and ubiquitous computing, he aims to help usher in a new age of ubiquitous augmented reality with a mixture of interactive real and virtual objects embedded in any environment. More recently, he has started to work on human-robot interaction interfaces with the aim of exploring and developing novel human-robot interaction methods.

Index